THE ROUTLEDGE HANDBOOK OF ELECTIONS, VOTING BEHAVIOR AND PUBLIC OPINION

Elections, voting behavior and public opinion are arguably among the most prominent and intensively researched sub-fields within political science. It is an evolving sub-field, in terms of both theoretical focus and, in particular, technical developments, and has made a considerable impact on popular understanding of the core components of liberal democracies in terms of election outcomes and the way these are affected by electoral systems, changes in public opinion and the aggregation of interests.

This handbook details the key developments and state-of-the-art research across elections, voting behavior and the public opinion by both providing an advanced overview of each core area and engaging in debate about the relative merits of differing approaches in a comprehensive and accessible way. Bringing geographical scope and depth, with comparative chapters that draw on material from across the globe, it will be a key reference point for both advanced level students and researchers developing knowledge and producing new material in these sub-fields and beyond.

The Routledge Handbook of Elections, Voting Behavior and Public Opinion is an authoritative and key reference text for students, academics and researchers engaged in the study of electoral research, public opinion and voting behavior.

Justin Fisher is Professor of Political Science and Director of the Magna Carta Institute at Brunel University London, UK. He was co-editor of the *Journal of Elections, Public Opinion and Parties* from 2004–2011.

Edward Fieldhouse is Professor of Social and Political Science at the University of Manchester, UK, and Director of the 2015 British Election Study. He was co-editor of the *Journal of Elections, Public Opinion and Parties* from 2012–2016.

Mark N. Franklin is a Director of the European Union Democracy Observatory at the European University Institute's Robert Schuman Centre for Advanced Studies. He was co-editor of the *Journal of Elections, Public Opinion and Parties* from 2012–2016.

Rachel Gibson is Professor of Political Science at the University of Manchester, UK, and Director of the Cathie Marsh Institute for Social Research. She was co-editor of the *Journal of Elections, Public Opinion and Parties* from 2012–2016.

Marta Cantijoch is a Q-Step Lecturer in Politics at the University of Manchester, UK. She was the editorial assistant of the *Journal of Elections, Public Opinion and Parties* from 2013–2016.

Christopher Wlezien is Hogg Professor of Government at the University of Texas at Austin, USA. He was co-editor of the *Journal of Elections, Public Opinion and Parties* from 2004–2011.

The handbook very nicely covers all the topics related to the study of elections, voting and public opinion: the most influential theories and methods, both turnout and vote choice, both the individual-level and the contextual determinants, the roles of both voters and parties. The review essays are written by top scholars in the field, with a crucial cross-national perspective. An essential reading for all those who study and/or teach political behavior.

André Blais, Université de Montréal, Canada

This handbook takes stock of 50 years of research into elections, voting behavior and public opinion. It is well structured and a stellar cast of authors presents the state of the art in a comprehensive fashion. This monumental volume is a true landmark. It is a must-read for all those interested in elections and democratic politics.

Hans-Dieter Klingemann, Social Science Research Center Berlin, Germany

THE ROUTLEDGE HANDBOOK OF ELECTIONS, VOTING BEHAVIOR AND PUBLIC OPINION

Edited by Justin Fisher, Edward Fieldhouse,
Mark N. Franklin, Rachel Gibson, Marta Cantijoch
and Christopher Wlezien

Routledge
Taylor & Francis Group

LONDON AND NEW YORK

First published 2018 by Routledge

2 Park Square, Milton Park, Abingdon, Oxfordshire OX14 4RN

52 Vanderbilt Avenue, New York, NY 10017

Routledge is an imprint of the Taylor & Francis Group, an informa business

First issued in paperback 2020

British Library Cataloguing in Publication Data
A catalogue record for this book is available from the British Library

Library of Congress Cataloging in Publication Data
A catalog record for this book has been requested

ISBN: 978-1-138-89040-4 (hbk)
ISBN: 978-0-367-50011-5 (pbk)

Typeset in Bembo
by Wearset Ltd, Boldon, Tyne and Wear

CONTENTS

Contents

Contents

FIGURES

TABLES

CONTRIBUTORS

Loes Aaldering is a Ph.D. candidate at the University of Amsterdam. Her research interests include political leadership, politics and gender, voting behavior (electoral volatility), political representation and media effects. She has published on these topics in *Quality & Quantity*, the *International Journal of Public Opinion Research* and *Political Studies*.

John H. Aldrich is the Pfizer-Pratt University Professor of Political Science, Duke University. He is past President of the Southern Political Science Association, the Midwest Political Science Association and the American Political Science Association. He has been a Guggenheim Fellow and is a Fellow of the American Academy of Arts and Sciences. His articles have appeared in the major journals. He is also the author or co-author of *Why Parties*, *Before the Convention*, *Linear Probability, Logit and Probit Models*, *Interdisciplinarity*, and a series of books on elections, the most recent of which is *Change and Continuity in the 2012 and 2014 Elections*. His and John Griffins' book, *Why Parties Matter: Political Competition and Democracy in the American South, 1832–2012*, is forthcoming in 2017.

R. Michael Alvarez is Professor of Political Science at Caltech, and is co-director of the Caltech/MIT Voting Technology Project. His research interests include political methodology, electoral and voting behavior, and voting technology.

Ksenia Northmore-Ball is a British Academy Post-doctoral Research Fellow in the School of Politics and IR at the University of Nottingham. Her research interests include voter turnout, the meaning of left-right, religiosity and authoritarian legacies in new democracies, particularly in Eastern Europe. Her recent work has been published in *Electoral Studies*, the *Journal for the Scientific Study of Religion* and *Social Science Research*.

Susan Banducci is Professor in Politics and Director of the Exeter Q-Step Centre at the University of Exeter, UK. She has contributed to a number of election and media projects, including the European Election Study. She is currently the co-editor of the *Journal of Elections, Public Opinion and Parties*.

Jørgen Bølstad is Assistant Professor at ARENA – Centre for European Studies at the University of Oslo and former Researcher and Lecturer at the Swiss Federal Institute of Technology, in Zürich. His publications appear in a number of leading international journals and address theoretical ambiguities and issues of causal inference in the areas of voting behavior, public opinion, political responsiveness and European politics.

Shaun Bowler is Professor of Political Science at UC Riverside. His work often addresses the link between political behavior and the institutions of representation. His most recent book, co-authored with Todd Donovan, is *The Limits of Electoral Reform* (Oxford University Press, 2013).

Marta Cantijoch is Lecturer in Politics at the University of Manchester. Her research interests include political behavior and engagement, political communication and the effects of new media.

Harold D. Clarke is Ashbel Smith Professor in the School of Economic, Political and Policy Sciences at the University of Texas at Dallas. His areas of interest involve social science data collection and analysis, survey research methodology, and public attitudes and participation. His recent books include *Affluence, Austerity and Electoral Change in Britain* (Cambridge University Press, 2013), *Austerity and Political Choice in Britain* (Palgrave Macmillan, 2016), and *Brexit – Why Britain Voted to Leave the European Union* (Cambridge University Press, 2017).

Lorenzo De Sio is Associate Professor at the LUISS Guido Carli University, Rome. His research interests are in elections, voting behavior and party competition in comparative perspective. He has authored and edited several books in Italian and English on these topics as well as internationally peer-reviewed articles in generalist and specialist journals. He has been a Visiting Research Fellow at UC Irvine, Jean Monnet Fellow at the Robert Schuman Centre of the European University Institute and a Campbell National Fellow at Stanford University. He is currently the coordinator of the CISE (Centro Italiano Studi Elettorali) and a member of the Scientific Council of the ITANES (Italian National Election Studies). As a member of the Methods Working Group of the "True European Voter" international research project (ESF-COST Action IS0806), he participates at the EUDO Observatory on Public Opinion, Political Elites and the Media.

Elias Dinas is Associate Professor of Comparative Politics and Tutorial Fellow at Oxford University and Brasenose College. His current research focuses on formation of political identities, looking at how past legacies are revived when stimulated by the current political context. He also examines the role of in-group victimhood on understanding out-group prejudice. His work has been published in various peer-reviewed journals and has been cited by various media outlets, including *The Economist*, the *New York Times* and *The Atlantic*. He is also co-director of the Oxford Spring School in Advanced Research Methods.

Keith Dowding is Professor of Political Science in the School of Politics and International Relations, Research School of Social Sciences, Australian National University. He has published over twenty books, most recently *Power, Luck and Freedom: Collected Essays* (Manchester University Press, 2017), *Policy Agendas in Australia* (with Aaron Martin; Palgrave, 2017) and *The Philosophy and Methods of Political Science* (Palgrave, 2016), and published widely in the fields of political philosophy, philosophy of social science, urban politics, public policy and administration, and comparative politics. He edited the *Journal of Theoretical Politics* from 1996–2013 and is now associate editor of *Research and Politics*.

Martin Elff is Professor of Political Sociology at Zeppelin University in Friedrichshafen, Germany. His research interests are the relation between social divisions and electoral behavior, the reconstruction of parties' positions from political texts, the impact of parties' political positions on electoral behavior and the methodology of political research.

Robert S. Erikson is a Professor of Political Science at Columbia University, specializing in public opinion, elections and representation in the US. He is the co-author of *Statehouse Democracy*, *The Macro Polity*, *The Timeline of Presidential Elections* and nine editions of *American Public Opinion*. He is the past editor of the *American Journal of Political Science* and *Political Analysis*. Erikson is a member of the American Academy of Science.

Geoffrey Evans is Official Fellow in Politics, Nuffield College and Professor of the University of Oxford. He has directed numerous large-scale research projects in Western and Eastern Europe, including the current British Election and EU Referendum Studies. He has published over 150 articles and chapters, and his books include: *The End of Class Politics?* (1999), *Political Choice Matters* (2013) and *The New Politics of Class: The Political Exclusion of the British Working Class* (2017).

Edward Fieldhouse is Professor of Social and Political Science at the University of Manchester, UK, and Director of the 2015 British Election Study. He was co-editor of the *Journal of Elections, Public Opinion and Parties* from 2012–2016. He has published widely on electoral behavior, including voter turnout, electoral geography and social influence on voting. Previous books include *Neither Left Nor Right: The Liberal Democrats and the Electorate*, with Andrew Russell.

Justin Fisher is Professor of Political Science and Director of the Magna Carta Institute at Brunel University London, UK. He was Principal Investigator of the ESRC-funded studies of constituency level campaigning at the 2010 and 2015 British general elections and has published widely on elections, campaigning, political parties and political finance. He was co-editor of the *Journal of Elections, Public Opinion and Parties* from 2004–2011.

Stephen D. Fisher is an Associate Professor in Political Sociology and Fellow and Tutor in politics at Trinity College in the University of Oxford. He is the author of various articles on electoral behavior, social attitudes and quantitative research methods. He has also produced forecasts at ElectionsEtc.com and election-night predictions for the BBC, ITV and Sky for various elections and referendums in the UK.

Mark N. Franklin, until he retired in 2007, was Professor of International Politics at Trinity College Connecticut, having previously taught at the Universities of Houston, Texas and Strathclyde, Scotland. In retirement he has held positions at the European University Institute (Florence, Italy), Nuffield College (Oxford, England) and the Massachusetts Institute of Technology (Cambridge MA, USA). He has published 20 books and some 150 articles, chapters, monographs and reports. A past Guggenheim Fellow, he has been advisor to British, Canadian, French and Italian election studies.

Rachel Gibson is Professor of Political Science and Director of the Cathie Marsh Institute for Social Research at the University of Manchester. Her research interests are in elections, parties and new forms of online communication and campaigning.

Donald P. Green is J. W. Burgess Professor of Political Science at Columbia University. Much of his research uses field experimentation to study the ways in which political campaigns mobilize and persuade voters. With Alan Gerber, he authored *Get Out The Vote: How to Increase Voter Turnout* (Brookings Institution Press, 2015) and *Field Experiments: Design, Analysis, and Interpretation* (W. W. Norton, 2012).

Oliver Heath is Reader in Politics in the Department of Politics and International Relations, Royal Holloway, University of London. His research interests include turnout, class voting, political representation and comparative politics. He has recently published articles in the *British Journal of Political Science, Journal of Politics, Electoral Studies, Party Politics*, and *Politics & Gender*. He is co-author of *Political Research: Methods and Practical Skills* (Oxford University Press, 2016).

Robert Huckfeldt is a Distinguished Professor in the Department of Political Science at the University of California, Davis. His research efforts address the implications of networks, contexts and political interdependence for the behavior of individuals and groups in democratic politics. He is author or co-author of a series of books and articles, including *Experts, Activists, and Democratic Politics* (Cambridge, 2014).

Vincent L. Hutchings is the Hanes Walton Jr. Professor of Political Science at the University of Michigan and a Research Professor at the Institute for Social Research. He received his Ph.D. from the University of California, Los Angeles. He is the author of *Public Opinion and Democratic Accountability* (2003), from Princeton University Press.

Hakeem J. Jefferson is a Ph.D. candidate in the department of political science at the University of Michigan. His primary research interests center around questions related to group identification and in-group heterogeneity, particularly among those who belong to stigmatized social groups

Libby M. Jenke is a Ph.D. candidate in Political Science at Duke University. Her articles have appeared in the *Journal of Conflict Resolution* and *Trends in Cognitive Sciences*.

Ron Johnston is a Professor in the School of Geographical Sciences at the University of Bristol. His main research interests are in electoral studies generally, and electoral geography more specifically: he has published extensively, for example, on constituency redistributions in the UK and their impact on election outcomes, on neighborhood and other spatial effects on voting behavior and on the geography of local campaigns. Much of that work is summarized in his 2006 book with Charles Pattie, *Putting Voters in Their Place*.

D. Roderick Kiewiet is Professor of Political Science at Caltech. His research interests include voting behavior, legislative politics, state and local government, and public school finance.

Oddbjørn Knutsen is Professor of Political Science at the University of Oslo. His research interests are in the fields of comparative politics with a special interest in Western Europe, political sociology and electoral behavior, value orientations and ideology, and methodology and statistics. He has published comparative articles in international journals on value change, value orientations and party choice, political cleavages and political ideology.

Pedro C. Magalhães is a Research Fellow of the Institute of Social Sciences of the University of Lisbon. His research covers a broad spectrum that includes public opinion, elections, and political attitudes and behavior.

Michael Marsh is a member of the Royal Irish Academy and Emeritus Professor of Political Science in Trinity College University of Dublin. He was principal investigator for the Irish National Election Study 2002–2007, 2011 and 2016, and has written extensively about parties and electoral behavior both in Ireland and in Europe. He is co-editor of *How Ireland Voted 2016: The Election That Nobody Won* (Palgrave, 2016) and *A Conservative Revolution? Electoral Change in Twenty First Century Ireland* (Oxford University Press, 2017).

Jonathan Mellon is a Research Fellow at Nuffield College, University of Oxford, working on the British Election Study. Jonathan is a Senior Data Scientist with the World Bank, works on the BBC's election night forecasts and has worked as a Data Scientist with the OSCE and Carter Center. He was awarded his DPhil in Political Sociology from the University of Oxford. His research interests include electoral behavior, cross-national participation, developing tools for working with big data in social science and social network analysis.

Ian McAllister is Distinguished Professor of Political Science at The Australian National University. His most recent books are *Conflict to Peace: Society and Politics in Northern Ireland Over Half a Century* (Manchester University Press, 2013), *The Australian Voter* (University of New South Wales Press, 2012) and *Political Parties and Democratic Linkage* (Oxford University Press, 2011). He has been director of the Australian Election Study since 1987, a large national post-election survey of political attitudes and behavior. His scholarly research covers Australian politics, comparative political behavior and post-communist politics. He is currently completing a book on Russian voting and elections.

Andrew McCall is a graduate student in Political Science at UC Berkeley. His research focuses on the relationship between mass beliefs, mass attitudes and criminal justice policies in the US.

Iain McLean is Professor of Politics, Oxford University, and a fellow of Nuffield College. He has worked on electoral systems for many years, and with co-authors was the first person to discover the pioneers of voting theory, including Ramon Llull, Nicolas of Cusa and J. I. Morales. These early works, in Catalan, Latin, French and Spanish, are now available in English; see I. McLean and A. B. Urken, *Classics of Social Choice* (Michigan, 1995) and I. McLean and F. Hewitt, *Condorcet* (Elgar, 1994).

Anthony Mughan is Professor of Political Science and Director of the Undergraduate International Studies Program at the Ohio State University. He has published extensively in leading political science journals in the United States, Australia and Western Europe and is the author or editor of eight books. His areas of research interest include public opinion, the media, political parties and elections.

Pippa Norris is the McGuire Lecturer in Comparative Politics at Harvard University, Australian Laureate and Professor of Government at the University of Sydney, and Director of the Electoral Integrity Project. Her most recent publications are a trilogy for Cambridge University Press, *Why Electoral Integrity Matters* (2014), *Why Elections Fail* (2015) and *Strengthening Electoral Integrity* (2017).

Lucas Núñez is a Ph.D. candidate in Social Science at the California Institute of Technology. His research interests include statistical methods, political methodology, and political behavior and participation.

Charles Pattie is a Professor in the Department of Geography at the University of Sheffield. He is an electoral geographer, and has worked on local economic and social contexts and their effect on the geography of the vote, the impact of constituency campaigning, political participation, the impact of individuals' social networks on their political views and decisions, electoral redistricting and the electoral politics of devolution in the UK.

B. Guy Peters is Maurice Falk Professor of Government at the University of Pittsburgh, and also President of the International Public Policy Association. He is also the author or editor of more than seventy books, most recently *Governance and Comparative Politics* (with Jon Pierre).

Matthew T. Pietryka is an Assistant Professor of Political Science at Florida State University. His research examines how individuals' social contexts and communication patterns influence their political attitudes and behavior. His most recent work has appeared in the *American Political Science Review*, *Political Psychology* and *Public Opinion Quarterly*.

Eric Plutzer is Professor of Political Science and Scientific Director of the Mood of the Nation Poll sponsored by the Center for American Political Responsiveness at Penn State. He serves as editor (with Patricia Moy) of *Public Opinion Quarterly*. He is the author (with Michael Berkman) of *Ten Thousand Democracies* (2005) and *Evolution, Creationism, and the Battle for America's Classrooms* (2010), as well as papers on social cleavages and on voter turnout.

Christopher Prosser is a Research Associate at the University of Manchester, and a Non-Stipendiary Research Fellow at Nuffield College, Oxford. He works on the British Election Study and his research focuses on political behavior and party competition in Britain and Europe, EU referendums, the effects of electoral systems and survey research methodology.

John B. Ryan is Associate Professor in the Department of Political Science at Stony Brook University. He is a faculty affiliate in the university's interdisciplinary Center for Behavioral Political Economy. His research focuses on communication in social networks as well as political campaigns. He is the co-author of *Experts, Activists, and Democratic Politics* (Cambridge, 2014), as well as articles appearing in journals such as the *American Journal of Political Science*, *Political Behavior* and *Political Communication*.

Luana Russo is a Lecturer in Research Methods at Maastricht University. She is a quantitative political science scholar with significant experience of working with ecological and geographical data, which she employs to investigate topics such as geography of political and electoral behavior, volatility and nationalization of voting behavior.

Holli A. Semetko is Asa Griggs Candler Professor of Media & International Affairs, Emory University. Her research interests include campaigns, technology and influence. She co-edited *The Sage Handbook of Political Communication* (2012), and was Fulbright Nehru Scholar at IIT-Bombay in 2013–2014.

Hermann Schmitt is a Professor of Political Science. He holds a Chair in Electoral Politics at the University of Manchester and is a research fellow of the MZES and a Professor at the University of Mannheim. He was a visiting professor at the University of Michigan (1996–1997), Science Po Paris (2001–2002), the Australian National University (2003), the IAS in Vienna (2005) and the UAM in Madrid (2008). He received his doctorate from the University of

Duisburg, and holds a *venia legendi* from both the Free University of Berlin and the University of Mannheim. He has been participating in a number of comparative projects; perhaps most important is his involvement, from 1979 on, in the series of European Election Studies. He received substantial research grants from European, German and British institutions. He is the author and editor of numerous books and articles on electoral behavior in multilevel systems, and on political representation in the European Union.

Marianne C. Stewart is a Professor in the School of Economic, Political and Policy Sciences at the University of Texas at Dallas. Her areas of interest involve the logic, methodology and scope of political science; political attitudes, electoral choice and political participation; the political economy of regime change and development; and survey research data collection and analysis. Her recent books include *Affluence, Austerity and Electoral Change in Britain* (Cambridge University Press, 2013) and *Austerity and Political Choice in Britain* (Palgrave Macmillan, 2016).

Laura Stoker is an Associate Professor of Political Science at UC Berkeley. Her research focuses on the development and change of political attitudes and behavior employing data drawn from surveys and experiments.

Eftichia Teperoglou is a Lecturer at the Department of Political Science, Aristotle University, Thessaloniki. She was a researcher at MZES, University of Mannheim and at the Centre for Research and Studies in Sociology, University Institute of Lisbon. Her main research interests are in the fields of political and electoral behavior with a focus on European elections, comparative politics and public opinion. She is one of the founders of the Hellenic National Election Study (ELNES). She has published work in international journals and in edited volumes. She is the author of the book *The Other 'National' Elections. Analyzing the European Elections in Greece 1981–2014* (Papazisis, 2016).

Hubert Tworzecki is Associate Professor of Political Science, Emory University. His research interests include parties and elections in new democracies. He is a Fulbright Scholar in Poland in 2016–2017.

Jan W. van Deth was Professor of Political Science and International Comparative Social Research at the University of Mannheim (Germany) and is Project Director at the Mannheim Centre for European Social Research (MZES). He has published widely in the fields of political culture and participation, social change and comparative research methods. He was Director of the MZES, convenor of the international network Citizenship, Involvement, Democracy (CID) and national coordinator of the German team for the European Social Survey. He is a Corresponding Member of the Royal Netherlands Academy of Arts and Sciences (KNAW).

Jennifer vanHeerde-Hudson is Associate Professor of Political Behaviour, University College London. Her research focuses on candidates, elections and representation in the UK (www.parliamentarycandidates.org) and comparative study of public opinion and attitudes toward development/aid (www.devcommslab.org).

Wouter van der Brug is Professor and Chair of Political Science at the University of Amsterdam. His research interests focus on comparative research in political behavior, in particular electoral processes, populism, political trust and support, and party system change. He publishes regularly in various international political science journals. His most recent (co-authored/co-edited) books are *The Politicisation of Migration* (Routledge, 2015) and *(Un)intended Consequences of European Parliament Elections* (Oxford University Press, 2016).

Cees van der Eijk is Professor of Social Science Research Methods at the University of Nottingham, and former Professor of Political Science at the University of Amsterdam. He has been Principal Investigator of National Election Studies in the Netherlands and Great Britain, and of the European Election Studies. He has authored or co-authored 18 books and over 100 articles and chapters, many of which are on electoral research and its methods.

Jack Vowles' research is primarily in comparative political behavior and New Zealand elections and party politics. He has previously worked at the University of Auckland, the University of Waikato and the University of Exeter. He has led the New Zealand Election Study since 1996.

Stephen Ward is a Reader in Politics, School of Arts & Media, University of Salford. His research interests are in digital politics campaigns and political participation.

Christopher Wlezien is Hogg Professor of Government at the University of Texas at Austin. He has previously been on the faculties of Oxford University, the University of Houston and Temple University, and holds or has held visiting positions at various universities. He has published numerous articles and chapters as well as a number of books, including *Degrees of Democracy, Who Gets Represented*' and *The Timeline of Presidential Elections*.

Erin A. York is a Ph.D. candidate in Political Science at Columbia University with a focus on field experiments and political economy. Her research explores ethnic politics, political participation and electoral accountability in the Middle East and North Africa.

ACKNOWLEDGMENTS

Putting together a large volume such as this creates many debts of gratitude. First and foremost, we would like to thank Andrew Taylor from Routledge for approaching us in the first instance to put the volume together, and for his friendly and helpful encouragement throughout. We would also like to thank Sophie Iddamalgoda from Routledge for her invaluable assistance, design ideas and her patience. Patrick English from the University of Manchester also deserves significant praise – he greatly assisted us in formatting the chapters in the final stages before submission. Finally, we would like to thank all our authors. We were delighted to recruit such a stellar group of international scholars. Each and every one produced excellent work and responded to our various questions and queries quickly and with the utmost professionalism. We have greatly enjoyed producing this handbook and hope that readers will find it useful; but above all, stimulating and a springboard for new ideas.

EDITORS' INTRODUCTION –
IN DEFENSE OF POLITICAL
SCIENCE

*Justin Fisher, Edward Fieldhouse, Mark N. Franklin, Rachel Gibson,
Marta Cantijoch and Christopher Wlezien*

Elections, voting behavior and public opinion are arguably among the most prominent and intensively researched sub-fields within political science. That said, each continues to evolve rapidly in theoretical and methodological terms. Each has also impacted on popular understanding of the core components of liberal democracies in terms of electoral systems and outcomes, changes in public opinion and the aggregation of interests. This handbook provides an up-to-date and authoritative "go to" guide for researchers looking to understand key developments in these important areas. It aims to provide an advanced level overview of each core area and also to engage in debate about the relative merits of differing approaches.

The handbook is edited by scholars who have served as past editors of the *Journal of Elections, Public Opinion and Parties* (*JEPOP*). As former editors, we were fortunate to be able to choose from a range of outstanding authors, reviewers and readers, who together provide the wealth of expertise and insights needed for such a handbook. Between them they provide wide-ranging, thoughtful, erudite, succinct and, above all, readable treatments of the major topics covered by *JEPOP*. Each chapter is written especially for the handbook with the objective of familiarizing political science scholars with core debates, past and present, in the areas of electoral and public opinion research. While its coverage is broad and we fully expect readers to approach it selectively, the chapters are designed to link together and reinforce one another to provide a comprehensive "360 degree" statement on the state of contemporary research in the field.

As we put the finishing touches to this handbook, democratic politics and political science is experiencing significant challenges. The largely unexpected outcome of the Brexit referendum in the United Kingdom and the election of Donald Trump as US President have led some to challenge the utility of political science research. Yet, as this handbook will show, these criticisms are largely without foundation. Far from being a time when we are morosely looking inwards, this is an exciting time for political science; a time when rapid advances are being made across the discipline and especially in these sub-fields. Recent developments in causal analysis have put an end to a period where authors were spending much time re-inventing the wheel or (if you like) going around in circles, obtaining results that were treated as "findings," only to be disproved by later new results. The adoption of new approaches, especially experimental methods, has led to a flood of findings that definitively confirm or disprove earlier contentions that many had found it hard to perceive as advances in knowledge. A recent pessimistic account of such advances in what we have learned about representation processes can be found in Achen and Bartels (2016). We take a very different view than the authors of that book, believing that what they describe is a world of political science now thankfully moving into our past. A decade or so ago it could indeed have at least been argued, as they do, that virtually nothing had been learned since the establishment of a social group basis for politics some sixty years ago. Partly we feel that their pessimistic view is due to their excessive focus on the United States, where their claimed lack of progress might seem perhaps more plausible than elsewhere, but mainly we feel that their view is so damning to the political science profession because they focus on topics that have been prominent both now and sixty years ago, largely ignoring competing approaches that have developed in the meantime. This handbook tries to avoid both these limitations, adopting a comparative view of new as well as classic topics that fall within its remit. The United States figures in its pages, but what we know about the United States is here illuminated by what we know about other countries as well as the other way around, quite in contrast to the prevailing norm. In our view, this makes the handbook both distinctive as well as comprehensive. We hope that readers agree.

Topics

The handbook is structured into six sections under which are grouped the individual chapters that address the state of play in each sub-field (though some sub-fields are addressed by more than one chapter). The book begins with a section on the different theoretical approaches that have been employed in recent years, starting with an approach based on political theory and moving on through the sociological, rational choice and institutionalist approaches, each of these giving rise to somewhat different research questions addressed by somewhat different methodologies. The strategy here is deliberate. Too often in the past, political scientists have approached topics such as electoral behavior from only one perspective, perhaps grudgingly accepting that an alternative theoretical approach is needed to deal with effects that have not yet been fitted into their preferred worldview. In our view, the modern student of elections and public opinion needs to adopt a multi-perspective position, especially in light of fundamental changes over time in the relative importance of different causal mechanisms. Political circumstances evolve, and the approaches taken by political scientists need to evolve in step. These chapters help illuminate what for many are a priori assumptions. Why, for example, might we consider that electoral systems would have an effect on voter behavior? And why might a person's social circumstances be in any way relevant to their political opinions? What is the underlying theoretical position suggesting that parties are likely to compete for the much vaunted "center ground"?

From there the handbook dives straight into the question of why people vote and what determines how many of them do so, using each of the theoretical approaches already introduced in the first section. From there it moves in much the same fashion into the determinants of vote choice, with two sets of themes on this topic – the first focusing on long-term factors such as social cleavages and partisanship and the second focusing on short-term factors such as government performance, strategic voting and economic voting.

The handbook then moves on to considering the role of context, focusing on the institutional, systemic, social, technological and electoral context. We then look at public opinion: its nature, the problems involved in understanding its effects, and its impact. The handbook ends with a long section on methodological challenges and new developments. Again, the inclusion of this last section is quite deliberate. As the handbook shows, the discipline has made significant advances over the last seven decades. And there is no better indication of the intellectual health of the discipline than the recognition of what our data can and can't tell us and how new methodological and technological developments can be harnessed to further enhance our – and the rest of the world's – understanding. Political science must not stand still. What our authors show is that the methods that political scientists have adopted have shaped how people think about explanations. Political science has indeed not stood still. As this book shows, in response to criticism, it has significantly diversified the way we collect data, from cross-sectional survey, to longitudinal surveys; from big data to experimental methods. Far from political science being in crisis, this book is testament to its rude health in studies of public opinion, voting and elections more generally.

Scholars are increasingly expected to engage with non-academic audiences and we are confident that political science is well positioned to address this need. This is no more apparent than during election campaigns, when experts in voting behavior are often required to become on-hand media pundits. The challenge for political science is that while the media are keen on providing predictions, scientific findings tend not to be obtained before Election Day but rather in the months and years which follow (see, however, Chapter 39 by Stephen D. Fisher on election forecasting in this handbook). Elections are increasingly difficult to predict. What the chapters in this handbook demonstrate, however, is that research in elections, voting and public opinion has produced, and continues to produce, a strong base of knowledge which can inform the public debate in meaningful and important ways.

Focus

The handbook sets out to address the fundamental question of how elections serve as the instruments that enable public opinion to be channeled by parties into decisions as to who will constitute the government and what policies that government will pursue. But we hope the handbook will do more than that. When reading this book, either as selected chapters or as a whole, there are some important questions that will give pause for thought. We focus here on six key areas:

First, macro and micro level explanations do not speak with each other as frequently as they might, or perhaps, should. Neither the characteristics of individual citizens, nor the macro economic, social and political conditions alone can fully explain election outcomes. Yet many studies – including those described in this volume – have focused either on the social-psychological determinants of voter behavior, or on the role of (aggregate) national and institutional characteristics on election outcomes, without attempting to bridge the two. We need to feel much freer to move between levels of analysis and of conceptualization than has been customary in past political science research. This handbook perhaps does not constitute much of a corrective since it summarizes that past research, yet we try to ensure that its authors are transparent about limitations deriving from the approaches that they report. Recently we have seen an increase in "contextual" approaches to election studies which recognize the interplay between individual citizens on the one hand and the social, economic and political context on the other and these also feature in many of the chapters in this volume.

Second, the handbook covers a literature spanning more than fifty years and during that time some ideas have come and gone whilst others have remained remarkably persistent. To a large extent, these shifts in the dominant paradigm in the study of elections and voters have reflected more-or-less secular trends in some of the phenomena under study: for example, the increasing volatility of voters, the weakening of social cleavages in determining party support, and the decline of party identification. These fundamental changes in context have meant that the applicability of different theories and models has also changed. This does not mean some models are right and that others are wrong, but rather that there is no one-size-fits-all model. Citizens are heterogeneous across space and time and our theory and models of electoral behavior should reflect that.

Third, in some ways, change can be helpful, giving us leverage in determining the importance of the factors that change. But in other ways change creates much potential for confusion unless scholars are very clear about what period they are thinking of in regard to different research questions. This complication is made worse by the fact that political realities do not necessarily evolve at the same rates or in the same directions in different countries. In this handbook, we have taken especial care to ensure that different chapters, in which scholars may have different periods in mind, speak to each other across the potential gulfs involved. We have tried to do the same regarding divisions between different theoretical approaches (which often are coterminous with temporal gulfs), as mentioned earlier.

Fourth, public opinion is a powerful influence both on election outcomes and on government actions between elections. Parties look to public opinion when deciding what policies will be attractive to voters and governments look to public opinion for guidance regarding the generality (and often even the details) of public policy. Yet much doubt surrounds the question of whether the public is sufficiently sophisticated (in terms of both information and cognitive skills) to provide the guidance that party and government leaders look for.

Fifth, turnout is a vitally important contributor to election results, since levels of turnout can skew electoral outcomes – often in very unexpected ways. This was really well illustrated by one of the great political earthquakes of 2016, the Brexit referendum in the UK, which delivered a higher turnout than any general election since 1992 because the Leave campaign managed to mobilize so many citizens who would not normally cast a ballot. It is well established that some groups are normally under-represented among voters (see Eric Plutzer's chapter, Chapter 6). Turnout has the potential to skew outcomes against clear sections of the population, particularly if politicians and parties adjust public policies accordingly. Age is a good example here. Because it takes time for younger voters to acquire habits of party support, older voters are commonly much more likely to vote and many governments as a partial consequence have struggled to confront future problems in pensions and health care. Such examples illustrate the potential for differential turnout to skew not only election results, but also public policy – often in favor of already privileged social groups. Such outcomes inevitably raise the question of whether voting should be a requirement of citizenship – not so much to compel citizens to act in a particular way, but to help ensure that election outcomes better reflect the average citizen's preferences and that the benefits of public policies are less asymmetrically distributed.

Finally, the question raised regarding turnout reflects a broader issue, which we hope will stimulate thought and debate – the extent to which citizens have democratic obligations as well as democratic rights. For example, if turnout is low, or the quality of campaign debate substandard, the fault is assumed to lie with the parties, candidates or media messengers. From this perspective, it is the responsibility of parties, politicians and governments to set the parameters and tone of the debate and to ensure that citizens are adequately informed. But, there is a strong case that citizens should play less of a passive role, taking responsibility for being better informed and holding politicians to account, along lines implicit in Wlezien's chapter (Chapter 32; cf. Bølstad's chapter, Chapter 30). This has never been more the case than in the new era of so-called "post-truth" politics in which apparently false or "fake news" is spread by citizens or possibly even government agencies via social media. This tendency, as Semetko and Tworzecki's chapter reveals (Chapter 24), may in fact point to an important new reverse trend and "fourth wave" in election campaigning whereby practices honed in the newer democracies are adopted by voters, parties and candidates in more established polities.

On the broader question of responsibility for the problems we now witness in contemporary democracies, it is clear that political scientists differ as to who they regard as the chief "culprits." However, one consistent line of argument within scholarship on elections, voting behavior and public opinion (and one that is certainly present in the chapters comprising this edited volume) is that to understand election outcomes and their impact on social well-being one must look at both political supply and public demand. As our authors here and more generally in the field make clear, a two-way relationship exists between the choices made by citizens and what the parties offer. That is, the choice sets open to voters are constrained and shaped by the strategic decisions made by parties and candidates in terms of the amount of policy differentiation. At the same time, parties are hemmed in by the ideological preferences of their grass-roots and of the electorate at large, and by pressure to achieve electoral success. Thus, the professionalization of parties and increased focus on stylistic issues of image management, while no doubt driven by the understanding that voters do not respond well to divided parties, present a challenge to their credentials as authentic representatives committed to a core set of principles. As well as being interdependent, the opportunity structures and choices faced by both political parties and voters are shaped by systemic factors including electoral rules and systems. Our goal is to ensure this volume adequately reflects that tension, giving regard to parties, voters and the wider electoral context. In doing this, we hope that this handbook shows how political science makes a significant contribution to our understanding of these tensions, but also how it helps us arrive at some possible solutions.

Reference

Achen, C. H. and Bartels, L. M. (2016) *Democracy for Realists: Why Elections Do Not Produce Responsive Government*, Princeton: Princeton University Press.

PART I

Theoretical approaches to the study of voter behavior

1

DEMOCRATIC THEORY AND ELECTORAL BEHAVIOR[1]

Ian McAllister

Normatively, democracy is a system of institutions, procedures and conventions. In practice, however, democracy is nothing without the citizens who provide it with form and substance. At democracy's core are the beliefs, behavior and actions of citizens who make up the actual or potential democratic polity. As Angus Campbell and his colleagues put it in the seminal *The American Voter* study, "our approach is in the main dependent on the point of view of the actor" (Campbell et al. 1960: 27). Placing the citizen at the core of our understanding of democracy therefore provides a different perspective on how democracy operates, how it is changing, and perhaps most important of all, how it may change in the future. The purpose of this chapter is to outline how recent advances in the study of electoral behavior are altering democratic theory.

The backdrop to understanding the role that electoral behavior plays in shaping democratic theory is the rapid post-war advances in social science methodology. These advances have made it possible to explore, among other things: what citizens understand about democracy and what their expectations of it are; how citizens behave within a democracy and the political consequences of their behaviors; and what political actions citizens might take under certain hypothetical conditions. The rise of public opinion surveys in the 1950s and 1960s provided an early and strong empirical base for analyzing these changes. Based on more than half a century of opinion research, we know an immense amount about how citizens think and behave politically.

In contrast to much recent research, many of the early scholars of political behavior were as interested in the normative implications of their work as they were in its substantive findings. Bernard Berelson's famous 1952 *Public Opinion Quarterly* article first gave voice to this approach by arguing that "opinion research can help a democracy to know itself, evaluate its achievements, and bring its practices more nearly in accord with its own fundamental ideals" (Berelson 1952: 313).[2] Another earlier pioneer of this approach was V. O. Key, who was particularly concerned about the role of public opinion in constraining political elites, and about elite responsiveness to citizen demands (Key 1966).

Despite this early and vigorous attempt to integrate theory with empirical research, it is fair to say that democratic theory, with some notable exceptions, has signally failed to keep pace with advances in electoral behavior.[3] Rather than post-war advances in methodology heralding a new collaboration between theorists and behaviorists, both sides have largely followed independent intellectual paths. The first section of this chapter examines how we define democracy as it relates to electoral behavior, while the second section focuses on the consequences of electoral system design for behavior and theory. The third section examines four fields of electoral behavior which have specific implications for democratic theory, while the conclusion highlights the benefits of a closer relationship between behavioral and normative approaches to democracy.

Defining democracy

Before we can evaluate how advances in electoral behavior affect democratic theory, we need to arrive at an understanding of what is meant by democracy, and what constitutes its main components. Such an exercise has obviously occupied many academic studies and a review of the relevant literature is beyond the scope of this chapter. Briefly, we can identify two general approaches.

The first approach is to see democracy in terms of institutions and procedures. One of the earliest expressions was Schumpeter's (1976 [1942]) definition of democracy as a competitive struggle for the popular vote. This view was further developed by Robert Dahl (1971), who saw democracy as involving contestation or competition on the one hand, and participation or inclusion on the other. Later studies have focused on outcomes, such as freedom and liberty, which can be defined in terms of the legal protections that citizens rely on (for reviews, see Diamond 1999; Ringen 2009).[4] Whatever the focus, electoral behavior has relatively little role to play in this approach since it sees democracy as consisting of a framework of rules, rather than as a pattern of behavior.

A second approach has viewed democracy in terms of the social benefits that it can deliver, such as providing access to welfare and ensuring a basic standard of living. This view that democracy acts as a social safety net has been especially popular in low-income societies; there it is argued that political rights are meaningless in the absence of clearly demarcated social rights (see, for example, Przeworski 1985). Moreover, following Sen's (1999) argument that democracy is more likely to increase living standards compared to other systems – since governments will have an electoral incentive to ensure fewer of its citizens remain in poverty – political and economic freedoms are often bracketed together. In this approach, too, behavior is seen to be of secondary importance to democracy when compared to social and economic performance.

One response to these varying definitions of democracy, and the implication that citizen opinions and behaviors are of secondary importance, has been to ask citizens themselves what they understand by the concept of democracy (Dalton, Shin and Jou 2007). This research has found that the public's understanding of democracy is driven as much by political history as by a society's economic development. Another response has been to use large-scale comparative surveys to measure various aspects of democracy (see Elkins 2000; Munck and Verkuilen 2002). Ferrín and Kriesi (2015), for example, show that Europeans mostly associate democracy with the rule of law and with free and fair elections. However, much of this research has been concerned with methodology rather than conceptualization. This has resulted in a poor fit between the normative and empirical aspects of democracy, and makes it difficult to arrive at agreed measures of democratic performance.

The approach taken by these studies is to define liberal democracy in terms of four key concepts which relate directly to electoral institutions; all four also overlap to a greater or lesser degree. First, *accountability* ensures that citizens can use regular elections to hold governments responsible for their performance while in office. Following O'Donnell (1998), vertical accountability is often distinguished from horizontal accountability. The former refers to the ability to hold elected representatives publicly accountable for their decisions while in office (Schedler 1999; Schmitter and Karl 1991), while the latter refers to the ability of government agencies to sanction one another for breaches of law or procedure. The ability of citizens in this way to steer governments toward policies they prefer has been a preoccupation of a large literature on dynamic representation (sometimes referred to as "thermostatic governance").[5]

The second aspect of democracy is *responsible government*, which means that governments are appointed by a popularly elected legislature, remain answerable to them and can be removed from office by them. This system had its roots in the nineteenth-century Westminster system of government. In the mid-twentieth century, the concept of responsible government was revised to take into account a third aspect of democracy: *political parties*. In this approach, political parties are identified as the central agents of mass mobilization and the mechanism through which the system of responsible government operates (American Political Science Association 1950). In turn, responsible party government exists to ensure that the system performs to the satisfaction of its citizens; thus *system performance* is the fourth aspect of democracy focused on in this chapter. Before turning to how advances in electoral behavior have revised these four key concepts of democracy, the next section examines the key role of the electoral system and its impact on political behavior.

Electoral systems and democracy

What citizens think about democracy is agreed to be a key driver of the health of a democracy. If citizens are generally supportive of democracy, then it should thrive; if citizens are equivocal, then democracy may be under threat, particularly during periods of existential crisis. A large literature has examined public opinion during the transition from authoritarianism to democracy – what is called the process of democratic consolidation (see, for example, Bratton, Mattes and Gyimah-Boadi 2004; Diamond 1999). Once citizens come to hold a widespread view that democracy is what Linz and Stepan (1996: 5) characterize as "the only game in town," then it can be properly said to have consolidated. But what constitutes widespread public support for democracy? And what are its mainsprings and how does public support vary according to differing institutional arrangements?

While scholars disagree about many aspects of public support for democracy, there is broad agreement that popular support for democracy is a highly complex phenomenon which is in a constant state of change (Klingemann 1999). This is especially the case in new democracies, which frequently retain elements of authoritarianism and where the norms, values and practices of democracy are often unfamiliar to many citizens. Measuring public support for democracy is therefore complex, and has to take into account different histories, cultures and institutional settings. Much of this complexity can be reduced to the distinction between whether the electoral system is majoritarian or proportional in its design. This is a distinction that was first highlighted by Lijphart (1999), who showed that it had particular consequences for the public's views of democracy.

In the majoritarian model of government, the goal of the political system is to satisfy the demands of the majority of the electorate, and the selection of a government becomes the first priority of the electoral system. The majority controls the government through two mechanisms. The first is by providing the government with a mandate, so that they have the popularly-derived authority to implement the legislative program on which they won the election. The second mechanism is via accountability, so that political elites are held accountable by citizens for their actions while in office. These mechanisms have been criticized by electoral behavior scholars as unrealistic in terms of how party policies guide voters' choices, and because winning parties rarely secure support from a majority of the electorate (see Thomassen 1994, 2014).[6]

In contrast to the majoritarian model, a proportional model of government is based on the assumption that elections produce elected representatives who reflect as closely as possible the characteristics of the electorate. Since it is rare under such a system for one party to achieve a governing majority, it is almost always the case that two or more parties must come together to form a governing coalition. An inevitable consequence of coalition government is that clarity of responsibility becomes blurred since it is never clear which party has been responsible for government policy (Aarts and Thomassen 2008). The ability of citizens to deliver an electoral reward or punishment for government performance is therefore weakened.

How do these two models of government shape the public's view of democracy? This question has generated considerable research. In general, proportional or consensual models of government seem to work more efficiently than majoritarian models, at least from the electorate's perspective. Powell (2000) argues that if elections are seen as a mechanism for linking citizen preferences with government outcomes, then the proportional model is more effective. Lijphart (1999) comes to similar conclusions, and he finds that the public's satisfaction with their democracy is around 17 percentage points higher in proportional systems compared to majoritarian ones (see also Klingemann 1999, but cf. Aarts and Thomassen 2008).

Along with the public's views of democracy, voting rules also have a wide range of consequences for electoral behavior. However, the interactions are complex and often intertwined with a country's history and culture (for reviews, see Klingemann 1999; Norris 2004). In general, majoritarian systems have higher thresholds for election, which encourages political parties to aggregate their support and adopt a "catch-all" strategy in seeking votes. In proportional systems, the threshold for election is usually lower, which produces a larger number of parties that are then encouraged to pursue a narrower base of support around a more particularistic range of issues. This, in turn, has consequences for how parties mobilize opinion, and for partisanship, which is generally weaker in countries with multiple parties. This can lead to higher levels of electoral volatility (see Heath, this volume; Bowler, this volume).

Electoral behavior and democracy

While the framework of democratic theory is ever changing, this chapter argues that our understanding of citizens' behavior and attitudes has advanced at a much greater pace. The period that has elapsed since the start of the quantitative revolution in the study of electoral behavior in the 1950s has resulted in numerous insights, and the last two decades have seen an unprecedented increase in the breadth and depth of such studies. Space prevents a detailed consideration of this research, but four areas are outlined here where developments have already fundamentally revised current theoretical approaches to democracy, or are likely to in the future. For each of these four areas, an outline of the findings of recent studies is provided, together with an evaluation of how and in what ways they influence democratic theory.

Political competency

One of the assumptions of liberal democratic theory is the existence of a competent electorate which is capable of making informed choices. Without a competent electorate, the public's ability to use elections to hold governments accountable for their performance while in office will be limited. This, in turn, will undermine the core assumptions of a liberal democracy. As Berelson, Lazarsfeld and McPhee (1966: 308) put it half a century ago:

> The democratic citizen is expected to be well informed about political affairs ... to know what the issues are, what their history is, what the relevant facts are, what alternatives are proposed, what the party stands for, what the likely consequences are.

This optimistic view of the public's political competency has been challenged by the evidence. Ever since opinion surveys began to collect information on political knowledge in the 1940s, a consistent finding has been that most citizens are anything but knowledgeable about politics (for a review, see Delli Carpini and Keeter 1996). Most citizens know little about politics and possess minimal factual information about the operation of the political system. Moreover, these persistently low levels of political knowledge have been impervious to advances in civic education, the huge post-war expansion of tertiary education and an increasingly sophisticated mass media.

One theoretical response to the lack of competency among the mass public is democratic elitism. The most famous advocate of this theory, Joseph Schumpeter (1976 [1942]), argued that democratic electorates were too ill-informed and superficial to identify the common good and that, as a result, citizens should be restricted to a single, periodic choice between competing elites. This view was supported by later empirical research by Herbert McCloskey (1964: 374), who argued that political elites "serve as the major repositories of the public conscience and as carriers of the Creed." In short, the role of citizens should be restricted to voting for members of competing political elites and they should have no role in the complexities of policy making.

In parallel with the research on political knowledge, a large literature has examined the level of political sophistication within the electorate. While much of the literature is discordant and has focused on different ways of measuring the concept of sophistication (see, for example, Luskin 1990), there is a dominant view that, while citizens may possess low levels of political knowledge, they are nevertheless able to reach well-informed judgments about leaders and issue positions based on limited information. Key (1966: 7) put it succinctly when he commented that "voters are not fools." In this view, then, citizens can still make balanced decisions on the basis of minimal information (see Bølstad in this volume; Erikson in this volume).

Serving to increase political competency among the public is the rise of educational attainments across almost all of the advanced democracies (Highton 2009). In addition to better cognitive skills, studies have also shown that election campaigns provide an important source of political information and learning for voters (Arceneaux 2006; Erikson and Wlezien 2012), with campaigns providing particularly useful information on economic matters. Leaders' debates conducted during campaigns are also an important source of information, particularly if the debate is held earlier in the campaign and if one or more of the leaders are unfamiliar to voters (Benoit and Hansen 2006).

The internet

Arguably the internet represents the greatest change to the political systems of the advanced societies since democratization. Traditional accounts of political communication show that the advent of television fundamentally changed the nature of politics in the 1960s and 1970s. It is now becoming clear that the internet will reshape the operation of the modern political system in ways which are at least as profound as television half a century earlier. More importantly, the interactivity of the internet has major consequences for democratic theory and will fundamentally alter how parties and voters view politics (for reviews, see Bimber 2003; Coleman and Blumler 2009; Farrell 2012). Three major political implications of the internet are examined here: democratic competency; e-voting; and e-participation.

In principle, the internet should deliver higher democratic competency by providing greater access to political information; this is reflected in the transition from a low-choice media environment to a high-choice one. For most of the post-war period, there were relatively few choices in whatever media sources citizens preferred, whether it was newspapers, radio or TV. The net effect was that citizens were exposed to low but constant levels of political information, which could not be ignored save for avoiding the media altogether (Prior 2007). The effect of this exposure was a low but consistent level of political involvement, which provided a degree of stability.

The rise of the internet has disrupted this decades-long stable relationship between voters and parties. Citizens now have unprecedented choice in the political information that they choose to access: at one extreme, citizens may choose to access no information; at another extreme, they can access highly detailed information for 24 hours a day. In many cases, the information that they choose to access reinforces rather than challenges their views. The interactivity, which is integral to the internet, means that citizens can increasingly have their views heard, rather than simply being passive recipients of information. Since internet use is disproportionately concentrated among the young, it provides a unique opportunity to convey political information to a group whose knowledge is low. A range of studies have confirmed that the internet is indeed having a significant impact on the levels of political information and democratic competency among the young (Gibson and McAllister 2015a; Gronlund 2007).

E-voting or digital democracy is a second area in which the internet can change democratic politics. With the ability to consult citizens about legislative changes interactively, the internet could in principle undermine the need for representative democracy altogether. The traditional objection to e-voting, the lack of internet security, is rapidly being solved by technological change (Lindner, Aichholzer and Hennen 2016). Studies have, however, focused less on giving citizens a direct say in decision-making through the internet and more on the development of online communications. This often occurs through the creation of virtual public spaces where citizens can exchange ideas and preferences, occasionally with the involvement of elected representatives (Coleman and Shane 2012).

Third, the internet facilitates interactive e-participation, to a degree that is unparalleled in modern times – almost akin to a continuous town hall meeting in the nineteenth century. Political parties have been slow to exploit this new opportunity for mobilization and conversion. Initial studies suggested that the major parties dominated the area, with their ability to design sophisticated multifunctional websites that delivered more information and greater opportunities for participation and financial donations (Schweitzer 2008). More recent research has shown that minor parties, such as those stressing the environment, have become highly effective in promoting e-participation, reflecting the medium's low entry costs (Gibson and McAllister 2015b).

Globalization

Vertical accountability in democracies depends on elections that are free, fair and competitive. Citizens then make judgments about the performance of governments while in office and, on that basis, can choose to either reward or punish them. But what if government performance has been shaped by factors that are outside the government's control? Globalization presents just such a challenge for democracy, since a country's economic performance may have been influenced by international events and policies, perhaps thousands of miles away, which are not under the control of the national government.

In practice, of course, a government can always shape policy outcomes to some degree. For example, even during the 2007–08 global financial crisis a government could be judged on its policy responses to the crisis, even though the crisis itself originated internationally. But when decision-making transcends the nation-state, it raises questions about how and under what circumstances transnational institutions can be held accountable to the people whose lives they affect (Sperling 2009: 8). Should a European government be punished for poor economic performance when the economic crisis that caused it began in the United States? Such questions raise fundamental issues for our ideas of accountability which are at the core of liberal democracy theory.

One case of democratic accountability within a global context is economic voting. A large literature has demonstrated that voters make judgments at elections about the economic performance of incumbent governments (for reviews see Duch and Stevenson 2008; Lewis–Beck and Stegmaier 2007). Such judgments can be made retrospectively or prospectively, and can be about citizens' own household economies ("egocentric") or about the nation's economy as a whole ("sociotropic"). However, if citizens do not see their national government as instrumental in shaping economic performance ("attribution"), and instead see international and/or market forces as being the important determinants, then accountability through the mechanism of an election cannot take place.

Studies suggest that globalization does indeed influence how voters approach accountability. Hellwig and Samuels (2007: 283; see also Kayser 2007) analyzed elections from 75 countries over 27 years to show that "exposure to the world economy weakens connections between economic performance and support for political incumbents." Other work has indicated that parties may adapt their positions in response to changing economic conditions. In particular, political incumbents are more likely to move toward the positions of their political opponents, thus blurring accountability and avoiding potential blame for a poorly performing economy (Hellwig 2011, 2016). The net effect is that voters have reduced information about who to blame or reward for economic performance.

A second example in which international changes are affecting traditional views of democratic accountability is the growth of governance beyond the nation-state, what is variously termed "transnational" or "supranational" governance. An example of such a change is the European Union, which exercises an increasing amount of power among its members over what were once exclusively domestic issues.[7] Such advances leave a "democratic accountability deficit" which is difficult to fill; remedial measures include greater openness and transparency in decision-making; clearer identification of decision-makers so that they can be held to account; and regular EU elections (Curtin, Mair and Papadopoulos 2010). However, even in the case of elections, they rarely act as sanctions since votes against the incumbent government are often difficult for political leaders to interpret (Hobolt, Spoon and Tilley 2009).

Party decline

Political parties act as a crucial linkage between citizens and policy outputs, through their ability to organize what Neumann (1956: 397) has called "the chaotic public will." In this view, parties are central to the model of responsible party government first articulated by the American Political Science Association's Committee on Political Parties in 1950. The apparent decline of political parties appears to undermine this ability to ensure accountability through elections. Mair (2005: 7) has noted the failure of parties "to engage ordinary citizens" and as evidence to support his case highlights declining electoral turnout, the rise of voter volatility, falling levels of party identification and the dramatic decline in party membership. Indeed, party membership is now so low in many countries that parties "have all but abandoned any pretensions to being mass organizations" (van Biezen, Mair and Poguntke 2012: 42).[8]

All of these trends – which are largely uncontested in the literature – would suggest that, at the very least, political parties are experiencing significant change, with major implications for the operation of liberal democracy (for a review, see Webb 2005). One consequence is a weakening link between the citizen and the government, with elections becoming less effective as a mechanism for holding governments to account. If this link were to significantly weaken, it would undermine the whole system of responsible party government.

Various objections have been made against the decline of parties thesis (for a review, see Dalton, Farrell and McAllister 2011). One objection is that, while the long-term trends show decline, the patterns are more modest than many have suggested. For example, while voter turnout has declined, it is often from a relatively high base, and in some countries has now begun to increase (Franklin 2004). A second objection is that parties have, in fact, been in decline in terms of their membership since the "golden age" of the mass party, which was first popularized by Duverger (1964). Parties may therefore be returning to a "steady state" level of mass membership following an abnormal heyday.

While overstating the trends is one argument against the decline of parties thesis, more important is the view that parties have begun to adapt to these changes (Dalton, Farrell and McAllister 2011: Chapter 9; Mair 2003). In response to an existential electoral threat, many parties have radically altered their policy appeals. This was the route the British Labour Party took in the early 1990s when it was rebranded as "New Labour" under the leadership of Tony Blair. The party ditched its outmoded class appeal and instead stressed equality of opportunity, thus skillfully retaining Labour's traditional working class supporters while recruiting disaffected Conservative voters. There are numerous other examples around the world of this form of party adaptation.

A second form of party adaption has been organizational. One approach has been to democratize the selection of the party leader, as has occurred, for example, in the British Labour Party. Giving the mass membership a greater say in the selection of the leader has been seen as one way of trying to arrest the decline in the mass party membership. However, the risk is that the membership will select a leader who is attractive to their own (more extreme) policy positions, but not to that of the median voter. The British Labour Party membership's two-time election of the left-wing Jeremy Corbyn as its leader is a case in point.

Another party tactic has been to exploit the rise of television through the promotion of leaders with attractive visual images and sophisticated communication skills. While there is a vigorous debate about the veracity of the "personalization of politics" thesis (McAllister 2007; Karvonen 2010), there is little dispute that a popular leader can communicate a party's message more effectively than a policy statement. In turn, voters prefer to hold a personality accountable for performance rather than an abstract entity such as a political party. And not least, a popular leader can appeal to the public over the heads of their political party. Such a tactic can be particularly effective when the leader runs into resistance from their party about strategy and direction.

Finally, parties have sought to redesign political institutions – "the rules of the political game" – with the aim of excluding competitors, such as newly emerging parties which could erode the party's electoral base. This interpretation of party adaptation has been most closely associated with Katz and Mair's (1995) "cartel party" model. In this view, major parties often collude in order to change the rules to best serve their interests and to exclude potential competitors. The best example of cartel behavior by the major political parties is the allocation of state finance for political parties, with the rules typically designed to exclude new entrants.

Conclusion

With some notable exceptions, democratic theory has tended to focus on the role of institutions and procedures, rather than on patterns of political behavior. Yet, it is the attitudes and behavior of citizens that give democracy form and meaning, so understanding how these attitudes and behaviors are shaped should inform our current understanding of theory. To date, this complementarity has not taken place, and research on democratic theory and research on political behavior have largely followed their own, independent paths. This chapter has examined how advances in electoral behavior across four main areas – political competence, the internet, globalization and party decline – present challenges to our current thinking about democratic theory.

A central theme of this chapter has been that democratic theory has been slow to respond to advances in our understanding of electoral behavior. This is understandable; the formulation of a theory requires the accumulation of a robust body of evidence that largely reaches similar conclusions. When this condition is met, theory can be revised. In many areas of electoral behavior, this requirement is as yet unfulfilled; we know, for example, that citizens have low levels of political knowledge, but views are divided on whether this ultimately affects the quality of the choices that citizens make at the ballot box. Similarly, we know that most indicators of the health of political parties are in long-term decline, but we also know that parties are beginning to adapt to these changes. In short, much of the empirical evidence that might result in revisions to democratic theory is, at a minimum, contestable.

Where there is broad agreement in the electoral research, there are clear implications for democratic theory. We know, for example, that citizens are more likely to use elections to reward governments, based on sound performance, rather than to punish them. This has implications for the operation of accountability and responsible party government. We also know that citizens support greater political involvement through the internet and the opportunity to have an enhanced say in government decision-making. This has implications for theories of representation, and for democratic elitism. In these and a host of other areas of electoral research, advances in our understanding of the attitudes and behavior of citizens have major implications for democratic theory.

Above all of these debates is the relentless pace of technological change, which is rapidly changing most of the assumptions on which liberal democratic theory rests. The advent of television in the 1960s was one of the main drivers of the personalization of politics, which has arguably fundamentally changed its nature. The rise of the internet will result in political changes that are expected to be many times more profound than television. The immediacy, interconnectivity and information-sharing that the internet brings to politics have implications for all aspects of democracy, from the accountability of governments to citizen competence and political participation, to responsible party government. How institutions and actors respond to these profound changes will shape twenty-first century democratic theory.

Notes

1 I am indebted to Keith Dowding for insightful comments on an earlier draft of the chapter. Also thanks to Rachel Gibson and the other editors for their valuable comments.

2 The tools of social research have made it possible, for the first time, to determine with reasonable precision and objectivity the extent to which the practice of politics by the citizens of a democratic state conforms to the requirements and the assumptions of the theory of democratic politics (insofar as it refers to decisions by the electorate). (Berelson 1952: 314)

3 There are, of course, exceptions to this. Prominent theorists who have made extensive use of empirical material relating to electoral behavior include Fishkin (1995) and Brennan and Lomasky (1993).

4 There is also a large literature dealing with the fairness and integrity of electoral practices, which is not considered here. (See Norris in this volume for an overview.)

5 For a seminal, wide-ranging and authoritative survey of this literature, see Franklin, Soroka and Wlezien (2014).

6 A further criticism of the clarity of responsibility mechanisms is when a governing party changes its policy position after an election (Quinn 2016).

7 Other examples include the G20 of nations or the United Nations.

8 A contrary argument is that formal membership figures are not a reliable measure of party health, since they largely ignore non-members who are nevertheless supporters. See Fisher, Fieldhouse and Cutts (2014) and Gauja (2015). Declining partisanship and increased volatility are viewed as by-products of other developments by van der Brug and Franklin (in this volume).

References

Aarts, K. and Thomassen, J. (2008) "Satisfaction with Democracy: Do Institutions Matter?" *Electoral Studies*, vol. 27, no. 1, March, 5–18.

American Political Science Association (1950) "Toward a More Responsible Two-Party System: A Report of the Committee on Political Parties," *American Political Science Review*, vol. 39, no. 11, December, 581–582.

Arceneaux, K. (2006) "Do Campaigns Help Voters Learn? A Cross-National Analysis," *British Journal of Political Science*, vol. 36, no. 1, January, 159–173.

Benoit, W. L. and Hansen, G. J. (2006) "Presidential Debate Watching, Issue Knowledge, Character Evaluation, and Vote Choice," *Human Communication Research*, vol. 30, no. 1, January, 121–144.

Berelson, B. R. (1952) "Democratic Theory and Public Opinion," *Public Opinion Quarterly*, vol. 16, no. 3, Autumn, 313–330.

Berelson, B. R., Lazarsfeld, P. F. and McPhee, W. N. (1966) *Voting*, Chicago: University of Chicago Press.

Biezen, I. van, Mair, P. and Poguntke, T. (2012) "Going, Going, … Gone? The Decline of Party Membership in Contemporary Europe," *European Journal of Political Research*, vol. 51, no. 1, January, 24–56.

Bimber, B. (2003) *Information and American Democracy: Technology in the Evolution of Political Power*, Cambridge: Cambridge University Press.

Bratton, M., Mattes, R. and Gyimah-Boadi, E. (2004) *Public Opinion, Democracy, and Market Reform in Africa*, New York: Cambridge University Press.

Brennan, G. and Lomasky, L. (1993) *Democracy and Decision: The Pure Theory of Electoral Preference*, Cambridge: Cambridge University Press.

Campbell, A., Converse, E., Miller, W. and Stokes, D. (1960) *The American Voter*, Chicago: University of Chicago Press.

Coleman, S. and Blumler, J. G. (2009) *The Internet and Democratic Citizenship: Theory, Practice and Policy*, Cambridge: Cambridge University Press.

Coleman, S. and Shane, P. M. (eds.) (2012) *Connecting Democracy: Online Consultation and the Flow of Political Communication*, Cambridge, Mass: MIT Press.

Curtin, D., Mair, P. and Papadopoulos, Y. (2010) "Positioning Accountability in European Governance: An Introduction," *West European Politics*, vol. 33, no. 5, August, 929–945.

Dahl, R. (1971) *Polyarchy*, New Haven: Yale University Press.

Dalton, R. J., Farrell, D. M. and McAllister, I. (2011) *Political Parties and Democratic Linkage: How Parties Organize Democracy*, Oxford: Oxford University Press.

Dalton, R. J., Shin, D. C. and Jou, W. (2007) "Understanding Democracy: Data from Unlikely Places," *Journal of Democracy*, vol. 18, no. 4, October, 142–156.

Delli Carpini, M. X. and Keeter, S. (1996) *What Americans Know About Politics and Why It Matters*, New Haven: Yale University Press.

Diamond, L. (1999) *Developing Democracy: Toward Consolidation*, Baltimore: Johns Hopkins University Press.

Duch, R. M. and Stevenson, R. T. (2008) *The Economic Vote: How Political and Economic Institutions Condition Election Results*, New York: Cambridge University Press.

Duverger, M. (1964) *Political Parties*, London: Methuen.

Elkins, Z. (2000) "Gradations of Democracy? Empirical Tests of Alternative Conceptualizations," *American Journal of Political Science*, vol. 44, no. 2, April, 287–294.

Erikson, R. S. and Wlezien, C. (2012) *The Timeline of Presidential Elections: How Campaigns Do (and Do Not) Matter*, Chicago: University of Chicago Press.

Farrell, H. (2012) "The Consequences of the Internet for Politics," *Annual Review of Political Science*, vol. 15, June, 35–52.

Ferrín, M. and Kriesi, H. (2015) "Democracy – the European Verdict," in Ferrín, M. and Kriesi, H. (eds.) *How Europeans View and Evaluate Democracy*, Oxford: Oxford University Press: 1–20.

Fisher, J., Fieldhouse, E. and Cutts, D. (2014) "Members Are Not the Only Fruit: Volunteer Activity in British Political Parties at the 2010 General Election," *British Journal of Politics and International Relations*, vol. 16, no. 1, January, 75–95.

Fishkin, J. S. (1995) *The Voice of the People: Public Opinion and Democracy*, New Haven: Yale University Press.

Franklin, M. N. (2004) *Voter Turnout and the Dynamics of Electoral Competition in Established Democracies Since 1945*, Cambridge: Cambridge University Press.

Franklin, M. N., Soroka, S. and Wlezien, C. (2014) "Elections," in Bovens, M., Goodin, R. E. and Schillemans, T. (eds.) *The Oxford Handbook of Public Accountability*, Oxford: Oxford University Press: 389–404.

Gauja, A. (2015) "The Construction of Party Membership," *European Journal of Political Research*, vol. 54, no. 2, May, 232–248.

Gibson, R. and McAllister, I. (2015a) "New Media, Elections and the Political Knowledge Gap in Australia," *Journal of Sociology*, vol. 51, no. 2, June, 337–353.

Gibson, R. and McAllister, I. (2015b) "Normalizing or Equalizing Party Competition? Assessing the Impact of the Web on Election Campaigning," *Political Studies*, vol. 63, no. 3, August, 529–547.

Gronlund, K. (2007) "Knowing and Not Knowing: The Internet and Political Information," *Scandinavian Political Studies*, vol. 30, no. 3, September, 397–418.

Hellwig, T. (2011) "Constructing Accountability: Party Position Taking and Economic Voting," *Comparative Political Studies*, vol. 45, no. 1, December, 91–118.

Hellwig, T. (2016) "The Supply Side of Electoral Politics: How Globalization Matters for Public Policy," in Vowles, J. and Xezonakis, G. (eds.) *Globalization and Domestic Politics: Parties, Elections, and Public Opinion*, Oxford: Oxford University Press: 31–51.

Hellwig, T. and Samuels, D. (2007) "Voting in Open Economies: The Electoral Consequences of Globalization," *Comparative Political Studies*, vol. 40, no. 3, March, 283–306.

Highton, B. (2009) "Revisiting the Relationship Between Educational Attainment and Political Sophistication," *Journal of Politics*, vol. 71, no. 4, October, 1564–1576.

Hobolt, S. B., Spoon, J. and Tilley, J. (2009) "A Vote Against Europe? Explaining Defection at the 1999 and 2004 European Parliament Elections," *British Journal of Political Science*, vol. 39, no. 1, January, 93–115.

Karvonen, L. (2010) *The Personalisation of Politics: A Study of Parliamentary Democracies*, Colchester: ECPR Press.

Katz, R. S. and Mair, P. (1995) "Changing Models of Party Organization and Party Democracy: The Emergence of the Cartel Party," *Party Politics*, vol. 1, no. 1, January, 5–28.

Kayser, M. A. (2007) "How Domestic is Domestic Politics? Globalization and Elections," *Annual Review of Political Science*, vol. 10, June, 341–362.

Key, V. O. (1966) *The Responsible Electorate*, Cambridge, Mass: Harvard University Press.

Klingemann, H. (1999) *The Comparative Study of Electoral Systems*, Oxford: Oxford University Press.

Lewis-Beck, M. S. and Stegmaier, M. (2007) "Economic Models of Voting," in Dalton, R. J. and Klingemann, H. (eds.) *The Oxford Handbook of Political Behavior*, Oxford: Oxford University Press: 518–537.

Lijphart, A. (1999) *Patterns of Democracy: Government Forms and Performance in Thirty-Six Democracies*, New Haven: Yale University Press.

Lindner, R., Aichholzer, G. and Hennen, L. (eds.) (2016) *Electoral Democracy in Europe*, Geneva: Springer.

Linz, J. J. and Stepan, A. C. (1996) *Problems of Democratic Transition and Consolidation: Southern Europe, South America, and Post-Communist Europe*, Baltimore: Johns Hopkins University Press.

Luskin, R. C. (1990) "Explaining Political Sophistication," *Political Behavior*, vol. 12, no. 4, December, 331–361.

Mair, P. (2003) "Political Parties and Democracy: What Sort of Future?" *Central European Political Science Review*, vol. 4, May, 6–20.

Mair, P. (2005) "Democracy Beyond Parties," Unpublished Manuscript, University of California.

McAllister, I. (2007) "The Personalization of Politics," in Dalton, R. J. and Klingemann, H. (eds.) *Oxford Handbook of Political Behavior*, Oxford: Oxford University Press: 571–588.

McClosky, H. (1964) "Consensus and Ideology in American Politics," *American Political Science Review*, vol. 58, no. 2, June, 361–382.

Munck, G. L. and Verkuilen, J. (2002) "Conceptualizing and Measuring Democracy: Evaluating Alternative Indices," *Comparative Political Studies*, vol. 35, no. 1, February, 5–34.

Neumann, S. (1956) *Modern Political Parties*, Chicago: University of Chicago Press.

Norris, P. (2004) *Electoral Engineering: Voting Rules and Political Behavior*, Cambridge: Cambridge University Press.

O'Donnell, G. (1998) "Horizontal Accountability in New Democracies," *Journal of Democracy*, vol. 9, no. 3, July, 112–126.

Powell, G. B. (2000) *Elections as Instruments of Democracy: Majoritarian and Proportional Visions*, New Haven: Yale University Press.

Prior, M. (2007) *Post-Broadcast Democracy*, Cambridge: Cambridge University Press.

Przeworski, A. (1985) *Capitalism and Social Democracy*, Cambridge: Cambridge University Press.

Quinn, T. (2016) "Throwing the Rascals Out? Problems of Accountability in Two-Party Systems," *European Journal of Political Research*, vol. 55, no. 1, February, 120–137.

Ringen, S. (2009) *What Democracy is For: On Freedom and Moral Government*, Princeton: Princeton University Press.

Schedler, A. (1999) "Conceptualizing Accountability," in Schedler, A., Diamond, L. and Plattner, M. F. (eds.) *The Self-Restraining State: Power and Accountability in New Democracies*, Boulder: Lynne Rienner: 13–28.

Schmitter, P. and Karl, T. L. (1991) "What Democracy Is … and Is Not," *Journal of Democracy*, vol. 2, no. 3, Summer, 75–88.

Schumpeter, J. A. (1976) [1942] *Capitalism, Socialism and Democracy*, 5th edition, London: Allen and Unwin.

Schweitzer, E. J. (2008) "Innovation or Normalization in E-Campaigning? A Longitudinal Content and Structural Analysis of German Party Websites in the 2002 and 2005 National Elections," *European Journal of Communication*, vol. 23, no. 4, December, 449–470.

Sen, A. (1999) *Development as Freedom*, New York: Knopf.

Sperling, V. (2009) *Altered States: The Globalization of Accountability*, Cambridge: Cambridge University Press.

Thomassen, J. (1994) "Empirical Research into Political Representation: Failing Democracy or Failing Models?" in Jennings, M. K. and Mann, T. E. (eds.) *Elections at Home and Abroad: Essays in Honor of Warren Miller*, Ann Arbor: University of Michigan Press: 237–264.

Thomassen, J. (2014) "Representation and Accountability," in Thomassen, J. (ed.) *Elections and Democracy: Representation and Accountability*, Oxford: Oxford University Press: 1–19.

Webb, P. (2005) "Political Parties and Democracy: The Ambiguous Crisis," *Democratization*, vol. 12, no. 5, December, 633–650.

2

THE SOCIOLOGICAL AND SOCIAL-PSYCHOLOGICAL APPROACHES

Vincent L. Hutchings and Hakeem J. Jefferson

Early proposed determinants of the vote choice

Why do citizens vote for one candidate rather than another? Various explanations have been offered over the roughly 70-year history of voting behavior research, but two explanations in particular have garnered the most attention and generated the most debate in the literature on voting behavior. These explanations are known as the Columbia Model and the Michigan Model, and describing these two theories – including their respective strengths and weaknesses – is the subject of this chapter.

Before summarizing these two foundational theories, it is important to first understand the prevailing view about the origins of candidate preference prior to the scientific study of this issue. Before the advent of voting behavior research, many believed that ordinary citizens, much like elites, viewed the parties and candidates in ideological terms and made their political judgments largely on this basis. At the time that research on voting behavior was first developing, and indeed long before this time, this explanation held considerable weight. Even today, variants of this explanation remain in political science and such views are often implicit in standard political reporting, which reflects a powerful, though empirically unsupported, view of the ordinary citizen as ideologically committed and attentive to the particulars of the American political system (Achen and Bartels 2016). Thanks in part to the pioneering scholarship of the authors of the Columbia and Michigan Models and earlier work by journalist Walter Lippman, we now know that voters are not typically motivated by ideology and are often ignorant of the most basic facts of politics (Campbell et al. 1960; Lazarsfeld, Berelson, and Gaudet 1944; Lippmann 1922). Indeed, even those familiar with public policy debates are often unaware of the position of the candidates and the parties on the issues (Converse 1964).

The Columbia Model – described as such because of the contributions of Paul Lazarsfeld, Bernard Berelson, and other scholars at Columbia University – helped to explain how voters make sense of the political world despite their general inattentiveness to politics. This groundbreaking theory was first articulated in *The People's Choice*, the first study to rely on representative sample surveys to explain what factors motivated individual voting decisions (Lazarsfeld, Berelson, and Gaudet 1944). The Columbia scholars examined survey respondents in Ohio from May to November of the 1940 presidential election. They found that exposure to the election campaign essentially had two effects: it *reinforced* the choices made by early deciders and it *motivated* the latent predispositions of uncommitted voters. These predispositions were associated with three types of social characteristics: (1) a citizen's class status; (2) a citizen's racial or religious identification; and (3) the region of the country a citizen lived in and whether they resided in an urban or rural setting. The social characteristics that were activated by the campaign were described as the *Index of Political Predispositions* (IPP) and this index predicted the 1940 vote quite accurately. For example, the IPP predicted that rural, middle class Protestants would vote for the Republican candidate and in fact this held true for about 74 percent of this group.

The Columbia scholars followed up on *The People's Choice* with the equally impressive book *Voting* (Berelson, Lazarsfeld, and McPhee 1954). As with *The People's Choice*, *Voting* argues that one's social identification, or political predispositions, largely accounts for how citizens think and act with regard to politics. In *Voting*, Berelson and his co-authors surveyed the citizens of a moderate-sized community, in Elmira, New York in 1948. In this study, Berelson and his colleagues provide much greater evidence, than in the previous study, of the importance of the social characteristics outlined above. Because their study focuses on only one community, however, they could not fully explore the role that place of residence plays in shaping political attitudes.

The Columbia Model was an important first step to answering the question posed at the beginning of this chapter and many of its insights regarding the political significance of social groups remains relevant today. Still, in spite of its strengths, the theory suffered from a very serious weakness. A model of vote choice based on social-demographic categories does not account very well for swings in election results over time. In other words, how could the Index of Political Predispositions explain the vote for Truman in 1948 (a very close Democrat victory) and the subsequent landslide victory of the Republican presidential nominee, Dwight Eisenhower, in 1952? The social characteristics of the voters could not account for these shifting preferences since the demographics changed little from 1948 to 1952. For this reason, an additional explanation was needed to account for over-time change in voting preferences.

Although the Columbia school's perspective on voting behavior proved influential, it was insufficiently dynamic, thus giving rise to an alternative model of voting. This newer model, proposed by scholars at the University of Michigan, offered a somewhat different explanation of voting behavior and it eventually became the dominant model of voting in the scholarly literature. Unlike the Columbia Model, which emphasized the social characteristics of voters, the Michigan Model – as this approach came to be known – focused on the individual attitudes of the voters as well as their identification with one of the major political parties. Briefly, the argument of *The American Voter* (Campbell et al. 1960) can be summarized into three larger points. First, the Michigan scholars argued that people identify psychologically with political parties just as they do with religious, class, racial, and ethnic groups. Second, identification with a political party should be viewed as a long-term component of the political system and therefore this identification should persist even when people vote for a candidate representing the opposing party. Lastly, party identification is powerful not merely for its direct effects on vote choice, but also for its indirect influence on attitudes associated with the vote. These attitudes include evaluations of the major party candidates, the issues of the day, and the political parties.

The Michigan scholars offered a distinctive definition of party identification. They defined it as a sense of psychological attachment to one of the major parties. Importantly, this did not mean that one officially belonged to the party in the sense that one held formal membership in the party. By attachment they meant a sense of attraction (or repulsion) similar to the sense of attachment one feels to one's class, racial, or religious group. According to Campbell and his co-authors, party identification has two characteristics: direction and strength. By direction, they simply meant whether one is a Democrat, Independent, or Republican. By strength, they meant the intensity of one's attachment to the parties. Thus, in this formulation, one's attachment to the party is either strong, not very strong, or one is an Independent who usually leans toward one of the two parties.

It is important to note that party identification could have been defined as one's prior voting record, and in fact other researchers had previously described it this way. The Michigan scholars rejected this definition because they did not want to confuse one's attachment to the party with how one votes at election time. They are not, strictly speaking, the same thing. Although not common, Republican identifiers can, under some circumstances, vote for a Democrat, and vice versa. If partisan attachment were not defined as something other than the vote this could not be recognized, let alone explained. In other words, the authors were interested in the extent to which the one (attachment) explains the other (voting behavior) and they could not explore this relationship unless the concepts were conceptually distinct.

As we have noted, the Michigan Model offered an explanation of vote choice based on a psychologically oriented perspective. This model was different from previous models because it did not locate explanations in the (relatively) immutable social characteristics of the voter, or in their presumed ideological sophistication, but in a broader set of individual attitudes. It is in this sense that *The American Voter* offers a "psychological" explanation of voting, although it does not strictly rely upon models developed in the field of psychology.

As indicated previously, the authors of *The American Voter* argued that attitudes about the candidates, issues, and parties predicted the subsequent vote choice. More importantly, however, levels of partisan identification predicted these attitudes. In other words, to a large extent, knowing which party a citizen identified with (and how strongly) determined how they would evaluate the candidates, and what position they would take on the issues. Thus, for example, citizens identifying with the Republican Party should also favorably evaluate Republican candidates and generally agree with Republican leaders on the major issues.

An obvious criticism of this formulation is that policy positions and candidate evaluations can also affect party identification, just as party identification can influence them. As plausible as this may sound, the Michigan scholars mostly reject the alternative proposition that issues affect partisanship. They adopt this view in part because of the relatively low levels of political knowledge in the electorate and the general lack of ideological sophistication. In making their argument, they also point out that party identification typically develops in adolescence and tends to be stable over time, while issue preferences and candidate evaluations usually arise much later and are more ephemeral (see Carsey and Layman 2006 for more recent evidence largely consistent with this view).

As evidence for the power of their theory, the authors of *The American Voter* examined nationally representative survey data from the 1952 and 1956 presidential elections. Their results are generally consistent with their expectations. They find that their measure of partisanship is strongly correlated with a variety of political attitudes about the candidates, parties, and current issues. Without exception, the stronger one's attachment to the parties is the more the respondent tends to view the political world in ways consistent with that attachment. For example, "strong Republicans" are much more likely to view Republican presidential nominee – and, later president – Dwight Eisenhower favorably, agree with the Republicans on domestic and foreign policy issues, and regard the Republican Party as a more effective manager of government than Republicans with moderate attachment to their party, Independents, moderately attached Democrats, and especially strong Democrats.

In their second test, Campbell and his co-authors argue that if party identification affects attitudes so deeply, the more partisan members of their sample should have more ideologically consistent issue positions than less partisan respondents. In other words, respondents' attitudes about the candidates, issues, and parties should more consistently favor the Republican/ Democratic Party as the strength of partisan attachment increases. They find that the evidence supports these hypotheses. Finally, they show that their measure of partisanship is strongly related to respondent vote choice in both 1952 and 1956.

According to the authors of *The American Voter*, issue preferences and ideological principles are not the source of party identification. Instead, partisanship is the result of pre-adult socialization. Attachments to political parties, they argue, typically form in mid-to-late childhood largely as a result of parental influence (similar to the acquisition of one's religious affiliation). As evidence for this claim, they use their survey data to show that respondents whose parents belong to the same party were overwhelmingly likely to also identify with that party. If parents disagreed with one another, the pattern was less consistent. An obvious problem with their evidence is that it is based on respondent recall. It is possible that strong partisans recall their parents having a similar party identification even though this is not the case. This is called "projection," and there is certainly evidence in the literature that citizens tend to erroneously assume that others (e.g., candidates, friends, relatives) have political views similar to their own. However, later work by Jennings and Niemi (1968) examined high-school students and their parents' partisanship and found that there was considerable agreement.

Although the authors of *The American Voter* argue that partisanship is mostly stable over time – at the individual level and in the aggregate – they do not argue that it never changes. Sometimes it does and they identify two causes of these changes. The first is what they call personal forces or changes in an individual's social environment. This was the least common explanation for the roughly 20 percent of the respondents in their sample who indicated that they had changed their party identification.

They refer to the more common explanation as emanating from social forces. Unlike personal forces that depend purely on personal circumstances, social forces involve experiences shared across a large number of citizens. There are essentially two ways that social forces can affect partisanship. The first is through life-cycle changes. For example, young people are more likely than older individuals to identify as Independents, whereas older people are more likely to identify as partisans. The second way that social forces can affect partisanship is through massive societal dislocations on the order of the Civil War or the Great Depression. From the vantage point of the Michigan Model, issues can influence partisanship only when they achieve this level of intensity.

In summary, the explanation for voting behavior offered by the Michigan Model can be summarized into three larger points: (1) people identify with political parties just as they do with their religious, class, racial, and ethnic group identity; (2) identification with political parties should be viewed as a long-term component of the political system that persists even when people vote contrary to their identification; and finally (3) partisanship is powerful not merely for its direct effect on vote choice, but also for its indirect influence on attitudes associated with the vote. The Michigan Model also holds that party identification is typically formed before citizens become adults (largely through parental influence) and that typically issues affect partisanship only when they reach catastrophic proportions (e.g., during the Great Depression).

Partisanship and the normal vote

The concept of partisanship was refined somewhat by Phil Converse, one of the co-authors of *The American Voter*, some six years after the publication of this landmark book. In an article entitled "The Concept of a Normal Vote," Converse (1966) pointed out that there were often large fluctuations in presidential election outcomes from one year to the next with no corresponding change in the overall distribution of party identification. Converse interpreted this to mean that the election outcomes could be characterized as fitting into two categories: the normal vote and short-term deviations from the normal vote. By the term "normal vote," Converse meant election results that simply reflected the voter's stable commitment to either of the two parties. In other words, since the majority of voters identified with the Democrats one could expect the Democrats to win every presidential election if the electorate voted only on the basis of their party attachment.

By "short-term deviations" from the normal vote, Converse meant that election outcomes were sometimes influenced by fleeting circumstances, such as scandals or international crises, which did not substantially affect the overall balance of partisan support in the electorate. Sometimes short-term forces worked to the benefit of the Republicans (as in 1952 when General Dwight Eisenhower, a war hero, was the Republican presidential nominee) and sometimes to the benefit of the Democrats (as in 1964 when the Democratic presidential nominee was the former Vice-President of the recently assassinated President Kennedy). When these short-term forces cancel out, or when they are essentially equal for both parties, Democrats were estimated to receive 54 percent of the two-party vote.

Contemporary socio-psychological perspectives on voting

In the aftermath of its publication, *The American Voter* generated considerable controversy and disagreement. In time, however, researchers focused less attention on the dominant role of partisan identification and more attention on the psychological underpinnings of the theory. In particular, a number of scholars relied on social identity theory to help adjudicate long-standing questions about partisanship and to reorient how we think about the concept. Green, Palmquist, and Schickler (2002) were at the forefront of this effort, along with Greene (1999), and Huddy, Mason, and Aarøe (2015).

In their 2002 book entitled *Partisan Hearts and Minds*, Green, Palmquist, and Schickler develop an argument they had originally introduced years earlier in several influential articles. In general, they argue that partisanship is a social identity and should be thought of in ways consistent with our understanding of other salient social identities. Building on the arguments put forth by the authors of *The American Voter*, Green and his co-authors also note that individuals consider salient social groups when they think of the political parties and subsequently determine their partisan loyalties by assessing which party most closely reflects their own unique set of identities. Beyond this grounding of party identification as a social identity, the authors present evidence suggesting that partisanship demonstrates levels of stability akin to other social identities. This stability is demonstrated at both the individual and the aggregate levels. On the occasions when we observe shifts in partisan identification, this is usually because individuals perceive changes in the identities of those who belong to the party. For example, we may expect shifts in partisan identification if one of the two major parties were to become newly associated with a different set of racial or ethnic groups. Interestingly, although their focus is clearly on America, the authors demonstrate that partisanship in places like Great Britain and Germany also operates similarly. The battles between Democrats and Republicans, or the more complicated multi-party competition in other democracies around the world, are not merely a fight over ideas; they are also fights between members of distinct social groups engaged in the same kind of conflict we observe between members of other social groups (for an opposing view, see Abramowitz and Saunders 2006).

In a similar vein, Greene (1999) posits that we should consider party identification through the lens of social identity theory. That is, individuals derive a sense of their own self-worth from

their self-perceived membership in partisan groups. Consistent with early work on social identity theory, Greene (1999: 394) suggests that partisan identifiers have an incentive to distinguish
their in-group from partisan out-groups, and engage in a style of social comparison that
"heighten[s] differences between the groups." Using a psychological measure of group identification, Greene gauged the extent to which Democrats, Republicans, and partisan leaners
expressed a partisan social identity. Unsurprisingly, Greene finds that partisan social identity is
most pronounced for strong partisans relative to weak partisans and leaners. He also finds that
higher degrees of social identification with a given party correspond with more negative perceptions of the out-party relative to the in-party. This measure of partisan social identity was also
related to an engagement in partisan political behavior and an individual's likelihood of
turning out.

Huddy and her colleagues (2015) have also sought to apply social identity theory to the issue
of partisan attachments. More specifically, they ask whether partisan identity is instrumental or
expressive. An instrumental understanding of partisan identity would suggest that individuals
collect some running tally of how well the parties have done and attend to questions of how
closely aligned the party's goals and preferences are with one's own. Focusing on the expressive
nature of partisan identity, however, builds on the idea that partisan identification, like other
social identities, motivates individuals to behave in ways that protect the image of the group and
maintains its high regard relative to the out-group. To explore the alternative explanations of
partisan identity, the authors use campaign activity as their main outcome variable of interest.
Across different studies, respondents noted whether they planned to contribute money to pres-
idential/congressional candidates, and political organizations, and whether they planned to volunteer. Whereas a measure of expressive partisan identity is related to the participatory behaviors
across the various studies, they find that an ideological intensity measure (the authors' measure
of instrumental partisanship) has a more limited influence.

In the past few years, scholars have reexamined the original perspectives outlined in the
Columbia and Michigan Models. In 2008, a new group of scholars – Michael Lewis-Beck,
William Jacoby, Helmut Norpoth, and Herbert Weisberg – sought to revisit the groundbreaking arguments of *The American Voter*. Specifically, they sought to subject the theories introduced
in this volume to examination with more recent survey data (i.e., the 2000 and 2004 American
National Election Studies). This replication was a bold effort. If the groundbreaking results of
The American Voter are as enduring as the original authors believed, they should hold up even
when examined with survey evidence collected almost 50 years after the data used in the original study. This updated test of the Michigan Model was explored in a book called *The American Voter Revisited*.

Lewis-Beck and his co-authors designed their book to mirror the same set-up as the original,
with chapters mostly following the same pattern and addressing the same subject matter as the
original book. One interesting point highlighted in the replication is that, although the authors
of *The American Voter* emphasized individual attitudes, they did not neglect the role of social-
demographic groups. Echoing results from *Voting*, as well as the original Michigan Model, the
authors of *The American Voter Revisited* find that group members who identify strongly with the
group are more likely to vote in accordance with the group. These effects are particularly strong
for some voters (e.g., Jewish voters and, to a somewhat lesser extent, union members, Hispanics
and women) but much weaker for others (e.g., blacks and Catholics).

Lewis-Beck and his colleagues, again building on the model developed by the Michigan
scholars, argued that the influence that is exerted by social groups is done largely through
their impact on party identification. In other words, just as the Columbia Model suggested,
social group attachments inevitably lead to partisan group attachments. However, once these

socio-demographic affiliations lead to the "appropriate" partisan identification, it becomes exceedingly difficult to dislodge this attachment. And, typically partisan group attachments exert more influence on political judgments than the social group memberships that give rise to it. If interest group leaders try to change the party identification of their members, for whatever reasons, they are likely to have a difficult time doing so – especially for older group members.

In 2016, Christopher Achen and Larry Bartels also addressed the fundamental question of what motivates voters. In their book, *Democracy for Realists*, they deconstruct what they refer to as the "folk theory of democracy" – the notion that citizens evaluate political leaders on the basis of ideology or issue preferences. The authors review a broad range of scholarship on this question, both within and outside of the US. Consistent with the early Columbia and Michigan Models, Achen and Bartels conclude that voters fail to meet even the more limited expectations of the retrospective model of voting (i.e., rewarding and/or punishing elected officials based on assessments of their performance in office rather than their adherence to abstract ideological principles). Given their condemnation of the "folk theory of democracy," the authors turn to a more realistic basis for political judgment – salient social groups. Again echoing the pioneering work of Lazarsfeld, Campbell, and their respective colleagues, Achen and Bartels conclude that the vast majority of voters develop their attachment to the parties based on social group loyalties (and pre-adult socialization from their parents). Similarly, they argue that the actions of political figures are primarily interpreted through a partisan or social group lens.

Although there is considerable evidence in support of the foundational works in public opinion, most of this evidence is derived from the US (although see Achen and Bartels 2016). Research on both stable and emerging democracies suggest that the concept of partisanship does not always perform as anticipated in other parts of the world. Holmberg (2007) provides an excellent review of this literature. He notes, for example, that the concept of party identification translates better in some parts of Europe than others. More specifically, partisanship is more volatile in the Netherlands than in Britain or Sweden. Moreover, the number of strong partisan identifiers is mostly stable in the US, but has been declining in Sweden. In the case of emerging democracies in Eastern Europe, Holmberg reports that partisan identifiers are also rare and – more troubling for the standard Michigan Model – such attachments that are developing seem mostly based on cognitive rather than affective factors.

Conclusion

Here, we have attempted to provide a broad overview of the early history of scholarship pertaining to candidate choice and some of the more recent examinations of these theories both domestically and internationally. In particular, we focused on two complementary, though distinct, schools of thought that laid the foundation for much of our contemporary understanding of how individuals come to make political decisions.

To recap, the Columbia Model, with its focus on the role of socio-demographic factors, including social class and membership within salient social groups, brings to the fore a consideration of how political decision-making is informed by one's place in the social hierarchy and one's connection to others who share in their social identity. Focusing more directly on the attitudes individuals hold toward political objects (e.g., candidates, parties, and issues), the Michigan Model adopted a more social-psychological understanding of individuals' decision-making calculus. Describing partisan identification as a psychological attachment to one of the political parties, akin to the attachment one might have to one's racial or religious group, the Michigan Model placed at the center of our theorizing a concern with party identification as a key predictor of individual-level behavior. Remarking on its stability, the authors concede that partisan identification is not immune to change, but note that change requires either a shift in an individual's personal situation or the occurrence of a large-scale, salient social or political event. With few exceptions, the claims put forth by the Michigan Model are replicated and extended by the authors of *The American Voter Revisited*, published more than 50 years after the original text.

Finally, as the other chapters of this handbook demonstrate, there is a great deal of new and exciting work being done that both clarifies and complicates our understanding of the nature of individuals' political beliefs and behaviors. And while much of this work warrants careful consideration by readers, we are particularly excited by scholarship that bridges literature in political science and social psychology to interrogate partisan identification as a meaningful social identity that forms the foundation for citizens' interactions in the political world. The chief tenets of social identity theory, which center on the connection between one's sense of self and her membership in a salient social group, not only provide an interesting lens through which to consider this important feature of the American political system. These tenets also allow us to make sense of deep and persistent divides between individuals for whom a partisan identity is about more than electoral choice, but occupies a central role in a broader set of social identities that motivates behaviors across a range of domains. In fact, this way of thinking about partisan identity takes us full circle to the Michigan Model's early sense that there was an important psychological underpinning to this politically meaningful construct.

In focusing on these two schools of thought and some of the subsequent scholarship they have inspired, we hope we have provided the reader with a useful starting place for grappling with the ideas and debates highlighted in other chapters of this handbook. And though many scholars appreciate both the role of social groups and the centrality of partisanship in the American political system, debates will undoubtedly continue in the literature about the relative stability or dynamism of partisanship, the influence of context on political identity, the role of social identities on political choice, and, in the case of new immigrants and emerging democracies, the very roots of partisan attachment. Clearly, the work we have endeavored to describe in the preceding pages represents the very beginning of what continues to be an exciting and growing area of study in our discipline.

References

Abramowitz, A. I., and Saunders, K. L. (2006) "Exploring the Bases of Partisanship in the American Electorate: Social Identity vs. Ideology," *Political Research Quarterly*, vol. 59, no. 2, June, 175–187.

Achen, C. H., and Bartels, L. M. (2016) *Democracy for Realists: Why Elections Do Not Produce Responsive Government*, Princeton: Princeton University Press.

Berelson, B. R., Lazarsfeld, P. F., and McPhee, W. N. (1954) *Voting: A Study of Opinion Formation in a Presidential Campaign*, Chicago: University of Chicago Press.

Campbell, A., Converse, P. E., Miller, W. and Stokes, D. (1960) *The American Voter*, New York: Wiley.

Carsey, T. M., and Layman, G. C. (2006) "Changing Sides or Changing Minds? Party Identification and Policy Preferences in the American Electorate," *American Journal of Political Science*, vol. 50 no. 2, April, 464–477.

Converse, P. E. (1964) "The Nature of Belief Systems in Mass Publics," in Apter, D. E. (ed.) *Ideology and Discontent*, New York: The Free Press: 206–261.

Converse, P. E. (1966) "The Concept of a Normal Vote," in Campbell, A., Converse, P. E., Miller, W., and Stokes, D. (eds.) *Elections and the Political Order*, New York: Wiley: 9–39.

Green, D., Palmquist, B., and Schickler, E. (2002) *Partisan Hearts and Minds: Political Parties and the Social Identities of Voters*, New Haven: Yale University Press.

Greene, S. (1999) "Understanding Party Identification: A Social Identity Approach," *Political Psychology*, vol. 20, no. 2, June, 393–403.

Holmberg, S. (2007) "Partisanship Reconsidered," in Dalton, R. J. and Klingemann, H. D. (eds.) *The Oxford Handbook of Political Behavior*, New York: Oxford University Press: 557–570.

Huddy, L., Mason, L., and Aarøe, L. (2015) "Expressive Partisanship: Campaign Involvement, Political Emotion, and Partisan Identity," *American Political Science Review*, vol. 109, no. 1, February, 1–17.

Jennings, M. K. and Niemi, R. G. (1968) "The Transmission of Political Values from Parent to Child," *American Political Science Review*, vol. 62, no. 1, March, 169–184.

Lazarsfeld, P., Berelson, B., and Gaudet, H. (1944) *The People's Choice*, New York: Duell, Sloane, and Pearce.

Lewis-Beck, M., Jacoby, W. G., Norpoth, H., and Weisberg, H. F. (2008) *The American Voter Revisited*, Ann Arbor: University of Michigan Press.

Lippmann, W. (1922) *Public Opinion*, New York: Free Press Paperbacks.

3

RATIONAL CHOICE THEORY AND VOTING

Keith Dowding

Political economy

Political economy, in studies of voter and party behavior, usually refers to a specific method: the economic or rational choice method. Sometimes termed "positive political theory," because its aim is to explain political behavior rather than tell us how we should run our political regimes (which is the job of normative political philosophy), it nevertheless has a strongly normative bent. Underlying political economy models are axiomatic principles that enable deductive model building and formally derived hypotheses. These principles – usually called "rationality assumptions" – can be considered normative desiderata for consistent behavior. They actually have very little to do with "rationality" or reasonableness as normally understood. We might be able to predict the behavior of an agent, be it a person or an institution, without considering that behavior to be in the least reasonable, prudent or sensible. Normatively an agent can be consistently irrational or unreasonable, but as long as they are consistent then their behavior can be modeled.

The tenets of "methodological individualism" are also usually associated with rational choice models. Karl Popper (1957: 136) was probably the first to link methodological individualism with economic methods, mis-citing Friedrich Hayek as his source (Hayek was actually saying that economics ought to be methodologically individualist, not that it is). In fact, the modern critics of classical economic methods, behavioral economists, are the true methodological individualists, with the claim that human agents do not behave with the consistency that classical economics assumes. In fact, as we shall see, whilst we can interpret political economy models in behavioral terms, they can more plausibly be seen as providing structural constraints or incentives for agents to behave within certain bounds. They provide structural explanation as much as methodologically individualist explanation.

The axioms of rational choice or revealed preference under certainty include reflexivity, completeness and transitivity (Austen-Smith and Banks 1999). The first ensures that someone is indifferent between two identical items; the second that all items enter into a person's preference function; and the third ensures the consistency that enables prediction. The idea of revealed preference is that we can observe behavior under some conditions in order to predict behavior under other conditions. The final continuity assumption is more technical, but is designed to convert ordinal preferences into cardinal utility functions.

The point of the assumptions of revealed preference is prediction. The idea is that if we can construct a utility function for an agent in one situation, we can then use the utility function to predict how they will behave in a different situation. Utility functions can include any type of argument. So individual utility functions do not need to be composed of material self-interest, but can include the welfare of the family, the group, society at large, refugees or the foreign needy. Adding any sort of social benefit can, within individual applications, provide trivial predictions but the idea of revealed preference theory is to take a utility function constructed in one situation and apply it to other situations to provide predictions there. This can work in practice if the situations are not too dissimilar. In fact, political science models are rarely if ever applied to "an" agent, but rather to sets of agents defined by their type, and so the assumption is that the important elements of the utility function are those that refer to the endogenous interests of that type. The important point is that the rationality assumptions are used for predictive and hence explanatory purposes. What we find – and this is not unimportant in applications to voting and party behavior – is that for collectives sometimes we cannot make a prediction, at least for single events, for it turns out there are no pure equilibrium strategies and/or there are multiple equilibriums.

Applications to voting

The two classic texts of political economy in relation to voters and elections are Kenneth Arrow's (1951) *Social Choice and Individual Values* and Anthony Downs' (1957) *An Economic Theory of Democracy*. Duncan Black's (1948) median voter theorem (often misattributed to Downs) was also seminal, though his argument for a similar conclusion takes an importantly different form.

Arrow is important normatively. He shows that there is no such thing as a social welfare function. In terms of elections, we can interpret this as saying that the result of any preference-aggregation mechanism (any voting system) depends upon the mechanism itself as well as on the preferences of the voters: same mechanism, different preferences: (potentially) different outcome; same preferences, different mechanism: (potentially) different outcome. Arrow's result can be considered a generalization of the Condorcet cycle with at least three alternatives and three voters – x beats y, y beats z and z beats x in pairwise votes. So every alternative loses to another alternative in a simple majority vote (see also Iain McLean's chapter in this volume).

Another way of thinking about this is that, just given the preferences of the collective alone, we cannot predict the result. Normatively this suggests that there is no perfect electoral system; in practice it entails that one can construct results from any electoral system that somehow seem paradoxical or wrong. More importantly, however, corollaries of Arrow's theorem show that electoral systems are manipulable (Gibbard 1973; Satterthwaite 1975). We sometimes see in legislatures that agenda setters can manipulate the order of votes to affect outcomes and enable heresthetic politicians to break up winning coalitions to form a new voting bloc (Riker 1982, 1986; McLean 2001). Voters can also vote strategically in order to scupper what would otherwise be winning alternatives. Such manipulation is usually considered to be normatively bad, some claiming that it means electoral results are arbitrary (Riker 1982), though others suggest that manipulation is just the game of politics (Dowding and van Hees 2008), not so different from behavior in market and other social situations. These essentially normative results are important in models of voter behavior only because they demonstrate the strategic possibilities and show the basic unpredictability of politics *even when we have full information*.

Black's median voter theorem is from the same academic stable as Arrow. It demonstrates that in one-dimensional ideological space, where voters have single-peaked preferences, the ideal point of the median voter is a Condorcet winner (Black 1948). Since a Condorcet winner is the alternative that beats all other alternatives in pairwise votes, the conditions of the proof discount the Arrow problem. As a Condorcet winner is a simple majority winner against each of the other alternatives, the median voter theorem can be given the normative praise that it truly defines a democratic result. Thus any voting system that picks a Condorcet winner will provide winners that satisfy the median voter.

In fact, few voting systems used in major elections ensure that winners are Condorcet winners, though any direct voting system will do so where there are only two candidates. Nevertheless, the median voter theorem is used in many contexts in political economy. Where issues are democratically decided and can be reasonably represented in one dimension, political economy models often assume that the median voter theorem will hold and that, accordingly, in committees, cabinets, parliaments, courts, and so on, the median voter can force a result that reflects their ideal point. Of course, conditions might not allow this to obtain. Votes are often not taken, for example, in cabinets. In parliaments with strong party systems, agenda setters (the government or prime minister) can ensure that the alternatives do not coincide with the ideal point of the median voter. But we can model the dynamics of what agenda setters can get away with given the ideological makeup of backbenchers of vying parties. So the median voter theorem is used to see how agenda setting and other strategic manipulation are constrained under democratic conditions. It becomes a structural condition or incentive constraining the possible maneuvers of powerful agents.

Spatial models

The Downsian model of voter and party behavior is rather different, and is confused with the median voter theorem simply because it utilizes the result that if there are only two parties then the winning party must secure the vote of the pivotal voter. Assuming a single ideological dimension, that voter will be a median voter. Downs' argument is based on the Hotelling model, which explains why similar businesses, such as shoe shops or electrical goods stores, tend to abide in the same location. The answer lies in competition for the best location – where most people will find it convenient to shop. A business that occupies the second-best location, assuming its products are no better, will always competitively be second. Translated to party competition, the party that will do best is the party that locates in ideological space closest to where most voters are also located – assuming, that is, that voters vote for the party closest to them in ideological space. Parties that locate elsewhere would always do worse.

Downs applied his model with most effect to the then contemporary two-party situation in the USA and the UK. Where there are two parties, each vying to become the majority party that controls the government or legislature, Downs argues that there is a logic for candidates or parties to converge on the center of the ideological spectrum if that center is understood as the median voter (Downs 1957; Hotelling 1929). This entails that if the median voter shifts ideological position over time, the ideological spectrum will also shift over time. But in a multiparty setting, especially when taking into consideration more proportional systems, whilst parties must be aware of the ideological shifts in parties close to them, such dynamic forces can lead to almost any set of shuffling up and down the single dimension. No long-term or point predictions are thus possible.

From that simple informal model, many more formal results have developed. In plurality systems, Palfrey (1984) demonstrates that two-party systems could deter third-party entrants by keeping away from the median voter, thus explaining non-convergence. The possibility of third-party entry can mean neither of the original two parties will locate at the median.

He demonstrates equilibrium where both parties locate away from the median, giving third parties no incentive to enter the contest. In more proportional systems, a third party can be guaranteed representation in parliament and possibly a share of power. Here again divergence is likely. Electoral systems do have determinative effects on party systems (Cox 1997; Grofman 2006), though not straightforwardly. In other words, we do not have to change the structural conditions very much to generate very different predictions. One of the strengths of formal modeling is that we can often see how robust conclusions are to the specific assumptions of the models. And where those assumptions do not hold, we can see why the conclusions of models do not follow. The models here provide a normative or ideal standard by which to judge reality.

Stephen Ansolabehere (2006: 35) suggests that the median voter theorem performs for political scientists the role of the Hardy–Weinberg model for evolutionary biologists. Hardy–Weinberg shows that allele and genotypic frequencies in a population will remain constant over generations in the absence of other evolutionary forces. However, other forces *are* always present, so the model acts as a reference point for measuring their effects. Ansolabehere's point is that the assumptions of the median voter theorem are rarely if ever satisfied, but we can examine what departures from those assumptions mean for voter and party behavior. In that sense, the median voter theorem is a reference point for comparative analysis to explain why it is that the parties are not at the median or the winning party did not capture the median voter.

Almost none of the conditions of the median voter theorem standardly hold. Not every person's preference is single-peaked and, whilst some divergence does not entail that Hotelling/ Black forces cannot operate, it can lead to cycling. Increasing the number of dimensions also brings problems of predictability. If preferences over issues cannot be summarized into a single ideological dimension, then voters might choose parties or candidates by the basket of policies each offers. The basket can be thought of as a vector product across n-dimensions. The McKelvey–Schofield theorem demonstrates that, as the number of dimensions increases and with relatively small numbers of voters, any basket of policies can be beaten by at least one other basket (McKelvey 1976; Schofield 1978). Whilst this theorem suggests that politics can be unpredictable, empirical research suggests that most voting decisions seem to be reducible to one or two dimensions and often, whilst the major issues can shift across elections, one or two issues tend to dominate (Poole 2005; Poole and Rosenthal 2007). However, perhaps a bigger problem for the assumptions of spatial models is valence issues (Stokes 1963).

Valence and trust

A valence issue is one where all voters want the same thing – less crime, lower inflation, peace, and so on. So the candidates will not differ much in their promises over valence issues, though they might disagree on how to go about, for example, reducing crime rates. In that case, there will be little ideological divergence over the policies that matter in an election, so voters must select their candidates on other grounds. They are likely to choose on the basis of how much they trust them. Trust can mean several things in this context. It could be an issue of competence or it could be related to how the voter thinks the candidate will respond to unforeseen contingencies.

On the first, voters might choose candidates or parties based on how competent they are on valence issues, and that might depend on how well the candidates have fared in the past. So a lot of voting depends upon rewarding or punishing past behavior, thinking about the future, how much they trust candidates. This can lead to votes of a personal nature for known candidates. Valence issues thus also affect the prediction that candidates or parties will converge on the median voter. If the candidates are close together, then the personal vote should count for more than when candidates are ideologically separated. If one candidate in a two-candidate contest has valence advantage, then his opponent has an incentive to move further away ideologically to reduce that advantage. That still holds, even though the candidate with valence advantage can locate at the median and so win with certainty (Ansolobehere and Snyder 2000; Wittman 2005).

These models all assume that voters know where in ideological or policy space the parties are located, and that the parties know where the electorate is situated. Even with certainty, we do not necessarily get convergence on the median voter; but with uncertainty we can also get divergence. If parties locate too close to each other, voters might not be able to distinguish them; this will reduce turnout and voting can be random (Hinich and Munger 1994). Such uncertainty can, as Downs (1957) first suggested, open up a role for ideology. Rather than striving to get voters to understand in detail their policy positions, the party creates a brand name associated with a particular ideological position, from which voters can estimate its likely policies. Meanwhile the parties target groups of voters whose policy positions they can best estimate, which means that some groups are left out of the competition for votes.

This leads to the second issue of trust. Ideology can serve as a signal as to how a candidate or party is likely to respond to some issue that has not arisen. One feature of the success of Donald Trump's bid for the Republican candidacy that has puzzled many commentators is why his many wild, implausible and false claims do not seem to damage him. Perhaps by making these claims, wild and false as they might be, he is providing a strong signal to a particular constituency that he thinks as they do on these issues, and so as president will behave as they would like to do if they had that role. The signal is one of political or social disposition, rather than of competence or actual policy preference. What he is saying is, "whatever the constraints, I am like you, so I will do the best that you could do if you were president."

Information

Uncertainty over spatial location shows the need for campaigning to provide information and provide such signals. However, given uncertainty about what voters want, candidates have incentives to try to create variance in their rivals' position by mud-slinging and character assassination, trying to make opponents seem more extreme. This predicts that negative campaigning will be more effective than positive (Hinich and Munger 1994: 216–219). On the other hand, the more ideological the groups, the less likely they are to be swayed. This implies that the battle, at least in two-party systems, will revolve around swing voters, those most likely to shift their votes. These will be the most ideologically neutral, so parties will concentrate their attention on those voters, who might not be the median as defined. Such voters might be swayed more by valence issues, particularly economic issues (Persson and Tabellini 2000: 52–58).

Whilst voting is often portrayed as irrational in terms of collective action, since a single vote is unlikely to be pivotal, the broader problem, and the one Downs (1957) first recognized, was rational ignorance. Again, the fact that many voters know little about the specific policy positions of candidates shows that ideology or signals about dispositions can take on great importance. Most of the models assume that politicians enter politics in order to win. Indeed, contestation is the heart of political economy models. Nevertheless, we should expect that candidates, like voters, have policy preferences. The fact that candidates have policy preferences also explains policy divergence (Besley and Coate 1997; Wittman 1983).

Parties should act as gatekeepers for candidates. On the one hand, parties, at least in strong party systems, should ensure that party leaders follow the ideology of the party, whilst keeping in check candidates who are likely to be electorally unsuccessful. To the extent that the procedures for choosing leaders are democratic, we should expect new leaders to win by gaining the votes of the median party voter. May's law of curvilinear disparity suggests the most ideological members of a party are the sub-leaders with ordinary members and those at the top, due to electoral consideration, the most moderate (May 1973). Whilst evidence on the claim is mixed (Kitschelt 1989; Norris 1995), we can know that the median member of left parties will be to the left of the median voter in the electorate, and the median member of a right party to the right of the median in the electorate. Given ideological divergence across parties, we should expect party leaders to take up divergent policy positions. However, once elected, new leaders have incentives to maximize their appeal across the broader electorate. We should expect therefore that new leaders will seem more radical than the outgoing incumbents, since they had to appeal to a more radical electorate, but over time they will soften their stance to appeal to the electorate more broadly. However, where a party has suffered a major electoral setback, the need to appeal more broadly might lead it to choose a leader more in keeping with the electorate's policy preferences.

We should also expect parties whose parliamentarians choose their leader to be more aware of electoral contingencies than those whose leadership electoral base is much broader. A major problem in US presidential elections, for example, is that the choice of candidate is broad-based, and occurs only a few months prior to the presidential campaign itself. Candidates must first appeal to their partisan base, but then do not have enough time to moderate their positions without seeming hypocritical when facing the national electorate.

Constructing utility functions

We saw that the rationality assumptions provide consistency that enables prediction, but utility functions must be constructed from behavior. When the four conditions hold, we can represent agents' preferences by a utility function unique up to a positive monotonic transformation. Roughly speaking, this means that two different mathematical functions can both represent the same choice behavior, as long as one increases whenever the other does. The precise interpretation of those functions might not matter for the behavior under analysis, but might do so under different structural incentives.

"Utility" in this formulation is a completely empty concept. It does not represent anything "experienced," such as "happiness," or "satisfaction," or "desire." It simply represents the behavior of the person. We assume that the behavior is going to be consistent – that is, when a person strictly prefers x to y, they will always choose x from the opportunity set $\{x, y\}$. In other words, "utility" does *not* provide a *reason* for choosing x over y. Someone might vote for a conservative party rather than a radical one for all sorts of reasons – they fear radicalism, they trust the conservative leader, distrust the radical leader, and so on. These are the person's *reasons* for voting for the conservative and not the radical party. But the fact they have those reasons means that when they vote conservative (they choose x over y), they maximize their utility. A person's reasons for choosing x over y are arguments in the person's utility function; the function itself simply represents the conclusion of those arguments.

Prediction is a necessary but not a sufficient condition for explanation; and explanation of behavior requires inputting an interpretation on to that behavior. Such interpretations can go astray. Again, though, this is no greater a problem for formal methods than for non-formal ones that also have to make these interpretative moves. For interpretation, further assumptions about the nature of preferences are required. Standard assumptions include material self- or group-interest and knowledge of the policy positions of the candidates or parties. Political economy models standardly assume that voters vote for parties or candidates whose policy positions are closest to the voter's own position. The models assume thereby that voters vote in their own interests, though those interests can be broadly defined not only in personal but also in family, group or class terms. Material self-interest, even understood broadly, brings the first oft-noted challenge to political-economic models of voter behavior. Of course, such assumptions are not simply those of classic political economy. Many social psychologists also work with such group-oriented self-interest. Weeden and Kurzban (2014) reconstruct party support in the USA across diverse subsets of voters, arguing that interest is what motivates all ideological and partisan support.

Nevertheless, the material self-interest assumption motivates the first important issue for political economy. How do we explain collective action, given underlying material self-interest? The collective action or free-rider problem arises because many actions to attain certain goals that require a large number of people also do not need everyone who would gain from the attainment of those goals to take part. If taking part is costly, then it is in each person's interest to be in the free-riding subgroup that does not actually engage in the collective act. Each person can assume or hope that others, because it is in their interest to secure some outcome, will work to attain it, allowing the individual herself to spend her time on other activities also to her benefit. If all reason in that way, no one will act and the collective interest will not be assured.

Rational turnout

We can easily recast this problem as a strategic game with multiple possible outcomes, some optimal, some sub-optimal. One of the earliest solutions for such collective action problems is the provision of selective benefits giving individuals private as well as collective benefits (Olson 1965, 1971). Such selective incentives need not be positive; much state regulation that, arguably, exists for the collective interest provides punitive incentives. Voting can also be seen as a collective action problem, but one not simply solvable through selective benefits. There are two related questions. First, is relatively high turnout explicable in rational choice terms? Second, are rational choice models consistent with high turnout? The second question enables us to admit that rational choice theory cannot get people to the polls – but once voters are in the polling booth it provides good explanations of their behavior there. Most rational choice scholars want to take on the first question.

So can political-economic models explain why people bother to vote at all? The rational turnout problem has long been associated with rational choice models (Dowding 2005; Fedderson 2004). Given that the chances of being pivotal or decisive in any election are so small and that voting has costs, why would anyone vote (Riker and Ordeshook 1968; Tullock 1967)? Olson's solution for general collective action is selective incentives, but there are few selective incentives on offer for voters.

The problem of getting rational actors to the polls has been tackled on many fronts. Some writers address the calculation associated with the problem, arguing that the probabilities of pivotality are higher than generally thought (Gelman et al. 1998) or that the costs of voting are too low for most people to consider at all (Aldrich 1993; Olson 1965, 1971; Palfrey and Rosenthal 1983). Others suggest that there are potential costs of not voting that can lead some to the polls (Ferejohn and Fiorina 1974). Rather than relying on the decision-theoretic logic of the simple calculation, game-theoretic models suggest that strategic consideration can lead people to vote. After all, if no one votes, then a single individual's voter would be decisive. Following such logic demonstrates that a mixed strategy for voting or not voting is a Nash equilibrium. However, these models predict levels of turnout far below those than actually witnessed (Ledyard 1984).

One early and standard solution is to return to a selective incentive, but an internal rather than an externally provided one. Riker and Ordeshook (1968), among the first to examine the turnout problem, suggest that people believe in a duty to vote. Empirical evidence supports this; and those who say that there is a duty to vote are both more likely to vote and less likely to be deterred by marginal increases in the costs of voting, such as bad weather (Blais 2000). Some believe that adding duty to a utility function trivializes the answer to the question (Barry 1976); however, to the extent that it captures a real factor in a utility function, there is no reason for not so adding it. Taking non-instrumental factors into account is further extended by those who argue that voting brings participation benefits (Brennan and Lomasky 1993). Such models have some important normative implications that I will explore below, but they are perfectly compatible with the spatial models that form the heart of most political–economic modeling.

The turnout problem is in many respects orthogonal to the ways in which political economy models are used to explain voting patterns and party behavior. The models are used for marginal predictions – differences that are made by changing costs and benefits or through shifting party position in ideological space. The strategic considerations are relevant for those concerned about whom to vote for rather than whether to vote at all. The rationale of voting depends in part upon the voter's party or candidate differential: that is, what it would mean for the voter if one or another side won the election. That party differential need not be simply self-interest narrowly understood, but also what the voter understands more broadly for the country as a whole (Weeden and Kurzban 2014). Certainly there is evidence that the greater the ideological divergence amongst candidates in two-horse races, the higher the turnout. Turnout is also higher in elections which matter more, measured by the power of the relevant government; and increases too with the closeness of the expected result (Blais 2000: 58). Conversely, small increases in the cost of voting reduce turnout, again showing that marginal factors matter. Policy makers have tried to reduce the costs of voting with the strategic placement of polling booths, making postal voting easier and so on. Even in countries where voting is compulsory with fines for not voting, such as Australia, turnout is about 80 percent of the voting age population. These suggest that, for at least part of the population, voting costs are not trivial. These considerations suggest that, even if political–economic models cannot explain why people vote, they are useful for helping to explain the way people vote.

One factor might simply be that people do not much consider the costs if they develop the habit of voting and if they do not really understand the probabilities. It has been shown that, whilst people have a good understanding of high probability estimates, they are very bad at behaviorally distinguishing low probability estimates.[1] Furthermore, parties and candidates do not want to win by a single vote: they want large majorities for both safety and stability and also for legitimacy – and voters might feel the same. The problem with the turnout paradox is that it is set up with the wrong utility function.

Alongside these considerations, for many people voting should be understood less instrumentally than expressively (Brennan and Lomasky 1993; Schuessler 2000). When people vote, they are expressing their views in a public forum. Some take that to mean elections are not necessarily Pareto-efficient signals in the same manner as purchasing in markets (Caplin 2007). This seems to downgrade the legitimacy of democratic decision-making. Whilst republicans, for example, might argue that people have a duty to vote, others suggest that the ignorant have a duty not to vote, since their participation reduces the rationality of the decision (Brennan 2012). However, if some people vote with due consideration and others vote randomly, the random voters will not affect the direction of the decision. Only if the ignorant systematically voted against their own interests could we believe that the quality of voting is reduced by ignorance.

Some simple agent-based models applied initially to turnout decision, but also to informational cascades which lead people to behave simply according to utility post their decision, even if the utility level is not causally determined by their behavior. So one might vote for an incumbent government if one's standard of living has risen during its tenure, but for an opposition party if it has stagnated. Surprisingly, such simple decision models show robust results in terms of more complex decision processes. These models can be considered rival to standard political economy models, as they depart from any assumptions over completeness of preference orderings. However, the utility functions they contain are still well-behaved.

Such considerations do not create problems for spatial modeling, since empirically both voter and candidate locations in policy space are based upon assessments made by voters. The major theoretical results of spatial voting are thus not affected by the nature of voter preferences.

Conclusions

Rational choice or political economy models are often thought to be based upon the idea that voters and politicians act out of material self-interest, and such assumptions do lead to the rational turnout problem. However, most models assume some form of spatial calculation where voters vote for the parties closest to them in ideological space. Where voters located themselves will be based upon considerations of their family interest, but that is not unrelated to the interests of most of the country when it comes to economic interests, and not unrelated to ideology. Indeed ideology is an important fact given the issue of rational ignorance. Voters do not know the detailed policies of candidates or parties and so work out what their views are likely to be over a range of issues based upon signals they receive. Signals over the ideology of the candidates and parties are important for voters. Other signals, for example, over the honesty and consistency of candidates, are important, though if candidates play fast and loose with facts but in a way that mirrors the attitudes of voters, the signal that voters receive is that this candidate thinks like they do. Thus they might be expected to behave in power as the voter would, whatever the facts are. This might explain why personal dishonesty is punished more than dishonesty over general facts about the economy, immigration or other social-economic issues. A bigger problem for the spatial models is valence issues where competence is the key factor in voting decisions rather than spatial position. Where valence issues dominate, spatial position as usually measured will not be predictive of outcomes, and specifically we should not expect candidate or party convergence.

The strength of political-economic models is the clarity of the theory and the prediction that the models produce. Often these models use stylized facts or make assumptions that are much simpler than the complex reality. In doing so, the models are normative comparators providing a standard by which to judge reality, where departures from the model predictions provide the explanations of outcomes as much as the models themselves. Some of the models are normative in a stronger sense revealing problems with basic assumptions in the normative desiderata of democracy and show how strategic manipulation becomes possible. All of these issues suggest that, whilst political economy models are an important explanatory technique in our understanding of electoral and party competition, they constitute a weapon that is best used alongside other methods.

Note

1 The fact that academics cannot agree over the probabilities only serves to reinforce this point (Brennan and Lomasky 1993; Gelman et al. 1998; Mueller 2003; Owen and Grofman 1984; Riker and Ordeshook 1968 – to name but a few).

References

Aldrich, J. (1993) "Rational Choice and Turnout," *American Journal of Political Science*, vol. 37, no. 1, February, 246–278.

Ansolabehere, S. (2006) "Voters, Candidates, and Parties," in Weingast, B. R. and Wittman, D. A. (eds.) *The Oxford Handbook of Political Economy*, Oxford: Oxford University Press: 29–49.

Ansolabehere, S. and Snyder, J. M. (2000) "Valence Politics and Equilibrium in Spatial Election Models," *Public Choice*, vol. 103, no. 3, June, 327–336.

Arrow, K. J. (1963) [1951] *Social Choice and Individual Values*, 2nd edition, New Haven: Yale University Press.

Austen-Smith, D. and Banks, J. S. (1999) *Positive Political Theory I*, Ann Arbor: University of Michigan Press.

Barry, B. (1976) *Sociologists, Economists and Democracy*, 2nd edition, Chicago: Chicago University Press.

Besley, T. and Coate, S. (1997) "An Economic Model of Representative Democracy," *Quarterly Journal of Economics*, vol. 112, no. 1, February, 85–114.

Black, D. (1948) "On the Rationale of Group Decision-making," *Journal of Political Economy*, vol. 56, no. 1, February, 23–34.

Blais, A. (2000) *To Vote or Not to Vote: The Merits and Limits of Rational Choice Theory*, Pittsburgh: University of Pittsburgh Press.

Brennan, J. (2012) *The Ethics of Voting*, Princeton: Princeton University Press.

Brennan, G. and Lomasky, L. (1993) *Democracy and Decision: The Pure Theory of Electoral Preference*, Cambridge: Cambridge University Press.

Caplin, B. (2007) *The Myth of the Rational Voter*, Princeton: Princeton University Press.

Cox, G. W. (1997) *Making Votes Count*, Cambridge: Cambridge University Press.

Dowding, K. (2005) "Is It Rational to Vote? Five Types of Answer and a Suggestion," *British Journal of Politics and International Relations*, vol. 7, no. 3, August, 1–18.

Dowding, K. and van Hees, M. (2008) "In Praise of Manipulation," *British Journal of Political Science*, vol. 38, no. 1, January, 1–16.

Downs, A. (1957) *An Economic Theory of Democracy*, New York: Harper and Row.

Fedderson, T. J. (2004) "Rational Choice Theory and the Paradox of Not Voting," *Journal of Economic Perspectives*, vol. 18, no. 1, Winter, 99–112.

Ferejohn, J. A. and Fiorina, M. P. (1974) "The Paradox of Not Voting: A Decision Theoretic Analysis," *American Political Science Review*, vol. 68, no. 2, June, 525–536.

Gelman, A., King, G. and Boscardin, W. J. (1998) "Estimating the Probability of Events That Have Never Occurred: When Is Your Vote Decisive?" *Journal of the American Statistical Association*, vol. 93, no. 441, March, 1–9.

Gibbard, A. (1973) "Manipulation of Voting Schemes: A General Result," *Econometrica*, vol. 41, no. 4, July, 587–601.

Grofman, B. (2006) "The Impact of Electoral Laws on Political Parties," in Weingast, B. R. and Wittman, D. A. (eds.) *The Oxford Handbook of Political Institutions*, Oxford: Oxford University Press: 102–118.

Hinich, M. J. and Munger, M. C. (1994) *Ideology and the Theory of Political Choice*, Ann Arbor: University of Michigan Press.

Hotelling, H. (1929) "Stability in Competition," *The Economic Journal*, vol. 39, no. 153, March, 41–57.

Kitschelt, H. (1989) "The Internal Politics of Parties: The Special Law of Curvilinear Disparity Revisited," *Political Studies*, vol. 37, no. 3, September, 400–421.

Ledyard, J. O. (1984) "The Pure Theory of Large Two-Candidate Elections," *Public Choice*, vol. 44, no. 1, January, 7–41.

May, J. D. (1973) "Opinion Structure of Political Parties: The Special Law of Curvilinear Disparity," *Political Studies*, vol. 21, no. 2, June, 135–151.

McKelvey, R. D. (1976) "Intransitivities in Multi-dimensional Voting Models and Some Implications for Agenda Control," *Journal of Economic Theory*, vol. 12, no. 3, June, 472–482.

McLean, I. (2001) *Rational Choice and British Politics: An Analysis of Rhetoric and Manipulation from Peel to Blair*, Oxford: Oxford University Press.

Mueller, D. C. (2003) *Public Choice III*, Cambridge: Cambridge University Press.

Norris, P. (1995) "May's Law of Curvilinear Disparity Revisited: Leaders, Officers, Members and Voters in British Political Parties," *Party Politics*, vol. 1, no. 1, January, 29–47.

Olson, M. (1965) *The Logic of Collective Action: Public Goods and the Theory of Groups*, Cambridge, MA: Harvard University Press.

Olson, M. (1971) *The Logic of Collective Action: Public Goods and the Theory of Groups*, 2nd edition, Cambridge, MA: Harvard University Press.

Owen, G. and Grofman, B. (1984) "To Vote or Not to Vote: The Paradox of Not Voting," *Public Choice*, vol. 42, no. 3, January, 311–325.

Palfrey, T. R. (1984) "Spatial Equilibrium with Entry," *Review of Economic Studies*, vol. 51, no. 1, January, 139–156.

Palfrey, T. R. and Rosenthal, H. (1983) "A Strategic Calculus of Voting," *Public Choice*, vol. 41, no. 1, January, 7–53.

Persson, T. and Tabellini, G. (2000) *Political Economics: Explaining Economic Policy*, Cambridge, MA: MIT Press.

Poole, K. T. (2005) *Spatial Models of Parliamentary Voting*, Cambridge: Cambridge University Press.

Poole, K. T. and Rosenthal, H. (2007) *Ideology and Congress*, New Brunswick: Transaction Publishers.

Popper, K. R. (1957) *The Poverty of Historicism*, London: Routledge and Kegan Paul.

Riker, W. H. (1982) *Liberalism against Populism: A Confrontation between the Theory of Democracy and the Theory of Social Choice*, San Francisco: W. H. Freeman & Co.

Riker, W. H. (1986) *The Art of Political Manipulation*, New Haven: Yale University Press.

Riker, W. H. and Ordeshook, P. C. (1968) "A Theory of the Calculus of Voting," *American Political Science Review*, vol. 62, no. 1, March, 25–43.

Satterthwaite, M. (1975) "Strategy Proofness and Arrow's Conditions: Existence and Correspondence Theorems for Voting Procedures and Social Welfare Functions," *Journal of Economic Theory*, vol. 10, no. 2, April, 187–217.

Schofield, N. (1978) "Instability of Simple Dynamic Games," *Review of Economic Studies*, vol. 45, no. 3, October, 575–594.

Schuessler, A. A. (2000) *A Logic of Expressive Choice*, Princeton: Princeton University Press.

Stokes, D. (1963) "Spatial Models of Party Competition," *American Political Science Review*, vol. 57, no. 2, June, 368–377.

Tullock, G. (1967) *Toward a Mathematics of Politics*, Ann Arbor: University of Michigan Press.

Weeden, J. and Kurzban, R. (2014) *The Hidden Agenda of the Political Mind: How Self-Interest Shapes Our Opinions and Why We Won't Admit It*, Princeton: Princeton University Press.

Wittman, D. A. (1983) "Candidate Motivations: A Synthesis of Alternative Theories," *American Political Science Review*, vol. 77, no. 1, March, 368–377.

Wittman, D. A. (2005) "Valence Characteristics, Costly Policy and the Median-Crossing Property: A Diagrammatic Exposition," *Public Choice*, vol. 124, no. 4, September, 365–382.

4

INSTITUTIONS AND VOTING BEHAVIOR

B. Guy Peters

The study of political institutions and voting behavior are generally kept far apart in contemporary political science theory. This separation is unfortunate, given that the two aspects of political life are, in practice, closely linked and an understanding of one can inform the understanding of the other. Elections are generally about the capacity to control an institution or multiple institutions. And institutions – notably legal institutions – shape the manner in which elections are conducted and can directly influence the outcomes. While some academic division of labor is inevitable, that division should not go so far as to exclude important factors arising in different elements of the discipline, or allied disciplines.

As well as the more empirical justifications for linking institutions and mass political behavior such as voting, there are theoretical reasons as well. Most obviously, these are the two sides of the classic structure versus agency problem in the social sciences (Giddens 1979; Thornton and Ocasio 2003). Do we explain observed outcomes based on the nature of institutions and other formal structures or do we explain those outcomes through the behaviors of individuals? The most satisfying answer to this somewhat false dichotomy is both. But that answer requires elaboration, and the interactions between structure and agency must be developed theoretically as well as empirically.

For the study of voting behavior and other forms of mass politics, the usual assumption about explanation has been agency, with individual voters being the relevant actors. These actors may be embedded in a social and political system but their attitudes, partisan identifications and perceptions of self-interest have dominated the discussion of voting (but see Blais, Singh and Dumitrescu 2014). While accepting that individual choice is central in voting and other forms of mass participation, we should also consider the role that political institutions have in shaping the opportunities for participation, and in providing incentives and disincentives for voting, and even for voting in certain ways.

This chapter will look at the reciprocal influences of structure and agency on political participation. The impact of voting and other aspects of political behavior on institutions is perhaps the more obvious direction of influence, given that voting will determine the occupants of institutional positions, at least in democratic regimes. I will, however, begin by attempting to demonstrate how the nature of institutions influences the behavior of individuals as well as the collective behavior of interest groups and political parties. In this perspective, institutions comprise the locus in which political participants engage in order to shape policy and the performance of the political system. Or, in the terms of Douglass North (1990; see also Khalil

1995), institutions are the rules of the game and political parties and other organizations are the teams playing the game. Also, for elections, individual voters can be conceptualized as participating in the "game" that is structured by the institutions.

The discussion to this point has been primarily in terms of formal institutions and their capacity to shape political behavior. But informal institutions, including norms, values and organizational routines can also be important in shaping the behaviors of individuals.[1] For example, campaigning for office may have relatively few formal rules but the behavior of candidates is constrained by understandings and informal protocols. Likewise, within formal institutions of government there are informal expectations and standards of behavior that also shape how individuals perform their roles.[2]

Institutional effects on individual and group behavior

Individuals are, by definition, the primary actors in mass politics but they are always acting in a context defined by formal and informal political institutions. In addition to the effects of those institutions on individuals, the institutions influence the behavior of organizational actors such as political parties and interest groups. Further, we can also conceptualize the political parties and interest groups themselves as institutions (see Peters 2010) that in turn interact with one another and also shape the behavior of individual citizens.[3]

I will be arguing that institutions have two primary effects on political participation and voting. The first is that institutions are *opportunity structures*, and the more open these structures are to the involvement of citizens then the greater encouragement they will provide for participation. The other effect of institutions on participation will be through *information*. To the extent that institutions can reduce the information costs of potential participants in the political process, the more likely those citizens are to actually participate.

Institutions as opportunity structures

One general way of conceptualizing the impact of institutions on individuals is to think of them as opportunity structures for individuals. That is, the formal institutions in the public sector can provide opportunities for political action, or they may be designed in ways that discourage or actively repress participation and involvement. These opportunities, or lack thereof, can be developed from the level of macro-constitutional structures all the way down to the structures of political parties and interest groups themselves. Further, the institutional features affecting behavior need not be formal organizations, but rather may also be legal prescriptions or proscriptions on behavior that affect the opportunities for involvement.[4]

In his conceptualization of opportunity structures, Kitschelt (1986) focused on the openness of institutions, as well as the effectiveness of institutions in making and implementing policy, to define types of structures. In this model, open systems, and especially those with effective governments, provide the greatest opportunities for participation, and have a style which attempts to assimilate social movement or other attempts to influence policy. On the other hand, more closed and ineffective political systems tend to provide fewer real opportunities and produce more confrontational styles of governing.

The term of opportunity structure has been employed in a variety of ways in the literature on political participation. The dominant use of the idea of opportunity structures has been in relationship to the development and success of social movements (McAdam, McCarthy and Zald 1996). In this perspective, the openness of the state to its citizens and their articulation of interests will influence the capacity, and the necessity, of those social movements to form and to have demonstrable effects on policy. On the other hand, the capacity of the state to employ repression to prevent mobilization of movements will obviously limit the opportunities for those movements to have any success.

I tend to subscribe to Giovanni Sartori's (1970) tenets about the dangers of concept "stretching." There is an inherent danger that by stretching the concept it loses meaning and is applied in circumstances in which it is inappropriate and may, in fact, cloud meaning rather than contribute to understanding. In this case, however, I do think it may be useful to extend the discussion of opportunity structures to encompass the various ways in which political institutions shape the opportunities available to citizens for participation. This stretching does not undermine the basic content of that concept in any significant manner, even though it does apply the concept to a much wider range of phenomena, in terms of both the institutions and the actors, than originally intended.[5] This should also be understood in a context in which some versions of institutionalism may themselves be considered "stretched" when compared to a formal, structural conception of that term.

In the following discussion, I will be examining the influence of institutions on opportunity structures for individuals and groups in society. The same logic that has been applied to social movements can be extended to a range of phenomena. While the study of social movements has tended to focus on the movements themselves, this analysis will focus more on the institutions that present the opportunity structures for participation, and which may even shape the direction of participation for citizens. The primary "dependent variable" for this discussion will be voter turnout, but other patterns of participation will also be considered.

Opportunity structures at the macro-level

As noted above, the concept of opportunity structures can also be applied at the macro-institutional or constitutional level as well as for mass participation. Several of the conventional institutional differences among political systems can be conceptualized as differences in opportunity structures for participation. While institutional differences such as those between presidential and parliamentary systems, and between federal and unitary regimes, are usually discussed in terms of their impacts on governance capacities (Lijphart 2012; Weaver and Rockman 1993), these different institutional structures also can be argued to influence levels and types of political participation of individuals.

If we begin with the classic distinction of presidential and parliamentary systems, we could posit several potentially contradictory hypotheses about the effect of these institutional structures on mass participation. On the one hand, the presence of two independent structures in presidential systems that have influence over policy provides citizens with multiple opportunities for voting, and for voting that actually does influence the policies being adopted by government. Parliamentary regimes, on the other hand, allow only one set of votes that in the end determine the occupants of both executive and legislative offices.

The alternative hypothesis would be that voters want the chance to actually choose policy when they vote, and therefore parliamentary regimes, especially parliamentary regimes with the opportunity to produce a one-party government, or a coalition with a limited number of parties, may provide them greater opportunities to shape policy directly. Voting for the parliament that in turn will determine the nature of the executive does not confront the voter with as great a probability of gridlock and dilatory institutional politics as is possible, or even likely, with presidential governments and their checks and balances.

The opportunities provided voters to make decisions about both executive and legislative officials in presidential governments appear to be taken by voters, and often result in divided government (Mayhew 1991). Divided governments emerge frequently at both the federal and the state government levels in the United States. There is a seemingly disproportionate number of elections that result in divided governments, with voters – whether consciously or subconsciously – choosing the legislature from one party and the executive from the other. If this outcome is intentional on the part of voters, then those choices would appear to contradict the assumption that voters like to choose governments and thereby to select public policy. Rather, these voters appear to be selecting inaction and gridlock.

Divided governments are not, however, solely an American phenomenon (Elgie 2001). In semi-presidential regimes such as France, there have been several periods of *cohabitation* since the formation of the Fifth Republic (Tsai 2008). Likewise, other countries copying the French model, especially in Eastern and Central Europe, have also had periods of divided government, sometimes with negative consequences for governing (Gerghina and Mosciou 2013). Leaving the governance consequences aside for the moment, the capacity to vote separately for the legislature and for the president provides more opportunities for participation and perhaps for differentiated choices by voters.

There are several possible effects on participation of having a presidential form of government. On the one hand, voting for president appears to focus attention on that election and to make voters believe that their participation is particularly important (Blais 2000). With the presidentialization of parliamentary systems (Poguntke and Webb 2007), the connections between voting for candidates and the choice of executive appear to have become clearer in many parliamentary systems, notably those with a limited number of possible post-election coalitions. However, when the coalition possibilities are not known *ex ante* the connections between voting in parliamentary elections and the governmental and policy outcomes of the election may be more difficult for voters to identify.[6]

At an extreme, the numerous elective positions in many American state and local governments can provide both opportunities for participation and a source of potential confusion for voters (see, for example, Green and Gerber 2015). Some American states in the South and Midwest provide for up to a dozen statewide elected officials in the executive branch – not counting legislators or judges. And then there are numerous local government officials to vote for as well, especially when local governments are nested within larger units.[7] These multiple opportunities for participation can at some point impose such great information demands on voters that they may opt out of voting. The multiple elections can also produce voter fatigue, especially with, as in Switzerland, multiple referendums (Rallings, Thrasher and Borisyuk 2003).

Federalism

The division of powers among levels of government, and the degree of autonomy available to sub-national governments, is another standard institutional question in the public sector. This question is usually phrased as federalism but the formal constitutional differences between federal and unitary systems tell only part of the story. For example, there are marked differences in the powers available to the provinces or states within federal regimes (Fenna and Hueglin 2010). Likewise, in some instances, sub-national governments in nominally unitary regimes may have more autonomy to raise taxes and make autonomous policy decisions than do those in federal regimes.[8]

We should therefore tend to think of this question of sub-national government more in terms of the degree of decentralization existing within a regime (Falleti 2005). What powers are decentralized – whether to provincial or local governments – and what powers are retained in the center? And to what extent are political powers decentralized? This division of power among various levels of government presents opportunities and barriers to voters attempting to control public policy. On the one hand, more decentralized forms of governance present more opportunities for citizens to participate. On the other, however, more decentralized regimes may make influencing overall patterns of policy more difficult; a party or an interest group would have to be successful in a number of different venues to shape national policy.

Although decentralization is the more generic concept for addressing the question of the allocation of powers among tiers of government, the formal institutions associated with federalism also have some relevance. In particular, having a sub-national tier of government with some degree of sovereignty and having autonomy over some aspects of governing – especially when that involves own-source revenues – creates arrangements that can influence the utility of voting, as well as the pattern of voting.

To be more precise, federalism creates the possibility of another form of divided government. Voters can, if they wish, create patterns in which the central government is controlled by one party or coalition and the states or *Länder* are controlled by another political group. These voting opportunities have special relevance when, as in the case of Germany and Austria, those *Land* governments send representatives to the second chamber of parliament. These second chambers cannot dismiss a government formed in the lower house, but they can make the life of that government rather difficult, as is true in any form of divided government.

The bureaucracy and participation

Bureaucracy and democracy are usually thought of as antithetical concepts, albeit both having substantial relevance for governing. However, the structure of bureaucracies may have some impact, albeit very indirectly, on the behavior of voters and the politicians whom they elect. The accountability function is central to any democratic regime (Brandsma and Schillemans 2013) and elections are far from irrelevant for promoting that accountability. This is especially true if, as Keane (2009) has argued, democracy is increasingly about monitoring government activities rather than voting to attempt to make grand policy decisions.

In addition to the argument concerning the monitory nature of contemporary democracy, the increased presidentialization of governments (see Poguntke and Webb 2007; Savoie 2008; but see Norton 2013 on the United Kingdom) may also emphasize voting as a mechanism for accountability rather than for policy choice. If in parliamentary regimes power is moving toward the executive and parliamentary democracy has in essence become prime ministerial democracies, then voting may be an even blunter instrument than in the past for controlling policy. That is especially true for multi-party systems in which the coalition that will emerge after an election is not known.[9]

The diminished capacity to control policy through the election appears to be a reality of contemporary democracies, and with it there may be a decrease in the real and/or perceived efficacy of voting for many citizens. That said, the necessity of controlling governments retrospectively will, if anything, have been increased by executive dominance in government. With the powers of the political executive parliaments increasing significantly, voters can react to perceived poor policy choices, or other perceived failures, through replacing that executive through a subsequent election.

At the same time that political executives have been increasing their powers relative to parliaments, there have been significant changes in the nature of public bureaucracy that also have made the voting act seemingly less efficacious in controlling the bureaucracy. As early as the 1980s (Day and Klein 1987), it had become clear that the classic form of parliamentary accountability was becoming less dominant and other forms of accountability depending more on the use of social actors and stakeholders were ascendant.

The shift in accountability is only one manifestation of changes in the public bureaucracy that may have some effect on voting, at least indirectly. Part of the logic of the New Public Management (see Christensen and Laegreid 2011) has been to emphasize the role of public administrators in making policy and denigrating their nominal political masters. As well as a general cultural shift within the public sector, structural changes, such as the use of agencies, tended to reduce the control of political leaders over the bureaucracy (Verhoest 2010).

While this shift in the linkage of voting to accountability over the public bureaucracy may tend to devalue voting, the positive side of the story is that these transformations may open different opportunities for participation. Although reforms of the public sector have tended to emphasize the autonomy of the bureaucracy, that autonomy is also limited by increased powers for clients and participants at the level of the individual facility (Gilley 2009). If voting does not provide the public with the type of influence over the executive that should exist in a democracy, there may still be effective forms of participation available for those citizens.

Information costs and voting

Information costs can be a second major variable affecting voting, and especially voting turnout. High information costs can be considered a major deterrent to potential participants in the political process. If voters have to invest heavily in acquiring information then they will be less likely to participate. Either the costs will be too high and they will not seek out the information, or they will not want to consider themselves ignorant when they go to the polls, so will not go. Institutions in the political system, and especially party systems and the nature of political parties, can raise or lower information costs, and hence affect turnout.

Campaign laws themselves may increase information costs for voting. In some countries, such as the United Kingdom, there are limits to the distribution of campaign information, and an inability to purchase media time. In others, campaigning may end a day or several days before the poll, so that last-minute potential voters have less information. And in the interest of preventing bandwagon effects, opinion poll information can be restricted. While done in the interest of fairness in most cases, these mechanisms do impose greater information costs.

While lowering information costs for voters may in general be a positive value for the political system, like so many aspects of designing institutions there will be trade-offs with other important values (Smith 2009). For example, lowering information costs for voting by reducing the number of parties and making the party system more stable (see below) will tend to reduce the representativeness of the party system and the parliament. Likewise, lowering information costs for voters through reducing the number of elective offices, or by reducing opportunities for referendums and initiatives, will potentially have a negative effect on democratic controls over government.

Credible commitment

The concept of credible commitment has been used to describe the need for public sector institutions, such as central banks and regulatory agencies, to make policy choices that will survive beyond a single term of office (Majone 2002; North 1993). Again, if we stretch the concept of credible commitment further, we can argue that political parties as institutions should make credible commitments to policy positions and ideology to reduce the information costs of voters. And if they can reduce those information costs then citizens will find it easier to make choices and to vote.

To some extent, the choice to maintain consistent policy positions is the decision of the party itself. If it wishes to maintain a stable approach to policy across time, there are few constraints on its doing so, other than perhaps electoral success. That said, the electoral systems and electoral laws may also influence the capacity of the party to maintain a predictable position. If we return to Duverger's (1951) classic distinction between parties of maneuver and parties of position, we could argue that parties of maneuver, usually parties in two-party or limited multi-party systems, will provide more unstable, or perhaps merely ambiguous, policy positions. In contrast, parties in more extreme multi-party systems will maintain more consistent positions and thus lower information costs for voters.

Proportional representation also tends to reduce the need for tactical or "sophisticated" voting. Perhaps only when there are questions of getting an allied party over a threshold is there much reason to vote for the party representing the voters' real preferences. In single-member districts, however, there are often significant incentives to vote for a less preferred alternative in order to prevent the least preferred party from winning (see Kiewiet 2013). The possible advantages of this type of voting in turn require higher levels of information from voters than would be true in other voting systems.

Unfortunately, there appears to be an equally viable alternative hypothesis about the role of multi-party systems. More extreme multi-party systems offer fewer barriers to entry for new parties, whether these be personalistic "flash" parties or attempts to create more stable and enduring parties. When there are a number of new parties entering the electoral market, then voters will have to sort through more options and acquire more information in order to make a rational choice among the options. Or they may simply opt not to participate.

The above discussion assumes that voters are indeed making their voting choices based primarily on their policy preferences. We have assumed the same already in some of the discussion of opportunity structures, with the argument being that when multi-party coalition systems obscure the connection between voting, the coalition that is formed, and policy choices, then potential voters may think that their vote is too blunt an instrument to affect the final choices made by government (see Selb 2009). In this case, the necessity of frequently renewing one's stock of relevant political information to take into account new parties that come, and may soon go, may lead potential voters to spend their time and energy elsewhere.

Electoral laws and voting behavior

I have already discussed some general analytic and theoretical approaches concerning the role of institutions in affecting voting. I will now look more specifically at the most significant institution affecting voting, namely electoral laws. These laws will influence voting behavior through both of the mechanisms mentioned above, and may have some more specific effects on the behavior of individuals as they become involved in the political process, as well as on the role of political parties that have an indirect effect on individual behavior.

Law is a fundamental institution of society, and for the political system. For the purposes of defining the opportunities for participation, and defining the impacts of voting behavior, electoral laws represent a crucial legal framework (Bowler 2006). From at least the time of Maurice Duverger (1951), we have understood clearly that electoral laws affect the party system, with two-party systems being likely to occur only in electoral systems with first-past-the-post systems. More recent scholarship (Taagapera and Shugart 1999) has refined the linkage between electoral laws and the capacity of electoral systems to produce outcomes that represent closely the division of votes among parties, and have discussed the effects of various electoral systems on the outcomes of elections.

We can hypothesize that this basic impact of electoral laws on the number of parties and the diversity of the ideologies (or at least electoral platforms) offered by the parties will affect the behavior of voters, as well as their political activities beyond voting. For example, the general argument – supported by some evidence – is that proportional representation systems are related to higher levels of turnout than are single-member district, first-past-the-post systems (Ladner and Milner 1999). This linkage between electoral law and the representativeness of parliaments is a manifestation of the logic of opportunity structures discussed above. If the electoral laws provide more opportunities for parties to enter politics, and therefore make it easier for voters to select parties whose policies they support, then citizens may be more likely to participate.[10]

The general assumption has been that proportional representation is linked to higher levels of turnout (see Brockington 2004, for a nuanced perspective). The effects of proportional representation on turnout appear to be manifested through several paths. The most obvious is that, with multiple parties running for office, the voter is likely to find a party that is close to his or her political views than in the more constrained selection of parties available under other electoral systems. In addition, the voter may feel more efficacious in a proportional representation system, knowing that their party or candidate has a greater opportunity to gain at least some representation.

There may, however, be some point at which the electoral institutions can permit too many parties to participate, and with that cause confusion and impose significant information costs on voters. Leaving aside small and obviously idiosyncratic parties, the Dutch general election of 2012 had 20 parties participating, while the Peruvian elections of 2016 for president had candidates representing 18 parties.[11] Especially if the party system is not well-institutionalized and there are numerous shifts in party names and composition between elections, this proliferation of parties can impose a major information burden on voters.

As well as the possible negative effects of a large number of parties on turnout, the informational demands imposed by more complex electoral systems, such as the Single Transferable Vote (STV), may also suppress participation. If a voter has to rank all candidates in a multi-party election then all but the best informed and most diligent of voters may feel somewhat reluctant to participate. Thus, those electoral systems that provide voters the greatest power over outcomes may also demand the most from those voters. Thus, in this setting there may be a conflict between the opportunities provided to, and the information required of, the voters.

Even in single-member districts, however, there may be effects of other aspects of electoral law on voter turnout. For example Jackman (1987) found that in the United States elections in competitive districts tend to have higher turnout than in those that are less competitive. The same appears to be true in most British elections (Denver 2015). In the competitive districts there was something to vote for, while in less competitive districts there may be little reason to vote, other than to express systemic support. Thus, in American elections with congressional districts and state legislatures increasingly gerrymandered to ensure one party or the other wins consistently, already low levels of turnout should be expected to worsen (Angstrom 2013). The relative absence of gerrymandered and safe seats in proportional representation systems provides voters with greater incentives to turn out to vote on a more consistent basis.

While these two basic notions of the linkage between electoral institutions and voting are useful, there may be several more detailed points that should also be made. The first is that the relationship between electoral laws and turnout is more suggestive than conclusive, and there are certainly cases in which the effects are the opposite of those argued above. The degree of representativeness produced by electoral laws and the capacity of voting to ensure the formation of government are inversely related. Therefore, voters may be deterred from voting if they think that their vote will not be related to the outcomes of the election. That said, however, majoritarian political systems tend to have lower levels of political participation than do proportional representation, arguing that voters appear to value having their views represented more than they do producing winners.

The presence of threshold values for the representation of a party in the parliament may affect the strategies of voters more than it affects the level of turnout. For example, if a political party A likely requires another particular party B as a coalition partner, then voters who actually prefer A may decide, or even be encouraged, to vote for B in order to ensure that B surpasses the electoral threshold. For example, the rather high threshold of 5 percent in German elections may encourage Christian Democratic Union adherents to vote for the Free Democrats in order to ensure that their usual coalition partner is indeed present in parliament.[12]

The threshold requirement may also affect turnout. If adherents of a particular party do not think their party can surpass the needed proportion of votes, then they may choose not to vote unless one of the other available parties is acceptable to them. While the presence of a threshold was intended to deter, at least in part, the representation of radical and anti-systemic parties in parliament, it may have a more pervasive effect of institutionalizing a particular cartel of parties and in the process discouraging voters who want to move away from the status quo, even if in benign directions.

Finally, other changes in electoral laws may also be able to influence turnout, and in a positive direction. Mechanisms such as postal voting, early voting, extending the time period for voting and Sunday elections all appear to increase turnout (Franklin 2001). These mechanisms appear to be especially important in the United States for increasing the electoral participation of members of minority groups.

Other reasons for voting

The above discussion has been premised on an assumption that voters choose parties, or candidates, for policy reasons. We know, however, that voters in many countries tend to be more interested in the capacity of politicians to provide constituency service, and to "bring home the bacon," than they are in their policy stances. That is, voters want representatives who will serve as intermediaries with the bureaucracy, and who can bring public money (whether as infrastructure or government contracts for local firms) to their area. For politicians, then, taking policy stances runs the risk of alienating voters while successful constituency service only makes friends.[13]

If we leave aside for a moment the more clientelistic forms of relationship between voters and their elected representative (Piattoni 2001), we can still identify the presence of an interaction among electoral laws, the provision of benefits for individuals and districts, and voting. First, for this relationship to function, there needs to be some close connection between the voter and the representative, something that is more likely to exist in first-past-the-post majoritarian systems.[14] The relationship is, however, confounded by the tendency for these voting systems to produce incumbency and safe districts, reducing the incentive for voters to turn out. Voters can therefore be free riders, taking the benefits of constituency service when needed but not having to invest time and effort in voting.

Political parties and participation

Not only do electoral laws affect the participation of individuals in politics, as I have argued above, political parties themselves may, as one type of institution, offer more or fewer opportunities for individuals to participate and to be effective in that participation.[15] At one extreme, one can find the American party system in which the leadership of the party has little control over the party and who can run for office in the name of the party. The primary system allows outsiders who have not worked their way up the hierarchy within the party – namely, Donald Trump and Ben Carson – to parachute into candidacy and, especially in state and local elections, even to win office. While the endorsement of the party may still be necessary for election – if nothing else being assured of places on the ballot – that endorsement is possible for an extremely wide array of individuals.

At the other end of this spectrum of political parties, those that function in closed list electoral systems can control not only who runs in their name but also the order in which they appear on the ballot. These more formalized structures and roles for political parties in the electoral process enable them to control political recruitment, but may also provide fewer opportunities for voters to express their views, especially of individual candidates. The capacity to control recruitment and placement of candidates strengthens parties as institutions, but also provides greater predictability for voters and thus lowers the information costs for those voters.

This powerful role assigned to the leadership of parties will be effective when there are strong party loyalties and commitments, as has been true for traditional parties in Europe and, to some extent, Latin America. But the commitment of voters to parties has been decreasing significantly for the past several decades (van Bizen, Mair and Poguntke 2012) and appears likely to continue. The former cartel parties (Katz and Mair 2009) are facing increased competition from "flash parties" and other less institutionalized parties (Barr 2009).

Summary

This chapter has attempted to demonstrate the connection between the institutional design of political systems and the behavior of voters. Although these institutional effects may appear far removed from more proximate causes of voting, such as attitudes and policy preferences, they are nonetheless important for understanding patterns of behavior at an aggregate level. These connections also point to the interactions between individuals and institutions that are important for institutional theory.

As well as the importance for institutional theory, this discussion is obviously very relevant for understanding how political participation – and most notably, voter turnout – can be shaped. While affecting attitudes toward government and a sense of civic duty toward voting may be difficult, institutions can be manipulated more readily. But, as already noted, attempts to affect levels of public participation may be only one of a number of criteria that institutional designers may consider when shaping institutions. Political institutions are complex structures with a wide range of effects on their members and on politics as a whole, and their role in political participation should not be underestimated.

Notes

1 The sociological approach to institutionalism (March and Olsen 1989) defines institutions in terms of these concepts, and does not differentiate clearly between formal and informal institutions. For the purposes of this analysis, I will focus on formal institutions defined in more legalistic and structural terms.
2 One of the best examples of this influence is Matthews (1960).
3 One of the standard understandings of institutional theory is that the environment of any one institution is composed of other institutions.
4 Elinor Ostrom (1990) defined institutions as structures of rules that permit, prescribe and proscribe behaviors by individuals.

5 In Sartori's terminology, this application of the concept of opportunity structures involves increased extension of the concept, although in this case there is not any significant reduction of the intension of the concept.

6 Richard Rose (1976) developed a model of party government that linked voting choices, the characteristics of the individuals occupying government positions and policy choices. He argued that even in majoritarian political systems such as the United Kingdom the linkage between voting and the choices of governments was tenuous.

7 For example, I vote for officials at the county level as well as for the borough in which I reside. And I also vote for school board members.

8 For example, Swedish local governments have substantially more taxing powers than do sub-national governments in federal regimes such as Germany.

9 Of course in some moderate multi-party systems, to use Sartori's term, there may be only a limited number of possible coalitions so that voters would have a much better chance of assessing *ex ante* likely policy choices.

10 For an analysis of the effects of proportional representation as opposed to the first-past-the-post system, see Dunleavy et al. (1998).

11 Perhaps the tradition of compulsory voting in the Netherlands mitigates some of the effects of so many choices for the voters.

12 In the 2013 election, this strategy failed and the Free Democratic Party did not pass the threshold. The Social Democrats have had a somewhat similar relationship with the Green Party, especially at the Land level.

13 This logic is at least part of the reason for high levels of reelection of sitting members of legislatures. For the classic statement, see Fiorina (1977).

14 That said, the STV voting system in Ireland, with the capacity of voters to rank candidates, may create some of the same patterns. See Collins (1985).

15 On political parties as institutions, see Peters (2010, Chapter 8).

References

Angstrom, E. J. (2013) *Partisan Gerrymandering and the Construction of American Democracy*, Ann Arbor: University of Michigan Press.

Barr, R. R. (2009) "Populists, Outsiders and Anti-Establishment Politics," *Party Politics*, vol. 15, no. 1, January, 23–48.

Bizen, I. van, Mair, P. and Poguntke, T. (2012) "Going, Going … Gone? The Decline of Party Membership in Contemporary Europe," *European Journal of Political Research*, vol. 51, no. 1, January, 24–56.

Blais, A. (2000) *To Vote or Not to Vote: The Merits and Limits of Rational Choice Theory*, Pittsburgh: University of Pittsburgh Press.

Blais, A., Singh, S. and Dumitrescu, D. (2014) "Political Institutions, Perceptions of Representation, and the Turnout Decision," in Thomassen, J. (ed.) *Elections and Democracy: Representation and Accountability*, Oxford: Oxford University Press: 99–112.

Bowler, S. (2006) "Electoral Systems," in Rhodes, R. A. W., Binder, S. A. and Rockman, B. A. (eds.) *The Oxford Handbook of Political Institutions*, Oxford: Oxford University Press: 577–594.

Brandsma, G. J. and Schillemans, T. (2013) "The Accountability Cube: Measuring Accountability," *Journal of Public Administration Research and Theory*, vol. 23, no. 4, October, 953–975.

Brockington, D. (2004) "The Paradox of Proportional Representation: The Effects of Party Systems and Coalitions in Individuals' Electoral Participation," *Political Studies*, vol. 52, no. 3, October, 469–490.

Christensen, T. and Laegreid, P. (2011) *Ashgate Research Companion to New Public Management*, Burlington: Ashgate.

Collins, C. A. (1985) "Clientelism and Careerism in Irish Local Government: The Persecution of Civil Servants Revisited," *The Economics and Social Review*, vol. 16, no. 4, July, 273–286.

Day, P. and Klein, R. (1987) *Accountabilities: Five Public Services*, London: Tavistock.

Denver, D. (2015) "The Results: How Britain Voted," *Parliamentary Affairs*, vol. 68, no. 4, October, 5–24.

Dunleavy, P., Margetts, H., O'Duffy, B. and Weir, S. (1998) "Remodelling the 1997 General Election: How Britain Would Have Voted Under Alternative Electoral Systems," *British Elections and Parties Review*, vol. 8, no. 1, 208–231.

Duverger, M. (1951) *Les Partis Politiques*, Paris: Armand Colin.

Elgie, R. (2001) *Divided Government in Comparative Perspective*, Oxford: Oxford University Press.

Falleti, T. G. (2005) "A Sequential Theory of Decentralization: Latin American Cases in Comparative Perspectives," *American Political Science Review*, vol. 99, no. 3, August, 327–346.

Fenna, A. and Hueglin, T. (2010) *Comparative Federalism: A Systematic Inquiry*, North York: University of Toronto Press.

Fiorina, M. (1977) *Congress: Keystone of the Washington Establishment*, New Haven: Yale University Press.

Franklin, M. N. (2001) "The Dynamics of Electoral Participation," in LeDuc, L., Niemi, R. and Norris, P. (eds.) *Comparing Democracies 2: Elections and Voting in Comparative Perspective*, Thousand Oaks: Sage: 148–168.

Gerghina, S. and Mosciou, S. (2013) "The Failure of Cohabitation: Explaining the 2007 and 2012 Institutional Crises in Romania," *East European Politics and Societies*, vol. 23, no. 4, November, 668–684.

Giddens, A. (1979) *Central Problems in Social Theory: Action, Structure and Contradiction in Social Analysis*, Cambridge: Cambridge University Press.

Gilley, B. (2009) *The Right to Rule: How States Win and Lose Legitimacy*, New York: Columbia University Press.

Green, D. P. and Gerber, A. S. (2015) *Get Out the Vote: How to Increase Voter Turnout*, Washington, DC: The Brookings Institution.

Jackman, R. W. (1987) "Political institutions and Voter Turnout in the Industrial Democracies," *American Political Science Review*, vol. 81, no. 2, June, 405–423.

Katz, R. S. and Mair, P. (2009) "The Cartel Party Thesis: A Restatement," *Perspectives on Politics*, vol. 7, no. 4, December, 753–766.

Keane, J. (2009) *Life and Death of Democracy*, New York: W. W. Norton.

Khalil, E. S. (1995) "Organizations Versus Institutions," *Journal of Theoretical and Institutional Economics*, vol. 151, no. 3, September, 445–466.

Kiewiet, D. R. (2013) "The Ecology of Tactical Voting in Britain," *Journal of Elections, Public Opinion and Parties*, vol. 23, no. 1, January, 86–110.

Kitschelt, H. P. (1986) "Political Opportunity Structures and Political Protest: Anti-Nuclear Movements in Four Democracies," *British Journal of Political Science*, vol. 16, no. 1, January, 57–85.

Ladner, A. and H. Milner (1999) "Do Voters Turn Out More Under Proportional than Majoritarian Systems? The Evidence from Swiss Communal Elections," *Electoral Studies*, vol. 18, no 2, June, 235–250.

Lijphart, A. (2012) *Patterns of Democracy: Government Forms and Performance in Thirty-Six Countries*, New Haven: Yale University Press.

Majone, G. (2002) "Delegation of Regulatory Powers in a Mixed Polity," *European Law Journal*, vol. 8, no. 3, September, 319–339.

March, J. G. and Olsen, J. P. (1989) *Rediscovering Institutions: The Organizational Basis of Politics*, New York: Free Press.

Matthews, D. R. (1960) *U.S. Senators and Their World*, Chapel Hill: University of North Carolina Press.

Mayhew, D. R. (1991) *Divided We Govern: Party Control, Lawmaking and Investigations 1946–1990*, New Haven: Yale University Press.

McAdam, D., McCarthy, J. D. and Zald, M. Y. (1996) *Comparative Perspectives on Social Movements: Political Opportunities, Mobilizing Structures and Cultural Framings*, Cambridge: Cambridge University Press.

North, D. C. (1990) *Institutions, Institutional Change and Economic Performance*, Cambridge: Cambridge University Press.

North, D. C. (1993) "Institutions and Credible Commitment," *Journal of Institutional and Theoretical Economics*, vol. 149, no. 1, March, 11–23.

Norton, P. (2013) "Parliament: A New Assertiveness?" in Jowell, J. L., Oliver, D. and O'Cinneide, C. (eds.) *The Changing Constitution*, Oxford: Oxford University Press: 171–193.

Ostrom, E. (1990) *Governing the Commons: The Evolution of Institutions of Collective Action*, Cambridge: Cambridge University Press.

Peters, B. G. (2010) *Institutional Theory in Political Science: The New Institutionalism*, London: Bloomsbury.

Piattoni, S. (2001) *Clientelism, Interests and Democratic Representation: The European Experience in Comparative Perspective*, Cambridge: Cambridge University Press.

Poguntke, T. and Webb, P. (2007) *Presidentialization of Politics: A Comparative Study of Modern Democracies*, Oxford: Oxford University Press.

Rallings, C., Thrasher, M. and Borisyuk, G. (2003) "Seasonal Factors, Voter Fatigue and the Costs of Voting," *Electoral Studies*, vol. 22, no. 1, March, 65–79.

Rose, R. (1976) *The Problem of Party Government*, London: Macmillan.

Sartori, G. (1970) "Concept Misformation in Comparative Politics," *American Political Science Review*, vol. 64, no. 4, 1033–1053.

Savoie, D. J. (2008) *Court Government and the Collapse of Accountability in Canada and the United Kingdom*, Toronto: University of Toronto Press.

Selb, P. (2009) "A Deeper Look at the Proportionality-Turnout Nexus," *Comparative Political Studies*, vol. 42, no. 4, April, 527–558.

Smith, G. (2009) *Democratic Innovations: Designing Institutions for Citizen Participation*, Cambridge: Cambridge University Press.

Taagapera, R. and Shugart, M. S. (1999) *Seats and Votes: The Effects and Determinants of Electoral Systems*, New Haven: Yale University Press.

Thornton, P. H. and Ocasio, W. (2003) "Institutional Logics," in Greenwood, R., Oliver, C., Suddaby, R. and Sahlin-Andersen, K. (eds.) *Sage Handbook of Organizational Institutionalism*, London: Sage: 99–129.

Tsai, J-H. (2008) "Sub-types of Semi-Presidentialism and Political Gridlock," *French Politics*, vol. 6, no. 1, April, 63–84.

Verhoest, K. (2010) *Autonomy and Control of State Agencies*, Basingstoke: Macmillan.

Weaver, R. K. and Rockman, B. A. (1993) *Do Institutions Matter?: Government Capabilities in the United States and Abroad*, Washington, DC: The Brookings Institution.

PART II

Turnout
Why people vote (or don't)

5

THE BIG PICTURE

Turnout at the macro-level

Jack Vowles

This chapter examines the "big picture" of electoral turnout: research at the aggregate or macro-level in search of temporal, contextual, and institutional explanations of variation in turnout. It begins with a brief review of the field and its methodology, moving on to assess the extent of change over time. It reviews debates and empirical evidence about the possible consequences of variation in turnout for partisan politics, public policy, and social and economic inequality. It concludes by addressing the reasons for variation in turnout, with particular attention to the order of elections, competitiveness, and electoral systems.

Development of the field and its methodology

Systematic aggregate-level cross-national analysis of electoral turnout began in the 1980s as a growing time series of continuously democratic elections began to accumulate (see, for example, Powell 1980). Countries and the elections nested within them could be treated as "country-election" cases. By the 1990s, as the number of individual-level sample-survey election studies multiplied around the world, research mixing aggregate and individual-level data began to emerge. Since 1996, the Comparative Study of Electoral Systems (CSES) has been collecting data from election studies around the world, providing easy access.[1] Multi-level models make it possible to combine analysis at both the aggregate and individual levels, estimating not only the direct effects of macro-variables but also the extent to which their effects run through and interact with other explanatory variables at the individual level. This approach is now at the cutting edge of both aggregate and individual-level observational electoral research on turnout. This chapter will therefore address the use of macro-level explanatory variables both in aggregate-level and in some multi-level analyses of turnout.

From the research so far, one set of findings stands out. Between-country differences in turnout cannot be explained by individual-level differences within them: indeed between-country differences in turnout exceed differences that are the consequence of individual-level characteristics. Change over time within countries is strongly shaped by processes of generational replacement that can be modeled at both the individual and aggregate levels (Franklin 2004; Franklin, Lyons, and Marsh 2004; van der Brug and Franklin in this volume). But between-country differences also are generally much greater than those associated with change over time.[2]

Aggregate-level electoral research presents methodological challenges. Countries differ in their cultures, in their social and economic development, and in their institutions. Change in these variables is slow. Institutional change is rare. Change within countries occurs more in the character of elections: in how much elections are perceived to matter, changes in the nature and strategies of actors, and in consequent voter perceptions of efficacy. Examining temporal change, one can cautiously make causal inferences. But because many country characteristics are within-country constants, modeling those relies on cross-sectional variation (for important exceptions, see Franklin 2004; Vowles, Katz, and Stevens 2015), and thus there is rarely empirical evidence of causality: such inferences rely largely on theory.

Time series analysis within cross-sectional panels presents further challenges. Trending in dependent and independent variables presents dangers of spurious correlation. Autocorrelation and the possible presence of unit roots in dependent variables add to the difficulties, as does the risk of heteroscedasticity. All these can be addressed through batteries of diagnostic tests and "fixes" (Beck and Katz 1995; Beck 2001; Wooldridge 2002; Wilson and Butler 2007). Over the years, awareness of such problems has grown and standards in recent research (following the hugely influential Beck and Katz 1995) are higher than in the past.

Up, down, or trendless?

Debate continues about electoral turnout trends. The Institute for Democracy and Electoral Assistance (IDEA) maintains a valuable database on electoral turnout around the world. The IDEA data estimate turnout as a percentage of those registered to vote, and also on an age-eligible population basis. These distinct statistics are the focus of another debate in the literature. Turnout on a registration basis excludes those not registered, which can be a significant number. Some people may be registered more than once. The list may contain people who have died or left the country. Turnout on an age-eligible population basis requires census data based estimates, and in many countries the denominator of the fraction will contain non-citizens, non-residents, and others ineligible to vote. The choice between the two means of estimation is difficult: some analysts choose one, some the other, and increasingly both (Geys 2006: 638–640).

Some may argue that seeking to generalize about turnout trends internationally is pointless: there is too much inexplicable country-level variation, and too much potential for error. Nonetheless, there remains a demand for systematic descriptions of this kind. IDEA provides further information in its database: the type of election (European Union, parliamentary, or presidential), whether or not voting is compulsory, and the Freedom House score of political and civil rights, the latter only available in the data from the beginning of Freedom House data collection from the early 1970s.

For national presidential and parliamentary elections, Figure 5.1 shows the trend of turnout change over this period in countries that have consistently scored one or two on the Freedom House Index, and in which an uninterrupted time series begins at some point in the 1970s or earlier: 31 relatively long-term free or full democracies with populations over 200,000.[3] The data are averaged over five-year time periods, allowing most countries to contribute at least one election to each estimate. Regardless of use of the registration or age-eligible base, average turnout is down by 11–12 percent from a peak in the period around 1980 to the present: by 77 to 65 percent on an age-eligible base, and 82 to 71 percent on a registration base. The peak is not at the beginning of the time series, but part way in. Examination of data prior to the 1970s suggests increasing turnout to about 1980 from a somewhat lower level in 1945, but the mix of countries in the earlier period is a smaller subset. In various regressions unreported here, fixed

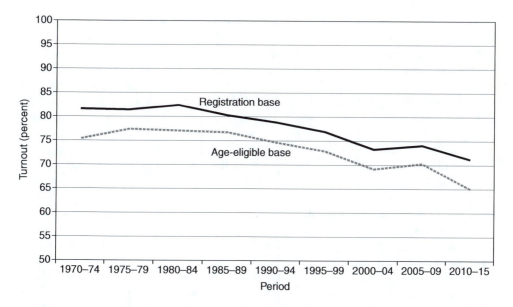

Figure 5.1 Turnout 1971–2014, 31 consistently free countries

country effects models controlling for lagged turnout, compulsory voting, parliamentary versus presidential, and population show that variation between countries is far greater than change over time, but change over time is highly significant, its slope after those controls closely reflecting those in Figure 5.1.

The consequences of turnout variation

Does the level of turnout matter, and if so, how and why? Normative debates inevitably enter the picture. For some, high turnout is intrinsically a "good" that maximizes inclusiveness, a key conceptual element of democracy (Dahl 1973). For others, high turnout is to be valued or not valued because of its consequences, with normative principles still very much in the debate.

From evidence indicating that many people know little about politics, some infer that the votes of people who are ill-informed about politics are not worth having, and the democratic process might be better off without them (for example, Caplan 2006; Rosema 2007; Brennan 2009). In a canonical contribution, Converse (1964) reported that repeated survey research indicates low levels of ideological consistency among many citizens, over time and even within an interview. In response to survey questions to which they did not know how to respond, people were sometimes prone to construct "non-attitudes." There are very few people who know enough about politics to fit into a model of the fully informed citizen (Delli Carpini and Keeter 1996; Bartels 2008; but see Bølstad in this volume, and Erikson in this volume). Low knowledge is also found among many people who vote regularly. Claims about "low quality voters" fail to consider the threshold below which, on those assumptions, one might decide that even people who vote now might be better off not doing so.

The majority of citizens are not perfect deliberators. Even the most informed often fail to change their opinions when confronted by contrary evidence (Kuklinski et al. 2000; Taber and Lodge 2006). High levels of knowledge do not guarantee well-considered choices. Given this, there is a case for valuing everyone's preferences: the more who are counted, the more likely a collective choice will be better for everyone (Surowiecki 2004). While a high number of completely random choices among the uninformed would do nothing to enhance elections (Katz 1997: 245), if those choices are random they are unlikely to create bias. There may be very few choices made that are completely random: voters can often get by with very little information and still make the choices that they would have made with more information (Popkin 1991; Page and Shapiro 1992; Lupia 1994). Such cues may be biased, but so may be the sources of information from which more knowledgeable voters draw: they too may have cognitive biases. The debate about whether or not we should value maximum or minimum turnout in terms of vote "quality" is at heart normative, and cannot be resolved by empirical analysis.

However, empirical research can seek to uncover the consequences of differential turnout on which basis some judgments might be made. Key (1949: 527) observed that politicians are "under no compulsion to pay much heed to classes and groups of citizens that do not vote." As Burnham (1987: 99) put it, "if you don't vote, you don't count." In the United States and elsewhere, those who are less likely to vote are to be found among the young, those on low incomes, and those with low levels of education (Verba, Scholzman, and Brady 1995; Leighley and Nagler 2013) – often the same individuals. One might therefore expect less government attentiveness to the young, the poor, and the less educated, among whom low turnout is concentrated (Solt 2010). Studies of turnout and policy bias across the American states confirm the claim that unequal participation, income inequality, and policy bias are linked, some pointing the causal arrow in one direction, some in the other, and some denying a relationship. Avery (2015) reviews the literature. Using a variety of robustness tests, he confirms that the strongest evidence supports causality from turnout bias through policy bias to inequality.

Drawing on international evidence, the debate is more strongly contested. Many argue that low turnout tends to generate a bias among those who can or do vote toward those on higher incomes (for example, references in Lijphart 1997; Giger, Rosset, and Bernauer 2012). Again, policy consequences are identified. As in the American literature, these are not necessarily reflected in the partisan composition of governments or legislatures (Grofman, Owen, and Collet 1999; Bernhagen and Marsh 2007). Instead, the case is made in terms of policy outcomes. Governments of left or right alike will deliver public policy in the interests of the young and poor if those groups vote at levels comparable to the rest of the population (Kenworthy and Pontusson 2005; Mahler 2008; Boix 2003: 184–191). Otherwise, policies will target the better off (Griffin and Newman 2013). Policies aimed to benefit the young and poor reduce inequality and provide incentives for people in those groups to vote, potentially breaking the cycle of inequality in both participation and incomes. Compulsory voting is often recommended to achieve better representation of those on lower incomes (Fowler 2013; Carey and Horuichi 2014).

There are findings that more equal societies tend to have higher turnout (Mahler 2002). However, the relationship between inequality and turnout remains contested. In a study containing data from 101 countries between 1970 and 2010, Stockemer and Scruggs (2012) find no such relationship, whether for developed countries separately or throughout their full dataset. Their estimate of inequality comes from Gini coefficients. Solt's (2008) study is a multi-level analysis based on 23 developed countries merging aggregate and survey data from the 1980s and 1990s. Developed countries are the focus. Solt argues that in less developed countries clientelistic politics will distribute goods to groups powerful enough to claim them, not promoting equality. Because his analysis is multi-level, Solt can interact the Gini coefficient with household income and estimate effects on the basis of income quintiles. He finds that inequality minimizes turnout most among the poor.

This is the key claim in the debate: not so much that inequality is associated with low turnout overall, but that inequality is associated with lower turnout among the poor. Kasara and

Suryanarayan (2015) argue that under conditions of high state capacity and redistribution of incomes that reduce inequality, the rich may be disposed to vote more than the poor in order to reduce their tax exposure. But they question Solt's finding that the poor are less likely to vote in developed countries where inequality is high. In less developed countries, where state capacity to redistribute is low and inequality is high, the rich have less need to vote, and the poor may be more likely to do so because of vote-buying and clientelism. The relationships between inequality, state capacity, redistribution, and turnout therefore remain unclear. At high levels of inequality, redistributive spending is low, and turnout has slightly negative effects on the size of government (Ansell and Samuels, 2014: 141–170; Boix 2003: 191). Progress toward greater consensus in this debate requires multi-level models because both macro- and micro-level data are needed.

Before turning to review three of the main areas of research in the aggregate-level study of turnout, one should note the very useful meta-analysis of the literature up to 2006 provided by Geys (2006). Summarizing findings about which there is no space to discuss here, Geys found that the majority of studies that included it found an effect for population size: turnout is lower in larger countries, higher in smaller ones. Population concentration in urban versus rural areas is much less frequently found to have an effect. Work based on aggregate measurements of individual-level characteristics indicates that stability of population and asset ownership as measured by the proportion of home-owners also had consistent effects when tested. Ethnic heterogeneity tends to reduce turnout, in proportion to the size of minority groups. Past levels of turnout are also a good predictor of present turnout. Campaign expenditure is another good predictor, with some effects for its tone and negative/positive balance. Compulsory voting delivers one of the most robust positive findings for turnout, depending on its level of enforcement. Ease of registration and ease of voting generally also tend to have consistent positive effects.

The differences of "order"

The establishment of direct elections to the European Parliament was a landmark in the development of electoral politics: the first major experiment in cross-national democracy. In terms of turnout, the result has been disappointing. This experience led analysts to the concept of "second-order elections," those deemed to be of relatively low importance by voters, parties, and the mass media (Reif and Schmitt 1980; Van der Eijk and Franklin 1996). National elections determining the holders of state executive power are "first order." Lower-level federal, regional, and local elections also fall into the "second-order" category. Second-order election behavior is shaped by the politics of the related first-order elections, citizens taking cues from the performance of their national governments, not so much from politics at the second-order level.

Second-order election theory is most applied to European Parliamentary elections. Low turnout is a major indicator of second-order status, raising issues of circularity given that low turnout is one of the theory's key predictions. Research in the Netherlands indicates that the prediction of low turnout, while confirmed at the aggregate level, is less well supported by individual-level data. Because turnout in second-order elections is more affected by mobilization, the absence of mobilization may be more important than perceptions of voters and non-voters themselves (Lefevre and Van Aelst 2014). The alternative claim that apathy and skepticism about the European project itself may outweigh perceptions of "less at stake" is either refuted (Franklin and Hobolt 2011) or shown to be weak (Schmitt, Sanz, and Braun 2008). Switching into non-voting is also related to discontent among those who had voted for the incumbent national government, although only where party systems are most institutionally entrenched in Western

Europe, where the European election was timed near the middle of the national electoral cycle, and found more strongly under single-party governments (Schmitt, Sanz, and Braun 2008).

Outside the politics of the European Parliament, local government provides opportunities for second-order analysis. From the beginnings of the systematic analysis of local elections (Morlan 1984), findings of lower turnout are consistent with the theory. However, the categories of first and second order may be too blunt. In the United Kingdom, turnout has tended to be higher in local than European elections because it is perceived that there is more at stake locally than across Europe (Heath et al. 1999). Cross-national comparison including both European and non-European countries indicates that turnout in local elections is not always lower than in national elections. Coining the term "turnout twist," Horiuchi (2004) has operationalized an independent indicator of how much is at stake from tax revenues and government expenditures that explains such cases.

Second-order election theory comes down to two claims: first, that high-stake elections will affect behavior at low-stake elections. This assumes that the same actors are in play at the different levels: non-partisan local elections do not fit in this picture. Another possibility has also been investigated: behavior at low-stake elections could have marginal but significant effects on those with high stakes. Turnout at United States presidential elections is correlated with that at previous mid-term elections, more so than with turnout at the previous presidential election (Franklin 2004: 107). Direct elections to the European Parliament have reduced turnout in European national parliamentary elections (Franklin and Hobolt 2011). Another "twist" comes from findings that in parliamentary systems where the Head of State is independently elected, turnout in parliamentary elections is adversely affected, although offset if those elections are concurrent (Tavits 2009). Concurrent presidential and legislative elections may boost turnout generally (Fornos, Power, and Garand 2004; Geys 2006: 652).

The second important claim of second-order theory is that people will vote or not vote according to how much is at stake, usually communicated to the electorate by party mobilization and media coverage. As developed by Horiuchi (2004), independent estimates of what is at stake seem the best way forward. Analysis linking the effects of the character of elections to turnout within individual countries use manifesto data or survey-based perceptions of party differences to show that turnout is higher where elections matter in these terms (see for examples Heath 2007; Vowles, Katz, and Stevens 2015).

The competitiveness model

Theoretically and empirically, the most comprehensive research on turnout at both aggregate and individual levels remains Mark Franklin's *Voter Turnout and the Dynamics of Electoral Competition in Established Democracies Since 1945* (2004). Franklin develops the insight that elections must matter to encourage people to vote and incorporates it within a general theory of electoral competitiveness. That competition should matter follows from the classic Downsian model where "p," the probability of one's vote having an effect, interacts with "b," the benefits one might anticipate if one's preferred candidate or party were elected (Downs 1957). Competitiveness is usually identified as the closeness of the race perceived by voters and parties. In district-based systems, parties will tend to target their mobilization efforts in the most competitive areas, reducing "c," the costs of voting, the third element on the right-hand side of the Downsian equation. Defined broadly, competitiveness tends to particularly encourage young people first entering the electorate to vote, and helps establish a habit of voting or not voting that subsequently "sticks," reducing the effects of later short-term influences, and establishing the foundations of variations in turnout between generations or age cohorts.

Ups and downs in the development of habits of voting or non-voting might remain relatively constant around a mean without any clear trend toward higher or lower competitiveness. However, in countries where elections have become less competitive and policy differences between parties more narrow, turnout decline is highly likely and non-competitiveness may be the most important driving force. For example, in the case of Britain, it has been claimed that there has been no trend toward lower competitiveness in terms of election margins that can be linked to turnout decline (Heath 2007) or that changes in electoral margins have had little or no effect on turnout (Blais and Rubenson 2013). Contrary evidence also taking account of generational replacement (see van der Brug and Franklin in this volume) is provided by Vowles, Katz, and Stevens (2015).

Much depends on how the electoral margins are used to define competition in terms of the closeness of the race. Most analysts use the vote share gap between first and second place at the election in question, measured at the national level, and the vast majority of studies up to 2006 have found a significant relationship (Geys 2006: 647). Where competition takes place in districts, margins can also be estimated at that level. Even when the race is not close nationally, a close local contest will still have effects (Franklin and Evans 2000). Most analysts calculate an "ex post" margin from the results of the election in question, effectively assuming that voters and non-voters could predict it exactly, thus biasing estimates. "Ex ante" margins work better (Geys 2006: 648). These can come from two sources: the margins from the previous election, or an average of polls, usually taken in the last week of the campaign. However, polls can only be used at the national level as even if there is any district-level polling it is usually fragmentary. The almost invariable choice of vote margins at the national level is, however, peculiar, particularly in non-proportional systems where seat margins at the previous election are a much better guide to the possibility of a change of government. Because there are multiple indicators of closeness, it makes sense to use as many as can be estimated in order to specify the full effects (for example, see Vowles, Katz, and Stevens 2015).

For example, Franklin (2004) incorporates an additional measure in his concept of competitiveness, a measure he later refers to as one of clarity of choices: the size of the largest party relative to 50 percent. Where the largest party receives half the votes, the contest is simplified to one of that party against the rest. As the gap between the largest party and 50 percent increases, the stakes in the contest become harder to assess, so this aspect of competition is also linked to the measure of electoral stakes already discussed.

Where PR systems operate entirely with national lists, there is no district margin to add to the mix. Yet many PR systems do use districts, and/or regional lists, and in these cases district margins can also be estimated. Indeed, at least three means of doing so have been suggested, one angle being to most closely approximate the first/second-place margin approach (Blais and Lago 2009; Grofman and Selb 2009), another being to estimate the chances of the previous plurality party losing its position (Kayser and Lindstadt 2015). Competitiveness can also be measured on a multi-party basis (Endersby, Galatas, and Rackaway 2002). So far, these new and more sophisticated measures of competitiveness have not been applied widely. It remains to be seen whether they will make much difference to what now must be approaching a consensus: close elections do matter.

A question remains: why do they matter? Is it the expectation that a governing executive may be dismissed (Kayser and Lindstadt 2015)? Or is the key mechanism a more general perception of uncertainty? Where polls indicate an incumbent government will be re-elected, or a candidate is strongly entrenched in a safe electoral district, those considering their vote will be very certain that it will make no difference. Where the margin is close, one cannot rule out the chance that one's vote could make a difference, unlikely though it may be. One might think of casting a vote in such circumstances as like buying a lottery ticket: one becomes a minor participant in the game. There may be a payoff by way of anticipation of the result and vicarious engagement. However, party elites do most of the thinking of this nature. They mobilize the vote and provide cues, targeting their campaigns in order to maximize turnout among their supporters according to the logic of the system in their country.

The PR debate

One of the most strongly contested debates in the literature on electoral turnout is about the effects of electoral systems. Systematic comparative empirical analysis kicked off in the 1980s, with work by Powell (1980, 1986). Powell found a positive effect for "nationally competitive electoral districts." Jackman (1987) took up that challenge, adding a variable measuring electoral disproportionality. He also included an estimate of party system fragmentation. While proportionality enhanced turnout, party system fragmentation had the opposite effects. Party system fragmentation increases uncertainty that votes will directly affect executive power, also true of Franklin's clarity of choices measure. In such circumstances, government formation may be determined more by elite bargaining.

Following Jackman, Blais and Carty (1990) took the analysis further, including elections back to the nineteenth century and employing a pooled time series model, setting the standard for all subsequent studies. They estimated the effects of electoral institutions formally, rather than in terms of proportionality. They estimated the effects of plurality, majority, and majority multi-member districts against PR systems as the reference category. On top of controls including compulsory or voluntary voting, and the logged size of the legislature as proxy for population, they found a 7 percent positive effect for PR against their defined alternatives.

The next step was to expand the analysis beyond the old established democracies, and here the consensus began to break down. Analysis of post-communist countries confirmed the finding (Kostandinova 2003) but no effects were found in Latin America (Pérez-Linàn 2001; Fornos, Power, and Garand 2004). Blais and Dobrzynska (1998) found only a weak 3 percent positive effect for PR when incorporating both old-established and more recently established democracies. Reviewing the findings, Blais and Aarts (2006) summarized a set of positive effects for turnout under PR, with the exception of Latin America, but were skeptical because of the weakness of the findings and uncertainty about their micro-level foundations.

The PR debate inevitably draws on the analysis of electoral competitiveness. If competitiveness is about expectations that a government might be dismissed, those expectations could be weaker under PR where party system fragmentation is high. On the other hand, if competitiveness is about uncertainty, PR maximizes uncertainty, particularly in terms of a vote affecting a single seat shift. PR also means that those wishing to vote for small parties unlikely to win single-member districts can vote without the certainty of knowing their parties will be unsuccessful. For the most part, PR systems abolish safe districts, again removing a source of certainty that many votes will not effectively count.

Indeed Selb (2009) has found the lack of competitiveness in safe districts under plurality systems to be largely responsible for lower turnout than under PR. His data was from aggregate district-level turnout data from 28 national parliamentary elections and 1113 electoral districts. To compare ex post margins comparable with single member plurality districts for multi-member PR districts, for the PR districts he estimated the margin for the contest for the last seat to be allocated (Selb 2009: 537). The data were confined to the old democracies with the addition of a scattering of newer democracies: Hungary, Mexico, Poland, Portugal, Spain, and Romania.

The problem of inconsistencies between the old and the new democracies was addressed by Endersby and Krieckhaus (2008). They criticized the use of registration-base turnout figures. Using an age-eligible base, they found that in fully democratic countries PR increases turnout by 5–10 percentage points compared to plurality-majority systems. The effects are higher in fully democratic countries. PR has no effects in partially democratic countries. This may explain the paucity of findings for Latin America. The use of a registration-based turnout estimate in earlier research also reduces the PR effect. The authors argue strongly for an age-eligible base estimation. Disaggregating non-PR systems, they find that it is majority systems and non-compensatory mixed systems that have the lowest turnout as compared to PR systems. The sign for simple plurality systems is negative but not significant.

However, most of this research has a major weakness. Because systems rarely change, most analysts draw their leverage almost entirely from cross-sectional country differences. Marking further progress in this debate, Cox, Fiva, and Smith (2015) investigate Norway's 1921 electoral reform and confirm the logic of Selb's (2009) findings: after change, variance in turnout across districts contracts toward an intermediate level. Where under the previous system the majority of districts were noncompetitive, a change of system to PR will increase average turnout. Turnout goes down in formerly competitive districts where elite mobilization was high, but rises elsewhere to more than compensate.

On the other hand, Vowles' (2010) macro-micro analysis of New Zealand elections, six before and four after the country's change to mixed-member PR in 1996, finds no robust electoral system effects. After a short-lived initial upturn, turnout continued to go down in conditions of lower overall vote mobilization, lower levels of national vote competition, disruptive electoral boundary changes, and the replacement of higher-voting earlier generations by lower-voting recent generations. Consistent with the findings of Cox, Fiva, and Smith (2015), district-level variation in turnout was reduced to insignificance. Some models indicated somewhat higher voting among those entering the electorate after the change compared to those beginning to vote before, but these findings were not robust or consistent. Consistent with the finding that "habit" matters (see Dinas in this volume), more elections under the new system may be needed for an identifiable difference to emerge. As things stand, the claim that PR enhances turnout still has the most support, but the debate will continue.

Conclusions

This review of macro-level explanations of variance in turnout illustrates both the strengths and the weaknesses of aggregate-level explanations, despite their strong explanatory power. We can confirm that turnout is declining in countries that have generated a sufficiently long time series for measurement. There is now a reasonable consensus that closeness of electoral margins matters, as well as policy differences between parties. PR does probably promote turnout if it abolishes non-competitive districts. Turnout can be low among the poor, but might be offset by higher turnout among the rich who vote to reduce their tax liabilities where market incomes are unequal but income redistribution is high. Bias in turnout probably does have public policy consequences, with less government attention paid to those who do not vote. But the international findings remain somewhat inconclusive. Aggregate-level analysis alone is insufficient to address many of these problems: the future lies in multi-level analyses bringing together and interacting variables at the macro- and micro-levels.

Notes

1 The CSES website can be accessed at www.cses.org.
2 Countries that have, during the period under study, experienced multiple changes in election rules and practices (e.g., Switzerland) can show turnout variations that rival between-country differences (Franklin 2004: 11, Table 1.1).
3 The countries are Australia, Austria, Bahamas, Barbados, Belgium, Canada, Costa Rica, Cyprus, Denmark, Finland, France, Germany, Greece, Iceland, Ireland, Israel, Italy, Japan, Luxembourg, Malta, Mauritius, Netherlands, New Zealand, Norway, Portugal, Spain, Sweden, Switzerland, Trinidad and Tobago, the United Kingdom, and the United States.

References

Ansell, B. and Samuels, D. (2014) *Inequality and Democratization: An Elite-Competition Approach*, New York: Cambridge University Press.

Avery, J. (2015) "Does Who Votes Matter? Income Bias in Voter Turnout and Economic Inequality in the American States from 1980 to 2010," *Political Behavior*, vol. 37, no. 4, December, 955–976.

Bartels, L. (2008) *Unequal Democracy: The Political Economy of the New Gilded Age*, Princeton: Princeton University Press.

Beck, N. (2001) "Time-Series-Cross-Section Data: What Have We Learned in the Past Few Years?" *Annual Review of Political Science*, vol. 4, June, 272–293.

Beck, N. and Katz, J. N. (1995) "What to Do (and Not to Do) with Time-Series Cross-Section Data," *American Political Science Review*, vol. 89, no. 3, September, 634–647.

Bernhagen, P. and Marsh, M. (2007) "The Partisan Effects of Low Turnout: Analyzing Vote Abstention as a Missing Data Problem," *Electoral Studies*, vol. 26, no. 3, September, 548–560.

Blais, A. and Aarts, K. (2006) "Electoral Systems and Turnout," *Acta Politica*, vol. 41, no. 2, July, 180–196.

Blais, A. and Carty, R. K. (1990) "Does Proportional Representation Foster Voter Turnout," *European Journal of Political Research*, vol. 18, no. 2, March, 167–181.

Blais, A. and Dobrzynska, A. (1998) "Turnout in Electoral Democracies," *European Journal of Political Research*, vol. 33, no. 2, March, 239–261.

Blais, A. and Lago, I. (2009) "A General Measure of District Competitiveness," *Electoral Studies*, vol. 28, no. 1, March, 94–100.

Blais, A. and Rubenson, D. (2013) "The Source of Turnout Decline: New Values or New Contexts?" *Comparative Political Studies*, vol. 46, no. 1, January, 95–117.

Boix, C. (2003) *Democracy and Redistribution*, Cambridge: Cambridge University Press.

Brennan, J. (2009) "Polluting the Polls: When Citizens Should Not Vote," *Australasian Journal of Philosophy*, vol. 87, no. 4, December, 535–549.

Burnham, W. D. (1987) "The Turnout Problem," in Reichley, A. J. (ed.) *Elections American Style*, Washington, DC: Brookings Institution: 97–133.

Caplan, B. (2006) *The Myth of The Rational Voter: Why Democracies Choose Bad Policies*, Princeton: Princeton University Press.

Carey, J. and Horuichi, Y. (2014) "Compulsory Voting and Income Inequality," Paper presented at 2014 Annual Meeting of the American Political Science Association, Washington, DC, August 28–31.

Converse, P. (1964) "The Nature of Belief Systems in Mass Publics," in Apter, D. E. (ed.) *Ideology and Discontent*, New York: Free Press of Glencoe: 206–261.

Cox, G. W., Fiva, J. H., and Smith, D. M. (2015) "The Contraction Effect: How Proportional Representation Affects Mobilization and Turnout," Working Paper, September 8.

Dahl, R. (1973) *Polyarchy: Participation and Opposition*, New Haven: Yale University Press.

Delli Carpini, M. X. and Keeter, S. (1996) *What Americans Know About Politics and Why It Matters*, New Haven: Yale University Press.

Downs, A. (1957) *An Economic Theory of Democracy*, New York: Harper and Row.

Eijk, C. van der and Franklin, M. N. (1996) *Choosing Europe? The European Electorate and National Politics in the Face of Union*, Ann Arbor: University of Michigan Press.

Endersby, J. W. and Krieckhaus, J. T. (2008) "Turnout Around the Globe: The Influence of Electoral Institutions on National Voter Participation, 1972–2000," *Electoral Studies*, vol. 27, no. 4, December, 601–610.

Endersby, J. W., Galatas, S. E., and Rackaway, C. B. (2002) "Closeness Counts in Canada: Voter Participation in the 1993 and 1997 Federal Elections," *Journal of Politics*, vol. 64, no. 2, May, 610–631.

Fornos, C. A., Power, T. J., and Garand, J. C. (2004) "Explaining Voter Turnout in Latin America, 1980–2000," *Comparative Political Studies*, vol. 37, no. 8, October, 909–940.

Fowler, A. (2013) "Electoral and Policy Consequences of Voter Turnout: Evidence from Compulsory Voting in Australia," *Quarterly Journal of Political Science*, vol. 8, no. 2, April, 159–182.

Franklin, M. N. (2004) *Voter Turnout and the Dynamics of Electoral Competition in Established Democracies Since 1945*, Cambridge: Cambridge University Press.

Franklin, M. N. and Evans, D. (2000) "The Low Voter Turnout Problem," in Zimmerman, J. F. and Rule, W. (eds.) *The US House of Representatives: Reform or Rebuild?* Westport: Praeger: 97–113.

Franklin, M. N. and Hobolt, S. B. (2011) "The Legacy of Lethargy: How Elections to the European Parliament Depress Turnout," *Electoral Studies*, vol. 30, no. 1, March, 67–76.

Franklin, M. N., Lyons, P., and Marsh, M. (2004) "The Generational Basis of Turnout Decline in Established Democracies," *Acta Politica*, vol. 39, no. 2, July, 115–151.

Geys, B. (2006) "Explaining Voter Turnout: A Review of Aggregate-Level Research," *Electoral Studies*, vol. 25, no. 4, December, 637–663.

Giger, N., Rosset, J., and Bernauer, J. (2012) "The Poor Political Representation of the Poor in a Comparative Perspective," *Representation*, vol. 48, no. 1, April, 47–61.

Griffin, J. D. and Newman, B. (2013) "Voting Power, Policy Representation, and Disparities in Voting's Rewards," *Journal of Politics*, vol. 75, no. 1, December, 52–64.

Grofman, B. N. and Selb, P. (2009) "A Fully General Index of Political Competition," *Electoral Studies*, vol. 28, no. 2, June, 291–296.

Grofman, B. N., Owen, G., and Collet, C. (1999) "Rethinking the Partisan Effects of Higher Turnout: So What's the Question?" *Public Choice*, vol. 99, no. 3, June, 357–376.

Heath, A., McLean, I., Taylor, B., and Curtice, J. (1999) "Between First and Second Order: A Comparison of Voting Behavior in European and Local Elections in Britain," *European Journal of Political Research*, vol. 35, no. 3, May, 389–414.

Heath, O. (2007) "Explaining Turnout Decline in Britain 1964–2005: Party Identification and the Political Context," *Political Behavior*, vol. 29, no. 4, December, 493–516.

Horuichi, Y. (2004) *Institutions, Incentives, and Electoral Participation in Japan*, Abingdon: Routledge.

International IDEA (2015) Voter Turnout Database, [Online], available: www.idea.int/data-tools/data/voter-turnout [accessed: December 1, 2015].

Jackman, R. W. (1987) "Political Institutions and Voter Turnout in the Industrial Democracies," *American Political Science Review*, vol. 81, no. 2, June, 405–423.

Kasara, K. and Suryanarayan, P. (2015) "When Do the Rich Vote Less Than the Poor and Why? Explaining Turnout Inequality across the World," *American Journal of Political Science*, vol. 59, no. 3, July, 613–627.

Katz, R. (1997) *Democracy and Elections*, New York: Oxford University Press.

Kayser, M. and Lindstadt, R. (2015) "A Cross-National Measure of Electoral Competitiveness," *Political Analysis*, vol. 23, no. 2, Spring, 242–253.

Kenworthy, L. and Pontusson, J. (2005) "Rising Inequality and the Politics of Redistribution in Affluent Countries," *Perspectives on Politics*, vol. 3, no. 3, September, 449–471.

Key, V. O. (1949) *Southern Politics in State and Nation*, Knoxville: University of Tennessee Press.

Kostadinova, T. (2003) "Voter Turnout Dynamics in Post-Communist Europe," *European Journal of Political Research*, vol. 42, no. 6, October, 741–759.

Kuklinski, J. H., Quirk, P. J., Jerit, J., Schwieder, D., and Rich, R. F. (2000) "Misinformation and the Currency of Democratic Citizenship," *Journal of Politics*, vol. 62, no. 3, August, 790–816.

Lefevere, J. and Van Aelst, P. (2014) "First-Order, Second-Order or Third-Rate? A Comparison of Turnout in European, Local and National Elections in the Netherlands," *Electoral Studies*, vol. 35, September, 159–170.

Leighley, J. E. and Nagler, J. (2013) *Who Votes Now? Demographics, Issues, Inequality, and Turnout in the United States*, Princeton: Princeton University Press.

Lijphart, A. (1997) "Unequal Participation: Democracy's Unresolved Dilemma," *American Political Science Review*, vol. 91, no. 1, March, 1–14.

Lupia, A. (1994) "Shortcuts Versus Encyclopedias: Information and Voting in California Insurance Reform Elections," *American Political Science Review*, vol. 88, no. 1, March, 63–76.

Mahler, V. A. (2002) "Explaining the Subnational Dimensions of Income Inequality: An Analysis of the Relationship Between Inequality and Turnout in the Developed Countries," *International Studies Quarterly*, vol. 46, no. 1, March, 117–142.

Mahler, V. A. (2008) "Electoral Turnout and Income Redistribution by the State: A Cross-National Analysis of the Developed Democracies," *European Journal of Political Research*, vol. 47, no. 2, March, 161–183.

Morlan, R. L. (1984) "Municipal vs. National Election Voter Turnout: Europe and the United States," *Political Science Quarterly*, vol. 99, no. 3, Autumn, 457–470.

Page, B. I. and Shapiro, R. Y. (1992) *The Rational Public: Fifty Years of Trends in Americans' Policy Preferences*, Chicago: University of Chicago Press.

Pérez-Linàn, A. (2001) "Neo-Institutional Accounts of Voter Turnout: Moving Beyond Industrial Democracies," *Electoral Studies*, vol. 20, no. 2, June, 281–297.

Popkin, S. L. (1991) *The Reasoning Voter: Communication and Persuasion in Presidential Campaigns*, Chicago: University of Chicago Press.

Powell, G. B. (1980) "Voting Turnout in Thirty Democracies: Partisan, Legal, and Socio-Economic Influences," in Rose, R. (ed.) *Electoral Participation: A Comparative Analysis*, Beverly Hills: Sage: 5–34.

Powell, G. B. (1986) "American Voter Turnout in Comparative Perspective," *American Political Science Review*, vol. 80, no. 1, March, 17–43.

Reif, K. H. and Schmitt, H. (1980) "Nine Second-Order National Elections – A Conceptual Framework for the Analysis of European Election Results," *European Journal of Political Research*, vol. 8, no. 1, March, 3–44.

Rosema, M. (2007) "Low Turnout: Threat to Democracy or Blessing in Disguise? Consequences of Citizens' Varying Tendencies to Vote," *Electoral Studies*, vol. 26, no. 3, September, 612–623.

Schmitt, H., Sanz, A., and Braun, D. (2008) "The Micro-Foundations of Second-Order Election Theory: Theoretical Reconstructions and Empirical Tests Based Upon the European Election Study 2004," Paper presented at the Citizen Politics Workshop, University of Manchester, December 9–11, 2008.

Selb, P. (2009) "A Deeper Look at the Proportionality-Turnout Nexus," *Comparative Political Studies*, vol. 42, no. 4, April, 527–558.

Solt, F. (2008) "Economic Inequality and Democratic Political Engagement," *American Journal of Political Science*, vol. 52, no. 1, January, 48–60.

Solt, F. (2010) "Does Economic Inequality Depress Electoral Participation? Testing the Schattschneider Hypothesis," *Political Behavior*, vol. 32, no. 2, June, 285–301.

Stockemer, D. and Scruggs, L. (2012) "Income Inequality, Development and Electoral Turnout – New Evidence on a Burgeoning Debate," *Electoral Studies*, vol. 31, no. 4, December, 764–773.

Surowiecki, J. (2004) *The Wisdom of Crowds: Why the Many Are Smarter Than the Few*, London: Abacus.

Taber, C. S. and Lodge, M. (2006) "Motivated Skepticism in the Evaluation of Political Beliefs," *American Journal of Political Science*, vol. 50, no. 3, July, 755–769.

Tavits, M. (2009) "Direct Presidential Elections and Turnout in Parliamentary Contests," *Political Research Quarterly*, vol. 62, no. 1, March, 42–54.

Verba, S., Schlozman, K. L., and Brady, H. (1995) *Voice and Equality: Civic Voluntarism in American Politics*, Cambridge: Harvard University Press.

Vowles, J. (2010) "Electoral System Change, Generations, Competitiveness and Turnout in New Zealand, 1963–2005," *British Journal of Political Science*, vol. 40, no. 4, October, 875–895.

Vowles, J., Katz, G., and Stevens, D. (2015) "Electoral Competitiveness and Turnout in British Elections, 1964–2010," *Political Science Research and Methods*, available online: https://doi.org/10.1017/psrm.2015.67.

Wilson, S. E. and Butler, D. M. (2007) "A Lot More to Do: The Sensitivity of Time-Series Cross-Section Analyzes to Simple Alternative Specifications," *Political Analysis*, vol. 15, no. 2, Spring, 101–123.

Wooldridge, J. M. (2002) *Econometric Analysis of Cross-Section and Panel Data*, Cambridge, MA: MIT Press.

6

DEMOGRAPHICS AND THE SOCIAL BASES OF VOTER TURNOUT

Eric Plutzer

Demographics as the essential core of political behavior research

The term "demographics" conjures up the idea of personal characteristics whose categories are typically reported in national censuses and government reports. In every nation, sex, age, marital status, educational attainment and some measure of economic status comprise the core concepts typically reported. In addition, the "essential core" might include language spoken at home in Canada and Switzerland; race, religion and residential mobility in the United States; or ethnicity in Uganda and Nigeria.

For scholars of political behavior generally, demographic characteristics represent highly accessible data that are often correlated with behaviors such as turnout, participation, issue preferences and party affiliation. Although scholars may consider different approaches to coding and measurement, the operationalization of demographic concepts has been relatively uncontroversial in comparison to the definition and measurement of concepts such as efficacy, alienation and other psychological traits believed to be causes of political behavior. The relative stability of many demographic characteristics also makes them attractive because reverse causality is (often) less plausible. For example, voting in a recent election is unlikely to fundamentally alter a citizen's reported age, sex, education or income.

For these reasons – ease of access, uncontested conceptualization and exogeneity – demographic characteristics have formed the essential core of any analysis that seeks to explain why citizens differ in their political behaviors.

The roots of this can be seen in all the classic studies of political behavior. Lazarsfeld, Berelson and Gaudet (1944), for example, examined age, education, occupation, age, place of residence and sex as predictors of political participation and engagement. Demographic predictors were used at least to some extent by Centers (1949) in *The Psychology of Social Classes*, Key's (1961) *Public Opinion and American Democracy* (1961), *The American Voter* (Campbell et al. 1960) and most notably in the essays Lipset published in the volume *Political Man* (1960).

The declining usefulness of simple demographics

Demographic variables' ease of use, however, can easily lull even experienced scholars into superficial – dare I say lazy – social research. Indeed, there are five common and recurring threats to valid inference.

First, lurking beneath the apparent consensus on measurement are multiple and conflicting meanings – for example, what exactly do we mean when we say one citizen is more highly educated than another? Might someone who attended Oxford for two years without attaining a degree have "higher" education than a graduate of my own Penn State University? Is a degree earned in 1980 comparable to a degree from the same school in 2015?

Second, observed differences such as gender *gaps*, ethnic *cleavages* and socio-economic *gradients* are the result of complex social processes that ideally should be understood and modeled directly.

Third, differences in measurement quality can sometimes tip the scales in favor of the better measured concept, leading researchers to incorrectly conclude that one variable is "more important" than another (for a modern review and some novel solutions, see Blackwell, Honaker and King 2015).

Fourth, some demographics are less stable than others, which can mislead scholars in interpreting their apparent effects. Instability can be of two types. First, there is instability in the actual construct – when a citizen is classified as married, divorced or single this might reflect a condition that has influenced current behavior for a few weeks, a few years or a few decades. In short, two individuals with the same demographic classification could have very different exposures to the actual causal factors that the demographic proxies are designed to capture.

Instability can also be a function of survey response – as in answering questions about sexual, racial or religious identification differently from time to time. Someone may identify today as African American and tomorrow as mixed race and this type of instability poses a different challenge to inference – with implications for questionnaire design as well as interpretation.

Fifth, and most fundamentally, society has changed dramatically since the pioneers of behavioral research began using demographics to predict political behavior. Social life was more rigid in 1950s and 1960s Europe and North America than it is today. Four examples illustrate this well.

First, men's and women's ideal roles were highly proscribed, and this gave the binary variable "sex" a clear referent that was reflected in observable differences in political engagement (Andersen 1975). Second, a sizable blue collar work force was not only a "class in itself" but, because of strong unions and labor-oriented political parties, blue collar workers comprised a class "for itself." For these reasons, the blue–white collar distinction was highly predictive of many political behaviors, such as political party affiliation, and authoritarian attitudes (Lipset 1960). Third, in Europe especially, university education was restricted to a small group and connoted privileged status. But the democratization of higher education and the growing diversity of higher education options create significant heterogeneity within traditional groupings of educational attainment. Finally, race and ethnicity tended to also put individuals "in their place" with relatively rigid expectations; in contrast, a growing number of citizens now claim multiple racial and ethnic identities – identities that might differ in salience from one day to another. This, along with rapidly changing competition and coalitions among cultural minorities, complicates any attempt to measure and assess the political consequences of racial and ethnic affiliation.

In short, simple demographic classifications were never perfect, but they represented justifiable ways of operationalizing the social bases of politics in the 1950s and 1960s. They may still be useful, but we have graduated beyond their uncritical use.

If "demographic effects" are not as simple as they seem, they remain essential to any effort to understand political behavior. Humans are social animals and the political choices we make are arguably circumscribed by the social worlds we inhabit. For example, our workplaces structure political information we receive (Mutz and Mondak 2006); our neighborhoods and our income determine the extent to which political parties seek to mobilize us (Huckfeldt and Sprague 1995) or seek contributions (Verba, Schlozman and Brady 1995). Thus my goal in writing this chapter is to provide a guide to the social bases of political behavior that will help scholars – both novice and established – to engage in rigorous research that does justice to the complexity of social life and the group affiliations that demographic variables connote. Scholars armed with an appreciation for the complexity underlying these deceptively simple variables will be better equipped to conduct research that is creative, that more closely models the underlying social processes, and is more useful in guiding reforms in public policy.

Ascription, achievement and the fluidity of identity

Anthropologists and sociologists traditionally (see, for example, Foner 1979) distinguish between ascribed traits that do not change (e.g., year of birth, sex) from achieved traits that are the result of individual and social processes (such as education and occupation). That distinction may have been useful as a simplification, but now obscures the importance of *identity* in translating social location into politics. The binary distinction between male and female has given way to sexual and gender identities that challenge traditional roles and challenge traditional notions of biological determinism (Waylen 2013). While European Jews and African Americans in the 1930s had little power over the categories that others placed them in, racial and religious identities are now more fluid (Huddy 2001; Junn and Masuoka 2008; Putnam and Campbell 2012) and more personal (Bellah et al. 2007).

While binary distinctions may be useful as *simplifying assumptions* for empirical research, we can no longer assume uncritically that these distinctions do a good job of capturing the *politically relevant* aspects of personal characteristics. Yet this is exactly what a good deal of contemporary research does. Whether as "control variables" or as potential causes of political behavior, many contemporary scholars continue to use traditional demographic variables and interpret them along outdated, culturally conventional lines.

In that light, my goal in this chapter is to provide readers with a review that empowers them to engage in research that does justice to the underlying social dynamics that give many demographics their explanatory power. Demographics matter – but determining how and why is hard work that can no longer rely on social conventions about "people's place" in the social order.

To do so, I will focus on four of the core clusters of variables that animate politics today. (1) I will begin with demographics that help us to understand political development over the life course: variables such as age, family formation, retirement. (2) I then discuss the cluster of demographics that comprise socio-economic status (SES): especially social status, education and income. (3) We will then move to variables that often interact in domestic life: sex, gender, family structure and labor force participation. (4) Finally, I turn to variables that represent national and geographic heritage – race, ethnicity and national origin. In each case, issues of conceptualization, operationalization and measurement are key considerations.

This is not, of course, an exhaustive list. This chapter will not discuss religion, residential mobility or place of residence (e.g., the urban–rural nexus). However, these variables are strongly illustrative of the key demographic variables that influence political behavior and the general principles that have led to major advances in the other clusters can be applied to other domains.

Scholars armed with an appreciation for the complexity underlying these deceptively simple variables will be better equipped to conduct research that is creative, that more closely models the underlying social processes and that will be more useful in guiding public policy.

Political participation over the life course

Of all demographic factors, none is more prevalent than age. Writing more than 50 years ago, Milbrath (1965: 134) cited eight papers that showed the same empirical pattern: very low turnout characterized the youngest eligible voters, followed by a steep rise in young adulthood followed by gradual increases until voters reach their sixties. Similar patterns are seen in all established democracies (Franklin 2004; Melo and Stockemer 2014) and emerging democracies (Potgieter 2013). Recently, fine-grained analyses suggest a slight fall in turnout when young voters leave the homes of their parents rather than a uniform monotonic rise (Bhatti and Hansen 2012a), but the broad pattern remains. This broad pattern, however, probably over-estimates the causal impact of age because age-specific mortality is higher for low-SES, low-turnout citizens, so each cohort becomes slightly more economically advantaged as it ages (Rodriguez 2012).

Whether and to what extent turnout falls off during old age is less often examined than the rise in young adulthood. This is partly due to the fact that many electoral surveys limit their sampling frame to the non-institutionalized population, thereby excluding citizens who live in nursing facilities. The result of this exclusion is that the small number of surveyed respondents who are among the old and oldest-old are disproportionately healthy, mobile and fit. For this reason, analyses of American National Election Studies, for example, fail to find a falling off in old age (Miller and Shanks 1996). However, when scholars have access to government electoral data that can be linked to census and health statistics, there is clear evidence of a steep decline in old age as well (Bhatti and Hansen 2012b).

Three broad explanations have been advanced to account for age effects. The first lies in the gradual clarification of interests and preferences. Younger citizens may not have a clear sense of their own current and future political interests (Achen 2006) – at the age of 18–20 they may be in university, in military service or in an apprentice position and lacking a clear sense of whether they are on track to benefit or not from high tax rates, tough workplace regulations or most government policies. These clarify over time, and seem to do so in ways consistent with Bayesian updating (Achen 2006). Likewise, new citizens may not fully appreciate how political parties differ (Plutzer 2002) so, even with clear values, it is difficult to map those values on to particular candidates or parties – diminishing the motivation to vote.

The second broad explanation is the gradual internalization of societal norms – adults are expected to start a family, keep up with the news, settle into a permanent residence of their own and participate in the civic life of the community. Markers of maturation and the adoption of adult roles, therefore, may be better predictors of turnout than age, per se (Highton and Wolfinger, 2001). The challenge of examining key "life cycle" events, however, is that many are not simply markers of maturation, but also of competing demands for time and attention (such as the raising of young children – Stoker and Jennings 1995; Plutzer 2002).

The third explanation focuses on how aging is associated with changes in social networks and peer groups. Young adults may first become eligible to vote while living with parents and while in schools that encourage civic engagement. But they soon find themselves living among other young people who lack electoral experiences – they go from a high turnout context to a low turnout context, with a corresponding reduction in social cues and expectations of civic participation (Bhatti and Hansen 2012a). As citizens near the ends of their lives, this process reverses as frailty and mortality both reduce the size of networks and impair the political involvement of close ties (Bhatti and Hansen 2012b).

No doubt, these three processes are all in play, sometimes in ways that are mutually reinforcing. The demographic variable of age, therefore, provides a window into the operation of key social and cognitive determinants of voting. There are important opportunities to enhance our understanding of participation by focusing theories on these underlying dynamics and seeking to model them directly, rather than by inferring their impact via the variable of age.

Of course, while "age" has a clear theoretical connotation, the variable of age in a cross-sectional data set is confounded with generational effects. For example, we often refer to "baby boomers," children of the welfare state, or Thatcher's or Reagan's children. Coming of age in particular political epochs has been explored extensively with respect to values (see, for example, Inglehart 1990), and vote choice (see, for example, van der Brug 2010), but less so for turnout (though see Miller and Shanks 1996).

The S in SES: social status

Socio-economic status, or SES, is not a variable but, rather, a catch-all term that encompasses a wide range of potential characteristics. In the 1960s and 1970s, when data and computational capacity exploded to create the modern discipline of political behavior, most researchers assumed that the various aspects of SES were so highly correlated that it made sense to think of them as comprising a single, unidimensional concept (Duncan 1961). For example, the occupational gradient of unskilled, skilled blue collar, clerical, management/professional was highly correlated with education and income (and, in the US, race as well). Scholars found it attractive to subsume these characteristics into a single concept because this would simplify both theory and analysis. Indeed, many data sets shipped with pre-calculated composite measures of SES – such as "Duncan's SEI." Today, few scholars find the unidimensional concept useful and our understanding of political behavior has been enhanced by close examination of the various components.

Social status and social exclusion

Max Weber famously wrote that collective political power can derive from *class* (the control of capital), *status* (one's group-based social standing), and *party* (the power of numbers) (Weber 1978 [1922]). For the purposes of political behavior research, however, these are amorphous concepts. The "S" in SES has given rise to many different concepts and operational variables. It is useful to recognize that, for Weber, "status" was a categorical variable. He used the word, "*standt*," which is best translated as "estate," and Weber was likely thinking of the political power that was wielded by the first estate (monarchs ruling by the social convention that they have a "divine right"), the second estate (clergy, to whom people defer even when they lack coercive power of the state or the power of money) and the third estate (landowners, who derive certain rights, most notably suffrage, as a consequence of their status).

The concept was later Americanized. America, many believed, had no social classes and no state church, but a continuum of statuses based on occupation – white collar professionals derived *prestige* and influence that was not necessarily linked to their income. A school teacher held more prestige than a unionized factory worker who might actually have higher earnings.

The key takeaway is that power and privilege can derive from the formal and informal prestige that a society grants to groups because of esteem, respect or tradition; and that this power and privilege is analytically distinct from power deriving from the group's economic resources.

Recently, this idea has found its expression most clearly in studies of *social exclusion* – when societal norms discourage the active participation of groups deemed to be outsiders or insufficiently integrated into the dominant culture. For example, Heath and his colleagues (2013, Chapter 8) show that ethnic minorities in the United Kingdom abstain from voting at especially high rates even after accounting for differences due to lower education, class and age; Aasland and Fløtten (2001) show similar impacts of Slavic minorities in Estonia and Lativa. The notion of social exclusion also has motivated former felons (Pettit and Sykes 2015; Bevelander and Pendakur 2011) and alienated youth (Bentley and Oakley 1999).

Education

Other than age, no demographic variable has received as much attention as education (see Burden 2009 for an excellent review). It is almost always the first or second strongest predictor of voter turnout and political participation, and education's presumed *causal* influence was unchallenged for four decades in spite of the obvious paradox that turnout in many Western nations declined even as educational attainment soared (Brody 1978; Franklin 2004). As late as 1992, Miller and Shanks (1996: 84) could write of the pre-New Deal generation that "education completed a half century earlier apparently subsumes all other social differentials as an influence promoting turnout." Miller and Shanks (1996: 85–92) similarly report education to be the strongest influence on turnout for New Dealers and the largest effects were found among the post-New Deal generation.

Early attempts to discern the causal influence of education by instrumental variable methods produced numerous contradictory findings. Milligan, Moretti and Oreopolus (2004) and Dee (2004) showed statistically significant net effects of education, while Tenn's (2007) analysis shows education's impact to be spurious – at least during the period of completing one's education.

Some analyses show that the impact of education is not absolute but apparently relative. Persson's (2013) cross-sectional analysis of 37 countries shows relative education is more predictive than absolute. At the individual level, Nie, Junn and Stehlik-Barry (1996) show that education effects are relative to one's generational cohort. The notion that education effects are relative can be interpreted in both causal and non-causal terms.

Hence it is relevant that a series of empirical analyses in the last decade have seriously undermined the idea that education has a causal effect on turnout. Persson's (2013) panel analysis of Swedish voters shows education effects present *before education is complete*. Highton (2009), looking at political sophistication using US panel data, finds exactly the same thing. Berinsky and Lenz's (2011) clever use of regression discontinuity designs shows no causal impact of education among young Americans in the Vietnam generation. While more research is yet to come, it seems that the stronger the research design in terms of causal inference, the less likely it is to find any impact of education whatsoever.

This then raises the question of what accounts for the strong *correlation* between education and turnout. It does not seem to be the result of *products* of education, such as cognitive ability or future earnings – for if it were, unmediated causal analysis would show an impact of education. Rather, it points us to precursors of education located in the family of origin, in personality and early socialization. In short, at this time, it appears that education effects likely reflect selection mechanisms and social forces that sort people into tracks of relative privilege.

The E in SES: class analysis and income effects

The *economic* components of SES have received considerably less attention than education in recent decades, with studies usefully located in two broad traditions. The first is more commonly employed in European political science and in North American political sociology, and relies heavily on the traditional notion of social class. The second is focused on *consumption* and therefore typically focuses on family or household income.

Class analysis

The Weberian and Marxist tradition of class analysis views politics in historical context and social classes as *collective actors* that make political history. Most of the research on social class derives from the presumed conflicts of interest that are created by an individual's location in the economic order. Anticipating Marx, Madison (1787) famously wrote in *Federalist #10* that "The most common and durable source of factions has been the various and unequal distribution of property. Those who hold and those who are without property have ever formed distinct interests in society."

During the 1960s, 1970s and 1980s, class was most typically operationalized based on whether the head of a household could be classified as a white collar or blue collar worker (see, for example, Burnham 1987). Starting in the late 1980s, the operationalization of social class became more nuanced. The two leading approaches augmented occupational titles with information on where a worker fit in the class structure, such as whether a worker owned a business, or whether she/he supervised lower level workers (see Manza, Hout and Brooks 1995 for a review). By and large, class effects on turnout tend to be modest in size in the United States and minimal in Europe. Drawing on three decades of evidence, Gallego (2010: 239) concluded "inequality in election turnout is not universal." According to records, in many countries, particularly European democracies, education and income are not associated with voter turnout. The small effect of class is in part due to the effective mobilization by trade unions and union-based political parties. Class effects are more evident for broader measures of civic participation (e.g., Li, Pickles and Savage 2005).

A second aspect of class analysis is class identification – do individuals *think of themselves* as being members of a particular class? The classical notion that class identity creates a class "for itself" implies that when lower income individuals self-identify with a working class movement, the group identification can be empowering (Mann 1973). Yet, the limited empirical evidence does not support this idea. For example, Walsh, Jennings and Stoker (2004) examined a multi-generational panel study and found that political participation was *negatively* related to working class identification (though they did not directly test the implied class × class identification interaction).

Income effects

Individual-level income effects are small or non-existent in Europe (Franklin 2002). When such effects are identified, they are typically modest or conditional on other factors – for example, Martikainen, Martikainen and Wass (2005) show small income effects on turnout among older Finnish citizens.

In contrast, income matters quite a bit for political participation in the United States. Leighley and Nagler (2013) demonstrate persistent effects of income on turnout in the United States over a 40-year span. In the US, the role of economic status has seen something of a renaissance in recent research. All scholars working in this area recognize that money is not a resource that can be *directly* utilized to increase participation, except in the narrow case of campaign contributions (Verba, Schlozman and Brady 1995). Rather, income is a proxy for more difficult-to-measure factors that directly or indirectly impact on participation in general and the turnout decision in particular.

Most of this work has focused on the lower end of the income distribution. Pacheco and Plutzer (2007, 2008) argue that economic hardship in young adulthood is a precursor to brushes with the law, crime victimization, interrupted education and early parenthood, all of which – in turn – disrupt the development of habits of civic engagement. Recent work by Holbein (2017) suggests that these experiences likely presage low turnout through their correlation with social skills such as inter-personal problem solving, emotional and impulse control, and overall life management – a finding consistent with Plutzer and Wiefek's (2006) speculation that income mobility effects on turnout might reflect non-cognitive traits such as personal organization and perseverance, and with Ojeda's (2015) demonstration that mental illness – in this case, depression – can impact voter turnout.

In short, recent advances have sought to unpack the complex social and psychological processes that are the proximal causes of observed income gradients in political participation. As Holbein shows, doing so can uncover actionable findings – methods to address the underlying causes may be far more practical than seeking to enhance participation by changing national distributions of income.

Measuring income

Even as income's effect is presumed to be indirect, the presence of substantial total effects of income is important, because it has important implications for the functioning of democracy and social justice (Bartels 2009). Ojeda (2017) posited that if income effects reflect an individual's or family's purchasing power, then political science research might benefit from work in economics that seeks to better measure this accurately. In particular, Ojeda shows that operationalizing income in terms of the ability to meet basic needs reveals larger income effects than would be the case using traditional ordinal or log-scaled measures. His approach of adjusting income by creating a ratio of current income to the relevant poverty threshold for an individual's family represents a promising approach that can be implemented in most electoral data sets.

Sex and gender, work and family

As recently as 1975, Kristi Anderson (1975: 439) could observe that "politics almost everywhere is a male dominated enterprise. … Sex differences in political participation are enormous." Yet even a half century ago, sex differences in most forms of participation were small. Indeed, Campbell et al. (1960: 484) show only a 10 percent difference in turnout in the 1956 presidential election. Ten years ago, Paxton, Kunovich and Hughes (2007: 264) could review the extant literature and conclude that "Women's fight for formal political representation is mostly won … women are more likely to vote than men in the United States … and across most countries women vote at rates fairly similar to men."

If turnout differences are small, there are some additional gender gaps in other dimensions of participation. For example, women are less expressive in open-ended questions and more likely to give "don't know" answers in political surveys (Atkeson and Rapoport 2003), they are less active in deliberative forums (Karpowitz, Mendelberg and Shaker 2012) and they score lower on scales measuring political knowledge, political interest and political efficacy (Verba, Burns and Schlozman 1997).

Family structure is another topic that has been investigated, with consistent findings that married citizens have higher turnout than unmarried citizens (Stoker and Jennings 1995; Denver 2008), with especially low levels for single parents (Wolfinger and Wolfinger 2008; Plutzer and Wiefek 2006). In addition, parental divorce during childhood can have lasting impacts that depress turnout in young adulthood (Sandell and Plutzer 2005).

By and large, these factors – gender, family structure and work life – have been studied in isolation, even though it might be expected that marriage, divorce, parenthood and career orientation are experienced quite differently for men and women. It is surprising then, that few have examined within-gender differences through the lens of a gendered society that differentially channels politically relevant resources to men and women. The major exception is the groundbreaking book by Burns, Schlozman and Verba (2001). They found that women whose work life was more career oriented had higher levels of participation than those with jobs that were less demanding or who had no employment at all. Though frequently cited, however, few have sought to build on this approach to develop a mature and cumulative research program on how the intersection of these factors may impact upon political participation.

Race and ethnicity

The enslavement of African Americans, their systematic disenfranchisement under Jim Crow laws and the slow implementation of the Voting Rights Act of 1965 creates a particular historical context for the study of race and politics in the United States. Not surprisingly, the electoral participation of African Americans lagged behind that of whites at the dawn of the era of behavioral political science. The authors of *The American Voter*, for example, estimated that black turnout was less than half the rate of whites even in the northern United States (Campbell et al. 1960: Table 11–6). Based on data from the American National Election Studies, Rosenstone and Hansen (2003) estimate an average 15-point racial gap in turnout between 1952 and 1988. That gap, however, has closed with African American turnout exceeding that of whites in the 2008 presidential election.

Critically, however, early studies examining the black–white gap in participation found that the effect disappeared or reversed after accounting for the much lower SES of African American voters (see, for example, Guterbock and London 1983). This then represented a puzzle: why did African Americans "outperform" the levels of participation that might be expected for white Americans of similar age, education and income? The research that sought to solve this puzzle is broadly generalizable. Though empirical results have been mixed, they represent approaches that have been applied to other minority groups in the United States, and have the potential for application to minority politics throughout the world.

Linked fate

The concept of linked fate was initially proposed in Dawson's seminal book, *Behind the Mule*. Gay, Hochschild and White (2014) describe it this way:

> due to historical and contemporary experiences of group disadvantage and discrimination, one's own life chances depend heavily on the status and fortunes of Black Americans as a whole. That perception has led, in turn, to the rational substitution of group utility for individual utility in political decision-making, and often to a strong moral and emotional commitment to the group.

The similarity of linked fate to the earlier ideas of class consciousness – how a class transforms from the class in itself to a class for itself – is clear, and the concept can in principle be applied to any group in any country that has endured periods of disadvantage and discrimination. Indeed, it has been applied to many groups in the United States by adapting Dawson's original question, "Do you think what happens generally to *Black* people in this country will have something to do with what happens in your life?," by substituting other groups in place of the word "Black." The empirical results, however, have been mixed. Effects for African Americans (Philpot, Shaw and McGowen 2009; Gay, Hochschild and White 2014), Latinos (Stokes 2003; Stokes-Brown 2006; Sanchez 2006; Gay, Hochschild and White 2014) and Asians (Kim 2015; Junn and Masuoka 2008; Gay, Hochschild and White 2014) have typically been small or not statistically significant in the expected direction.

Political empowerment

A long-standing argument is that members of racial and ethnic minorities may be mobilized by political empowerment – that is, descriptive representation can lead to feelings of pride and efficacy, and a reduction in cynicism, thereby spurring higher turnout (Bobo and Gilliam 1990). This argument is more complicated than it seems at first glance, however, because of feedback to majority member citizens. The political empowerment model is silent on (for example) the impact of an African American office holder on the mobilization of white voters (Washington 2006). If the political empowerment thesis is tested by examining black–white gaps, a significant effect could be due to larger black mobilization, white demobilization, or both. Likewise, a conclusion of "no effect" could be the result of black political empowerment and white reaction of similar magnitudes.

Most recently, Logan, Darrah and Oh (2012) confirmed the empowerment thesis for African Americans, showing a small but significant effect for Latinos, but a negative impact for Asian Americans.

Religious mobilization

A third explanation with broader applicability focuses on religious mobilization. When racial and ethnic groups attend religious institutions that cater specifically to members of their own members, the mobilization effect of religious attendance may be amplified – a conclusion reached by Segura and Bowler (2012) based on their review of the empirical literature (see Harris 1994 and Jones-Correa and Leal 2001).

In sum, every racial and ethnic minority group has a unique history – a history that may begin with enslavement, escape from war or civic violence, or in economic migration. The social and political exclusion of the first generations of the group are also critical in establishing patterns of political participation – and of course the institutional framework of the national and subnational governments play outsized roles. Amidst such diversity, can we build a broader theoretical framework that can guide our research and interpretation of racial and ethnic demographic variables? The three approaches reviewed here – linked fate, political empowerment and religious mobilization – represent promising ideas on which to build.

Summary and conclusion

Demographic variables represent an essential core of quantitative research in political behavior. Despite the rapid pace of social change, we *continue* to observe turnout gaps related to age, ethnicity and education. As a consequence, any serious analysis must control for these key variables, which structure opportunities, mobilization and information acquisition in modern democracies. Yet in every instance, a close look at the best empirical research suggests that no demographic variable embodies a simple causal story. In some cases, such as education, new research is overturning decades of political wisdom. In other cases, such as the linked fate and class consciousness paradigm, the empirical effects are relatively small in comparison to qualitative accounts of these processes. In every instance, we are reminded that society never holds "all else equal" so it becomes difficult to isolate the effects of age from income, income from race, race from class, class from work status, or work status from gender.

Because it is not possible to experimentally manipulate demographic variables, advances will necessarily come from unpacking the mechanisms that link social group membership to political engagement – mechanisms that will vary within demographic groups and which, in some cases, might be good candidates for experimental research. Better use of longitudinal research may also be promising, and clever exploitation of quasi-experiments (e.g., changes in voter context due to redistricting) may provide the basis to better specify theories such as those related to political empowerment. Finally, attention to measurement – especially for income, education and group identity – has substantial promise to enhance our understanding of how and why demographic variables consistently predict differences in voter turnout.

References

Aasland, A. and Fløtten, T. (2001) "Ethnicity and Social Exclusion in Estonia and Latvia," *Europe-Asia Studies*, vol. 53, no. 7, November, 1023–1049.

Achen, C. H. (2006) "Expressive Bayesian Voters, Their Turnout Decisions, and Double Probit: Empirical Implications of a Theoretical Model," Unpublished Manuscript, Princeton University.

Andersen, K. (1975) "Working Women and Political Participation, 1952–1972," *American Journal of Political Science*, vol. 19, no. 3, August, 439–453.

Atkeson, L. R. and Rapoport, R. B. (2003) "The More Things Change the More They Stay the Same: Examining Gender Differences in Political Attitude Expression, 1952–2000," *Public Opinion Quarterly*, vol. 67, no. 4, Winter, 495–521.

Bartels, L. M. (2009) *Unequal Democracy: The Political Economy of the New Gilded Age*, Princeton: Princeton University Press.

Bellah, E. R. N., Tipton, S. M., Sullivan, W. M., Madsen, R. and Swidler, A. (2007) *Habits of the Heart: Individualism and Commitment in American Life*, Berkeley: University of California Press.

Bentley, T. and Oakley, K. (1999) *The Real Deal: What Young People Really Think About Government, Politics and Social Exclusion*, London: Demos.

Berinsky, A. J. and Lenz, G. S. (2011) "Education and Political Participation: Exploring the Causal Link," *Political Behavior*, vol. 33, no. 3, September, 357–373.

Bevelander, P. and Pendakur, R. (2011) "Voting and Social Inclusion in Sweden," *International Migration*, 49, no. 4, August, 67–92.

Bhatti, Y. and Hansen, K. M. (2012a) "Leaving the Nest and the Social Act of Voting: Turnout Among First-Time Voters," *Journal of Elections, Public Opinion and Parties*, vol. 22, no. 4, November, 380–406.

Bhatti, Y. and Hansen, K. M. (2012b) "Retiring from Voting: Turnout Among Senior Voters," *Journal of Elections, Public Opinion and Parties*, vol. 22, no. 4, November, 479–500.

Blackwell, M., Honaker, J. and King, G. (2015) "A Unified Approach to Measurement Error and Missing Data Overview and Applications," *Sociological Methods and Research*, available online: http://gking. harvard.edu/files/gking/files/measured.pdf.

Bobo, L. and Gilliam, F. D. (1990) "Race, Sociopolitical Participation, and Black Empowerment," *American Political Science Review*, vol. 84, no. 2, June, 377–393.

Brody, R. A. (1978) "The Puzzle of Political Participation in America," in Beer, S. H. (ed.), *The New American Political System*, Washington, DC: American Enterprise Institute: 287–324.

Brug, W. van der (2010) "Structural and Ideological Voting in Age Cohorts," *West European Politics*, vol. 33, no. 3, May, 586–607.

Burden, B. C. (2009) "The Dynamic Effects of Education on Voter Turnout," *Electoral Studies*, vol. 28, no. 4, December, 540–549.

Burnham, W. D. (1987) "The Turnout Problem," in Reichley (ed.) *Elections American Style*, Washington, DC: Brookings Institution: 97–133.

Burns, N., Schlozman, K. L. and Verba, S. (2001) *The Private Roots of Public Action*, Cambridge, MA: Harvard University Press.

Campbell, A., Converse, E., Miller, W. and Stokes, D. (1960) *The American Voter*, Chicago: University of Chicago Press.

Centers, R. (1949) *The Psychology of Social Classes*, Princeton: Princeton University Press.

Dawson, M. C. (1994) *Behind the Mule: Race and Class in African American Politics*, Princeton: Princeton University Press.

Dee, T. S. (2004) "Are There Civic Returns to Education?" *Journal of Public Economics*, vol. 88, no. 9, August, 1697–1720.

Denver, D. (2008) "Another Reason to Support Marriage? Turnout and the Decline of Marriage in Britain," *British Journal of Politics and International Relations*, vol. 10, no. 4, November, 666–680.

Duncan, O. D. (1961) "A Socioeconomic Index for All Occupations," in Reiss, A. J. (ed.) *Occupations and Social Status*, New York: Free Press: 109–139.

Foner, A. (1979) "Ascribed and Achieved Bases of Stratification," *Annual Review of Sociology*, vol. 5, August, 219–242.

Franklin, M. N. (2002) "The Dynamics of Electoral Participation," in Ludec, L., Niemi, R. and Norris, P. (eds.) *Comparing Democracies 2: Elections and Voting in Global Perspective*, Thousand Oaks: Sage: 148–168.

Franklin, M. N. (2004) *Voter Turnout and the Dynamics of Electoral Competition in Established Democracies Since 1945*, Cambridge: Cambridge University Press.

Gallego, A. (2010) "Understanding Unequal Turnout: Education and Voting in Comparative Perspective," *Electoral Studies*, vol. 29, no. 2, June, 239–248.

Gay, C., Hochschild, J. L. and White, A. (2014) "Americans' Belief in Linked Fate: A Wide Reach but Limited Impact," Unpublished Manuscript, Harvard University.

Guterbock, T. M. and London, B. (1983) "Race, Political Orientation, and Participation: An Empirical Test of Four Competing Theories," *American Sociological Review*, vol. 48, no. 4, August, 439–453.

Harris, F. C. (1994) "Something Within: Religion as a Mobilizer of African-American Political Activism," *Journal of Politics*, vol. 56, no. 1, February, 42–68.

Heath, A. F., Fisher, S. D., Rosenblatt, G., Sanders, D. and Sobolewska, M. (2013) *The Political Integration of Ethnic Minorities in Britain*, Oxford: Oxford University Press.

Highton, B. (2009) "Revisiting the Relationship Between Educational Attainment and Political Sophistication," *Journal of Politics*, vol. 71, no. 4, October, 1564–1576.

Highton, B. and Wolfinger, R. E. (2001) "The First Seven Years of the Political Life Cycle," *American Journal of Political Science*, vol. 45, no. 1, January, 202–209.

Holbein, J (2017) "Childhood Skill Development and Adult Political Participation." American Political Science Review, 1–12. doi:10.1017/S0003055417000119

Huckfeldt, R. R. and Sprague, J. (1995) *Citizens, Politics and Social Communication: Information and Influence in an Election Campaign*, Cambridge: Cambridge University Press.

Huddy, L. (2001) "From Social to Political Identity: A Critical Examination of Social Identity Theory," *Political Psychology*, vol. 22, no. 1, March, 127–156.

Inglehart, R. (1990) *Culture Shift in Advanced Industrial Society*, Princeton: Princeton University Press.

Jones-Correa, M. A. and Leal, D. L. (2001) "Political Participation: Does Religion Matter?" *Political Research Quarterly*, vol. 54, no. 4, December, 751–770.

Junn, J. and Masuoka, N. (2008) "Asian American Identity: Shared Racial Status and Political Context," *Perspectives on Politics*, vol. 6, no. 4, December, 729–740.

Karpowitz, C. F., Mendelberg, T. and Shaker, L. (2012) "Gender Inequality in Deliberative Participation," *American Political Science Review*, vol. 106, no. 3, August, 533–547.

Key, V. O. (1961) *Public Opinion and American Democracy*, New York: Knopf.

Kim, D. (2015) "The Effect of Party Mobilization, Group Identity, and Racial Context on Asian Americans' Turnout," *Politics, Groups, and Identities*, vol. 3, no. 4, November, 592–614.

Lazarsfeld, P. F., Berelson, B. and Gaudet, H. (1944) *The People's Choice: How the Voter Makes Up His Mind in a Presidential Campaign*, New York: Duell, Sloan and Pearce.

Leighley, J. E. and Nagler, J. (2013) *Who Votes Now? Demographics, Issues, Inequality, and Turnout in the United States*, Princeton: Princeton University Press.

Li, Y., Pickles, A. and Savage, M. (2005) "Social Capital and Social Trust in Britain," *European Sociological Review*, vol. 21, no. 2, April, 109–123.

Lipset, S. M. (1960) *Political Man: The Social Bases of Politics*, Garden City: Doubleday.

Logan, J. R., Darrah, J. and Oh, S. (2012) "The Impact of Race and Ethnicity, Immigration and Political Context on Participation in American Electoral Politics," *Social Forces*, vol. 90, no. 3, March, 993–1022.

Madison, J. (1787) "The Federalist No. 10," *The New York Packet*, November 22, available online: www.congress.gov/resources/display/content/The+Federalist+Papers#TheFederalistPapers-10.

Mann, M. (1973) *Consciousness and Action Among the Western Working Class*, London: Macmillan.

Manza, J., Hout, M. and Brooks, C. (1995) "Class Voting in Capitalist Democracies Since World War II: Dealignment, Realignment, or Trendless Fluctuation?" *Annual Review of Sociology*, vol. 21, August, 137–162.

Martikainen, P., Martikainen, T. and Wass, H. (2005) "The Effect of Socioeconomic Factors on Voter Turnout in Finland: A Register-Based Study of 2.9 Million Voters," *European Journal of Political Research*, vol. 44, no. 5, August, 645–669.

Melo, D. F. and Stockemer, D. (2014) "Age and Political Participation in Germany, France and the UK: A Comparative Analysis," *Comparative European Politics*, vol. 12, no. 1, January, 33–53.

Milbrath, L. W. (1965) *Political Participation: How and Why Do People Get Involved in Politics?*, Chicago: Rand McNally.

Miller, W. E. and Shanks, J. M. (1996) *The New American Voter*, Cambridge, MA: Harvard University Press.

Milligan, K., Moretti, E. and Oreopoulos, P. (2004) "Does Education Improve Citizenship? Evidence from the United States and the United Kingdom," *Journal of Public Economics*, vol. 88, no. 9, August, 1667–1695.

Mutz, D. C. and Mondak, J. J. (2006) "The Workplace as a Context for Cross-Cutting Political Discourse," *Journal of Politics*, vol. 68, no. 1, February, 140–155.

Nie, N. H., Junn, J. and Stehlik-Barry, K. (1996) *Education and Democratic Citizenship in America*, Chicago: University of Chicago Press.

Ojeda, C. (2015) "Depression and Political Participation," *Social Science Quarterly*, vol. 96, no. 5, November, 1226–1243.

Ojeda, C. (2017) "The Measurement of Income in the Study of Political Behavior." Working paper, Knoxville: University of Tennessee.

Pacheco, J. S. and Plutzer, E. (2007) "Stay in School, Don't Become a Parent: Teen Life Transitions and Cumulative Disadvantages for Voter Turnout," *American Politics Research*, vol. 35, no. 1, January, 32–56.

Pacheco, J. S. and Plutzer, E. (2008) "Political Participation and Cumulative Disadvantage: The Impact of Economic and Social Hardship on Young Citizens," *Journal of Social Issues*, vol. 64, no. 3, September, 571–593.

Paxton, P., Kunovich, S. and Hughes, M. M. (2007) "Gender in Politics," *Annual Review of Sociology*, vol. 33, August, 263–284.

Persson, M. (2013) "Is the Effect of Education on Voter Turnout Absolute or Relative? A Multi-Level Analysis of 37 Countries," *Journal of Elections, Public Opinion and Parties*, vol. 23, no. 2, March, 111–133.

Pettit, B. and Sykes, B. L. (2015) "Civil Rights Legislation and Legalized Exclusion: Mass Incarceration and the Masking of Inequality," *Sociological Forum*, vol. 30, no. S1, June, 589–611.

Philpot, T. S., Shaw, D. R. and McGowen, E. B. (2009) "Winning the Race: Black Voter Turnout in the 2008 Presidential Election," *Public Opinion Quarterly*, vol. 73, no. 5, 995–1022.

Plutzer, E. (2002) "Becoming a Habitual Voter: Inertia, Resources, and Growth in Young Adulthood," *American Political Science Review*, vol. 96, no. 1, March, 41–56.

Plutzer, E. and Wiefek, N. (2006) "Family Transitions, Economic Status, and Voter Turnout Among African-American Inner-City Women," *Social Science Quarterly*, vol. 87, no. 3, September, 658–678.

Potgieter, E. (2013) *Predictors of Political Participation in New Democracies: A Comparative Study*, MA Thesis, Stellenbosch University.

Putnam, R. D. and Campbell, D. E. (2012) *American Grace: How Religion Divides and Unites Us*, New York: Simon and Schuster.

Rodriguez, J. M. (2012) *The Effects of Mortality and Health Inequalities Over Disparities in Political Behavior*, Doctoral Dissertation, University of California.

Rosenstone, S. J. and Hansen, J. M. (2003) *Mobilization, Participation, and Democracy in America*, New York: Longman.

Sanchez, G. R. (2006) "The Role of Group Consciousness in Political Participation Among Latinos in the United States," *American Politics Research*, vol. 34, no. 4, July, 427–450.

Sandell, J. and Plutzer, E. (2005) "Families, Divorce and Voter Turnout in the US," *Political Behavior*, vol. 27, no. 2, June, 133–162.

Segura, G. and Bowler, S. (2012) *The Future is Ours: Minority Politics, Political Behavior, and the Multiracial Era of American Politics*, Thousand Oaks: Sage.

Stoker, L. and Jennings, M. K. (1995) "Life-Cycle Transitions and Political Participation: The Case of Marriage," *American Political Science Review*, vol. 89, no. 2, June, 421–433.

Stokes, A. K. (2003) "Latino Group Consciousness and Political Participation," *American Politics Research*, vol. 31, no. 4, July, 361–378.

Stokes-Brown, A. K. (2006) "Racial Identity and Latino Vote Choice," *American Politics Research*, vol. 34, no. 5, September, 627–652.

Tenn, S. (2007) "The Effect of Education on Voter Turnout," *Political Analysis*, vol. 15, no. 4, Autumn, 446–464.

Verba, S., Burns, N. and Schlozman, K. L. (1997) "Knowing and Caring About Politics: Gender and Political Engagement," *Journal of Politics*, vol. 59, no. 4, November, 1051–1072.

Verba, S., Schlozman, K. L. and Brady, H. E. (1995) *Voice and Equality: Civic Voluntarism in American Politics*, Volume 4, Cambridge, MA: Harvard University Press.

Walsh, K. C., Jennings, M. K. and Stoker, L. (2004) "The Effects of Social Class Identification on Participatory Orientations Towards Government," *British Journal of Political Science*, vol. 34, no. 3, July, 469–495.

Washington, E. (2006) "How Black Candidates Affect Voter Turnout," *The Quarterly Journal of Economics*, vol. 121, no. 3, August, 973–998.

Waylen, G. (2013) *The Oxford Handbook of Gender and Politics*, Oxford: Oxford University Press.

Weber, M. (1978) [1922] "The Distribution of Power Within the Political Community: Class, Status, Party," in Roth, G. and Wittich, C. (eds.) *Economy and Society: An Outline of Interpretive Sociology*, Berkeley: University of California Press: 926–940.

Wolfinger, N. H. and Wolfinger, R. E. (2008) "Family Structure and Voter Turnout," *Social Forces*, vol. 86, no. 4, June, 1513–1528.

7

TURNOUT AND THE CALCULUS OF VOTING

Recent advances and prospects for integration with theories of campaigns and elections

John H. Aldrich and Libby M. Jenke

The "calculus of voting" is the rational-choice based theory of turnout and vote choice that has been at the base of the choice-theoretic studies of campaigns and elections since its first formal statement by Downs (1957) and especially by Riker and Ordeshook (1968). Perhaps because of its initial formal results about turnout that are ordinarily understood to be both pessimistic and empirically wrong, a number of years passed with relatively little theoretical advancement, while theories of voting, political parties, and campaigns and elections developed, often with little to no attention to the voters' calculus.

In this chapter, after a review of the basics of the calculus of voting with respect to turnout, we consider two relatively new theoretical advances: the development of a fully articulated theory of expressive voting; and specification of the (spatial) utility function, to consider a theoretically coherent account of "abstention due to alienation," and its relationship to the (spatial) account of moral convictions.

Turnout and decision theory

Rational choice theoretic accounts understand political behavior as a series of choices made by individuals. The choices they make are assumed to be considered and deliberate (but not necessarily *carefully* considered or *deeply* deliberated) and thus choices seen as applications of decision theory. The question is: what form of decision theory?

Downs (1957) began the systematic inquiry into rational choice and turnout by posing the problem as one in expected utility. This was a perfectly sensible move and led to a rich research tradition, but that is actually the second step in applying decision theory to turnout. A second step is needed because basic decision theory (especially under certainty) yields an incomplete theory. That is, in some circumstances the basic decision problem yields no answer, and it does so in an especially important circumstance, that of close elections. Using the logic of expectations is only one way to complete the answer to the question of when to vote. So, we begin with the basic problem and consider alternatives.

All decision theoretic accounts model choices as a balance of the costs and benefits associated with the actions the decision maker is choosing among. Costs and benefits are understood as the utility derived from outcomes, and these are used to associate the comparative costs and benefits of voting or abstaining – that is, the utility associated with the various available actions. One then takes the action associated with highest utility. In the US election case, the standard choice over actions is whether to vote for one of two candidates or to abstain.[1] By convention (and without loss of generality), let 1 be the utility gained when the preferred candidate wins and 0 when the other candidate wins.[2] While those are the entire set of possible (collective) outcomes, each outcome is differently valued if the preferred candidate wins (yielding 1 utile) and the citizen abstains, compared to the case where the preferred candidate wins (also yielding a net benefit of 1) and the citizen votes. They are different because there are differential costs and differential benefits associated with turning out to vote compared to abstaining. In addition, it is plausible to suppose that these comparative costs and benefits of the act of voting are relatively high in relation to the costs and benefits of the collective outcomes.[3] This would be unlike the case of, say, ordering at a restaurant, where the costs of ordering are treated as relatively tiny and inconsequential compared to getting versus not getting the preferred meal.

The costs of voting can be understood as the difference in decision making costs and in performing the act of voting (actually registering and going to the polls, etc.) compared to abstaining. Whatever the differential costs are, it is usually assumed that the costs are higher for turning out than for abstaining. These differential costs may be denoted Cv, $Cv > 0$ (for the difference between the costs of voting and of abstaining), although we follow convention by simply writing the costs as C. Similarly, there may be differential benefits for the act of voting compared to abstaining. Downs (1957) suggested such benefits of voting flow from helping assure the continuation of democracy. Riker and Ordeshook (1968) associated these benefits with the already well-known social-psychological concept of citizen duty, as employed by Campbell et al. (1960). Fiorina (1976) associated these benefits with the act of supporting one's preferred candidate (or opposing a detested candidate), regardless of whether the candidate wins or loses. In each of these cases, the voter realized these differential benefits (or, perhaps, avoids costs, such as guilt in failing to do one's duty) which the abstainer does not realize. By assumption these differential benefits from voting, say D, are positive, $D > 0$ for turning out, regardless of the outcome (and for whom one votes). C and D may be large or small relative to the 1 associated with the preferred candidate winning compared to losing.

In this simple, stylized case there are five distinct combinations of costs and benefits, associated with five sets of outcomes, as seen in the decision table in Table 7.1. One case combines all instances in which the preferred candidate is winning by more than one vote before considering this citizen's action. A second case is where the preferred candidate is winning by exactly one vote, and another is where that candidate is exactly tied. The final two cases are the reverse of the first two, where the preferred candidate is losing by exactly one vote and losing by two or more votes.

Table 7.1 Turnout: basic decision matrix for the two-party case

Vote for	Preferred candidate is:				
	Winning by more than one vote	Winning by exactly one vote	Tied	Losing by exactly one vote	Losing by more than one vote
1	$1 - C + D$	$1 - C + D$	$1 - C + D$	$\frac{1}{2} - C + D$	$0 - C + D$
2	$1 - C + D$	$\frac{1}{2} - C + D$	$0 - C + D$	$0 - C + D$	$0 - C + D$
Abstain	1	1	$\frac{1}{2}$	0	0

The decision problem yields some conclusions. As noted in Aldrich (1993: 251):

1   Never vote for the less preferred candidate. Voting for the less preferred candidate is "dominated" by voting for the preferred candidate – the latter always yields at least as much utility, and sometimes more;
2   If $D-C$ is low, $(D-C) \leq -0.5$, which means the costs outweigh the benefits by an amount greater than the value of a tied outcome, always abstain;
3   If $D-C$ is zero or even positive (i.e., when the benefits are greater than the costs of voting), always vote for the preferred candidate, as that choice dominates abstaining;
4   If $0 > D-C > -0.5$, the basic model is silent.

Thus, decision theory, per se, is silent in at least some cases involving the middle columns, and alternative rational choice models of turnout differ over ways to handle those middle cases.

The "calculus of voting," or the expected utility model of turnout

Downs developed a specific way to close the theory, expected utility, which was proving fruitful in economics and other social sciences, and like so much in his case, he did so in a way to translate popular discussions of turnout into a scientific form. In his case, the popular idea was that you should vote when your vote matters, that is, if the election is close. Scientifically, Downs used expected utility theory to formalize this idea: The benefits one gets from the electoral outcome are conditional on the chances that one's vote makes a difference in the outcome. Consider the probability of being in each of those cases in Table 7.1, and from that probability, consider the *expected* benefit of the outcome, PB. Since D is about the performance of the act, it is independent of the closeness of the election. The calculus of voting (as Riker and Ordeshook 1968 dubbed their extension of Downs) has been tested extensively, and three terms – the valuation of the outcomes, the costs of voting, and the benefits associated with voting – have been found to be strongly and consistently related to the choice. Closeness of the outcome has led to mixed results, strongly associated with turnout in aggregate data models and often weakly related (if related at all) to turnout in individual level models.[4] Moreover, because the theoretical concept of closeness is whether one's vote makes or breaks an exact tie, and because so many millions vote in elections, the "P" term, properly understood, seems to require that P, and likely therefore PB, be vanishingly small. And if it is so vanishingly small, then the middle columns are essentially irrelevant to turnout, and the expected utility terms never "really" make a difference.

Minimax regret and game theoretic models of turnout

Aldrich (1993) provides a more detailed consideration of two other models of the turnout decision that are consistent with decision theory but differ from expected utility maximization. Ferejohn and Fiorina (1974; 1975) apply minimax regret to the turnout decision problem (akin to Table 7.1, and indeed from which we developed Table 7.1). The minimax regret notion is that probabilities are not and perhaps cannot meaningfully be calculated, and thus expected utility is not meaningful. But one could imagine asking the question, "How would you feel if you woke up on the day after the election having not bothered to vote and heard that your favored candidate lost by a single vote?" Minimax regret formalized that feeling and uses it to close the remaining gap in the decision theoretic account, as Downs did with the P term. Expected utility maximization extends decision making theory from "under certainty" (in which one knows exactly what outcome occurs, given one's choice of actions) to "under risk" (in which one's actions lead to a set of outcomes with a known probability distribution over each element in the set). Minimax regret is the most useful of the various ways of dealing with decision making "under uncertainty" (in which case one's actions lead to a set of outcomes, but one does not know their probability of occurring). It has its own disadvantages, in that, like the calculus of voting, minimax regret hinges on the same existence of an exact tie or of a one-vote lead, even if these are not given specific probabilities. Also, applying it to the three or more candidate/party case, minimax regret leads to no "strategic voting" at all, whereas the calculus of voting does (and in ways that are empirically supported, where "closeness" does matter). Both models, that is, are not fully satisfying to most voting theorists, and both models have problematic empirics. These disadvantages do not rule out either model, but both do point toward areas for theoretical improvement.

The most important way in political science to resolve the indeterminacy from decision making under uncertainty is not typically to use decision-theoretic concepts such as minimax regret, but to apply game theory. Of course, that means that the indeterminacy needs to be due to the actions of others, but that is true in this case. As Aldrich (1993) reviews, there are important game theoretic models of turnout. They have complications of their own. The most important one here is that most rest on a base of the calculus of voting, or more accurately, they assume "modern" game theory, in which citizens are assumed to be Bayesian decision makers, à la Harsanyi (1977), and thus fully capable of generating well-behaved probabilities, such as the Downsian P.

We believe that the most important theories of democratic choice are game theoretic models that have candidates and other "elite" actors understanding their choices as contingent not only on the choices of these other elite actors (e.g., the other candidates) but also on those of the citizens. Similarly, citizens' choices should be understood as contingent on elite behavior, and possibly on the choices of the rest of the citizenry. However, to the extent that the Harsanyi-based understanding of game theory in which the players in the game can calculate well-formed probability distributions (applying Bayes' rule to virtually anything applies), game theoretic models of turnout, per se, at least as they are currently developed, also do not fully let us get around the same problems as affect the calculus of voting and minimax regret. Or, at least, these are the arguments that underlie a new development in rational choice models of turnout, expressive voting.

A note on strategic voting

Our account has focused on the case in which there are exactly two serious candidates. Even in the US, there are regular instances in which a third candidate enters with enough strength to attract attention and enter into citizens' calculations, and this is not only a strength of the calculus of voting, but also such matters as the scientific explanation of Duverger's Law (1959) which rest on accounts that assume the calculus of voting (see, for example, Cox 1997). Here, we consider a small part of the decision matrix and how the calculus of voting for three, rather than two, choices yields not only an explanation of turnout but one of strategic voting as well.

In Table 7.2, we provide a partial representation of the decision matrix for the three-party case, where we denote the candidates as 1, 2, and 3, in order of the citizen's preferences, and in particular we present the cases in which, as one contemplates voting, there is one or another sort of tie in the election. We continue to assign utility to the election of the most preferred candidate (candidate 1) as 1 and candidate 3 as 0. The second-ranked candidate has a value of S, where S is "in between" that of candidates 1 and 3, $0 < S < 1$. Here, we separate out (in anticipation of

Table 7.2 Turnout: partial decision matrix for the three-party case

Vote for	1–2 tie	1–3 tie	2–3 tie	1–2–3 tie
1	$1 - C + D + B$	$1 - C + D + B$	$S/2 - C + D + B$	$1 - C + D + B$
2	$S - C + D$	$\frac{1}{2} - C + D$	$S - C + D$	$S - C + D$
3	$\frac{1}{2} + S/2 - C + D$	$- C + D$	$- C + D$	$- C + D$
Abstain	$\frac{1}{2} + S/2$	$\frac{1}{2}$	$S/2 - C + B$	$(1 + S)/3$

expressive voting) the positive return one gets for voting for one's favorite, call it B, and leave all costs and any other benefits for voting (e.g., acting on one's duty) as C and D. We do so because expressing support for one's favorite candidate comes only if one votes for that candidate. All other costs and benefits of voting come from voting, per se, regardless of whom one votes for.

The key point is that it is no longer true that voting for the preferred candidate dominates voting for the second choice candidate, as it does in the two-candidate case (although voting for 1 does dominate voting for 3). In particular, if candidates 2 and 3 are tied, voting for the preferred candidate may or may not be the better choice. If $S/2 < B$, then one should vote for the most preferred candidate. If, however, $S/2 > B$ – that is, the value of having the second choice win is greater than twice the value of supporting your first preference, regardless of outcome – then one should "defect" from voting for one's first choice and vote for the second choice, which is what we mean by strategic voting (for more formal presentation, see McKelvey and Ordeshook 1972; Ksleman and Niou 2010; Niou 2001). That is to say, if you back a hopeless candidate you might support your second choice who is apparently running a close race against the least-liked alternative.

Expressive voting

Fiorina (1976) notes the terms "instrumental" and "expressive" were first used for understanding voting behavior by Butler and Stokes (1969) in their magisterial account of British voting. It appears to be Fiorina, however, who first developed the formal accounting of the two concepts for understanding turnout. Schuessler (2000a, 2000b) developed this logic further. Brennan and colleagues extended the logic in two important ways. One was to provide a substantive economic and philosophic foundation for justifying expressive voting, and the other was to embed it in a spatial context.

Fiorina argued for a model that combines instrumental and expressive components, just as we do here. Indeed, he laid out the basic parameters that are the key for such a model. The decision-theoretic matrix in Table 7.3 presents the account in our notation, and it is quite

Table 7.3 Turnout: basic decision matrix for the two-party case with expressive rewards

Vote for	Preferred candidate is:				
	Winning by more than one vote	Winning by exactly one vote	Tied	Losing by exactly one vote	Losing by more than one vote
1	$1 - C + D + B$	$1 - C + D + B$	$1 - C + D + B$	$\frac{1}{2} - C + D + B$	$- C + D + B$
2	$1 - C + D$	$\frac{1}{2} - C + D$	$- C + D$	$- C + D$	$- C + D$
Abstain	1	1	$\frac{1}{2}$	0	0

simple. Voters care about the election outcome, the 1, 0, or, in case of a tie, the 0.5 values in each cell. The instrumental part is that they may be simply Downsian/Riker-and-Ordeshook voters, that is, expected utility maximizers. Like their accounts, there are non-outcome-terms, those associated with the costs and benefits of voting, per se. That is, there are the C and D terms of long-standing. Fiorina added a value, we call it here B, to denote an expressive benefit that comes from being able to express one's support for the favored party or candidate.[5] He focused particularly on B as a benefit that comes to partisan identifiers for voting for the candidate of the party that forms the major part of their political identity, and he drew some interesting and important derivations from this account. That expressive benefits come only to partisans is an assumption that narrows the potential generality of the B term. We could imagine non-partisans being so enthused in support of, say, Barack Obama in 2008 – the first opportunity for African-Americans to vote for an African-American with a real chance of winning – regardless of their partisanship. Or we could imagine voting for, say, George Washington or Dwight Eisenhower as genuine war heroes, to support their election regardless of party. Fiorina finds his (slightly less general) model rich enough to derive 16 testable hypotheses from it.

Brennan and colleagues maintain the Fiorina account of expressive voting but break apart the hybrid nature of the account so they can contrast the "pure theory" of instrumental voting (where there is no expressive B term, i.e., B = 0 for all) from the "pure theory" of expressive voting (where P = 0 for all). Doing so allows them to make two important additions that have not fully penetrated into the study of voting, and thus we attend to their consequences by way of arguing not for the "pure theory" of expressive voting, but for serious attention to the hybrid account. Brennan and Hamlin (1998) embed this mixed calculus of voting into a spatial model of elections (drawn from a different chapter in Downs 1957), so we begin there and then treat the topics of alienation and indifference and of pragmatic versus moral issue preferences.

Brennan and Hamlin (1998) compare their expressive voting model of an election with Ledyard's (1984) famous voting game that uses the calculus of voting in a spatial policy setting.[6] In it, Ledyard concluded that candidates converge to the policy that maximizes the sum of citizens' utilities (or in other models converge to the median or even to the mean citizen ideal point), and no one votes (see Brennan and Hamlin 1998: 153). Their model, by contrast, yields reasonably high levels of turnout in most cases, candidates tend to converge to modes in citizen preferences, and there are equilibria in many, rather than few, cases (Brennan and Hamlin 1998: 72–3).[7] Convergence is not guaranteed.[8] As they note, they see these two models not as rival models but as "… distinct aspects of a more complex whole" (Brennan and Hamlin 1998: 173), a point with which we agree.

The idea is that turnout is higher if voters are expressive rather than instrumental. This is so because the positive benefits come from voting whether the favored candidate wins or not, and whether the election is close or not. An expressive-oriented citizen will vote when the most preferred candidate is valued sufficiently (and undiscounted by P) to outweigh the costs of voting. As Brennan and Hamlin (1998: 157) point out, "More generally, some citizens would be willing to vote in an election even when there is little or no doubt about the result of the election." As a result, we would ordinarily anticipate that turnout in a purely expressive electorate will be rather high, but it will be quite low in a purely instrumental electorate.

We note that this model could be used to predict moderately high turnout in two-party contests, such as in the US and (sometimes!) the UK, because parties would try to pick policies and candidates attractive to voters, that is, with reasonably high B values for many. Expressive models should be expected to predict even higher turnout in truly multi-party systems. This would be so because of the greater number and diversity of parties and candidates and of policy platforms presented to the public. Expressive voting occurs as long as there is at least one candidate with a high B value for the citizen, so with many contenders, there would be many such voters.

Alienation and indifference

Substantively, it is common to say that someone might fail to vote because they do not care whether one candidate or the other wins. The outcome is simply immaterial to them; they are indifferent. That may be a characteristic of a single citizen, but it also may be a characteristic of the entire electorate. If Downs is correct, the two candidates will offer exactly the same platform, that is, converge to each other.[9] If so, every citizen receives exactly the same value if candidate one wins as they receive if candidate two wins. This form of abstention is referred to as "indifference."

It is also widely argued that people may abstain if there is a better alternative but even this "better" candidate offers an abhorrent possibility. In that case, we say that people abstain due to "alienation." Hinich and Ordeshook (1969) developed the spatial accounting. Brody and Page (1973) tested these two notions systematically.

The "pure" theories of the instrumental voting (as we now call the calculus of voting) and of expressive voting have very different approaches to alienation in particular.[10] In the traditional spatial model, alienation is measured by the distance between the closer candidate's location and the voter's ideal point. The idea is that if the closer candidate is far away from the voter, the voter will be disenchanted by both candidates and find the "lesser of two evils" too evil to support.

That concept makes intuitive sense, but it is not consistent with the standard spatial model. From Davis, Hinich, and Ordeshook (1970) on, the most common assumption about how spatial position is translated into utility for the voter is that utility is quadratic in distance. This reflects not just standard spatial modeling, but standard economics in general, where it is argued that most decision makers, most of the time, are risk averse, and quadratic utility is the standard way to formulate that notion.[11] In Table 7.1, *et seq.*, the choice is how much better is one candidate compared to the other? If, say, the first candidate is one unit from the voter, that would be a utility from that candidate's election of -1 ($-[1^2]$) whereas, if the other candidate is 2 units away, that would be a utility of -4 ($-[2^2]$), for a difference in the choice of 3 units of utility. If, however, both candidates are quite far away, say 5 and 6 units from the voter, the difference is $(-25) - (-36)$ or 9 units of utility. There is more than twice the outcome-based-utility reasoning for supporting the closer, if far away, contender. This is general, so that alienation in the design as traditionally used in spatial modeling is inconsistent with the verbal description of alienation. In fact, Brennan and Hamlin (1998: 154–155) note that "there is no scope for the idea of citizen alienation in [the Downsian] model … Indifference rather than alienation is the key to non-participation." But they do not make it a central focus of their analysis. In the next section, we develop a different account of utility which is consistent with spatial modeling of this traditional form and also consistent with the intuition underlying alienation.

Brennan and Hamlin, by contrast, have the easier case. With B being a utility for supporting the preferred candidate, per se, it is easy to translate the "lesser of two evils is too evil to support" into expressive voting terms. Since B is simply the utility for the preferred candidate and not a difference between the utilities for the two candidates, the farther the voter is from the preferred candidate, the less the voter likes that candidate, and at some point (e.g., when expressive benefits are less than the costs of voting), the expressive voter will not turn out. They just don't like the best choice enough to vote for her.

Spatial voting with moral and non-moral preferences

Spatial modeling derives from the thinking of rational-choice-based micro-economic reasoning. The standard good, whether that be an economic good like apples or a political good like government health insurance policies is understood to be amenable to trading off with other goods. It is thus reasonable to imagine an overall utility function over numerous goods (policies in the spatial voting case) with some sort of distance metric defined over it, capturing the smooth nature of trading off one dimension or policy for another. Some goods in politics, however, may admit no trade off at all, or do so only under very extreme conditions. These are likely to deal with issues that are directly tapping voter's ethical, moral preferences, such as abortion, measuring the valuation of the life of the fetus and/or of the rights of the mother. People may not be sure just what the government can or should do to control, say, inflation, but they value – and can evaluate – life and liberty. This suggests a different structure for preferences over issues about which voters have strong moral convictions, and this different structure has consequences for how the intuition about alienation can be derivable from the traditional spatial model.

This difference in voters' ability to trade off issues that are moral versus those that are not can be captured by changing their utility functions. This idea of different functional forms for utility builds on previous work. For example, Poole and Rosenthal base their NOMINATE model on a utility function that is shaped like a normal distribution (Poole 2005). However, in order for this to be precise, we would still need justification for such a conceptual expansion in terms of psychological intuition. Two cognitive mechanisms could explain alienation according to a logic based in indifference. It could be that alienated voters perceive little to no difference in utility between distant candidates. That is, alienated voters are just distant, indifferent voters. If this is the case, then quadratic utility is not applicable and another way of equating distance with a voter's utility is needed. Alternatively, it could be that these voters do perceive a difference between two far-away candidates but feel disinclined to vote. That is, alienated voters are not indifferent, but something gained from abstention makes up for the potential utility loss in the case that one's favored candidate loses. If this is the case, it is not sufficient to say that the voter is just alienated; as explained already, this formulation is inconsistent with the spatial model. So a theory of why voters stop caring about the difference between candidates, and at what proximity this variable begins to affect the participation calculus, is needed.

Jenke (2017)[12] proposes a theory in the vein of the first argument – that "alienated" voters are simply indifferent voters who are far away from all available candidates. She suggests this specification is appropriate for voters with a high level of moral conviction. These voters are of particular interest in regards to alienation, since they tend to locate at the extremes of the policy spectrum (Ryan 2014) and are thus the section of the electorate traditionally held to be alienated. Most importantly, previous research on moral conviction provides a psychological basis for the idea that such voters are unique in terms of their utility loss.

Recent research in political psychology has defined a moral conviction as an opinion rooted in beliefs about an absolute sense of right and wrong that transcends normative conventions and cultural context (Skitka and Bauman 2008). Moral conviction is associated with a propensity to view political issues in a one-sided manner: voters with moral convictions show an increased animosity toward candidates and individuals who disagree with their opinions (Skitka, Bauman and Sargis 2005; Tetlock et al. 2000). Such respondents are also uniquely unwilling to compromise: moral conviction predicts opposition to politicians willing to compromise with the opposition (Skitka, Bauman and Sargis 2005; Toner et al. 2013; Ryan 2017). These findings are related to those by Tavits (2007), who examines the electoral effect of policy shifts on pragmatic versus principled issues.[13] She finds that candidates who shift their policies on principled issues experience an overall decrease in votes, while policy shifts on pragmatic issues lead to an increase in votes. This finding suggests that voters may dislike even small movements on the policy spectrum away from their ideal points when the issues connect with their value systems.

Moral judgments by definition defy the assumption of gradual utility loss inherent in linear or quadratic models. They are "evaluations *(good vs. bad)* of the actions or character of a person that are made with respect to a set of virtues held to be obligatory by a culture or subculture." And moral reasoning "consists of transforming given information about people in order to reach a moral judgment" (Haidt 2001). Thus, we can think of a model of moral conviction as the transformation of the policy space into a binary utility space: high utility for the "right" thing and low utility for the "wrong" thing. As specified by Haidt, a moral judgment has only two outcomes; a moral judgment of right or wrong does not lend itself to magnitudes, such as the "really right (wrong) thing," "somewhat right (wrong) thing," or "neither right nor wrong thing."

This binary view of utility translates directly into a step function, where the step (down) occurs at the point where the individual switches from viewing the policy as the right thing to do to the wrong thing to do. For the policies that an individual deems "right," she has a high and relatively flat level of utility; for those that she deems "wrong," she has a similarly flat but low level of utility.

This type of utility function has an important application to theories of voter alienation. A utility function with a long, flat tail offers a theoretically coherent explanation as to why one group of extreme voters may abstain due to alienation: once candidates are located outside of the realm of policies that the individual deems "right," the voter sees little difference between them and abstains. At the decision theoretic level, the cause of abstention is indifference between two "wrong" policies. But the result is consistent with the intuitions of the alienation hypothesis. Unlike quadratic utility, it predicts that indifference (and thus abstention) is higher when voters are far removed from candidates. Thus, this explanation yields the predictions of what looks like "alienation" in the common language origin of the term, but flows from the decision-theoretic logic of indifference.

Figure 7.1 demonstrates the difference in utility loss that a voter has between two candidates as their location moves from two versus three policy units away from the voter's ideal point to eight versus nine units away (their distance from each other remaining the same). The figure contains three utility functions: a quadratic function, a linear function, and a step function. On the quadratic function, the voter loses only five points of utility by moving from a candidate one unit away to a candidate two units away. But when the candidates are eight and nine units away, there is a difference in utility of 17 points between them. Thus, the voter will be more motivated to vote for the closer candidate when the candidates are further removed from her. The linear function similarly does not support the idea of alienation, having a constant slope. The voter is no more likely to abstain when the candidates are far removed, since the utility loss between them remains constant. Only in the step function is the idea of alienation supported: the difference in utility between the candidates *decreases* from 100 units when they are close to 0 units when they are further away. Thus, such a function supports the idea that a voter will choose not to vote for anyone when all candidates are far away, but it does so through the logic of indifference.

Thus, Jenke (2017) proposes that there are two types of voters. Morally convicted voters have a flat tail of utility loss, and are often indifferent ("alienated") when presented with distant choices. All other voters have the commonly assumed quadratic utility. This interpretation stems directly from the idea of what alienation is: the threshold is the policy that voters deem morally acceptable. The alienation is derivative of the utility function, which is derivative of a theory of how morals function in a decision.

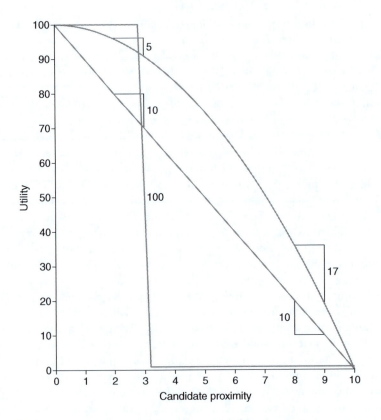

Figure 7.1 Utility losses over quadratic, linear, and sigmoidal utility functions

Note
Shown on the left side are differences in utility for candidates who are two unit and three units away from the voter's ideal point (here, zero) under each of the three utility functions, and on the right side are differences for candidates eight and nine units away.

This is therefore a different kind of explanation of alienation from the Brennan–Hamlin expressive voting form. Of course the moral–preference explanation is based on the transformation of distance into preferences over a Downsian-style policy space. It is therefore an explanation that is fully consistent with the pure theory of instrumental voting, the pure theory of expressive voting, and the hybrid model that combines the two, as Fiorina, Brennan and Hamlin, and we prefer.

Conclusion

The purposes of this chapter have been to review the nature of rational choice models of the turnout decision and to present two theoretical developments to such models. A basic decision theoretic account of turnout gets us only so far. In cases in which the difference between the costs and benefits of voting is between –0.5 and 0.5, decision theory is silent on whether the individual should turn out. Because the difference in utility from having your more preferred candidate win or lose is 1 unit, that indeterminate range spans a great deal of the space, at least in terms of voter utility. Alternative rational choice theories of voting are distinguished by the way in which they close this decision problem. These include transforming the decision problem into one of expected utility maximization (Downs 1957), transforming it into a minimax regret formulation (Ferejohn and Fiorina 1974), or embedding the expected utility account in a game theoretic analysis. One problem with these accounts is that they depend on the existence of an exact tie or a one-vote lead, whether or not these are given specific probabilities.

A third option is to expand the theory from its instrumentalist roots to develop a theory of expressive voting (Fiorina 1976; Brennan and Hamlin 1998). This option may be done in a stand-alone fashion (the "pure theory of expressive voting") or in combination of the two theories. As the name suggests, voters gain an expressive benefit, that is, one that comes simply and directly from the act of supporting their favored candidate or party. Brennan and Hamlin's (1998) hybrid account, mixing instrumental and expressive voting, is particularly beneficial when embedded in a spatial model of elections. It predicts relatively high levels of turnout, movement of candidates to modes in citizen preferences, and equilibria in many, rather than few, cases.

We then turned to examine a contradiction between the verbal statement of alienation as a form of abstention and its formal representation. At least in the "pure theory" of instrumental voting, and as long as utility functions are assumed to be linear or quadratic in distance, the standard spatial model yields either no decrease in relative utility for two candidates as the ideal point becomes farther removed from the closer candidate's position (under linear utility) or even makes the relative utility increase (under quadratic utility). Thus, while it seems intuitively reasonable to assert that the farther away the closer candidate is in spatial distance, the more "alienated" the voter becomes, it actually happens that voting for the preferred candidate becomes more, not less, important to the voter. Here we offer two accounts that can be used to transform the intuition of alienation into an appropriate theoretical form. One is expressive voting, in which it follows straightforwardly that voters become increasingly less happy with their preferred option, the farther away it is from their ideal point. We offer a second account, one developed by Jenke (2017), which assumes that voters whose choice is based on policies that, to them at least, are based in moral convictions yield a different functional relationship between policy distance and utility than in the standard spatial model. Instead of linear or quadratic-based transformations of distance to utility, morally convicted voters have a unique utility function which drops off more quickly than other (what we refer to here as "pragmatic") voters, and then it turns to have a flat tail at great distances. This function captures the behavior of such respondents, who view politics through a lens of "right" and "wrong." Such voters are more likely to be indifferent between distant candidates, thus explaining the behavior predicted by the alienation hypothesis through the logic of indifference.

Downs (1957) presented his account as a way to transform common political understandings into scientifically rigorous form: candidates in that era sought the policy center, offering "tweedle dee and tweedle dum" policies. The public is (and ought to be) largely ignorant of politics. Citizens should vote only if the election matters to them and the candidates are engaged in a close contest. Riker and Ordeshook (1968) completed this formalization of the calculus of voting in particular by building on the already well-established empirical work of social scientists to justify their formalization. It sometimes seems that this interaction between observations of the real political world and that of theoretical social science has too often been lost.

This chapter is an attempt to revive this creative synthesis – to the benefit not only of theoretical political science but also to generate new political insights. Here we develop two relatively new versions of such a synthesis: the theory of expressive voting (actually not very new, Fiorina 1976 but newly developed into an integrated theory of voting and democratic politics, such as in Brennan and Hamlin 1998), and the theory of moral sentiments.

We believe that these help reopen an opportunity to embed an expanded version of a calculus of voting into a richer theory of democratic politics. Brennan and Hamlin (1998) provide an exemplar of this strategy. They embedded the pure theory of expressive voting into a spatial model and were able to not only make better sense of the voters' decision problem but also developed new and different derivations about candidate behavior. This was the motivation underlying Downs' original work, and we conclude by encouraging development of these models such that we approach a richer and deeper understanding of the workings of democracy, not just of individual behavior.

Notes

1 If there is at least one consequential third candidate, then the calculus of voting needs to be expanded (see McKelvey and Ordeshook 1972) and strategic voting considered; see below.
2 Ties are assumed to be broken randomly, and the outcome of a tie is therefore worth 0.5.
3 Or, looked at from a different direction, the differential utility associated with who wins and who loses is relatively small.
4 See Aldrich (1993) for citations and consideration of the reasons that macro- and micro-data results differ.
5 Note that this concept implies that D and perhaps at least parts of C are also "expressive" components of the vote decision. We reserve the term "expressive" in the rest of this chapter for expressing support for a particular party or candidate, not, say, expressing support for the health of democracy, as Downs (1957) defined the D term.
6 Part of the importance of Ledyard's model is due to the fact that he was the first to have a fully developed equilibrium model of voting and candidate strategy.
7 Turnout is highest among those closest to a candidate in their model, rather than from extremists in the Ledyard model, if any vote in his model at all.
8 In the traditional spatial model, convergence is "guaranteed" in the sense that if there are any equilibriums at all, there are ones in which both candidates converge, that is, take the same spatial position. See McKelvey (1972) for proof.
9 For the original formalization and generalization of Downs' spatial model, see Davis, Hinich, and Ordeshook (1970) and McKelvey (1975).
10 Indifference, however, seems simply to be indifference, no matter how the decision problem is formulated.
11 While quadratic utility is often employed in spatial models (as was true from their earliest formalization, reviewed in Davis, Hinich, and Ordeshook 1970), and while many economists prefer risk aversion formulations, there is nothing in particular that favors quadratic utility over other forms, especially linear utility. McKelvey (especially 1972; 1975) derives his results from "quadratic-based," which is a much more general formulation, including all forms studied here, including the curvilinearity of moral utility functions. Empirically, there is some support for linear and some for quadratic formulations. However, Singh (2014: 47) provides perhaps the most rigorous testing between these two forms and finds as one of his three major conclusions: that "Third, on average, over all countries, the linear loss function also outperforms the quadratic loss function in terms of voter turnout."
12 Much of the following text is taken from Jenke (2017).
13 We took the term "pragmatic" from her work.

References

Aldrich, J. H. (1993) "Rational Choice and Turnout," *American Journal of Political Science*, vol. 37, no. 1, February, 246–278.
Brennan, G. and Hamlin, A. (1998) "Expressive Voting and Electoral Equilibrium," *Public Choice*, vol. 95, no. 1, April, 149–175.
Brody, R. A. and Page, B. I. (1973) "Indifference, Alienation and Rational Decisions," *Public Choice*, vol. 15, no. 1, June, 1–7.
Butler, D. and Stokes, D. (1969) *Political Change in Britain: Forces Shaping Electoral Choice*, New York: St. Martins.
Campbell, A., Converse, P. E., Miller, W. E., and Stokes, D. E. (1960) *The American Voter*, New York: John Wiley.

Cox, G. W. (1997) *Making Votes Count: Strategic Coordination in The World's Electoral Systems*, Volume 7, Cambridge: Cambridge University Press.

Davis, O. A., Hinich, M. J., and Ordeshook. P. C. (1970) "An Expository Development of a Mathematical Model of the Electoral Process," *American Political Science Review*, vol. 64, no. 2, June, 426–448.

Downs, A. (1957) *An Economic Theory of Democracy*, New York: Harper and Row.

Duverger, M. (1959) *Political Parties: Their Organization and Activity in the Modern State*, London: Methuen.

Ferejohn, J. and Fiorina, M. P. (1974) "The Paradox of Not Voting: A Decision Theoretic Analysis," *American Political Science Review*, vol. 68, no. 2, June, 525–536.

Ferejohn, J. and Fiorina, M. P. (1975) "Closeness Counts Only in Horseshoes and Dancing," *American Political Science Review*, vol. 69, no. 3, September, 920–925.

Fiorina, M. P. (1976) "The Voting Decision: Instrumental and Expressive Aspects," *Journal of Politics*, vol. 38, no. 2, May, 390–413.

Haidt, J. (2001) "The Emotional Dog and Its Rational Tail: A Social Intuitionist Approach to Moral Judgment," *Psychological Reviews*, vol. 108, no. 4, October, 814–834.

Harsanyi, J. C. (1977) *Rational Behavior and Bargaining Equilibrium in Games and Social Situations*, Cambridge: Cambridge University Press.

Hinich, M. J. and Ordeshook, P. C. (1969) "Abstentions and Equilibrium in the Electoral Process," *Public Choice*, vol. 7, no. 1, September, 81–106.

Jenke, L. (2017) "The Unique Utility Function of Morally Convicted Voters," February 16, 2017. Available online at SSRN: https://ssrn.com/abstract=2919036 or http://dx.doi.org/10.2139/ssrn.2919036.

Kselman, D. and Niou, E. (2010) "Strategic Voting in Plurality Elections," *Political Analysis*, vol. 18, no. 2, Autumn, 227–244.

Ledyard, J. O. (1984) "The Pure Theory of Large Two-Candidate Elections," *Public Choice*, vol. 44, no. 1, January, 7–41.

McKelvey, R. D. (1972) *Some Extensions and Modifications of Spatial Models of Party Competition*, Doctoral dissertation, University of Rochester.

McKelvey, R. D. (1975) "Policy Related Voting and Electoral Equilibrium," *Econometrica*, vol. 43, no. 6, September, 815–843.

McKelvey, R. D. and Ordeshook, P. C. (1972) "A General Theory of the Calculus of Voting," in Herndon, J. F. and Bernd, J. L. (eds.) *Mathematical Applications in Political Science*, Charlottesville: University of Virginia Press: 32–78.

Niou, E. (2001) "Strategic Voting Under Plurality and Runoff Rules," *Journal of Theoretical Politics*, vol. 13, no. 1, April, 209–227.

Poole, K. T. (2005) *Spatial Models of Parliamentary Voting*, Cambridge: Cambridge University Press.

Riker, W. H. and Ordeshook, P. C. (1968) "A Theory of the Calculus of Voting," *American Political Science Review*, vol. 62, no. 1, March, 25–42.

Ryan, T. J. (2014) "Reconsidering Moral Issues in Politics," *Journal of Politics*, vol. 76, no. 2, February, 380–397.

Ryan, T. J. (2017) "No Compromise: Political Consequences of Moralized Attitudes," *American Journal of Political Science*, vol. 61, no. 2, April, 409–423.

Schuessler, A. A. (2000a) *A Logic of Expressive Choice*, Princeton: Princeton University Press.

Schuessler, A. A. (2000b) "Expressive Voting," *Rationality and Society*, vol. 12, no. 1, February, 87–119.

Singh, S. (2014) "Linear and Quadratic Utility Loss Functions in Voting Behavior Research," *Journal of Theoretical Politics*, vol. 26, no. 1, January, 35–58.

Skitka, L. J. and Bauman, C. W. (2008) "Moral Conviction and Political Engagement," *Political Psychology*, vol. 29, no. 1, February, 29–54.

Skitka, L. J., Bauman, C. W., and Sargis, E. G. (2005) "Moral Conviction: Another Contributor to Attitude Strength or Something More?," *Journal of Personality and Social Psychology*, vol. 86, no. 6, June, 895–917.

Tavits, M. (2007) "Principle vs. Pragmatism: Policy Shifts and Political Competition," *American Journal of Political Science*, vol. 51, no. 1, January, 151–165.

Tetlock, P. E., Orie, V., Kristel, S., Elson, B., Green, M. C., and Lerner, J. S. (2000) "The Psychology of the Unthinkable: Taboo Trade-Offs, Forbidden Base Rates, and Heretical Counterfactuals," *Journal of Personality and Social Psychology*, vol. 78, no. 5, May, 853–870.

Toner, K., Leary, M., Asher, M., and Jongman-Sereno, K. (2013) "Feeling Superior Is a Bipartisan Issue: Extremity (Not Direction) of Political Views Predicts Perceived Belief Superiority," *Psychological Science*, vol. 24, no. 12, December, 2454–2462.

8

VOTING AND THE EXPANDING REPERTOIRE OF PARTICIPATION

Jan W. van Deth

Introduction: expanding repertoires

Since elections are the hallmark of democracy voting occupies a unique position among the many ways people can be engaged in politics. Only elections have formal consequences for the distribution of political power and the legitimacy of political decisions and decision-making procedures. Democracy, therefore, cannot exist without general suffrage. The widely recognized significance and uniqueness of voting and elections for the quality of democracy have been challenged by two seemingly related developments: whereas citizens in many countries are staying away from the polls in record numbers, other forms of political participation have become increasingly popular. By now, the repertoire of participation is virtually endless covering forms as different as casting a vote, signing petitions, demonstrating, donating money, attending flash mobs, contacting public officials, buying fair-trade products, signing petitions, boycotting, guerrilla gardening, volunteering, organizing blogs, and suicide protests.

The downward trends in voting turnout in many countries and the continued rise of new forms of engagement attracted the attention of many scholars and pundits. Do these processes imply a transformation "From Voters to Participants" (Gundelach and Siune 1992) and is voting crowded out by the evident appeal of these new modes in "Zero Sum Democracy" (Peters 2016)? Can the spread of new modes of participation be seen as a kind of "compensation" for declining turnout? Are we confronted with parallel but causally unrelated developments or with flip sides of the same coin? At first sight, these questions can be easily answered by referring to broad processes of societal, social, and political change implying the weakening of the nation-state in a globalized world. As the scope of government activities and responsibilities expanded considerably since the 1960s, the domain of political participation grew too; that is, political participation became relevant in areas that would be considered private, social, or economic only a few decades ago. Furthermore, with the rapidly increasing interdependencies and complexities in a globalized world "nongovernmental politics" and non-state actors are becoming increasingly important (Feher 2007; Hutter 2014; Sloam 2007; Walker et al. 2008), especially to deal with the immense ecological, socioeconomic, and demographic challenges facing mankind (Bauman 1998). Consequently, the decline of voting and the rise of new forms of participation are both stimulated by the expansion of government interventions and especially by the rise of non-state actors.

Plausible and enticing as these broad interpretations might be they usually avoid offering explanations for the exact mechanisms that would enforce people to withdraw from conventional government activities or nation-state politics. In his seminal article on profound political changes in democratic societies, Ronald Inglehart (1971) probably presented the most famous and widely used approach to explain these developments comprehensively. In his view, declining voter turnout and the rise of new modes of participation are clearly connected because they both rely on the combined effects of the spread of postmaterialist value orientations and the rise of cognitive competences among the populations of advanced democracies. According to Inglehart, this mainly generationally driven change will increasingly result in a decline of support for authorities, conventions, and material advantages as well as a downward trend in voting turnout.

In this chapter, four aspects of these debates are considered. First, the main developments in political participation in the last decades – declining electoral participation and expansions of the repertoire – are depicted. Second, the distinctions between the various modes of participation are explored in order to see whether casting a vote has lost its initial uniqueness with the growth of all-embracing repertoires of political participation. Third, the empirical soundness of the widely accepted idea of a generationally based process of value change counting for both declining turnout and increasing popularity of newer modes of participation is evaluated. Finally, the evidence for a direct relationship between casting a vote and other forms of participation is considered: do protest and voting strengthen or exclude each other? The findings all suggest that voting and other modes of participation should neither be studied separately nor should they be considered simply as substitutable specimen of political engagement: "When we conceptualize political engagement only as periodic voting we miss the richness and dynamic potential of democratic citizenship" (Berger 2011: 41).

Changing participation

As can be easily illustrated with the publication of a few landmark studies in empirical political participation research, a continuous expansion of the repertoire of participation is hard to overlook.[1] More specifically, the introduction of new forms and modes of participation gradually lessened the initial strong focus on elections as the main arena for democratic participation. This emphasis is evident in the seminal voting studies of the 1940s and 1950s that restricted political participation mainly to casting a vote, campaigning, and further party- or election-related activities (Berelson et al. 1954; Lazarsfeld et al. 1948). For the authors of "The American Voter," political participation was broadly understood as activities concerned with constitutional political institutions – mainly related to electoral activities by politicians and parties – but also included public contacts between citizens and government officials (Campbell et al. 1960). Because of the growing relevance of community politics these forms of participation were expanded with direct contacts between citizens, public officials, and politicians in empirical studies in the late 1960s and early 1970s (Verba and Nie 1972; Verba et al. 1978). The repertoire of political participation covered by these seminal works in the first post-war decades includes all accepted activities in representative democracies which later became known as *conventional* or *institutionalized* modes of participation.

Even if one does not buy the romantic and exaggerated depictions of the late 1960s as a revolutionary area, it is clear that the waves of protest in many countries established a major shift in political engagement. Obviously, political participation could no longer be restricted to broadly accepted forms or "proper" activities. Protest, opposition, and rejection are clear expressions of citizens' interests and opinions and therefore should be included in the repertoire of political participation (Barnes et al. 1979; Marsh 1977). Because these protest forms of participation were not in line with social norms of the early 1970s they have been labeled *unconventional* modes of participation – a depiction that continued to be used long after social norms changed in favor of these activities. New social movements such as women's or pacifists' groups also belong to this category (Dalton and Küchler 1990). Many protest actions and activities by new social movements challenge the conventional understanding of the scope and nature of politics and stress political struggles. To underline this character labels such as *contentious politics* (Tarrow 1998) or *elite-challenging* modes of participation (Inglehart 1990; Inglehart and Catterberg 2002) are used.

The rise of new social movements in the early 1970s already indicated that the traditional understanding of politics as being limited to governments, politicians, and electoral processes rapidly vanished. Recent expansions of the repertoire of political participation all show the further dissolution of the borderline between political and non-political spheres in many countries. First, in the early 1990s the revival of Tocquevillean and communitarian approaches lead to an expansion of the repertoire with civil activities such as volunteering and social engagement in all kinds of voluntary associations (Verba et al. 1995). In these approaches, the quality of democracy is directly related to the existence of a vibrant *civil society* (Putnam 1993). Second, many citizens detected that their power as consumers could be used successfully to achieve social or political goals by boycotting or "buycotting" certain products or firms (Micheletti 2003). In a relatively short period of time *political consumerism* became one of the most popular forms of participation (Stolle and Micheletti 2013). A third major development concerns the spread of internet-based technologies – especially social media – as means for political participation. Because of their extremely low opportunity costs, these technologies appear to be efficient ways to raise public awareness and the visibility of all kind of causes and issues almost instantly (Shirky 2008). Moreover, the production and dissemination of political news on the internet hardly can be restricted or manipulated by authorities. Several authors argue that these implications and consequences of the use of internet technologies already gave rise to a new type of "connective action" replacing "collective action" (Bennett and Segerberg 2013).

With these recent expansions of the repertoire, the nature of political activities changed. Whereas older forms of participation such as voting or demonstrating are specific activities mainly devised and used to influence political decision-making processes, newer modes such as political consumption or guerrilla gardening are non-political activities used for political aims (van Deth 2010). These activities do not require any organization or collective action and establish what Micheletti (2003: 25; see c.f. Stolle and Micheletti 2013: 36–39) nicely depicted as "individualized collective action": to be effective, a large number of people should behave in a similar way, but they can all act individually, separately, and with distinct aims and motivations. Usually these activities have an unmistakable emphasis on the expression of moral and ethical standpoints, which gradually seem to replace the older, more instrumentally based motivations for political engagement. The spread of internet-based technologies strongly facilitates these non-private, individualized, and expressively motivated actions.

The uniqueness of the vote

The continued expansions of the repertoire of political participation since the Second World War have increasingly dissolved the distinctions between political and non-political activities and by now almost every conceivable form of non-private activity can be understood as a mode of political participation sometimes (van Deth 2001, 2014). As mentioned, the initial strong focus on elections as the main arena for democratic participation gradually diminished with the introduction of new forms of participation. Although the rise of each new activity implies the expansion of the general repertoire of political participation, it does not mean that we simply observe the addition of new forms of participation to available ones. In fact, empirical research consistently shows that the repertoire of political participation encompasses distinct forms – or actions – grouped into several modes of participation.[2] More importantly, empirical analyses of these (latent) structures largely show similar results in many countries. After Milbrath (1965: 18) had suggested a pyramid-shaped distribution of active and passive forms of participation, already Milbrath and Goel (1977: 20f.) and Verba and Nie (1972: 60–75) applied advanced statistical methods to distinguish four major modes of political participation in the US: "voting," "campaign activity," "communal activity," and "particularized contacting." The distinction between conventional and unconventional modes was also based on the application of data reduction techniques (Barnes et al. 1979: 540–550). Parry et al. (1992: 50–62) found six modes of participation in Britain: "voting," "party campaigning," "collective action," "contacting," "direct action," and "political violence." In a similar vein, Verba et al. (1995) expanded the list of four modes of participation developed by Verba and Nie more than twenty years earlier with "protest" and divided campaign activities and contacting further into subcategories. Moreover, they added activities in voluntary associations and volunteering to the repertoire of participation. These last-mentioned activities also show up in Norris' three-dimensional space distinguishing "civic activism," "protest activism," and "voting turnout" (2002: 196). In the most extensive empirical study in Europe, Teorell et al. (2007: 344–345) grouped the many forms of participation they found into five modes: "voting," "contacting," "party activity," "protest activity," and "consumer participation." Recent analyses of the structure of the repertoire of participation also report five modes: "voting," "conventional participation," "protest," "consumer participation," and "digitally networked participation" (Theocharis and van Deth 2016).

The specific number and depictions of the various dimensions reflect the forms of participation considered relevant for these studies – obviously this relevance varies by time and place. Yet, if we look behind the different labels used, probably the most remarkable and consistent empirical result is the fact that casting a vote is not only the most widely used form of engagement, but always arises as a distinct mode of participation. No matter how many other forms of participation are included in the analyses voting apparently cannot be combined with other forms of participation into a more general mode of participation. Besides, casting a vote is the only form of participation that requires such an exclusive position; all other forms of participation can be combined to establish specific modes of participation. It should be noticed, however, that these conclusions are all based on the application of data reduction procedures aiming to find independent dimensions of the latent spaces constructed.[3] The use of item response models (especially stochastic cumulative scaling techniques) allowing for multiple instead of independent scales suggests that voting is related to several other forms of participation. In a unique and very extensive study, García-Albacete (2014) reviewed all cross-national surveys since the 1970s and painstakingly developed equivalent instruments for political participation in various countries based on the use of item response models (Mokken scaling). These analyses show that "voting" is included in an identical scale for "institutional participation" together with "contacting politicians" and "working for a political party." For the construction of equivalent measures this scale can be expanded with "membership in a traditional organization" and "donating money" in several countries. The inclusion of casting a vote in these scales causes several minor problems – especially in Denmark and Italy – but does not challenge the idea that voting can be considered to be a specimen of an "institutional" mode of participation (García-Albacete 2014: 25–39). The use of scale models instead of dimensional analyses, then, shows that, on the one hand, casting a vote is associated with a few forms of participation directly related to the main actors in the electoral process. On the other hand, it is clear that voting definitely *does not* belong to the larger "non-institutional" mode of participation, which includes forms such as demonstrating or signing petitions.

A second way to explore the relationships between voting and other forms of participation is to compare their respective antecedents. The study by Parry et al. in Britain follows this design and shows that the "pattern" of individual resources determining participation is very similar for all modes of participation, but "only voting shows a different pattern" (1992: 84). Using sophisticated models, Oser (2016) is able to show that predictors of being a "high-voting engaged participant" differ clearly from those for other groups. The seminal study of Verba and his colleagues (1995) on political and social involvement in the US covers many forms of participation and a large number of antecedents. Summarizing the huge amounts of information they collected the authors strongly stress the "uniqueness of the vote" and conclude their empirical analyses with a clear warning:

> with respect to every single aspect of participation we scrutinize, voting is fundamentally different from other acts. (…) To repeat, on every dimension along which we consider participatory acts, voting is *sui generis*. For this reason, it is a mistake to generalize from our extensive knowledge about voting to all forms of participation.
>
> *(Verba et al. 1995: 23–24; emphasis original)*

This "uniqueness of the vote" probably stimulated the separate development of voting studies and participation research in the last decades[4] and the spread of terms such as "non-institutional" or "non-electoral" participation.

Looking at contextual impacts provides a third way to study differences and similarities between casting a vote and other modes of participation. A growing number of studies argue that voting and these other modes of participation are essentially different because they depend on the institutional and political contexts in different ways. Although these studies are usually based on a rather limited number of actions – five or six forms of participation typically being the maximum amount available – the conclusions consistently underline the need to distinguish between casting a vote on the one hand and all other forms of participation on the other (Bolzendahl and Coffé 2013: 72; Brunton-Smith and Barrett 2015: 203). Typical specimens of this work are the cross-national analyses of Weldon and Dalton (2013) of the impact of the degree of "consensualism" – the attempts to integrate various interests instead of applying majority rule – in advanced democracies on participation. Confirming very similar findings from other studies (Peters 2016; van der Meer et al. 2009; Vráblíková 2013, 2016; Vráblíková and van Deth 2017), they report contrary effects for different actions: "Consensual party-based electoral systems may stimulate turnout in elections – but they also appear to discourage an active and more robust democratic citizenship" (Weldon and Dalton 2013: 127).

These three distinct approaches of the relationships and (dis)similarities between voting and other forms of participation – (i) dimensional analyses, and exploratory analyses of (ii) antecedents and (iii) contextual impacts – do not have much in common. Nonetheless each of the analyses concerned corroborates the idea that casting a vote is not only a distinct form but also a distinct mode of political participation. Only incidentally voting is shown to be associated with a few forms of participation directly related to the electoral process, together establishing an "electoral" or "institutionalized" mode of participation. Even if casting a vote is not considered to be "the holy grail of political engagement" (Berger 2011: 164), it certainly is a unique specimen of being involved.

The impact of values and institutions

The parallel developments of declining voter turnout and expansions of the participatory repertoire can be seen as different phenomena to be explained by different theoretical approaches. For instance, Mair (2013) strongly argued that the "failures of contemporary parties" are mainly responsible for much of the problems representative democracies face today, including growing political indifference among the populations. As with globalization theories focusing on the decline of the nation-state and the implied move toward non-governmental politics to explain waning turnout (see above), Mair's explanation emphasizes the relevance of supply-side factors for the explanation of political participation. In these approaches, the rise of new modes of participation is simply implied by assuming that, in a rapidly changing world, people will move from the nation-state to other areas and targets that are considered to be more relevant to express their political demands and opinions.

Despite their intuitive plausibility, supply-side approaches to explain political participation have a modest empirical record. Therefore, explanations take situational and contextual factors into account increasingly, but emphasize demand-side factors; that is, circumstantial factors and characteristics of individual citizens and their micro-contexts are combined in integrated multi-level models. For the study of changing political participation, probably the most influential approach following this recommendation is Ronald Inglehart's theory of a "Silent Revolution" (1971). According to this theory, unprecedented economic prosperity and a lack of social turmoil after the Second World War triggered a process of value change in many countries. Especially among young people the satisfaction of existential needs gradually was taken for granted; consequently they increasingly attached priority to self-fulfillment and the satisfaction of social needs. According to Inglehart, this generationally based transformation from "materialist" to "postmaterialist" value orientations affects all aspects of life ranging from changes in religious beliefs, work motivation, parental goals, and attitudes toward divorce and homosexuality, to changes in the nature of political conflicts, the rise of Green parties, and the spread of cosmopolitan attitudes in a globalizing world. On average, these younger generations will also be much higher educated and will have much easier access to information than their predecessors. Postmaterialist value orientations, therefore, will be articulated by young citizens with a relatively high level of cognitive skills, which enable them to deal with political abstractions and phenomena that are remote in time and space. In this way, value change and "cognitive mobilization" are very closely interrelated (Inglehart, 1971, 1977, 1981, 1990; Inglehart and Catterberg, 2002).

Already in the first extensive presentation of his theory, Inglehart dealt with the "apparent contradiction" (1977: 314) that the predicted increase in social and political engagement among postmaterialists very clearly does not hold for voting turnout, which is notoriously low among young people. According to Inglehart, the postmaterialist desire to move from "elite-directed" to "elite-challenging" modes of participation is strongly stimulated by the process of "cognitive mobilization" – together they provide the key to solve the "contradiction":

> This change does not imply that mass publics will simply show higher rates of participation in traditional activities such as voting but that they may intervene in the political process on a qualitatively different level. Increasingly, they are likely to demand participation in *making* major decisions, not just a voice in selecting the decision-makers.
>
> *(Inglehart 1977: 293; emphasis original)*

In combination with the weakening of party identification and the declining attractiveness of conventional mobilization agencies such as parties, churches, and unions, these emerging demands drive the dual developments of decreasing voter turnout and the spread of new forms of participation (Dalton 2012). In fact, the generationally based nature of this process implies a continuously declining trend in voting as well as a parallel but continuously increasing tendency in the use of newer modes of participation. While almost each aspect of Inglehart's theory of value change has been criticized (c.f. Abramson 2015; Davis et al. 1999; Scarbrough 1995) the initial idea of a "Silent Revolution" has been further developed and expanded into a general theory of human development (Inglehart and Welzel 2005; Welzel 2013). Besides, it has been shown that values also have a substantial impact on political behavior as a(n) (aggregated) feature of a political culture and not just as individual properties (Jakobsen and Listhaug 2015; Welzel and Deutsch 2012).

The impact of values on political behavior has been empirically demonstrated in a number of studies. However, the effects on political participation outside the ballot box are much clearer than effects on voting. Whereas, for instance, Gundelach concludes that "…postmaterialism plays a notable role in stimulating grass-roots activity" (1995: 432), Borg found that "…post-materialist values have little impact on turnout levels" (1995: 459). Unfortunately, most studies available focus on a single aspect of these processes, use a very limited number of determinants, or do not compare potential effects on various modes of participation systematically (Vráblíková and Císař 2015). More importantly, most studies do not compare the impact of values with the impact of other, non-attitudinal determinants at both the micro and the macro level and, therefore, cannot be used for empirical evaluations of the idea that changes in participation are mainly driven by value change.

In a rare combined comparative analysis of individual and contextual determinants of various modes of participation, Vráblíková (2016) studies the relative effects of institutional arrangements and value orientations. Her main conclusion is that contextual factors need to be taken into account in combination with cultural aspects, but that institutional arrangements such as the separation of powers and the degree of competition frequently overshadow the impact of values. In other words: although the notion of a generationally based transformation of values and competences triggering changes in many areas of life in many countries is widely accepted by now, it is also clear that this transformation is not the only relevant, and probably not the most important, factor to explain changes and cross-national differences in political participation.

A different logic

The analyses presented by Vráblíková (2016) also allow for an important conclusion on the relationships between voting and other forms of participation. When country-specific effects – including differences in institutional arrangements and value orientations – are taken into account, it becomes clear that casting a vote and other modes of participation do not exclude each other:

> In contrast to the notion of displacement, which theorizes that non-electoral activism is driving out electoral participation, the literature and results reviewed above suggest that the structure of people's political action repertoire is cumulative. The vast majority of people who get involved in non-electoral activities also vote, and this repertoire composition holds regardless of the specific country context.
>
> *(Vráblíková 2016: 169)*

On this crucial point, however, other researchers are less positive. Whereas, for instance, Stolle and Micheletti conclude that "the rise of political consumerism does not necessarily compensate for the decline in traditional participation" (2013: 265), other scholars report modest but negative correlations between voting and new modes of participation (Norris 2002: 205; Theocharis and van Deth 2016: 16) or no correlation at all when "radical protest" is considered (Bean 1991: 267).[5] An extensive discussion of a "reciprocal relationship" is presented by McAdam and Tarrow (2010).

Moving the focus of the analyses from the participation repertoires of citizens toward the study of political actors in various societies, a different type of analysis has risen recently. In a highly original study of the relationships between "electoral politics" and "protest politics" in Western Europe, Hutter (2012, 2014) stresses that the saliency of issue positions for newly emerging issues related to globalization, migration, and European integration plays a key role in our understanding of the roles and positions of political actors. He distinguishes three possible interpretations of the relationships: the "congruence thesis" (postulating a positive correlation between electoral and protest politics), the "counterweight thesis" (postulating that salient issues in the electoral arena will be less salient in protest politics – and vice versa), and the "different logics thesis" (postulating that the direction of the relationship depends on the political orientations of the actors involved: left-wing actors will show a positive relationship, right-wing a negative one) (Hutter 2012: 189–191; 2014: Chapter 2; see also Císař and Vráblíková 2015). The last interpretation is clearly corroborated by the empirical evidence available:

> there are different logics at work with respect to the relationship between electoral and protest mobilization on the political left and right. The left can be expected to wax and wane at the same time in both arenas, while for the right, when its actors and issue positions become more salient in one arena their salience should decrease in the other.
>
> *(Hutter 2014: Introduction; see also Hutter 2012: 203)*

The findings presented by Vráblíková and by Hutter suggest rather complex mechanisms relating voting to other modes of participation with conditional effects replacing simple direct impacts. Although dealing with political actors instead of individual citizens, the "distinct logic" stressed by Hutter (2012, 2014), however, once again shows that casting a vote should be distinguished from other activities if we want to understand political engagement in a globalizing world.

Conclusions and discussion

Elections establish the core of democracy and so voting should be at the center of discussions about political participation among mass publics. In this chapter, the seemingly related processes of downward trends in voting turnout and the increasing popularity of other forms of participation have been considered. Four conclusions can be based on the available evidence. First, it is clear that the repertoire of political participation rapidly expanded in the last few decades: by now, almost every non-private act can be used for political purposes and voting is only one of the many options available to citizens. Second, the repertoire of participation appears to be fairly similarly structured in many studies with voting always establishing a distinct mode of participation. This "uniqueness of the vote" (Verba et al. 1995) is corroborated by analyses of the antecedents of different modes of participation as well as their contextual determinants. Third, generationally based shifts in values play an important role in approaches advocating that declining turnout and the spread of other modes of participation are flip sides of the same coin. Yet extensive analyses taking into account both value orientations and institutional arrangements at the micro and macro level show a relatively stronger impact of institutional arrangements than values. Finally, empirical evidence does not support displacement or crowding out effects: citizens using one or more of the available newer forms of participation are likely to visit the ballot box too, but a "distinct logic" (Hutter 2012, 2014) explains the relationships differently for left- and right-wing politics.

The popularity of new forms or participation clearly refutes the idea of a general decline in political involvement or a general shift away from social and political issues among the populations in many countries. Downward trends in voter turnout, however, suggest that also among activists electoral participation gradually becomes less important or attractive. The fact that voting apparently establishes a distinct mode of participation implies that a decline in turnout cannot be easily counteracted or compensated by the proliferation of other forms of participation. Even studies relying on a large number of different forms of participation do not reveal a reduction of the number of dimensions or the inclusion of voting into some broader range of forms of participation. On the other hand, it is clear that representative democracy without sizeable voter turnout and some party work cannot function. These findings all suggest that voting and other modes of participation should neither be studied separately nor should they be considered as substitutable specimen of political engagement.

This delicate relationship between voting and other modes of participation also indicates that terms such as "Zero Sum Democracy" or "Positive Sum Democracy" (Peters 2016) correctly point to inherent relationships between various modes of participation but are probably too broad to be used for evaluations of the challenges democracies face. A vibrant democracy clearly necessitates the widespread willingness to cast a vote as well as broad support for other forms of citizens' involvement. What is required, therefore, is that at least a part of the other forms of participation are integrated into institutionalized democratic policy-making processes to avoid that the erosional trend in electoral participation challenges the legitimacy of representative democracy. Several authors called for a "second transformation" of democracy that should entail exactly this integration (Cain et al. 2003). The complicated interdependencies between voting and other forms of participation summarized in this chapter should be taken as an incitement and stimulus for further work in this direction.

Notes

1 Whereas a "form" of participation is a specific activity, several forms sharing some feature are called a "mode" or "type" of participation. A "repertoire" of political participation unites all available forms (and modes) of participation.

2 That is, each form of participation can be depicted as a point in a latent space (the repertoire) defined by several directions or dimensions (the modes of participation).

3 Reducing data on participation using principal components analysis (PCA) with orthogonal rotation is standard praxis in the field. The use of orthogonal rotation procedures, however, is questionable because various modes of participation have shown to be correlated. For a different approach, see Oser (2016).

4 This split comes with distinct projects such as the Comparative Study of Electoral Systems (CSES) vs. the Citizenship, Involvement, Democracy project (CID), and with distinct journals such as *Electoral Studies* or the *Journal of Elections, Public Opinion and Parties* vs. more general journals such as *Comparative Political Studies* or *Political Behavior*.

5 Researchers using cluster-analytic or typological approaches instead of correlational analyses usually show that small numbers of voters are also engaged in other activities. See Oser (2016) for a very interesting study along these lines.

References

Abramson, P. R. (2015) "Value Change Over a Third of a Century. The Evidence for Generational Replacement," in Dalton, R. J. and Welzel, C. (eds.) *The Civic Culture Transformed: From Allegiant to Assertive Citizens*, Cambridge: Cambridge University Press: 19–34.

Barnes, S. H., Kaase, M., Allerbeck, K. R., Farah, B. G., Heunks, F., Inglehart, R., Jennings, M. K., Klingemann, H-D., Marsh, A., and Rosenmayr, L. (1979) *Political Action: Mass Participation in Five Western Democracies*, Beverly Hills: Sage.

Bauman, Z. (1998) *Globalization: The Human Consequences*, Cambridge: Polity Press.

Bean, C. (1991) "Participation and Political Protest: A Causal Model with Australian Evidence," *Political Behavior*, vol. 13, no. 3, September, 253–283.

Bennett, W. L. and Segerberg, A. (2013) *The Logic of Connective Action. Digital Media and the Personalization of Contentious Politics*, Cambridge: Cambridge University Press.

Berelson, B. R., Lazarsfeld, P. F., and McPhee, W. N. (1954) *Voting: A Study of Opinion Formation in a Presidential Campaign*, Chicago: University of Chicago Press.

Berger, B. (2011) *Attention Deficit Democracy: The Paradox of Civic Engagement*, Princeton: Princeton University Press.

Bolzendahl, C. and Coffé, H. (2013) "Are 'Good' Citizens 'Good' Participants? Testing Citizenship Norms and Political Participation across 25 Nations," *Political Studies*, vol. 61, no. S1, April, 45–65.

Borg, S. (1995) "Electoral Participation," in van Deth, J. W. and Scarbrough, E. (eds.) *The Impact of Values*, Oxford: Oxford University Press: 441–460.

Brunton-Smith, I. and Barrett, M. (2015) "Political and Civic Participation. Findings from the Modelling of Existing Survey Data Sets," in Barrett, M. and Zani, B. (eds.) *Political and Civic Engagement: Multidisciplinary Perspectives*, New York: Routledge: 195–212.

Cain, B. E., Dalton, R. J., and Scarrow, S. E. (eds.) (2003) *Democracy Transformed? Expanding Political Opportunities in Advanced Industrial Democracies*, Oxford: Oxford University Press.

Campbell, A., Converse, P. E., Miller, W. E., and Stokes, D. E. (1960) *The American Voter*, New York: John W. Wiley & Sons.

Císař, O. and Vráblíková, K. (2015) "At the Parliament or in the Streets? Issue Composition of Contentious Politics in the Visegrad Countries," Paper presented at the 2015 meeting of the American Political Science Association, San Francisco, September 2–6.

Dalton, R. J. (2012) *The Apartisan American: Dealignment and Changing Electoral Politics*, Thousand Oaks: CQ Press.

Dalton, R. J. and Küchler, M. (eds.) (1990) *Challenging the Political Order: New Social and Political Movements in Western Democracies*, Cambridge: Polity Press.

Davis, D. W., Dowley, K. M., and Silver, B. D. (1999) "Postmaterialism in World Societies: Is it Really a Value Dimension?," *American Journal of Political Science*, vol. 43, no. 3, July, 935–962.

Feher, M. (ed.) (2007) *Nongovernmental Politics*, New York: Zone Books.

García-Albacete, G. M. (2014) *Young People's Political Participation in Western Europe: Continuity or Generational Change?*, Houndmills: Palgrave.

Gundelach, P. (1995) "Grass-roots Activity," in van Deth, J. W. and Scarbrough, E. (eds.) *The Impact of Values*, Oxford: Oxford University Press: 412–440.

Gundelach, P. and Siune, K. (eds.) (1992) *From Voters to Participants*, Aarhus: Politica.

Hutter, S. (2012) "Congruence, Counterweight, or Different Logics? Comparing Electoral and Protest Politics," in Kriesi, H., Grande, E., Dolezal, M., Helbling, M., Höglinger, D., Hutter, S., and Wüest, B. (eds.) *Political Conflict in Western Europe*, Cambridge: Cambridge University Press: 182–203.

Hutter, S. (2014) *Protesting Culture and Economics in Western Europe: New Cleavages in Left and Right Politics*, Minneapolis: University of Minnesota Press.

Inglehart, R. (1971) "The Silent Revolution in Europe: Intergenerational Change in Post-Industrial Societies," *American Political Science Review*, vol. 65, no. 4, December, 991–1017.

Inglehart, R. (1977) *The Silent Revolution: Changing Values and Political Styles Among Western Publics*, Princeton: Princeton University Press.

Inglehart, R. (1981) "Postmaterialism in an Environment of Insecurity," *American Political Science Review*, vol. 75, no. 4, December, 880–900.

Inglehart, R. (1990) *Culture Shift in Advanced Industrial Society*, Princeton: Princeton University Press.

Inglehart, R. and Catterberg, G. (2002) "Trends in Political Action: The Developmental Trend and the Post-Honeymoon Decline," *International Journal of Comparative Sociology*, vol. 43, no. 3, October, 300–316.

Inglehart, R. and Welzel, C. (2005) *Modernization, Cultural Change, and Democracy: The Human Development Sequence*, Cambridge: Cambridge University Press.

Jakobsen, T. G. and Listhaug, O. (2015) "Social Change and the Politics of Protest," in Dalton, R. J. and Welzel, C. (eds.) *The Civic Culture Transformed: From Allegiant to Assertive Citizens*, Cambridge: Cambridge University Press: 213–239.

Lazarsfeld, P. M., Berelson, B., and Gaudet, H. (1948) *The People's Choice: How the Voter Makes Up His Mind in a Presidential Campaign*, New York: Columbia University Press.

Mair, P. (2013) *Ruling The Void: The Hollowing Of Western Democracy*, London: Verso.

Marsh, A. (1977) *Protest and Political Consciousness*, Beverly Hills: Sage.

McAdam, D. and Tarrow, S. (2010) "Ballots and Barricades: On the Reciprocal Relationship Between Elections and Social Movements," *Perspectives on Politics*, vol. 8, no. 2, June, 529–542.

Micheletti, M. (2003) *Political Virtue and Shopping. Individuals, Consumerism and Collective Action*, New York: Palgrave Macmillan.

Milbrath, L. W. (1965) *Political Participation: How and Why Do People Get Involved in Politics?*, Chicago: Rand McNally.

Milbrath, L. W. and Goel, M. L. (1977) *Political Participation: How and Why Do People Get Involved in Politics?*, Chicago: Rand McNally.

Norris, P. (2002) *Democratic Phoenix: Reinventing Political Activism*, Cambridge: Cambridge University Press.

Oser, J. (2016) "Assessing How Participators Combine Acts in Their 'Political Tool Kits': A Person-Centered Measurement Approach for Analyzing Citizen Participation," *Social Indicators Research*, available online: http://link.springer.com/article/10.1007/s11205-016-1364-8.

Parry, G., Moyser, G., and Day, N. (1992) *Political Participation and Democracy in Britain*, Cambridge: Cambridge University Press.

Peters, Y. (2016) "Zero-Sum Democracy? The Effects of Direct Democracy on Representative Participation," *Political Studies*, vol. 64, no. 3, October, 593–613.

Putnam, R. D. (1993) *Making Democracy Work. Civic Traditions in Modern Italy*, Princeton: Princeton University Press.

Scarbrough, E. (1995) "Materialist-Postmaterialist Value Orientations," in van Deth, J. W. and Scarbrough, E. (eds.) *The Impact of Values: Beliefs in Government*, Volume 4, Oxford: Oxford University Press: 123–159.

Shirky, C. (2008) *Here Comes Everybody: The Power of Organizing without Organizations*, New York: Penguin.

Sloam, J. (2007) "Rebooting Democracy: Youth Participation in Politics in the UK," *Parliamentary Affairs*, vol. 60, no. 4, October, 548–567.

Stolle, D. and Micheletti, M. (2013) *Political Consumerism: Global Responsibility in Action*, Cambridge: Cambridge University Press.

Tarrow, S. G. (1998) *Power in Movement. Social Movements and Contentious Politics*, 2nd Edition, Cambridge: Cambridge University Press.

Teorell, J., Torcal, M., and Montero, J. R. (2007) "Political Participation: Mapping the Terrain," in van Deth, J. W., Montero, J. R., and Westholm, A. (eds.) *Citizenship and Involvement in European Democracies: A Comparative Analysis*, London: Routledge: 334–357.

Theocharis, Y. and van Deth, J. W. (2016) "The Continuous Expansion of Citizen Participation: A New Taxonomy," *European Political Science Review*, available online: https://doi.org/10.1017/S17557739 16000230.

van der Meer, T. W. G., van Deth, J. W., and Scheepers, P. L. H. (2009) "The Politicized Participant: Ideology and Political Action in 20 Democracies," *Comparative Political Studies*, vol. 42, no. 11, November, 1426–1457.

van Deth, J. W. (2001) "Studying Political Participation: Towards a Theory of Everything?," Paper presented to the 2001 Joint Sessions of Workshops of the European Consortium for Political Research, Grenoble, April 6–11.

van Deth, J. W. (2010) "Is Creative Participation Good for Democracy?," in Micheletti, M. and McFarland, A. S. (eds.) *Creative Participation. Responsibility-Taking in the Political World*, Boulder: Paradigm: 146–170.

van Deth, J. W. (2014) "A Conceptual Map of Political Participation," *Acta Politica*, vol. 49, no. 3, July, 349–367.

Verba, S. and Nie, N. (1972) *Participation in America: Political Democracy and Social Equality*, New York: Harper and Row.

Verba, S., Nie, N. H., and Kim, J-O. (1978) *Participation and Political Equality: A Seven-Nation Comparison*, New York and London: University of Chicago Press.

Verba, S., Schlozman, K. L., and Brady, H. E. (1995) *Voice and Equality: Civic Voluntarism in American Politics*, Cambridge, MA: Harvard University Press.

Vráblíková, K. (2013) "How Context Matters? Mobilization, Political Opportunity Structures, and Non-electoral Political Participation in Old and New Democracies," *Comparative Political Studies*, vol. 47, no. 2, February, 203–229.

Vráblíková, K. (2016) *What Kind of Democracy? Participation, Inclusiveness and Contestation*, London: Routledge.

Vráblíková, K. and Císař, O. (2015) "Individual Political Participation and Macro Contextual Determinants," in Barrett, M. and Zani, B. (eds.) *Political and Civic Engagement. Multidisciplinary Perspectives*, London and New York: Routledge: 33–53.

Vráblíková, K. and van Deth, J. W. (2017) "Conducive Contexts: The Impact of Collective and Individual Social Capital on Democratic Citizenship," *Acta Politica*, vol. 51, no. 1, January, 23–42.

Walker, E. T., Martin, A. W., and McCarthy, J. D. (2008) "Confronting the State, the Corporation, and the Academy: The Influence of Institutional Targets on Social Movement Repertoires," *American Journal of Sociology*, vol. 114, no. 1, July, 35–76.

Weldon, S., and Dalton, R. J. (2013) "Democratic Structures and Democratic Participation: The Limits of Consensualism Theory," in Thomassen, J. J. A. (ed.) *Elections and Democracy: Representation and Accountability*, Oxford: Oxford University Press: 113–131.

Welzel, C. (2013) *Freedom Rising. Human Empowerment and the Quest for Emancipation*, Cambridge: Cambridge University Press.

Welzel, C., and Deutsch, F. (2012) "Emancipative Values and Non-Violent Protest: The Importance of 'Ecological' Effects," *British Journal of Political Science*, vol. 42, no. 2, April, 465–479.

9

THE ACQUISITION OF VOTING HABITS

Elias Dinas

A stubborn stylized fact that has been established in the voting behavior literature is that young people vote at lower rates than older people. This age gap seems so persistent across a variety of political contexts and periods as to be often given the status of truism. Evidence abounds, both at the individual (Powell 1986; Highton and Wolfinger 2001; Wattenberg 2007) and the aggregate level (Franklin 2004).[1]

Although there is hardly any disagreement about the presence of this gap, its origins remain contested. Even if implicitly, most explanations draw on the calculus of voting (Riker and Ordeshook 1968). According to the classic rational choice paradox, voting represents a collective action problem. One the one hand, individual votes cast cannot affect the outcome and thus any utility derived from the implementation of the desired policy remains independent from individual participation. On the other hand, casting a ballot has non-zero opportunity costs. Taken together, these two conjectures render voting irrational.

Seen from the perspective of rational choice theory, most attempts to account for the age gap in voting point to age-related differences in the cost attached to this action. For example, one set of studies attributes the importance of age to the role of resources (Blais 2007; Martikainen et al. 2005). As people move away from early adulthood, they accumulate life achievements (Plutzer 2002), extend their social networks (Zuckerman 2005), augment their stores of political knowledge (Jennings 1996) and develop their political skills (Glenn and Grimes 1968). These resources can potentially reduce the cost of collecting political information and turning out to vote. Since these attributes tend to correlate positively with age, older people are expected to vote more frequently than younger ones.

An alternative mechanism points to the role of residential mobility (Squire, Wolfinger and Glass 1987). People tend to be more mobile at early adulthood than in later stages of their life trajectory. Voting necessitates information about where and how registration and actual voting take place. This information remains constant for those residing in the same location but varies as individuals change residence. Moreover, residential mobility weakens social ties, which serve as catalysts of electoral mobilization (Franklin 2005). Taken together, these mechanisms explain why the cost of voting is likely to be higher among young voters than among their older counterparts.[2]

While still targeting the reduction in the cost accompanying the act of voting, a relatively recent literature on turnout has moved away from the standard cost–benefit framework, providing instead a more behavioral explanation for the age gap. The locus of these studies lies in their conceptualization of voting as "habit forming." Voting in one election facilitates voting in the next consequent election and thus makes turnout more likely (Fowler 2006). As elections accumulate, individuals, it is argued, gradually develop inertia, which results into continuity in their voting trajectories. Voting becomes then a habitual response to the same contextual stimulus (Cebula, Durden and Gaynor 2008; Aldrich, Montgomery and Wood 2011). Those who start participating in elections are thus likely to end up becoming regular voters. Those who do not will find it more difficult to develop such voting habits.

Using both observational and experimental data, various studies have tested the habit hypothesis and tried to unpack its underlying roots. Although most of the evidence is favorable to the habit thesis, the mechanism driving the habit hypothesis remains unclear. How are voting habits formed? Is this habit formation process symmetric, yielding regular non-voters in the same way as it yields regular voters? Finally, the idea that early electoral experiences leave a long-standing imprint on people's voting records implies that shocks that may affect turnout at a given point in time are likely to also have long-term effects. This pattern invites a reappraisal of the role of period, life cycle and cohort effects on the probability of voting.

The chapter revisits these questions under the light of the new developments in the literature. The first section reviews the findings of the habit formation hypothesis. The second section builds on these findings to examine the role of early voting experiences. The third section draws on this evidence to assess interventions that have been either suggested or even adopted as an attempt to increase turnout and reduce inequality in electoral participation. As we will see, the habit thesis has informed the debate among policy analysts and commentators. The concluding section highlights a few new directions in this literature.

Voting as habit forming

Although the habit thesis rests on a very simple premise – that voting once increases the chances of voting in the future – testing this idea has been methodologically challenging. People choose whether to vote or not and the factors that explain this decision in one election apply also in the next election. Disentangling their effect from that of previous voting experience is very difficult with observational data. Two different research designs have been employed to overcome this selection problem.[3]

The first strategy is based on the usage of the downstream benefits of experimentation (Gerber and Green 2002). The key idea here is that the selection problem can be addressed by randomly assigning a mobilization treatment (via a personal, telephone or mail Get-Out-The-Vote [GOTV] message) to induce exogenous variation in turnout in an election at time t_1. If one is willing to assume that the mobilization impact of the treatment wanes after this election, any remaining gap in the turnout between the treated and the control group over the course of future elections can be attributed to prior voting experience. In other words, the initial boost to vote as a result of a GOTV message translates itself into a persistent gap in turnout rates as a result of the self-reinforcing nature of the act of voting. By responding to their treatment status, units receiving GOTV messages are also assumed to build voting habits.

Gerber, Green and Shachar (2003) were the first to put this idea to the test. They randomly assigned a GOTV message to induce turnout variation in New Haven in the 1998 midterm election. Those who received the treatment appeared approximately 10 percentage points more likely to vote in that election than the control group. What is more important, however, they also kept voting at higher rates in the 1999 local election, one year after the previous election and without any further treatment having been assigned between the two elections. While trying to rule out the possibility of the GOTV message having had lasting mobilization effects, the authors attribute the 1999 difference to the self-reinforcing nature of the act of voting. They find that having voted in 1998 increases the chances of voting also in 1999 by approximately 50 percent. Similar effects were found in Britain, when Cutts, Fieldhouse and John (2009) replicated this design, looking at the long-term impact of a GOTV experiment. Bedolla and Michelson (2012) extend this evidence by tracing the long-term effects of GOTV campaigns among ethnic minorities in California. The authors look at a series of primary and general elections between 2006 and 2008 and find that a significant part of the mobilization effect that is evident in the former type of election lasts up until the general election. Contrary to this evidence, Michelson (2003) finds no evidence that voting in a municipal election in California (as a result of a successful GOTV campaign) increases turnout in the coming primary election (one year later). Hill and Kousser (2015) report similar null findings, combined with significant first-stage GOTV effects.

A key assumption in these studies is that of exclusion: the GOTV treatment does not impact turnout in election t_2 in any other way than by increasing the propensity to vote in election t_2. This assumption can be problematic, especially when the GOTV treatment aims at inducing mobilization by triggering specific attributes that are deemed to correlate with high turnout. Examples include GOTV setups that attempt to induce social pressure or civic duty (Gerber, Green and Larimer 2008, 2010; Panagopoulos 2010). As a way to address this concern, a different research design has been employed to isolate the effect of prior voting on future turnout from possible confounders.

Instead of making use of randomly assigned mobilization shocks, a few studies have used the discontinuities arising from voter eligibility status. The key idea here is to compare two groups, the first of which being marginally older than the second, yet sufficiently older so as to be eligible to vote in election t_1. If the age gap is small enough so as not to leave room for aging-related confounding, one can assume that in expectation eligibles and non-eligibles are similar in all other respects but for the fact that only the former could vote in election t_1. Since some eligibles have voted in t_1 but none of the non-eligibles did, eligibility operates in a similar way as the GOTV treatment, that is, by inducing as-good-as-random variation in turnout at election t_1. Comparing these two groups in the next elections could then allow researchers to examine the impact of turnout at election t_1 on voting at election t_2. Once again, the key assumption upon which the design is based is that eligibility at election t_1 affects turnout at t_2 only via its effect on turnout in t_1.[4]

The pioneering work in this strand of the literature belongs to Meredith (2009), who compares cohorts of voters in California, showing that cohorts just eligible to vote in 2000 were five percent more likely to vote in 2004 than those born only a few weeks later but not eligible to vote in 2000. Similar findings have been reported by Dinas (2012), who uses a class-cohort study to compare 21-year old survey respondents who were just eligible to vote in the 1968 presidential election with their classmates who were only a few months younger and thus not of age in that election. The author finds that the first group votes at higher rates not only in the 1970 midterm election but also in future presidential elections. Extending this line of research to the study of vote choice, Dinas (2014a) finds that voting in 1968 also resulted into an enduring increase in the strength of partisanship, which lasted at least until 1973. This finding echoes the results from Mullainathan and Washington (2009), who also employed eligibility-based comparisons to examine the attitudinal consequences of voting. The authors found that having voted in a presidential election strengthens support for the chosen candidate and reduces support for the non-voted alternative.

That said, few studies have also reported negative eligibility effects. In particular, using the Florida voter file, Holbein and Hillygus (2016) find that those narrowly ineligible to vote in

2008 voted at higher rates in 2012 than 2008–eligibles. A re-analysis of these data by Nyhan, Skovron and Titiunik (forthcoming) confirm this seemingly counterintuitive pattern.[5] De Kadt (2017) provides an interesting qualification to previous studies by looking at heterogeneity in first-voting effects according to whether the first election was considered a positive or negative experience. He uses data from South Africa and finds that the relatively low average treatment effects of first-time eligibility in the 1994 South African election are driven by the negative effects among the white South Africans. As the author explains, if the first electoral experience is dominated by a negative emotional state, it can leave a demobilizing shadow on future voting patterns.

In an attempt to systematically combine the two strands of this literature, Coppock and Green (2015) assemble evidence from both GOTV experiments and eligibility-based discontinuity designs. In both sets of analysis, the authors test the impact of voting in the upstream election (in which the encouragement-to-vote treatment has been applied) on the probability of also voting in the downstream election. They find overwhelming evidence in favor of the habit formation thesis. Although voting effects seem stronger when both upstream and downstream elections are of similar type, they hold for all combinations of elections – midterm to midterm; midterm to presidential; presidential to presidential; and presidential to midterm. The authors also try to explore whether the self-reinforcing pattern in turnout is due to internalized habit or alternative mobilization effects stemming from induced vote in election t_1.[6] Voting in the upstream election might increase political engagement, which in turn leads to information-seeking behavior and attitudes. Such change is sufficient to encourage turnout in future elections even in the absence of habit. To test this possibility, Coppock and Green (2015) look at heterogeneity in eligibility effects according to the saliency of the upstream election. Being of age to vote in a more salient election should be accompanied by higher mobilization effects. However, there seems to be no substantive difference in the magnitude of eligibility effects on voting in subsequent elections between low- and high-saliency elections. By the same token, the authors report results from previous analyses (Rogers et al. 2014; Dinas 2012) showing negligible change in turnout-inducing campaign contact as a result of voting in election t_1. Taken together, these findings lend support to the idea that at least in part continuity in voting patterns is driven by internalized habit.

An intriguing finding from Coppock and Green (2015) is that the eligibility analysis denotes more durable effects than the GOTV analysis. A meta-analysis of eligibility-based discontinuities reveals enduring voting habits, which persist over a period of at least 20 years. The GOTV effects, on the other hand, appear to dissipate over time. As Coppock and Green note, a potential explanation for this divergence relates to the subgroup affected by the encouragement-to-vote treatment. By definition, eligibility thresholds apply to first-time voters. In contrast, mobilization messages are assigned to the electorate as a whole. As a consequence, eligibility estimates voting effects for young voters whereas GOTV experiments provide a weighted average of treatment effects across the full range of age.

The question that naturally follows from this explanation is why voting treatments exert stronger influence on young voters than older ones. The next section addresses this question, looking at new developments in social psychology, sociology and the voting behavior literature.

Early voting experiences

Applying the standard intuition of Bayesian inference, past research on political change has envisioned political attitudes as evolving through a process of continuous updating. Individuals, it is argued, weight the information available to them and form political preferences based on this information (Achen 1992). More recent shocks are weighted more heavily than earlier information that has accumulated into individuals' mental storage (Gerber and Green 1998). Under this perspective, change is likely to occur at any point during the life cycle and to reflect more vividly the impact of current events, which gradually replace past experiences (Grynaviski 2006).

This idea has been challenged by a strand of literature that sees non-trivial differences in the propensity for attitude change across different stages of the life trajectory. Individuals, according to the so-called impressionable years hypothesis, are more likely to change their political attitudes and voting patterns when they are still in their adolescence and early adulthood (Sears and Funk 1999, Krosnick and Alwin 1989, Osborne et al. 2011). Two reasons have been provided. The first is related to changes in the social and political environment. Early adulthood is characterized by increased levels of residential mobility, often accompanied by change in peers and the social context within which individuals operate. More often than not, these life developments introduce new political stimuli, which might question people's priors (Huckfeldt and Sprague 1995). The second explanation points to age-related differences in the weight attached to political messages. Being still in the process of attitude formation, young individuals are more susceptible to new information and thus more likely to alter their views under the light of new political influences (Dinas 2014b).

Empirical evidence seems to provide considerable support to this hypothesis. Sears and Valentino (1997) show that electoral campaigns serve to crystallize political attitudes among adolescents, especially toward salient political objects, such as parties and their candidates. In so doing, elections operate as periodic catalysts of political socialization, leaving an enduring imprint on young individuals' attitudinal and behavioral outlooks. Similar evidence is provided by Bartels and Jackman (2014), who use presidential elections as political shocks and develop a flexible model to allow differential weights on people's partisan profiles. They find that shocks taking place in earlier stages of the life span are more powerful in coloring people's partisanship. As they argue, the weight of the past is simply too heavy to be accounted for by tidy Bayesian learning models. This conclusion is echoed also in Ghitza and Gelman's (2015) generational analysis, which shows that the dominant partisan tides during teenage and early adult years are pivotal in shaping enduring partisan predispositions. Looking at a more concrete example of the impact of political environment during early adulthood, Erikson and Stoker (2011) have demonstrated the long-term implications of policy interventions. The authors show that young individuals with higher probability of being drafted to join the American army in the Vietnam war developed long-standing anti-Republican sentiments.

Research in social psychology has explicitly tried to unpack the psychological mechanism explaining why young adults are more prone to attitudinal change. Schuman and Corning (2012) have used surveys in which respondents are asked which political events come closer to mind. On the one hand, Bayesian updating would lead to the expectation that more recent events are more easily sampled from the storage of political information. The formative years hypothesis, on the other hand, would lead to the expectation that events taking place during the period of adolescence and early adulthood exert a more notable impact on attitude crystallization and are thus more likely to remain rigid in people's memories. They provide ample evidence in favor of the second hypothesis. Even at the advent of 9/11, respondents socialized during the 1960s referred to political events from that period. Dinas (2013) uses the Watergate scandal as a way to isolate the increased sensitivity mechanism from the change in social environment mechanism. He finds that the Watergate scandal altered people's beliefs and attitudes about Reagan and the Republicans, but its effect was markedly more prominent among young adults (aged between 18 and 30 in 1972). Taken together these studies seem to provide solid evidence about the increased sensitivity of young adults to political stimuli.

This research has important implications about the habit formation thesis. It suggests that early electoral experiences are critical in establishing long-term voting patterns. Anticipating this idea, Plutzer (2002) developed a growth curve model of turnout that allows key predictors to exercise a differential impact on the probability of voting across different stages in people's life trajectory. He found that all key predictors of turnout, such as life achievements, socioeconomic background and parental influence, play a fundamental role in bringing young voters into the polls. After a series of electoral experiences, however, their importance diminishes under the weight of inertia, generated by applying the same response to the same electoral stimuli. Using aggregate data, Franklin (2004) extends this evidence, showing that contextual predictors of turnout are more important among young adults, operationalized as those having experienced up to three general elections. More significantly, Franklin illustrates the gradual but long-term implications of policy interventions for aggregate turnout rates. Indicatively, he shows how the lowering of voting age from 21 to 18 increased the pool of first-time abstainers. Since some of them developed into habitual non-voters, this policy was partly conducive to the gradual decline in turnout rates that has been frequently reported and commented upon by media analysts and political commentators alike.

Extending further this idea, Hobolt and Franklin (2011) reverse the logic of habit formation by examining the long-term effect of early low-mobilization experiences. Applying the logic of the vote eligibility design, the authors make use of variation in the saliency of first-eligible elections to explore the long-term impact on turnout of early low-saliency elections. In particular, they compared European voters according to whether their first-eligible election was a national general election or whether it was an election for the European Parliament (EP) – also known as a second-order election (Reif and Schmitt 1980). The key hypothesis is that early electoral experiences matter not only positively, by boosting turnout, but also negatively, by suppressing it. A national election, which attracts media attention, generates a context that favors turnout to a higher extent than an election of less importance both for elites and for the media. Consistent with the idea of negative early voting experiences, the authors found that, all else being equal, coming of age to vote in an EP election lowers the probability of voting in such an election later in the life span than when coming of age during a national election. Extending the field of enquiry to encompass party choice, Dinas and Riera (forthcoming) report similar findings. Using a similar identification strategy, the authors find that EP eligibles are more likely to vote for small parties in national elections than those first eligible to vote in a national election.

The importance of early voting experiences becomes particularly evident when we compare the impact of policy interventions among younger and older cohorts. A classic example in this respect relates to the study by Firebaugh and Chen (1995), who use theoretical insights from the socialization literature to account for the evolution of the gender gap in turnout in the US. The authors find that women socialized well before the nineteenth amendment (enacted in 1920), were not affected very much by the policy, hence retaining high levels of abstention. Younger cohorts, socialized during and after this important policy intervention, however, were particularly affected, denoting significantly higher levels of turnout. According to this logic, the closing of the gender gap in turnout is the result of generational replacement, with the younger cohorts, socialized in an environment in which women have the right to vote, gradually replacing their older counterparts, who were socialized without voting rights. Dinas (2014c) extends this evidence, looking at the downstream impact of electoral disenfranchisement. He finds that the offspring of women socialized before 1920 denote lower levels of turnout than offspring of women socialized after the nineteenth amendment was enacted.

Taken as a whole, these studies point to the same conclusion. Similar to partisanship and other attitudinal responses, turnout levels are marked by cohort effects, conceptualized as the interaction between age and period effects. Shocks, which can take the form of elections, political events or policy interventions, hit the young members of the electorate to a greater extent than the rest of the population (cf. van der Brug and Franklin in this volume). In so doing, these influences generate snowball effects, leaving a long-term shadow on young people's political outlooks. Even if other influences intervene later in life, the long-term shadow of these initial experiences remains often apparent in people's turnout profiles. This pattern leads to the formation of distinctive cohorts, which might keep their commonalities, even if partially eroded, over their life span. The next section reviews the lessons we can draw from these findings about the long-term impact of policy interventions designed to combat the decline in turnout and the associated rising inequality in electoral participation.

Policy interventions and habit formation

Irrespective of its analytical vigor, academic research often fails to disseminate its findings within the public discourse. This is not the case for the habit formation literature, however. Perhaps an indication of its policy relevance, the findings from this research seem to have informed policy proposals, sparking an interesting interchange between academics, the media and policy makers. Two increasingly popular policy changes have been frequently discussed among political elites and the media: compulsory voting and lowering voting age.[7] In what follows I illustrate how the habit formation literature has informed the public discussion on both policies.

Statistics provided by the Institute for Democracy and Electoral Assistance (IDEA) suggest that voting has fallen across OECD countries from around 85 percent in the 1940s to around 65 percent in 2015 (The Economist 2015). Apart from the fact that this decline is in itself worrisome, it also generates rising concerns because it drives increasing inequality in electoral participation. Differential abstention rates among various socioeconomic strata can significantly affect the quality of policy representation. Since resources tend to correlate positively with turnout, abstention is unevenly distributed, mainly affecting below-median-income citizens. In means-tested welfare worlds, these citizens would be in favor of redistribution and thus more likely to support the left. As a consequence, the idea of introducing (or reviving) compulsory voting has acquired significant support. Bechtel, Hangartner and Schmid (2016) demonstrate nicely the long-term policy implications of compulsory voting by comparing Vaud, a Swiss canton that retained compulsory voting until 1948, with other cantons, in which compulsory voting was abolished in the early twentieth century. They find that leftist proposals put into federal referendums received stronger levels of support in this canton than in cantons without compulsory voting. Similar evidence is provided by Miller (2008), who showed that women's enfranchisement caused a shift in legislative behavior, resulting in growth in public health spending which in turn reduced child mortality by up to 15 percent.

The problem with compulsory voting, however, is that to be binding it requires the activation of sanctions to non-compliers. Monitoring of compliance and application of sanctions are both costly. Applying the findings from the habit formation research can be potentially helpful in reducing such costs. Limiting compulsory voting to individuals' first-eligible election can save resources while ensuring that the first-time voting boost will apply to most of the electorate. Without necessarily approaching the very high levels of turnout observed under compulsory voting, this idea can still generate habitual voters who might have otherwise failed to develop such habits.

Building on the habit formation research, Lodge, Gottfried and Birch (2014), among others, suggested the enactment of compulsory first-eligible voting as a way to increase participation and reduce inequality of participation in the British general elections. This idea has been given serious consideration by think-tanks and political commentators, sparking a fruitful debate and coming close to becoming Labour's official policy proposal in its 2015 manifesto (Guardian 2014).

Another policy suggestion that has drawn on the literature of voting as habit formation is the lowering of the voting age to 16. This idea has been also popular among pundits and electoral analysts and is based on the assumption that, if voting is habit forming, bringing individuals earlier into the polls will accelerate the formation of voting habits. The problem with this line of argument, however, is that it tends to neglect the mirror image of voting habits, that is, the formation of non-voting habits. As discussed in the previous section, evidence from low-saliency elections points to the long-term repercussions of early demobilizing experiences. Since age appears to correlate negatively with turnout, lowering voting age could exacerbate the problem it is designed to address, especially if the voting age is lowered only for certain types of elections, as has been enacted in Estonia and as was the subject of a government-sponsored experiment in Norway (in both countries voting age was lowered only for municipal elections).

There is, however, a missing parameter that, if taken into consideration, qualifies the pessimistic prediction about the impact of lowering the voting age on aggregate levels of turnout. Focusing on the very first years of adulthood, Bhatti, Hansen and Wass (2012) find a monotone negative relationship between age and turnout. Turnout is higher among eligibles aged 18 or 19 than those aged 20 or 21. Their analysis is based on government records from Denmark, which contain turnout information about the whole population of eligible residents in 44 municipalities. The authors have tried to account for this seemingly counterintuitive pattern, pointing to the importance of parental and peer influence in the decision to cast a ballot in these elections. The first group appears significantly more likely to reside still in their parental home. Parental mobilization seems to be a key factor in explaining turnout during this age. In contrast, those aged 20 or 21 are more likely to have left their parental home and their turnout is now influenced more by the turnout of their peers – typically of approximately the same age (Bhatti and Hansen 2012). Establishing voting age at 16 enhances the chances of finding first-eligible voters in their parental home, thus being more likely to be mobilized to vote. Most of them are still at school, which also serves as an additional force of mobilization. Without having many examples of voting age set at 16, a recent example from Austria seems to confirm this view, showing remarkably high rates of turnout among first-time eligible voters (Zeglovits and Aichholzer 2014). Following the logic of habit formation, this policy might help not only in boosting turnout among first-time voters but also in forming new cohorts of habitual voters. In so doing, it might have significant downstream effects on overall turnout rates.

New directions

Having sparked a voluminous literature, the idea of voting as habit forming, opens a wide array of new questions about the impact of the political context on the formation of voting regularities. Most of the empirical evidence stems from established democracies, characterized by relatively stable party systems, in which political actors have a long history in party competition and easily predictable issue stances and coalition strategies. Extending this evidence to new democracies would help to examine the impact of elections under conditions of uncertainty about the issue stances and coalition strategies of political elites. Since many of these democracies have adopted a semi-presidential system, this research might also help to shed light on the heterogeneity in treatment effects according to different types of elections. While retaining their statues of high-saliency elections, direct elections for the head of state invite more majoritarian electoral systems and often result in ad hoc coalition strategies among parties (Kitschelt 1995).

These characteristics allow researchers to draw inferences about the varying effect of voting beyond a binary distinction between low- and high-saliency elections.

A related line of research involves a closer insight into the mechanism driving continuity in voting patterns. According to Gerber, Green and Shachar (2003), voting habits stem from a process of social identity formation. By casting their vote, individuals come to classify themselves as voters and thus respond to the next electoral campaign by following their group identity. Dinas (2014a) offers a complementary mechanism of group identification. The author finds significant gains in the strength of partisanship as a result of voting in one's first-eligible election (see also van der Brug and Franklin in this volume). Partisanship is well-known to induce turnout (Clarke et al. 2004). It might thus be that both partisanship and turnout represent two habits, formed hand-in-hand. Future research on the interplay between the attitudinal and behavioral consequences of voting would help to disentangle further the mechanism of habit formation. Indeed, given the importance of partisanship in guiding the acquisition of policy preferences (Heath, this volume; Bowler, this volume) it is possible that the act of voting is central to the formation of attitudes and even of ideological beliefs.

Extending the attitudinal implications of early voting experiences beyond partisanship could allow researchers of democratic representation to explore the potential impact of electoral participation on attitudes toward democracy. Does voting in early democratic elections leave an imprint on people's perceptions of regime legitimacy? Even more interestingly, how does the electoral experience affect people's views on subsequent attempts to break the democratic rule? To name just one example, it would be interesting to examine whether voting in the 2012 Egyptian election generates polarization in people's views about the subsequent military regime. Finding that this is the case would constitute interesting evidence about the possible normative implications stemming from the act of voting.

Notes

1 The binary distinction between young and older voters should not be interpreted as a monotone relationship between aging and voting. This relationship is in fact curvilinear, as the gains in the probability of voting that accompany increases in age have a threshold, beyond which aging leads to lower turnout rates. This threshold appears in late adulthood, typically due to physical infirmities (Milbrath 1965).

2 More than reducing the cost of voting, social ties increase the probability of voting mainly by introducing selective incentives for participation, via peer pressure and the diffusion of social norms (Gerber and Rogers 2009).

3 The rationale behind my focus on these two designs – Get-Out-The-Vote (GOTV) experiments and eligibility-based discontinuities – is that they capture the dominant trend in the literature and are based on more solid identification assumptions than most other studies. That said, this categorization ignores alternative designs that have been employed to address identification concerns. There are at least two such studies, falling outside either of the two categories, which need to be mentioned. Denny and Doyle (2009) use residential mobility before a general election in Britain as an instrument of voting in that election to explore the impact of voting on future turnout rates. They find that voting in one election significantly increases the likelihood of also voting in subsequent national elections. Similar findings are reported by Green and Shachar (2000), who use perceived closeness of the race and ideological distance of candidates as instruments of voting in the treatment election.

4 Both GOTV- and eligibility-based designs can be treated as ways of instrumenting turnout at election t_1. Seen in this way, the instrument in GOTV campaigns satisfies ignorability by design and denotes stronger first stage in low-salience elections. Eligibility satisfies ignorability in an as-good-as-random fashion (by construction, the two groups differ in terms of age, but such differences are typically nonconsequential) and typically performs better in terms of first stage in high-saliency elections. Exclusion can in principle be violated in both designs (both the GOTV message and eligibility itself might exert a long-term impact on turnout).

5 Nyhan, Skovron and Titiunik (forthcoming) find similar negative eligibility effects when using voter file data from 42 states (plus the District of Columbia), but as they show, these effects are sensitive to differing registration rates between the two groups. Assuming that eligibles were only 5 percent more likely to register than non–eligibles would turn this negative effect into a positive one.

6 It is worth emphasizing that these tests do not directly address problems of exclusion; instead, they try to disentangle the habit mechanism from other alternative mechanisms through which voting in the upstream election might have induced higher turnout rates in the downstream election.

7 As an indication of the saliency of these proposals, it might be worth noting that: a) Barack Obama has suggested that it might be a good idea to consider making voting mandatory (The Economist 2015); and b) both the Electoral Reform Society and the Labour Party in the UK suggested the lowering of voting age to 16.

References

Achen, C. H. (1992) "Social Psychology, Demographic Variables, and Linear Regression: Breaking the Iron Triangle in Voting Research," *Political Behavior*, vol., 14, no. 3, September, 195–211.

Aldrich, J., Montgomery, J. and Wood, W. (2011) "Turnout as a Habit," *Political Behavior*, vol. 33, no. 4, December, 535–563.

Bartels, L. M. and Jackman, S. (2014) "A Generational Model of Political Learning," *Electoral Studies*, vol. 33, March 7–18.

Bechtel, M. M., Hangartner, D. and Schmid, L. (2016) "Does Compulsory Voting Increase Support for Leftist Policy?," *American Journal of Political Science*, vol. 60, no. 3, July, 752–767.

Bedolla, L. G. and Michelson, M. R. (2012) *Mobilizing Inclusion: Transforming the Electorate through Get-Out-the-Vote Campaigns*, New Haven: Yale University Press.

Bhatti, Y. and Hansen, K. M. (2012) "Leaving the Nest and the Social Act of Voting: Turnout Among First-Time Voters," *Journal of Elections, Public Opinion and Elections*, vol. 22, no. 4, November, 380–406.

Bhatti, Y., Hansen, K. M. and Wass, H. (2012) "The Relationship Between Age and Turnout: A Roller-Coaster Ride," *Electoral Studies*, vol. 31, no. 3, September, 588–593.

Blais, A. (2006) "What Affects Voter Turnout?," *Annual Review of Political Science*, vol. 9, June, 111–125.

Cebula, R. J., Durden, G. C. and Gaynor, P. E. (2008) "The Impact of The Repeat-Voting-Habit Persistence Phenomenon on the Probability of Voting in Presidential Elections," *Southern Economic Journal*, vol. 75, no. 2, October, 429–440.

Clarke, H., Sanders, D., Stewart, M. and Whiteley, P. (2004) *Political Choice in Britain*, Oxford: Oxford University Press.

Coppock, A. and Green, D. P. (2015) "Is Voting Habit Forming? New Evidence from Experiments and Regression Discontinuities," *American Journal of Political Science*, vol. 60, no. 4, October, 1044–1062.

Cutts, D., Fieldhouse, E. and John, P. (2009) "Is Voting Habit Forming? The Longitudinal Impact of a GOTV Campaign in the UK," *Journal of Elections, Public Opinion and Parties*, vol. 19, no. 3, August, 251–263.

De Kadt, D. (2017) "Voting Then, Voting Now: The Long Term Consequences of Participation in South Africa's First Democratic Election," *Journal of Politics*, vol. 79, no. 2, April, 670–697.

Denny, K. and Doyle, O. (2009) "Does Voting History Matter? Analyzing Persistence in Turnout," *American Journal of Political Science*, vol. 53, no. 1, January, 17–35.

Dinas, E. (2012) "The Formation of Voting Habits," *Journal of Elections, Public Opinion and Politics*, vol. 22, no. 4, November, 431–456.

Dinas, E. (2013) "Opening 'Openness to Change': Political Events and the Increased Sensitivity of Young Adults," *Political Research Quarterly*, vol. 66, no. 4, December, 868–882.

Dinas, E. (2014a) "Does Choice Bring Loyalty? Electoral Participation and the Development of Party Identification," *American Journal of Political Science*, vol. 58, no. 2, April, 449–465.

Dinas, E. (2014b) "Why Does the Apple Fall Far from the Tree? How Early Political Socialization Prompts Parent-Child Partisan Dissimilarity," *British Journal of Political Science*, vol. 44, no. 4, October, 827–852.

Dinas, E. (2014c) "The Long Shadow of Parental Political Socialization on the Development of Political Orientations," *The Forum*, vol. 12, no. 3, October, 397–416.

Dinas, E. and Riera, P. (forthcoming). "Do European Parliament Elections Impact National Party System Fragmentation?," *Comparative Political Studies*.

Erikson, R. S. and Stoker, L. (2011) "Caught in the Draft: The Effects of Vietnam Draft Lottery Status on Political Attitudes," *American Political Science Review*, vol. 105, no. 2, May, 221–237.

Firebaugh, G. and Chen, K. (1995) "Voter Turnout of Nineteenth Amendment Women: The Enduring Effect of Disenfranchisement," *American Journal of Sociology*, vol. 100, no. 4, January, 972–996.

Fowler, J. H. (2006) "Habitual Voting and Behavior Turnout," *Journal of Politics*, vol. 65, no. 2, May, 335–344.

Franklin, M. N. (2004) *Voter Turnout and the Dynamics of Electoral Competition in Established Democracies Since 1945*, Cambridge: Cambridge University Press.

Franklin, M. N. (2005) "You Want to Vote Where Everybody Knows Your Name: Anonymity, Expressive Engagement, and Turnout Among Young Adults," Paper presented to the 2005 Annual Meeting of the American Political Science Association, Washington DC, August 31–September 3.

Gerber, A. S. and Green, D. P. (1998) "Rational Learning and Partisan Attitudes," *American Journal of Political Science*, vol. 42, no. 3, July, 794–818.

Gerber, A. S. and Green, D. P. (2002) "The Downstream Benefits of Experimentation," *Political Analysis*, vol. 10, no. 4, Autumn, 394–402.

Gerber, A. S. and Rogers, T. (2009) "Descriptive Social Norms and Motivation to Vote: Everybody's Voting and So Should You," *Journal of Politics*, vol. 71, no. 1, January, 178–191.

Gerber, A. S., Green, D. P. and Larimer, C. W. (2008) "Social Pressure and Voter Turnout: Evidence from a Large-scale Field Experiment," *American Political Science Review*, vol. 102, no. 1, February, 33–48.

Gerber, A. S., Green, D. P. and Larimer, C. W. (2010) "An Experiment Testing the Relative Effectiveness of Encouraging Voter Participation by Inducing Feelings of Pride or Shame," *Political Behavior*, vol. 32, no. 3, September, 409–422.

Gerber, A. S., Green, D. P. and Shachar, R. (2003) "Voting May Be Habit-Forming: Evidence from a Randomized Field Experiment," *American Journal of Political Science*, vol. 47, no. 3, July, 540–550.

Ghitza, Y. and Gelman, A. (2015) "The Great Society, Reagan's Revolution, and Generations of Presidential Voting," Unpublished Manuscript, Columbia University.

Glenn, N. D. and Grimes, M. (1968) "Aging, Voting, and Political Interest," *American Sociological Review*, vol. 33, no. 4, August, 563–575.

Green, D. P. and Shachar, R. (2000) "Habit Formation and Political Behavior: Evidence of Consuetude in Voter Turnout," *British Journal of Political Science*, vol. 30, no. 4, October, 561–573.

Grynaviski, J. (2006) "A Bayesian Learning Model with Applications to Party Identification," *Journal of Theoretical Politics*, vol. 18, no. 3, July, 323–346.

Guardian (2014) "Labour Plans to Lower Voting Age to 16," January 23, 2014, available online: www.theguardian.com/politics/2014/jan/23/labour-voting-age-16-mayoral-elections.

Highton, B., and Wolfinger, R. E. (2001) "The First Seven Years of the Political Life Cycle," *American Journal of Political Science*, vol. 45, no. 1, January, 202–209.

Hill, S. J. and Kousser, T. (2015) "Turning Out Unlikely Voters? A Field Experiment in the Top-Two Primary," *Political Behavior*, vol. 38, no. 2, June, 413–432.

Hobolt, S. and Franklin, M. (2011) "The Legacy of Lethargy: How Elections to the European Parliament Depress Turnout," *Electoral Studies*, vol. 30, no. 1, March, 67–76.

Holbein, J. B. and Hillygus, D. S. (2016) "Making Young Voters: The Impact of Preregistration on Youth Turnout," *American Journal of Political Science*, vol. 60, no. 2, April, 364–382.

Huckfeldt, R. and Sprague, J. (1995) *Citizens, Politics, and Social Communication: Information and Influence in an Election Campaign*, Cambridge: Cambridge University Press.

Jennings, M. K. (1996) "Political Knowledge Over Time and Across Generations," *Public Opinion Quarterly*, vol. 60, no. 2, Summer, 228–252.

Kitschelt, H. (1995) "Formation of Party Cleavages in Post-Communist Democracies Theoretical Propositions," *Party Politics*, vol. 1, no. 4, October, 447–472.

Krosnick, J. A., and Alwin, D. F. (1989). "Aging and susceptibility to attitude change." *Journal of personality and social psychology*, vol. 57, no. 3, 416.

Lodge, G., Gottfried, G. and Birch, S. (2014) *The Political Inclusion of Young Citizens, Policy Report*, London: Democratic Audit.

Martikainen, P., Martikainen, T. and Wass, H. (2005) "The Effect of Socioeconomic Factors on Voter Turnout in Finland: A Register Based Study of 2.9 Million Voters," *European Journal of Political Research*, vol. 44, no. 5, August, 645–669.

Meredith, M. (2009) "Persistence in Political Participation," *Quarterly Journal of Political Science*, vol. 4, no. 3, October, 187–209.

Michelson, M. R. (2003) "Dos Palos Revisited: Testing the Lasting Effects of Voter Mobilization," Presented at the Annual Meeting of the Midwest Political Science Association.

Milbrath, L. W. (1965) *Political Participation: How and Why Do People Get Involved in Politics?*, Chicago: Rand McNally.

Miller, G. (2008) "Women's Suffrage, Political Responsiveness, and Child Survival in American History," *Quarterly Journal of Economics*, vol. 123, no. 3, August, 1287–1327.

Mullainathan, S. and Washington, E. (2009) "Sticking With Your Vote: Cognitive Dissonance and Political Attitudes," *American Economic Journal: Applied Economics*, vol. 1, no. 1, January, 86–111.

Nyhan, B., Skovron, C. and Titiunik, R. (forthcoming) "Differential Registration Bias in Voter File Data: A Sensitivity Analysis Approach," *American Journal of Political Science*, available online: www-personal. umich.edu/~titiunik/papers/NyhanSkovronTitiunik2017-AJPS.pdf.

Osborne, D., Sears, D.O., and Valentino, N.A. (2011) "The end of the solidly democratic South: The impressionable-years hypothesis." *Political Psychology*, vol 32, no. 1, 81–108.

Panagopoulos, C. (2010) "Affect, Social Pressure and Prosocial Motivation: Field Experimental Evidence of the Mobilizing Effects of Pride, Shame and Publicizing Voting Behavior," *Political Behavior*, vol. 32, no. 3, September, 369–386.

Plutzer, E. (2002) "Becoming a Habitual Voter: Inertia, Resources and Growth in Young Adulthood," *American Political Science Review*, vol. 96, no. 1, March, 41–56.

Powell, G. B. (1986) "American Voter Turnout in Comparative Perspective," *American Political Science Review*, vol. 80, no. 1, March, 17–43.

Reif, K., and Schmitt, H. (1980) "Nine Second-Order National Elections – A Conceptual Framework for the Analysis of European Election Results," *European Journal of Political Research*, vol. 8, no. 1, March, 3–44.

Riker, W. H. and Ordeshook, P. C. (1968) "A Theory of the Calculus of Voting," *American Political Science Review*, vol. 62, no. 1, March, 25–42.

Rogers, T., Green, D., Ternovski, J. and Ferrerosa-Young, C. (2014) "Social Pressure and Voting: A Field Experiment Conducted in a High-Salience Election," Working Paper, Harvard Kennedy School and Columbia University.

Schuman, H. and Corning, A. D. (2012) "Generational Memory and the Critical Period: Evidence for National and World Events," *Public Opinion Quarterly*, vol. 76, no. 1, Spring, 1–31.

Sears, D. O. and Funk, C. L. (1999) "Evidence of the Long-term Persistence of Adults' Political Predispositions," *Journal of Politics*, vol. 61, no. 1, February, 1–28.

Sears, D. O. and Valentino, N. A. (1997) "Politics Matters: Political Events as Catalysts for Preadult Socialization," *American Political Science Review*, vol. 91, no. 1, March, 45–65.

Squire, P., Wolfinger, R. E. and Glass, D. P. (1987) "Residential Mobility and Voter Turnout," *American Political Science Review*, vol. 81, no. 1, March, 45–65.

The Economist (2015) "Mandatory Voting: Want to Make Me?," May 20, 2015, available online: www. economist.com/blogs/democracyinamerica/2015/03/mandatory-voting.

Wattenberg, M. P. (2007) *Is Voting for Young People? With a Postscript on Citizen Engagement*, Great Questions in Politics Series, New York: Pearson/Longman.

Zeglovits, E. and Aichholzer, J. (2014) "Are People More Inclined to Vote at 16 than at 18? Evidence for the First-Time Voting Boost Among 16- to 25-Year-Olds in Austria," *Journal of Elections, Public Opinion and Politics*, vol. 24, no. 3, August, 351–361.

Zuckerman, A. S. (2005) *The Social Logic of Politics: Personal Networks as Contexts for Political Behavior*, Philadelphia: Temple University Press.

PART III

Determinants of vote choice

10

LONG-TERM FACTORS

Class and religious cleavages

Geoffrey Evans and Ksenia Northmore-Ball

Introduction

The extent to which party choices are structured by social divisions and the origins of these divisions, as well as change in their strength over time, is important for understanding the politics of contemporary democracies. The Michigan Model stresses that class position helps account for perceptions and attitudes which in turn shape political choices (see Hutchings and Jefferson, this volume). It can explain, for example, why some people endorse income redistribution while others do not. Moreover, changes in the sizes of classes, the evolution of the class structure, can help explain the menu of party choices available to voters, as well as the consequences this has for their choices and whether they vote at all. Similarly, religious denomination and religiosity continue to form prominent cleavages in several societies; religion is after all one of the "triumvirate" of social bases of cleavages (class, religion, and language) identified in Lijphart's seminal article (1979) and is identified as the oldest prominent cleavage in Lipset and Rokkan's (1967) classic analysis. In the same way that class position can shape perceptions and attitudes, so does religion, though in areas such as abortion, euthanasia, and gay marriage rather than distribution of economic resources. Changes in levels of religiosity can likewise be expected to influence the nature of party competition and the political choices presented to voters. Most research into the social bases of political divisions has been of a descriptive nature, focusing on the strength of cleavages across time and space. This chapter addresses that approach, but also covers a newer body of work that aims to address explanations for variations in the strength of these cleavages.

In the rest of the chapter, we first consider what we mean by cleavages. We then examine class politics and class voting, considering first what we mean by class. Finally, we examine research into religious denomination, religiosity, and voting.

The theory of cleavages

The related but separate concepts of *social* and *political* cleavages are central to understanding how class and religion can inform political choice. Social cleavages refer to distinctions in social and political values held between different social groups such as social classes as well as ethnic and religious groups that may or may not be relevant as the basis of political competition and hence political choice. Political cleavages, on the other hand, refer to divisions in political and social values that are directly relevant to political competition and thus political choice. Differences in values are usually conceptualized along two dimensions: the economic and social. The economic dimension is usually understood to provide a contrast between pro-market and anti-market views (for example, one being for lower taxation and the other for greater redistribution), whereas the social dimension is understood as a contrast between liberal and authoritarian/conservative values.

Although the study of the social and political cleavages is often combined in empirical work, the study of *social* cleavages primarily relates to purely social stratification and divisions and, in the case of religion, to conflicts in social values in societies and their impact on political behavior, whereas the study of *political* cleavages tends to focus on political institutions and their ability to shape social values (Bartolini and Mair 1990: 215). The first is very much a "bottom-up" approach that focuses on long-term social change such as the secularization of societies as they modernize or the changes in class identities driven by the rising dominance of service industries over traditional sectors such as manufacturing and agriculture. In contrast, the second emphasizes the "top-down" influence of political institutions and elites on shaping and activating a latent division in the population. These two perspectives, although combined in empirical studies, represent distinct theoretical traditions that have shaped debate on the social bases of politics. We first examine how they are manifest in the study of class and politics.

What do we mean by class?

Characterizations of class position have included numerous occupational classifications, employment status (e.g., owner versus employee), status rankings, income level, educational level, various combinations of education and income and occupation, and subjective class identification. In American voting studies, it has not been unusual to treat current income as a measure of class position, typically trichotomized into upper/middle/lower income classes (see, for example, Bartels 2008; Leighley and Nagler 1992, 2007). Outside of the USA, however, researchers have typically focused on occupational class position. A simple manual versus nonmanual occupational class distinction was used extensively in the mid–late twentieth century, but has since tended to give way to more complex classifications. Most contemporary researchers studying voting behavior have tended to adopt a validated and widely-used measure of occupational class position originally developed by sociologists, particularly Goldthorpe, Llewellyn, and Payne (1987; Erikson and Goldthorpe 1992). The main classes identified in this measure are the higher and lower professional and managerial classes (classes I and II), the "routine nonmanual class" (typically lower-grade clerical "white-collar workers," class III), the "petty bourgeoisie" (small employers and self-employed, class IV), and the "working class" (foremen and technicians, skilled, semi-, and unskilled manual workers, classes V, VI, and VII). These classes differ significantly in terms of wages, job security, flexible working hours, pension provision, sickness benefits, autonomy, future career prospects, and life-time expected income, and have been rigorously validated (e.g., Evans 1992; Evans and Mills 1998; Goldthorpe and McKnight 2006). As a result, they now form the basis of both the UK Census measure of class position (Rose and Pevalin 2003) and the European Socio-Economic Classification (Rose and Harrison 2010).

Going beyond two classes and two parties

Classic texts in political sociology saw elections as the expression of "the democratic class struggle" (Anderson and Davidson 1943) between just two classes, the working and the middle, and their representatives, the parties of the left and right. Early surveys observed that, in general, working class voters were more likely to vote for left-wing political parties than were those in the middle class, though with substantial cross-national differences. Scandinavia and Britain displayed the highest levels of class voting and the United States and Canada the lowest, though the cross-national comparability of such studies was limited by a lack of standardized measures of social class (see, for example, Lipset 1981 [1960]; Rose 1974). The first study to undertake a more directly comparable assessment of class voting was Alford's (1963) analysis of Australia, Britain, Canada, and the US between 1936 and 1962 in which he introduced the commonly used "Alford index." The Alford index is the difference between the percentage of manual workers that voted for left-wing parties on the one hand and the percentage of nonmanual workers that voted for these parties on the other. This became the standard instrument in many studies in ensuing decades, most of which found that class voting was in decline (Lipset 1981 [1960]: 505; Inglehart 1990: 260; Sainsbury 1987; Listhaug 1993; Lane and Ersson 1994: 94).

This position was further endorsed by two extensive cross-national studies of electoral change and cleavage politics: Nieuwbeerta (1995) and Franklin, Mackie, and Valen (1992). As a result, by the 1990s many commentators agreed that class voting in modern industrial societies had all but disappeared (see, for example, Clark and Lipset 1991: 408). Class was thought to have lost its importance as a determinant of life-chances and political interests because either the working class had become richer, white-collar workers had been "proletarianized," or social mobility between classes had increased. At the same time, post-industrial cleavages such as gender, race, ethnicity, public versus private sector, and various identity groups had emerged and replaced class-based conflict, while new post-material values had supposedly led to the "new left" drawing its support from the middle classes, thus weakening the class basis of left–right divisions. More-over, rising levels of education had ostensibly produced voters who were calculating and "issue oriented" rather than being driven by collective identities such as class (Franklin, Mackie, and Valen 1992).

Although these studies have been influential, during the 1980s a body of research emerged that questioned the robustness of their findings, arguing that reliance on the manual/nonmanual distinction obscured important variations in the composition of these highly aggregated classes (Heath, Jowell, and Curtice 1985). For example, if skilled manual workers are more right-wing than unskilled workers and the number of skilled workers increases, the Alford estimate of dif-ference between manual and nonmanual workers will decline even if the relative political posi-tions of skilled, unskilled, and nonmanual workers remain the same. Accordingly, studies using the Goldthorpe class schema and more extensive categories of political choice found little evid-ence of declining class voting in Britain (see, for example, Heath, Jowell, and Curtice 1985; Heath et al. 1991; Evans, Heath, and Payne 1991), but only "trendless fluctuations." Com-parative research found that the linear decline in left versus non-left voting proposed, most notably, by Nieuwbeerta (1995) was not universal. In Norway (Ringdal and Hines 1999), the decline in traditional class voting is confined to a short period in the 1960s. The decline in Denmark disappears (Hobolt 2013). There is also evidence of *rises* in levels of class voting. In Britain, levels of class voting increased in the 1940s and 1950s before falling again in the 1960s (Weakliem and Heath 1999). Also, in some of the new post-communist democracies, the pres-sures of marketization and increasing economic inequalities strengthened class voting (Mateju, Rehakova, and Evans 1999; Evans 2006; Evans and Whitefield 2006).

The discussion below of the "bottom-up" and "top-down" approaches will show, however, that the cleavage decline and "trendless fluctuation" stories can be viewed as different aspects of a greater process of "unfreezing" of the traditional links between social groups and parties. This "unfreezing" process occurs through several interacting mechanisms, such as the phasing out of traditional party loyalties through generational replacement of voters (see van der Brug and

Franklin in this volume) as well as changes in the social structure and political elite strategies, which will be discussed further.

In recent years, the debate about the decline of class voting has arguably lost its intensity: there is evidence of decline (Jansen, Evans, and De Graaf 2013), but the cross-national picture shows considerable variation with little or no evidence of a fall in class voting in some societies (see Brooks, Nieuwbeerta, and Manza 2006, and relevant case studies in Evans and De Graaf 2013). Interest instead has turned to *explanations* for variations in the strength of the class–vote relationship across time and societies.

Explaining the evolution of class politics: bottom-up or top-down?

Most early scholars assumed a sociological, relatively deterministic "bottom-up" explanation in which the transition to a post-industrial society was accompanied by a diffusing of the class structure resulting in weaker patterns of voting between classes. However, an opposing view to this socially deterministic argument emphasizes the role of the political elite in the structuring of class political divisions. This approach claims that "variations in class voting are argued to derive from differences in the redistributive policy choices offered to voters" (Evans 2000: 411). Often referred to as a "top-down" approach, variations in the strength of social divisions in political preferences are argued to derive from the choices offered to voters by politicians and parties. Studies focus primarily on the extent to which parties take differing positions along dimensions of ideologies or values and thus shape voters' political choice sets. To the degree that voters are responsive to the programs offered by parties, rather than simply voting on the basis of habit, or long-term party attachment, differentiation between parties on relevant ideological dimensions increases the strength of the association between class position and party choice. Conversely, where parties do not offer different choices, class divisions are weaker. In short, voter responses to party polarization and the extent to which this drives changes in the class bases of party preference depend upon the choices voters are offered (the supply side), as well as the presence of differences in ideological and value preferences within the electorate (the demand side).

The thesis is not new (see, for example, Converse 1958; Kelley, McAllister, and Mughan 1985; Przeworski and Sprague 1986; Kitschelt 1994) but only recently has there been extensive empirical analysis of the impact of the choices offered by parties on social divisions in voting. Moreover, it differs from some earlier top-down arguments in that it moves away from the assumption that class-based values and preferences are themselves shaped by the way parties frame choices and talk about politics (see, for example, Sartori 1969). Such "preference shaping" implies that parties influence the attitudes of their supporters, so that class differences in ideology and values derive from the positions taken by the parties associated with different social classes. However, recent studies (see, for example, Baldassarri and Gelman 2008; Adams, Green, and Milazzo 2012) indicate that sorting takes place rather than "indoctrination" – thus on issues where voters differ from their party they will, over time, shift away from that party. In the British case, for example, the distancing of the political left from the working class occurs because the Labour Party failed to carry the working class with it as it moved to more liberal positions on economic and social issues, resulting in increased defection to parties such as UKIP (Ford and Goodwin 2014; Evans and Mellon 2016). Class divisions in preferences are robust even when the parties shift their positions (Evans and Tilley 2012b). A similar resistance to preference shaping explains the emergence of a working class basis to radical right rather than left-wing parties as the latter have shifted to court the votes of the new middle classes (e.g., McGann and Kitschelt 2005; Spies 2013; Rennwald and Evans 2014).

Evidence for the impact of changes in parties' left–right ideological positions on levels of class voting was initially provided in Britain by Evans, Heath, and Payne (1999), who show a close relationship over a 20-year period between left–right polarization in parties' manifesto positions and the extent of class voting. A further study extended this analysis to more than 40 years and estimated that without convergence in party programs no convergence in class voting would have been observed (Evans and Tilley 2012a). Studies by Oskarson (2005) and Elff (2009) suggest that this pattern is found elsewhere in Europe. Most recently, the "political choice" model of class voting has been consolidated by a broad-ranging comparative combination of case studies and cross-nationally pooled over-time analyses of the relationship between party manifesto positions and the strength of class voting (Evans and De Graaf 2013). A 15-nation analysis combining up to 50 years of evidence finds a correlation of 0.42 between left–right polarization in party manifesto programs and the strength of class voting, even when controlling for other aspects of social change (Jansen, Evans, and De Graaf 2013). This growing body of evidence points to the importance of political choices for patterns of class voting, in addition to any social changes that might influence them.

Whether to vote or not: the new class cleavage?

An interest in how the choices offered by parties influence voting has also led to a focus on the political consequences of the shape of the class structure: specifically, the declining size of the working class. Early voting research focused on the working class, especially in Britain (see, for example, Butler and Stokes 1969), where studies explored in detail the phenomenon of "working class Conservatives" (McKenzie and Silver 1968; Nordlinger 1967), as it was assumed that it was only the failure of such voters to fully express their "true" class interests electorally that prevented a left-wing, working class electoral hegemony. Since then, however, the reduction in the size of the working class, as industrial societies have become post-industrial, has led to it no longer constituting the largest class, nor being the primary source of left-party support. This process has been argued to lead to a vicious circle in which parties stop representing working class people, who in turn stop turning out to vote, further reducing the incentive for parties to appeal to them (Evans and Tilley 2017). Whereas the social attitudes and policy preferences of the working class were at one time considered mainstream by virtue of the working class constituting a significant proportion of the population, they have become increasingly marginal as the working class has become a minority. This marginalization has been exacerbated by changes in the recruitment patterns of the parties: even parties of the left are now dominated by professional politicians with middle class backgrounds, an elite university education, and the values associated with such milieu (Carnes 2012; Heath 2015; Evans and Tilley 2017). Increasingly, these politicians are socially alien to working class voters. Arguably an important growing class cleavage therefore is between voting or not voting: political parties aim their campaigns at a new middle class constituency who are more likely to turn out at the polls (Evans and Tilley 2017), while ignoring working class voters and further dis-incentivizing their participation. This process was identified in the US some time ago by Hill and Leighley (1996), who linked state-level left policy programs to class differences in turnout. Once the habit of voting is lost it is difficult to reinstate: Leighley and Nagler (2014) find no increase in poor/working class participation since the late twentieth century, despite the ideological polarization of the main US parties, thus shifting the center of political gravity toward a new, middle class electoral hegemony.

The waning influence of religion?

There are similarities in the debates about class and those about our other significant social cleavage, religion. Until quite recently the dominant consensus has been that religion is declining in importance across modern societies and thus of little relevance to understanding political competition. The modernization of societies has been said to lead to the gradual secularization of societies. In what is very much a "bottom–up" approach, the secularization thesis argues that the rising levels of urbanization and education have increased the dominance of scientific rationality (Swatos and Christiano 1999); economic development, on the other hand, is said to alleviate the economic vulnerabilities that underpin the attractiveness of religion as a source of social support and security to marginalized socio-economic groups (Norris and Inglehart 2004). On the whole, the gradual secularization of Western societies leads to the loss of religious identity as a source of distinct social and political values such as social conservatism.

Although most scholars throughout the twentieth century tended to agree that secularization characterizes most European societies irrespective of denomination (Dobbelaere 1985; Lechner 1991; Tschannen 1991; Wilson 1982), the secularization paradigm has been challenged on various fronts. There seems to be little evidence of secularization in competitive religious "markets" such as the United States (Finke and Stark 1998; see Gill 2001 for a review) or in Eastern European societies undergoing religious revivals (Evans and Northmore-Ball 2012; Northmore-Ball and Evans 2016). Several authors have also pointed out flaws in the secularization argument such as the use of a "romanticized" religious past as a reference point and excessive Eurocentrism (Swatos and Christiano 1999) as well as a restrictive focus on formal expressions of religiosity such as affiliation and church attendance (Davie 1994).

Religiosity and religious denominations have formed the basis of cleavages in several societies, with political parties stressing traditional moral issues such as abortion, euthanasia, and gay marriage (De Graaf, Heath, and Need 2001; Bolzendahl and Brooks 2005). These issues have been conceptualized as the social dimension of political competition contrasting moral traditionalism and conservatism with "progressive" liberal positions. Studies of the impact of religion on politics focus primarily on this dimension.

Top-down versus bottom-up drivers of religious cleavages: mechanisms and agents of change

The study of religious cleavages and political choice very much falls into two perspectives, which differ in their understanding of sources of the influence of religious cleavages on political choice, how they change, and most importantly the mechanism linking religious cleavages and political choice. These perspectives echo the "bottom–up" versus "top–down" perspectives already presented for class voting. The earlier "bottom–up" perspective is rooted in three main bodies of research: first, that stemming from Lipset and Rokkan's (1967) seminal work on the historical origins of cleavages in Europe, the sociological work on the general process of secularization and waning of religion in Western societies, and finally the literature on the effects of economic modernization on social change. The second and newer perspective is based in the studies of the recent changes in party competition on Western democracies and focuses very much on the ability of political parties and elites to activate/de-activate the relevance of religious social divisions for political competition as well as the diversity in the strength of religious cleavages across countries and time (Evans and De Graaf 2013).

Lipset and Rokkan (1967) trace the origin of religious cleavages as the basis of political competition in Western societies to the Reformation and the ensuing conflict between the newly ascendant nation-states and the Catholic Church. They show how today's political competition between religious voters who support conservative parties (particularly Social Democratic parties), which are often linked to the Catholic Church, and non-religious voters who support secular liberal parties can be traced back to the "frozen" church-state conflict of the Reformation. More recent work in this tradition looks at the legacies of communism in Eastern Europe for creating a secular-religious/nationalist cleavage thus creating competition between reformed communist parties and nationalist parties (Kitschelt 1994, 1999). The two later bodies of literature focus on the declining role of religion in society as scientific rationality becomes mainstream and increasing economic security reduces the attractiveness of religion as a source of social support. Overall, the "bottom-up" perspective emphasizes the blurring of religious divisions as the key mechanism of change: as religion loses its significance, the values of the nominally religious become increasingly similar to those of the non-religious. These changes are driven by large-scale, socio-structural processes such as modernization or industrialization, or major historical events such as the European Reformation (Lipset and Rokkan 1967) or the rise and collapse of Communism (Kitschelt 1999; Evans and Whitefield 1993; Whitefield 2002). The emphasis on these macro-level slow-moving processes and "frozen" social conflicts, however, limits the ability of the "bottom-up" approach to explain shorter term fluctuations in the relevance of religion for political choice; the "bottom-up" approach is fundamentally unidirectional.

The second "top-down" approach emphasizes that political elites determine the relevance of religion to political choice through their strategic considerations and position on ideological dimensions. The most recent version of the "top-down" approach focuses on the restriction of electoral choices rather than preference shaping as the mechanisms linking religiosity to political choice (Evans and De Graaf 2013). This supply-side approach emphasizes that political parties need to diverge on moral issues in order to make religion relevant. With a wider variety of options along the social dimension, the value differences between religious and non-religious people take on importance for political choice; these value differences will matter even if the overall numbers of religious voters may have declined due to secularization. Party polarization on the relevant value dimension should increase the magnitude of the association between religiosity and party choice, whereas convergence should weaken the association. The pressures for convergence tend to be more apparent in majoritarian than PR systems. The agents of change are political parties, although the impetus for the strategic behavior of political elites can lie in long-term social change.

Empirical considerations: the measurement of religiosity and religious cleavages

The measurement of the effect of religiosity on vote choice, particularly in a comparative context, is complicated by difficulties in measuring religiosity itself. The common measures of denominational affiliation and church attendance vary in their meaning in different countries and for different denominations. For example, in Catholic contexts there is far greater social pressure for people to attend church, raising overall church attendance rates. Denominational affiliation as a measure raises the possibility of failing to capture religiosity due to "believing but not belonging" (Davie 1994, 2000) or over-estimating religiosity in contexts where nominal affiliation may have a strong presence (Evans and Northmore-Ball 2012). Also denomination is not a useful indicator in countries dominated by one religion (i.e., Catholicism in Poland or Spain, or Eastern Orthodoxy in Bulgaria or Russia). Church attendance however has not been found to under-estimate religiosity (Aarts et al. 2010) and church attendance levels have been found to be associated with levels of traditional religious belief (De Graaf and Te Grotenhius 2008).

The issues of measuring religiosity are related to the complexity in conceptualizing the idea of religious cleavage. The concept of religious cleavage can be said to capture two aspects: the individual and contextual. At the individual level, religiosity is related to how religious a person is; this can be captured by the frequency of church attendance or some measure of the intensity of religious belief (for example, the World Values Survey religious belief measures used in Norris and Inglehart 2004). The contextual effects of shared group consciousness can be captured by denomination. Presumably the contextual effects can persist even in the presence of declining levels of religiosity, for example, through the politicization of collective social identities.

Empirical evidence: a general decline or a diverse set of patterns?

After a few decades of much attention being devoted to religious cleavages by the likes of Lijphart, Lipset, and Rokkan, the study of religious cleavages entered a phase of neglect; in the 1980s and early 1990s most studies concluded that religion was in general decline and therefore irrelevant as a basis of competition for religious parties and even right-wing parties (Franklin, Mackie, and Valen 1992: 40; Franklin 1992), mirroring the general consensus on the decline of class and other social cleavages at the time (see Evans 1999; Evans and Norris 1999 for summaries of debate). This consensus on religious cleavages was challenged in the mid-1990s by arguments about the limits of the secularization thesis as well as the documented rise of "religious issues" in politics. Several studies began to show evidence for the persistence of religious cleavages (i.e., Elff 2007; van der Brug, Hobolt, and De Vreese 2009; Tilley 2015).

The latest empirical evidence on the impact of religiosity on voting shows a variety of patterns across both established and new democracies. The evidence shows that religion matters to vote choice overall but not in every country and to varying degrees. In several countries, religion is a more relevant cleavage than social class; these include the Netherlands, the United States, West Germany, and France (Evans and De Graaf 2013). The trends in religious voting show a decline in France, West Germany, Italy, and the Netherlands (Heath and Bellucci 2013; De Graaf, Jansen, and Need 2013; Gougou and Roux 2013; Elff 2013), but, in newer democracies such as Poland, Spain, and East Germany, religious voting appears stable (Orriols 2013; Letki 2013; Elff 2013). The United States stands alone among established democracies in displaying both strong evidence of religious voting as well as an absence of any decline; rather, there is evidence of a realignment as, for example, Catholic voters switched from the Democratic to the Republican Parties (Weakliem 2013).

The "top-down" political choice and "bottom-up" social change explanations apply to varying extents across the different countries, reflecting the variety of political and cultural conditions. Overall, however, recent empirical evidence favors the political choice explanation; with the exception of a few new democracies, the ideological differences between parties explain the strength of religious voting (Evans and De Graaf 2013). The effects of social change, in particular secularization, are clearly apparent in all Western European democracies as religion loses its importance. Secularization is even evident in the United States (Aarts et al. 2010; Evans and De Graaf 2013). However, the evidence on effects of secularization on political choice is not unequivocal given the lack of clarity in the links between social conservatism and religious attendance. Furthermore, the classic secularization thesis which points to the blurring of social heterogeneity and consequent decline in religiosity as societies modernize (Norris and Inglehart 2004) is of more limited relevance in countries outside Western Europe, such as Romania, Bulgaria, and Russia (Evans and Northmore-Ball 2012; Northmore-Ball and Evans 2016).

Conclusions

Until recently, studies on class and religious cleavages have argued that both have progressively faded as societies have undergone modernization and secularization; however, recent work on class and religious cleavages has displayed a more complex picture of fluctuations and varied trends. Current studies are more explanatory than descriptive, focusing on a "top-down" approach to cleavages which demonstrates the ability of party elites to activate and de-activate *political* cleavages by offering more or less choice on relevant issue dimensions. This "top-down" approach indicates that the strength and over-time changes in cleavages are country-specific and can fluctuate depending on the dynamics of party competition. The ability of parties to shape cleavages is connected with the decline of the intergenerational transmission of partisanship (see van der Brug and Franklin, this volume), thus enabling party signals to more effectively influence voter decision-making. Though class voting is less pronounced than during the late-industrial era, economic and social differences between classes (namely *social* cleavages; see earlier discussion on the distinction between cleavages types) have persisted, and what the parties do and say to maintain or minimize class *political* cleavages, or to re-shape those cleavages with the rise of radical right parties and the decline of working class electoral participation, is significant. To summarize: the contributions of the seemingly contradictory approaches all point to a more general shift from vote choices being made based on long-term party loyalties to more fluid issue-based voting; class remains relevant but as the basis for issue positions rather than party loyalty.

Turning to religion, we find that, despite evidence of a general process of secularization in many Western societies, recent studies indicate that religious cleavages continue to be an important basis of party choice across many societies. In new democracies, particularly in Eastern Europe, religion has even undergone a revival, possibly providing a renewed basis of party preference. Again, party signals matter for levels of religious voting as they do for class.

In conclusion, the general pattern of development in this research tradition has been from descriptive concerns with more or less class/religious voting to an understanding of the sources of those differences in terms of the choices offered to voters, the dynamics of the relationships between parties and voters and, rather more weakly, examination of the mechanisms accounting for the relationship between social classes, religious groupings, and parties. These explanatory rather than descriptive concerns are likely to be the focus of new class and religious voting research in coming decades.

References

Aarts, O., Need, A., Te Grotenhuis, M., and De Graaf, N. D. (2010) "Does Duration of Deregulated Religious Markets Affect Church Attendance? Evidence from 26 Religious Markets in Europe and North America Between 1981 and 2006," *Journal for the Scientific Study of Religion*, vol. 49, no. 4, December, 657–672.

Adams, J., Green, J., and Milazzo, C. (2012) "Has the British Public Depolarized Along with Political Elites? An American Perspective on British Public Opinion," *Comparative Political Studies*, vol. 45, no. 4, April, 507–530.

Alford, R. (1963) *Party and Society: The Anglo-American Democracies*, Westport: Greenwood Press.

Anderson, D. and Davidson, P. (1943) *Ballots and the Democratic Class Struggle*, Stanford: Stanford University Press.

Baldassarri, D. and Gelman, A. (2008) "Partisans Without Constraint: Political Polarization and Trends in American Public Opinion," *American Journal of Sociology*, vol. 114, no. 2, September, 408–446.

Bartels, L. M. (2008) *Unequal Democracy*, Princeton: Princeton University Press.

Bartolini, S. and Mair, P. (1990) *Identity, Competition, and Electoral Availability: The Stabilization of European Electorates 1885–1985*, Cambridge: Cambridge University Press.

Bolzendahl, C. and Brooks, C. (2005) "Polarization, Secularization, or Differences as Usual? The Denominational Cleavage in US Social Attitudes Since the 1970s," *The Sociological Quarterly*, vol. 46, no. 1, February, 47–78.

Brooks, C., Nieuwbeerta, P., and Manza, J. (2006) "Cleavage-Based Voting Behavior in Cross-National Perspective: Evidence from Six Postwar Democracies," *Social Science Research*, vol. 35, no. 1, March, 88–128.

Brug, W. van der, Hobolt, S. B., and de Vreese, C. H. (2009) "Religion and Party Choice in Europe," *West European Politics*, vol. 32, no. 6, October, 1266–1283.

Butler, D. E. and Stokes, D. E. (1969) *Political Change in Britain: Forces Shaping Electoral Choice*, New York: St. Martin's Press.

Carnes, N. (2012) "Does the Numerical Underrepresentation of the Working Class in Congress Matter?," *Legislative Studies Quarterly*, vol. 37, no. 1, February, 5–34.

Clark, T. N. and Lipset, S. M. (1991) "Are Social Classes Dying?," *International Sociology*, vol. 6, no. 4, December, 397–410.

Converse, P. E. (1958) "The Shifting Role of Class in Political Attitudes and Behavior," in Maccoby, E. E., Newcomb, T. M., and Hartley, E. L. (eds.) *Readings in Social Psychology*, 3rd Edition, New York: Holt: 388–399.

Davie, G. (1994) *Religion in Britain Since 1945: Believing Without Belonging*, New York: John Wiley & Sons.

Davie, G. (2000) *Religion in Modern Europe: A Memory Mutates*, Oxford: Oxford University Press.

De Graaf, N. D. and Te Grotenhuis, M. (2008) "Traditional Christian Belief and Belief in the Supernatural: Diverging Trends in the Netherlands Between 1979 and 2005?," *Journal for the Scientific Study of Religion*, vol. 47, no. 4, December, 585–598.

De Graaf, N. D., Heath, A., and Need, A. (2001) "Declining Cleavages and Political Choices: The Interplay of Social and Political Factors in the Netherlands," *Electoral Studies*, vol. 20, no. 1, March, 1–15.

De Graaf, N. D., Jansen, G., and Need, A. (2013) "The Political Evolution of Class and Religion," in Evans, G. and De Graaf, N. D. (eds.) *Political Choice Matters: Explaining the Strength of Class and Religious Cleavages in Cross-National Perspective*, Oxford: Oxford University Press: 205–242.

Dobbelaere, K. (1985) "Secularization Theories and Sociological Paradigms: A Reformulation of the Private-Public Dichotomy and the Problem of Societal Integration," *Sociology of Religion*, vol. 46, no. 4, Winter, 377–387.

Elff, M. (2007) "Social Structure and Electoral Behavior in Comparative Perspective: The Decline of Social Cleavages in Western Europe Revisited," *Perspectives on Politics*, vol. 5, no. 2, June, 277–294.

Elff, M. (2009) "Social Divisions, Party Positions, and Electoral Behavior," *Electoral Studies*, vol. 28, no. 2, June, 297–308.

Elff, M. (2013) "Social Divisions and Political Choice in Germany," in Evans, G. and De Graaf, N. D. (eds.) *Political Choice Matters: Explaining the Strength of Class and Religious Cleavages in Cross-National Perspective*, Oxford: Oxford University Press: 277–308.

Erikson, R. and Goldthorpe, J. H. (1992) *The Constant Flux: A Study of Class Mobility in Industrial Societies*, Oxford: Clarendon Press.

Evans, G. (1992) "Testing the Validity of the Goldthorpe Class Schema," *European Sociological Review*, vol. 8, no. 3, December, 211–232.

Evans, G. (ed.) (1999) *The End of Class Politics? Class Voting in Comparative Context*, Oxford: Oxford University Press.

Evans, G. (2000) "The Continued Significance of Class Voting," *Annual Review of Political Science*, vol. 3, June, 401–417.

Evans, G. (2006) "The Social Bases of Political Divisions in Post-Communist Eastern Europe," *Annual Review of Sociology*, vol. 32, August, 245–270.

Evans, G. and De Graaf, N. D. (2013) *Political Choice Matters: Explaining the Strength of Class and Religious Cleavages in Cross-National Perspective*, Oxford: Oxford University Press.

Evans, G. and Mellon, J. (2016) "Working Class Votes and Conservative Losses: Solving the UKIP Puzzle," *Parliamentary Affairs*, vol. 69, no. 2, April, 464–479.

Evans, G. and Mills, C. (1998) "Identifying Class Structure: A Latent Class Analysis of the Criterion-Related and Construct Validity of the Goldthorpe Class Schema," *European Sociological Review*, vol. 14, no. 1, March, 87–106.

Evans, G. and Norris, P. (eds.) (1999) *Critical Elections: British Parties and Voters in Long-Term Perspective*, London: Sage.

Evans, G. and Northmore-Ball, K. (2012) "The Limits of Secularization? The Resurgence of Orthodoxy in Post-Soviet Russia," *Journal for the Scientific Study of Religion*, vol. 51, no. 4, December, 795–808.

Evans, G. and Tilley, J. (2012a) "How Parties Shape Class Politics: Explaining the Decline of the Class Basis of Party Support," *British Journal of Political Science*, vol. 42, no. 1, January, 137–161.

Evans, G. and Tilley, J. (2012b) "The Depoliticization of Inequality and Redistribution: Explaining the Decline of Class Voting," *Journal of Politics*, vol. 74, no. 4, October, 963–976.

Evans, G. and Tilley, J. (2017) *The New Politics of Class: The Political Exclusion of the British Working Class*, Oxford: Oxford University Press.

Evans, G. and Whitefield, S. (1993) "Identifying the Bases of Party Competition in Eastern Europe," *British Journal of Political Science*, vol. 23, no. 4, October, 521–548.

Evans, G. and Whitefield, S. (2006) "Explaining the Emergence and Persistence of Class Voting for Presidential Candidates in Post-Soviet Russia, 1993–2001," *Political Research Quarterly*, vol. 59, no. 1, March, 23–34.

Evans, G., Heath, A., and Payne, C. (1991) "Modelling Trends in the Class/Party Relationship, 1964–87," *Electoral Studies*, vol. 10, no. 2, June, 99–117.

Evans, G., Heath, A., and Payne, C. (1999) "Class: Labour as a Catch-All Party?" in Evans, G. and Norris, P. (eds.) *Critical Elections: British Parties and Voters in Long-term Perspective*, London: Sage: 87–101.

Finke, R. and Stark, R. (1998) "Religious Choice and Competition," *American Sociological Review*, vol. 63, no. 5, October, 761–766.

Ford, R. and Goodwin, M. J. (2014) *Revolt on the Right: Explaining Support for the Radical Right in Britain*, London: Routledge.

Franklin, M. N. (1992) "The Decline of Cleavage Politics," in Franklin, M. N., Mackie, T. T., and Valen, H. (eds.) *Electoral Change: Responses to Evolving Social and Attitudinal Structures in Western Countries*, Cambridge: Cambridge University Press: 383–405.

Franklin, M. N., Mackie, T. T., and Valen, H., (Eds.) (1992) *Electoral Change: Responses to Evolving Social and Attitudinal Structures in Western Countries*, Cambridge: Cambridge University Press.

Gill, A. (2001) "Religion and Comparative Politics," *Annual Review of Political Science*, vol. 4, June, 117–138.

Goldthorpe, J. H. and McKnight, A. (2006) "The Economic Basis of Social Class," in Morgan, S. L., Grusky, D. B., and Fields, G. S. (eds.) *Mobility and Inequality: Frontiers of Research in Sociology and Economics*, Stanford: Stanford University Press: 109–136.

Goldthorpe, J. H., Llewellyn, C., and Payne, C. (1987) *Social Mobility and Class Structure in Modern Britain*, Oxford: Clarendon.

Gougou, F. and Roux, G. (2013) "Political Change and Cleavage Voting in France," in Evans, G. and De Graaf, N. D. (eds.) *Political Choice Matters: Explaining the Strength of Class and Religious Cleavages in Cross-National Perspective*, Oxford: Oxford University Press: 243–276.

Heath, A., Jowell, R., and Curtice, J. (1985) *How Britain Votes*, Oxford: Pergamon Press.

Heath, A., Jowell, R., Curtice, J., Evans, G., Field, J., and Witherspoon, S. (1991) *Understanding Political Change: The British Voter, 1964–1987*, Oxford: Pergamon Press.

Heath, O. (2015) "Policy Representation, Social Representation and Class Voting in Britain," *British Journal of Political Science*, vol. 45, no. 1, January, 173–193.

Heath, O. and Bellucci, P. (2013) "Class and Religious Voting in Italy: The Rise of Policy Responsiveness," in Evans, G. and De Graaf, N. D. (eds.) *Political Choice Matters: Explaining the Strength of Class and Religious Cleavages in Cross-National Perspective*, Oxford: Oxford University Press: 309–336.

Hill, K. Q. and Leighley, J. E. (1996) "Political Parties and Class Mobilization in Contemporary United States Elections," *American Journal of Political Science*, vol. 40, no. 3, August, 787–804.

Hobolt, S. B. (2013) "Enduring Divisions and New Dimensions: Class Voting in Denmark," in Evans, G. and De Graaf, N. D. (eds.) *Political Choice Matters: Explaining the Strength of Class and Religious Cleavages in Cross-National Perspective*, Oxford: Oxford University Press: 185–204.

Inglehart, R. (1990) *Culture Shift in Advanced Industrial Society*, Princeton: Princeton University Press.

Jansen, G., Evans, G., and De Graaf, N. D. (2013) "Class Voting and Left-Right Party Positions: A Comparative Study of 15 Western Democracies, 1960–2005," *Social Science Research*, vol. 42, no. 2, March: 376–400.

Kelley, J., McAllister, I., and Mughan, A. (1985) "The Decline of Class Revisited: Class and Party in England, 1964–1979," *American Political Science Review*, vol. 79, no. 3, September, 719–737.

Kitschelt, H. (1994) *The Transformation of European Social Democracy*, Cambridge: Cambridge University Press.

Kitschelt, H. (1999) *Post-Communist Party Systems: Competition, Representation, and Inter-Party Cooperation*, Cambridge: Cambridge University Press.

Lane, J. and Ersson, S. O. (1994) *Politics and Society in Western Europe*, London: Sage.

Lechner, F. (1991) "The Case Against Secularization: A Rebuttal," *Social Forces*, vol. 69, no. 4, June, 103–119.

Leighley, J. E. and Nagler, J. (1992) "Socioeconomic Class Bias in Turnout, 1964–1988: The Voters Remain the Same," *American Political Science Review*, vol. 86, no. 3, September, 725–736.

Leighley, J. E. and Nagler, J. (2007) "Unions, Voter Turnout, and Class Bias in the U.S. Electorate, 1964–2004," *Journal of Politics*, vol. 69, no. 2, May, 430–441.

Leighley, J. E. and Nagler, J. (2014) *Who Votes Now? Demographics, Issues, Inequality, and Turnout in the United States*, Princeton: Princeton University Press.

Letki, N. (2013) "Do Social Divisions Explain Political Choices? The Case of Poland," in Evans, G. and De Graaf, N. D. (eds.) *Political Choice Matters: Explaining the Strength of Class and Religious Cleavages in Cross-National Perspective*, Oxford: Oxford University Press 337–359.

Lijphart, A. (1979) "Religious vs. Linguistic vs. Class Voting: The 'Crucial Experiment' of Comparing Belgium, Canada, South Africa, and Switzerland," *American Political Science Review*, vol. 73, no. 2, June, 442–458.

Lipset, S. M. (1981) [1960] *Political Man: The Social Bases of Politics*, London: Heinemann.

Lipset, S. M. and Rokkan, S. (1967) "Cleavage Structures, Party Systems and Voter Alignments: An Introduction," in Lipset, S. M. and Rokkan, S. (eds.) *Party Systems and Voter Alignments: Cross National Perspectives*, New York: The Free Press: 1–64.

Listhaug, O. (1993) "The Decline of Class Voting," in Strøm, K. and Svåsand, L. G. (eds.) *Challenges to Political Parties: The Case of Norway*, Ann Arbor: University of Michigan Press: 77–91.

Mateju, P., Rehakova, B., and Evans, G. (1999) "The Politics of Interests and Class Realignment in the Czech Republic, 1992–96" in Evans, G. (ed.) *The End of Class Politics? Class Voting in Comparative Context*, Oxford: University of Oxford Press: 231–253.

McGann, A. J. and Kitschelt, H. (2005) "The Radical Right in the Alps: Evolution of Support for the Swiss SVP and Austrian FPO," *Party Politics*, vol. 11, no. 2, March, 147–171.

McKenzie, R. T. and Silver, A. (1968) *Angels in Marble: Working Class Conservatives in Urban England*, London: University of Chicago Press.

Nieuwbeerta, P. (1995) *The Democratic Class Struggle in Twenty Countries, 1945–1990*, Amsterdam: Thesis Publishers.

Nordlinger, E. A. (1967) *The Working-Class Tories: Authority, Deference and Stable Democracy*, Berkeley: University of California Press.

Norris, P. and Inglehart, R. (2004) *Sacred and Secular: Religion and Politics Worldwide*, Cambridge, MA: Cambridge University Press.

Northmore-Ball, K. and Evans, G. (2016) "Secularization Versus Religious Revival in Eastern Europe: Church Institutional Resilience, State Repression and Divergent Paths," *Social Science Research*, vol. 57, May, 31–48.

Orriols, L. (2013) "Social Class, Religiosity, and Vote Choice in Spain 1979–2008," in Evans, G. and De Graaf, N. D. (eds.) *Political Choice Matters: Explaining the Strength of Class and Religious Cleavages in Cross-National Perspective*, Oxford: Oxford University Press: 360–390.

Oskarson, M. (2005) "Social Structure and Party Choice," in Thomassen, J. (ed.) *The European Voter*, Oxford: Oxford University Press: 84–105.

Przeworski, A. and Sprague, J. (1986) *Paper Stones: A History of Electoral Socialism*, Chicago: University of Chicago Press.

Rennwald, L. and Evans, G. (2014) "When Supply Creates Demand: Social-Democratic Party Strategies and the Evolution of Class Voting," *West European Politics*, vol. 37, no. 5, September: 1108–1135.

Ringdal, K. and Hines, K. (1999) "Changes in Class Voting in Norway 1957–1989," in Evans, G. (ed.) *The End of Class Politics? Class Voting in Comparative Context*, Oxford: University of Oxford Press: 181–202.

Rose, R. (1974) *Electoral Behavior: A Comparative Handbook*, New York: Free Press.

Rose, D. and Harrison, E. (eds.). (2010) *Social Class in Europe: An Introduction to the European Socio-Economic Classification*, London: Routledge.

Rose, D. and Pevalin, D. (2003) *A Researcher's Guide to the National Statistics Socio-Economic Classification*, London: Sage.

Sainsbury, D. (1987) "Class Voting and Left Voting in Scandinavia: The Impact of Different Operation-alizations of the Working Class," *European Journal of Political Research*, vol. 15, no. 5, September, 507–526.

Sartori, G. (1969) "From the Sociology of Politics to Political Sociology," in Lipset, S. M. (ed.) *Politics and the Social Sciences*, Oxford: Oxford University Press: 195–214.

Spies, D. (2013) "Explaining Working–Class Support for Extreme Right Parties: A Party Competition Approach," *Acta Politica*, vol. 48, no. 3, July, 296–325.

Swatos, W. H. and Christiano, K. J. (1999) "Introduction – Secularization Theory: The Course of a Concept," *Sociology of Religion*, vol. 60, no. 3, Autumn, 209–228.

Tilley, J. (2015) "'We Don't Do God'? Religion and Party Choice in Britain," *British Journal of Political Science*, vol. 45, no. 4, October, 907–927.

Tschannen, O. (1991) "The Secularization Paradigm: A Systematization," *Journal for the Scientific Study of Religion*, vol. 30, no. 4, December, 395–415.

Weakliem, D. (2013) "United States: Still the Politics of Diversity," in Evans, G. and De Graaf, N. D. (eds.) *Political Choice Matters: Explaining the Strength of Class and Religious Cleavages in Cross-National Perspective*, Oxford: Oxford University Press: 114–136.

Weakliem, D. L. and Heath, A. (1999) "The Secret Life of Class Voting: Britain, France, and the United States Since the 1930s," in Evans, G. (ed.) *The End of Class Politics? Class Voting in Comparative Context*, Oxford: Oxford University Press: 97–136.

Whitefield, S. (2002) "Political Cleavages and Post-Communist Politics," *Annual Review of Political Science*, vol. 5, no. 1, June, 181–200.

Wilson, B. (1982) *Religion in Sociological Perspective*, Oxford: Oxford University Press.

11

IDEOLOGY AND ELECTORAL CHOICE

Martin Elff

Introduction

Few topics in Political Science appear as burdened with difficulties as the term "ideology." On the one hand, the term "ideological" is often used in political discussions to criticize or vilify opponents either as irrational and intransigent – as sticking to principles beyond reason – or as insincere – as masquerading special interests as a common good. On the other hand, the meaning of the term "ideology" in Political Science seems to have been "thoroughly muddied by diverse uses" (Converse 1964: 207). Yet the diversity of uses does not indicate that it is impossible to associate a meaning with the term. While "ideology" is used to refer to different phenomena in different areas of scholarship, this does rarely lead to disagreements about its denotation *within* a particular field. Furthermore, despite this diversity, the usages of the term are not unrelated. Usually they refer to a set of *abstract* or *general* ideas, distinct from parties', candidates' or citizens' positions on particular issues or from specific policy plans. Disregarding the more polemic uses of the term, "ideology" has been used to refer to (see also Sartori 1969a; Jost 2006; Knight 2006):

1. a set of ideas that justify a social or political state of affairs
2. a set of ideas that give the (usually economic) interests of a certain social group a moral or (more generally) normative appeal
3. a particular line or tradition of political thought, such as Liberalism, Conservatism, Socialism, Fascism, etc.
4. the set of ideas that determine the political aims and policy positions of a political party
5. factors that structure citizens' attitudes and values.

While the first four of these uses are coherent with Downs' definition of ideology as "a verbal image of the good society and of the chief means of constructing such a society" (Downs 1957: 96), it is the fifth of these that appears to be immediately relevant for voting behavior. But the third and the fourth uses of the term "ideology" are also relevant for voting behavior and its analysis, though in a less obvious way. Their relevance comes from the consideration that it would be surprising to find persistent and coherent patterns of voting if not for persistent and coherent differences between parties in terms of the polices they announce or promise to voters. These differences between parties may be related to their membership in a party family – for example, of the liberal, conservative or social democratic parties – which are each rooted in one of the grand traditions of political thought that emerged in the nineteenth century – that is, Liberalism, Conservatism, Socialism, etc. (see Heywood 2003). Yet while categorizing parties in party families may facilitate the comparative description of class voting or voting along religious-secular lines, it masks out the variability of parties' policy positions. If parties that compete for voters in a country become more similar in terms of their policy positions, announcements and promises, they give fewer incentives to voters from different social groups to diverge in terms of voting behavior. Thus the political convergence of parties of the left and the center/right has been suggested as an explanation of the decline in class voting in Western Europe (see, for example, Elff 2009 and Evans and Northmore-Ball in this volume).

The spatial theory of party competition in the tradition of Downs (1957) views parties' ideologies as positions in an abstract unidimensional space, the principal directions of which are typically identified with the labels "left" and "right" (when applied to European politics) or "liberal" and "conservative" (when applied to American politics). The idea of such an overarching political dimension that lies behind the various policy or issue positions is however not confined to the spatial theory of party competition, but also common in the empirical analysis of patterns in citizens' political opinions and attitudes. Therefore, the question of whether such "citizen ideologies" (as distinguished from party ideologies) are adequately described by a single dimension or by multiple dimensions will be a central one in this chapter as well as the question about the origins of such dimensions. Another question addressed in this chapter is whether ideologies can be the foundation of new lines of cleavage, especially if traditional social cleavages based on class and religion have faded away. Yet the first question to be addressed is to what degree citizens have ideologies at all, since it was argued early on (Converse 1964) that ideologically coherent patterns of citizens' attitudes and values are a rare phenomenon and that – at least in the United States of the 1950s – most citizens are (or were) "innocent of ideology" (but see Jost 2006; Bølstad in this volume).

The question of coherence in belief systems

In his seminal contribution "The Nature of Belief Systems in Mass Publics," Philip Converse suggested substituting the "muddied" concept of ideology with the concept of a belief system, which he defines as "a configuration of attitudes and ideas in which the elements are bound together by some form of constraint or functional interdependence" (Converse 1964: 207). While such a "constraint" is understood as an *intra-individual* connection between these beliefs and ideas, so that the change of one idea or attitude would "psychologically" require the change of another idea or attitude, in actual empirical research such constraint is usually operationalized as a *correlation* between attitudes or ideas. Based on the low correlation among attitudes toward political issues that are related in content or in terms of their ideological significance, Converse argues that such belief systems in the (then) contemporary American public are quite rare, restricted to a thin elite of highly involved political activists and experts.

Intra-individual connections between beliefs and ideas are however not sufficient for the existence of correlations between ideas or attitudes in the general public, which poses a problem for the operationalization of constraint in terms of correlations. That is, if there is a high variety of *different* belief systems – each with a different pattern of constraint – the correlation among measurements of ideas and attitudes from different people may be quite low. For strong correlations to exist there must also be a high level of *polarization* between a small number of types of individual belief systems. Indeed, Converse's pessimistic assessment has been questioned and criticized repeatedly, if only for slightly different reasons. The first type of criticism was methodological. One argument, which goes back to Achen (1975), is that the low correlation among issue attitudes that Converse found were not indicative of a lack of constraint, but of a lack of reliability in attitude measures. The idea of inter-individually differing belief systems has led other authors to posit the existence of "hierarchical" or "vertical" patterns of constraint. These are constraints between abstract principles and attitudes toward the issues in a particular policy area that citizens might be particularly interested or engaged in (Peffley and Hurwitz 1985). The other type of criticism questioned the general relevance of the finding of low constraint. Thus it has been suggested that the apparent low level of constraint was a phenomenon of the halcyon American politics of the 1950s and that attitude constraint and polarization was much higher in the more turbulent 1970s (see, for example, Nie and Andersen 1974) and in the highly polarized politics of the current decade (see, for example, Jewitt and Goren 2016). Yet there are also disagreeing voices that state that partisan polarization and issue polarization between parties has increased, but not issue constraint (see, for example, Mason 2015). A result that still stands, however, is that ideological constraint is related to political sophistication and to education and indeed the gains in constraint appear to be restricted to the educated and politically engaged (see, for example, Jewitt and Goren 2016); but ideological constraint varies not only systematically across individuals but also across countries. For example, a high visibility of the welfare state also increases the constraint among attitudes toward the welfare state (Gingrich 2014).

As just discussed, there is evidence of systematic differences between individuals in terms of belief system constraint, at least if measured in terms of correlations among attitudes. Those correlations are however inter-individual patterns, while constraint really is a concept that concerns intra-individual patterns of attitudes. Thus the findings of variations over time and across countries may be the artifacts of variations in the polarization of attitudes, which in turn may be affected by the polarization at the level of political elites. On the other hand, it is quite plausible that the variations across individuals, in so far as they are related to education and political involvement, may indeed reflect variations in intra-individual constraint. To uncover these effects of political context and individuals' political sophistication, it is necessary to find ways to measure intra-individual constraint of political attitudes independent from correlations across individuals, which is still an unmet challenge (but see Erikson this volume).

Ideology as a means to facilitate electoral choice

A fundamental idea of the spatial theory of ideologies, which goes back to Downs' *Economic Theory of Democracy* (1957), is that they can be represented by locations on a single dimension, usually identified with a left–right or liberal–conservative axis: The more similar two ideologies are, the closer to each other they are on this axis. Extreme ideologies are more distant from the middle of the axis than centrist ideologies. In so far as ideology is relevant for citizens' voting decisions, they choose the party or candidate that has the closest to their own ideological position.

In Downs' version of the theory (1957), neither parties nor voters are interested in ideologies themselves. For parties and candidates, ideologies are just means to win elections. For voters, ideologies are means for the reduction of information costs. They simplify the choice between parties, because voters do not need to acquire detailed information about parties' potential government activities and to evaluate these in terms of their own well-being. Instead, voters can identify a party's notion of the good society and what place they themselves would have in it. That is, parties' or candidates' ideological positions are some sort of heuristics.

It is not immediately clear how this spatial notion of ideologies can be reconciled with the idea that they are descriptions of "good societies" and the way toward them. In order to be able to compare parties' ideological positions with their own position, they need to be able to have such ideological positions, and that means to have their own notion of a good society. This seems to require a certain degree of abstract thinking, which, as we saw previously, not many citizens are capable of or engaged in. Alternatively, one could assume that citizens do not care about the ideologies in themselves. Instead they look at ideologies only in terms of those aspects they are affected by. These aspects then do not need to lie on the same dimension as the ideologies. This idea was formalized by Hinich and Pollard (1981) and Enelow and Hinich (1982), who posit that voters care about parties' or candidates' positions on issues, but find it costly to learn about these positions directly. Instead, they use linear mappings to predict these positions from parties' or candidates' ideological positions. While this idea has nice mathematical properties, it actually begs the question of how citizens construct these mappings. Irrespective of whether these mappings are the product of logical inference or of learning from experience, they would constitute a considerable cognitive achievement. In fact, this idea of linear mappings between ideological positions and particular issue positions seem to fit together with the idea of attitude constraint manifested in correlations among attitudes: Like in the general factor analysis model, the less "noisy" individuals' mappings between ideological positions and issue positions are, the higher the absolute correlation among issue attitudes will be.

The idea of ideological distinctions as inferential devices is not restricted to research motivated by the spatial theory of voting. From cognitive psychology comes the idea of the left–right distinction as a *schema* (Conover and Feldman 1984). A schema is a cognitive structure that helps individuals to organize diverse experience. Schemas can have different levels of abstraction and are typically domain-specific, that is, used (only) in a particular area of experience. But this means that if the notions of "left" and "right" each refer to a schema or if the left–right axis is a schema, as it appears to be in West European politics (Fuchs and Klingemann 1990), it is not necessarily the only one. There may be other, general or domain-specific, schemata that are used as an alternative or as a supplement to the left–right schema to make sense of political information and to take positions on particular issues (see, for example, Medina 2015).

If voters do not care for each and every implication that an ideology has, then a complete and coherent belief system may not be necessary for ideological cues to be useful for them. But at least they will need a basic understanding of what it means for a party or candidate to be either "left" or "right," "liberal" or "conservative." Again it was Converse who brought dismal tidings: Only a small section of the citizenry – at least at the time of his writing – actively used ideological categories explicitly in their evaluation of parties and an only somewhat broader section appeared able to make sense of ideological labels when presented with them (Converse 1964). While results for West European countries are somewhat more favorable, there are still differences between educational groups in terms of recognition and understanding of "left" and "right," even though they appear small in comparison to the differences between the West European countries and the US (Klingemann 1972). Yet respondents in the study by Fuchs and Klingemann (1990) often use dichotomies of "progressive" vs. "conservative" and "communism" vs. "fascism" as interpretations of "left" and "right" and thus use categories no less abstract than the original terms, while they rarely use more concrete meanings such as "worker" vs. "entrepreneur" or "poor" vs. "rich." But if citizens are only able to paraphrase abstract terms with different abstract terms, there is room for doubt that they are able to make any specific inferences with regards to parties' or candidates' policy positions.

Even if a citizen is able to associate substantial issue content with labels such as "left" and "right" in a wide range of policy areas, and place themselves and parties correctly on a left–right scale, this will not prove that he or she uses left–right positions to *infer* positions on particular issues. While such a finding would be consistent with such a use, it is also possible that he or she has just merely learned, *after* picking up a certain set of positions, that certain positions and the use of "left" and "right" go together. To prove his or her inferential use of left–right positions, one will need to provide him or her with left–right positions of (fictitious) parties and candidates and record whether he or she makes correct predictions about these parties' issue positions. It appears that no research in this direction has been undertaken yet.

The content and dimensionality of "left" and "right"

It would be a fallacy to conclude from the ubiquity of the use of "left" and "right" as political categories that there exists a consensus about their issue content. This insight has led many scholars to look into the correlates of citizens' left–right self-placement. If these correlates are indicative of the content of "left" and "right," then there is ample evidence that it varies considerably across space (i.e., countries) and time (see, for example, van Elsas and van der Brug 2015).

Further, there is evidence that ideological positions cannot or can no longer be adequately described by positions on a single axis. A growing literature (see, for example, Hooghe, Marks and Wilson 2002; Feldman and Johnston 2014) suggests that there are instead at least two ideological dimensions:

- an economic left–right or "materialist" dimension that contrasts

  - demands for redistribution of assets and income toward more equality, public provision of welfare benefits and an active role of the state in controlling the economy, with
  - an affirmation of the freedom from interventions into property rights and demands for the state to let markets run their course

- a "non-materialist," "post-materialist," "social," "authoritarian-libertarian" or "GAL/ TAN" dimension that contrasts

  - the affirmation of citizens' political rights and individuals' liberties to choose their way of life, with
  - an emphasis of authority of the state to constrain or coerce citizens in the name of public security and an affirmation of traditional norms of piety and modesty.

The notion of two ideological dimensions has become popular in the literature that postulates that a value change from materialist to post-materialist priorities has occurred. This value change is supposed to have led to a confrontation between "old politics" and "new politics," which cuts across traditional left–right alignments based on economic interests and class divisions (see, for example, Inglehart 1984). But this second dimension is arguably a quite old one, which derives from religious-secular divisions and conflicts about the contrast between individual freedom and the authority of the national state, conflicts that go back to the late nineteenth and early twentieth century and that have become manifest in the divergent ideological movements of Liberalism and Conservatism. Considering that in some cases the authority of the nation-state could get into conflict with Catholic church religiosity, it might be reasonable to distinguish *two* non-economic ideological dimensions (see, for example, Elff 2009), one contrasting individual way-of-life liberties with traditional-religious norms and one contrasting citizens' rights with the authority of the nation-state (Lipset and Rokkan 1967; Elff and Rossteutscher 2017).

So how many dimensions of ideology exist? The significance of the answer to this question depends on whether ideological dimensions are genuine (latent) factors or epiphenomenal to clusters of ideas. In the first case, if ideologies are genuine latent factors, they will restrict the degrees of freedom of positional changes by parties – for example, by restricting them to movements on a single left–right axis. The number of ideological dimensions could then be determined by a combination of theoretical reasoning and sophisticated analysis of data on parties' electoral platforms and/or voters' issue preferences. In the second case, if ideologies are primarily sets or clusters of ideas, each cluster being held together by a common origin and/or logical or factual coherence, then ideological dimensions are a mere means for the description of differences among these idea clusters. Sophisticated data analysis may still lead to results that suggest a representation of ideologies by a small number of dimensions, but the implications of such findings will be limited and likely to be dependent on context and time. But the different clusters/dimensions may also be ephemeral side-effects of an evolution of the meaning of left–right itself as new issues arise that will eventually be absorbed into the left–right dimension (van der Brug and Franklin in this volume), perhaps as a pre-condition for their having effects on party support.

Operational and symbolic ideology

It is tempting to equate citizens' self-placement on a scale with ideological labels such as "left" and "right" or "liberal" and "conservative," etc. with actually having corresponding ideological orientations. Yet if someone reports a "moderately leftist" score of 3 on a 10-point left–right scale, for example, then this does not imply that he or she will support all the issue stances that a party or candidate with such an ideological position will assume. Instead, respondents' left–right or liberal–conservative self-placements and their issue positions may empirically diverge and in some instances they do. Ellis and Stimson (2009) therefore distinguish between an "operational ideology" and a "symbolic ideology." An operational ideology is a coherent set of attitudes and beliefs similar to Converse's concept of a belief system. An individual's symbolic ideology is his or her self-identification with ideological labels, such as "left" or "right," or with groups denoted by such labels, such as "liberals" or "conservatives." The phenomenon of "conflicted conservatives," who identify themselves with an ideological symbol without actually supporting any of the policies that members of the political elite would ascribe to it (Ellis and Stimson 2012), are an instructive example for such a divergence.

While the concept of symbolic ideology suggests that it is causally prior to vote decisions and to some degree also to operational ideology, other interpretations of ideological self-identification view it as a *consequence* of partisanship and/or party preference. Thus when Inglehart and Klingemann (1976) examine the relative influence of value orientations and partisanship on left–right self-placement, they find that the latter dominates. Thus the question may arise about the relative priority of party identification and partisanship on the one hand and ideological self-placement or symbolic ideological identification on the other. Both causal pathways appear equally plausible. If partisanship is a product of socialization (by parents and perhaps also by peer groups) and the meanings of ideological "labels" are learned from their application to the policy positions of the party one identifies with, then partisanship is causally prior. This is likely to be the case in the US where the ideological polarization between parties used to be low (even if it has increased recently). In contrast, if political socialization does not lead so much to the identification with parties than with ideological labels or ideologically labeled groups, then ideological self-identification is likely to condition individuals' adoption of issue positions and electoral choices, which may then coagulate into partisan attachments. This is more likely to be the case in countries with several small to medium-size parties that sort themselves into ideological "camps," such as in pre-1990 Italy. The causal relation between partisanship and ideological identification may however be reciprocal if the party system is sufficiently concentrated so that certain parties can, at least in public perception, be the exclusive "owners" of particular ideological brands. For example, if there is a major party calling itself the "Socialist Party" or similar and if this party describes itself as "moderate leftist" – as in many West European countries before 1990 – then partisan attachments and ideological identifications are likely to develop in tandem. It is of course difficult to disentangle these causal pathways empirically, because this requires panel survey studies with the right instruments. These are quite rare, with the various studies conducted by Michael Lewis-Beck and his co-workers on France as exceptions (e.g., Fleury and Lewis-Beck 1993). They find ideology to be a cause of partisanship rather than the other way around – though the findings are consistent with a view that party choice is a cause of both (see Dinas in this volume).

Psychological underpinnings

Much of the discussion about the concept of ideology and the causes and consequences of ideological thought and conceptualization considered so far can be characterized by a "top-down" perspective, where ideologies are originally systems of thought adopted by parties and political elites, which then color the perceptions of those who identify with those parties (see Heath in this volume). A more psychologically oriented "bottom-up" perspective can be contrasted with this (Jost, Federico and Napier 2009). In this perspective, ideologies are patterns of sentiments and cognition, rooted in individuals' personality, their particular situation or experience, or even their genetic makeup.

Much of the research tradition on the psychological underpinnings of ideology goes back to Adorno et al.'s (1950) *Authoritarian Personality* and focuses on personality traits that dispose individuals toward right-wing authoritarian attitudes (see, for example, Altemeyer 1981) or hierarchical relations between groups (see, for example, Pratto et al. 1994). This research thus favors a uni-polar conception of ideologies or is restricted to a particular ideological content. Later authors focus on more general attitudes such as (in)egalitarianism and resistance to change and their relation to liberal–conservative or left–right self-placement (see, for example, Thorisdottir et al. 2007). Explanations of these phenomena appear to draw from the full inventory of psychological factors. They include situational factors such as perceived threat (see, for example, Jost 2009), psychological needs (see, for example, Thorisdottir et al. 2007), experiences during youth and childhood (see, for example, Block and Block 2006), personality factors such as the "Big Five" (Jost 2006), or even physiological and genetic factors (Smith et al. 2011; Funk et al. 2013).

Another area of psychological research is less focused on the content of ideological thinking than on the psychological foundation of what Sartori (1969b) calls the ideological mind-set. The central concept of this research is "motivated reasoning" (Redlawsk 2002), which involves not so much the deductive search for implications and consequences from certain premises as it tries to find reasons to justify a given and predetermined political decision – that is, to *rationalize* them. In particular, such research focuses on to what degree and under what conditions individuals retain certain political positions or preferences, despite being faced with factual information that contradicts the reasons that appear to justify these positions or preferences (see, for example, Kahan 2012).

While these lines of research contribute important insights into phenomena that are related to ideologies in the various meanings discussed at the beginning of this chapter, care must be taken that phenomena such as resistance to change are not confused with ideologies themselves. Furthermore, it seems worthwhile to explore the relation of psychological factors to politics in more refined ways than with reference to left–right or liberal–conservative self-placements. Finally, it appears that psychological factors are perhaps rather moderators than primary factors since, for example, the need for security varies between Eastern and Western Europe in terms of the relation with left–right self-placements (Thorisdottir et al. 2007).

Outlook: an ideology-based cleavage structure?

Apart from giving an overview of the role played by ideology in shaping electoral choices, a main purpose of this chapter is to examine whether ideologies can be the basis of new political cleavages after the traditional ones based on social structure have faded away, as often is claimed (see Evans and Northmore-Ball in this volume). As it turns out, the answer is (as ever so often) "it depends." In the present case, it depends on the meaning of the terms "cleavage" and "ideology."

While the concept of cleavage is no more clear than that of ideology, for reasons of space the following "minimal" definition will have to suffice: A cleavage is a persistent division of groups with systematically divergent patterns in political behavior, including patterns of voting (this minimal definition is inspired by Rae and Taylor 1970). A "social cleavage" is a group division where members of different groups differ in their position in the system of social stratification or other major aspects of their social life – such as religiosity or church attendance or religious non-affiliation. An "ideological cleavage" then would be a division between groups that differ in their ideologies, irrespective of their social position. Since one can distinguish between symbolic ideology and operational ideology, one can analogously distinguish between symbolic ideological cleavages and operational ideological cleavages.

While stable programmatic divisions between parties may be important for the existence of social cleavages, they are obviously even more important for cleavages based on operational ideology. It will be hard to understand why voters with different operational ideologies vote for different parties, if not for differences between parties in terms of ideological messages or ideologically relevant policy proposals. But the existence of such cleavages also requires a sufficient amount of constraint among voters' political opinions and attitudes to produce such coherent responses to parties' messages. Clearly, the dependence of such cleavages on party agency makes it unlikely that such cleavages will be uniform across countries and over time. If most citizens lack the necessary structuration of opinions and attitudes, it will be unlikely that such cleavages will range deep into society, if they occur at all. The matter may be different in the case of cleavages based on symbolic ideology, at least at first glance. If there are groups defined by the identification with ideological symbols and if certain parties can be associated with these symbols, then a more or less stable pattern of voter alignments may result. But it is possible that symbolic and operational ideology do not match, and it is plausible that such a mismatch undermines such ideological cleavages. Whether this is empirically the case is still an open question.

Another question is whether the psychological dispositions that are at the center of the "bottom-up" perspective could form the basis of new political cleavages. On the one hand, being affective dispositions, they are less cognitively demanding than operational ideologies and thus potentially more widespread. On the other hand, the psychological dispositions on which the "bottom-up" approach focuses are not really ideologies in any of the senses discussed at the beginning of this chapter. It is however plausible that these dispositions contribute to the psychological underpinnings of the value conflicts that lead to the tension between liberal and conservative ideologies.

The discussion so far focused on the possibility that ideological cleavages emerge at all. This leaves open the question about the content of potential ideological cleavages, provided that the conditions are met for their manifestation: If ideological cleavages substituted social cleavages, what would they be about? While inventive scholars will always try to demonstrate otherwise, it does not seem plausible that ideological cleavages will result in the emergence of something radically new. First, ideologies with mass appeal cannot be invented out of the blue, but take time to evolve, so that socialism, liberalism, conservatism, Christian democracy, etc. are likely here to stay. Second, the major issues of the day, inequality and immigration, are far from alien to the historical currents of ideology. Inequality has always been a foundational concern of socialism, and ethnic divisions, which are created or highlighted by immigration, have been exploited by right-wing nationalism since the beginning on the twentieth century. The new populist movements virulent in certain European countries and elsewhere are thus not much more than old wine in new bottles, while socialism may again become resurgent should the parties of the moderate left cease or undo their attempt to re-define themselves in terms of a "New Center" or a "Third Way." The only genuinely new ideological current that has emerged in the last few decades is ecologism. Yet its electoral impact has remained limited, even though demands for fighting pollution and wildlife protection have often been picked up by the "traditional" political left or even addressed by supranational regulations. Whether further climate change lends new fervor to this movement remains a matter of future research.

References

Achen, C. H. (1975) "Mass Political Attitudes and the Survey Response," *American Political Science Review*, vol. 69, no. 4, December, 1218–1231.

Adorno, T. W., Frenkel-Brunswik, E., Levinson, D. J. and Sanford, R. N. (1950) *The Authoritarian Personality*, New York: Harper and Row.

Altemeyer, B. (1981) *Right-Wing Authoritarianism*, Winnipeg: University of Manitoba Press.

Block, J. and Block, J. H. (2006) "Nursery School Personality and Political Orientation Two Decades Later," *Journal of Research in Personality*, vol. 40, no. 5, October, 734–749.

Conover, P. J. and Feldman, S. (1984) "How People Organize the Political World: A Schematic Model," *American Journal of Political Science*, vol. 28, no. 1, February, 95–126.

Converse, P. E. (1964) "The Nature of Belief Systems in Mass Publics," in Apter, D. E. (ed.) *Ideology and Discontent*, New York: The Free Press: 206–261.

Downs, A. (1957) *An Economic Theory of Democracy*, New York: Harper and Row.

Elff, M. (2009) "Social Divisions, Party Positions, and Electoral Behaviour," *Electoral Studies*, vol. 28, no. 2, June, 297–308.

Elff, M. and Rossteutscher, S. (2017) "Religion," in Arzheimer, K., Evans, J. and Lewis-Beck, M. S. (eds.) *The SAGE Handbook of Electoral Behaviour*, London: Sage: 199–219.

Ellis, C. and Stimson, J. A. (2009) "Symbolic Ideology in the American Electorate," *Electoral Studies*, vol. 28, no. 3, September, 388–402.

Ellis, C. and Stimson, J. A. (2012) *Ideology in America*, New York: Cambridge University Press.

Elsas, E. van and Brug, W. van der (2015) "The Changing Relationship Between Left–Right Ideology and Euroscepticism, 1973–2010," *European Union Politics*, vol. 16, no. 2, June, 194–215.

Enelow, J. M. and Hinich, M. J. (1982) "Ideology, Issues, and the Spatial Theory of Elections," *The American Political Science Review*, vol. 76, no. 3, September, 493–501.

Feldman, S. and Johnston, C. (2014) "Understanding the Determinants of Political Ideology: Implications of Structural Complexity," *Political Psychology*, vol. 35, no. 3, June, 337–358.

Fleury, C. J. and Lewis-Beck, M. S. (1993) "Anchoring the French Voter: Ideology Versus Party," *Journal of Politics*, vol. 55, no. 4, November, 1100–1109.

Fuchs, D. and Klingemann, H. D. (1990) "The Left–Right Schema," in Jennings, M. K. and Van Deth, J. (eds.) *Continuities in Political Action: A Longitudinal Study of Political Orientations in Three Western Democracies*, Berlin: Walter de Gruyter: 203–234.

Funk, C. L., Smith, K. B., Alford, J. R., Hibbing, M. V., Eaton, N. R., Krueger, R. F., Eaves, L. J. and Hibbing, J. R. (2013) "Genetic and Environmental Transmission of Political Orientations," *Political Psychology*, vol. 34, no. 6, October, 805–819.

Gingrich, J. (2014) "Visibility, Values, and Voters: The Informational Role of the Welfare State," *Journal of Politics*, vol. 76, no. 2, February, 565–580.

Heywood, A. (2003) *Political Ideologies: An Introduction*, 3rd Edition, Basingstoke: Palgrave Macmillan.

Hinich, M. J. and Pollard, W. (1981) "A New Approach to the Spatial Theory of Electoral Competition," *American Journal of Political Science*, vol. 25, no. 2, May, 323–341.

Hooghe, L., Marks, G. and Wilson, C. J. (2002) "Does Left/Right Structure Party Positions on European Integration?," *Comparative Political Studies*, vol. 35, no. 8, October, 965–989.

Inglehart, R. (1984) "The Changing Structure of Political Cleavages in Western Society," in Dalton, R. J., Flanagan, S. C. and Beck, P. A. (eds.) *Electoral Change: Realignment and Dealignment in Advanced Industrial Democracies*, Princeton, NJ: Princeton University Press: 25–69.

Inglehart, R. and Klingemann, H-D. (1976) "Party Identification, Ideological Preference and the Left–Right Dimension Among Western Mass Publics," in Castiglione, D. and Hoffmann-Martinot, V. (eds.) *Party Identification and Beyond: Representations of Voting and Party Competition*, London: John Wiley & Sons: 243–273.

Jewitt, C. E. and Goren, P. (2016) "Ideological Structure and Consistency in the Age of Polarization," *American Politics Research*, vol. 44, no. 1, January, 81–105.

Jost, J. T. (2006) "The End of the End of Ideology," *American Psychologist*, vol. 61, no. 7, October, 651–670.

Jost, J. T. (2009) "'Elective Affinities': On the Psychological Bases of Left–Right Differences," *Psychological Inquiry*, vol. 20, no. 2–3, April, 129–141.

Jost, J. T., Federico, C. M. and Napier, J. L. (2009) "Political Ideology: Its Structure, Functions, and Elective Affinities," *Annual Review of Psychology*, vol. 60, no. 1, January, 307–337.

Kahan, D. M. (2012) "Ideology, Motivated Reasoning, and Cognitive Reflection: An Experimental Study," *Judgment and Decision Making*, vol. 8, no. 4, July, 407–424.

Klingemann, H. D. (1972) "Testing the Left-Right Continuum on a Sample of German Voters," *Comparative Political Studies*, vol. 5, no. 1, April, 93–106.

Knight, K. (2006) "Transformations of the Concept of Ideology in the Twentieth Century," *American Political Science Review*, vol. 100, no. 4, November, 619–626.

Lipset, S. M. and Rokkan, S. (1967) "Cleavage Structures, Party Systems, and Voter Alignments: An Introduction," in Lipset, S. M. and Rokkan, S. (eds.) *Party Systems and Voter Alignments: Cross-National Perspectives*, New York: Free Press: 1–64.

Mason, L. (2015) "'I Disrespectfully Agree': The Differential Effects of Partisan Sorting on Social and Issue Polarization," *American Journal of Political Science*, vol. 59, no. 1, January, 128–145.

Medina, L. (2015) "Partisan Supply and Voters' Positioning on the Left–Right Scale in Europe," *Party Politics*, vol. 21, no. 5, September, 775–790.

Nie, N. H. and Andersen, K. (1974) "Mass Belief Systems Revisited: Political Change and Attitude Structure," *Journal of Politics*, vol. 36, no. 3, August, 540–591.

Peffley, M. A. and Hurwitz, J. (1985) "A Hierarchical Model of Attitude Constraint," *American Journal of Political Science*, vol. 29, no. 4, November, 871–890.

Pratto, F., Sidanius, J., Stallworth, L. M. and Malle, B. F. (1994) "Social Dominance Orientation: A Personality Variable Predicting Social and Political Attitudes," *Journal of Personality and Social Psychology*, vol. 67, no. 4, October, 741–763.

Rae, D. W., and Taylor, M. (1970) *The Analysis of Political Cleavages*, New Haven: Yale University Press.

Redlawsk, D. P. (2002) "Hot Cognition or Cool Consideration? Testing the Effects of Motivated Reasoning on Political Decision Making," *Journal of Politics*, vol. 64, no. 4, November, 1021–1044.

Sartori, G. (1969a) "From the Sociology of Politics to Political Sociology," in Lipset, S. M. (ed.) *Politics and the Social Sciences*, Oxford: Oxford University Press: 195–214.

Sartori, G. (1969b) "Politics, Ideology, and Belief Systems," *American Political Science Review*, vol. 63, no. 2, June, 398–411.

Smith, K. B., Oxley, D., Hibbing, M. V., Alford, J. R. and Hibbing, J. R. (2011) "Disgust Sensitivity and the Neurophysiology of Left-Right Political Orientations," *PLoS ONE*, vol. 6, no. 10, October, 1–9.

Thorisdottir, H., Jost, J. T., Liviatan, I. and Shrout, P. E. (2007) "Psychological Needs and Values Underlying Left-Right Political Orientation: Cross-National Evidence from Eastern and Western Europe," *Public Opinion Quarterly*, vol. 71, no. 2, Spring, 175–203.

12

PARTY IDENTIFICATION

Shaun Bowler

Introduction

The classical definition of party identification is that it is a "sense of personal attachment which the individual feels towards the [party] of his (*sic*) choice" (Campbell, Gurin and Miller 1954: 88–89). That is, voters have long-running attachments to particular parties regardless of candidates or issues in specific elections. Voters may defect from "their" party every now and then – they may choose a candidate from another party – but over the long run, more often than not, voters will have a homing tendency and return to support "their" party for which they have a sense of attachment. Party identification is probably the central conceptual building block in behavioral research and is a standard, one might even say required, factor to be included in models of vote choice, being seen as a precursor to the vote and party preference. One crude indication of its importance is found in Google Scholar where a search for the terms "party identification" AND "political science" produces over 27,000 results. Clearly, such a large literature presents challenges for any review. This chapter on party identification is therefore necessarily limited and organizes a discussion of party identification around three main questions. The first question is: what does party identification do? The second is: how (and why) do people develop party identification? And the third question asks: what kinds of variations do we see in party identification?

What does party identification do?

One of the more important features of party identification is that it not only helps to shape choices directly by capturing a long-term loyalty or standing decision to support a given party, it also shapes choices indirectly by helping make sense of information we receive. Perhaps the clearest way in which this happens is when considering economic information. We know that voters take government performance into account when making their choices: incumbents are punished for bad performance news, rewarded for good. But what makes performance "good" or "bad" is not simply a matter of an objective number but may also be subject to interpretation. Once there is room for interpretation there is room for information to be filtered by party identification. A 7 percent unemployment rate under a Conservative government may be seen as a good level of unemployment so far as Conservative identifiers are concerned, not so good if the voter identifies with Labour (see, for example, Wlezien, Franklin and Twiggs 1997). It is not just economic news that is filtered in this way. Anduiza, Gallego and Muñoz (2013) show that party identifiers are even willing to turn a blind eye toward corruption.

Party identifications also provide short cuts that reduce the amount of information voters need to process. Voters do not need to develop complex ideologies or think out positions for specific issues; using parties as heuristics allows people to develop information short cuts and to cue-take from party leaders. Brader, Tucker and Duell (2013), for example, demonstrate some of the limits to cue-taking but also show it in action, concluding that more established parties are likely to be able to send cues that voters respond to with regard to specific policies.

Party identifications are also associated with several positive attributes that help support what was termed in early literature as a "democratic political culture." We know that party identification is associated with interest in politics and elections. Those with strong identifications are more likely to be engaged in the system – to pay attention to politics and to turn out and vote. That said, one of the difficulties of this list of functions is that the direction(s) of causal relationships are not always clearly established or simple. Take, for example the relationship between party identification and interest in politics: is it the case that those who are interested in politics develop a party identification? Or does party id strengthen an interest in politics? Or does the relationship go both ways? At the very least, what this discussion suggests is that the familiar model specifications in which party is included side by side with interest, or, alternatively, where interest is predicted by partisanship, probably over-states the size of the relationship.

Party identification is also useful at the level of the system as well as individual voters. Party loyalties help promote turnout and also provide a tie between individuals and the political system and gives people a way of locating themselves in the wide political context. These effects, in addition to the individual level effects on interest, attention and turnout, are all consistent with a vibrant and active democratic process and so are valuable from a system perspective. Consequently, aggregate levels of party identification among the electorate are often seen as a marker for the overall health of a democratic system since those levels are associated with levels of engagement and turnout.

Take, for example, the pattern we see in Figure 12.1, which shows the relationship between party identification and a sense of whether people feel elections make a difference.

Figure 12.1 displays aggregate level data from CSES 2 and CSES 3.[1] We find a bivariate correlation of 0.41 (p = 0.0002, N = 75) between the national level percentage of people who identify with a party and the national level percentage of people who respond that elections make a difference. A similar, if somewhat weaker, relationship exists between the aggregate level percentage of those who say they are close to a party with the percentage of those responding that they are "very" satisfied with democracy (correlation = 0.26, p = 0.019, N = 78). We will return to definitional issues relating to "closeness" to a party and other issues arising from Figure 12.1 below. For the moment, the point made by Figure 12.1 is simply to provide some evidence that there is indeed a relationship between partisanship and system level indicators of democratic health.

The short answer to the question of what do party identifications do is that "they do a lot." Given the value of partisanship to both citizens and political systems alike it is not surprising that a large body of literature has considered how citizens acquire partisanship.

Why (and how) do we have party identifications?

One of the major distinctions to be made is whether partisanship is either a consequence of socialization or simply a matter of habituation. Both strands of thought are present in the

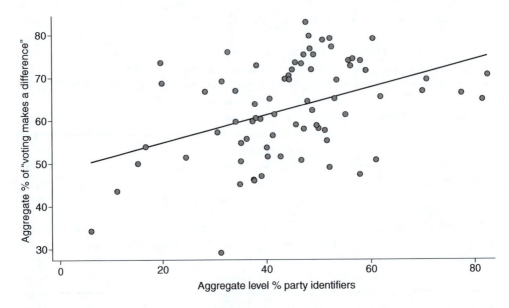

Figure 12.1 Who people vote for makes a difference

literature and, as we will see, both are able to point to evidence in their support. Although the degree to which party identification is seen as a property of one rather than the other does seems to depend in part on where, and when, we look. We begin, however, where the literature on party identification began, which is an understanding of party id in terms of socialization.

The earliest work on party identification, that of the 1960s and 1970s, emphasized childhood socialization and that children "acquired" the party loyalties of their parents. Research shows that children share the party loyalties of their parents to a surprising degree. One set of scholars highlight that the size of effect is comparable to religiosity:

> The high levels of concordance [between parents and children] found for partisan orientations compare favorably with those for levels of religiosity, as indexed by frequency of church attendance and beliefs about the inerrancy of the Bible. Parents are expected to exert a powerful influence on the religious practices and beliefs of their children.
>
> *(Jennings, Stoker and Bowers 2009: 796)*

A more recent body of work has begun to revisit those earlier findings and found that those earlier findings largely persist (Jennings and Markus 1984: Jennings, Stoker and Bowers 2009)

> As expected (…), children are more likely to adopt their parents' political orientations if the family is highly politicized and if the parents provide consistent cues over time. The direct transmission model is robust, as it withstands an extensive set of controls. Early acquisition of parental characteristics influences the subsequent nature of adult political development.
>
> *(Jennings, Stoker and Bowers 2009: 782)*

Other work on the psychology of vote choice anchored an understanding of partisanship in social identity theory in which citizens chose to identify with a group and/or the relationship between parties and groups (left parties and labor unions; center-right parties and religious affiliation) meant that voters would acquire partisanship more or less as part of their group-based social identity. To the extent that groups in society are becoming more complex and/or people join multiple groups then we may see these kinds of relationships shift. While there has been some renewal of interest in childhood and adolescent socialization processes, there has been less new work on the social identity basis of partisanship. Green, Palmquist and Schickler (2004) represent something of an exception but there is less work done in the comparative context (Green, Palmquist and Schickler 2004; Sapiro 2004). One exception is that of Huber, Kernell and Leoni (2005) with a study that uses a 25-country sample from CSES 1 and concludes that: "We find that voters are most likely to form party attachments when group identities are salient and complimentary" (Huber, Kernell and Leoni 2005: 365).

If partisanship is seen as something that develops from fundamental social contexts like family or group this suggests that citizens acquire – and so hold onto – partisanship in an almost unthinking and unconscious way. To borrow a phrase from Medeiros and Noël, these works reinforce the sense that party identification can be seen as a "prepolitical and arational" foundation of political behavior, a "psychological attachment" based on affect more than on cognition, and one likely to stand the test of time because it was anchored in "a person's self-concept" (Medeiros and Noël 2013: 3–4).[2]

To the extent that party identifications are rooted in "arational" factors there may be no need to explain why people choose to have them. The answer is that it simply is not a choice for people. Yet, despite the socialization processes and identifications and despite the usefulness of party identification, it is less clear why voters have them in the first place. That is, it is worth asking whether, left to themselves, voters would choose to acquire a party identification. While party identifications have many benefits once acquired, those benefits may not provide sufficient reason for an individual to acquire a party identification to begin with. It would likely seem to be the case that individual voters may care very little for system level functions – for example, they may care little that get out the vote campaigns are easier for parties if voters are staunch partisans. Voters may even not care too much about how party identifications may make them feel better about the political system. After all, a body of evidence shows that, for many people, politics is not just low salience but an irritant (Hibbing and Theiss-Morse 2002). In acquiring a party identification voters choose a number of frustrations – including the frustration for many minor party supporters of supporting a party that never wins. To borrow an analogy from the sporting world, it is almost as if someone who does not like soccer becomes a fan of a team perennially at the bottom of the league. On the face of it, then, it is surprising that voters keep hold of party identification, especially in the face of repeated frustrations and irritations. Yet the evidence suggests voters not only hold on to party identifications but that those identifications strengthen over the life cycle.

It is possible, however, to see voters developing party identifications without having the need to invoke social identity theory or childhood socialization as explanations. Before moving on to develop this point, it is important to note that, even in the earlier work on party identification socialization, life experiences had some role to play. Someone's life experiences could interrupt and in some instances over-ride early socialization. Dinas' (2014) work is perhaps the best recent example of demonstrating this point. For Dinas, the combination of politically engaged parents with politically engaged children can lead to changes in political views later in life that may lead people to differ from their parents. Nevertheless, despite the role of experiences, the received view of partisanship often emphasized socialization processes within the family, or within social groups.

A consideration of life experiences helps to open the door to explanations of party identification not grounded in socialization but grounded more in habituation. While socialization

processes of various kinds may provide a sufficient explanation for the existence of party identification, such processes may not provide a necessary explanation. After all, parties and party
government are a highly visible, even ever-present, part of society. Even between elections it is
hard to avoid seeing or hearing from the main political parties. It is thus hard for citizens to
avoid having some response to political parties as agents or actors in the society. At election time
the prominence of political parties in the media and public debate peaks. This prominence of
political parties must go some way to explaining why people may acquire partisanship independent of the kind of long-term socialization/social identity processes.

One group of voters that is interesting in terms of whether/how voters develop partisanship
separate from socialization are citizens in the new democracies. In these countries party systems
were formed anew, implying that there is no relevant childhood socialization experience.[3] In
the wave of democratizations in the 1990s and 2000s, people were suddenly asked about their
relationship to parties. Again referring back to Figure 12.1 and the CSES aggregate level data,
simply distinguishing between "old" and "new" (< 25 years old) democracies with a dummy
variable produces a correlation of -0.31 (p$=0.005$, N$=78$). Dalton and Weldon (2007: 192)
rightly note the chicken and egg problem for new democracies: partisanship promotes stable
party systems, which in turn promote partisanship, but when party systems are unstable and/or
electoral volatility is high there may be a less stable set of party identifications among individual
votes. Mainwaring and Zoco (2007) highlight the importance of the conditions at the start of
democratic formation as a factor shaping the stability of party systems: they find that newer
democracies tend to have higher levels of volatility, which is consistent with there being lower
levels of partisanship in newer democracies.

Even if we see party identification as a response to circumstance – to "nature" not "nurture"
– there still remains a role for socialization in the acquisition of party id. For example, "the
third-wave democracies also display evidence of latent socialization carried over from the old
regime. The results suggest that party identities can develop in new democracies if the party
system creates the conditions to develop these bonds" (Dalton and Weldon 2007: 179). But
citizens in new democracies do eventually begin to acquire partisanship, even absent socialization processes of the kind seen in more established democracies, in part because elections are
held, and so parties become prominent mobilizing forces (Dalton and Weldon 2007: 192). A
version of this pattern is also seen in Kroh (2014), who shows that partisanship is endogenous to
the system, coming about as a consequence of holding elections.

Adult immigrants are also interesting from the point of view of understanding whether partisanship can develop absent socialization. Such voters do not have childhood experiences that
socialize them into the party system of their new home. Immigrants may bring with them party
leanings from their previous home (Wals 2011, 2013) – hence there is still scope for a version
of the socialization argument – but obviously that scope is limited. In new democracies, some
families still have memories of pre-dictatorship political patterns and some immigrants may
remember the affiliations/orientations of their native country. In both instances, those memories may persist and color current orientations. But, while there may be some similarities between
ideology of parties between the old and new countries, or the same country in a previous generation, the current set of parties facing voters will be quite different. Even immigrants from one
established democracy to another and with similar institutions – say Canada to the UK or vice
versa – will face a very different choice set: the NDP is not the same as the Labour Party and the
Canadian Conservative Party has a different set of concerns than the UK Conservative Party.
Once in their new home, however, it is expected that people will acquire party attachments as
part of their new citizenship. In fact, acquiring a party identification is almost seen as part and
parcel of citizenship for new citizens.

A body of literature in the US case has begun to address the question of how people orient themselves to their new home (see, for example, Cain, Kiewiet and Uhlaner 1991; Wong 2000; Hajnal and Lee 2011). As we saw in the case of new democracies, the longer a person is in the political system the more likely it is that s/he will develop a party predisposition. Wong (2000), for example, finds that:

> A strong relationship between the number of years an immigrant has lived in the US and the acquisition of partisanship is found. Further analysis shows that naturalization, gains in English language skills, and media use also contribute to immigrants' acquisition of partisanship. This study reveals that a process of reinforcement through exposure to the political system underlies the development of political attitudes across diverse immigrant groups.
>
> *(Wong 2000: 341)*

The experience from both new democracies and new citizens shows that early socialization is not a necessary condition for the acquisition of party affiliation. People can, and do, develop party identifications simply as a consequence of being in the system itself. To use the phrase from Medeiros and Noël, there can be a "cognitive basis" to partisanship. In itself this should not be surprising; parties and elections are prominent features of news and life in any democracy. It seems reasonable, then, to expect people to develop some kind of response to political parties. While there is scope for an argument based in socialization processes, it seems that a socialization argument is unlikely to offer a complete understanding of party identification. Nevertheless, it does seem that a cognitive argument may also fail to offer a complete explanation of party identification; a point we return to below.

How does party identification vary?

We consider two sources of variation: variation across countries and over time.

As the simple descriptive patterns in Figure 12.1 show, the level of attachment to political parties varies considerably across nations. Averaged across all countries, 44 percent of people said they were close to a political party. The range around that average, however, is substantial, spreading from around 6 percent at the low end (Thailand) to 80 percent at the high end (Australia). As we noted above, some of that variation is attributable to variation in the stage of democratic development. But other cross-system variations are attributable to other factors.

One misleadingly simple issue is that of translating party identification into languages other than English. Schickler and Green (1997: 454) and Sinnott (1998), for example, document issues with translation between countries. Appendix A lists some notes on question wording taken from the CSES 3 survey, which give a sense of the different wording across nations. Even accepting that the phrasing "close to" is a reasonable representation of party identification as a concept we can see that the concept does not always travel easily across linguistic boundaries.

For Blais et al. (2001), survey responses on party identification are strongly affected by question wording and the relationship between party identification and variables such as party and leader ratings and voting behavior "does not quite conform to theoretical expectations" (Blais et al. 2001: 5). The results of Blais et al. are worth quoting at some length:

> The traditional question wording suggests that somewhere between two thirds (in Canada) and seven eighths (in Britain) of the electorate think of themselves as partisans. Yet, when the same people are asked if they think of themselves as close to

a party, the percentages of identifiers drop to between two and three fifths (Canada and the United States respectively). The overall average for the three countries goes from 76% to 48%.

(Blais et al. 2001: 18)[4]

At least one part of the issue is what to do with respondents who say they have "no identification" (Blais et al. 2001: 18). In the US case this has also surfaced in terms of how to address "independents" or those who "identify" as Independent. In 1954, the time of *The American Voter*, roughly 97 percent of the Californian electorate were registered either Democrat or Republican. By 2014 the share of registration by the two main parties had dropped to around 72 percent with roughly 25 percent of Californians reporting that they were "Independent." Independent voters are a source of some discussion within the US literature. For the most part, these have been interpreted as being partisans "really." In surveys, Independents are pushed to respond to a question over which of the two parties they really prefer. In this way the standard 5-point scale (Strong Democrats, Weak Democrats, Independents, Weak Republicans, Strong Republicans) can become a one-dimensional 7-point scale (Strong Democrats, Weak Democrats, Leaning Democrat, Independents, Leaning Republican, Weak Republicans, Strong Republicans). Part of the problem with doing this, even if Independents are "really" some form of partisan, is it undermines the argument to the effect that partisanship is a meaningful or appealing form of social identity. If social identity is an important component of partisanship then if a sizable share of voters see a social desirability bias pressing toward denying that identity it is hard to see how partisanship overall functions in the way it was originally thought. More worrisome for those who see partisanship in largely one-dimensional terms is that many Independents simply are not "really" partisans. Some Independents are quite critical of parties and the party system and their independent status does not so much reflect a lack of affect so much as disaffection from the choices on offer. In other words, in the US context, it seems that while some Independents are "really" partisan supporters of the two main parties some others are quite different. In practice, however, voters are generally presented with just two parties from which to choose, meaning that when we look at voting, Independents appear partisan.

Comparative work raises the question of whether the concept of party identification travels outside the US. Thomassen (1993) goes furthest to unsettle the value of party identification as a concept outside the US by arguing that, at least in the Dutch case, "party identification is not causally prior to the vote but simply a reflection of the vote and therefore causally posterior" (Thomassen 1993: 266) in part because there is instability over time – partisanship will track vote choice. Possibly related to Thomassen's concern, the long-standing discussion in political science relates to whether party identification is multi-dimensional or not, even in the US case. In the US the existence of a two-party system means that partisanship is sometimes represented as an interval level scale ranging from Strong Democrat to Strong Republican. In multiparty systems, such a representation does not make much sense (are weakly identifying German Greens to the left of or the right of strongly identifying SPD supporters?) but even in the US case the argument is persuasive that there is, in effect, both a policy distance dimension and also an affective dimension.

Other sources of cross-national variation are more systematic. At least some of the differences involve institutional variation: some institutions reinforce partisanship. At its simplest, ballots can differ in their presentation of what voters are choosing between – parties or candidates. Electoral systems will also permit or deny voters the opportunity to vote for one or many candidates. Furthermore, electoral systems – through their effects on the incentives facing parties and candidates – will offer many or few choices. Where voters are given multiple choices over candidates and parties – as under the Single Transferable Vote – it is likely that they will be less dug in on party choices. Huber, Kernell and Leoni (2005) find "that institutions that assist voters in retrospectively evaluating parties – specifically, strong party discipline and few parties in government – increase partisanship" (Huber, Kernell and Leoni 2005: 365). We see institutional effects, too, within the US. Norrander, for example, finds that "cross-state variation in independent identification is due to variations in state political characteristics such as interparty competition organizational strength of parties, type of primary, and primary turnout" (Norrander 1989: 516; see also Burden and Greene 2000).

Change over time is the other element of how partisanship may vary. Different schools of thought emphasize different sides of this coin: those grounded more in psychology and sociology emphasizing the stability of party attachments. Not surprisingly, if one's relationship to parties is anchored in one's sense of self then it is likely to be more stable than unstable over time. Sources of change in party id within an individual have, then, tended to come from models more grounded in economics. The standard way of seeing change at work is in Fiorina's "retrospective voting" model in which partisanship is seen as a summary measure updated by performance assessments. If – as does seem to be the case – party operates as a strong perceptual filter, then the rate of updating will necessarily be affected: strong partisans will only very slowly take on board negative information about their party. Neundorf and Adams (2015) show that issue preferences both influence partisanship but are, in turn, influenced by partisanship.

Neundorf, Stegmueller and Scotto (2011) use German panel data to show that the electorate – perhaps not surprisingly – is heterogeneous: there are groups of stable partisans with a strong affective attachment and others who are more performance driven and – hence – more fluid or "flexible." These authors argue for a concept of bounded partisanship in which voters stay within a particular party but with varying degrees of attachment. So, in a sense, they rely on multidimensionality to explore variation in affect as much as variation across party. Flexible partisans do not necessarily move to another party but, rather, to some version of "independence" (Neundorf, Stegmueller and Scotto 2011: 476). This is evidence that is, at least in passing, consistent with the idea that partisanship is two- and not one-dimensional. That is, partisan Social Democrats may blow hot and cold on their party over time, but remain Social Democrats; which means, in turn, that what we mean by stability or instability in party identification turns, at least in part, on whether we are considering change in the degree of affect toward the same party over time a measure of instability or just wish to consider change in party preference over time.

Discussion

This review has highlighted several persistent difficulties about the measure and use of party identification as a concept. There are, for example, questions about measurement which, at the very least, mean that it is probably not appropriate to treat party identification as an interval measure in statistical models (see in particular Neundorf, Stegmueller and Scotto 2011 and the literature reviewed there) in part because the measure is multi- rather than uni-dimensional. There is also a lot to be said for a cognitive approach to partisanship because such a model offers a way to explain change in partisanship over time by an individual. Arguments about socialization and generational change can help us understand change at the level of the cohort or possibly level of the electorate but seem less well-suited to helping understand change at the level of the individual. More to the point, experience of both adult immigrants and newly emerged democracies suggest that while socialization arguments may well explain party identification they fail to specify necessary conditions. That is, it is possible for party identification to develop absent socialization. Moreover, one of the consistent patterns we see in the literature is that party identification is endogenous to many features of the system. At its narrowest, party identification is endogenous to choosing from the set of parties running. This choice set obviously varies cross-nationally but can also vary within a nation across federal boundaries: the Scottish National Party does not run in England, the Christian Social Union does not run candidates outside Bavaria and so on. But it also seems to be the case that features of party loyalty vary by electoral system and other institutional arrangements. These variations in party identification by context would seem more amenable to analysis based on a cognitive approach to party identification. They are also, to some extent, under-studied. How and why voters change party allegiance – and the role of the parties themselves in conditioning those changes – seem to be not well understood.

While a more cognitive approach does have considerable promise, especially when it comes to understanding changes in identification, such an approach cannot help explain the affective component of party identification. If there is anything distinctive about partisanship as a concept it is that affective component. We know from work in other areas of political behavior (e.g., Valentino et al. 2011) that the emotional aspect to politics is an important one. At the risk of some over-simplifying, there are at least some analogies between party identification and sport fandom, although it is possible to over-state the correspondence. For example:

> When sports fans identify strongly with a team, they tend to experience more extreme feelings than those who identify weakly with a team. Among the affective consequences of sports fan identification … are level of arousal, sympathy, post-game affect and enjoyment.
>
> *(Dietz-Uhler and Lanter 2008: 106)*

All of which translate fairly readily into reactions at election time and relate to the politically relevant factors noted earlier, such as interest in and engagement with the political process, although the analogy does fall down when pushed too far. Nevertheless, discussing these issues is easier if we do conceptualize partisanship as multi-dimensional rather than uni-dimensional since that does allow us to break apart the question of party choice from the question of affect. It is entirely possible, of course, that ideology and affect are correlated: more extreme parties may be associated with more extreme affect. But we can only explore these issues if we adopt a more multi-dimensional approach to party identification.

Party identification has been an invaluable construct in helping us to understand a range of political behaviors among mass publics since its introduction into the discipline. But there are some difficulties to be aware of even as we continue to rely on party identification as a concept. Despite its flaws, however, there seems to be no construct in the literature ready to rival party identification as a guide to vote voice. Party identification will remain a central component of our understanding political behavior for the foreseeable future.

Appendix A: selected notes on wording of "close to a party" question from CSES 3 codebook

ELECTION STUDY NOTES – AUSTRALIA (2007):
This variable was reconstructed from party identification question B1: "Generally speaking, do you usually think of yourself as Liberal, Labor, National or what?"

ELECTION STUDY NOTES – BRAZIL (2010):
The wording in the Brazilian questionnaire slightly deviates from the original CSES question. It was asked as follows: "In general, is there any political party that you like?"

ELECTION STUDY NOTES – LATVIA (2010):

The wording in the Latvian questionnaire deviates from the CSES standard. The question asked was: "Do you feel yourself a little closer to one of the political parties than the others?"

ELECTION STUDY NOTES – MEXICO (2009):

Note that the Mexican wording deviates from the original CSES question. It was asked as follows: "Regardless of which party you voted for during the last election, in general, do you sympathize with any political party in particular?"

ELECTION STUDY NOTES – NETHERLANDS (2010):

Question text: "Do you think of yourself as an adherent to a certain political party?"

ELECTION STUDY NOTES – TAIWAN (2008):

Note that in the Taiwanese election study specific parties were named within the question text. It was asked as follows: "Among the main political parties in our country, including the KMT, DPP, NP, PFP and TSU, do you think of yourself as leaning towards any particular party?"

ELECTION STUDY NOTES – UNITED STATES (2008):

1   "Generally speaking, do you usually think of yourself as a Democrat, a Republican or an Independent?"
2   "If R considers self a Democrat/Republican: Would you call yourself a strong or a not very strong Democrat/Republican?"
3   "If R's party preference is Independent, no preference, other, don't know: Do you think of yourself as closer to the Republican Party or to the Democratic Party?"

Notes

1 Available from: www.cses.org/datacenter/download.htm. Party identifiers are those coded as replying yes to the question "Do you usually think of yourself as close to any particular party?" The variable "elections make a difference" is the percentage of people who respond with a 4 or 5 to the question: "Some people say that no matter who people vote for, it won't make any difference to what happens. Others say that who people vote for can make a big difference to what happens. Using the scale on this card (where ONE means that voting won't make any difference to what happens and FIVE means that voting can make a big difference), where would you place yourself?"
2 Some work suggests even more fundamental processes at work. Gerber et al. (2012) note the role of personality and partisanship. A somewhat more extreme version of this is found in the current literature on the genetic basis of politics. Settle, Dawes and Fowler (2009), for example, discuss the inheritability of party identifications – that is, there is a component of partisanship due to nature and not simply nurture. The findings on heritability are new and not uncontroversial. The more standard view of partisanship invokes processes of socialization.
3 One exception would be socialization into Communist parties in the case of post-Communist societies.
4 Although Schickler and Green (1997) find a great deal of stability over panels (see, for example, Tables 2a and 2b: 469–470), they generally report stability for Germany and the UK slightly different for Canada – average $R2$ between panels in the high 0.9s for Germany and UK, more like 0.8 for Canada.

References

Anduiza, E., Gallego, A. and Muñoz, J. (2013) "Turning a Blind Eye: Experimental Evidence of Partisan Bias in Attitudes Toward Corruption," *Comparative Political Studies*, vol. 46, no. 12, December, 1664–1692.

Blais, A., Gidengil, E., Nadeau, R. and Nevitte, N. (2001) "Measuring Party Identification: Britain, Canada, and the United States," *Political Behavior*, vol. 23, no. 1, March, 5–22.

Brader, T., Tucker, J. A. and Duell, D. (2013) "Which Parties Can Lead Opinion? Experimental Evidence on Partisan Cue Taking in Multiparty Democracies," *Comparative Political Studies*, vol. 46, no. 11, November, 1485–1517.

Burden, B. C. and Greene, S. (2000) "Party Attachments and State Election Laws," *Political Research Quarterly*, vol. 53, no. 1, March, 63–76.

Cain, B. E., Kiewiet, D. R. and Uhlaner, C. J. (1991) "The Acquisition of Partisanship by Latinos and Asian Americans," *American Journal of Political Science*, vol. 35, no. 2, May, 390–422.

Campbell, A., Gurin, G. and Miller, W. E. (1954) *The Voter Decides*, Oxford: Row, Peterson, and Co.

Dalton, R. J. and Weldon, S. (2007) "Partisanship and Party System Institutionalization," *Party Politics*, vol. 13, no. 2, March, 179–196.

Dietz-Uhler, B. and Lanter, J. R. (2008) "The Consequences of Sports Fan Identification," in Hugenberg, L. W., Haridakis, P. M. and Earnheardt, A. C. (eds.) *Sports Mania: Essays on Fandom and the Media in the 21st Century*, London: McFarland & Company: 103–113.

Dinas, E. (2014) "Why Does the Apple Fall Far from the Tree? How Early Political Socialization Prompts Parent-Child Dissimilarity," *British Journal of Political Science*, vol. 44, no. 4, October, 827–852.

Gerber, A. S., Huber, G. A., Doherty, D. and Dowling, C. M. (2012) "Personality and the Strength of Direction of Partisan Identification," *Political Behavior*, vol. 34, no. 4, December, 653–688.

Green, D. P., Palmquist, B. and Schickler, E. (2004) *Partisan Hearts and Minds: Political Parties and the Social Identities of Voters*, London: Yale University Press.

Hajnal, Z. L. and Lee, T. (2011) *Why Americans Don't Join the Party: Race, Immigration, and the Failure (of Political Parties) to Engage the Electorate*, Princeton: Princeton University Press.

Hibbing, J. R. and Theiss-Morse, E. (2002) *Stealth Democracy: Americans' Beliefs About How Government Should Work*, Cambridge, UK: Cambridge University Press.

Huber, J. D., Kernell, G. and Leoni, E. L. (2005) "Institutional Context, Cognitive Resources and Party Attachments Across Democracies," *Political Analysis*, vol. 13, no. 4, Autumn, 365–386.

Jennings, M. K. and Markus, G. B. (1984) "Partisan Orientations Over the Long Haul: Results from the Three-Wave Political Socialization Panel Study," *American Political Science Review*, vol. 78, no. 4, December, 1000–1018.

Jennings, M. K., Stoker, L. and Bowers, J. (2009) "Politics Across Generations: Family Transmission Reexamined," *Journal of Politics*, vol. 71, no. 3, July, 782–799.

Kroh, M. (2014) "Growth Trajectories in the Strength of Party Identification: The Legacy of Autocratic Regimes," *Electoral Studies*, vol. 33, March, 90–101.

Mainwaring, S. and Zoco, E. (2007) "Political Sequences and the Stabilization of Interparty Competition: Electoral Volatility in Old and New Democracies," *Party Politics*, vol. 13, no. 2, March, 155–178.

Medeiros, M., and Noël, A. (2013) "The Forgotten Side of Partisanship: Negative Party Identification in Four Anglo-American Democracies," *Comparative Political Studies*, vol. 47, no. 7, June, 1–24.

Neundorf, A. and Adams, J. (2015) "The Micro-Foundation of Party Competition and Issue Ownership: The Reciprocal Effects of Citizens' Issue Salience and Party Attachments," *British Journal of Political Science*, available online: https://doi.org/10.1017/S0007123415000642.

Neundorf, A., Stegmueller, D. and Scotto, T. J. (2011) "The Individual-Level Dynamics of Bounded Partisanship," *Public Opinion Quarterly*, vol. 75, no. 3, Autumn, 458–482.

Norrander, B. (1989) "Explaining Cross-State Variation in Independent Identification," *American Journal of Political Science*, vol. 33, no. 2, May, 516–536.

Sapiro, V. (2004) "Not Your Parents' Political Socialization: Introduction for a New Generation," *Annual Review of Political Science*, vol. 7, June, 1–23.

Schickler, E., and Green, D. P. (1997) "The Stability of Party Identification in Western Democracies: Results from Eight Panel Surveys," *Comparative Political Studies*, vol. 30, no. 4, August, 450–483.

Settle, J. E., Dawes, C. T. and Fowler, J. H. (2009) "The Heritability of Partisan Attachment," *Political Research Quarterly*, vol. 62, no. 3, September, 601–613.

Sinnott, R. (1998) "Party Attachment in Europe: Methodological Critique and Substantive Implications," *British Journal of Political Science*, vol. 28, no. 4, October, 627–650.

Thomassen, J. A. (1993) "Party Identification as a Cross-National Concept: Its Meaning in the Netherlands," in Niemi, R. G. and Weisberg, H. F. (eds.) *Classics in Voting Behavior*, London: Sage: 263–266.

Valentino, N. A., Brader, T., Groenendyk, E. W., Gregorowicz, K. and Hutchings, V. L. (2011) "Election Night's Alright for Fighting: The Role of Emotions in Political Participation," *Journal of Politics*, vol. 73, no, 1, January, 156–170.

Wals, S. C. (2011) "Does What Happens in Los Mochis Stay in Los Mochis? Explaining Postmigration Political Behavior," *Political Research Quarterly*, vol. 64, no. 3, September, 600–611.

Wals, S. C. (2013) "Made in the USA? Immigrants' Imported Ideology and Political Engagement," *Electoral Studies*, vol. 32, no. 4, December, 756–767.

Wlezien, C., Franklin, M. and Twiggs, D. (1997) "Economic Perceptions and Vote Choice: Disentangling the Endogeneity," *Political Behavior*, vol. 19, no. 1, March, 7–17.

Wong, J. S. (2000) "The Effects of Age and Political Exposure on the Development of Party Identification Among Asian American and Latino Immigrants in the United States," *Political Behavior*, vol. 22, no. 4, December, 341–371.

13

TRENDS IN PARTISANSHIP

Oliver Heath

Introduction

Party identification, defined as an enduring commitment or attachment to a particular political party, has for more than half a century been at the heart of research on electoral behavior in many countries around the world. The traditional view is that party identification develops at an early age, largely through the influence of parents, is remarkably stable throughout life, is relatively unaffected by short-term forces, and acts as a central organizing force for other political perceptions and preferences (Campbell et al. 1960).

Although the concept of party identification has been the subject of vigorous debate (see Chapter 12), it is thought to serve a number of important functions that help to integrate citizens with political processes. It serves as a "perceptual screen" that helps voters to organize their political evaluations and judgments. That is, once voters acquire a partisan identity, they tend to view politics from a more partisan perspective. A sense of party identification also performs a mobilizing function. It creates and reinforces a sense of loyalty toward a given political party and thereby encourages individuals to vote for their party. In doing so, party identification helps to incorporate and stabilize social demands and facilitate participation in the electoral system.

Whereas it has long been recognized that partisanship tends to be weak in new democracies; it has also been observed that in many established democracies partisanship has been on the wane. As partisanship has weakened, elections have become less stable and more unpredictable. Voters no longer have a standing decision for which party to vote; and make up their mind who to vote for (or whether to vote at all) late in the campaign. This chapter provides a brief overview of research on these different themes. The first part of the chapter documents the changes that have taken place in partisan attachments over the last 50 years or so in different established democracies. The second part considers a range of different explanations for why partisanship has weakened. Finally, the third part of the chapter considers some of the more notable consequences of partisan dealignment for electoral behavior.

Measuring party identification

Comparative research on partisanship has been hampered by a number of methodological challenges. The idea of party identification means different things in different countries – and so it is not always possible to compare like with like. Moreover, self-reported levels of party identification are very sensitive to question wording – and even slight changes in how questions are worded (including how they are translated) can have a substantial effect on the number of people who declare an identification (or attachment).

The concept of party identification was first developed in the USA, where voters have to register as supporters of either the Democrats or the Republicans in order to vote in Presidential primaries. Because voters declare themselves as either "Democrats," "Republicans," or "Independents" – even if they occasionally vote for other parties – the idea of party identification as something separate from vote choice has a clear intuitive meaning, which is not always so apparent in other countries.

The traditional measure of party identification, developed in the US context, bluntly asks "Generally speaking, do you usually think of yourself as a Republican, a Democrat, an Independent, or what?" Respondents who reply Republican or Democrat are then asked to say how strongly they think of themselves in that way. By and large this question has not been asked in the same way in comparative research; partly because it becomes somewhat cumbersome to ask in multi-party systems, and partly because it is a somewhat leading question, which presupposes that respondents have an identification to declare in the first place (Heath and Johns 2010). A second, more widely used measure of party attachment is "Do you usually think of yourself as close to any particular political party?" Respondents who answer "yes" are then asked a follow-up question: "What party is that?" Respondents are said to hold a "party attachment" if they answer "yes" to the first question and can then name a valid party.

Trends in partisanship over time

A growing body of research has shown that in many Western democracies the level of partisanship has noticeably declined over the last few decades (Dalton 1984, 2006, 2012; Mair and Biezen 2001; Schmitt 2009). This process is often referred to as partisan dealignment. In one of the first comparative studies on the topic, Dalton and Wattenberg (2000) found a substantial decline in partisan identification between 1976 and 1992 in Western Europe, and in an updated and expanded analysis, Dalton (2012) shows that the trend continues into the 2000s.

Dalton's (2012) table is reproduced below (Table 13.1). The data come from the National Election Studies of the respective countries. The first column of data in the table shows how many people in each country declared a partisan affiliation at the start of the time period (averaged across the first two time points). Not too much should be read in to differences between countries, as the questions used to measure party attachment vary somewhat between studies. The second column – which is more revealing – shows how much the level of partisanship has changed over time. In all the countries the change has been negative, indicating that the level of partisanship has declined. For example, Dalton (2012: 178) reports that in Sweden 65 percent of the public expressed a partisan attachment in 1968, compared to just 28 percent in 2010. The per annum change of –0.86 indicates that in a typical decade the level of partisanship declined by 8.6 percentage points. Overall, in practically all the countries, the level of partisanship is lower in the 2000s than it was in the 1960s and early 1970s. This apparently common trend has attracted a great deal of attention. As Putnam et al. (2000: 17–18) note, "seldom does such a diverse group of nations reveal so consistent a trend. The only major variation is in the timing of the decline." An observation echoed by Dalton (2012: 178), who writes "seldom does the public opinion evidence from such a diverse group of nations follow such a consistent trend."

However, it is also worth noting that there is considerable variation between countries both in terms of the extent of the decline and the speed of the decline (Berglund et al. 2005). For

Table 13.1 Trends in party identification across countries

Country	% with PID	Per annum change	Period	Time points
Australia	92	−0.20	1967–2010	13
Austria	67	−0.56	1969–2009	9
Britain	93	−0.32	1964–2010	12
Canada	90	−0.54	1965–2006	12
Denmark	52	−0.03	1971–2005	11
Finland	57	−0.26	1975–2007	6
France	73	−0.79	1967–2002	6
Germany	78	−0.51	1972–2009	11
Italy	80	−0.78	1975–2008	9
Japan	70	−0.59	1962–2000	12
Netherlands	38	−0.19	1971–2006	11
New Zealand	87	−1.12	1975–2008	12
Norway	66	−0.66	1965–2005	11
Sweden	64	−0.85	1968–2010	14
Switzerland	61	−0.63	1971–2007	10
United States	77	−0.33	1952–2008	15

Source: Reproduced from Dalton (2012: 178). Original source: National Election Studies in each country.

Note
The percentage with a party identification is the average of the percentage expressing a party identification in the first two surveys in each series.

example, whereas partisanship has dramatically declined in Sweden since the 1960s it has barely changed in Denmark. Whereas partisanship has declined in the UK, over the last few decades it has in fact increased in the USA (Bartels 2000). To illustrate some of these divergent trends, Figures 13.1 and 13.2 depict the level of partisanship in the UK and USA over time, using data from their respective National Election Studies. These two countries have been the subject of a great deal of research on partisanship; but also exhibit rather different trends.

The concept of party identification was imported to the UK by Butler and Stokes (1969). Party identification in Britain had a clear class basis – working class people tended to be Labour identifiers and middle class people tended to be Conservative identifiers, and when voters went to the polls they expressed their "tribal loyalties." However, as early as the 1970s, Crewe et al. (1977) noticed that these party identifications were weakening. Clarke et al. (2004) document that this process of partisan dealignment has been ongoing. As Figure 13.1 shows, in Britain the average strength of party identification has substantially declined. The percentage of the electorate who identified "very strongly" with a political party has fallen from 45 percent in 1964 to 11 percent in 2010. At the same time, the proportion of non-identifiers has increased from 5 percent to 19 percent during the same period.

By contrast, Figure 13.2 shows in the USA the strength of partisanship declined very sharply from the 1960s to the late 1970s, but since then has in fact increased (see also Bartels 2000). During the 1970s, a raft of publications drew attention to the increasing proportion of "independents" and the increasing prevalence of split-ticket voting as indicators of partisan decline (Broder 1971; DeVries and Tarrance 1972). Niemi and Weisberg (1976: 414) went as far as to say that these developments signified "the end of parties." However, these authors were writing at a particular low point in the history of partisanship in the USA. Since then

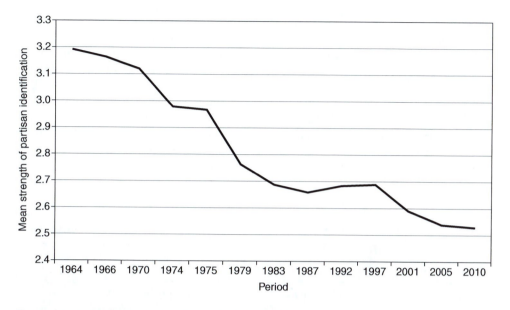

Figure 13.1 Strength of party identification in the UK, 1964–2010

Source: British Election Study, 1964–2010.

Note

Strength of party identification is measured on a 1–4 scale; where 1=no party ID; 2=not very strongly; 3=fairly strongly; 4=very strongly.

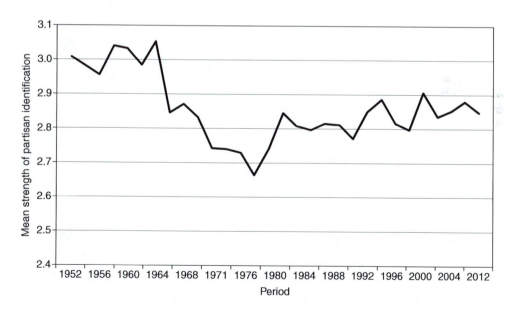

Figure 13.2 Strength of party identification in the USA, 1952–2012

Source: ANES cumulative file.

Note

Strength of party identification is measured on a 1–4 scale; where 1=independent; 2=leaning independent; 3=weak partisan; 4=strong partisan.

party identification has not only increased, but has also become a better predictor of vote choice (Bartels 2000).

As Holmberg (2007) concludes, there is no uniform, secular trend downwards for partisanship in Western democracies, and the pattern differs rather dramatically by country. Although some countries have witnessed a pronounced decline in partisanship others have not. With respect to the USA in particular, Bartels (2000) cautions that the conventional wisdom regarding the "decline of parties" is both exaggerated and outdated. To understand why partisanship declines (or not) we must therefore be sensitive to the different trends that are evident between countries as well as the different trends that are evident within countries, where levels of partisanship can go both up and down.

Explaining partisan dealignment

Why were voters once so willing to name a preferred party, and why – in so many democracies – are they so unwilling to do so in the present? Answers to these simple questions remain a matter of dispute. Broadly speaking, previous research on the decline of partisanship has tended to fall into one of two camps: those that emphasize social changes that have taken place within the electorate, such as the spread of education, and those that emphasize political changes that have taken place within political parties (such as policy convergence or polarization). These two accounts provide very different explanations for why partisanship has declined, and also suggest very different implications for the consequences of this decline (which I discuss in the next section).

Cognitive mobilization

One influential explanation for partisan dealignment argues that changes that have occurred within the electorate, such as rising living standards, the spread of affluence, and, particularly, the expansion of higher education, have led to an electorate that is more sophisticated, more demanding and critical of government activity, less deferential, and more likely to challenge authority than in the past (Norris 1999; Dalton 2002, 2006). This thesis posits that there has been gradual decline in partisanship over time, and that this decline is driven by social change. Citizens now possess the political resources and skills that help them to deal with the complexities of politics without reliance on party cues (Dalton 1984, 2007) and as a consequence people have become less likely to identify with a political party.

According to this perspective, the spread of education in advanced industrial democracies has increased the political sophistication of citizens. At the same time, these countries have also experienced an "information explosion" through the mass media (Holmberg 2007). Because of this "cognitive mobilization" (CM) more voters are now able to deal with the complexities of politics and make their own political decisions (Dalton 1984, 2007). Thus, the functional need for partisan cues to guide voting behavior is declining for a growing number of citizens (Dalton 1984, 2007).

This account draws on the argument made by Shively (1979) that party identification serves a functional role in helping citizens with low levels of political information to make decisions about how to vote. Becoming well-informed bears costs, and these costs are higher for those who are poorly educated and who receive little exposure to information about current events (Albright 2009). If the functional model is correct, then one should expect partisanship to decline as mass publics become better educated and as the mass media become more prevalent.

Although this argument provides a compelling narrative, the evidence to support the narrative is hotly contested. In a series of articles, Dalton charts the growth of what he terms the cognitive partisan and the decline of the ritual partisan. Cognitive partisans are attached to a political party but importantly also possess the cognitive resources (measured in terms of education and political interest) to be involved in politics even when party cues are lacking. By contrast, ritual partisans are attached to a political party but lack cognitive sophistication. Over time, in a number of different countries, the proportion of cognitive partisans within the electorate has increased and the proportion of ritual partisans has decreased. Yet showing this is not quite the same as demonstrating that the spread of education has weakened partisanship. Rather, it shows that partisans are now better educated than they were previously, which – given the spread of education – is hardly a surprise.

However, the theory of a CM argues that citizens are likely to abandon partisan attachments as they become better informed about politics and gain exposure to mass media. A number of comparative studies have directly tested this hypothesis. Berglund et al. (2005) show the decline of party identification in North Europe has in fact been sharper among the less well-educated than it has been among the university educated, the opposite of what CM would suggest. Lupu (2015) shows that partisanship is stronger among the well-educated; Albright (2009) shows that CM actually increases the probability that a respondent expresses an attachment to a specific party, and this positive relationship does not change across cohorts. Similarly, Huber et al. (2005) show that partisan attachments *increase* with cognitive resources.

A number of single-country case studies have also tested the CM hypothesis. Examining partisan dealignment in Germany, Arzheimer (2006: 799) observes that CM can be "quickly ruled out" since the relationship between education and partisanship was not statistically significant during the late 1970s, and in fact became significantly *positive* toward the end of the period under study. Thus, if anything, the so-called "educational revolution" hampered the decline of partisanship. Also in Germany Dassonneville and Dejaeghere (2014) find that, although at the aggregate rising levels of political sophistication have occurred simultaneously with decreasing partisanship, individual level analysis clearly suggests that the least sophisticated are most likely to feel alienated from the party system. Studies in Italy (Poletti 2015) and France (Marthaler 2008) also find results that contradict the CM hypothesis.

This body of work presents something of a challenge to CM. There is little evidence to support the idea that the spread of education has had a direct negative impact on partisanship, and a number of studies suggest that it may have had a positive impact. Moreover, CM does not explain why partisanship has declined in some developed democracies (such as Sweden) but not others (such as Denmark), or why in some circumstances partisanship has increased (such as in the USA).

In order to appreciate the differences between countries – as well as within them – it is necessary to consider the role that the political context plays in shaping partisanship. As previously noted, in many democracies, notably Britain, partisan identity had a strong class component. But in many of these same democracies the impact of class as an electoral cleavage has declined over time. This has led to a decline in the strength of partisanship, particularly among young people, who – since they no longer grow up in such partisan households – are not socialized in the same way into a specific partisan identity (van der Eijk and Franklin 2009: 180). In order to understand the decline of partisanship we must therefore also understand the changing political context to do with the decline of social cleavages, which is discussed in detail in Evans and Northmore-Ball in this volume (see also van der Brug and Franklin in this volume).

Policy polarization

The political context may also have a more direct effect on party identification, which brings us to the second main approach to explaining the decline of party identification that relates to the supply side of what parties offer voters and what parties stand for. The policy polarization thesis contends that the extent to which citizens identify with a political party depends at least in part upon how distinctive the parties are with respect to their policy platforms. If all the parties in a country adopt similar policies, then voters might not care very much which party wins. But if parties adopt very distinctive policies, citizens may also form stronger party attachments. Party polarization may therefore strengthen party brands and clarify voters' choices (Lupu 2015), and presented with a clearer set of choices among parties, citizens may also form stronger party attachments (Lupu 2015).

The idea that party identification is related to the political context is somewhat at odds with the orthodox perspective on party identification as originally developed by the Michigan school (Campbell et al. 1960). According to this perspective, party identification is a psychological attachment rooted in early-adult socialization experiences, and is relatively immune from changes in the political context. However, a more revisionist view treats party identification as a "running tally" of retrospective evaluations of party performance (Fiorina 1981). According to this perspective, party identification is supposed to vary with the political–institutional context rather than with the social structure of society (see Huber et al. 2005).

One reason, then, why partisanship may have declined more in some countries rather than others, or declined at certain times, is to do with how parties have changed, rather than how the voters have changed. A number of studies on the United States show that people perceive more policy differences between Democrats and Republicans today than in the 1970s (Wattenberg 1998; Hetherington 2001). The American parties have become more different and distinct in the eyes of the voters, making it easier and more meaningful to identify strongly with one of them. This period of party polarization coincides with a resurgence of mass partisanship since the 1970s (Abramowitz and Saunders 2008; Bartels 2000; Brewer 2005; Hetherington 2001; Levendusky 2009). By contrast, data from Sweden, where the strength of party identification is falling, show that people over the last 20 years perceive fewer and fewer ideological differences between the parties, especially between the Social Democrats and the largest non-socialist party, the Conservatives (Holmberg 2007).

A number of early comparative studies gave support to this idea. Schmitt and Holmberg (1995) found that the decline in the strength of party identification tended to be related to weakening party polarization, declining ideological conflicts, diminished issue differences, and increases in the number of political parties. Berglund et al.'s (2005) study on six north European countries finds that the more polarized a party system is, the more numerous party identifiers are. They conclude that there is clear evidence that party polarization leads to a higher level of party identification. Lupu's (2015) study of over 30 democracies from across the world supports this view and finds that party polarization correlates with partisanship across time and across countries. Lastly, Huber et al. (2005) find that party attachments increase with greater clarity of party responsibility (a low number of legislative parties).

In sum, although it is clear that partisan attachments have weakened considerably in a number of Western democracies, it is less clear why. Part may be due to the changing media environment, and the volume and tone of information that is now available to citizens in advanced democracies. Part may also be due to how voters have changed. But importantly parties and politicians have also changed. In the USA, parties have become more polarized, whereas in many other democracies they have become more socially and politically similar (Evans and

De Graaf 2013). There is now growing evidence that this social and political similarity has weakened the class basis of party support in many European democracies (Heath 2015; Evans and Tilley 2012; Elff 2009), which historically formed the basis for partisan attachments.

The consequences of partisan dealignment

What impact does partisan dealignment have on the functioning of democracy and the ways in which citizens participate in the political system? Has partisan dealignment led to the emergence of sophisticated and critical citizens who are more likely to hold the government to account for what it has delivered (or failed to deliver)? Or has it led to political alienation and withdrawal from the political process? The answers to these questions have important implications for the long-term health of democracy, and are also a topic of lively debate and controversy.

It is well known that partisanship has a number of behavioral consequences. People with a strong sense of party identification are more likely to vote (Heath 2007), more likely to participate in election campaigns (Finkel and Opp 1991), and more likely to vote consistently for a particular political party (Dalton et al. 2000). By contrast non-partisans are more likely to vote for different parties from one election to the next, and to make a final decision closer to the date of the election (Dalton et al. 2000).

The weakening of partisan attachments therefore has important implications for the functioning of democratic politics. Parties no longer act as such an important source of political information or perceptual screen for many voters, who in turn are likely to be more easily swayed by cues from other sources, such as the media. Perhaps more importantly, (at least some) voters are less tribal, and their sense of loyalty to political parties has gradually given way to a more conditional form of support, based on governments' performance and management of the economy (Sanders et al. 2001; Clarke et al. 2009), although this could be a feature of younger voters whose partisanship increases with age (see van der Brug and Franklin in this volume).

In addition, since non-partisans are more likely to switch their vote between elections – and there are now many more non-partisans than there used to be – elections are more volatile and less predictable. Dalton and Wattenberg (2000) present evidence consistent with this hypothesis, and show that electoral volatility has increased across a wide range of democracies. High levels of partisanship thus reduce electoral volatility and encourage party system stability (see Mainwaring and Zoco 2007). However, it is also possible that electoral volatility could be a source of partisan dealignment. Party identity not only strengthens with age, but also strengthens with the repetition of voting for the same party over successive elections (Butler and Stokes 1969). During periods of high electoral volatility, this repetition is interrupted, which could delay the formation of a strong party identity. In particular, young people who have not yet developed a strong party identification may be more likely to vote for a new party or to change which party they support, which may prevent them from forming strong bonds with any one party in particular.

Lastly, since non-partisans tend to make up their mind about who to vote for later in the campaign, and there are now more non-partisans than there used to be, election campaigns have become more important for helping people decide which party to vote for (Kosmidis and Xezonakis 2010). In the era of strong partisan attachments, election outcomes could be predicted on the basis of prior dispositions, and so campaigns were thought to matter little (Campbell et al. 1960). However, as Dalton and Wattenberg (2000: 48) report, the proportion of people who decide who to vote for during an election campaign has substantially increased in many democracies. For example, according to British Election Study data just 11 percent of voters were undecided about who to vote for at the start of the campaign in 1964; whereas in

2005 approximately 35 percent were undecided. Kosmidis and Xezonakis (2010) show that these undecided voters tend to be particularly sensitive to short-term issues, such as the economy. Whereas previously election campaigns were primarily about mobilizing existing supporters to turn out and vote, now they are also opportunities for persuasion.

This development has led to a subtle shift in the determinants of election outcomes. It has long been recognized that strong partisans are less responsive to short-term factors in making their voting decision (Converse and Dupeux 1962). Building on this insight, Kayser and Wlezien (2011) argue that if partisanship does inure the electorate to short-term shocks, partisan decline should imply a greater responsiveness to such shocks, be they economic or otherwise. Kayser and Wlezien (2011) show that the rising proportion of non-partisans (individuals without an affinity toward a political party) in European electorates means that voters respond more to the economy than in the past. They interpret this as a positive development, which enhances mechanisms of accountability.

Whereas some of these developments sound positive, partisan dealignment may also have a number of less desirable consequences. For example, according to Dassonneville and Dejaeghere (2014), the decline of party identification in Germany represents a form of alienation from the political system in general, and more specifically toward the party system. This withdrawal from the political process is evident in a number of ways. Since partisans tend to be more likely to vote than non-partisans, the increase of non-partisans within the electorate may have led to a decline in turnout (Heath 2007). According to Heath (2007), partisan dealignment in Britain between 1964 and 2005 is responsible for a decline in turnout of almost 7 percentage points.

Moreover, the decline of party attachments may have also made voters more responsive to outsider or niche parties. In recent years, a number of anti-politics parties have gained electoral success, from the 5 Star Movement in Italy to UKIP in the UK. With respect to UKIP in particular, Evans and Mellon (2016) show that the party was particularly successful at attracting the votes of people who *used to be* partisans, but had become disenfranchised with Labour's move to the "Liberal Consensus" on the EU and immigration (which occurred before UKIP became an electoral force).

There is also evidence that non-partisans are more swayed by personality and candidate traits than they are by party labels. One the one hand, this had led to the emergence of "leadership effects" – where voters pay particular attention to the credibility and competence of party leaders. This is often understood within a valence framework (Clarke et al. 2004) that emphasizes the politics of competence and performance. According to Hayes and McAllister (1997: 3), election outcomes are now, more than at any time in the past, determined by voters' assessments of party leaders. The reasoning is that if the number of partisans tends to decline, there is greater room for other factors, especially political leaders, to affect vote choice (Aarts et al. 2013: 5).

But on the other hand non-partisans may also be receptive to charismatic populist leaders too. In democracies where partisanship is strong, elections tend to be relatively stable and predictable. In contrast, in democracies where partisanship is weak, elections often become an arena for charismatic or demagogic leaders to seize power without any real advancement of the public good or long-term policy commitments (Kitschelt et al. 1999; Hicken and Kuhonta 2011). Weak partisanship greatly reduces the quality of representation and the predictability of policies, both of which are necessary for the stable development of a polity (Kitschelt et al. 1999).

Conclusion

Partisanship has weakened in many advanced democracies – though by no means all of them. This finding alone is enough to cast doubt on some of the more popular explanations for partisan decline. If – as many scholars have argued – modernization undermines partisanship, why then has party identification declined so much in Sweden but not Denmark? And why has partisanship in the USA increased over the last 20 years? And if the spread of education is responsible for declining party attachments, why are party attachments stronger among the well-educated than the lower-educated? Clearly social change can, at best, only be part of the story.

Perhaps then a more fruitful line of inquiry is to consider the role that parties themselves have played in the process of partisan dealignment. When parties provide the electorate with clear choices and there are clear differences between the parties, it is easier for voters to identify with one party over another. As parties in many advanced democracies have become more similar, and converged on the mythical center ground, voters have become less able to distinguish between parties – and as a consequence are less likely to express a partisan attachment. These different accounts have important implications for our understanding of why partisanship has declined, but also have important implications for the potential consequences of this decline.

The modernization approach does not necessarily regard partisan dealignment as a negative development for the functioning of democracy. The rise of cognitive mobilization means that voters now make more informed decisions based on policy positions and economic performance, both of which augur well for strengthening chains of accountability. By contrast, the policy polarization perspective implies that partisan dealignment stems from disillusionment with the mainstream alternatives, and perhaps even alienation from the political process. If the parties all look the same, people do not identify with a party, are less likely to vote, and are perhaps also more responsive to the appeals of outsider or fringe parties and charismatic politicians.

References

Aarts, K., Blais, A., and Schmitt, H. (eds.) (2013) *Political Leaders and Democratic Elections*, Oxford: Oxford University Press.

Abramowitz, A. I. and Saunders, K. L. (2008) "Is Polarization a Myth?," *Journal of Politics*, vol. 70, no. 2, April, 542–555.

Albright, J. J. (2009) "Does Political Knowledge Erode Party Attachments? A Review of the Cognitive Mobilization Thesis," *Electoral Studies*, vol. 28, no. 2, June, 248–260.

Arzheimer, K. (2006) "Dead Men Walking? Party Identification in Germany, 1977–2002," *Electoral Studies*, vol. 25, no. 4, December, 791–807.

Bartels, L. M. (2000) "Partisanship and Voting Behavior, 1952–1996," *American Journal of Political Science*, vol. 44, no. 1, January, 35–50.

Berglund, F., Holmberg, S., Schmitt, H., and Thomassen, J. (2005) "Party Identification and Party Choice," in Thomassen, J. (ed.) *The European Voter: A Comparative Study of Modern Democracies*, Oxford: Oxford University Press: 106–124.

Brewer, M. D. (2005) "The Rise of Partisanship and the Expansion of Partisan Conflict Within the American Electorate," *Political Research Quarterly*, vol. 58, no. 2, June, 219–229.

Broder, D. S. (1971) *The Party's Over: The Failure of Politics in America*, New York: Harper and Row.

Butler, D. and Stokes, D. (1969) *Political Change in Britain*, New York: St. Martin's Press.

Campbell, A., Converse, P. E., Miller, W. E., and Stokes, D. E. (1960) *The American Voter*, New York: Wiley.

Clarke, H. D., Sanders, D., Stewart, M. C., and Whiteley, P. (2004) *Political Choice in Britain*, Oxford: Oxford University Press.

Clarke, H., Sanders, D. Stewart, M., and Whiteley, P. (2009) *Performance Politics and the British Voter*, Cambridge: Cambridge University Press.

Converse, P. E. and Dupeux, G. (1962) "Politicization of the Electorate in France and the United States," *Public Opinion Quarterly*, vol. 26, no. 1, January, 1–23.

Crewe, I., Särlvik, B., and Alt, J. (1977) "Partisan Dealignment in Britain 1964–1974," *British Journal of Political Science*, vol. 7, no. 2, April, 129–190.

Dalton, R. J. (1984) "Cognitive Mobilization and Partisan Dealignment in Advanced Industrial Democracies," *Journal of Politics*, vol. 46, no. 1, February, 264–284.

Dalton, R. J. (2002) "Cognitive Mobilization and Partisan Dealignment," in Dalton, R. J. (ed.) *Citizen
Politics: Public Opinion and Political Parties in Advanced Industrial Democracies*, London: Chatham House
Publishers: 264–284.

Dalton, R. J. (2006) *Citizen Politics: Public Opinion and Political Parties in Advanced Industrial Democracies*, 4th
Edition, Washington, DC: CQ Press.

Dalton, R. J. (2007) "Partisan Mobilization, Cognitive Mobilization, and the Changing American Electorate," *Electoral Studies*, vol. 26, no. 2, June, 274–286.

Dalton, R. J. (2012) *The Apartisan American: Dealignment and Changing Electoral Politics*, CQ Press: Washington DC.

Dalton, R. J. and Wattenberg, M. P. (2000) *Parties Without Partisans: Political Change in Advanced Industrial
Democracies*, New York: Oxford University Press.

Dalton, R. J., McAllister, I., and Wattenberg, M. P. (2000) "The Consequences of Partisan Dealignment,"
in Dalton, R. J. and Wattenberg, M. P. (eds.) *Parties Without Partisans: Political Change in Advanced
Industrial Democracies*, New York: Oxford University Press: 37–63.

Dassonneville, R., and Dejaeghere, Y. (2014) "Bridging the Ideological Space: A Cross-National Analysis of
the Distance of Party Switching," *European Journal of Political Research*, vol. 53, no. 3, August, 580–599.

DeVries, W. and Tarrance, V. L. (1972) *The Ticket-Splitter: A New Force in American Politics*, Grand Rapids,
MI: William B. Eerdmans.

Eijk, C. van der and Franklin, N. (2009) *Elections and Voters*, London: Palgrave Macmillan.

Elff, M. (2009) "Social Divisions, Party Positions, and Electoral Behaviour," *Electoral Studies*, vol. 28, no.
2, June, 297–308.

Evans, G. and De Graaf, N. D. (eds.) (2013) *Political Choice Matters: Explaining the Strength of Class and
Religious Cleavages in Cross-National Perspective*, Oxford: Oxford University Press.

Evans, G. and Mellon, J. (2016) "Working Class Votes and Conservative Losses: Solving the UKIP Puzzle,"
Parliamentary Affairs, vol. 69, no. 2, April, 464–479.

Evans, G. and Tilley, J. (2012) "How Parties Shape Class Politics: Explaining the Decline of Class Party
Support," *British Journal of Political Science*, vol. 42, no. 1, January, 137–161.

Finkel, S. and Opp, K-D. (1991) "Party Identification and Participation in Collective Political Action,"
Journal of Politics, vol. 53, no. 2, May, 339–371.

Fiorina, M. (1981) *Retrospective Voting in American Elections*, New Haven: Yale University Press.

Hayes, B. and McAllister, I. (1997) "Gender, Party Leaders, and Election Outcomes in Australia, Britain,
and the United States," *Comparative Political Studies*, vol. 30, no. 1, February, 3–26.

Heath, O. (2007) "Explaining Turnout Decline in Britain, 1964–2005: Party Identification and the Political Context," *Political Behavior*, vol. 29, no. 4, December, 493–516.

Heath, O. (2015) "Policy Representation, Social Representation, and Class Voting in Britain," *British
Journal of Political Science*, vol. 45, no. 1, January, 173–193.

Heath, O. and Johns, R. (2010) "Measuring Political Behaviour and Attitudes," in Bulmer, M. (ed.) *Social
Measurement Through Social Surveys: An Applied Approach*, Farnham: Ashgate: 47–68.

Hetherington, M. J. (2001) "Resurgent Mass Partisanship: The Role of Elite Polarization," *American Political Science Review*, vol. 95, no. 3, September, 619–631.

Hicken, A. and Kuhonta, E. (2011) "Shadows from the Past: Party System Institutionalization in Asia,"
Comparative Political Studies, vol. 44, no. 5, May, 572–597.

Holmberg, S. (2007) "Partisanship Reconsidered," in Dalton, R. and Klingermann, H. (eds.) *The Oxford
Handbook of Political Behavior*, Oxford: Oxford University Press: 557–570.

Huber, J. D., Kernell, G., and Leoni, E. L. (2005) "Institutional Context, Cognitive Resources, and Party
Attachments Across Democracies," *Political Analysis*, vol. 13, vol. 4, July, 365–386.

Kayser, M. and Wlezien, C. (2011) "Performance Pressure: Patterns of Partisanship and the Economic
Vote," *European Journal of Political Research*, vol. 50, no. 3, May, 365–394.

Kitschelt, H., Lange, P., Marks, G., and Stephens, J. D. (1999) "Convergence and divergence in advanced
capitalist democracies," in Kitchelt, H., Lang, P., Marks, G., and Stephens, J. (eds.) *Continuity and
Change in Contemporary Capitalism*, Cambridge: Cambridge University Press: 427–460.

Kosmidis, S. and Xezonakis, G. (2010) "The Undecided Voters and the Economy: Campaign Heterogeneity in the 2005 British General Election," *Electoral Studies*, vol. 29, no. 4, December, 604–616.

Levendusky, M. S. (2009) *The Partisan Sort: How Liberals Became Democrats and Conservatives Became Republicans*, Chicago: The University of Chicago Press.

Lupu, N. (2015) "Party Polarization and Mass Partisanship: A Comparative Perspective," *Political Behavior*, vol. 37, no. 2, June, 331–356.

Mainwaring, S. and Zoco, E. (2007) "Political Sequences and the Stabilization of Interparty Competition Electoral Volatility in Old and New Democracies," *Party Politics*, vol. 13, no. 2, March, 155–178.

Mair, P. and van Biezen, I. (2001) "Party Membership in Twenty European Democracies, 1980–2000," *Party Politics*, vol. 7, no. 1, January, 5–21.

Marthaler, S. (2008) "The Paradox of the Politically-Sophisticated Partisan: The French Case," *West European Politics*, vol. 31, no. 5, August, 937–959.

Niemi, R. G. and Weisberg, H. F. (1976) "Are Parties Becoming Irrelevant?," in Niemi, R. G. and Weisberg, H. F. (eds.) *Controversies in American Voting Behavior*, San Francisco: W. H. Freeman and Company: 413–421.

Norris, P. (1999) *Critical Citizens: Global Support for Democratic Government*, Oxford: Oxford University Press.

Poletti, M. (2015) "The Cognitive Mobilization of Organizational Participation: Missing Evidence from Italy (1972–2006)," *Electoral Studies*, vol. 40, December, 245–255.

Putnam, R. D., Pharr, S. J., and Dalton, R. J. (2000) "Introduction: What's Troubling the Trilateral Democracies?," in Pharr, S. J. and Putnam, R. D. (eds.) *Disaffected Democracies: What's Troubling the Trilateral Democracies*, Princeton: Princeton University Press: 1–3.

Sanders, D., Clarke, H., Stewart, M., and Whiteley, P. (2001) "The Economy and Voting," *Parliamentary Affairs*, vol. 54, no. 4, October, 789–802.

Schmitt, H. (2009) "Partisanship in Nine Western Democracies: Causes and Consequences," in Bartle, J. and Bellucci, P. (eds.) *Political Parties and Partisanship: Social Identity and Individual Attitudes*, London: Routledge: 75–87.

Schmitt, H. and Holmberg, S. (1995) "Political Parties in Decline?," in Klingemann H-D. and Fuchs, D. (eds.) *Citizens and the State*, Oxford: Oxford University Press: 95–133.

Shively, W. P. (1979) "The Development of Party Identification Among Adults: Exploration of a Functional Model," *American Political Science Review*, vol. 73, no. 4, December, 1039–1054.

Wattenberg, M. (1998) *The Decline of American Political Parties 1952–1988*, Cambridge, MA: Harvard University Press.

14

POLITICS, MEDIA AND THE ELECTORAL ROLE OF PARTY LEADERS

Anthony Mughan and Loes Aaldering

Introduction

The leaders of political parties are seen as key figures in the democratic political process as they take primary responsibility for organizing their parties' efforts to win elections and, if victorious, for governing the people and the country they have been chosen to serve. Interestingly, however, the conventional wisdom has been that, with the exception of presidential candidates in the US, these same key political figures exert very little influence on election outcomes given their limited impact on individuals' vote choice. Essentially indistinguishable in the eyes of voters from the party they represented, party leaders failed to influence the vote independently of the strong, social cleavage-based partisan loyalties that were the norm for much of the post-1945 period. Put differently, party leaders in parliamentary systems of government were dismissed as at best bit players in the larger election drama (Butler and Stokes 1969). More recently, however, perceptions have changed dramatically and the study of the electoral effects of party leaders is a growth area in the study of democratic mass political behavior (Bean and Mughan 1989; Aarts, Blais and Schmitt 2011; Bittner 2011).

Two particular developments are generally offered to explain the emergence of parliamentary party leaders as electoral forces in their own right. The first concerns a fundamental change in the electorate and the second in the media environment in which elections take place. Let us take the changing electorate first. Over the last several decades, voters' loyalties to political parties have generally weakened as the social cleavages on which those affiliations were based have become less salient. In addition, many voters have become disillusioned with established parties' performance in office (Franklin, Mackie and Valen 1992; Pharr and Putnam 2000). Commonly referred to as "partisan dealignment," this process undermined the tendency to vote out of long-term habitual party loyalty and made way for election-specific, or short-term, forces to exercise a greater influence on the vote decision (Dalton and Wattenberg 2000). As originally expounded in the context of US presidential elections, prominent among these short-term forces were policy issues and candidates (with parliamentary party leaders being the functionally equivalent competitors for the position of chief executive) (Campbell et al. 1966). The door was thus opened wider to election-specific influences on the vote decision and party leaders stepped over the threshold (McAllister 2007).

The second common reason given for enhanced leader effects in parliamentary elections is the transformed media environment in which these contests now take place. In particular, television gradually displaced newspapers and other communication forms as political parties' preferred campaigning medium and voters' principal source of political information. This shift partly reflected changing media consumption patterns in the country at large and partly reflected the desire of increasingly catch-all political parties to reach beyond their traditional support base to attract votes. Not only did television allow them to reach unprecedented numbers of voters, but it did so when they were in the comfort of their living rooms with their partisan defenses relatively low. The cost, though, was that parties had to adapt their campaigning strategies to the presentational "logic" of their new communications medium of choice (Altheide and Snow 1979). In particular, parties had to come to terms with television being a medium of communication that is better suited to the projection of personality than the discussion of complex issues. Thus, the foundations of a new prominence role for party leaders in a television age were laid.

Leaving these foundations aside, the key question that these developments pose for political scientists relates ultimately to the nature of leader effects. What is it about party leaders that gives them "added value" in the eyes of voters and what determines the extent of this value? The answers to these questions are not simple since electoral effects vary according to the leaders themselves, as well as across space and time. It is the purpose of this chapter to explore some of the major sources of this variation.

Leader effects

If only by virtue of their position of institutional leadership, party leaders can influence any number of political outcomes. They are usually, for example, the principal driving force behind government formation as well as policy proposals and outcomes. In specifically electoral terms, however, there are two major effects that they can have on voters. On the one hand, there is a reinforcement effect whereby, through their personality or actions, they strengthen partisan loyalties to the party that they lead in the election. On the other hand, there is a defection effect. This can be defined as the "added value, in electoral terms, that a specific … candidate is able to bring his/her party or coalition through the effectiveness of his/her public image as appraised at that specific time" (Barisione 2009: 474). That is, through their personality or actions, a party leader persuades partisans of other parties to leave the party for which they usually vote (or for which they voted in the last election) to cast their ballot for the party he/she leads. Given that the conventional wisdom is that election campaigns, and the specific medium of newspapers in particular, reinforce political attitudes and behaviors rather than change them (Berelson, Lazarsfeld and McPhee 1954; Butler and Stokes 1969), this chapter focuses primarily on the dynamics of defection. Our starting point is that this dynamic is now common, but it is not uniform in strength across all leaders, at all times or in all places. Rather, we argue, the magnitude of leader effects varies with the personalities of the leaders themselves, their institutional environment and media coverage of them.

Personality

The unanimous consensus is that it is the psychological variable of personality that draws voters to party leaders. The public values certain personality characteristics in its political leaders and these can be sufficiently attractive to persuade voters to deviate from habitual voting choices and cast their ballot for another party. Personality itself is conceptualized either as overall affect for the leader or as a set of character traits that, for voters at least, suit her/him to the position of chief executive and leader of the government. In the former case, affect is measured by voters giving each party leader a score on a thermometer scale ranging from 0 to 10 and usually anchored by "strongly dislike" and "strongly like" respectively. In the latter case, voters ascribe to party leaders' individual character traits, like competence, deemed desirable in a chief executive.

This emphasis on leader personality has led to their coming to enjoy an increased electoral influence over time, a process labeled the "personalization" (or sometimes even "presidentialization") of politics. This "personalization" thesis has sometimes been misinterpreted as implying that the electoral impact of party leaders increases with each passing election. But while there is some evidence of such an upward trend in leader effects over certain periods of time in Australia (Hayes and McAllister 1997), Britain (Mughan 2000) and the United States (Wattenberg 1994), other studies have challenged this conclusion and claim to show a decrease or no change in their magnitude either within single countries over time (Clarke et al. 2004; Gidengil and Blais 2007) or cross-nationally (Aardal and Binder 2011). Even when the attractiveness of leaders to voters is measured in the same way, this disagreement is only to be expected. For a start, there is variation in the popularity of party leaders both relative to each other and over time for the same individual. Such variance means that, depending on the larger context of specific elections, the ability of a leader to attract defectors from another party can go down as well as up. It may be, for example, that other electoral forces, like the state of the economy or involvement in a foreign war, can come to the fore and overshadow party leaders in one election more so than was the case previously.

When it comes to the character traits that attract voters to the leaders of parties other than the one they consider to be their own, no definitive list of such traits has been identified so that different studies rely on different traits to measure the attractiveness of leaders to voters. However, one comprehensive attempt to compile a set of traits from the literature and to test for their presence in Dutch newspaper articles has come up with the following list: political craftsmanship (including competence), vigorousness (including strong leadership), integrity, communicative skills and consistency (Aaldering and Vliegenthart 2015). When it comes to the question of the electoral impact of specific character traits, however, there are several areas of disagreement in the literature. One such area pits those who take the view that voters look for the same uniform set of traits in all party leaders (Miller, Wattenberg and Malanchuk 1986) against those taking the position that the traits that are important for voters can vary over leaders and for the same leader over time (Hayes 2005). A second area of disagreement concerns which traits matter most to voters who fall prey to the influence of a leader of a party other than the one that usually commands their loyalty. One side advocates for the primacy of performance-related traits as competence and reliability (Miller, Wattenberg and Malanchuk 1986) and others claim to show the greater persuasive power of character-related traits, like integrity and empathy (Bittner 2011). Finally, there is the question of the relative potency of perceived positive or negative leader traits in encouraging voting defection among party loyalists. Those who opt for the primacy of negative evaluations base their argument on prospect theory in social psychology, which holds that voters respond more strongly to negative impressions of political parties and their leaders than to positive ones (Klein 1991). Other studies, in contrast, show empirically that the pull-factors in a party leader's image are more influential for voters than the push-factors (see, for example, Aarts and Blais 2011).

But commonly being based on studies of single elections at single points in time, these contrasting conclusions tend to ignore change over time in either leader images or the impact of specific leader traits on voters. If only for this reason, they probably represent false dichotomies that disguise a more complex reality. Put differently, the characteristics desired in a leader likely change with the circumstances of individual election contests. Being competent might be a trait valued in a context taking place in hard times, but being caring could well trump competence when times have improved. In the bitterly fought 1983 British general election, for instance, the perception that the prime minister, Margaret Thatcher, and opposition leader, Michael Foot, were caring mattered little for voting patterns. By contrast, the same perception of Prime Minister Thatcher in the less polarized 1987 contest played a significant and substantial role in persuading Labour identifiers to vote Conservative (Mughan 2000: 67–68). It is probably no coincidence that contributing to this change were Mrs. Thatcher's great efforts between the two contests to moderate her public image so as to appear less strident, more understanding and more sympathetic to voters. Among these efforts were changes in dress and hair style as well as voice lessons to lower her natural pitch level and moderate what was described as a "grating, relentless monotone that drove half the nation into paroxysms of irritation" (Young 1991: 429).

Political institutions

If the party leaders themselves are an important source of variation in the magnitude of leader effects in democratic elections, so too is the institutional architecture within which those elections take place. This architecture is, of course, highly complex and many parts of it may offer opportunities for party leaders to influence voters. Compulsory voting, for example, is likely to bring to the polls a considerable number of voters who lack deep party loyalties or interest in the election. Under such conditions, one might expect the impact of factors such as the personality of the party leaders to have a greater influence on voting behavior. There is any number of such possible institutional influences so limitations of time and space lead us to focus on three of the most widely recognized of them: regime type, electoral/party systems and political parties.

Regime type

Institutions matter for leader effects and perhaps the most important institutional difference conditioning them is form of government, presidential or parliamentary (Ohr and Oscarsson 2011). Two dimensions of difference would seem to be particularly relevant here. First, in presidential systems, the party leader stands for the position of chief executive separately from the rest of the party's office seekers and voters choose directly between the competing candidates in a nationwide vote. In parliamentary systems, by contrast, the road to the position of chief executive (prime minister, chancellor, or whatever) is indirect. The would-be chief executives stand for election in just one single- or multi-member district and as one among many representatives of a political party seeking office; voters do not get the chance to vote directly for their next head of government. Instead, the choice is made after the election is over and the distribution of parliamentary seats determined. The leader of the party best able to command a majority is elevated to the position of chief executive by the parliamentary majority. In other words, leader effects are likely to be stronger in presidential than parliamentary systems because voters choose an individual, who is nonetheless the most prominent representative of a party, in the former, and a party in the latter (Wattenberg 1991).

Second, presidents are elected for a fixed period, can claim to have received a personal mandate and need not always carry their party along if they are to govern effectively. Prime ministers, in contrast, need to maintain majority support in the legislature to govern, which means that they are less autonomous and less easily held responsible for the actions or inactions of the government they head. Blame is relatively easily shifted to the likes of incompetent cabinet colleagues, recalcitrant coalition partners or an uncooperative legislature. Relatively isolated, presidents are less able to shift blame in this way and are more readily held accountable by voters for political outcomes, thereby functioning under normal circumstances as a bigger influence on the vote for themselves or their party. The notion of "presidentialization" captures the argument that prime ministers have become like presidents in terms of now having the possibility of enjoying an electoral influence in their own right and of being far more important cues for voters than other senior figures in their party (Mughan 2000; Poguntke and Webb 2007).

Electoral/party systems

Institutional differences within parliamentary regimes can also influence whether the magnitude of leader effects is more or less similar to that found in presidential regimes. Majoritarian electoral systems tend to produce two-party systems and single-party governments, whereas proportional systems promote multiple parties and coalition governments. Leader effects are stronger in the former precisely because the leaders of single-party governments can be held more readily accountable for the successes or failures of their government; blame cannot be diverted onto others so easily and, in addition, there is no need to share the credit for political successes (Curtice and Hunjan 2011).

A second characteristic of party systems potentially relevant to the magnitude of leader effects is the ideological character of the parties themselves. Where parties are deeply rooted in social cleavages and ideologically distinctive, there is little likelihood that relatively transient influences like party leaders will disrupt habitual voting loyalties. This is probably the main reason these leaders were not taken seriously as electoral forces prior to the onset of partisan dealignment. Starting in the last part of the twentieth century, however, political parties in most Western democracies became more alike in terms of their political ideologies and goals for society (Franklin, Mackie and Valen 1992). This transition from "mass-based" to "catch-all party" systems weakened habitual voting loyalties and encouraged the emergence of party leaders as potentially potent electoral forces in their own right (Costa Lobo 2014). The converse is also true, of course. The greater the ideological divergence between parties, the less room there is for short-term influences on the vote, like party leaders (Holmberg and Oscarsson 2011).

Parties still matter

The focus on party leaders implies a diminished role for the institution of the political party in shaping the electoral calculus of voters, but its decline should not be overstated. Partisan dealignment notwithstanding, the majority of voters continue to demonstrate a long-term commitment to a particular party and this identification still has a very strong influence on their vote (Bittner 2011). Along with leader evaluations, for example, party identification lies at the core of the recently floated valence model of voting (Clarke et al. 2004). But party is also an important short-term influence on the vote and election-specific evaluations of parties have non-trivial implications for the magnitude of leader effects. The norm is for individual party leaders to be treated as separate entities in the leader effects literature, but it turns out that electoral impact is substantially stronger when they are conceptualized not as stand-alone stimuli, but as objects that voters evaluate relative to the parties on offer in the election. Of course, leaders affect the vote when they are treated as stand-alone stimuli, but defection is substantially more likely when voters like the leader of another party in that election more than they like their own party; the greater this gap, the greater the likelihood of defection at the polls to the favored leader's party (Mughan 2015). To be sure, leaders matter, but the fact that political parties remain a continuing multifaceted reference point for voters should not be lost from sight in discussions of leader effects.

Media

As the principal information source for voters, the mass communications media lie at the heart of the electoral calculus of voters. Initially, the dominant medium of communication between governors and governed was the newspaper and early research found that it tended to reinforce long-standing political predispositions and behaviors rather than to change them. The reason was a combination of voters exposing themselves only to newspapers that echoed their existing political biases and their having defensive psychological mechanisms, like selective recall, that shielded these biases against discordant information (Berelson, Lazarsfeld and McPhee 1954; Butler and Stokes 1969). With the primary intent of reinforcing their electoral support rather than changing it in a world where partisan loyalties ran deep, political parties mostly controlled their media environment.

In more recent years, this control has been seriously eroded by the emergence of television as voters' preeminent source of political information and, consequently, as an important influence on their attitudes and behaviors. The essential problem for political parties generally is that they cannot control this medium and state-licensed broadcasters are commonly required by law to be impartial between them in their political coverage (Gunther and Mughan 2000). Thus, not being able to control the new medium, parties had to adapt to its logic as the first step in harnessing its power to their own electoral ends. This adaptation entailed above all a shift from a pattern of political communication dominated by a party logic in which political parties played the major role in determining what is politically newsworthy to a media logic in which a wholly different style of political communication built around personalized coverage, visualization, simplification, negative coverage, horse race coverage and framing politics as conflict is the norm (Altheide and Snow 1979; Mazzoleni 1987). For the purposes of this chapter, the most important consequence of this switch in the pattern of political communication was an enhanced role for party leaders in the media coverage of politics in general and election campaigns in particular. The reasons for this "personalization" of television coverage of politics are simple. The majority of political coverage takes place through news programs and television newscasts that lend themselves to short, snappy sound bites and the projection of personality more than to the outline and discussion of complex political issues. Additionally, television needs a (familiar) visual image to cover political news stories (McAllister 2007). Moreover, the more authoritative the person behind the visual image, the better the television so that party leaders became preferred over other senior political figures. Inevitably, the party leader became the spokesperson and public face of the party. In the process, the content of media coverage of election campaigns shifted. Less attention was paid to parties' proposals, performance and policy plans and more to their leaders, but with a focus less on their political credentials, issue positions and promises and more on such non-political characteristics as family, personal appearance, life-style, upbringing and religion (Langer 2007).

The upshot of these changes in the media landscape is that the party choice of the many voters has come to be influenced by televised leader images. The strongest direct evidence for such a media effect comes from the United States where sophisticated experiments have demonstrated not only that presidential candidates have an electoral impact through voters' exposure to them on television, but they have also identified the psychological mechanisms through which this impact makes itself felt. These mechanisms are labeled priming and framing. Priming entails that "news content suggests to news audiences that they ought to use specific issues as benchmarks for evaluating the performance of leaders and governments" (Scheufele and Tewksbury 2007: 11). Framing, by contrast, involves television in presenting political and social problems in such a way as to place blame on different sets of actors and institutions. For example, unemployment can be framed in the media as a product of presidential policies or as the result of economic developments. In the case of the former, voters could well lay the blame for unemployment at the president's door and decide not to vote for him (Iyengar and Kinder 1987; Iyengar 1992). Although comparable systematic evidence regarding the role of priming and framing on leader effects in parliamentary elections is lacking, there are indications that here too television plays an important role in shaping voters' perceptions of politicians and the credibility of their messages. One quasi-experimental study of BBC and ITV news broadcasts in Britain, for example, found that leader effects were not dependent on the informational content in the news reports. Instead, if a party succeeds in convincing voters that the television news is biased in favor of a rival, then this perception of bias will result in a stronger electoral impact for the leader whose party is deemed the victim of this bias (Mughan 1996).

The importance of television for leader effects is nowhere more apparent than in the evolution of the institution of the televised leader debate. Starting with the famous 1960 confrontation in the US between John Kennedy and Richard Nixon, debates have been a continuous and integral part of presidential election campaigns there since 1976. As well, the contagion has spread. A clear indication that political parties now give a more prominent electioneering role to their leader is that debates between party leaders have now taken root in 14 other democracies, most of them parliamentary systems without the popular election of a president (Argentina, Australia, Brazil, Canada, France, Germany, Ireland, Kenya, Malta, Mexico, the Netherlands, New Zealand, the United Kingdom and Uruguay). There is also convincing evidence that these debates are important and consequential for voters. For example, they help voters to position parties on policy issues more accurately (Van der Meer, Walter and Aelst 2016). Additionally, they influence how heavily voters rely on their perception of leaders' personalities in their evaluations of them (Druckman 2003). There is even some preliminary evidence to suggest that televised debates might constitute the most influential television broadcast form for voters, albeit perhaps only in a system where paid political advertising is illegal. Despite 2015 being only the second British general election to include leader debates, a survey of over 3,000 people found that 38 percent of them claimed to be influenced by them as compared to 23 percent who were influenced by TV news coverage and 10 percent by party political broadcasts (BBC News 2015). This pattern of responses is, of course, no more than suggestive, not least because the "influence" it measures does not indicate whether, and in what measure, these debates reinforce or undermine long-standing attitudes and behaviors. Nonetheless, it does suggest that the interaction between party leaders and the media has become a potent electoral force that we are only beginning to understand.

A good starting point might be the improved specification of the characteristics of voters who are susceptible to mediatized leader images when making their vote decision. To be sure, something is known about the psychological processes, like priming and bias perception, that help to translate leader evaluations into an actual voting decision, but there is little agreement on the political and sociological characteristics of those succumbing to the pull of the party leaders. The conventional wisdom used to be that political leaders are most central to the decision making of unsophisticated voters: "The common – indeed universal – view has been that voting choices based on policy concerns are superior to those based on party loyalty or candidate images. Only the former represents clearly sophisticated behavior" (Carmines and Stimson 1980: 79). Some empirical evidence is consistent with this view, showing that leader effects are indeed strongest among less educated or politically sophisticated voters (Gidengil 2011). The explanation of this finding is usually that leader effects can be considered as heuristics or shortcuts for voters who lack the reasoning capacity and/or political knowledge to make a decision based on "policy concerns." However, other scholars find precisely the opposite and show that leader effects are actually strongest for more highly educated and politically sophisticated voters (Bittner 2011; Lachat 2014). Their explanation is that leader effects are not just shortcuts. Rather, the evaluation of a leader is based on the voter's assessment of how well the leaders performed, or would perform, in office so that the "process of leader evaluation is complex – perhaps more so than we think" (Bittner 2011: 54). Closer analysis of the increasingly popular televised leader debates should help to adjudicate between such conflicting conclusions.

Future research

One of the more consequential electoral developments in recent decades has been the generalized growth of the importance of party leaders as electoral forces in their own right. From an initial consensus that they used to matter little to not at all in parliamentary elections in particular, the argument has been made that they can even be the difference between victory and defeat for their party in closely fought elections (Bean and Mughan 1989, but see King 2002). To argue for leaders' independent electoral impact, however, is not to imply that this impact is uniform across them, time or space. Rather, the central theme of this chapter is that the magnitude of leader effects is conditional on a number of factors and, among them, we have examined briefly the personalities of the leaders themselves, the political institutions in which leaders operate, the parties in the election and the media. But this "conditionality research" is only in its infancy; much remains to be done to specify the conditions shaping the magnitude of leader effects and we would like to conclude this chapter with some suggestions for future areas of research. Reflecting much of what has already been written on the subject of leader effects, we will focus on the personalities of the party leaders and the media, both old and new.

Dating from at least Max Weber's writings on charismatic leadership, the importance of personality for the political relations between leaders and led has been recognized and this tradition has defined leader effects studies to this point. Voters respond to party leaders as individuals they like or dislike, respect or disrespect, and so on. But if leaders have increasingly become the public face of the party, then the question inevitably arises as to whether voters' reactions to them have a political as well as personality content. Especially the longer they stay at the head of their party, do leaders' images become defined by their party's traditional ideological stance or its current policy positions as much as (or even more than) by their personalities? A case in point is if voters do indeed defect because, in the context of a specific election, they like the leader of another party more than they like their own party (Mughan 2015), what can be the basis of their choice to defect? After all, if political parties do not have personalities, it can't be personality that is being compared in the voter's mind. Voter preferences must be based, at least partly, on other criteria and surely political criteria can be expected to loom large here.[1] Thus, future research should "politicize" leader effects instead of just continuing to "psychologize" them. This is not to say that the latter are not important to voters, but the possibility should be entertained that both politics and psychology play a role in conditioning leader effects so that the interesting question becomes under what conditions one becomes more powerful than the other in affecting the vote decision.

A second area in which we still need to learn a lot more is the interaction between media, party leaders and the vote. Media can be divided into "old" and "new" forms. Television is the predominant "old" medium and we still know little about its role in promoting leader effects in parliamentary elections in particular. Part of the reason is methodological. Experiments (commonly used in the United States but less so outside) could be used, for example, to investigate the relative potency of negative and positive character traits. The effects of debates are also largely unknown. It was mentioned earlier that many more British voters claimed to be influenced by them than by other televised political broadcasts, but is their effect to reinforce habitual party loyalties, promote defection from them or both? "New" media are more commonly referred to as social media and are becoming more central components of parties' campaign strategies and tools for communicating (often interactively) with voters (Druckman, Kifer and Parkin 2007). In addition, we know that voters use them to discuss political issues and express their political preferences (Tumasjan et al. 2011). But how does the use of social media relate to leader effects? To be sure, leaders' use of social media affects voters; for example, candidates for political office in the Netherlands won more votes when they used Twitter (Kruikemeier 2014). The early evidence suggests, however, that they may personalize the voting decision less than television insofar as online news seekers are systematically less likely to base their voting decision on presidential candidates' personality assessments as compared to television viewers (Holian and Prysby 2014). But many interesting and important questions remain unaddressed. How, for example, do parties and their leaders use social media? What form does the presentation of party leaders take in them? And with what effect? Which methods of internet use are most conducive to the promotion of leader effects? These are some of the pressing questions in the study of social media and leader effects.

Note

1 There may be a relationship, for example, insofar as perceptions of a leader's character influences perceptions of her/his performance in office. Another take comes from Costa Lobo and Curtice (2014), who conclude that leader personality evaluations originate largely in political considerations so that voters are more influenced by those evaluations in political environments where leaders are more influential, i.e., that it is rational behavior for voters to be influenced by leaders' personalities.

References

Aaldering, L. and Vliegenthart, R. (2015) "Political Leaders and the Media: Can We Measure Political Leadership Images in Newspapers Using Computer-Assisted Content Analysis?," *Quality and Quantity*, vol. 50, no. 5, September, 1871–1905.

Aardal, B. and Binder, T. (2011) "Leader Effects and Party Characteristics," in Aarts, K., Blais, A. and Schmitt, H. (eds.) *Political Leaders and Democratic Elections*, Oxford: Oxford University Press: 108–126.

Aarts, K. and Blais, A. (2011) "Pull or Push? The Relative Impact of Positive and Negative Leader Evaluations on Vote Choice," in Aarts, K., Blais, A. and Schmitt, H. (eds.) *Political Leaders and Democratic Elections*, Oxford: Oxford University Press: 165–188.

Aarts, K., Blais, A. and Schmitt, H. (eds.) (2011) *Political Leaders and Democratic Elections*, Oxford: Oxford University Press.

Altheide, D. and Snow, R. (1979) *Media Logic*, Beverly Hills: Sage Publications.

Barisione, M. (2009) "Valence Image and the Standardisation of Democratic Political Leadership," *Leadership*, vol. 5, no. 1, February, 41–60.

BBC News (2015) "Election 2015: TV Debates 'Most Influential' for Voters," May 9, 2015, www.bbc.co.uk/news/election-2015-32673439, [accessed February 10, 2017].

Bean, C. and Mughan, A. (1989) "Leadership Effects in Parliamentary Elections in Australia and Britain," *American Political Science Review*, vol. 83, no. 4, December, 1165–1179.

Berelson, B., Lazarsfeld, P. and McPhee, W. (1954) *Voting*, Chicago: Chicago University Press.

Bittner, A. (2011) *Platform or Personality? The Role of Party Leaders in Elections*, Oxford: Oxford University Press.

Butler, D. and Stokes, D. (1969) *Political Change in Britain: Forces Shaping Electoral Choice*, New York: St. Martin's Press.

Campbell, A., Converse, P., Miller, W. and Stokes, D. (1966) *Elections and the Political Order*, New York: Wiley.

Carmines, E. and Stimson, J. (1980) "The Two Faces of Issue Voting," *American Political Science Review*, vol. 74, no. 1, March, 78–91.

Clarke, H., Sanders, D., Stewart, M. and Whiteley, P. (2004) *Political Choice in Britain*, Oxford: Oxford University Press.

Costa Lobo, M. (2014) "Party Dealignment and Leader Effects," in Costa Lobo, M. and Curtice, J. (eds.) *Personality Politics? The Role of Leader Evaluations in Democratic Elections*, Oxford: Oxford University Press: 148–167.

Costa Lobo, M. and Curtice, J. (eds.) (2014) *Personality Politics? The Role of Leader Evaluations in Democratic Elections*, Oxford: Oxford University Press.

Curtice, J. and Hunjan, S. (2011) "Elections as Beauty Contests: Do the Rules Matter?," in Aarts, K., Blais, A. and Schmitt, H. (eds.) *Political Leaders and Democratic Elections*, Oxford: Oxford University Press: 91–107.

Dalton, R. and Wattenberg, M. (eds.) (2000) *Parties Without Partisans: Political Change in Advanced Industrial Democracies*, Oxford: Oxford University Press.

Druckman, J. (2003) "The Power of Television Images: The First Kennedy-Nixon Debate Revisited," *Journal of Politics*, vol. 65, no. 2, May, 559–571.

Druckman, J., Kifer, M. and Parkin, M. (2007) "The Technological Development of Congressional Candidate Websites: How and Why Candidates Use Web Innovations," *Social Science Computer Review*, vol. 25, no. 4, Winter, 425–442.

Franklin, M., Mackie, T. and Valen, H. (eds.) (1992) *Electoral Change: Response to Evolving Social and Attitudinal Structures in Western Countries*, Cambridge: Cambridge University Press.

Gidengil, E. (2011) "Voter Characteristics and Leader Effects," in Aarts, K., Blais, A. and Schmitt, H. (eds.) *Political Leaders and Democratic Elections*, Oxford: Oxford University Press: 147–164.

Gidengil, E. and Blais, A. (2007) "Are Party Leaders Becoming More Important to Vote Choice in Canada?," in Michelmann, H., Clarke, D. and Steeves, J. (eds.) *Political Leadership and Representation in Canada: Essays in Honour of John C. Courtney*, Toronto: University of Toronto Press: 39–59.

Gunther, R. and Mughan, A. (eds.) (2000) *Democracy and the Media: A Comparative Perspective*, Cambridge: Cambridge University Press.

Hayes, B., and McAllister, I. (1997) "Gender, Party Leaders, and Election Outcomes in Australia, Britain, and the United States," *Comparative Political Studies*, vol. 30, no. 1, February, 3–26.

Hayes, D. (2005) "Candidate Qualities Through a Partisan Lens: A Theory of Trait Ownership," *American Journal of Political Science*, vol. 49, no. 4, October, 908–923.

Holian, D. and Prysby, C. (2014) *Candidate Character Traits in Presidential Elections*, Abingdon: Routledge.

Holmberg, S. and Oscarsson, H. (2011) "Party Leader Effects on the Vote," in Aarts, K., Blais, A. and Schmitt, H. (eds.) *Political Leaders and Democratic Elections*, Oxford: Oxford University Press: 36–52.

Iyengar, S. (1992) *Is Anyone Responsible? How Television News Frames Political Issues*, Chicago: University of Chicago Press.

Iyengar, S. and Kinder, D. (1987) *News that Matters: Television and American Opinion*, Chicago: University of Chicago Press.

King, A. (ed.) (2002) *Leaders' Personalities and the Outcomes of Democratic Elections*, Oxford: Oxford University Press.

Klein, J. (1991) "Negativity Effects in Impression Formation: A Test in the Political Arena," *Personality and Social Psychology Bulletin*, vol. 17, no. 4, August, 412–418.

Kruikemeier, S. (2014) "How Political Candidates use Twitter and the Impact on Votes," *Computers in Human Behavior*, vol. 34, no. 1, May, 131–139.

Lachat, R. (2014) "Leader Effects and Party Polarization," in Lobo, M. C. and Curtice, J. (eds.) *Personality Politics? The Role of Leader Evaluations in Democratic Elections*, Oxford: Oxford University Press: 105–124.

Langer, A. (2007) "A Historical Exploration of the Personalisation of Politics in the Print Media: The British Prime Ministers (1945–1999)," *Parliamentary Affairs*, vol. 60, no. 3, July, 371–387.

Mazzoleni, G. (1987) "Media Logic and Party Logic in Campaign Coverage: The Italian General Election of 1983," *European Journal of Communication*, vol. 2, no. 1, March, 81–103.

McAllister, I. (2007) "The Personalization of Politics," in Dalton, R. and Klingeman, H. (eds.) *The Oxford Handbook of Political Behavior*, Oxford: Oxford University Press: 571–588.

Meer, T. van der, Walter, A. and Aelst, P. (2016) "The Contingency of Voter Learning: How Election Debates Influenced Voters' Ability and Accuracy to Position Parties in the 2010 Dutch Election Campaign," *Political Communication*, vol. 3, no. 1, January, 136–157.

Miller, A., Wattenberg, M. and Malanchuk, O. (1986) "Schematic Assessments of Presidential Candidates," *American Political Science Review*, vol. 80, no. 2, June, 521–540.

Mughan, A. (1996) "Television Can Matter: Bias in the 1992 General Election," in Farrell, D., Broughton, D., Denver, D. and Fisher, J. (eds.) *British Elections and Parties Yearbook 1996*, London: Frank Cass: 128–142.

Mughan, A. (2000) *Media and the Presidentialization of Parliamentary Elections*, Houndmills: Palgrave.

Mughan, A. (2015) "Parties, Conditionality and Leader Effects in Parliamentary Elections," *Party Politics*, vol. 21, no. 1, January, 28–39.

Ohr, D. and Oscarsson, H. (2011) "Leader Traits, Leader Image, and Vote Choice," in Aarts, K., Blais, A. and Schmitt, H. (eds.) *Political Leaders and Democratic Elections*, Oxford: Oxford University Press: 127–146.

Pharr, S. and Putnam, R. (eds.) (2000) *Disaffected Democracies: What's Troubling Trilateral Countries*, Princeton: Princeton University Press.

Poguntke, T. and Webb, P. (eds.) (2007) *The Presidentialization of Politics: A Comparative Study of Modern Democracies*, Oxford: Oxford University Press.

Scheufele, D. and Tewksbury, D. (2007) "Framing, Agenda Setting, and Priming: The Evolution of Three Media Effects Models," *Journal of Communication*, vol. 57, no. 1, March, 9–20.

Tumasjan, A., Sprenger, T. O., Sandner, P. G. and Welpe, I. M. (2011) "Election Forecasts with Twitter: How 140 Characters Reflect the Political Landscape," *Social Science Computer Review*, vol. 29, no. 4, November, 402–418.

Wattenberg, M. (1991) *The Rise of Candidate-Centered Politics: Presidential Elections of the 1980s*, Cambridge: Harvard University Press.

Wattenberg, M. (1994) *The Decline of American Political Parties, 1952–1992*, Cambridge: Harvard University Press.

Young, H. (1991) *One of Us: A Biography of Margaret Thatcher*, London: Macmillan.

15

PREFERENCES, CONSTRAINTS, AND CHOICES

Tactical voting in mass elections

R. Michael Alvarez, D. Roderick Kiewiet, and Lucas Núñez

Introduction

Voters have preferences over parties and candidates. Their ability to express these preferences in an election is constrained by the ballot choices that are presented to them and in the way in which ballots are aggregated into outcomes. In most cases voters do not sense the impact of these constraints, nor any tension between their preferences and their choices. In single member district systems with plurality rule (SMD), they simply vote for the candidate that they most prefer. In multi-candidate proportional representation (PR) elections, sincere voters' rankings of candidates mirror their preference orderings. Sometimes, however, voters do not act sincerely, and make choices that do not follow from a straightforward mapping of their preferences.

The most heavily studied departure from sincere voting is that of tactical voting in SMD systems. This occurs when voters, believing that their most preferred candidate has no chance of winning, vote instead for a less preferred candidate so as to counter another candidate whom they dislike. In PR systems, voters might also conclude that they would be "wasting" their vote on a party that is unlikely to get enough votes to win a seat. Considerations of how different party coalitions are likely to form can also lead voters to engage in different forms of tactical voting. In this chapter we discuss tactical voting in SMD systems and in PR systems. We review and evaluate previous research, and identify the major findings that have emerged. We then suggest avenues for future research that are important and promising.

Tactical voting in SMD systems

Farquharson (1964) provides a modern, game theoretic analysis of tactical voting, but, as he notes, it has a long and venerable heritage; Pliny the Younger describes an episode of tactical voting in the Roman Senate in the year 105. The most common formulation of tactical voting in SMD systems is associated with Duverger (1955). The winner-take-all nature of SMD contests strongly penalizes minor parties when votes are translated into seats. Voters are aware of the bias generated by this "mechanical factor," which is thereby reinforced by a "psychological factor": when voters perceive that their most preferred candidate is sure to lose, they often cast a tactical vote for a less preferred (but competitive and still acceptable) candidate in order to counter their least preferred candidate. Thus, according to Duverger's Law, minor parties are suppressed, and elections in SMD systems are generally contested by two major parties.

Duverger's Law is not a law, of course, but at most a general tendency. The factors he identifies apply to individual contests, and individual contests can aggregate into a wide variety of patterns. Britain, the US, Canada, and India all have SMD but very different party systems (Grofman, Blais, and Bowler 2009). In Britain the party system has become significantly more fractionalized over time even though SMD has remained in place. In any given election, moreover, tactical voting need not systematically help or hurt a particular party in all contests. Little about the nature and extent of tactical voting can be inferred from the nature of a country's party system or from the outcome of national elections.

There are studies of tactical voting in countries besides Britain, but because of a pattern of party competition that persisted for decades – two major parties and a significant third party contesting most constituencies – research on tactical voting has focused primarily on British parliamentary elections. Early efforts to estimate the extent of tactical voting in Britain used aggregate-level constituency returns to track changes in vote totals across successive elections. The hypothesis they entertained is that a party that finishes third in one election suffers a loss of votes in the subsequent election, as discouraged supporters switch to voting for one of the two top parties. Parties that finish first or second in the first election correspondingly experience an increase in vote share in the next election due to the infusion of tactical votes. In his "flow of the vote" study of British elections held between 1892 and 1966, Shively (1970) concludes that tactical voting can be detected, but that it was insignificant in magnitude and impact. In their study of the 1983 and 1987 elections, Curtice and Steed (1988) also report that the extent of tactical voting was quite limited, and changed the outcomes of only a handful of individual constituency elections. Johnston and Pattie (1991) report finding more tactical voting in 1987 than in 1983, but even in 1987 the rate of tactical voting they detected was limited in extent and of minor consequence for election outcomes.

A problem with flow-of-the-vote analyses is that of establishing a proper baseline. A party that finished third in the first of two elections could well have had its totals depressed by tactical voting in the first election as well as the second. Parties that finished first or second could correspondingly have had their totals enhanced by tactical voting in both elections. Comparisons of constituency results across pairs of elections can also be compromised by omitted variable bias – for example, by changes in party support traceable to economic and demographic trends that are not accounted for in the analysis (Johnston 1981).

Many political scientists are also skeptical of flow-of-the-vote analyses because they are based upon constituency-level vote totals. As Campbell et al. (1966: 2) put it, "... As long as one has only aggregate data at hand one can only speculate as to what moved the individual members of the collectivity" (see also Russo in this volume). Subsequent studies of tactical voting have relied heavily upon survey data, and, specifically, upon a question posed in the British Election Study (BES) in every election since 1983: "Which one of the reasons comes closest to the main reason you voted for the Party you chose?" The responses offered vary from study to study, but in all elections respondents could report that "I really preferred another party, but it had no chance of winning in this constituency." Those who chose this response are deemed to have voted tactically.

Analyses of BES survey data indicate that tactical voting is more prevalent than suggested by flow-of-the-vote studies (Niemi, Whitten, and Franklin 1992). Cain's (1978) study of 1970 BES survey data, based instead upon differences in party feeling thermometer scores, reports a remarkably high rate of tactical voting – nearly 20 percent. Subsequent studies, however, point to a number of problems in survey-based estimates of tactical voting. According to Heath et al.

(1991), some respondents said that they had voted tactically, but reported their favorite party to be the same party that they voted for. Others claim to have voted tactically but shifted their vote to another small party that had no better chance of winning than their favorite. The Heath et al. (1991) study, as well as Franklin, Niemi, and Whitten (1994), also find that nearly half the survey respondents who claim to have voted tactically most preferred a party that finished in first or second place. There is general agreement with Heath and Evans (1994) that "instrumental" tactical voting – that is, what Duverger had in mind – must be distinguished from an "expressive" version. In such cases voting decisions that respondents describe as tactical are motivated by idiosyncratic considerations that lead them to make a variety of often inexplicable choices.

These survey-based estimates of tactical voting, as well as estimates derived from flow-of-the-votes, pertain to the entire electorate. According to Cox (1997), however, one should expect to see tactical voting only in constituencies in which the two leading parties are clearly identifiable, and not where uncertainty clouds the expected order of finish. Consider the following. In the first constituency the Liberal Democrat (LD) is widely expected to run well behind Labour and the Conservatives. Here it will be reasonable for LD supporters to consider casting a tactical vote. In the other constituency the Liberal Democrat finished third by only a few percentage points behind the second-place party in the last election, and the LD candidate is currently running a vigorous campaign. In this case LD supporters have reason to believe that they will finish second, or perhaps even first. The rationale for voting tactically thus disappears.

More generally, for tactical voting to occur, and to thus undermine support for minor parties and enhance the vote shares of the two major parties, voters must have common expectations as to which parties are viable – that is, running either first or second – and which are not (Palfrey 1989; Myatt and Fisher 2002). When common expectations about viability are present, supporters of the top two parties remain loyal and vote sincerely, while tactical supporters of nonviable parties abandon ship and vote for one of the top two. When common expectations about viability are not present, voters are uncertain as to whether the party they support is going to finish third or whether it is going to be one of the top two. Here tactical voting does not occur.

A common intuition concerning tactical voting, usually referred to as the marginality hypothesis, is that it should be more prevalent in close elections. Minor party supporters are seen to be more comfortable voting sincerely if one party or candidate has such a commanding lead that the outcome of the election is a foregone conclusion. It could also be that a close election makes the choice between the top two alternatives more salient and third parties less relevant. But tactical voting will not occur even in very close elections if voters are unable to distinguish between which parties are viable – that is, headed for a first- or second-place finish – and which are not. Votes can remain splintered among three or more parties, and a party can win with much less than an absolute majority. In Britain parliamentary elections, there are usually dozens of constituencies in which the winning party garners less than 40 percent of the vote.

A pair of studies reveals the importance of confining estimates of the rate of tactical voting to those constituencies where it makes sense for voters to consider voting tactically. In their analysis of BES survey data, Alvarez and Nagler (2000) regress individuals' vote choices onto a wide range of variables, including demographics, issue distance measures, perceptions of economic conditions, and variables reflecting the pattern of party competition in the respondent's constituency. They then counterfactually predict how voters would have voted absent tactical considerations and compare their prediction to how respondents reported voting. They report a tactical voting rate of 7.3 percent in 1987 – a little higher than that suggested by the standard tactical voting question, but in the same neighborhood. Alvarez, Boehmke, and Nagler (2005) then refine this analysis by confining their attention solely to supporters of parties who finished third (or worse) in their constituency in the previous election. Among this subset of respondents, they estimate that the rate of tactical voting was 43 percent.

Kiewiet (2013), similarly, stipulates that voters consider casting a tactical vote only when their most preferred party faces a "dismal outlook." This occurs when their most preferred party (1) finished more than 10 percentage points behind the second-place party in their constituency in the previous election, and (2) fails to spend even half of the sum that could legally be spent on behalf of the individual candidate in the current election period. Research based upon the 1997–2001 British Election Panel Study strongly indicates that a poor third-place finish by a party in the previous election encourages its supporters to vote tactically (Fieldhouse, Shryane, and Pickles 2007) and that spending on behalf of individual candidates was consistent with tactical considerations by both parties and voters (Fieldhouse, Pattie, and Johnston 1996). Analyzing both NES survey data and constituency returns for all six parliamentary elections held in Britain between 1983 and 2005, Kiewiet finds that, in most elections, between one fourth and one third of the voters whose preferred party faced a dismal outlook cast tactical votes. Labour supporters appear to have voted tactically more frequently than LD supporters – in a couple of elections (1992 and 1997) at rates approaching 50 percent.

Kiewiet's findings are also consistent with Myatt and Fisher (2002), who show that the pattern of party competition in individual constituencies is such that the mechanical and psychological components of Duverger's Law can work in opposite directions. Liberal Democrats usually finished third and so were badly penalized by the translation of votes into seats. In many individual contests, however, they benefited from tactical votes that they received from supporters of Labour and other parties. Both of these effects result from the fact that they occupy the middle position on the ideological spectrum. Virtually all tactical votes cast by Labour and Conservative supporters went to the Liberal Democrats, while those cast by Liberal Democrats flowed both to the left (Labour) and to the right (Conservatives). In a recent, innovative study that utilizes Bayesian small sample estimation to infer district-level preferences from the inevitably small numbers of respondents sampled from each district, Hermann, Munzert, and Selb (2016) report finding similar patterns of tactical voting in the 1997 and 2001 British parliamentary elections.

As noted previously, several political scientists studying tactical voting have entertained the marginality hypothesis – that is, that it should be more prevalent in close elections. Early aggregate-level studies report some evidence favoring the marginality hypothesis in the 1966 and 1970 British general elections (Spafford 1972; Cain 1978). Since then, studies that have investigated this hypothesis with both BES and constituency-level data, with methodologies ranging from quite simple to highly sophisticated, have not found a consistent relationship between closeness and the rate of tactical voting (Lanoue and Bowler 1992; Fisher 2001; Alvarez, Boehmke, and Nagler 2005; Kiewiet 2013; Elff 2014).

Tactical voting in proportional representation (PR) systems

In contrast to winner-take-all SMD systems, proportional representation (PR) systems award seats to parties in proportion to the votes they receive in multi-member districts. A voter's most preferred party can finish third, fourth, or even worse, and still obtain a seat. For that reason Duverger (1955) doubted that voters would vote tactically in such systems. As Leys (1959) and Sartori (1968) note, however, if district magnitudes are low (i.e., only a few seats are allocated per district), it is common for small parties not to have enough votes to be awarded a seat. As in SMD systems, this could lead those who most prefer such a party to vote tactically for their most-preferred party that is likely to win at least one seat. The Leys–Sartori conjecture, then, is that the smaller the district magnitude in a PR election, the greater the extent of tactical voting that is likely to occur.

Analyzing the outcomes of small magnitude PR elections in Colombia and Japan, Cox and Shugart (1996) look for the presence of tactical voting by calculating "SF" ratios – that is, where F is the largest vote remainder and S the second largest vote remainder after assigning the final seat in the district. The SF ratio is a macro-level statistic, reflective of choices made by party elites and candidates as well as those of voters. An SF ratio approaching zero, however, signals the presence of tactical voting, and so is a useful diagnostic when more specific information about voters' preferences and choices is not available. Their findings suggest that voters in both countries exhibited some amount of tactical voting by deserting parties unable to win a seat.

Cox and Shugart also report that tactical voting could not be detected in larger magnitude districts, and there are two reasons to accept this verdict. Mathematically, the larger district magnitude is, provided there is a low threshold, the smaller the share of votes a party needs to win at least one seat. Another consideration is informational. As in SMD systems, tactical desertion here also requires widely shared expectations regarding which parties are likely to obtain a seat and which are not. When district magnitudes are large – typically seen as more than five – voters may find it difficult to form such expectations and thus vote sincerely.

Gschwend, Stoiber, and Günther (2004) do not accept this line of argument. They argue instead that there are not insurmountable informational costs to tactical voting in PR systems, as voters can condition their decision upon what happened in the last election. Just as those looking for tactical voting in SMD systems hypothesize that supporters of parties that came in third in the previous election should be the most inclined to vote tactically, they posit that tactical voting should be most prevalent in PR systems among supporters of parties that either barely won a seat in the previous election or failed to win a seat. They call this an "election history heuristic" because it is not seen to require much from the voters in the way of information or thought. The findings of their analysis of elections in Finland between 1991 and 2003 indicate that marginal parties suffered less from tactical voting in large districts than in small ones (district magnitude in Finland during this period ranged from 6 to 33), but that non-negligible amounts of tactical voting occurred even in large magnitude districts.

Lago (2008) agrees that voters can use an electoral history heuristic regardless of district magnitude. Analyzing survey data collected in Spain in the 1970s and 1980s, he finds that voters have no more difficulty forming expectations about party viability in large magnitude districts than in small ones. There is less tactical desertion away from small parties in large magnitude districts simply because it is more likely for small parties to win a seat. Analyses of Spanish elections in 1977 and 1982 (Gunter 1989) and 2000 and 2008 (García-Viñuela, Artés, and Jurado 2015) report similar findings: supporters of small parties are more likely to cast tactical votes for larger parties when district magnitude is small, but even in large magnitude districts smaller party vote totals are suppressed by their supporters voting tactically for parties that win seats.

Another major reason why small parties fail to win seats in parliament, other than being squeezed by low district magnitude, is the presence of a threshold – that is, the requirement to win a certain percentage of votes (often 5 percent) in order to obtain a seat. Tavits and Annus (2006) find that voters in the new democracies of Eastern Europe and the former Soviet Union were sensitive to threshold requirements and tended to avoid casting votes for parties that fell below the threshold. Their findings are also supportive of the hypothesis that voters adopt an election history heuristic, in that there was clear evidence of voter learning over the course of successive elections. In consecutive elections in these countries, voters increasingly deserted parties whose support was either barely above the threshold of representation or fell below it. Additional evidence that voters in new democracies have come to adopt Duvergerian tactical reasoning comes from Duch and Palmer's (2002) study of tactical voting in Hungary, which utilizes a complex three-layer, mixed member electoral system. Duch and Palmer ask voters whether they would be willing to switch their vote to another party if their most preferred party would get too few votes to get into parliament. About 14 percent of respondents answered this question positively, which they then use as an indicator of tactical voting. A probit analysis of these data shows that voters with stronger partisan attachments are less likely to behave tactically, and that those who are ideologically closer to their alternative party are more likely to vote tactically than those who are ideologically farther from it.

Political scientists have also sought to estimate the extent of tactical voting by comparing the choices voters make in mixed member district (MMD) systems, which have become common throughout the world. In the German MMD system, for example, about half the members of parliament are selected from party lists, with seats awarded in proportion to their national vote shares, and the other half from single member districts. Voters thus cast two votes, participating simultaneously in parallel PR and SMD elections. Assuming that voters vote sincerely when casting PR votes, votes cast for other parties' candidates at the district level are deemed to be tactical in nature. Fisher (1973), Jesse (1987), and Bawn (1999) find that, in Germany, major party candidates garner larger percentages of votes in the SMD elections than their parties receive in the PR election. Reed (1999), similarly, finds that in the 1996 MMD election in Japan, voters who supported smaller parties cast larger percentages of votes for them in the PR election than in the district election.

According to Gschwend, Johnston, and Pattie (2003), German parties that had done poorly in the SMD constituency contest in the previous general election were disproportionately hurt by tactical voting — more evidence that voters use an election history heuristic in deciding whether or not to cast a tactical vote. Unlike most studies of tactical voting in pure SMD systems, Bawn finds some support for the marginality hypothesis: the extent of tactical voting was positively correlated with how close the race was between the top two candidates in district-level elections.

Both Bawn (1999) and Gschwend, Johnston, and Pattie (2003) report that, in the German MMD system, remarkably large percentages of small party supporters split their votes across the two elections. In the 1983 election over two thirds of those who voted for the minor party Free Democrats in the PR election, as well as nearly half of those who voted for the Greens, voted for a CDU/CSU or SPD candidate in the SMD contest. One reason why these percentages are so high is because they likely reflect more than just Duvergerian tactical voting. Some of the votes won by the SMD winners in excess of their party's PR totals are "personal" votes reflecting their popularity with the local electorate (Moser and Scheiner 2005), or are due to an incumbency advantage (Bawn 1999).

SMD and PR systems aggregate votes into seats in a very different manner, but PR systems generally differ from SMD systems in another fundamental way: the election does not in and of itself determine who will and who will not be in the next government. This is determined instead by the nature of the party coalitions that form after the election. According to Hobolt and Karp (2010), in 17 Western European countries about two thirds of all governments formed since World War II have been coalitions. Voters presumably care about which parties end up in government, and not just about who gets elected. If so, they might well cast tactical votes based upon their expectations concerning which parties will form coalition governments in the post-election bargaining process.

Just as he had doubted that there would be tactical voting in PR systems motivated by the desire to avoid wasting a vote on a party unlikely to win a seat, Downs (1957) did not believe that voters' decisions would be influenced by considerations of which post-election coalitions would emerge. Tactical voting of this nature would require voters to assess which coalitions were likely to form given different election outcomes, the probability that a party would enter a coalition, and the policy compromises parties would be willing to accept to enter each possible coalition. Few voters, it seemed to Downs (1957: 300), would be able to work out this complicated chain of inferences: "…in systems usually governed by coalitions, most citizens do not vote as though elections were government-selection mechanisms."

Downs notwithstanding, Austen-Smith and Banks (1988) formally characterize the decision environment that voters (and parties) face in situations where coalitional governments are likely to occur, and define conditions under which some voters will engage in tactical voting motivated by coalitional considerations. It is also the case that voters can make use of informational shortcuts to reduce the potentially complex considerations involving election outcomes and coalition formation. Some possible coalitions can be discarded as practical impossibilities – for example, a partnership between the extreme right and extreme left parties. More generally, coalitions of parties that are close ideologically are more likely than ones in which the parties are further apart. There is the electoral history heuristic. Parties that formed a coalition in the past are more likely to form a coalition again. Armstrong and Duch (2010) document historical patterns of coalition governments in 34 countries and find that the composition of governing coalitions (and the prime minister's party in that coalition) is quite stable over time. Finally, in countries where coalition governments are common, party elites can provide information about which coalitions they are willing to enter. In their study of the 2002 election in the Netherlands, Irwin and van Holsteyn (2012) find that voters had reasonably accurate beliefs about the number of seats each party would get and about which coalitions were likely to emerge. A significant number of voters assigned a high likelihood to the coalition government that actually ended up forming. Depending on the party, between 8 and 17 percent of the voters who were in a position to cast a tactical vote based upon coalitional considerations did so. These findings are impressive, given the complexity of the Dutch party system and elite reluctance to make pre-electoral coalition arrangements (Blais et al. 2006).

Predicting what voters will do in response to coalitional expectations, however, is not as simple and straightforward as the Duvergerian hypothesis that they will seek to avoid wasting their votes on parties not in contention. In their study of Austrian elections, Meffert and Gschwend (2010) reason that tactical voting may take three different forms: (1) the standard "wasted vote" hypothesis that supporters of small parties not expected to exceed the electoral threshold defect to a larger party; (2) the "rental vote" hypothesis that some major party supporters vote for a junior coalition party in order to help it pass the minimum threshold for representation; and (3) tactical behavior aimed at influencing (balancing) the composition of the next coalition government. Their study relies on a pre-election survey that asked respondents about their party preferences, their vote intentions, and coalition preferences, as well as their expectations. Their findings show support for all three types of tactical behavior considered. Around 10 percent of small party supporters voted so as to not waste their vote, another 5–10 percent "rented" their vote out to a potential junior coalition partner, and a significant proportion was motivated by concerns about the composition of the governing coalition.

The results of Gschwend's (2007) multinomial logit analysis of survey data from the 1998 MMD German election also support the rental vote hypothesis, in that some CDU/CSU supporters cast votes in the PR contest for their junior coalition partner, the FDP. It does not appear, however, that SPD voters rented out votes to their junior partners, the Greens. The results of a highly sophisticated econometric analysis of data from the 1994 German election by Shikano, Hermann, and Thurner (2009) are similar. About a quarter of CDU/CSU supporters who feared the FDP's entry to parliament was at risk voted FDP, but they also failed to observe this type of behavior among supporters of the other large party, the SPD, which had a pre-electoral coalition arrangement with the Greens. The authors speculate that this difference in behavior among the supporters of the two major parties is due to the fact that the 1994 election was the first time the Green party made pre-election coalition agreements with the SPD. The FDP, in contrast, had often made pre-election coalition agreements, and thus once again electoral history informed voters' tactical behavior.

Bowler, Karp, and Donovan (2010) study the case of New Zealand during the 2002 general election. For this election, almost every New Zealander expected the Labour Party to be in the governing coalition, but there was uncertainty as to whom the junior coalition member would be, if any. Here, around 20 percent of the voters made tactical choices: if they believed their preferred party had little chance of being in government they were more likely to vote for their second most preferred party. If, on the other hand, they believed that their most disliked party had a good chance of being in government, they switched their vote to their second preference so as to block that outcome.

Blais et al. (2006) study tactical voting based upon coalitional considerations in what is probably the most challenging environment of all as far as information is concerned – the nationwide party list elections to the 120-member Israeli Knesset, where there is now a 3.25 percent threshold for representation (prior to 1988 the threshold was only 1 percent). In a national survey conducted prior to the 2003 election, respondents were asked to rate parties, to assess potential coalitions, and to indicate their vote preference. They defined tactical voting to occur in this situation when, instead of voting for their most preferred party, they voted instead for a party they believed would be a member of their most preferred coalition. Their analyses indicate that about 10 percent of Israeli voters voted tactically due to coalitional considerations. Individuals with stronger preferences for a particular party were less likely to cast tactical coalition votes, while those with stronger preferences for a particular coalition were more likely to do so.

Directions for future research

Many political scientists have seen tactical voting as evidence that voters are rational and instrumental; rather than utterly forego the chance of affecting the election, they instead narrow their choice to candidates where their vote might be pivotal. In large-scale elections, however, a voter has far less probability of affecting the outcome than they do of getting hit by lightning several times. The standard rational choice model of tactical voting based on potential pivotality thus hardly seems consistent with a theory that purports to be based upon principles of rationality. The zero likelihood of being pivotal has led some to argue that it makes no sense to cast a tactical vote, but *not* casting a tactical vote, or not voting at all, has the same, utterly inconsequential impact on election outcomes.

It is important, therefore, to learn more about what exactly voters are thinking when they consider casting a tactical or protest vote. They may indeed harbor the illusion of possibly being pivotal, but the consistent evidence that rates of tactical voting are not related to the closeness of the elections suggests they do not. Alvarez and Kiewiet (2009) characterize tactical voters as "rationalistic": they have well-behaved preference orderings, make choices that are consistent with these orderings, and sometimes vote for a lesser preferred candidate *as if* they were the pivotal voter. Another possibility is that tactical voters may see themselves as contributing a vote to a potentially pivotal voting bloc. But this of course does not lessen the problem that their single vote is inconsequential. Finally, tactical voters may not even be thinking in tactical terms at all, but may be simply restricting their voting choices to what they consider to be the feasible set of candidates (Elff 2014).

Although estimates vary considerably, available evidence indicates that in most cases around 15 percent to 40 percent of the voters who are in a position to cast a tactical vote actually do so. Those who strongly support their most preferred party or candidate are less likely to vote tactically and those who are more favorably disposed to a party in contention are more likely, but most potential tactical voters end up voting sincerely. Voters thus display what might be described as a sincerity bias. Why? Is it because they are simply unaware that tactical voting is an option? Or are they aware that they could vote tactically, but, like Pliny the Younger nearly 2,000 years ago, believe that it is morally wrong to misrepresent their preferences? What is needed, then, is more research on the psychology of tactical voting. It is an area of inquiry that is ripe for theoretical and empirical development.

References

Alvarez, R. M. and Kiewiet, D. R. (2009) "Rationality and Rationalistic Choice in the California Recall," *British Journal of Political Science*, vol. 39, no. 2, April, 267–290.

Alvarez, R. M. and Nagler, J. (2000) "A New Approach for Modeling Strategic Voting in Multiparty Elections," *British Journal of Political Science*, vol. 30, no. 1, January, 57–75.

Alvarez, R. M., Boehmke, F., and Nagler, J. (2005) "Strategic Voting in British Elections," *Electoral Studies*, vol. 25, no. 1, March, 1–19.

Armstrong, D. A. and Duch, R. M. (2010) "Why Can Voters Anticipate Post-Election Coalition Formation Likelihoods," *Electoral Studies*, vol. 29, no. 3, September, 308–315.

Austen-Smith, D. and Banks, J. (1988) "Elections, Coalitions, and Legislative Outcomes," *American Political Science Review*, vol. 82, no. 2, June, 405–422.

Bawn, K. (1999) "Voter Responses to Electoral Complexity: Ticket Splitting, Rational Voters, and Representation in the Federal Republic of Germany," *British Journal of Political Science*, vol. 29, no. 3, June, 487–505.

Blais, A., Aldrich, J. H., Indridason, I. H., and Levine, R. (2006) "Do Voters Vote for Government Coalitions? Testing Downs' Pessimistic Conclusion," *Party Politics*, vol. 12, no. 6, November, 691–705.

Bowler, S., Karp, J., and Donovan, T. (2010) "Strategic Coalition Voting: Evidence from New Zealand," *Electoral Studies*, vol. 29, no. 3, September, 350–357.

Cain, Bruce (1978) "Strategic Voting in Britain," *American Journal of Political Science*, vol. 22, no. 3, August, 639–655.

Campbell, A., Converse, P., Miller, W., and Stokes, D. (1966) *Elections and the Political Order*, New York: John Wiley and Sons.

Cox, G. W. (1997) *Making Votes Count: Strategic Coordination in the World's Electoral Systems*, Cambridge: Cambridge University Press.

Cox, G. W. and Shugart, M. S. (1996) "Strategic Voting Under Proportional Representation," *Journal of Law, Economics, and Organization*, vol. 12, no. 2, October, 299–324.

Curtice, J. and Steed, M. (1988) "Appendix 2: Analysis," in Butler, D. and Kavanagh, D. (eds.) *The British General Election of 1987*, New York: St. Martin's Press: 316–362.

Downs, A. (1957) *An Economic Theory of Democracy*, New York: Harper and Row.

Duch, R. M. and Palmer, H. D. (2002) "Strategic Voting in Post-Communist Democracy?," *British Journal of Political Science*, vol. 32, no. 1, January, 63–91.

Duverger, M. (1955) *Political Parties*, New York: Wiley.

Elff, M. (2014) "Separating Tactical from Sincere Voting: A Finite-Mixture Discrete-Choice Modelling Approach to Disentangling Voting Calculi," Paper presented at the 2014 Annual Meeting of the Midwest Political Science Association, Chicago, April 3–6.

Farquharson, R. (1964) *Theory of Voting*, New Haven: Yale University Press.

Fieldhouse, E., Pattie, C., and Johnston, R. (1996) "Tactical Voting and Constituency Campaigning at the 1992 General Election in England," *British Journal of Political Science*, vol. 26, no. 3, July, 403–439.

Fieldhouse, E., Shryane, N., and Pickles, A. (2007) "Strategic Voting and Constituency Context: Modelling Party Preference and Vote in Multiparty Elections," *Political Geography*, vol. 26, no. 2, February, 159–178.

Fisher, S. D. (2001) "Intuition Versus Formal Theory: Tactical Voting in England 1987–1997," Paper presented at the 2001 Annual Meeting of the American Political Science Association, Washington DC, August 30–September 2.

Fisher, S. L. (1973) "The Wasted Vote Thesis: West German Evidence," *Comparative Politics*, vol. 5, no. 2, January, 293–299.

Franklin, M., Niemi, R., and Whitten, G. (1994) "The Two Faces of Tactical Voting," *British Journal of Political Science*, vol. 24, no. 4, October, 549–557.

García-Viñuela, E., Artés, J., and Jurado, I. (2015) "Strategic Voting and Non-Voting in Spanish Elections," *Party Politics*, vol. 21, no. 5, September, 738–749.

Grofman, B., Blais, A., and Bowler, S. (2009) *Duverger's Law of Plurality Voting*, New York: Springer.

Gschwend, T. (2007) "Ticket-Splitting and Strategic Voting under Mixed Electoral Rules: Evidence from Germany," *European Journal of Political Research*, vol. 46, no. 1, January, 1–23.

Gschwend, T., Johnston, R., and Pattie, C. (2003) "Split-Ticket Patterns in Mixed-Member Proportional Election Systems: Estimates and Analyses of Their Spatial Variation at the German Federal Election, 1998," *British Journal of Political Science*, vol. 33, no. 1, January, 109–127.

Gschwend, T., Stoiber, M., and Günther, M. (2004) "Strategic Voting in Proportional Systems: The Case of Finland," Paper presented at the 2004 Annual Meeting of the Midwest Political Science Association, Chicago, April 15–18.

Gunther, R. (1989) "Electoral Laws, Party Systems, and Elites: The Case of Spain," *American Political Science Review*, vol. 83, no. 3, September, 835–858.

Heath, A. and Evans, G. (1994) "Tactical Voting: Concepts, Measurement and Findings," *British Journal of Political Science*, vol. 24, no. 4, October, 557–561.

Heath, A., Jowell, R., Curtice, J., Evans, G., Field, J., and Witherspoon, S. (1991) *Understanding Political Change: The British Voter 1964–1987*, Oxford: Pergamon Press.

Hermann, M., Munzert, S., and Selb, P. (2016) "Determining the Effect of Strategic Voting on Election Results," *Journal of Royal Statistical Society*, vol. 179, no. 2, February, 583–605.

Hobolt, S. B. and Karp, J. A. (2010) "Voters and Coalition Governments," *Electoral Studies*, vol. 29, no. 3, September, 299–307.

Irwin, G. A. and van Holsteyn, J. J. M. (2012) "Strategic Electoral Considerations Under Proportional Representation," *Electoral Studies*, vol. 31, no. 1, September, 184–191.

Jesse, E. (1987) "Split-Voting in the Federal Republic of Germany: An Analysis of the Federal Elections from 1953 to 1987," *Electoral Studies*, vol. 7, no. 2, August, 109–124.

Johnston, R. (1981) "Regional Variations in British Voting Trends – 1966–1979: Tests of an Ecological Model," *Regional Studies*, vol. 15, no. 1, January, 23–32.

Johnston, R. and Pattie, C. (1991) "Tactical Voting in Britain in 1983 and 1987: An Alternative Approach," *British Journal of Political Science*, vol. 21, no. 1, January, 95–128.

Kiewiet, D. R. (2013) "The Ecology of Tactical Voting in Britain," *Journal of Elections, Public Opinion and Parties*, vol. 23, no. 1, January, 86–110.

Lago, I. (2008) "Rational Expectations or Heuristics? Strategic Voting in Proportional Representation Systems," *Party Politics*, vol. 14, no. 1, January, 31–49.

Lanoue, D. and Bowler, S. (1992) "The Sources of Tactical Voting in British Parliamentary Elections, 1983–1987," *Political Behavior*, vol. 14, no. 2, June, 141–157.

Leys, C. (1959) "Models, Theories and the Theory of Political Parties," *Political Studies*, vol. 7, no. 2, June, 127–146.

Meffert, M. F. and Gschwend, T. (2010) "Strategic Coalition Voting: Evidence from Austria," *Electoral Studies*, vol. 29, no. 3, September, 339–349.

Moser, R. G. and Scheiner, E. (2005) "Strategic Ticket Splitting and the Personal Vote in Mixed-Member Electoral Systems," *Legislative Studies Quarterly*, vol. 30, no. 2, May, 259–276.

Myatt, D. and Fisher, S. D. (2002) "Tactical Coordination in Plurality Electoral Systems," *Oxford Review of Economic Policy*, vol. 18, no. 4, Winter, 504–522.

Niemi, R., Whitten, G., and Franklin, M. (1992) "Constituency Characteristics, Individual Characteristics and Tactical Voting in the 1987 British General Election," *British Journal of Political Science*, vol. 22, no. 2, April, 229–240.

Palfrey, T. (1989) "A Mathematical Proof of Duverger's Law," in Ordeshook, P. (ed.) *Models of Strategic Choice in Politics*, Ann Arbor: University of Michigan Press: 69–72.

Reed, S. R. (1999) "Strategic Voting in the 1996 Japanese General Election," *Comparative Political Studies*, vol. 32, no. 2, April, 257–270.

Sartori, G. (1968) "Political Development and Political Engineering," in Montgomery, J. D. and Hirschman, A. O. (eds.) *Public Policy*, Cambridge: Cambridge University Press: 261–298.

Shikano, S., Herrmann, M., and Thurner, P. W. (2009) "Strategic Voting Under Proportional Representation: Threshold Insurance in German Elections," *West European Politics*, vol. 32, no. 3, April, 634–656.

Shively, W. P. (1970) "The Elusive 'Psychological' Factor: A Test for the Impact of Electoral Systems on Voters' Behavior," *Comparative Politics*, vol. 3, no. 1, October, 115–125.

Spafford, D. (1972) "Electoral Systems and Voters' Behavior: Comment and a Further Test," *Comparative Politics*, vol. 5, no. 1, October, 129–134.

Tavits, M. and Annus, A. (2006) "Learning to Make Votes Count: The Role of Democratic Experience," *Electoral Studies*, vol. 25, no. 1, March, 72–90.

16

ECONOMIC VOTING

Marianne C. Stewart and Harold D. Clarke

The central importance of relationships among economy, polity and society to the wealth of nations and the well-being of people has attracted much interest among academic researchers and non-academic observers for many years (see, for example, Smith 1776; Keynes 1936; Acemoglu and Robinson 2012). Since at least the early 1970s, this interest has been heightened by the varying fortunes of governing parties and their opponents, of government policies and of economic conditions (see, for example, Vig and Schier 1985: Chapter 1; Clarke et al. 1992: Chapter 1; Clarke et al. 2016). One area of interest involves reaction functions and outcomes functions, whereas another is popularity-vote (V-P) functions (see, for example, Whiteley 1986; Clarke et al. 1992: Chapters 1 and 8; Lewis-Beck and Stegmaier 2013; Stegmaier, Lewis-Beck and Park 2017). Reaction functions refer to government effects on economic policies, as well as policy effects on economic outcomes, notably whether and how government policies can stimulate employment, growth and investment and reduce inflation and poverty. V-P functions pertain to the effects of economic conditions (the objective economy) and economic evaluations (the subjective economy) on people's party support, including their economic voting.

Economic-voting research has become a well-developed but a still-progressing program (for reviews, see Norpoth, Lewis-Beck and Lafay 1991; Lewis-Beck and Stegmaier 2000, 2007; van der Brug, van der Eijk and Franklin 2007; Duch and Stevenson 2008; Lewis-Beck and Costa Lobo 2017). This chapter reviews the contributions of this program, and offers several recommendations for its progress in terms of models, measures and methodologies.

Major models of economic voting

A major model of economic voting is *the reward-punishment model* (Downs 1957; Key 1968; for reviews, see Clarke et al. 1992 and Lewis-Beck and Stegmaier 2007). According to this model, people who evaluate economic conditions as getting better vote for, thereby "rewarding," a governing party or leader. But people who judge that these conditions have worsened vote for an opponent, thereby "punishing" an incumbent party or leader. This model involves at least three assumptions (see, for example, Clarke et al. 1992: Chapter 1). First, people apply a rational-choice, "optimizing" strategy by "rewarding" a governing party that pushes economic conditions toward, while "punishing" one that pulls such conditions away from, their preferred performance. Second, people use retrospective judgments by focusing on past or recent performance of the country's economy and/or their own economic circumstances during the time that a party is in government (see Kiewiet 1983; see also Healy and Malhotra 2013). This focus is sensible since economic performance that is currently "known" is presumably more reliable than that which requires future guessing. Third, people attribute responsibility to governing parties for the performance of the country's and/or their own economic circumstances. When doing so, they credit the government for better circumstances or blame it for worsening ones (see, for example, Powell and Whitten 1993; Anderson 1995).

Although the reward–punishment model is straightforward and has attracted much attention among academic researchers and non-academic observers, its coronation as the superior explanation of economic voting remains premature. There are two major reasons for this. One set of reasons involves the reward–punishment model itself (see, for example, Monroe 1979; Clarke et al. 1992; Lewis-Beck and Stegmaier 2007). The model is fundamentally misnamed because voters may not have reward/credit or punitive/blame motivations but, rather, a best-performance incentive of wanting the best economic conditions for their country and for themselves. Moreover, several assumptions that inform the model are not necessarily consistent with a rational-choice view (see, for example, Monroe 1991). According to this view, people should not be retrospective but, rather, prospective thereby using current or future-focused information to update their evaluations, with little or no discounting of this information by their past evaluations of economic performance. Indeed, other research shows that people can be more prospective than retrospective when making their vote decisions (see, for example, Lewis-Beck 1988; MacKuen, Erickson and Stimson 1992; Clarke and Stewart 1994; van der Brug, van der Eijk and Franklin 2007).

Responsibility attributions raise other considerations. Contexts that permit the formation of clear responsibility attributions tend to display stronger economic effects on vote choices (for discussion, see Lewis-Beck and Stegmaier 2007). But, responsibility attributions can be asymmetric with governing parties "blamed/punished" for bad performance but not necessarily "credited"/"rewarded" for good performance (see, for example, Bloom and Douglas Price 1975; Clarke et al. 1992; van Brug, van der Eijk and Franklin 2007). And people who live in institutionally complex settings, such as those with multiple parties in coalition governments or (con)federal systems with two or more government levels having overlapping economic-management jurisdictions, might be excused for lacking valid information about who is responsible for what (Powell and Whitten 1993; Anderson 1995; Schwindt-Bayer and Tavits 2016). In such settings, people's information and knowledge can be confused rather than clarified, because responsibility for economic performance is confused rather than clarified. A vote-seeking party in a governing coalition and/or a (con)federal system strategically shirks when it tries to offload responsibility for economic performance to another party or another level (Clarke et al. 1992; van Brug, van der Eijk and Franklin 2007).

Cognitive difficulties may be further imposed on people's economic evaluations (the subjective economy) when they try to obtain accurate information about economic conditions (the objective economy) from multiple, streaming sources. Thus, the links between evaluations and conditions might be best described as "through a glass darkly," with distorted evaluations based on incomplete information about economic conditions (see, for example, Stimson 1989; Clarke et al. 1992: Chapter 3). The linkage becomes blurrier when the conditions being considered are country-level (that is, sociotropic; see, for example, Kinder and Kiewiet 1981), rather than personal (that is, egocentric), since voters might be expected to know relatively less about the former than about the latter.

A second set of reasons why the coronation of the reward-punishment model is premature is that *rival models and alternative frameworks* lay claim to the crown of superior explanation of economic voting. According to the issue-priority model, public evaluations of political parties as "owning" particular issues influence voting choices (see Budge and Farlie 1983; Clarke et al. 1992: Chapter 1). For example, people would vote for, not against, a governing conservative/right-of-center party when they think that rising taxes are an important issue and that this party's proven record will guide it to lower taxes in comparison with that of a left-of-center/liberal party. In turn, people would support a governing left-of-center/liberal party when they think that rising poverty is a real problem and that this party's known reputation will guide it to reduce poverty much more than would that of a conservative/right-of-center alternative.

The spatial and valence models distinguish between economic issue types (see Downs 1957; Stokes 1963, 1992; for discussions, see Clarke et al. 1992: Chapter 1, 2004: 21–25, 2009, 2016; Whiteley et al. 2013). In a spatial (or positional or issue-proximity) model, parties express different issue preferences, people form specific issue preferences, and they estimate which party's preferences approximate their own when choosing how to vote. Income (re)distribution is an example of spatial issues. In a valence (or performance) model, parties and people agree on a preferred issue outcome, and people then assess which governing or opposition party is most able to produce this outcome when deciding how to vote. Two examples of valence issues are a good economy and a safe society.

Overall, the four models described above share several similarities (for additional discussion, see Clarke et al. 2004: 21–25). They acknowledge the role of economic performance evaluations in vote choices and they do not meet all of the strict requirements of rational-choice theory (see, for example, Monroe 1991). But, unlike the reward–punishment model, the issue-priority, spatial and valence models recognize that vote choices are influenced, albeit in sometimes counter-intuitive ways, by retrospective and/or prospective as well as by egocentric and/or sociotropic economic evaluations. These other models also allow that most voters' evaluations of economic performance are not based on full and perfect information. Rather, experimental economists and cognitive psychologists have conducted numerous experiments that have contributed important insights into how people make decisions, including their use of cognitive "short-cuts" or cues, in political-economic settings (see, for example, Sniderman, Brody and Tetlock 1991; Gigerenzer 2008; Gigerenzer, Hertwig and Pachur 2011; Kahneman 2011; Thaler 2016). These cues include, but are not limited to, their party (non)identifications and/or their attitudes about parties and candidates/leaders.

As is well known, party identification and candidate/leader attitudes are important factors in two major and alternative theoretical frameworks of voting behavior. According to the social-psychology framework, the "funnel of causality" begins with socialization learning and social groups leading to the formation of party identification as "the unmoved mover," which, in turn, affects candidate attitudes, issue attitudes and voting behavior (Campbell et al. 1960; Butler and Stokes 1969). This framework has received much attention, including challenges by empirical analyses of partisan change and by the individual choice framework. In this framework, the "running tally" operates when people update their candidate/leader and issue attitudes and, in turn, their party (non)identifications and electoral choices (Downs 1957; Key 1968; Fiorina 1981).

The above review leads to *three principal recommendations* for further progress in economic-voting research. One recommendation is that it develop and apply an "anthropology" of voters. This anthropology would recognize that people do think and they do form evaluations, but they are not omniscient and they do use cognitive short-cuts or cues about performance when forming their vote decisions. Second, multiple models – not one model – of economic voting exist and vie for analytical attention. This recommendation is not a plea for the proliferation of models and the rejection of none. Rather, the models and frameworks discussed above require ongoing collections of reliable and valid data and analyses having strong diagnostic tests. These enable assessment of which model is inferior, which model is superior since it can do what other models do and do not, or whether several models contribute coherently to the explanation of economic voting. A third and related recommendation recognizes that models of economic voting are fundamentally nested in models of electoral behavior. Accordingly, the former need to include, rather than ignore, economic attitudes as well as candidate/leader, other issue and party (non)identification attitudes to avoid the risk of misspecification error and its threat to causal inference.

Multiple measures of economic voting

In economic-voting research, the principal dependent variables are *vote intentions* and *vote choices*. The former is typically based on survey questions that ask people about whether they intend to vote and, if so, then for which candidate or party in a forthcoming election. Vote choices are usually based on survey questions that ask people whether they did vote and, if so, then for which candidate or party in a just-held election.

The principal explanatory or independent variables tend to be of two types. As discussed above, one type is the *objective economy*, which involves employment, inflation, investment or growth indicators based on government or other statistical data. These objective indicators have been argued to be the key drivers (see, for example, Kramer 1983; Hibbs 1987; Fair 1978), or to play an important role (see, for example, van der Brug, van der Eijk and Franklin 2007; van der Eijk et al. 2007), in people's voting and other party support decisions. However, and as also noted above, objective economic indicators say little about how voters think as well as form and act on attitudes about economic performance. Accordingly, another type pertains to the *subjective economy*. Since approximately the mid-1950s, various election studies and other major surveys have included one or more of several questions enabling multiple measures of economic evaluations. Some questions ask people about the economy in general or about inflation or unemployment in particular, whereas other questions ask them about their own personal economic circumstances. These questions inquire whether people think that the country's economy has gotten better, gotten worse or stayed the same over the past year (sociotropic retrospection); whether it will get better, get worse or stay the same over the upcoming year (sociotropic prospection); whether their personal economic circumstances have gotten better, gotten worse or stayed the same over the past year (egocentric retrospection); and whether these circumstances will get better, get worse or stay the same over the upcoming year (egocentric prospection) (see Lewis-Beck 1988; Lewis-Beck and Stegmaier 2007).

These four measures have provided valuable service to economic-voting research. However, further research progress depends in part on at least *two important recommendations*. First, survey instruments need to avoid periodically asking just one, two or three questions, or asking the two egocentric questions combined and the two sociotropic questions combined. Instead, all four evaluation questions need to be asked consistently for proper measurement construction and model testing. A second recommendation is related to the anthropology of the voter. It recognizes that people's attitudes are evaluative as well as affective and cognitive, and all three have experiential bases. In this regard, more attention needs to be paid to voters' emotional reactions, such as anger or happiness, and fear or confidence, regarding their own or the country's economic circumstances (see, for example, Conover and Feldman 1986). And more thought needs to be given to how people acquire economic information indirectly by accessing news provided by various media outlets (see, for example, Mutz and Kim 2017) and/or directly through economic experiences. These experiences include, but are not limited to, employment and income situations or prospects, purchases of food, clothing, shelter and other needs and wants, wealth assets and liabilities, as well as conversations with others that exchange information based on both news and experiences (see, for example, Conover, Feldman and Knight 1987; Feldman and Conley 1991; Lewis-Beck, Nadeau and Foucault 2013).

Methodological issues in economic voting

To date, economic-voting research has relied heavily on observational methods. Much of this research has used aggregate- or individual-level data and multivariate statistical models. These models typically have been single-equation specifications whose parameters are estimated using ordinary least squares regression or maximum likelihood techniques.

Some researchers have long advocated the use of *aggregate-level data* (see, for example, Kramer 1971, 1983). Indeed, path-breaking studies conducted during the revival of political-economy research in the 1970s and 1980s tended to be simple aggregate-level models that regressed party support in successive national elections (see, for example, Fair 1978) or vote intentions as measured in monthly public opinion polls (see, for example, Mueller 1970), on objective economic indicators involving employment, inflation and/or economic growth rates. The relative simplicity of these models and their promise of providing a tool for forecasting the future dynamics of party support conditional on economic outcomes stimulated considerable excitement in the research community.

However, initial enthusiasm waned when it became evident that these first-generation, aggregate-level models of party support suffered from several intertwined theoretical/modeling and methodological problems. As discussed above, a fundamental theoretical problem is that regressions with macroeconomic aggregates, such as unemployment, inflation or growth rates, as explanatory variables told researchers little about the psychology underpinning voters' party support decisions. Are voters primarily retrospectively or prospectively oriented? Are they ego-centric or sociotropic actors (see, for example, Kinder and Kiewiet 1981)? Are they a homogeneous group whose members all react the same way, or is there significant heterogeneity reflecting varying levels of cognitive capacity and political knowledge (Converse 1964; see also Luskin 1987; Lupia 2016)? Perhaps most basically, what is the anthropology of voters? Are they rational actors closely akin to the "homo economicus" who populates introductory economics texts, or "homo heuristicus" who is found in the experimental research of behavioral economists and cognitive psychologists? Answers to these questions have major implications for the specification and interpretation of models of economic voting and political choice (see van der Brug, van der Eijk and Franklin 2007; Clarke et al. 2009; Clarke, Elliott and Stewart 2015).

Related theoretical/modeling and methodological difficulties that occurred in early aggregate-level studies and continue to bedevil much contemporary scholarship deserve further mention. As discussed in the "Major models" section above, one difficulty involves "issue-priority" or "issue-ownership" considerations. It has long been evident that party reputations for competence in managing economic affairs, and for being concerned about and responsive to particular economic problems, such as unemployment or inflation (see, for example, Budge and Farlie 1983; Clarke et al. 1992: Chapter 1), can vary over time. Such variations occurred in Great Britain when the currency crisis in September 1992 and the Great Recession starting in 2008 both caused serious erosion in the economic competence reputations of governing parties of the day (see, for example, Whiteley et al. 2013; Clarke et al. 2016). Accordingly, the impact of economic conditions on party support can differ depending on these reputational variations. This can produce parameter instability in dynamic models for analyses conducted in single countries, as well as differences in parameter values in cross-national comparative studies.

A related difficulty is that economic issues are perennially important, but their salience on the political agenda changes over time, co-varying with other domestic and (less frequently) foreign policy issues. However, variables measuring the impact of these noneconomic issues on party support were not included in the early aggregate-level studies and attention to them remains quite uneven. A further difficulty is that individual-level data analyses have long shown that attitudes about party leaders are important explanatory variables in some political systems (Campbell et al. 1960; Clarke et al. 2004; Clarke, Kornberg and Scotto 2009). These variables also were noticeably absent from the early aggregate-level political economy models and, with few exceptions, their omission continues.

The basic point here is that extremely parsimonious specifications of aggregate-level economic-voting models are likely to be a serious liability for assessing the impact of the economy on the dynamics of party support within and across political systems. However technically sound their econometrics, regressions of party vote shares in successive elections or monthly/quarterly polling data on macroeconomic statistics are unlikely to tell us what we need to know about how variations in the economy affects party support within and across countries. Adequate specification of aggregate-level vote and popularity functions requires attention to voters' reactions to noneconomic events and conditions, but time series data on these events and conditions may be unavailable.

Aggregate-level economic-voting models also have encountered a variety of estimation problems. For example, famous simulations (see, for example, Granger and Newbold 1974) and formal analyses (see, for example, Phillips 1986; Sims, Stock and Watson 1990) convincingly show that regressions involving nonstationary (trending) measures of party support and non-stationary macroeconomic variables encounter "spurious regression" risks that pose serious threats to inference. As conjectured nearly a century ago (Yule 1926), type 1 errors are rife in such regressions. Although early studies typically ignored these risks, most researchers now employ a set of standard unit-root tests to determine whether their data are nonstationary and they difference variables as required before estimating economic-voting models.

Other problems exist. For example, when doing post-estimation diagnostics, researchers who find that residuals are serially correlated often try to "fix" this problem by inserting a lagged endogenous (dependent) variable as an additional predictor variable. If the data are stationary, this practice may be technically sound (if there is no simultaneity bias induced by the presence of the lagged endogenous variable), but it has a significant theoretical implication that may be overlooked. The revised model with the lagged endogenous variable implies that all of the explanatory variables have dynamic effects on the dependent variable, with the size of these effects eroding at the same rate at successively longer lags. Skeptics are right to require additional testing against rival specifications that permit dynamic effects to vary across predictors or to be absent entirely for some of them. Similar considerations regarding theory and interpretations of estimation results apply to other models, such as those estimated using feasible generalized least squares techniques (see, for example, Greene 2011), with implications that are hidden from naive analysts and their readers.

Economic-voting models that use time series data pooled across multiple groups (typically countries) also can be problematic. Like analyses of data for single groups, these panel studies require stationary data, and the use of lagged endogenous variables may be problematic for the reasons just stated. However, there are additional difficulties with panel designs. The most well-known is unit-induced heteroskedasticity, and researchers have long debated the advantages and disadvantages of using fixed- and random-effects estimators to address this difficulty (see, for example, Bell and Jones 2015).

A basic difficulty involves the pooling operation itself. This operation assumes that all predictor variables have exactly the same effects for all units, that is, there is parameter invariance across space and time. But this assumption is highly implausible since it is very unlikely that, for example, economic-voting effects are the same in different countries over time. Panel unit-root tests can help researchers to assess whether the dynamics of economic conditions or party support vary significantly across units. Moreover, rather than pooling data a priori, analysts often would be well advised to pool only if tests for parameter invariance provide a "green light" or, at a minimum, after "jack-knifing" to investigate whether particular units are driving theoretically interesting findings by exercising undue leverage on parameter estimates.

A final problem with aggregate-level economic-voting models concerns the aforementioned conjecture that endogeneity is causing simultaneity bias. Although critics seldom conjure the specter of endogeneity when party support variables are regressed on objective economic conditions, such as unemployment and inflation, they often do so when covariates are measures of voters' cognitive or emotional reactions to those conditions. This is especially the case if the model under consideration is an error correction specification that involves a long-run (co-integrating) relationship between economic attitudes and party support. Critics often recommend that the analyst should conduct Granger causality tests (Granger 1969) to check whether endogeneity is present and simultaneity bias poses a threat to inference. The check for endogeneity is prudent. But, Granger causality tests are relevant only for conditional forecasting exercises where the $t + i$ feedback from Y to X needs to be incorporated into a multi-equation specification for forecasts extending beyond the time horizon of the feedback loop.

Given the above, weak exogeneity tests have been recommended to determine whether Y is likely to affect X contemporaneously (see, for example, Charemza and Deadman 1997). But, such tests tend to have weak statistical power and are subject to misspecification because of the absence of strong theoretical rationale for the model of X. Accordingly, the specifications of vector autoregressive (VAR) and, if co-integration is present, vector error correction (VECM) models have been recently recommended (Whiteley et al. 2016; see also Sims 1980; Johansen 1996). The VECM approach has proven to be very useful for modeling the inter-related dynamics among economic evaluations and other key variables in a valence politics model of party support in Britain (Whiteley et al. 2016; see also Clarke et al. 2009). The approach is an attractive way of handling mutually endogenous relationships, but it requires relatively high frequency (e.g., monthly) time series data on all variables under consideration (e.g., economic evaluations, attitudes about other issues and about party leaders). Such data are available for Britain over the 1992–2015 period, but this often is not the case for other places and other times.

Still other economic-voting researchers have used *individual-level data* that typically rely on survey data, especially those gathered in national election studies. Since its inception nearly 70 years ago, the American National Election Study (ANES) has served as a template for these surveys in a wide range of established democracies as well as emerging ones, such as the Taiwan Election and Democratization Study (TEDS) (see Ho et al. 2013). The usefulness of these national election studies has been significantly enhanced by other survey data collections for conducting cross-national research on economic voting and other topics in comparative perspective. These include the Comparative Study of Electoral Systems (CSES), which places common modules of questions on successive national election studies in multiple countries; the Eurobarometers (see, for example, Lewis-Beck 1988); the European Parliament Election Studies involving 42 cross-sectional surveys conducted in all EC/EU countries after the 1989, 1994 and 1999 elections (van der Brug, van der Eijk and Franklin 2007); the European Social Surveys (ESS); and other projects (see, for example, Duch and Stevenson 2008; for a review, see Lewis-Beck and Stegmaier 2007).

Although many of these national surveys are either "one-shot" post-election cross-sections or two-wave pre- and post-election panels, some are multi-wave panels conducted over several months or entire election cycles. These panel designs were introduced several decades ago (see, for example, Campbell et al. 1960; Butler and Stokes 1969), and they help researchers to assess stability and change in party support and public attitudes about economic conditions and other theoretically relevant variables. This task is not as simple as it might appear because observed change in responses to survey questions at two or more points in time may reflect random measurement error rather than true change (Green, Palmquist and Schickler 2002). But, the task is not insuperable. Four or more waves of panel data permit estimation of parameters for mixed Markov latent class (MMLC) models that assess the magnitude of true (latent-level) change controlling for random measurement error (Clarke et al. 2004, 2009; Clarke and McCutcheon 2009). Estimates of the proportions of "movers" and "stayers" for theoretically important variables like party identification (see, for example, Fiorina 1981; Green, Palmquist and Schickler 2002; Clarke et al. 2004) can help researchers resolve longstanding controversies in the voting behavior literature that are relevant for understanding how economic conditions affect party support.

Using multi-wave panel surveys to estimate MMLC models of economic voting is an example of the more general point that panel surveys can provide significant leverage for addressing statistical issues that can threaten inference in research designs that rely on cross-sectional data. Although their statistical power makes multi-wave panel surveys attractive to economic-voting and other researchers, they are in short supply because they are very expensive. Multi-wave surveys also can suffer from sampling problems due to panel attrition and/or measurement problems due to panel-conditioning effects (see, for example, Weisberg 2005).

Persistent problems with cross-sectional designs also arise when a covariate in an estimating equation is correlated with the random error term in that equation. As is well known, this correlation will produce a biased and inconsistent estimate of the effect of that covariate (see, for example, Greene 2011). In economic-voting models, these biases may occur because of endogenous relationships between the dependent variable (a measure of party support) and a covariate (e.g., evaluations of national or personal economic conditions over retrospective or prospective time horizons). The "endogeneity conjecture" is that party support (partisan attachments, vote intention or the vote itself) influences voters' attitudes about economic conditions, and this reciprocal causal influence creates a simultaneity bias in models that seek to estimate the effects of those attitudes on party support (see, for example, Wlezien, Franklin and Twiggs 1997; Evans and Andersen 2006; van der Eijk et al. 2007).

Some economic-voting students have attempted to minimize or to eliminate endogeneity problems in several ways. One way uses pre-post election panel data, with all covariates measured in the pre-election wave panel and voting reports measured in the post-election wave. Assuming voters cast their ballots on election day (or any time after the first panel wave), it is argued that the act of voting could not have caused pre-election responses to queries about economic evaluations (see, for example, Lewis-Beck 1988). However, critics contend that the endogeneity problem has been inadequately controlled for in many studies that rely on cross-sectional or two-wave panel survey data (see, for example, Evans and Chzhen 2016). They further contend that statistical models using data drawn from three or more panel waves show that the dominant flow of influence is from party support to economic evaluations rather than vice versa. Another way uses objective measures rather than subjective assessments of economic conditions (van der Brug, van der Eijk and Franklin 2007). Still other ways of dealing with the problems exist (e.g., Duch and Stevenson 2008; but see Franklin 2009).

In response, researchers who argue that economic attitudes have sizable and consequential influences on party support also argue that the statistical models employed by proponents of the endogeneity hypothesis are seriously flawed for several reasons. These include model misspecification, mismeasurement of key variables and "timing problems" in the conduct of multi-wave surveys such that data are not gathered at points in time coordinated with the flow of economic information in the electorate (Whiteley et al. 2016). The latter problem also may cause these models to have their own unappreciated simultaneity biases.

Attempts to deal with endogeneity problems in individual-level economic-voting models via standard econometric instrumental variables procedures incur difficulties. These include the absence of suitable instruments (but see Nadeau, Lewis-Beck and Belanger 2013), the lack of statistical power of standard endogeneity tests and the absence of strong theory to mandate the specification of models used for endogeneity testing. The latter two problems can create a further problem if researchers join the "frequent regressors club" by conducting specification searches that continue until a preferred (exogeneity or endogeneity) test result is obtained.

Conclusion

Since the revival of political-economy research in the early 1970s, the economic-voting field has witnessed substantial progress as well as enduring controversies. Some scholars initially attracted to the field by the "promise of parsimony" discovered the field to be more difficult than originally thought. Similar to other areas of social-science inquiry, economic-voting studies experience theoretical, modeling and methodological challenges involving specification and analysis of multivariate models of observational data. The usefulness of these analyses depends on the quality of the theories guiding model specification and the availability of data that permit analysts to estimate parameters with confidence. In addition, and motivated by a desire to make broad generalizations across countries and over time, economic-voting students have encountered significant "contextual challenges" posed by varying combinations of economic, political and institutional differences between political systems and significant change within systems over time.

As discussed in this chapter, economic-voting researchers have reacted to these several challenges with industry and ingenuity and many valuable studies have appeared. More remains to be done. Particularly important will be the acquisition of high-frequency time series data that can facilitate dynamic analyses which address model specification and parameter estimation problems discussed above. Coordinated cross-national data collections of this type would be especially valuable for systematic analyses of the influence of contextual factors on economic voting.

Equally important, researchers need to address basic questions about the anthropology of the voter and their implications for theories and models of political choice. Doing so requires close attention to the results of research by behavioral economists and cognitive psychologists, as well as those by political psychologists that document significant heterogeneity of people's levels of political sophistication. This recommendation may be seen as a variant of the challenge that Herbert Simon (1956) posed over half a century ago when he scandalized fellow economists by daring to conjecture that the world is populated by real people who satisfice, rather than by abstract agents who optimize. A similar challenge is relevant today for students of economic voting who wish to advance their field of inquiry in theoretically interesting and reality-oriented ways.

References

Acemoglu, D. and Robinson, J. A. (2012) *Why Nations Fail: The Origins of Power, Prosperity and Poverty*, New York: Crown Publishers/Random House.

Anderson, C. J. (1995) *Blaming the Government: Citizens and the Economy in Five European Democracies*, Armonk: M. D. Sharpe.

Bell, A. and Jones, K. (2015) "Explaining Fixed Effects: Random Effects Modeling of Time-Series Cross-sectional and Panel Data," *Political Science Research and Methods*, vol. 3, no. 1, January, 133–153.

Bloom, H. and Douglas Price, H. (1975) "Voter Response to Short-Run Economic Conditions: The Asymmetric Effects of Prosperity and Recession," *American Political Science Review*, vol. 69, no. 4, December, 1240–1254.

Brug, W. van der, Eijk, C. van der and Franklin, M. N. (2007) *The Economy and the Vote: Economic Conditions and Elections in Fifteen Countries*, New York: Cambridge University Press.

Budge, I. and Farlie, D. J. (1983) *Explaining and Predicting Elections: Issue Effects and Party Strategies in Twenty-Three Democracies*, London: George Allen & Unwin.

Butler, D. and Stokes, D. E. (1969) *Political Change in Britain: Forces Shaping Electoral Choice*, London: Macmillan.

Campbell, A., Converse, P. E., Miller, W. E. and Stokes, D. E. (1960) *The American Voter*, New York: John Wiley & Sons.

Charemza, W. W. and Deadman, D. F. (1997) *New Directions in Econometric Practice*, 2nd Edition, Aldershot: Edward Elgar Publishing.

Clarke, H. D. and McCutcheon, A. (2009) "The Dynamics of Party Identification Reconsidered," *Public Opinion Quarterly*, vol. 73, no. 4, Winter, 704–728.

Clarke, H. D. and Stewart, M. C. (1994) "Prospections, Retrospections, and Rationality: The 'Bankers' Model of Presidential Approval Reconsidered," *American Journal of Political Science*, vol. 38, no. 4, November, 1104–1123.

Clarke, H. D., Elliott, E. W., Mishler, W., Stewart, M. C., Whiteley, P. F. and Zuk, G. (1992) *Controversies in Political Economy: Canada, Great Britain, the United States*, Boulder: Westview Press.

Clarke, H. D., Elliott, E. W. and Stewart, M. C. (2015) "Heuristics, Heterogeneity and Green Choices: Voting on California's Proposition 23," *Political Science Research and Methods*, available online: https://doi.org/10.1017/psrm.2015.39.

Clarke, H. D., Kellner, P., Stewart, M. C., Twyman, J. and Whiteley, P. (2016) *Austerity and Political Choice in Britain*, Basingstoke: Palgrave Pivot/Macmillan.

Clarke, H. D., Kornberg, A. and Scotto, T. J. (2009) *Making Political Choices: Canada and the United States*, Toronto: University of Toronto Press.

Clarke, H. D., Sanders, D., Stewart, M. C. and Whiteley, P. (2004) *Political Choice in Britain*, Oxford: Oxford University Press.

Clarke, H. D., Sanders, D., Stewart, M. C. and Whiteley, P. (2009) *Performance Politics and the British Voter*, Cambridge: Cambridge University Press.

Conover, P. J. and Feldman, S. (1986) "Emotional Reactions to the Economy: I'm Mad as Hell and I'm Not Going to Take It Anymore," *American Journal of Political Science*, vol. 30, no. 1, February, 50–78.

Conover, P. J., Feldman, S. and Knight, K. (1987) "The Personal and Political Underpinnings of Economic Forecasts," *American Journal of Political Science*, vol. 31, no. 3, August, 559–583.

Converse, P. E. (1964) "The Nature of Belief Systems in Mass Publics," in Apter, D. E. (ed.) *Ideology and Discontent*, Glencoe: The Free Press: 206–261.

Downs, A. (1957) *An Economic Theory of Democracy*, New York: Harper and Row.

Duch, R. M. and Stevenson, R. T. (2008) *The Economic Vote: How Political and Economic Institutions Condition Election Results*, New York: Cambridge University Press.

Eijk, C. van der, Franklin, M. N., Demant, F. and van der Brug, W. (2007) "The Endogenous Economy: 'Real' Economic Conditions, Subjective Economic Evaluations and Government Support," *Acta Politica*, vol. 42, no 1, April, 1–22.

Evans, G. and Andersen, R. (2006) "The Political Conditioning of Economic Perceptions," *Journal of Politics*, vol. 68, no. 1, February, 194–207.

Evans, G. and Chzhen, K. (2016) "Re-Evaluating the Valence Politics Model of Political Choice," *Political Science Research and Methods*, vol. 4, no. 1, January, 199–220.

Fair, R. C. (1978) "The Effects of Economic Events on Votes for President," *The Review of Economics and Statistics*, vol. 60, no. 2, April, 159–173.

Feldman, S. and Conley, P. (1991) "Explaining Explanations of Changing Economic Conditions," in Norpoth, H., Lewis-Beck, M. S. and Lafay, J-D. (eds.) (1991) *Economics and Politics: The Calculus of Support*, Ann Arbor: University of Michigan Press: 185–206.

Fiorina, M. P. (1981) *Retrospective Voting in American National Elections*, New Haven: Yale University Press.

Franklin, M. N. (2009) "Book Review – The Economic Vote: How Political and Economic Institutions Condition Election Results by Raymond M. Duch and Randolph T. Stevenson," *Perspectives on Politics*, vol. 7, no. 1, March, 202–203.

Gigerenzer, G. (2008) *Rationality for Mortals: How People Cope with Uncertainty*, Oxford: Oxford University Press.

Gigerenzer, G., Hertwig, R. and Pachur, T. (eds.) (2011) *Heuristics: The Foundations of Adaptive Behavior*, Oxford: Oxford University Press.

Granger, C. (1969) "Understanding Causal Relations by Econometric Models and Cross-Spectral Methods," *Econometrica*, vol. 37, no. 3, August, 424–438.

Granger, C. and Newbold, P. (1974) "Spurious Regression in Econometrics," *Journal of Econometrics*, vol. 2, no. 2, July, 111–120.

Green, D., Palmquist, B. and Schickler, E. (2002) *Partisan Hearts and Minds*, New Haven: Yale University Press.

Greene, W. (2011) *Econometric Analysis*, 7th Edition, Upper Saddle River: Pearson Education Ltd.

Healy, A. and Malhotra, N. (2013) "Retrospective Voting Reconsidered," *Annual Review of Political Science*, vol. 16, May, 285–306.

Hibbs, D. A. (1987) *The American Political Economy: Macroeconomics and Electoral Politics*, Cambridge, MA: Harvard University Press.

Ho, K., Clarke, H. D., Chen, L. K. and Weng, D. L-C. (2013) "Valence Politics and Electoral Choice in a New Democracy: The Case of Taiwan," *Electoral Studies*, vol. 32, no. 3, September, 476–481.

Johansen, S. (1996) *Likelihood-Based Inference in Cointegrated Vector Autoregressive Models*, Oxford: Oxford University Press.

Kahneman, D. (2011) *Thinking, Fast and Slow*, New York: Farrar, Strauss and Giroux.

Key, V. O. (1968) *The Responsible Electorate: Rationality in Presidential Voting, 1936–1960*, New York: Vintage Books.

Keynes, J. M. (1936) *The General Theory of Employment, Interest and Money*, London: Macmillan.

Kiewiet, D. R. (1983) *Macroeconomics and Micropolitics: The Electoral Effects of Economic Issues*, Chicago: University of Chicago Press.

Kinder, D. R. and Kiewiet, D. R. (1981) "Sociotropic Politics: The American Case," *British Journal of Political Science*, vol. 11, no. 2, April, 129–161.

Kramer, G. H. (1971) "Short-Term Fluctuations in U.S. Voting Behavior, 1896–1964," *American Political Science Review*, vol. 65, no. 1, March, 131–143.

Kramer, G. H. (1983) "The Ecological Fallacy Revisited: Aggregate- versus Individual-Level Findings on Economics and Elections and Sociotropic Voting," *American Political Science Review*, vol. 77, no. 1, March, 92–111.

Lewis-Beck, M. S. (1988) *Economics and Elections: The Major Western Democracies*, Ann Arbor: University of Michigan Press.

Lewis-Beck, M. S. and Costa Lobo, M. (2017) "The Economic Vote: Ordinary vs. Extraordinary Times," in Arzheimer, K., Evans, J. and Lewis-Beck, M. S. (eds.) *The Sage Handbook of Electoral Behaviour*, London: Sage Publications: 584–607.

Lewis-Beck, M. S. and Stegmaier, M. (2000) "Economic Determinants of Electoral Outcomes," *Annual Review of Political Science*, vol. 3, June, 183–219.

Lewis-Beck, M. S. and Stegmaier, M. (2007) "Economic Models of Voting," in Dalton, R. J. and Klingemann, H-D. (eds.) *The Oxford Handbook of Political Behavior*, New York: Oxford University Press: 518–537.

Lewis-Beck, M. S. and Stegmaier, M. (2013) "The V-P Function Revisited: A Survey of the Literature on Vote and Popularity Functions after over 40 Years," *Public Choice*, vol. 157, no. 3, December, 367–385.

Lewis-Beck, M. S., Nadeau, R. and Foucault, M. (2013) "The Compleat Economic Voter: New Theory and Evidence," *British Journal of Political Science*, vol. 43, no. 2, April, 241–261.

Lupia, A. (2016) *Uninformed: Why People Seem to Know So Little About Politics and What We Can Do About It*, New York: Oxford University Press.

Luskin, R. (1987) "Measuring Political Sophistication," *American Journal of Political Science*, vol. 31, no. 4, November, 856–899.

MacKuen, M. B., Erikson, R. S. and Stimson, J. A. (1992) "Peasants or Bankers: The American Electorate and the U.S. Economy," *American Political Science Review*, vol. 86, no. 3, September, 597–611.

Monroe, K. R. (1979) "God of Vengeance and Reward?: The Economy and Presidential Popularity," *Political Behavior*, vol. 1, no. 4, December, 301–329.

Monroe, K. R. (ed.) (1991) *The Economic Approach to Politics: A Critical Reassessment of the Theory of Rational Action*, New York: Harper Collins.

Mueller, J. E. (1970) "Presidential Popularity from Truman to Johnson," *American Political Science Review*, vol. 64, no. 1, March, 18–34.

Mutz, D. C. and Kim, E. (2017) "Economic Voting in a New Media Environment: Preliminary Evidence and Implications," in Arzheimer, K., Evans, J. and Lewis-Beck, M. S. (eds.) *The Sage Handbook of Electoral Behaviour*, London: Sage Publications: 733–758.

Nadeau, R., Lewis-Beck, M. S. and Belanger, E. (2013) "Economics and Elections Revisited," *Comparative Political Studies*, vol. 46, no. 5, May, 551–573.

Norpoth, H., Lewis-Beck, M. S. and Lafay, J-D. (eds.) (1991) *Economics and Politics: The Calculus of Support*, Ann Arbor: University of Michigan Press.

Phillips, P. (1986) "Understanding Spurious Regressions in Econometrics," *Journal of Econometrics*, vol. 33, no. 3, December, 311–340.

Powell, G. B. and Whitten, G. D. (1993) "A Cross-National Analysis of Economic Voting: Taking Account of the Political Context," *American Journal of Political Science*, vol. 37, no. 2, May, 391–414.

Schwindt-Bayer, L. and Tavits, M. (2016) *Clarity of Responsibility, Accountability and Corruption*, New York: Cambridge University Press.

Simon, H. A. (1956) "Rational Choice and the Structure of the Environment," *Psychological Review*, vol. 63, no. 2, May, 129–138.

Sims, C. A. (1980) "Macroeconomics and Reality," *Econometrica*, vol. 48, no. 1, January, 1–48.

Sims, C. A., Stock, J. H. and Watson, M. W. (1990) "Inference in Linear Time Series Models with Some Unit Roots," *Econometrica*, vol. 58, no. 1, January, 113–144.

Smith, A. (1776) *An Inquiry into the Nature and Causes of the Wealth of Nations*, Volume 1, London: W. Strahan & T. Cadell.

Sniderman, P. M., Brody, R. A. and Tetlock, P. R. (eds.) (1991) *Reasoning and Choice: Explorations in Political Psychology*, Cambridge: Cambridge University Press.

Stegmaier, M., Lewis-Beck, M. S. and Park, B. (2017) "The V-P Function: A Review," in Arzheimer, K., Evans, J. and Lewis-Beck, M. S. (eds.) *The Sage Handbook of Electoral Behaviour*, London: Sage Publications: 608–630.

Stimson, J. A. (1989) "Perceptions of Politics and Economic Policy: A Macroanalysis," in Clarke, H. D., Stewart, M. C. and Zuk, G. (eds.) *Economic Decline and Political Change: Canada, Great Britain, the United States*, Pittsburgh: University of Pittsburgh Press: 195–221.

Stokes, D. E. (1963) "Spatial Models of Party Competition," *American Political Science Review*, vol. 57, no. 2, June, 368–377.

Stokes, D. E. (1992) "Valence Politics," in Kavanagh, D. (ed.) *Electoral Politics*, Oxford: Clarendon Press: 141–164.

Thaler, R. H. (2016) *Misbehaving: The Making of Behavioral Economics*, New York: W. W. Norton & Company.

Vig, N. J. and Schier, S. E. (eds.) (1985) *Political Economy in Western Democracies*, New York: Holmes and Meier.

Weisberg, H. (2005) *The Total Survey Error Approach: A Guide to the New Science of Survey Research*, Chicago: University of Chicago Press.

Whiteley, P. (1986) *Political Control of the Macro-Economy*, London: Sage Publications.

Whiteley, P., Clarke, H. D., Sanders, D. and Stewart, M. C. (2013) *Affluence, Austerity and Electoral Change in Britain*, Cambridge: Cambridge University Press.

Whiteley, P., Clarke, H. D., Sanders, D. and Stewart, M. C. (2016) "Hunting the Snark: A Reply to 'Re-Evaluating Valence Politics Models of Political Choice,'" *Political Science Research and Methods*, vol. 4, no. 1, January, 221–240.

Wlezien, C., Franklin, M. N. and Twiggs, D. (1997) "Economic Perceptions and Vote Choice: Disentangling the Endogeneity," *Political Behavior*, vol. 19, no. 1, March, 7–17.

Yule, G. U. (1926) "Why Do We Sometimes Get Nonsense-Correlations Between Time-Series – A Study in Sampling and the Nature of Time-Series," *Journal of the Royal Statistical Society*, vol. 89, no. 1, January, 1–63.

PART IV

The role of context and campaigns

17

ELECTORAL SYSTEMS

Iain McLean

There is (usually) no best electoral system

In general, there is no best electoral system, but some are worse than others. Each electoral system appeals, openly or implicitly, to a concept of representation. There are two of these, explained in the second section of this chapter, namely the principal-agent concept, and the microcosmic concept. Both are valid, but they are incompatible with one another. Therefore, electoral system designers must choose a system appropriate for the context in which it is to be used. They must also decide whether the system is to aggregate judgments or to aggregate preferences, and whether it is to elect one person or a multi-member assembly.

This framework enables us to analyze the main varieties of electoral system. Within each family (e.g., majoritarian and proportional), some systems are no worse than their rivals, and are better in at least one respect.

Let us then start with some theorems, although we will not stay long with the mathematics of elections. The three theorems that every electoral system designer needs to know are:

- May's theorem (May 1952, 1953): simple majority rule is the only system that simultaneously satisfies some desirable conditions for choosing between two alternatives;
- The median voter theorem (Black 1948, 1958; popularized by Downs 1957): when voting opinion is one-dimensional, the position (person) preferred by the median voter will win in any well-designed voting system;
- Arrow's theorem (Arrow 1963 [1951]): no choice or aggregation system can simultaneously satisfy some minimal requirements of consistency and fairness.

May's theorem

An election rule is a mapping from many votes to a single decision, or choice. The first property we want it to satisfy is *decisiveness*. Imagine the rule as an obedient but cuddly robot charged with making the binary choice between X and Y. We want it always to be able to say "X won" or "Y won" or "X and Y have tied." No matter how numerous the individual votes that we have fed into it, we don't want it to keep on whirring and be unable to give us a result.

Next up is *anonymity*. A rule is anonymous if swapping the identity of two voters doesn't affect the result. Suppose I am one voter, and the King of Sweden is another. A rule is anonymous if, after I have cast the King of Sweden's vote and he has cast mine, the result is unaffected. Sometimes we may want a rule to be non-anonymous – for example, when we give the chair of a meeting a casting vote to break a tie. But in a democracy we would normally want my vote to be worth neither more nor less than the King of Sweden's.

Neutrality is to options what anonymity is to voters. Suppose the initial outcome is X. Then let everyone who voted for X vote for Y, and everyone who voted for Y vote for X. With a neutral rule, if the voters flip, so should the outcome, which will now be Y. As with anonymity, we would sometimes want a non-neutral rule. A majority rule for juries is an example. Suppose the rule says that at least 10 out of 12 jurors are required to convict. Then if nine say Innocent and three say Guilty, the result is Innocent. If we flip, with nine saying Guilty and three saying Innocent, the result is still Innocent. So a jury rule may be non-neutral. But normally, in a democracy, we want our rules to be neutral.

Finally, *positive responsiveness*. A rule is positively responsive if, when the outcome is a tie, a switch of a single vote suffices to switch the overall result in the direction of the switch. Qualified-majority rules are not positively responsive. If the rule requires (say) a two-thirds majority for a motion to pass, and stipulate that in the event of a tie the motion does not pass, then a switch of one voter from against to for does not cause the motion to pass. Once again, there are sometimes good reasons for qualified-majority rules, but generally in a democracy we want the majority to win.

It is easy to see that simple majority rule satisfies the four conditions. What requires some math is to prove that it is the *only* rule that satisfies the four conditions. But it is (May 1952, 1953). That seems to constitute a powerful argument for majority rule.

The median voter theorem

Suppose that every voter can be ranked by her position on some scale. It might be left–right, but it could be anything (musical tastes, say). Let us assume that those who most like the music of J. S. Bach most hate the music of Justin Bieber, and vice versa. A Bach-lover likes a piece of music the less, the further down the Bach-to-Bieber scale it lies. A Belieber is the mirror image. A person whose favorite composer is somebody else will like music less, the further it departs from her favorite toward either Bach or Bieber. The technical terms for this condition are "uni-dimensionality" and "single-peakedness" (Black 1958). When opinion is unidimensional and single-peaked, then with any good voting rule the favorite option of the median voter will beat all others. The median voter is the one with exactly as many voters to her "left" as to her "right." In the world of easy proofs, the number of voters is always odd. Like May's theorem, the median voter theorem (MVT) makes a powerful argument in favor of democracy.

Arrow's theorem

Unfortunately, it is not always so simple. In a stunning result, Arrow (1963 [1951]) proves that no system satisfies some minimal requirements of fairness and logicality. These are: decisiveness (as in May); transitivity (if A is preferred to B and B is preferred to C, then A is preferred to C); the Pareto condition (if everyone prefers X to Y, the system does not rank Y above X); independence of irrelevant alternatives (the choice between X and Y is a function only of voters' preferences between X and Y, and nothing else); and non-dictatorship (there is no voter whose preference automatically becomes the output of the system, regardless of others' preferences).

This may all be a bit of a mouthful for the average electoral system designer, so I will try to spell out how it arises, and some of its implications. It has been known since Condorcet (1785,

1995 [1788]) that when there are at least three voters and at least three options, majority rule may be intransitive. I prefer A to B and B to C. You prefer B to C and C to A. She, over there, prefers C to A and A to B. By majority rule A beats B (I and She against You). B beats C (I and You against Her). Transitivity requires A to beat C. But C beats A (You and She against me). This may seem trivial, but it is not. It is called a "cycle" – a name conferred by Lewis Carroll (Dodgson 1876). It is the reason why the nice results of May and Black do not carry over to the multi-person, multi-option case with more than one dimension. Arrow's theorem shows that there is no easy way out. Every system, tried, untried, or not yet invented, must violate at least one of Arrow's conditions. Yet most of us would want at least those conditions, and much more besides.

It follows that there is no such thing as a perfect electoral system. The comforting thing about Arrow is that we can abandon the search now. For all we know, life may exist on another planet. But we know for sure that a system that meets all Arrow's conditions does not exist, even on another planet.

That does not mean that any electoral system is as good as any other. It means that we have to decide, first, what an electoral system is *for*. Having decided that, we can say that some systems are better than others for that purpose.

Three sets of criteria for an electoral system

Two concepts of representation

The oldest meaning of the verb "to represent" in the authoritative *Oxford English Dictionary*, attested since 1390, is:

> To assume or occupy the role or functions of (a person), typically in restricted, and usually formal situations; to be entitled to speak or act on behalf of (a person, group, organization, etc.); (in later use esp.) to act or serve as the spokesperson or advocate of.
>
> *(Oxford English Dictionary Online 2017)*

I represent you if I stand for you in a place where you cannot: for example, if I am your lawyer, with expert knowledge that you lack; or if there are many of you, who cannot all attend parliament, so I attend it as your representative. This is now called the "principal-agent" conception. You are the principal(s), and I am your agent.

Almost as old (attested from 1400) is sense 8b: "To bring clearly and distinctly before the mind or imagination; to describe, evoke, conjure; to imagine, conceptualize" (Oxford English Dictionary Online 2017). This is the sense in which a painting or a play re-presents a character. When applied to a large body of people, it leads to the "microcosm" conception of representation. In the ferment of the French and American Revolutions, the Comte de Mirabeau and John Adams came (independently, I think) to the same idea: that in some sense the assembly should be a microcosm of the people who elected it (cited in McLean 1991: 173).

Etymologically, both senses are perfectly valid. But they are incompatible. One person cannot be a microcosm of many, as the many comprise different genders, different ages, different ethnicities, and have different interests and values. For legislative elections, the principal-agent conception points to single-member districts. The microcosm conception points to proportional representation (PR), and/or to quotas (requiring, for instance, that a minimum proportion of candidates have some gender or ethnic characteristic). Some PR systems, like the one used in Scotland, Wales, Germany, and New Zealand, combine a single-member and a proportional component. In those systems, it is only the proportional component that can bring about micro-cosmic representation.

Judgments vs. preferences

The second way to ask what a system is *for* is this: *Is it designed to aggregate people's judgments, or people's preferences?* Consider a jury. In principle, all the jurors want the same thing, which is to find out the unknown truth: did the accused commit the crime as charged, or not? There should be no difference between conservative and socialist jurors, or between Bachians and Beliebers: each in principle wants the same thing.

A less pure example is selecting somebody for a job. All members of the selection committee want the best person for the job. But they may have different ideas as to the qualities of the ideal candidate, so it is not a pure case of judgment aggregation.

A mass election is quite different. Some voters are moved by interests; some by ideology; many by both. Interests and ideologies differ. There is no sense in which the voters can be said to be groping toward an unknown truth.

Electing one vs. electing many

The third dimension for judging systems asks: is this an election of one person, or of more than one? Obviously, the concept of proportional representation has no meaning if there is only one post to fill. A president cannot be male, female, black, white, rich, poor, straight, gay … in the same proportions as the population. There is only one of him (of her).

If the task is to elect a multi-member body, such as a parliament, then the principal-agent and microcosmic conceptions point in different ways. As already noted, the former points to single-member districts, so that each group of principals knows for sure who their agent is. The latter points to proportional representation, which cannot be achieved in single-member districts for the reason just given.

The main system families

For aggregating judgments

When a judgment-aggregation task is truly binary, as in most jury systems (not in Scotland, where a third verdict labeled "not proven" exists), then the May and median voter theorems take us quickly to a result. Juries should use a form of majority rule. It should be anonymous, because each juror is assumed to be as well qualified as each other to discern the truth. Most jury rules, however, use a non-neutral procedure, in which more votes are required for a guilty verdict than for a not-guilty verdict. This is reasonable, on the basis that convicting an innocent person is regarded (by legal theorists) as worse than letting off a guilty person.

Most judgment-aggregation processes are not truly binary, however. When selecting some-body for a job or an honor, there are typically more than two candidates. Normally a rank-order is required, so that if the person at the top of the list declines an offer or fails a medical, the selec-tors can go to the next.

The modern foundations of the theory of elections were laid in the French Enlightenment, largely around the question of what electoral system academicians should use when voting in elections to the national academies. The debate was most intense in the *Académie royale des sciences*, of which the principal theorists Condorcet (1785) and Borda (1784) were both fellows.

They had radically different ideas of what sort of person should be elected (McLean, McMillan, and Monroe 1998: xxvii). Their radically different ideas hid behind a (superficially) polite disagreement about voting rules. The Condorcet rule makes pairwise comparisons among all pairs of candidates. A *Condorcet winner* is the candidate who beats every other in those comparisons. Unfortunately, because of the possibility of cycles, a Condorcet winner may not exist. Condorcet has a procedure to deal with this, but it is so complicated that it took two centuries to be understood (Young 1988). That rules out Condorcet procedures as a practical matter.

The Borda rule is well-known, although not necessarily under that name. It is used in the Eurovision Song Contest and some other sporting tournaments (also, it should properly be called the Cusanus rule, as it was proposed by Nicolas of Cusa in 1434 [McLean and Urken 1995: 77–78]). The Borda rule is a points rule. You award a fixed score (usually zero) to the candidate you like least, and a fixed interval (usually 1) for each candidate above that. Hence for n candidates, each voter scores them from $n - 1$ down to 0. Ties may be allowed, or may be forbidden. The Borda rule can be operated either way.

The Borda rule is very simple, but has an overwhelming defect, which is obvious to anyone who has watched the Eurovision Song Contest. If you want your favorite singer to prevail against her most dangerous rival, be sure to give the latter a score of 0. As it is common knowledge that sophisticated voters will do this, the Borda rule may quickly degenerate into a contest to see who is the smartest manipulator.

We know that something like this happened when the Borda rule was used to elect academicians to the *Académie royale des sciences*. When this defect was pointed out, Borda said (I assume plaintively), "My scheme is only intended for honest men" (Black 1958: 182). That the Borda rule is flagrantly manipulable arises from its violation of Arrow's axiom of independence of irrelevant alternatives (IIA). Under Borda, one can raise, or scupper, the chances of A by changing one's ranking of B and C. Alone of Arrow's conditions, the meaning and importance of IIA is not immediately obvious, and some serious scholars (see, for example, Saari 1990) doubt whether it should be a requirement. I (and probably most voting theorists) would condemn them to a lifetime of watching reruns of the Eurovision Song Contest.

Thus neither the Condorcet nor the Borda rule can usually be recommended directly. The first fails the decisiveness test. The second is extremely manipulable. But both of the Borda and Condorcet *principles* are valuable. One of the problems (which is really Arrow restated) is that the principles are not always compatible. When the Borda rule and the Condorcet rule yield different answers, which is the "true" winner? That cannot be settled by appealing to either principle.

A new procedure proposed by Balinski and Laraki (2010) may help to break this deadlock. Their "Majority judgment" procedure is designed, as the name suggests, for judgment-aggregation procedures. In their many applications, they show how the rules for wine-judging and figure-skating tournaments have evolved as participants have learned by bitter experience not to use the simple Borda (ranking) rule.

Balinski and Laraki (2010) point out that in a judgment aggregation, what voters are asked to do is not directly to rank the wines, skaters, or politicians, but to grade them against some mental standard. It is also what school and university examiners are asked to do. In some exam subjects, such as mathematics, it is easy to score the papers. In others, such as history, it is not. In math, a mark of 70 percent has a direct interpretation (the candidate got 70 percent of the answers right). In history, a mark of 70 percent has no direct meaning. But, in both cases, the examiners are grading the candidate against some unspoken criterion ("this is the threshold above which students are likely to be able to do math at university," or "this is the threshold for a good degree").

Electing a politician can be framed as a judgment-aggregation task. In their best-known experiment, Balinski and Laraki (2010) conducted an exit poll among people who had just voted in a French presidential election. The actual electoral system is a two-stage runoff, to be discussed later. But Balinski and Laraki offered voters leaving the polling station a mock ballot, in which they were asked to grade each candidate by completing the sentence: "To be president of France I judge in conscience that this candidate would be ...." The grades were the exam grades used to report French school results, which were therefore familiar to all voters. The rubric's mention of "in conscience" was designed to remind voters that they were not (only) being asked to choose the candidate whose politics they most liked but (also) the candidate most fitted to be president of France.

For judgment aggregation where there are only two possibilities (e.g., "Guilty" and "Not Guilty"), the theorems that we have reviewed give the answer. We should use majority rule: a non-neutral majority rule if we judged that the consequences of an error in one direction are worse than the consequences of an error in the other direction. Jury rules are binary. They may offer an exception to the generalization with which I started, that there is no best electoral system.

How big a majority should be required to validate an outcome? That is partly a matter of judgment, which an electoral systems expert cannot settle: how much worse is it that an innocent person should be convicted than that a guilty person should go free? But in other jury-like contexts, some further mathematics is available. Juries comprise people (or maybe computers or sensors) who make imperfect judgments about the true state of the world. If a sensor in a jumbo jet or a nuclear power station indicates a fault condition, there are two possibilities: that the plane (reactor) is faulty, and that the sensor is faulty. As with convicting the innocent, the possibilities are asymmetrical. A faulty sensor may lead the plane to make an unnecessary, unscheduled landing in South Dakota. A sensor that correctly warns of a fault, but is ignored, may lead to the plane crashing with the loss of all on board.

The Condorcet jury theorem (Condorcet 1785; Austen-Smith and Banks 1996; List and Goodin 2001) enables us to apply the theory of probability to situations like these. If we know the average reliability of a juror (sensor), then we can stipulate the required majority of observations above which we can be, for all practical purposes, certain that the true state of the world is that which the majority of sensors show.

When there are more than two options in a judgment-aggregation problem, the Condorcet jury theorem can be adapted to suit. Unfortunately, because of Arrow's result, the May majority rule theorem cannot be. For tasks such as selecting a shortlist of candidates for appointment, or choosing a president of France (if these are considered as judgment aggregations), how if at all can we get around the Arrow restrictions?

We could use a Condorcet procedure, comparing each candidate with each other, and ranking the candidates in descending order of the number of victories they score. That has the drawback that there may be a cycle. This rules out a Condorcet procedure for something like a presidential election. It may be acceptable for selecting a shortlist for appointment – but if the top candidates remain in a cycle, it will have to be broken somehow.

We could, but should not, use a Borda procedure. Even for the task of electing academicians, Borda found that his rule was subverted by dishonest men.

The Condorcet rule is almost never used in practice, and the Borda rule tends to be used only in relatively frivolous contexts such as song competitions. Better than either are two rules that are not as well-known as they should be.

Approval voting (Brams and Fishburn 1983) is very simple. You vote for as many candidates as you approve of – anything from one to all minus one. To choose one person, elect the person with the highest number of approvals. To elect more than one (e.g., a shortlist), do the same, going down the list until the predetermined number of places have been filled.

An attraction of approval voting is that it caters for the voter who has very strong views about who should (not) be chosen, and the voter who is content for a large number of candidates to be regarded as acceptable. Unlike Borda, it does not require the voter to make a strict ranking of the candidates. But that opportunity can be a curse as well as a blessing. Though it cannot wholly escape the Arrow trap, because no ranking procedure can, it beats direct use of either Condorcet or Borda. Unlike Condorcet, it always produces a result. It is less manipulable than Borda.

More radically, bodies such as shortlisting committees should consider the Balinski–Laraki procedure. Because it is a grading, not a ranking rule, it can plausibly claim to escape the Arrow trap. At least one national scientific academy uses a hybrid of the Balinski–Laraki and Borda rules for electing academicians (personal communication). This is the more striking, as the academy in question selected its rule before the Balinski–Laraki proposal was formally characterized. It seems to have lighted on it serendipitously.

None of these rules is much used in real-world procedures to elect a single person. These rules are discussed in the next section.

For electing one person: interest aggregation

It may be utopian to regard the voters in a presidential election as actually engaging in deciding "in conscience" who is best fitted to be the next president. No presidential election system uses either approval voting or the Balinski–Laraki rule. So let us start from the other end, and evaluate the rules that are actually used.

Some countries elect their president directly, others indirectly through an electoral college. In either case, proportional representation is irrelevant, for the reason already given, namely that the person elected cannot be male, female, black, white, straight, gay, Christian, or Muslim in the same proportions as the population. There is only one of him (her). The electoral rule for the election of the president of Ireland is described on a government website as follows: "The Presidential election is by secret ballot and based on proportional representation by the single transferable vote" (Government of Ireland 2016).

This is a category mistake. A presidential election cannot use proportional representation. The actual Irish system is what is known in the UK as alternative vote, in Australia as preferential voting, and in the USA as instant runoff. Under any of these names, each voter ranks the candidates. If one candidate wins more than 50 percent of the first places, s/he is elected. If not, candidates with the fewest first preferences are eliminated in succession and their supporters' next available preferences, if any, are transferred until one candidate has more than half of the remaining valid votes.

A cousin of this method is the French runoff system. In the first round anybody may stand. If nobody gets more than half of the votes cast, a second round is held a few days later, to which only the top two vote-getters from the first round go forward. The winner at the second round is elected.

Alternative vote and runoff systems are very similar. The main difference is that in a runoff system voters have more information. Before the second round, they know how the first-round ballots were cast. More information is good in itself, but it also gives more incentives to strategic behavior.

This subtle difference pales into insignificance, compared to the enormous defect of both systems, which is as follows: *There is no guarantee that the person elected is either the Condorcet or the (sincere) Borda winner.* As noted, the Condorcet and Borda principles are not wholly compatible, but nobody has suggested a credible rival criterion for determining the "true" majority winner when there are more than two candidates. To see why they violate both criteria, consider a candidate who is everyone's second preference. In a unidimensional world where the median vote theorem (above) applies, it is quite likely that such a person will exist: a centrist whose own first preferences are meagre, but whom both Bachians and Beliebers, left- and right-wing voters ..., prefer to the standard-bearer of the other side.

Such a candidate is likely to be the Borda winner because she scores, on average, highest on voters' ballot papers. She is likely to be the Condorcet winner because in a tournament of pairwise comparisons, she would win them all. This is an implication of the median vote theorem. But under either alternative vote or a runoff system, such a candidate is likely to be eliminated after the first round. Balinski and Laraki (2010) show from survey data that this has very likely happened in recent French presidential elections.

Although elimination rules are bad, they are not the very worst of rules which purport to be democratic. They are better than plurality rule ("first-past-the-post"), under which first preferences for all candidates are counted, and the modal candidate is elected. The modal candidate is the most popular single candidate, whether or not she has won over 50 percent of the vote. For an election to a single post, this is even worse than an elimination rule. At least an elimination rule cannot choose a Condorcet or Borda loser (namely, a candidate who loses every pairwise contest, and a candidate with the lowest average score. In the elimination round the successful candidate must have beaten one other, and therefore cannot be a Condorcet or Borda loser). First-past-the-post can select a Condorcet or Borda loser. It is therefore highly problematic for elections to a single post. It has a role in elections to a legislature, discussed below.

Therefore, for direct elections of one person, the systems to consider are either approval voting or Balinski–Laraki. Neither is clearly better than the other, but both are better than elimination systems or first-past-the-post.

Several democracies elect their president indirectly. Germany and the USA are two examples. Under the German Basic Law of 1949, which was enacted under the tutelage of the post-war Allied powers, the president is elected by a Federal Convention, which meets for that sole purpose: "The Federal Convention shall consist of the Members of the Bundestag and an equal number of members elected by the parliaments of the Länder on the basis of proportional representation" (Federal Law Gazette 2014). This is a huge advance on the US Constitution, which provides for an Electoral College to elect the president. The Electoral College was one of the most contested items in the Federal Convention in Philadelphia in 1787. It was intended to assemble an intermediate body of wise men who would elect the president. It has never worked like that. American voters, when they vote in a presidential election, are technically voting for their state's electors, not for the president. Since 1800, would-be electors have announced who they will support. This combines with the non-constitutional convention of winner-takes-all for Electoral College votes. In almost every state, the plurality-winning state wins that state's entire Electoral College vote. This is one reason (there are many) why *election inversions* occur. An election inversion occurs when the winner of the presidential election is not the popular vote winner. The most momentous such inversion was in 1860, when Abraham Lincoln not only got less than 40 percent of the popular vote, but would have won in the Electoral College even in a straight fight with Stephen Douglas, who was the Condorcet and Borda winner among the four candidates. There were election inversions in 2000 and 2016. In 2016, Hillary Clinton (Democrat) got more popular votes than Donald Trump (Republican), who was elected. The US Electoral College has no friends among electoral system scholars (if that matters), but because part of the arrangement is in the Constitution, it is unlikely to be revised (see further Peirce and Longley 1981; Miller 2012).

For electing many people: principal-agent systems

Finally, consider the case where the electoral system is aggregating interests, not judgments, and is used to choose a multi-member body such as a parliament. There are many handbooks to world electoral systems (see, for example, Colomer 2004). Here we have space only to concentrate on fundamentals. There cannot be a best electoral system, because of the incompatible conceptions of representation discussed above. The principal-agent conception requires single-member districts. The principals (voters) need to know who is their unique agent (legislator), if only so that they have the chance to "throw the rascals out" at the next election. When it is objected that single-member districts produce highly disproportionate results in all the countries which use them, including the USA, UK, France, Canada, and India, the principal-agent theorist replies that the objection is based on a category mistake – the system is not intended to be proportional.

Sometimes, a single-member system uses an elimination rule. This applies in Australia, where the House of Representatives is elected by preferential voting (alternative vote). This arose in a quite unprincipled way. In 1918 the governing Nationalists had split over support for World War I. They faced a resurgent Labor Party in a by-election. Between the election being called and taking place, they rushed through a change to a preferential system where (they hoped) National supporters would transfer their support among varieties of National candidates and keep Labor out (McLean 1996).

In 2011, the UK Coalition government held a referendum on changing the Westminster electoral system from plurality to alternative vote. This was a sort-of compromise between the Liberals' wish for proportional representation and the Conservatives' wish for no change. It was not much of a compromise and was heavily defeated. Minor variants of alternative vote (AV plus; supplementary vote) have been proposed or tried. Supplementary vote was introduced for London mayoral elections in the hope of keeping them a two-party game between the Conservative and Labour candidates. These variants are described by the Electoral Reform Society (2010). There is no need to discuss elimination systems in detail here, because they barely improve on plurality rule. They may produce an even more disproportional result; they can penalize a centrist party that might be the Borda or Condorcet winner in each seat; against that, they have the advantage that they cannot elect a Borda or Condorcet loser.

For electing many people: proportional systems

To implement a microcosmic conception of representation, a proportional (PR) electoral system is often needed. Each of these tries to ensure that, as closely as possible, the seat shares in the legislature match the vote shares in the country. They fall into three main classes: *list systems*; *additional member systems*; and the *single transferable vote* (STV) family.

List systems

In these, the voter votes for a single party. The parties are assigned as near as can be, after rounding, the correct number of seats each. List systems can be highly proportional. They face two objections: that control of who is elected lies more with the party than with the voter; and that some list systems use an incorrect rounding-off algorithm.

When the parties have complete control of the order of the candidates on their lists ("closed-list"), they in effect decide who will be elected and who will not, at least if they can make a reasonable guess at the number of seats they will win. The formula for this is:

$$Q_i = \left\lceil \frac{V_i}{M+1} \right\rceil$$

where Q_i denotes the quota of seats for party i, V_i denotes the votes it has received, M denotes the number of seats to be filled ("district magnitude"), and the one-ended brackets $\lceil \ \rceil$ denote the *upper integer bound* of the expression inside them. This means $V_i/(M+1)$ rounded up to the next whole number, or, if it is already a whole number, rounded up by 1.

Exactly how proportional a list system is depends on the district magnitude M. The larger is M, the more proportional the system. Therefore, the Netherlands and Israel, which treat the whole country as one district and M as the size of the whole legislature, have the most proportional electoral systems in the world.

To give less control to the parties and more to the voters, some countries use variants of "open-list," where voters may choose a candidate within a party. Such votes are assigned both to the party and to the candidate within the party, hence giving voters some control.

Most list systems use an incorrect algorithm for rounding off fractional entitlements to seats. These algorithms are biased, and they do not guarantee that the right number of representatives is selected without some further tweaks. They use either:

- a system invented in the 1870s by the Belgian voting theorist Victor D'Hondt, which is identical to the system proposed in 1790 by Thomas Jefferson for rounding off entitlements to state seats in the US House of Representatives, or
- a system of giving a seat for each quota and then awarding any remaining seats in descending order of the fractional part of the quotient for unsuccessful candidates (largest remainder systems, invented in the USA by Alexander Hamilton in 1790).

The D'Hondt formula favors large parties, sometimes giving them more seats than their quotas. It is popular with the political parties who introduce PR, since usually, by construction, they are large parties. Hamilton systems sound fair, but they are bedeviled by paradoxes of monotonicity (where a candidate becomes more popular and thereby reduces her chances of election).

The only fair and non-paradoxical rounding-off algorithm is the one proposed in 1910 by the French mathematician André Ste-Laguë. This system, homologous to the rule proposed by Daniel Webster in 1832 for the US House problem, is the only one that treats large parties and small parties equally. It is therefore the only one that is fair to both the large-party and the small-party voter. The fascinating homologies (i.e., identities) between the American and European rules were first discovered, and proven, by Balinski and Young (2001), which is the authoritative source for everything in this paragraph.

Single transferable vote

This system was devised by several Victorian electoral reformers, the most prominent being Thomas Hare. Whereas list systems concentrate first on parties, STV concentrates first on fairness to voters. Hare's idea was that every group of voters who amounted to at least a quota was entitled to a representative of their choice. In STV, voters cast ranked ballots. First preferences are counted, and any candidate(s) who have met the natural quota Q defined above are elected.

Their surpluses above Q are redistributed to the next available candidate listed on each ballot. When nobody else can be elected by this method, the candidates with fewest first preferences are (successively) eliminated until the required number of candidates is elected. STV is used in Ireland (both North and South), in Malta, for Scottish local government elections, and for the Australian Senate (although there a rule change in the 1980s, such that most voters choose their party's ranking rather than choosing their own, means that STV has mutated to open-list). Like largest remainder, it is non-monotonic, although in the case of STV that is not a serious practical objection for mathematical reasons (Bartholdi, Tovey, and Trick 1989). For more on STV in practice see, for example, Bowler and Grofman (2000).

STV can go wrong when it is applied in a judgment aggregation. For instance it is widely used in the internal elections of the Church of England. Since medieval times, voting theorists have characterized church elections as attempts to find out the will of God (Colomer and McLean 1998). But if opinions as to the will of God are incompatible and deeply entrenched, campaigners focus rather on the natural quota Q. A faction can obtain as many seats as it has quotas. Rather than discouraging factionalism, in a case like this STV may actually encourage it.

Single *non*-transferable vote (SNTV) was discussed by Lewis Carroll in the 1880s (McLean, McMillan, and Monroe 1996; Cox 1991). Under SNTV the voter has only one vote in a multi-member district. If voters and parties behave with full information and reasonable calculations about one another, however, its effects are similar to those of STV.

Additional member systems

List systems typically have large M and are responsive; STV has small M and achieves some of the advantages of single-member district systems at the expense of proportionality. A compromise between the two is to use a mixed-member system (MMS), as in Germany, New Zealand, Scotland, Wales, and the London Assembly. The details vary between these jurisdictions but the principle is the same. Part of the legislature is elected in single-member districts. The disproportionality that this produces is countered by electing the rest of the house in a regional or national party list, on a compensating rule such that the proportionality of the whole legislature is determined by the party share of the list vote. Since single-member district rules exaggerate the lead of the winning party, it follows that most of the list seats go to other parties.

There is a lot to be said for the MMS system as it tries to deliver the best of both worlds: preserve a principal-agent link while achieving (at least some) proportionality. It cannot of course achieve as much proportionality as a pure list system. This may have consequences as in Scotland in 2011, when the Scottish National Party (SNP) gained a majority of seats on about 44 percent of the votes. But this leads me to end where I began. No electoral system is perfect, but if the system designer starts by deciding the purpose of the votes and only then chooses an electoral system, she is proceeding in the right order.

Conclusion

So where have we reached? We have shown that there is no one answer to the question "What is the best electoral system?" That is because the question is incomplete. We should only ever ask, "What is the best electoral system *for this purpose?*" after deciding the purpose of the election. Is it to find out the truth? Is it to elect an executive? Is it to elect a parliament? Is it to choose a list, in order, of the best wines or the best figure-skaters? Is it to decide which candidate(s) for a job fit the essential criteria for that job, so that some of them are appointable, and others are not?

Electoral systems have consequences. We have seen that, with a given underlying structure of preferences, different electoral systems will produce different outcomes. Only one example is needed to make the point. The most important election in US presidential history, that of 1860, was won by Abraham Lincoln on less than 40 percent of the vote. He won because of the spatial distribution of the vote, because of the first-past-the-post system, and because of the Electoral College. Under Condorcet, Borda, or most other systems, the election would have gone to his great rival, Stephen A. Douglas (Riker 1982). The Civil War might or might not have taken place (Douglas died not long after the election), but it would have had a different course and perhaps a different outcome.

Thus electoral systems have fundamental implications for the effects of public opinion on policy-making and other activities of government. The public opinion that elected Lincoln was the same public opinion that would have elected Douglas under other systems. The history of the United States reached a fork in 1860. Every national election held since then has been held in the shadow of that contest. Equally, Balinski's and Laraki's experiments show that a different president would have been elected in France in 2002 had the electoral system been their majority judgment system. There is a huge downstream literature on the electoral effects of proportional versus majoritarian systems, which is out of scope for this chapter. But nobody should ever doubt the importance of the choices among the systems we have been discussing.

References

Arrow, K. J. (1963) [1951] *Social Choice and Individual Values*, 2nd Edition, New Haven: Yale University Press.

Austen-Smith, D. and Banks, J. (1996) "Information Aggregation, Rationality, and the Condorcet Jury Theorem," *American Political Science Review*, vol. 90, no. 2, March, 34–45.

Balinski, M. L. and Laraki, R. (2010) *Majority Judgment: Measuring, Ranking, and Electing*, Cambridge, MA: MIT Press.

Balinski, M. L. and Young, H. P. (2001) *Fair Representation: Meeting the Ideal of One Man, One Vote*, 2nd Edition, Washington, DC: Brookings Institution Press.

Bartholdi, J. J. III, Tovey, C. A., and Trick, M. A. (1989) "Voting Schemes for Which It Can Be Difficult to Tell Who Won the Election," *Social Choice and Welfare*, vol. 6, no. 2, April, 157–165.

Black, D. (1948) "On the Rationale of Group Decision-Making," *Journal of Political Economy*, vol. 56, no. 1, February, 23–34.

Black, D. (1958) *The Theory of Committees and Elections*, Cambridge: Cambridge University Press.

Borda, J-C. (1784) "Mémoire Sur les Élections au Scrutin," in McLean, I. and Urken, A. B. (1995) *Classics of Social Choice*, Ann Arbor, MI: University of Michigan Press: 83–90.

Bowler, S. and Grofman, B. (eds.) (2000) *Elections in Australia, Ireland, and Malta Under the Single Transferable Vote*, Ann Arbor, MI: University of Michigan Press.

Brams, S. J. and Fishburn, P. C. (1983) *Approval Voting*, 2nd Edition, New York: Springer.

Colomer, J. M. (ed.) (2004) *Handbook of Electoral System Choice*, Basingstoke: Palgrave-Macmillan.

Colomer, J. M. and McLean, I. (1998) "Electing Popes: Approval Balloting and Qualified-Majority Rule," *Journal of Interdisciplinary History*, vol. 29, no. 1, Summer, 1–22.

Condorcet, M. J. A. N. (1785) *Essai sur L'application de L'analyse à la Probabilité des Décisions Rendues à la Pluralité des Voix*, Paris: Imprimerie royale.

Condorcet, M. J. A. N. (1995) [1788] "Essai sur les Assemblées Provinciales," in McLean, I. and Urken, A. B. (1995) *Classics of Social Choice*, Ann Arbor, MI: University of Michigan Press: 139–168.

Cox, G. W. (1991) "SNTV and D'Hondt are 'Equivalent,'" *Electoral Studies*, vol. 10, no. 2, June, 118–132.

Dodgson, C. L. (1876) "A Method of Taking Votes on More Than Two Issues," in Black, D. (1958) *The Theory of Committees and Elections*, Cambridge: Cambridge University Press: 224–234.

Downs, A. (1957) *An Economic Theory of Democracy*, New York: Harper and Row.

Electoral Reform Society (2010) "Majoritarian Electoral Systems," www.electoral-reform.org.uk/majoritarian-electoral-systems, [accessed October 20, 2015].

Federal Law Gazette (2014) "Basic Law for the Federal Republic of Germany," www.gesetze-im-internet. de/englisch_gg/englisch_gg.html, [accessed October 10, 2015].

Government of Ireland (2016) "Presidential Election in Ireland," www.citizensinformation.ie/en/ government_in_ireland/elections_and_referenda/national_elections/presidential_election.html, [accessed February 7, 2017].

List, C. and Goodin, R. E. (2001) "Epistemic Democracy: Generalizing the Condorcet Jury Theorem," *Journal of Political Philosophy*, vol. 9, no. 3, September, 277–306.

May, K. O. (1952) "A Set of Independent Necessary and Sufficient Conditions for Simple Majority Decision," *Econometrica*, vol. 20, no. 4, October, 680–684.

May, K. O. (1953) "A Note on Complete Independence of the Conditions for Simple Majority Decision," *Econometrica*, vol. 21, no. 1, January, 172–173.

McLean, I. (1991) "Forms of Representation and Systems of Voting," in Held, D. (ed.) *Political Theory Today*, Cambridge: Polity Press: 172–196.

McLean, I. (1996) "E. J. Nanson, Social Choice, and Electoral Reform," *Australian Journal of Political Science*, vol. 31, no. 3, November, 369–385.

McLean, I. and Urken, A. B. (1995) *Classics of Social Choice*, Ann Arbor, MI: University of Michigan Press.

McLean, I., McMillan, A., and Monroe, B. L. (1996) *A Mathematical Approach to Proportional Representation: Duncan Black on Lewis Carroll*, Dordrecht: Kluwer.

McLean, I., McMillan, A., and Monroe, B. L. (1998) *The Theory of Committees and Elections by Duncan Black; and Committee Decisions with Complementary Valuation by Duncan Black and R. A. Newing*, 2nd Edition, Dordrecht: Kluwer.

Miller, N. R. (2012) "Electoral Inversions by the US Electoral College," in Felsenthal, D. S. and Machover, M. (eds.) *Electoral Systems: Paradoxes, Assumptions, and Procedures*, Berlin: Springer: 93–109.

Oxford English Dictionary Online (2017) "Represent," https://en.oxforddictionaries.com/definition/ represent, [accessed October 20, 2015].

Peirce, N. and Longley, L. D. (1981) *The People's President: The Electoral College in America and the Direct Vote Alternative*, New Haven, CT: Yale University Press.

Riker, W. H. (1982) *Liberalism against Populism*, San Francisco: W. H. Freeman.

Saari. D. (1990) "The Borda Dictionary," *Social Choice and Welfare*, vol. 7, no. 4, December, 279–317.

Young, H. P. (1988) "Condorcet's Theory of Voting," *American Political Science Review*, vol. 82, no. 4, December, 1231–1244.

18
ELECTORAL INTEGRITY

Pippa Norris

Over the course of the past decade a new sub-field of study has emerged on the topic of electoral integrity, which can be broadly defined as the overarching practical and normative context within which elections occur. This chapter reviews the growth of this literature to show how it departs from traditional approaches to understanding electoral behavior and institutions. In particular it highlights the commitment of scholars to a more normative, problem solving, and policy relevant agenda. After contextualizing this new body of work within the wider academic canon the chapter moves on to discuss how electoral integrity can be operationalized and sets out the key criteria that measures of electoral integrity need to meet in order to be considered valid and reliable. The final section of the chapter summarizes recent empirical work demonstrating the importance of perceptions of electoral integrity for levels of popular trust and confidence in the political system, and also for turnout and protest activity. The conclusion identifies the next steps for moving the contemporary research agenda on electoral integrity forward.

Conceptualizing electoral integrity

Electoral integrity can be conceived in several ways. The key difference centers on whether it is understood negatively or positively (van Ham 2015). On the former front studies have typically focused on whether contests are "manipulated" (Schedler 2002; Simpser 2013), "fraudulent" (Lehoucq and Jiménez 2002; Vickery and Shein 2012) or characterized by "malpractices" (Birch 2010). The latter more positive accounts center on whether elections can be considered as "free and fair" (Bjornlund 2004; Elkit and Reynolds 2005; Lindberg 2006; Goodwin-Gill 2006; Bishop and Hoeffler 2014), "genuine and credible" (observer reports), "competitive" (Hyde and Marinov 2012), or "democratic" (Munck 2009; Levitsky and Way 2010).

A human rights understanding of electoral integrity, and the preferred approach of this chapter, adopts this latter more positive stance and argues that it exists when electoral procedures meet agreed international conventions and global norms covering the full election cycle – that is, from the pre-election period, through to the campaign, polling day, and the immediate aftermath (Norris 2013, 2014, 2015). These conventions and norms are typically contained in written declarations, treaties, protocols, case law, and guidelines issued by inter-governmental organizations, and endorsed by member states worldwide. While some of these conventions are legally binding under international law, others are more customary in nature but in effect have the same compulsory status.

Article 21(3) of the 1948 Universal Declaration of Human Rights is widely seen as providing the cornerstone of the legal definition of electoral integrity. Namely that

> The will of the people shall be the basis of the authority of government: this will shall be expressed in periodic and genuine elections which shall be by universal and equal suffrage and shall be held by secret vote or by equivalent free voting procedures.

This framework was further developed through Article 25 of the 1966 UN International Convention for Civil and Political Rights. Since then, a series of conventions endorsed by member states of the United Nations and inter-governmental regional organizations such as OSCE and OAS have extended the framework to outlaw any form of discrimination based on race, sex, or disability.[1]

The growth of electoral integrity research agenda

A key driver behind the rise of the electoral integrity research agenda has been the surge in the use of elections around the world. Banks' Cross-National Time-Series dataset reports that, at the end of World War II, around 50 independent nation-states had a popularly elected legislature. This number has now roughly quadrupled (see Figure 18.1). With some exceptions, therefore,[2] almost all independent nation-states around the world now hold multi-party elections for the lower house of the national parliament.

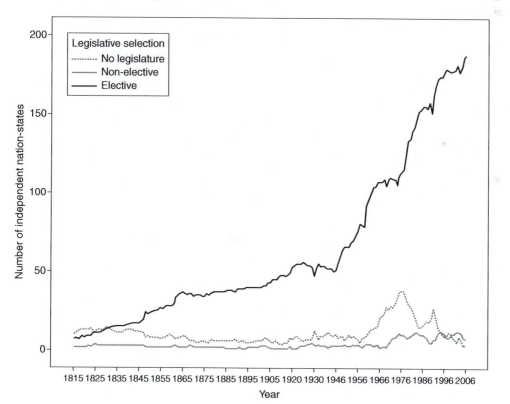

Figure 18.1 The growing number of elected national legislatures, 1815–2007

Source: Arthur Banks Cross-National Time-Series Dataset 1815–2007.

Electoral malpractices under autocracies

This diffusion of elections worldwide has led to burgeoning literature on the way these contests work (or fail to do so) in autocratic states. In the heyday of the Soviet Union, contests for the Duma were infrequent phenomenon with few significant consequences beyond conferring a patina of legitimacy upon Communist parties. By contrast, the last decade has seen rapidly growing interest in the role and function of electoral institutions in authoritarian states. Debate has centered on the consequences of multi-party elections for democratization with some scholars such as Lindberg (2006) arguing that they offer important opportunities for opposition parties to organize and mobilize support. Others such as Carothers (2002) have warned against assuming that elections *inevitably* lead to a progressive transition toward democracy. Recent evidence of an authoritarian push-back against democracy and signs that it may be "in retreat" (Kurlantzick 2014) or "in decline" (Diamond and Plattner 2015) are seen as supporting this more pessimistic view.

Recognition of this new constitutional fluidity has led scholars to abandon the dichotomous regime typologies developed by Przeworski et al. (2000) and since updated by Cheibub, Gandhi, and Vreeland (2010) in favor of more flexible schemas that focus on the intermediate or gray zone between democracy and autocracy. These efforts have resulted in identification of a more mixed set of regime types including "electoral democracies," "semi-democracies," and "semi-free" regimes (Freedom House 2017). Elsewhere, scholars have avoided references to democracy, preferring to talk about "hybrid states" (Diamond 2002), "anocracies" (Polity), or "electoral" or "competitive" autocracies. (Schedler 2006; Levitsky and Way 2002, 2010). Several sub-types have also been distinguished among the latter – for example, Magaloni (2006) draws a line between "hegemonic-party autocracies," which are thought to differ from military regimes and personal dictatorships.

The growth of these new hybrid states poses many new and interesting questions for scholars of elections, public opinion and parties. In particular they challenge the focus of conventional electoral behavioral research on the micro-level modeling of individual voter decision making and shift attention toward the role of broader contextual factors in explaining both elite and mass activities. Why, for example, would the ruling parties in these states allow any contests to occur given the risks they pose for destabilizing their power base? Why would the citizens living under these autocratic conditions actually turn out to vote in the first place? Finally, how can we explain popular support for hegemonic parties?

Electoral maladministration in democracies

A second factor that has prompted academic interest in questions of electoral integrity has been the growing recognition of problems in the regulation and administration of electoral procedures in established democracies. Concern over the performance of elections in Western democracies, and interest in policy reforms designed to strengthen the electoral process, have grown over the past quarter century. Since the 1990s several major reforms of electoral systems have been undertaken in many long-established democracies, such as Italy, Japan, and New Zealand (Renwick 2010). There have also been numerous legal and regulatory reforms imposed on various aspects of the electoral process such as campaign finance, term limits, direct democracy initiatives, and convenience voting procedures that have prompted scholarly attention in terms of analyzing their causes and effects (Bowler and Donovan 2013; Norris and Abel van Es 2016).

Within the US there has been a longstanding tradition of academic research into the impact of varying state-level registration and voting procedures on voter turnout (Rosenstone and

Wolfinger 1978; Wolfinger and Rosenstone 1980). Scrutiny of these procedures, however, increased dramatically following the Florida presidential vote count in 2000, which provoked a heated and heavily polarized debate over the fairness and integrity of US elections. The irregularities identified in the voting process prompted a series of major legal challenges and high-profile accusations of voter fraud against the Republican winner, George W. Bush. The 2014 report of the bipartisan Presidential Commission on Election Administration did little to calm these fears, setting out a long list of vulnerabilities in American elections (Bauer et al. 2014). Growing anxieties over the contemporary quality and performance of US electoral laws can also be seen in the number of recommendations being put forward for practical reforms of state and local public administration (Alvarez and Grofman 2014; Cain, Donovan, and Tolbert 2008; Hasen 2012; Streb 2004). It has also prompted action by state legislatures with controversial new laws being introduced typically under Republican majorities, designed to tighten the security of voter registration and balloting identification requirements. Such measures have since been copied by right-wing governments in other countries, leading to partisan battles over the "Fair Votes" Act in Canada and heated debate over the introduction of new individual voter registration procedures in the UK. These developments clearly present challenges to conventional studies of voting behavior in these countries in that they add in a new context and criteria to the choices being made. More specifically, how does one interpret a vote decision in the context of flawed and even failed election?

Electoral integrity and traditional studies of voting behavior

As the previous section suggests, the rapid changes and concerns arising in the electoral landscape of so many nations has meant that studies of voting behavior have struggled to keep pace with, and explain, recent developments. Much of the empirical research on elections and voting behavior from the mid-twentieth century onward has been conducted within a paradigm of scientific neutrality. Institutional studies of electoral reforms have come perhaps closest intellectually to the integrity paradigm, although these accounts typically seek to classify rules and explain procedural changes and their consequences from a neutral or relativistic standpoint, rather than explicitly advocating any single "best" system (Colomer 2004; Gallagher and Mitchell 2005; Renwick 2010). Academic engagement in normative debates about how elections should work and what policy reforms might help them perform better has thus been largely avoided. Micro-level studies of voter attitudes and behavior in established and newer democracies in particular have generally displayed very little interest in citizens' evaluations of the integrity of electoral processes and how this might influence voting choices and participation. Any problems arising from electoral malpractices have typically been left to legal scholars, historians, and policy analysts to analyze. Evidence of this lack of attention is evident from only a brief look at a wide range of cross-national surveys and national election studies. Items measuring trust and confidence in electoral procedures and authorities are rarely included on any regular basis.

By contrast, accounts within the electoral integrity perspective typically adopt an overtly critical and normative stance to the topic. Scholars typically begin with an explicit recognition that electoral procedures in many contests fail to meet certain desirable standards of human rights. This is then followed by the realization that these flawed and failed contests have important consequences for citizens and regimes. Analysis and conclusions then center on identifying the reforms of public policies and administrative procedures that are necessary to address these problems (Norris 2014, 2015).

Measuring electoral integrity

Given its breadth and complexity as a concept, operationalizing and measuring electoral integrity presents a challenging task. However, recent efforts have shown that it can be operationalized in ways that are precise, valid, and reliable (Norris 2013; van Ham 2015). The approaches that have been taken to date in measuring electoral integrity can be broadly divided into two types – those that utilize mass survey data and those relying on expert judgments.

Mass level studies

As noted earlier, measures of electoral integrity at the mass level are rare, particularly in cross-national studies and in repeated or longitudinal manner. The first wave of CSES in the mid-1990s monitored citizens' assessment of "free and fair" elections (Birch 2008, 2010). However, this item was not asked in subsequent waves of the study. Similarly isolated items about attitudes toward free and fair elections have fielded in the Global-barometers and the ISSP surveys, as well as in specific national election studies in countries such as Russia and Mexico. More promisingly, however, since 2005, the Gallup World Poll has regularly asked the public in over 100 societies around the world about the honesty of elections in their country. Most recently the sixth wave of the World Values Survey (2010–2014) carries the most extensive battery of nine items monitoring perceptions of electoral integrity and malpractices in around forty societies (Norris 2014).

Elite level studies

A more common approach to measuring electoral integrity is one that relies on expert judgments. Of these, the Freedom House and Polity IV indices are probably among the most widely used and recognized. These indices are designed to measure the level of democratization or democratic performance of a nation *writ large* rather than the quality of its electoral practices specifically. While there is clearly an argument for some linkage between the democratic status of a nation and the standard of its elections, as the evidence has increasingly shown there are cases where the two diverge and the former cannot form a proxy for the latter. Thus, these standard measures need some further nuancing and disaggregation.

The Perceptions of Electoral Integrity (PEI) index

The Perceptions of Electoral Integrity (PEI) index helps to fill this gap. The index emerged from the Electoral Integrity Project as a new tool to measure electoral practices worldwide. The index, fielded annually since 2012, uses expert evaluations to measure the perceived quality of elections. It is based on the central premise that elections can be broken down into eleven key sequential and inter-related steps. These are represented in Figure 18.2.

Like complex links in a chain, violating international standards at any one step in the process throws into question the integrity of the whole electoral process. Thus, rather than focus on particular acts of electoral fraud such as the occurrence of multiple voting or stuffing of ballot boxes, as previous indices have done, the PEI index captures multiple points where fraud and manipulation can occur. This can range from the drawing of district boundaries to advantage a particular party or candidate, to generating false criminal charges to disqualify opponents. Unequal access to media and money can also act as a significant and less visible barrier to open selection of candidates. Finally, once the results are announced, lack of impartial adjudication to resolve any disputes can trigger protest and violence.

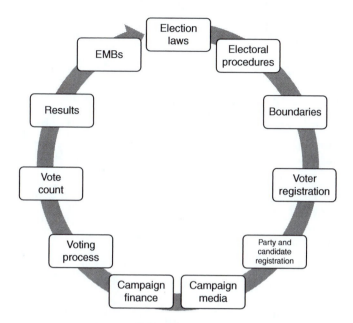

Figure 18.2   The stages in the electoral integrity cycle

The breadth and flexibility of the PEI index means that analysts are able to disaggregate it and pinpoint the issues that they regard to be of most concern in each context. This might involve a focus on the impartiality of the electoral authorities, equitable access to resources during campaigning, or conflict flaring up in the aftermath of the results. In addition, the PEI measures electoral integrity on a continuum rather than by adopting an arbitrary cut-off point. If need be, however, it can be calibrated to the mean to produce categorical distinctions of flawed contests (elections with moderate integrity) and failed contests (ranked lowest on the index). The PEI can also accommodate contests with varying degrees of electoral competition. Thus it can be used to measure integrity in national elections in one-party states such as Cuba where all opposition parties are banned, or where one specific type of party is restricted from ballot access, such as the Freedom and Justice Party in Egypt. It can also be applied to contests where restrictions on individual candidates standing are applied through vetting processes such as in Iran.

Data collection, as stated above, involves completion of a survey by a cross-section of electoral scholars with country-specific expertise.[3] Each of the eleven stages of the electoral process are broken down into more specific domains of activities and respondents are then asked to evaluate the perceived quality of practice in each domain. Findings from the first wave of the PEI (2012–2016) for the 153 countries holding national elections from mid-2012 to mid-2016 are presented in Table 18.1.

The results point to some expected global patterns in that many long-established democracies score well, especially countries in Scandinavia and Western Europe. Countries in the Middle East and Africa generally register much lower scores, as do many countries in the Asia-Pacific region and also in Central Asia. There are also some interesting findings among the more established democracies that underscore the evidence presented earlier about growing problems of electoral legitimacy in these nations. In particular, the United States and the United Kingdom both perform relatively poorly while many of the states in Central and Eastern Europe and the Baltics achieve comparatively healthy scores, as do several countries in Latin America, such as

Table 18.1 The Perception of Electoral Integrity index (PEI-5.0)

N&W Europe		Americas		C&E Europe		Asia-Pacific		Middle East & North Africa		Africa	
Country	PEI Index	Country	PEI Index	Country	PEI Index	Country	PEI Index	Country	PEI Index	Country	PEI Index
Denmark	86	Costa Rica	81	Estonia	79	New Zealand	76	Israel	74	Cape Verde*	70
Finland	86	Uruguay	75	Lithuania*	78	Korea, Rep.*	74	Tunisia	67	Benin*	69
Norway	83	Canada	75	Slovenia	77	Taiwan*	73	Oman	61	Ghana*	65
Iceland*	83	Brazil	68	Czech Rep.	76	Australia*	70	Morocco*	56	Mauritius	64
Sweden	81	Jamaica*	67	Slovak Rep.*	75	Japan*	68	Kuwait*	54	Rwanda	64
Germany	80	Chile	66	Poland	74	Tonga	68	Iran*	49	South Africa	63
Netherlands	79	Grenada	66	Latvia	72	Mongolia*	64	Jordan*	49	Lesotho	63
Switzerland	78	Argentina	64	Croatia*	65	Vanuatu*	63	Turkey	48	Namibia	60
Austria*	77	Barbados	63	Georgia*	59	Micronesia	62	Iraq	44	Botswana	58
Portugal*	75	Peru*	62	Bulgaria*	57	Bhutan	61	Algeria	43	Sierra Leone	56
Belgium	71	United States*	61	Moldova*	57	India	59	Egypt	43	Cote d'Ivoire*	56
Ireland*	71	Panama	61	Hungary	56	Solomon Islands	57	Bahrain	38	Guinea-Bissau	54
Cyprus*	70	Colombia	59	Romania*	56	Maldives	57	Syria*	25	Burkina Faso	53
Spain*	69	Mexico	57	Albania	54	Indonesia	57			Nigeria	53
Italy	67	Cuba	56	Kyrgyzstan	54	Samoa*	55			Central African Rep.*	53
Greece	66	Bolivia	56	Bosnia	53	Myanmar	54			Mali	53
Malta	65	Paraguay	55	Serbia*	52	Nepal	53			Sao Tome & Principe*	52
UK	65	Ecuador	55	Montenegro*	51	Fiji	53			Niger*	48
		El Salvador	54	Ukraine	51	Singapore	53			The Gambia*	48
		Belize	54	Macedonia*	48	Thailand	52			Malawi	46
		Guyana	53	Kazakhstan*	45	Sri Lanka	52			Cameroon	46
		Suriname	51	Russia*	44	Philippines*	49			Swaziland	45
		Guatemala	48	Armenia	44	Pakistan	48			Comoros*	45
		Venezuela	45	Belarus*	39	Laos*	48			Zambia*	44
		Honduras	45	Uzbekistan*	39	Bangladesh	39			Mauritania	44
		Dominican Rep.*	44	Turkmenistan	38	Malaysia	35			Tanzania	44
		Nicaragua*	36	Tajikistan	36	Vietnam*	34			Sudan	43
		Haiti*	31	Azerbaijan	35	Cambodia	32			Guinea	42
						Afghanistan	32			Kenya	41
										Madagascar	39
										Togo	38
										Uganda*	37
										Zimbabwe	35
										Angola	35
										Mozambique	35
										Gabon*	34
										Chad*	30
										Djibouti*	30
										Congo, Rep.*	28
										Eq. Guinea*	25
										Burundi	24
										Ethiopia	23
Regional mean 75		**57**		**56**		**55**		**50**		**47**	

Key:
- = Very High / High (60+)
- = Moderate (50-59)
- = Low / Very Low (less than 50)

Source: PEI-5.0.

Note
★ = election in 2016.

Costa Rica and Uruguay. There is, however, a wide dispersion around the mean in both of these regions.

As a final step to indicate the robustness of the PEI index we correlate the scores it produces against those generated through the alternative democratization indices discussed above. The results are reported in Figure 18.3.

The figure confirms that a significant degree of overlap exists across the indices but also reveals some important differences in the scores produced. Specifically we see a strong correlation in the top right-hand quadrant which confirms that more democratic states typically display more electoral integrity. A similar clustering exists in the bottom left-hand quadrant showing that autocratic states have a higher incidence of electoral malpractices as we might expect.

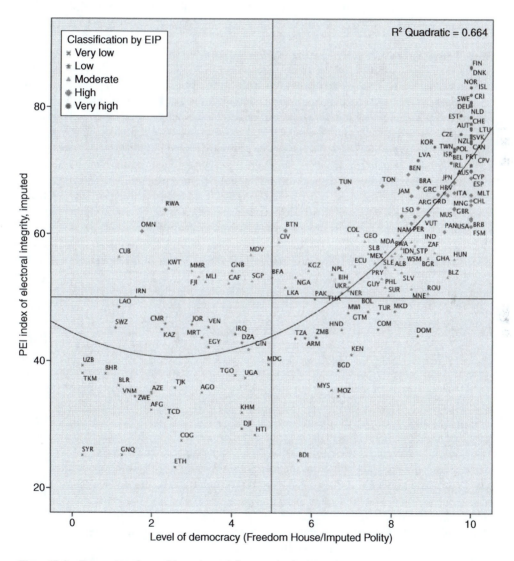

Figure 18.3 Comparing electoral integrity and democratization

Sources: Freedom House/Imputed Polity Quality of Government dataset; Perceptions of Electoral Integrity (PEI 4.5), www.electoralintegrityproject.com.

However, it is also clear that there are many democratic states located in the bottom right hand-quadrant, meaning they report low levels of electoral integrity. The findings thus support the contention that the PEI index is not simply a proxy for regime type and that it can discriminate subtle but important differences in the quality of elections worldwide.

Does integrity matter for political attitudes and voting behavior?

Repeated application of the PEI will provide the basis for examining important research questions central to many sub-fields of political science. For instance, do certain problems surface more frequently under particular regime types? When are malpractices most likely to occur in the electoral cycle? What are the structural, international, and institutional factors that drive flawed and failed contests (Norris 2015)? Finally, and perhaps most importantly, what can be done to fix failed elections? In developing this new research agenda it is important to establish what insights and conclusions existing empirical analyses of electoral integrity have drawn. In this final section of the chapter, therefore, a summary of the main questions and findings that this more applied work has generated is presented.

To date, while some attention has been given to specific events or actors within the electoral integrity cycle, such as the impact of international monitors on polling place fraud and ballot stuffing (Hyde 2011; Kelley 2012; Donno 2013), most of the empirical work on the topic has centered on the extent to which citizens' views of their electoral system affects levels of democratic legitimacy within a society. This is typically measured through indicators such as decreases or increases in levels of trust in the authorities and/or behavioral support for the system in terms of voter turnout. Such studies have been undertaken as large N comparative analyses (Birch 2010; Norris 2014) as well as more focused regional and national studies. On the latter front this has included studies of the usual suspects in North America and Western Europe. For example shortcomings in electoral laws and voting procedures were shown as lowering turnout in several American states (Burden and Stewart 2014; Alvarez and Grofman 2014). Furthermore the depressive effect of perceived malpractices was found to be particularly strong among African-American voters. In Western Europe, studies by Anderson and Tverdova (2003) and Gronlund and Setala (2011) found that perceptions of bribery and corruption generally depressed trust in political institutions.

Elsewhere, studies of African electorates have found that those who express greater confidence in the quality of their elections are more likely to give positive evaluations of democratic performance and to believe in the legitimacy of their regime (Moehler 2009; Robbins and Tessler 2012; Bratton 2013). In their analysis of Sub-Saharan Africa, Bratton and de Walle (1997) found that perceptions of the quality of elections were positively associated with voter turnout in a number of states. Moving to the Latin American region, McCann and Dominguez (1998) examined a series of public opinion polls in Mexico in the mid-1980s to the mid-1990s, a period of one-party rule by the PRI. They found that those citizens expecting electoral fraud were more likely to stay at home on election day, and this group was also more likely to support the opposition. Work by Simpser (2012) confirmed these conclusions through analysis of aggregate turnout data in the pre and post-reform eras. Finally these relationships have also been seen to hold among Eastern European voters. Rose and Mishler (2009), for example, report that Russians who thought that the Duma elections were unfair were less likely to express national pride, as well as proving more mistrusting of parties and parliament, and less likely to endorse the regime.

Looking beyond these conventional measures of democratic legitimacy, other studies have shown how general mistrust in electoral processes can have a contrary effect on less institutionalized methods of participation and particularly levels of protest activity. Based on the World

Values Survey data in many diverse societies, Norris (2014) found that public perceptions of electoral integrity slightly dampened the propensity to engage in direct action, while perceptions of malpractice strengthened protest activism. Indeed, disaffection with the procedural fairness of elections had a stronger direct effect on protest than standard demographic variables such as age and income and other political attitudes such as dissatisfaction with democracy or confidence in elected institutions.

Overall, therefore, the clear and consistent finding message emerging from contemporary empirical research on electoral integrity, and one that future studies can build on, is that mass perceptions of the fairness of elections matter for electorates' behavior and attitudes. This appears to hold regardless of regional context and the distinctiveness of local political culture.

Conclusions

The concept of electoral integrity can be seen as having introduced a new contextual and individual level variable relevant for models of political behavior. In doing so it has supplemented and enriched longstanding approaches to electoral research, and extended their normative and policy relevant quality. On the former front it offers the potential for fresh analytical insights into many classic issues, including how formal procedures shape party choice and turnout in voting behavior, and what determines citizens' confidence and trust in political authorities and satisfaction with democracy? On the latter front, the introduction of the concept has also raised important normative debates about the most desirable qualities of elections and policy-relevant questions about how to reform malpractices both at home (Bauer et al. 2014) and abroad (Bowler and Donovan 2013). The radical paradigm developing around issues of electoral integrity is still in the process of coalescing, but it promises to shake up a half century of electoral studies and political behavior. By addressing contemporary real-world problems well beyond academe, the emerging sub-field holds considerable promise of dissolving conventional divides between the practitioner and scholar and breaking down intellectual walls separating scholars of the West and the rest. Finally, from a disciplinary perspective, the electoral integrity agenda also has the potential to challenge the boundaries that typically characterize political science research, and forge a new and exciting interface between scholars of public administration, political participation, international relations, normative political theory, and comparative institutions.

Notes

1 Legally-binding commitments and state ratifications have been collated by Tuccinardi (2014) for International IDEA and codified in an integrated Elections Obligations and Standards (EOS) database maintained by The Carter Center. *Elections Obligations and Standards Database.* http://electionstandards. cartercenter.org/tools/eos/.

2 Only a handful of contemporary autocracies (including Saudi Arabia, Qatar, the United Arab Emirates, and Brunei) lack constitutional provisions for any direct elections to the lower house of the national parliament. In some cases, like Thailand, elections are currently suspended by the military junta, although promised to be restored eventually. A few one-party states remain, exemplified by China, Vietnam, North Korea, and Cuba, where only Communist party members can hold national legislative office. A few other states, such as Bahrain and Kuwait, also ban all political party organizations by law, although they allow "societies" or "blocs" and individual candidates to run for office. Other countries ban specific parties, such as the courts in Sisi's Egypt, which outlawed the Freedom and Justice Party, the Muslim Brotherhood's political wing.

3 The survey asks around forty electoral experts from each country, generating a mean response rate of around 28 percent across the survey with replies in PEI 4.5 from 2,417 experts covering 213 elections.

References

Alvarez, R. M. and Grofman, B. (eds.) (2014) *Election Administration in the United States: The State of Reform after Bush v. Gore*, New York: Cambridge University Press.

Anderson, C. J. and Tverdova, Y. V. (2003) "Corruption, Political Allegiances, and Attitudes Toward Government in Contemporary Democracies," *American Journal of Political Science*, vol. 47, no. 1, January, 91–109.

Bauer, R. F., Ginsberg. B. L., Britton, B., Echevarria, J., Grayson, T., Lomax, L., Coleman Mayes, M., McGeehan, A., Partick, T., and Thomas, C. (2014) *The American Voting Experience: Report and Recommendations of the Presidential Commission on Election Administration*, Washington DC: Presidential Commission on Election Administration.

Birch, S. (2008) "Electoral Institutions and Popular Confidence in Electoral Processes: A Cross-National Analysis," *Electoral Studies*, vol. 27, no. 2, June, 305–320.

Birch, S. (2010) "Perceptions of Electoral Fairness and Voter Turnout," *Comparative Political Studies*, vol. 43, no. 12, December, 1601–1622.

Bishop, S. and Hoeffler, A. (2014) "Free and Fair Elections: A New Database," Working Paper, Center for the Study of African Economies (CSAE), University of Oxford.

Bjornlund, E. C. (2004) *Beyond Free and Fair: Monitoring Elections and Building Democracy*, Washington, DC: Woodrow Wilson Center Press.

Bowler, S. and Donovan, T. (2013) *The Limits of Electoral Reform*, New York: Oxford University Press.

Bratton, M. (2013) *Voting and Democratic Citizenship in Africa*, Boulder: Lynne Rienner.

Bratton, M. and van de Walle, N. (1997) *Democratic Experiments in Africa: Regime Transitions in Comparative Perspective*, New York: Cambridge University Press.

Burden, B. C. and Stewart, C. III (eds.) (2014) *The Measure of American Elections*, New York: Cambridge University Press.

Cain, B. E., Donovan, T., and Tolbert, C. (2008) *Democracy in the States: Experimentation in Election Reform*, Washington, DC: Brookings Institution Press.

Carothers, T. (2002) "The End of the Transitions Paradigm," *Journal of Democracy*, vol. 13, no. 1, January, 5–21.

Cheibub, J. A., Gandhi, J., and Vreeland, J. R. (2010) "Democracy and Dictatorship Revisited," *Public Choice*, vol. 143, no. 2, April, 67–101.

Colomer, J. M. (2004) *Handbook of Electoral System Choice*, New York: Palgrave Macmillan.

Diamond, L. (2002) "Thinking About Hybrid Regimes," *Journal of Democracy*, vol. 13, no. 2, April, 21–35.

Diamond, L. and Plattner, M. F. (eds.) (2015) *Democracy in Decline?*, Baltimore: Johns Hopkins University Press.

Donno, D. (2013) *Defending Democratic Norms*, New York: Oxford University Press.

Elklit, J. and Reynolds, A. (2005) "A Framework for the Systematic Study of Election Quality," *Democratization*, vol. 12, no. 2, April, 147–162.

Freedom House (2017) www.freedomhouse.org.

Gallagher, M. and Mitchell, P. (eds.) (2005) *The Politics of Electoral Systems*, Oxford: Oxford University Press.

Goodwin-Gill, G. S. (2006) *Free and Fair Elections*, 2nd Edition, Geneva: Inter-Parliamentary Union.

Gronlund, K. and Setala, M. (2011) "In Honest Officials We Trust: Institutional Confidence in Europe," *American Review of Public Administration*, vol. 42, no. 5, September, 523–542.

Ham, C. van (2015) "Getting Elections Right? Measuring Electoral Integrity," *Democratization*, vol. 22, no. 4, June, 714–737.

Hasen, R. L. (2012) *The Voting Wars: From Florida 2000 to the Next Election Meltdown*, New Haven: Yale University Press.

Hyde, S. D. (2011) *The Pseudo-Democrat's Dilemma*, Ithaca: Cornell University Press.

Hyde, S. D. and Marinov, N. (2012) *Codebook for National Elections Across Democracy and Autocracy (NELDA) 1945–2010, Version 3*, available online: www.nelda.co/NELDA_codebook_2012.pdf.

Kelley, J. (2012) *Monitoring Democracy: When International Election Observation Works and Why It Often Fails*, Princeton: Princeton University Press.

Kurlantzick, J. (2014) *Democracy in Retreat: The Revolt of the Middle Class and the Worldwide Decline of Representative Government*, New Haven: Yale University Press.

Lehoucq, F. E. and Jiménez, I. M. (2002) *Stuffing the Ballot Box: Fraud, Electoral Reform, and Democratization in Costa Rica*, New York: Cambridge University Press.

Levitsky, S. and Way, L. A. (2002) "The Rise of Competitive Authoritarianism," *Journal of Democracy*, vol. 13, no. 2, April, 51–66.

Levitsky, S. and Way, L. (2010) *Competitive Authoritarianism: Hybrid Regimes after the Cold War*, New York: Cambridge University Press.

Lindberg, S. (2006) *Democracy and Elections in Africa*, Baltimore, MD: The Johns Hopkins University Press.

Magaloni, B. (2006) *Voting for Autocracy: Hegemonic Party Survival and Its Demise in Mexico*, Cambridge: Cambridge University Press.

McCann, J. A. and Dominguez, J. I. (1998) "Mexicans React to Electoral Fraud and Political Corruption: An Assessment of Public Opinion and Voting Behavior," *Electoral Studies*, vol. 17, no. 4, December, 483–503.

Moehler, D. C. (2009) "Critical Citizens and Submissive Subjects: Elections Losers and Winners in Africa," *British Journal of Political Science*, vol. 39, no. 2, April, 345–366.

Munck, G. L. (2009) *Measuring Democracy: A Bridge Between Scholarship and Politics*, Baltimore: The Johns Hopkins Press.

Norris, P. (2013) "Does the World Agree About Standards of Electoral Integrity? Evidence for the Diffusion of Global Norms," *Electoral Studies*, vol. 32, no. 4, December, 576–588.

Norris, P. (2014) *Why Electoral Integrity Matters*, New York: Cambridge University Press.

Norris, P. (2015) *Why Elections Fail*, New York: Cambridge University Press.

Norris, P. and A. Abel van Es. (2016) *Checkbook Elections*, New York: Oxford University Press.

Przeworski, A., Alvarez, M. E., Cheibub, J. A., and Limongi. F. (2000) *Democracy and Development: Political Institutions and Well-Being in the World, 1950–1990*, New York: Cambridge University Press.

Renwick, A. (2010) *The Politics of Electoral Reform*, New York: Cambridge University Press.

Robbins, M. D. H. and Tessler, M. (2012) "The Effects of Elections on Public Opinion Towards Democracy: Evidence from Longitudinal Survey Research in Algeria," *Comparative Political Studies*, vol. 45, no. 10, October, 1255–1276.

Rose, R. and Mishler, W. (2009) "How Do Electors Respond to an "Unfair" Election? The Experience of Russians," *Post-Soviet Affairs*, vol. 25, no. 2, April, 118–136.

Rosenstone, S. J. and Wolfinger, R. E. (1978) "The Effect of Registration Laws on Voter Turnout," *American Political Science Review*, vol. 72, no. 1, March, 27–45.

Schedler, A. (2002) "The Menu of Manipulation," *Journal of Democracy*, vol. 13, no. 2, April, 36–45.

Schedler, A. (ed.) (2006) *Electoral Authoritarianism: The Dynamics of Unfree Competition*, Boulder: Lynne Rienner.

Simpser, A. (2012) "Does Electoral Manipulation Discourage Voter Turnout? Evidence from Mexico," *Journal of Politics*, vol. 74, no. 3, July, 782–795.

Simpser, A. (2013) *Why Parties and Governments Manipulate Elections: Theory, Practice and Implications*, New York: Cambridge University Press.

Streb, M. J. (ed.) (2004) *Law and Election Politics*, 2nd Edition, New York: Routledge.

Tuccinardi, D. (ed.) (2014) *International Obligations for Elections: Guidelines for Legal Frameworks*, Stockholm: International IDEA.

Vickery, C. and Shein, E. (2012) *Assessing Electoral Fraud in New Democracies*, Washington, DC, IFES, available online: www.ifes.org/sites/default/files/assessing_electoral_fraud_series_vickery_shein_0.pdf.

Wolfinger, R. E. and Rosenstone, S. J. (1980) *Who Votes?* New Haven: Yale University Press.

19

VOTING BEHAVIOR IN MULTI-LEVEL ELECTORAL SYSTEMS

Hermann Schmitt and Eftichia Teperoglou

Across many countries a central element of political competition is arising from the multi-level dynamics of electoral politics. The evolution of this sub-field of electoral research has been especially relevant in electoral studies of federal states (e.g., Belgium, Canada, Germany, the US or Spain). Moreover, it is also related to a shift of authority from the national to the subnational or supranational level. This increased relocation of authority to govern is generally challenging the role of the democratic nation-state (Hooghe et al. 2010). This is all the more the case in the European Union (EU), which has become one of the most characteristic examples of multi-level politics, with supranational, national and subnational levels of jurisdiction cooperating and to some degree competing with one another. Under these circumstances, one research question for this chapter is about the relationship (or "interdependency") between elections at these different levels of government. Another question is whether "electoral actors" exhibit different motivations and behaviors depending on the level of jurisdiction at which an election is held (van der Eijk and Schmitt 2008). In order to explore these questions, many scholars have put forward two groups of contextual variables – one being the character and importance of the electoral contest, and the other being the political climate in the "main" political arena at the time of the election under study. The first group of contextual variables includes the perceived political importance (or salience) of the office(s) to be filled. National parliamentary elections or those for a president with executive powers are contests of "high salience" (or "high stimulus" elections), while all other types of elections are of "low salience" (or "low stimulus" elections) (see Campbell 1960 for this distinction). The political climate includes various short-term aspects related to the timing of the "low stimulus" election within the electoral cycle of the main political arena (such as the popularity of the government (see, for example, Stimson 1976); or the state of the economy (see, for example, Tufte 1975).

Indeed, the roots of a systematic study of the interdependence of political behavior in different types of elections were first proposed in the literature on US mid-term election results. The three main streams of that literature are the "surge and decline" theory of the Michigan school (Campbell 1960); the "referendum" theory (Tufte 1975); and the "balancing" theory (Alesina and Rosenthal 1989, 1995). These approaches have set out to explain one of the most regular trends in the electoral behavior of US politics. Compared with previous and subsequent "high stimulus" presidential elections, mid-term elections are characterized by lower levels of electoral

municipal elections, for instance, often serve less as a barometer of national government popularity simply because there are other issues and personalities at stake at the local level than at the national one (e.g., Sinnott 1995: 256; but see Curtice and Payne 1991).[2]

A second reason is related to the main assumption of the SOE model. The EP elections are "less important" contests because there is "less at stake"[3] than in FOEs. SOE results do not determine the composition of the executive in the main political arena (Reif and Schmitt 1980: 9). Based on this observation, some aggregate predictions about the outcome of SOEs are spelled out. A first regards electoral participation, following in this case mainly the theoretical argument by the "surge and decline" theory. The prediction is that participation is lower in a SOE compared both to the previous and the subsequent FOE. Moreover, and somehow related to that, the number of invalid and blank votes is expected to be higher in a SOE. But expectations are also specified regarding vote choices. Here we can find another point of innovation of the SOE model compared to the paradigm of mid-term losses. It is the inclusion of party properties beyond the government-opposition status. Irrelevant in the US two-party context, "party size" is of particular importance in the analysis of "low stimulus" elections in multi-party systems. Reif and Schmitt (1980) specify the following predictions: government parties are likely to lose support in a SOE compared with the previous and subsequent FOE, but big parties more generally are expected to perform worse. On the other hand, smaller parties are expected to perform better in a "low stimulus" election. A final main addition of the SOE model to the literature on "low stimulus" election is the analytical consideration of the position of the SOE in the national electoral cycle. As we have seen, Reif and Schmitt were not the first to observe an interaction of SOE results with their position in the national electoral cycle. However, their model along with some more recent studies (e.g., van der Eijk and Franklin 1996) introduced the analysis of voting patterns in EP elections based on the timing of this election within the first-order electoral cycle of the respective country.

The aggregate hypotheses of the SOE model repeatedly received empirical support (for European elections see, for example, Hix and Marsh 2011; Norris 1997; Reif 1985, 1997; Schmitt 2005, 2009; Teperoglou 2010; Teperoglou et al. 2015; Schmitt and Teperoglou 2015; van der Brug and van der Eijk 2007; van der Eijk and Franklin 1996; for regional elections see, for example, Pallarés and Keating 2003; Schakel and Jeffery 2013; Schakel 2014). Nevertheless, important exceptions are also documented which proved to be useful for identifying the theoretical limits of the SOE model. Some of the most striking evidence toward a shift in the second-order nature of the EP elections is observed at the occasion of the 2014 EP elections. Both the socio-political circumstances and the economic turmoil at the time of the 2014 EP election, as well as the fact that for the first time the results of the elections have been considered for the appointment of the president of the European Commission, had the potential to change the second-order character of the contest. In many EU countries, European governance appeared as a polarizing issue with indications of becoming significant in determining voting choices (Schmitt and Teperoglou 2015; Schmitt and Toygür 2016). In other words, there were signs that the 2014 EP elections could be considered as "critical" contests in the sense of the pioneering study by V. O. Key (1955).[4] Overall, it turned out that these developments could not profoundly change the second-order nature of the EP elections across all 28 EU member states. However, for the first time in the history of EP elections we can also identify some signs toward a critical realignment in European party systems on EU issues (Schmitt and Teperoglou 2015).

Having said that, however, it must be added that the most significant failure of the SOE model in predicting EP election results was observed in the EP election of 2004. Analyses of the European Election Study (EES) 2004 revealed that in the new post-communist member countries the losses of government parties did not follow the FOE cycle and in some of these countries, smaller parties did not perform better compared to the previous FOE (see Schmitt 2005; Marsh 2005; Koepke and Ringe 2006). The main explanation offered for these deviations is that the SOE model was built upon the assumption of stable and consolidated electoral and party systems, while in the East European member countries such a party system had and to some degree still has to develop (Schmitt 2005: 666).

Subnational elections as second-order contests

The application of the aggregate hypotheses of the SOE model is more questionable in the case of some municipal and local elections. Local politics often have their own dynamics. The local political arena, the candidates and their personality and local policy orientations are among the factors that could contribute toward a departure from the second-order voting mechanism (Magone 2004; Marien et al. 2015; Sinnott 1995). Moreover, studies focusing mainly on regional elections posit the question of a kind of "hierarchy" among the different types of SOE (e.g., see Heath et al. 1999; Lefevere and van Aelst 2014; Skrinis and Teperoglou 2008).

Various studies have tested the SOE model on regional elections across Europe and the Americas (among others, see Erikson and Filippov 2001; Jeffery and Hough 2003; Pallarés and Keating 2003; Schakel and Jeffery 2013; Dandoy and Schakel 2013; Thorlakson 2015; Remmer and Gélineau 2003). Most of these confirm that government parties tend to lose in regional elections, while opposition and small parties tend to gain. Participation is lower compared with the national election. Nevertheless, there is one important deviation from the SOE model hypotheses. The losses for the incumbent parties do not always follow the electoral cycle of the FOE arena (Schakel 2014: 4; Johnston 1999 for Canada; Schmitt and Reif 2003 for Germany). The provincial elections in Canada represent an important outlier, since the results clearly do not fit the SOE model (Jeffery and Hough 2009). Jeffery and Hough (2003) analyzed the losses for the governmental parties in relation to regional power and strong territorial cleavages. The greater variation in the institutional arrangements of regional elections calls for less uniformity and more deviations. Moreover, Schakel and Jeffery (2013) conclude that the SOE model is not confirmed in the case of regional elections which take place in powerful regions where strong regionalist parties instead of nation-wide parties stand for election.

Voting patterns in second-order elections

The first main amendment of the original SOE model regards a typology of voting in SOE (see mainly van der Eijk and Franklin 1996). The different forms of vote switching between SOE and FOE are partly linked to the timing of the SOE within the national electoral cycle. One important voting pattern in SOE is a protest vote against the incumbent government. The "low stimulus" elections offer voters the opportunity to express their current dissatisfaction with the party they usually vote for; and this dissatisfaction manifests itself in defection (i.e., votes for another party) or abstentions. Using a term from the lexicon of football hooliganism, protest voting has been characterized as "voting with the boot" (see, for example, Oppenhuis et al. 1996: 301–304; Franklin 2005). Some scholars (van der Eijk and Franklin 1996) argue that protest vote is mainly observed in EP elections that take place in the later-term of the electoral cycle. According to them, citizens are more likely to vote "with the boot" (or defect "strategically," see Schmitt et al. 2008, 2009) the closer an EP election comes to the next FOE. On the other hand, there is also the observation that the electorate treats later-term EP elections as quasi national elections and thus, government parties on average do not suffer severe losses (Reif and Schmitt 1980).

The other main voting pattern in SOE, actually the predominant one, is linked to the fact that there is less at stake in this type of election. Voters therefore can afford to cast a "sincere" vote for the party they prefer most. Voters are free to abandon strategic considerations (or "voting with the head," see Oppenhuis et al. 1996: 301–304, Marsh and Franklin 1996: 16–21; Franklin 2005) and cast a vote "with the heart." Van der Eijk and Franklin (1996) argue that this voting pattern is mainly observed during the "honeymoon" period of the electoral cycle. On the contrary, Reif and Schmitt (1980) suggest that a SOE shortly after a FOE is mainly characterized by a post-electoral euphoria and, therefore, government parties will receive near identical support in the EP election. Finally, at around mid-term of the electoral cycle strategic voting against the government is probably most widespread ("cyclical signaling," see Schmitt et al. 2008, 2009). Then, losses for the incumbent parties will be greater than either early or late in the electoral cycle (see, for example, Reif 1985; van der Eijk and Franklin 1996), following mainly the arguments of the original studies back in the US context. Overall, we can conclude that the electorate behaves differently when these elections are held early in the first-order election cycle or during the run-up to the next national election.

Voting patterns in "low stimulus" elections are further analyzed in another main amendment to the SOE model. This revision concerns the so-called "micro-foundations" of the SOE model (see, for example, Carrubba and Timpone 2005; Hobolt and Wittrock 2011; Hobolt and Spoon 2012; Schmitt et al. 2008, 2009; Weber 2011; Schmitt and Teperoglou 2015). Both the motivations of individual citizens and their political behaviors are at the core of the analysis. Three different processes are likely to affect inter-election vote patterns according to the SOE model: mobilization, sincere voting and strategic voting (Schmitt et al. 2008, 2009). Mobilization likely has an impact on SOE abstentions, while sincere and strategic motivations are affecting both SOE abstainers and SOE defectors (for a comprehensive analysis of the micro-level hypotheses, see mainly Schmitt et al. 2008, 2009 and also Schmitt and Teperoglou 2017).

It is important to stress that everything happens at once – probably due in part to the different loci of EP elections in the respective national electoral cycle. There are clear mobilization effects with regard to turnout; and there are both sincere and strategic effects on vote switching, with sincere motivations having a somewhat stronger impact.

The consequences of second-order elections for the first-order political arena

The SOE model entails that it is more likely that the first-order political arena affect electoral behavior in EP elections than vice versa. If we want to understand the results of EP elections, we first have to appreciate the decisive role of the political situation in the first-order political arena at the time when second-order elections are being held (Reif and Schmitt 1980: 8). Therefore, the model focuses mainly on the way in which national politics are influencing "less important" elections. However, the reverse outcome is also considered possible, and there is an emerging literature which tries to substantiate this claim. As noted by van der Brug and de Vreese (2016), EP elections might have unintended consequences for national politics. In the following, we attempt to identify such spillover effects from a SOE to a FOE. We can distinguish between three main groups of consequences, some of them more overt and direct while others more covert or even "hidden." At a first glance, we identify some very practical or procedural changes in the domain of EU decision-making. Over the years from the first EP election of 1979, the powers of the European Parliament have been amplified, a process which culminated in the co-decision procedure promoting the EP to an equal co-legislator next to the European Council. After the 2014 EP election, based on stipulations of the Lisbon Treaty, the

European Parliament even had a decisive say in the selection of the president of the European Commission when the lead candidate of the victorious European People's Party was appointed. In addition, we are witnessing an increasing politicization of EU politics. In many EU member states (in particular those directly affected by the economic crisis) a European dimension of political competition ranging from outright opposition to full support of EU integration has emerged as a relevant structure of party competition (Kriesi et al. 2008; Hooghe and Marks 2009; Teperoglou and Tsatsanis 2011; Hutter et al. 2016). Under these circumstances, the composition of the European Parliament and its balance of power is affecting the direction of EU policy making, which in turn might have an impact on domestic political decisions.

The direct election of the members of the European Parliament, from 1979 on, was expected to increase citizens' awareness of EU institutions and strengthen EU democracy as perceived by its citizens. Many politicians hoped that the elections of the members of the European Parliament would add legitimacy to the EU level of European multi-level governance. Such consequences of EP elections were consdiered as normatively positive and desireable (Marsh and Franklin 1996: 30). Thirty-seven years later, we cannot find any clear evidence pointing in this direction. While affecting the level of turnout somewhat, the nomination and campaign of lead candidates or Spitzenkandidaten in the EP elections of 2014 could not alter the "low stimulus" character of the election and change it in the direction of a more "genuine European contest" (Schmitt et al. 2015).

There are two other sets of potential consequences to which we will briefly turn to below: the impact of a second-order election on national party systems, and on the levels of electoral participation in national elections.

The impact of a SOE on national party systems

One of the main hypotheses of the SOE model is that "low stimulus" elections provide opportunities for small parties to perform better compared to the environment provided by national first-order elections. In particular, new small parties that enter the political arena first at the time of an EP election can profit from the fact that there is less at stake. EP elections have indeed been described as the "midwife assisting in the birth of new parties" (van der Eijk and Franklin 1996: 53). Different electoral systems being applied in national and EP elections may further facilitate the electoral performance of small and new parties. The question is whether these new parties will survive in the subsequent national election. The history of EP elections provides some prominent examples of a breakthrough of newcomers. In France, the performance of the Front National (Ysmal and Cayrol 1996) is one of them, and Die Republikaner in Germany (Schmitt 1996) and more recently UKIP in the UK (Ford and Goodwin 2014) are further examples from the far right. However, this mechanism does not only apply on the far-right of national party systems but also in the left-green spectrum: the rise of many new Green and ecological parties in different EU member-countries – like Die Grünen in Germany – is another example of the spillover of EP election successes into the arena of national electoral politics (Curtice 1989). Moreover, Dinas and Riera (2017) are able to show that the likelihood of voting for a small party in subsequent FOEs increases when the individual's first vote ever was cast in an EP election in which voting for a small party is easier.

Using data from the European Election Studies 2004 and 2009, Markowski (2016) identifies different factors (both at the individual and at the contextual level) that might contribute to the likelihood of a spillover of SOE electoral successes of small and new parties into the FOE electoral arena. A main finding from this study is that social cohesion is more important than ideological or political cohesion for the electoral success of the party in the subsequent FOE. The timing of an EP election within the first-order national electoral cycle does not seem to play a role. Markowski identifies differences between old and stable democracies and the new Eastern EU member states. In the latter group of countries, the possibilities for the new party to keep its electoral success are linked to the quality of political representation and social bonds. However, the limited number of observations in this particular study has led the author to acknowledge that these findings should not lead to far-reaching generalizations.

The impact of a SOE on electoral participation

An EP election might be consequential in terms of the mobilization of the electorate. Franklin and Hobolt (2010) identify that turnout in EP elections is particularly low in that part of the electorate the electoral participation of which is not yet "habitual" (see also Dinas 2012). This is relevant for the national electoral arena as citizens who become enfranchised first at the time of a second-order EP election are not only less likely to vote in a SOE, but also in the subsequent FOE. They get used to not voting: the early experience of an EP election does not contribute to the development of the habitual voting mechanism. Their analysis has shown that given the fact EP elections are only a "pale reflection" of a national contest, for young voters who have not yet had the opportunity to develop strong ties to parties, there is a spillover effect in terms of abstention from the second-order contest to the first-order one. Therefore, EP elections, in the long run, depress turnout in the FOE arena as well.

Concluding remarks

Starting from the early studies of mid-term elections in the US, a whole industry of studies into "less important" elections emerged. Upon that background, the conceptual framework developed around the SOE model was meant as an effort to broaden the earlier US centric mid-term elections perspective and include a wider variety of second-order elections into the theoretical discussion and empirical analysis. One of the major lessons from testing the SOE model not only for EP elections but also for other "low stimulus" contests is that the electoral behavior in different contexts is not restricted to one electoral and political arena, but to more than one and possibly to many. This is not a trivial observation as this simple fact has severe consequences for electoral participation and party choice. The original proposal by Reif and Schmitt concentrated on macro-level hypotheses, and on effects on second-order electoral results which originate in the first-order electoral arena. Micro-level processes were not ignored in the original statement – nor are they ignored in the mid-term election literature – but it took a while until the micro-foundations of SOE behavior became somewhat more systematized. Our literature review demonstrated that this path of research has received more attention recently, and it is expected to become more prominent in the future. Even more recent are efforts to understand the reverse flow of causation – the effects that SOE might have on FOE electoral politics – both in the aggregate with regard to party system change and at the individual one with regard to electoral participation. Again, we believe that more work has to be done in this research field. Times of economic turmoil and increasing xenophobia are marked by growing populism and Eurosceptical stances of political parties, increased de-alignment and high volatility of voters, and "earthquake" or "critical" elections in various first-order contests – including the recent referendum of British EU membership. By studying the spillover effects of SOE to the first-order electoral arena, perhaps we might detect further important pieces in the still unsolved multi-level electoral puzzle.

Notes

1 For the cyclical character of government popularity, see also, for the US, Goodhart and Bhansali (1970) and Stimson (1976), and for the UK, Miller and Mackie (1973).
2 In addition, it is hard to generalize from the findings of the heterogeneous field of local elections because of the very different rules and contexts under which they are held in Europe and beyond.
3 The original study by Reif and Schmitt included some other analytical dimensions: the specific-arena, the institutional-procedural, the campaign, the main-arena political change and, finally, social and cultural change (1980: 10–15). However, most of the subsequent studies have focused on the "less at stake" dimension.
4 According to Key (1955), elections are critical when the traditional coalitions between social groups and their political agents are subject to profound and lasting realignment.

References

Alesina, A. and Rosenthal, H. (1989) "Partisan Cycles in Congressional Elections and the Macroeconomy," *The American Political Science Review*, vol. 83, no. 2, June, 373–398.
Alesina, A. and Rosenthal, H. (1995) *Partisan Politics, Divided Government, and the Economy*, New York: Cambridge University Press.
Brug, W. van der and de Vreese, C. (eds.) (2016) *Unintended Consequences of European Parliamentary Elections*, Oxford: Oxford University Press.
Brug, W. van der and van der Eijk, C. (eds.) (2007) *European Elections and Domestic Politics: Lessons from the Past and Scenarios for the Future*, South Bend: University of Notre Dame Press.
Campbell, A. (1960) "Surge and Decline: A Study of Electoral Change," *Public Opinion Quarterly*, vol. 24, no. 3, Autumn, 397–418.
Carrubba, C. J. and Timpone, R. J. (2005) "Explaining Vote Switching Across First and Second Order Elections: Evidence from Europe," *Comparative Political Studies*, vol. 38, no. 3, April, 260–281.
Curtice, J. (1989) "The 1989 European Election: Protest or Green Tide," *Electoral Studies*, vol. 8, no. 3, December, 217–230.
Curtice, J. and Payne, C. (1991) "Local Elections as National Referendums in Great Britain," *Electoral Studies*, vol. 10, no. 1, March, 3–17.
Dandoy, R. and Schakel, A. (eds.) (2013) *Regional and National Elections in Western Europe: Territoriality of the Vote in Thirteen Countries*, Houndmills: Palgrave Macmillan.
Dinas, E. (2012) "The Formation of Voting Habits," *Journal of Elections, Public Opinion and Parties*, vol. 22, no. 4, November, 431–456.
Dinas, E. & Riera, P. (2017) "Do European Parliament Elections Impact National Party System Fragmentation?," *Comparative Political Studies*, 1–30.
Dinkel, R. (1977) "Der Zusammenhang Zwischen Bundes-und Landtagswahlergebnissen," in Kaase, M. (ed.) *Wahlsoziologie Heute. Analysen aus Anlass der Bundestagswahl 1976*, Opladen: Westdeutscher Verlag: 348–359.
Dinkel, R. (1978) "The Relationship Between Federal and State Elections in West Germany," in Kaase, M. and Von Beyme, K. (eds.) *Elections and Parties*, London: Sage: 53–65.
Eijk, C. van der and Franklin, M. (1996) *Choosing Europe? The European Electorate and National Politics in the Face of the Union*, Ann Arbor: University of Michigan Press.
Eijk, C. van der and Schmitt, H. (2008) (eds.) *The Multilevel Electoral System of the EU*, Mannheim: Mannheim Centre for European Social Research.
Eijk, C. van der, Franklin, M. and Marsh, M. (1996) "What Voters Teach Us About Europe-Wide Elections: What Europe-Wide Elections Teach Us About Voters," *Electoral Studies*, vol. 15, no. 2, May, 149–166.
Erikson, R. S. (1988) "The Puzzle of Mid-Term Loss," *Journal of Politics*, vol. 50, no. 4, November, 1011–1029.
Erikson, R. S. and Filippov, M. G. (2001) "Electoral Balancing in Federal and Sub-National Elections: The Case of Canada," *Constitutional Political Economy*, vol. 12, no. 4, December, 313–331.
Ford, R. and Goodwin, M. (2014) *Revolt on the Right. Explaining Support for the Radical Right in Britain*, London: Routledge.
Franklin, M. (2005) "The Fading Power of National Politics to Structure Voting Behaviour in Elections to the European Parliament," Paper presented at the 2004 Conference on European Elections, Central European University, May 20–23.

Franklin, M. and Hobolt, S. (2010) "The Legacy of Lethargy: How Elections to the European Parliament Depress Turnout," *Electoral Studies*, vol. 30, no. 1, March, 67–76.

Goodhart, C. A. E. and Bhansali, R. J. (1970) "Political Economy," *Political Studies*, vol. 18, no. 1, March, 43–106.

Heath, A., Mclean, I., Taylor, B. and Curtice, J. (1999) "Between First and Second-Order: A Comparison of Voting Behaviour in European and Local Elections in Britain," *European Journal of Political Research*, vol. 35, no. 3, May, 389–414.

Hix, S. and Marsh, M. (2011) "Second-Order Effects Plus Pan-European Political Swings: An Analysis of European Parliament Elections Across Time," *Electoral Studies*, vol. 30, no. 1, March, 4–15.

Hobolt, S. and Spoon, J. (2012) "Motivating the European voter: Parties, Issues and Campaigns in European Parliament Elections," *European Journal of Political Research*, vol. 51, no. 6, October, 701–727.

Hobolt, S. and Wittrock, J. (2011) "The Second Order Election Model Revisited: An Experimental Test of Vote Choices in European Parliament Elections," *Electoral Studies*, vol. 30, no. 1, March, 29–40.

Hooghe, L. and Marks, G. (2009) "A Post-Functionalist Theory of European Integration: From Permissive Consensus to Constraining Dissensus," *British Journal of Political Science*, vol. 39, no. 1, January, 1–23.

Hooghe, L., Marks, G. and Schakel, A. H. (2010) *The Rise of Regional Authority: A Comparative Study of 42 Democracies*, London: Routledge.

Hutter, S., Grande, E. and Kriesi, H. (eds.) (2016) *Politicising Europe: Integration and Mass Politics*, Cambridge: Cambridge University Press.

Jeffery, C. and Hough, D. (2001) "The Electoral Cycle and Multi-Level Voting in Germany," *German Politics*, vol. 10, no. 2, August, 73–98.

Jeffery, C. and Hough, D. (2003) "Regional Elections in Multi-Level Systems," *European Urban and Regional Studies*, vol. 10, no. 3, July, 199–212.

Jeffery, C. and Hough, D. (2009) "Understanding Post-Devolution Elections in Scotland and Wales in Comparative Perspective," *Party Politics*, vol. 15, no. 2, March, 219–240.

Johnston, R. (1999) "Business Cycles, Political Cycles and the Popularity of Canadian Governments, 1974–1998," *Canadian Journal of Political Science*, vol. 32, no. 3, September, 499–520.

Key, V. O. (1955) "A Theory of Critical Elections," *Journal of Politics*, vol. 17, no. 1, February, 145–155.

Koepke, J. R. and Ringe, N. (2006) "The Second Order Election Model in an Enlarged Europe," *European Union Politics*, vol. 7, no. 3, September, 321–346.

Kriesi, H., Grande, E., Lachat, R., Dolezal, M., Bornschier, S. and Frey, T. (2008) *West European Politics in the Age of Globalization*, Cambridge: Cambridge University Press.

Lefevere, J. and van Aelst, P. (2014) "First-Order, Second-Order or Third Rate? A Comparison of Turnout in European, Local and National Elections in the Netherlands," *Electoral Studies*, vol. 35, September, 159–170.

Magone, J. M. (2004) *Contemporary Spanish Politics*, London: Routledge.

Marien, S., Dassonneville, R. and M. Hooghe (2015) "How Second-Order Are Local Elections? Voting Motives and Party Preferences in Belgian Municipal Elections," *Local Government Studies*, vol. 41, no. 6, December, 898–916.

Markowski, R. (2016) "How European Elections Affect National Party Systems: On the Survival of Newly Established Parties," in van der Brug, W. and De Vreese, C. (eds.) *Unintended Consequences of European Parliamentary Elections*, Oxford: Oxford University Press: 125–147.

Marsh, M. (2005) "The Results of the 2004 European Parliament Elections and the Second-Order Model," in Niedermayer, O. and Schmitt, H. (eds.) *Europawahl 2004*, Wiesbaden: VS-Verlag: 142–158.

Marsh, M. (2008) "Vote Switching in European Parliament Elections: Evidence from June 2004," in van der Eijk, C. and Schmitt, H. (eds.) *The Multilevel Electoral System of the EU*, Mannheim: Mannheim Centre for European Social Research: 71–95.

Marsh, M. and Franklin, M. (1996) "The Foundations: Unanswered Questions from the Study of European Elections, 1979–1994," in van der Eijk, C. and Franklin, M. (eds.) *Choosing Europe? The European Electorate and National Politics in the Face of Union*, Ann Arbor: University of Michigan Press: 11–33.

Miller, W. L. and Mackie, M. (1973) "The Electoral Cycle and the Asymmetry of Government and Opposition Popularity," *Political Studies*, vol. 21, no. 3, September, 263–279.

Mughan, A. (1986) "Toward a Political Explanation of Government Vote Losses in Midterm By-Elections," *American Political Science Review*, vol. 80, no. 3, September, 761–775.

Norris, P. (1997) "Nomination: Second Order Elections Revisited," *European Journal of Political Research*, vol. 31, no. 1, February, 109–114.

Oppenhuis, E., van der Eijk, C. and Franklin, M. (1996) "The Party Context: Outcomes," in van der Eijk, C. and Franklin, M. (eds.) *Choosing Europe? The European Electorate and National Politics in the Face of Union*, Ann Arbor: University of Michigan Press: 287–306.

Pallarés, F. and Keating, M. (2003) "Multi-Level Electoral Competition: Regional Elections and Party Systems in Spain," *European Urban and Regional Studies*, vol. 10, no. 3, July, 239–255.

Reif, K. (1985) "Ten Second-Order National Elections," in Reif, K. (ed.) *Ten European Elections: Campaigns and Results of the 1979/81 First Direct Elections to the European Parliament*, Aldershot: Gower: 1–36.

Reif, K. and Schmitt, H. (1980) "Nine Second-Order National Elections; A Conceptual Framework for the Analyses of European Election Results," *European Journal of Political Research*, vol. 8, no. 1, March, 3–44.

Reif, K. (1997) "European elections as member state second-order elections revisited," *European Journal of Political Research*, vol. 31, no.1–2: 115–124.

Remmer, K. L. and Gélineau, F. (2003) "Subnational Electoral Choice: Economic and Referendum Voting in Argentina, 1983–1999," *Comparative Political Studies*, vol. 36, no. 7, September, 801–821.

Schakel, A. H. (2014) "How to Analyze Second-Order Election Effects? A Refined Second-Order Election Model," *Comparative European Politics*, vol. 13, no. 6, November, 636–655.

Schakel, A. H. and Jeffery, C. (2013) "Are Regional Elections Really 'Second-Order' Elections?," *Regional Studies*, vol. 47, no. 3, 323–341.

Schmitt, H. (1996) "Germany: A Bored Electorate," in van der Eijk, C. and Franklin, M. (eds.) *Choosing Europe? The European Electorate and National Politics in the Face of Union*, Ann Arbor: University of Michigan Press: 137–156.

Schmitt, H. (2005) "The European Parliament Elections of June 2004: Still Second Order?," *West European Politics*, vol. 28, no. 3, May, 650–679.

Schmitt, H. (2009) "Introduction," *Journal of European Integration*, vol. 31, no. 5, September, 525–536.

Schmitt, H. and Reif, K. (2003) "Der Hauptwahlzyklus und die Ergebnisse von Nebenwahlen," in Wüst, A. (ed.) *Politbarometer*, Opladen: Leske und Budrich: 239–254.

Schmitt, H. and Teperoglou, E. (2015) "The 2014 European Parliament Elections in Southern Europe: Second-Order or Critical Elections?," *South European Society and Politics*, vol. 20, no. 3, July, 287–309.

Schmitt, H. and Teperoglou, E. (2017) "The Study of Less Important Elections," in Arzheimer, K., Evans, J. and Lewis-Beck, M. (eds.) *The Sage Handbook of Electoral Behaviour*, Los Angeles, London, New Delhi, Singapore, Washington DC and Melbourne: Sage: 56–79.

Schmitt, H. and Toygür, I. (2016) "European Parliament Elections of May 2014: Driven by National Politics or EU Policy Making?," *Politics and Governance*, vol. 4, no. 1, 167–181.

Schmitt, H., Hobolt, S. and Popa, S. (2015) "Does Personalization Increase Turnout? 'Spitzenkandidaten' in the 2014 European Parliament Elections," *European Union Politics*, vol. 16, no. 3, September, 347–368.

Schmitt, H., Sanz, A. and Braun, D. (2008) "The Micro-Foundations of Second-Order Election Theory: Theoretical Reconstructions and Empirical Tests Based Upon the European Election Study 2004," Paper presented at the 2008 CSES Workshop, University of Manchester, December 9–11.

Schmitt, H., Sanz, A. and Braun, D. (2009) "Motive individuellen Wahlverhaltens in Nebenwahlen: Eine theoretische Rekonstruktion und empirische Überprüfung," in Falter, J. W., Gabriel, O. and Wessels, B. (eds.) *Wahlen und Wähler: Analysen aus Anlass der Bundestagswahl 2005,* Wiesbaden: Verlag für Sozialwissenschaften: 585–605.

Sinnott, R. (1995) *Irish Voters Decide: Voting Behaviour in Elections and Referendums Since 1918*, Manchester: Manchester University Press.

Skrinis, S. and Teperoglou, E. (2008) "Studying and Comparing Second-Order Elections: Examples from Greece, Portugal and Spain," in Van der Eijk, C. and Schmitt, H. (eds.) *The Multilevel Electoral System of the EU*, Mannheim: Mannheim Centre for European Social Research: 163–189.

Stimson, J. A. (1976) "Public Support for American Presidents: A Cyclical Model," *Public Opinion Quarterly*, vol. 40, no. 1, Spring, 1–21.

Teperoglou, E. (2010) "A Chance to Blame the Government? The 2009 European Election in Southern Europe," *South European Society and Politics*, vol. 15, no. 2, June, 247–272.

Teperoglou, E. and Tsatsanis, E. (2011) "A New Divide? The Impact of Globalization on National Party Systems," *West European Politics*, vol. 34, no. 6, November, 1207–1228.

Teperoglou, E., Tsatsanis, E. and Nicalokopoulos, E. (2015) "Habituating to the New Normal: The 2014 European Election in Greece in a Post-Earthquake Party System," *South European Society and Politics*, vol. 20, no. 3, 333–355.

Thorlakson, L. (2015) "Explaining the Federal-Provincial Turnout Gap in the Canadian Provinces," *Canadian Political Science Review*, vol. 9, no. 1, 164–176.

Tufte, E. (1975) "Determinants and Outcomes of Midterm Congressional Elections," *American Political Science Review*, vol. 69, no. 3, September, 812–826.

Weber, T. (2011) "Exit, Voice, and Cyclicality: A Micro-Logic of Midterm Effects in European Parliament Elections," *American Journal of Political Science*, vol. 55, no. 4, October, 907–922.

Ysmal, C. and Cayrol, R. (1996) "France: The Midwife Comes to Call," in van der Eijk, C. and Franklin, M. (eds.) *Choosing Europe? The European Electorate and National Politics in the Face of Union*, Ann Arbor: University of Michigan Press: 115–136.

20

LOCAL CONTEXT, SOCIAL NETWORKS AND NEIGHBORHOOD EFFECTS ON VOTER CHOICE

Ron Johnston and Charles Pattie

Most elections, both for the composition of a legislative body (a parliament, say, or a city council) and for a single legislator (such as a president or mayor), are contested across a territory that comprises a number of – if not a myriad – separate places. Overviews of election results often treat that territory as a homogeneous unit – relationships between voter characteristics and choices are assumed to be invariant across all of its constituent places. Much research has shown that this is rarely the case, however, and that there are significant differences between places in voter behavior. Such differences are often grouped together as neighborhood effects, and their cause associated with the flow of information through local social networks.

Much media and other commentary on voter behavior, and some academic studies, therefore (implicitly at least) treat members of the electorate as isolated atoms who make decisions on whether to vote and who or what to vote for without any reference to the places where they live and the people they interact with there. Many treat them as members of some idealized concept – such as a social class – but fail to recognize that none of those concepts are "natural"; they are social constructions and if people are both assigned to a group and accept its membership, they then have to learn what that membership involves and how they are expected to behave. Such learning – like all other forms of learning – involves interactions with others and, despite the growing importance of the internet and electronic communications, most of those interactions occur in places: they literally take place – we do not yet live in placeless worlds.

However important membership of particular groups – age, gender, ethnicity, social class, etc. – are in the structuring of society and as influences on patterns of behavior, therefore, place matters as a behavioral context as exemplified in a wide range of studies of public opinion and voting behavior. This chapter reviews that literature. Its main sections illustrate three separate – though in most cases inter-linked – place-based vote-winning strategies: inter-personal interactions in local contexts; local environmental effects; and organizational effects.

Neighbors and networks: the neighborhood effect

A very substantial component of the literature on voting patterns and local contexts concerns what has become known very widely as the neighborhood effect. The classic work was by Tingsten (1937), who noted that working-class support for the Swedish socialist party increased the more working-class the voting precinct in which class members lived. The implication was that people's political opinions are influenced by their neighbors', so that, for example, the more socialist party supporters individuals encountered in their neighborhood (or at their workplace, or in a range of other formal – such as churches and trade unions – and informal organizations and settings) the more likely they were to be influenced by them and vote socialist too.

Many have followed Tingsten's example and found evidence that where a party's support base was strong, in terms of an area's class structure, for example, it tended to attract above-average levels of support, but where it was weak its vote was below-average; electorates were spatially more polarized in their support for particular parties than they were in the social characteristics of the individual members. That this polarization came about through personal influence was in most cases only inferred, however, because the evidence was obtained from aggregate data only: Cox (1971), for example, knew how many manual workers (ouvriers) there were in each district in a sample of Parisian arrondissements, and what percentage of the votes cast there were won by the Communist party, but could only infer that the larger Communist vote in the districts with most ouvriers resident there resulted from inter-personal influence – what Miller (1977) referred to as "people who talk together vote together." But the findings were consistent with Cox's (1969; see Johnston and Pattie 2012) model of voting decisions in a spatial context. Individuals operate as nodes on social networks – receiving, processing and sending out information along their links. Many of those networks are spatially restricted, focused on the individuals' home neighborhoods, so that if (some) people (at least) are influenced in their political opinions by those they interact with, then where the weight of information in an area favors one party over others participants in its social networks are more likely to vote for the majority party than their contemporaries who may have similar individual characteristics but live in areas where the party has much less support.

Many patterns of voting consistent with this "contagion by contact" model have been identified, but the evidence presented is usually circumstantial only, and similar patterns could be the outcome of different processes: people favoring a particular party may choose to live in areas where it is already strong, for example, so that the observed neighborhood effect is a result of self-selection rather than "conversion by conversation" (Walks 2004, 2006, 2007; Gimpel and Hui 2015: that argument is also central to Bishop and Cumming's [2008] contention that the recent growing spatial polarization of voting in the USA reflects selective migration – an argument strongly countered by, among others, Abrams and Fiorina 2012; but see Johnston, Manley and Jones 2016). To counter that, researchers have sought more convincing evidence that the processes are as assumed. This has invariably involved using data obtained from individuals, taking advantage of small and large social surveys that include data on conversations and behavior. Work by, for example, Huckfeldt and Sprague (1995) and Mutz (2006) has provided convincing evidence of the "contagion by contact" model's veracity, and although not all of the applications of this approach have had locational data relating to the geography of the social networks involved (though see Pattie and Johnston 2000), it has become increasingly clear that the socio-spatial polarization of electorates is the norm.

The tendency for people to align their party support with that of their conversation partners is at the heart of the classic neighborhood effect, therefore, and research shows that people who talk together do, to a noticeable degree, vote together, as a result of conversion processes. However, this hardly ever results in complete unanimity within neighborhoods or within conversation networks: dissent persists. In part, this is because conversation networks are rarely politically homogeneous: most people talk to supporters of several different parties and of none. As a result, they are open to sometimes heterodox opinions. Not all conversations point in the same direction (Huckfeldt, Johnson and Sprague 2004). In part, too, it is because some voices are more influential than others. People pay more attention to those they know well than to strangers, to those whose opinions and judgments they trust, and to those who they think have expertise on the subject than on those whose views and judgments they trust less (Huckfeldt 2001; Huckfeldt, Pietryka and Reilly 2014). Not surprisingly, the stronger an individual's own political views and partisanship, the less likely he or she is to be influenced by divergent views coming from conversation partners (Cox 1969; McClurg 2006). Not all of the studies such as those discussed here have data on the geography of the conversation networks studied; those undertaken by Huckfeldt do, however, and a reworking of the data showed that most conversations took place between people living no more than three miles apart (Eagles, Bélanger and Calkins 2004; see also Johnston and Pattie 2006).

Of course, very few neighborhoods are exclusive to one social class, and many social networks contain individuals who differ in their political persuasions. All networks and districts are open to external – and challenging – influences, therefore, and although continuity is the dominant pattern in any area's voting over time change is possible as a result of new information flows, perhaps introduced through what Granovetter (1973) termed weak ties (as illustrated in Huckfeldt, Johnson and Sprague 2004). Area populations change too, as people die and others move out, and their replacements may bring new ideas and affiliations. Those who move away from a neighborhood where they spent their formative years may retain the attitudes learned there, however, as illustrated by Wright's (1977) study of voting for the American Independent Party (Southern populist and segregationist) candidate George Wallace in the 1968 US presidential election: the larger the black population of the area in which white voters lived, the more likely the latter were to vote for Wallace – but it was the level of black concentration where they lived in 1940, when many of those who voted for Wallace 30 years later were being politically, socially and culturally socialized, rather than where they lived in election year itself, that had the strongest impact on their political attitudes (in this example, the smaller the white minority in an area the greater the cohesion around attitudes against the local black majority).

When change is slow, new residents in an area may be strongly influenced by the majority opinion there – especially if they are both open to persuasion and participate in neighborhood activities. Many studies of political attitudes have found that, while some people are strongly committed to one set of ideas and one party, and vote for it whatever challenging information they may encounter, others (and an increasing proportion of the population in many countries) are less committed than their predecessors and open to considering alternative ideas and party manifestos. Research (see, for example, Johnston et al. 2005a) has found that those with strong levels of neighborhood social capital were more likely to conform to local electoral behavior patterns than those who were "spatial isolates"; joining local social networks encourages embracing local majority attitudes.

Many studies of neighborhood effects have, because of the nature of the available data, been constrained to analyses of its operation at one spatial scale only – basically, whatever data are available at a scale that seems to approximate that of the neighborhoods within which (many) people interact. As more data have become available and as it has become possible to merge social surveys comprising data on individuals with census and other data on aggregate populations at a variety of scales, so more sophisticated modeling of neighborhood effects – broadly defined – has become feasible. One scale largely omitted from most studies has been that of the individual household, yet this is the context within which most people are politically socialized. People who live together, and especially those who talk politics together at home, should show the effects of inter-personal influence – a hypothesis confirmed by studies using data on all members of households: not only do they vote together but they also tend to change their partisan preferences together (Johnston et al. 2005b; Zuckerman, Dasovic and Fitzgerald 2007). Not all research focuses on interactions within neighborhoods: Huckfeldt and Sprague (1995), for example, looked at church congregations as local contexts, and Mutz and Mondak (2006) explored workplace contexts, both with the same results – people who worship together, vote together, as also do people who work together.

The greater flexibility of modern datasets – many of which are now geocoded – has seen the introduction of what are known as "bespoke neighborhoods" to voting studies. Instead of relying on data at one scale only – such as the census tract – investigators have been able to compile data on the characteristics of either all individuals living within a prescribed distance of a survey respondent's home, or on those of the nearest number of individuals (say 2000) to that address. As many censuses now report data at very small spatial scales – with average populations of only a few hundred at most – it is possible to construct a spatial hierarchy of such bespoke neighborhoods (such as neighborhoods comprising the nearest 250 persons to a survey respondent's home, nested within neighborhoods with the nearest 1000 persons, nested in those with the nearest 2500, and so on ...). This enables an evaluation of at which scales neighborhood effects are most intensive. One early study, for example, found that in 1997 British working-class individuals were more likely to vote Labour the more working-class the parliamentary constituency in which they lived; within those constituencies, they were more likely to vote Labour the more working-class the district in which they lived; and within those districts, the more working-class the immediate neighborhood around their homes, the greater still the probability that they voted Labour (MacAllister at al. 2001). Investigations of such multi-scalar influences have been advanced by the adoption of multi-level modeling strategies (Jones, Johnston and Pattie 1992). Their application in analyses of two British general elections showed significant variations in voting behavior at two local scales (the immediate neighborhood – within 250 meters of the individual's home – and its wider locale – within 2000 meters) as well as between regions (Johnston et al. 2005c; similar findings were reported in a study of voting at Taiwanese elections: Weng 2015; and Bisgaard, Dinesen and Sonderskov 2016 have shown that individual Danish voters' perceptions of the state of the national economy were influenced most by the level of unemployment in their immediate neighborhoods – as the area was enlarged the effect of local context on perceptions diminished).

Friends and neighbors voting

In most elections voters are faced with a choice between rival political parties, even though the mark they make on the ballot paper may be against named candidates: most of the latter are supported not on the basis of their personal characteristics but rather because of the parties they represent. Nevertheless, there are some situations where the individual candidates' characteristics are among the major criteria influencing voters' decisions.

The classic study of such situations was V. O. Key's (1949) on *Southern Politics* in the USA. Many states there during the first half of the twentieth century were dominated by a single party and the main electoral contests were between candidates seeking its nomination for a local, state or national office. Key's examples showed that many performed better in the areas around their home than elsewhere within the territory being contested. He interpreted this as voters, in the absence of any other criteria on which to base their decisions, plumping for the local candidate (whom they may know), as a way of promoting local interests. This became known as friends and neighbors voting: people vote for local candidates because they either know them personally or know people who do – or they believe somebody with local links will best represent them in the relevant legislative body or office. Such personal knowledge is rarely extensive, however, especially in large territories, and voters depend on other cues to direct them to the characteristics of and likely benefits to accrue from support for local candidates – such as local media, as illustrated by Bowler, Donovan and Shipp (1993) in a Californian study. Candidates who get – and may seek – high profiles in local media which cover part of the electoral territory only may perform better there than in other parts of the territory as a consequence.

Given the predominance of parties in most elections, friends and neighbors voting may be considered a minor element to the geography of voting behavior, being characteristic of just those contests, many of them intra-party, where the choice set invites electors to deploy other criteria when determining which candidates to support – as illustrated by studies of city council elections in New Zealand (Johnston 1973). Particular voting systems may encourage such behavior. In both Australia and Ireland, for example, the single transferable vote system requires candidates to be rank-ordered. Where a voter is determining which of a party's candidates to rank first, a local candidate – if there is one – may be preferred (Johnston 1978; Parker 1982). More importantly, as clearly illustrated by some Irish studies, in order to maximize the number of its representatives who win election, a party's campaigning may focus on different candidates in different parts of a multi-member constituency (Gorecki and Marsh 2012, 2014).

The friends and neighbors effect was divided into three main components in a recent study of the 2010 contest for the leadership of the UK's Labour Party (Johnston et al. 2016a), in which one part of the electoral college involved voting by party members conducted in and reported for each of Great Britain's 632 Constituency Labour Parties (CLPs). Voting by party members in each candidate's home constituency was by people who almost certainly knew the candidate – they were local friends. Candidates were much less likely to be known personally to party members in adjacent constituencies, but the flow of information across constituency boundaries through social networks and via local media could promote their cause among neighbors. Finally, there was the potential influence of political friends in other constituencies. In order to contest the election, candidates had to be nominated by a number of their fellow MPs, and those who nominated a candidate may have influenced members of their own local parties to support the person they preferred. Analyses showed that all three were relevant; even though the contest was for the leadership of one of the country's largest political parties, and thus for a potential prime minister, these local effects were clearly discernible. For example, one candidate – Andy Burnham – averaged only 8.8 percent of the members' first preference votes across all 632 CLPs: he got 69.1 percent in his home constituency, an average of 34.1 percent in the five adjacent constituencies and 19.4 percent across the remaining 68 constituencies in the northwest region where his constituency was located; he also averaged 20.9 percent in the 33 constituencies whose MPs nominated him, and 25.0 percent in the 23 whose MPs gave him their first preference vote.

Recent work has also identified voting patterns consistent with the "friends and neighbors" argument at British general and local elections. At the 2010 general election, for example, Arzheimer and Evans (2012; see also Gimpel et al. 2008, for similar findings in the United States) found that the distance between survey respondents' home addresses and those of candidates in their constituency was negatively related to their propensity to vote for those candidates (other influences being held constant); similar results emerged from their study of voting at local government elections (Arzheimer and Evans 2014). But the effect doesn't always work. Some candidates for the American presidency choose vice-presidential running mates whom they hope can deliver substantial support from certain groups and/or areas: Devine and Kopko (2016), however, found no evidence of vice-presidential candidates making a significant difference to the outcome in their home states.

Local issues

Most election campaigns, especially those to national and regional legislatures and to leadership positions, focus on issues with a wide relevance across the electorate – those that large numbers of voters consider the most important (such as the economy and immigration) and on which the contestants are offering alternative perspectives and policies. Even so, many of these salient policy issues vary locally: an economy may be booming in some parts of the country but relatively depressed elsewhere; the housing market may be buoyant in some places but not elsewhere. If those situations are important to the voters, their responses may well vary according to the local circumstances. Thus, for example, Johnston and Pattie (2001) found that in 1997 British voters decided whether to punish or reward the incumbent Conservative government on the basis of both their personal financial situations and the performance of their local economy rather than the national situation; indeed other research showed that some people voted altruistically, against the incumbent government because many of their neighbors were suffering economically, even though they themselves were not (Johnston et al. 2000). Similarly, Pattie, Dorling and Johnston (1995) found that voters' likelihood to support the incumbent UK government at the 1992 general election was related to the performance of the local housing market during its slump in the preceding years; where that slump was deepest voters, especially those who themselves experienced negative equity, were less likely to vote for the government's candidates.

As well as these spatial variations in the nature of some of the key elements in an election campaign, local issues may be more influential on some voters in a place than the general ones, and may be linked to the local candidate(s). Incumbents seeking re-election, for example, may be punished by the local electorate for their performance – as to a small extent with the UK expenses scandal a year before the 2010 general election – and their party performs less well there than anticipated as a consequence (Pattie and Johnston, 2014; for a comparable US "scandal" which involved Congressmen writing checks on overdrawn accounts, and suffering in the subsequent polls as a consequence, see Banducci and Karp 1994; Williams, 1998). Others may be rewarded by local voters – as illustrated by the large American literature on pork barrel politics, with legislators who deliver benefits for their local community, such as a major infrastructure investment, getting electoral returns as a consequence (Ferejohn 1974; Johnston 1980). Legislators will sometimes reflect local issues when voting in parliamentary divisions, even if it means opposing the party line and whips. In late 2015, for example, UK Conservative MPs were whipped to abstain in the vote against a Labour amendment regarding changes in the tax credit regime, but 20 voted for that amendment, a number of them representing marginal constituencies where the proposed cuts could significantly reduce their majority.[1]

An example of the impact of a specific issue affecting parts of an area only was voting for the Mayor of Christchurch, New Zealand in 1971. The two main candidates – one representing a relatively right-wing group and the other a left-wing party – drew votes across the city largely reflecting the class composition of different neighborhoods. The city was to host the Commonwealth Games in 1974. The right-wing candidate (and incumbent mayor) backed one of the proposed sites for the main stadium, and he performed better than expected at the polling booths close to that site; his opponent favored an alternative site – and his performance around it was better than average (Johnston 1976). In a different context, research in Colombia has shown that people who move from a state-controlled part of the country to an area where right-wing militias hold sway are more likely to support a right-wing candidate for the country's presidency (García-Sánchez 2016).

In many countries – especially those using plurality electoral systems with single-member constituencies – tackling local issues, whether personal to individual voters, relating to a local community within the territory or concerning the area as a whole, is a major component of their representatives' workload, and what their constituents expect (Campbell and Lovenduski 2015). In the United Kingdom, for example, acting as a local caseworker and champion is seen as one of the MPs' two main roles (Speaker's Conference on Parliamentary Representation 2010; Morris 2012); they are expected to maintain an office and a home in their constituency and to be active in social, cultural and economic as well as political life there. This can bring electoral rewards: MPs perceived by the electorate as effective operators within and for their constituents can be rewarded by greater support when they seek re-election. British studies have shown that this benefit is especially conferred on new MPs seeking re-election for the first-time (Wood and Norton 1992; Buttice and Milazzo 2011; Curtice, Fisher and Ford 2015).

Some MPs are more assiduous at the constituency role than others, although in the UK a very large proportion now give it a great deal of attention, making regular and frequent visits to the area and holding regular surgeries there, as well as (through their staff) responding to an increasing number and range of requests for assistance (many of them by email). In addition, some parties are generally more assiduous than others in the local activities undertaken by their members, in local as well as national government. In Great Britain, for example, the Liberal Democrat party built its parliamentary vote share (to over 20 percent at the 1983–1987 and then the 2005–2010 general elections) on the foundations of local activism and local government performance (as illustrated for one constituency in a former leader's autobiography: Ashdown 2009; see also Dorling, Rallings and Thrasher 1998, and Cutts 2006a, 2006b). The MPs elected on this foundation had strong local roots, therefore, which were reflected in their electoral support. At the 2015 general election, for example, the Liberal Democrats' national vote share fell to 8.1 percent from 23.0 percent five years earlier. The party was defending 57 seats; in the 46 being contested by an incumbent MP, its vote share fell by 14.3 percentage points on average, whereas in the 11 where the incumbent had retired and was replaced by a new candidate the fall was much larger at an average of 21.8 points. A similar spatially-structured campaign was the centerpiece of the electoral strategy developed by the United Kingdom Independence Party for the 2015 general election (Goodwin and Milazzo 2015).

Parties and candidates seeking votes: campaign and canvass effects

The main actors in almost all elections are the parties and their candidates, who actively seek support from the voters. Many campaigns, especially at general elections, are dominated now by the print, radio and TV and, increasingly, electronic media and forms of communication: parties put out messages promoting themselves and their candidates (especially their leaders). Alongside that, their local organizations and candidates make direct contact with voters within their own electoral districts.

Although the procedure varies from country to country (and sometimes within countries) the main goal of the local campaigns is to identify the party's supporters and then contact them – personally at their home if possible – to encourage them to remain firm in their support, and to express that support by turning out to vote on election day. Over time, parties build up databases – annotated versions of the electoral register – of their supporters who will almost certainly vote for them, those who do not support and will not vote for them, and those who may support the party. These have to be regularly updated, because of population mobility and to ensure that people have not changed their predispositions. Thus in the months before an election is due parties – especially in marginal districts where a seat could be won or lost – canvass support through a variety of means, both personal contact (on the doorstep) and indirectly (through telephone calls and email contacts where numbers and/or addresses are known). To a considerable extent these "get out the vote" strategies are not random exercises: parties concentrate their efforts where they are more likely to get substantial rewards – in neighborhoods within districts where their supporters are concentrated, which they identify using geodemographic classifications of small-scale census and other data. (See Cutts 2006a, on the activities of the Liberal Democrats in one English city, Green and Gerber's 2004 account of controlled experiments designed to test the efficacy of such campaigns, and Barwell's 2016 detailed description of his own campaigning in a marginal constituency; see also, however, the negative findings reported by Cantoni and Pons 2016.) Leaflets are distributed in those areas to ensure voters know of the election, the party's candidate there and what policies are being promoted, and there are follow-up calls, particularly on polling day when get-out-the-vote tactics are deployed to check whether supporters have voted and, if not, encourage them to do so before polling closes. Increasingly, those local efforts are enhanced by direct contact with local voters from the party's central (or regional) campaign organization, usually through such channels as bespoke letters, emails and postings on social media sites (Cowley and Kavanagh 2015; Fisher 2015). But contact may not always be necessary; in one experiment, Green et al. (2016) showed that the density of posters on lawns in an area had an influence on the advertised candidates' success.

These campaigns have become increasingly sophisticated, as have the techniques deployed to explore their extent and efficacy. In the UK, for example, early studies had to use surrogate data for a campaign's intensity – such as the amount that candidates report having spent on their campaigns (relative to the legally-imposed limits), the number of members and activists working in the constituency and a range of other measures of campaign intensity (for an overview of much of this work, see Johnston and Pattie 2014). All reach the same conclusion: the more intensive a local party's campaign, however measured, the better its candidate's performance. But these provide circumstantial evidence only. The development of internet panel surveys has allowed more direct evidence to be elucidated. For example, the 2011 Welsh Election Study asked respondents whether they had been contacted by one or more of the parties during the campaign. Among them, 236 had voted Conservative at the previous National Assembly election in 2007; 181 of these had no contact from the party during the campaign; and 78.5 percent of them voted Conservative again. Of the remainder, of those whose only contact was to receive a leaflet, 83.3 percent voted Conservative, whereas among those contacted personally by the party – by a home visit, for example – 93.3 percent voted Conservative. Of Liberal Democrat voters in 2007, only 36.4 percent of those not contacted during the campaign supported the party again in 2011, whereas 71.4 percent of those contacted did so; those ignored by the party in 2011 were more likely to defect to another party. Even among those who supported a party in the past, therefore, those who were personally asked to again were more likely to do so; those not contacted were more likely to change their mind and vote for another – especially if it did contact them (Johnston et al. 2016b).

Although panel survey data provide much better insight into the impact of local campaigns they are not without problems: a party is more likely to contact its known supporters in the last weeks before an election, for example, and they are more likely to vote for it – for them, contact during the campaign may have little effect as they are already committed to it. Methods have been developed to circumvent this potential problem (the technical term is endogeneity) and confirm that campaign contact has an independent impact (Pattie, Whitworth and Johnston 2015). Parties and candidates expend much more effort in some places than others in seeking votes – they spend more money on leaflets and posters, they contact more voters in their homes and on the streets, and they visit more of their known supporters on polling day itself to ensure that they vote. It works: the more active a party is locally, the better its performance relative to places where they make much less effort.

Conclusions

The much-quoted adage, generally associated with former US House of Representatives Speaker Tip O'Neill, that "all politics is local" may be hyperbole: people vote in a particular way for a variety of reasons, some, if not many, of which may have little to do with their local context. But voters, all other things being equal (which, of course, they very rarely are), prefer local candidates (Campbell and Cowley 2014; Childs and Cowley 2011), especially local candidates who know their constituency, its residents and their concerns and represent those concerns, even if it means acting against their party's wider interests. Parties are, of course, aware of this, of how information about candidates flows through local social networks and influences their behavior and they act accordingly when seeking support. Election results thus reflect a continuing interplay between the parties and candidates, on the one hand, and the local context, on the other; as studies of an increasing number of countries demonstrate (Guigal, Johnston and Constantinescu 2011; Weng 2015; Amara and El Lagha 2016), geography is a fundamental component of many aspects of elections, their conduct and their outcomes. *All* politics may not be local: but where it is locally oriented, there are substantial rewards to be won.

Note

1 www.conservativehome.com/parliament/2015/10/20-conservatives-revolt-over-tax-credits-five-of-them-are-2015-intake-members.html?utm_medium=email&utm_campaign=Friday+30th+October+2015&utm_content=Friday+30th+October+2015+CID_c9c6e7f9b4b40aba7f0e84dfba4b668d&utm_source=Daily%20Email&utm_term=20%20Conservative%20MPs%20revolt%20over%20tax%20credits%20Five%20of%20them%20are%202015%20intake%20members.

References

Abrams, S. J. and Fiorina, M. P. (2012) "'The Big Sort' That Wasn't: A Sceptical Re-Examination," *PS: Political Science and Politics*, vol. 45, no. 2, April, 203–210.

Amara, M. and El Lagha, A. (2016) "Tunisian Constituent Assembly Elections: How Does Spatial Proximity Matter?," *Quality and Quantity*, vol. 50, no. 1, January, 65–88.

Arzheimer, K. and Evans, J. (2012) "Geolocation and Voting: Candidate-Voter Distance Effects on Party Choice in the 2010 UK General Election in England," *Political Geography*, vol. 31, no. 5, June, 301–310.

Arzheimer, K. and Evans, J. (2014) "Candidate Geolocation and Voter Choice in the 2013 English County Council Elections," *Research and Politics*, available online: http://journals.sagepub.com/doi/abs/10.1177/2053168014538769.

Ashdown, P. (2009) *A Fortunate Life: The Autobiography of Paddy Ashdown*, London: Aurum Press.

Banducci, S. A. and Karp, J. A. (1994) "Electoral Consequences of Scandal and Reapportionment in the 1992 House Elections," *American Politics Quarterly*, vol. 22, no. 1, January, 3–16.

Barwell, G. (2016) *How to Win a Marginal Seat: My Year Fighting for My Political Life*, London: Biteback Books.

Bisgaard, M., Dinesen, P. T. and Sonderskov, K. M. (2016) "Reconsidering the Neighborhood Effect: Does Exposure to Residential Unemployment Influence Voters' Perceptions of the National Economy?," *Journal of Politics*, vol. 78, no. 3, July, 719–723.

Bishop, B. and Cummings, R. G. (2008) *The Big Sort: Why the Clustering of Like-Minded America is Tearing Us Apart*, Boston: Houghton Mifflin.

Bowler, S., Donovan, T. and Shipp, J. (1993) "Local Sources of Information and Voter Choice in State Elections: Microlevel Foundations of the 'Friends and Neighbors' Effect," *American Politics Quarterly*, vol. 21, no. 4, October, 473–489.

Buttice, M. and Milazzo, C. (2011) "Candidate Positioning in Great Britain," *Electoral Studies*, vol. 30, no. 4, December, 848–857.

Campbell, R. and Cowley, P. (2014) "What Voters Want: Reactions to Candidate Characteristics in a Survey Experiment," *Political Studies*, vol. 62, no. 4, December, 745–765.

Campbell, R. and Lovenduski, J. (2015) "What Should MPs Do? Public and Parliamentarians' Views Compared," *Parliamentary Affairs*, vol. 68, no. 4, October, 690–708.

Cantoni, E. and Pons, V. (2016) *Do Interactions with Candidates Increase Voter Support and Participation? Experimental Evidence from Italy*, Cambridge, MA: Harvard Business School, Working Paper 16–080.

Childs, S. and Cowley, P. (2011) "The Politics of Local Presence: Is There a Case for Descriptive Representation?," *Political Studies*, vol. 59, no. 1, March, 1–19.

Cowley, P. and Kavanagh, D. (2015) *The British General Election of 2015*, Basingstoke: Palgrave Macmillan.

Cox, K. R. (1969) "The Voting Decision in a Spatial Context," in Board, C., Chorley, R. J., Haggett, P. and Stoddart, D. R. (eds.) *Progress in Geography 1*, London: Edward Arnold: 83–117.

Cox, K. R. (1971) "The Spatial Components of Urban Voting Response Surfaces," *Economic Geography*, vol. 47, no. 1, January, 27–35.

Curtice, J., Fisher, S. D. and Ford, R. (2015) "The Results Analysed," in Cowley, P. and Kavanagh, D. (eds.) *The British General Election of 2015*, Basingstoke: Palgrave Macmillan: 387–431.

Cutts, D. J. (2006a) "Continuous Campaigning and Electoral Outcomes: The Liberal Democrats in Bath," *Political Geography*, vol. 25, no. 1, January, 75–88.

Cutts, D. J. (2006b) "'Where We Work We Win': A Case Study of Local Liberal Democrat Campaigning," *Journal of Elections, Public Opinion and Parties*, vol. 16, no. 3, October, 221–242.

Devine, C. J. and Kopko, K. C. (2016) *How Running Mates Influence Home State Voting in Presidential Elections*, Manchester: Manchester University Press.

Dorling, D., Rallings, C. and Thrasher, M. (1998) "The Epidemiology of the Liberal Democrat Vote," *Political Geography Quarterly*, vol. 17, no. 1, January, 45–70.

Eagles, M., Bélanger, P. and Calkins, H. W. (2004) "The Spatial Structure of Urban Political Discussion Networks," in Goodchild, M. F. and Janelle, D. G. (eds.) *Spatially Integrated Social Science*, Oxford: Oxford University Press: 205–221.

Ferejohn, J. A. (1974) *Pork-Barrel Politics: Rivers and Harbors Legislation 1947–1968*, Stanford: Stanford University Press.

Fisher, J. (2015) "Party Finance: The Death of the National Campaign?," in Geddes, A. and Tonge, J. (eds.) *Britain Votes 2015*, Oxford: Oxford University Press: 133–152.

García-Sánchez, M. (2016) "Territorial Control and Vote Choice in Colombia: A Multilevel Approach," *Política y Gobierno*, vol. 23, no. 1, January, 53–96.

Gimpel, J. G. and Hui, I. S. (2015) "Seeking Politically Compatible Neighbors? The Role of Neighborhood Partisan Composition in Residential Sorting," *Political Geography*, vol. 48, no.1, September, 130–142.

Gimpel, J. G., Karnes, K., McTague, J. and Pearson-Merkowitz, S. (2008) "Distance-Decay in the Political Geography of Friends and Neighbors Voting," *Political Geography*, vol. 27, no. 2, February, 231–252.

Goodwin, M. and Milazzo, C. (2015) *UKIP: Inside the Campaign to Redraw the Map of British Politics*, Oxford: Oxford University Press.

Gorecki, M. and Marsh, M. (2012) "Not Just 'Friends and Neighbours': Canvassing, Geographical Proximity and Voter Choice," *European Journal of Political Research*, vol. 51, no. 5, August, 563–582.

Gorecki, M. and Marsh, M. (2014) "A Decline of 'Friends and Neighbours' Voting in Ireland: Local Candidate Effects in the 2011 Irish 'Earthquake Election'," *Political Geography*, vol. 41, July, 11–20.

Granovetter, M. S. (1973) "The Strength of Weak Ties," *American Journal of Sociology*, vol. 78, no. 6, May, 1360–1380.

Green, D. P. and Gerber, A. S. (2004) *Get Out the Vote! How to Increase Voter Turnout*, Washington, DC: The Brookings Institution.

Green, D. P., Krasno, J. S., Coppock, A., Farrer, B. D., Lenoir, B. and Zingher, J. N. (2016) "The Effects of Lawn Signs on Vote Outcomes: Results from Four Randomized Filed Experiments," *Electoral Studies*, vol. 41, March, 143–150.

Guigal, A., Johnston, R. J. and Constantinescu, S. (2011) "Democratic Musical Chairs? Romania's Post-1989 Electoral Geography," *Space and Polity*, vol. 15, no. 2, March, 143–161.

Huckfeldt, R. (2001) "The Social Communication of Political Expertise," *American Journal of Political Science*, vol. 45, no. 2, April, 425–438.

Huckfeldt, R. and Sprague, J. (1995) *Citizens, Politics and Social Communication*, Cambridge: Cambridge University Press.

Huckfeldt, R., Johnson, P. E. and Sprague, J. (2004) *Political Disagreement: The Survival of Diverse Opinions Within Communication Networks*, Cambridge: Cambridge University Press.

Huckfeldt, R., Pietryka, M. T. and Reilly, J. (2014) "Noise, Bias and Expertise in Political Communication Networks," *Social Networks*, vol. 36, no. 1, January, 11–121.

Johnston, R. J. (1973) "Spatial Patterns and Influences on Voting in Multi-Candidate Elections: The Christchurch City Council Elections, 1968," *Urban Studies*, vol. 10, no. 1, February, 69–81.

Johnston, R. J. (1976) "Political Behaviour and the Residential Mosaic," in Herbert, D. T. and Johnston, R. J. (eds.) *Social Areas in Cities: Volume 2: Spatial Perspectives on Problems and Policies*, London: John Wiley: 65–88.

Johnston, R. J. (1978) "On Elections, Voting, and Participation: Friends and Neighbours Voting in Australia: A Note," *Politics*, vol. 13, no. 1, May, 151–154.

Johnston, R. J. (1980) *The Geography of Federal Spending in the United States of America*, London: Research Studies Press.

Johnston, R. J. and Pattie, C. J. (2001) " 'It's the Economy, Stupid' – But Which Economy? Geographical Scales, Retrospective Economic Evaluations and Voting at the 1997 British General Election," *Regional Studies*, vol. 35, no. 4, 309–319.

Johnston, R. J. and Pattie, C. J. (2006) *Putting Voters in Their Place: Geography and Elections in Great Britain*, Oxford: Oxford University Press.

Johnston, R. J. and Pattie, C. J. (2012) "Kevin Cox and Electoral Geography," in Jonas, A. E. G. and Wood, A. (eds.) *Territory, the State and Urban Politics: A Critical Appreciation of the Selected Writings of Kevin R. Cox*, Farnham: Ashgate: 23–44.

Johnston, R. J. and Pattie, C. J. (2014) *Money and Electoral Politics: Local Parties and Funding in General Elections*, Bristol: The Policy Press.

Johnston, R. J., Dorling, D., Tunstall, H., Rossiter, D. J., MacAllister, I. and Pattie, C. J. (2000) "Locating the Altruistic Voter: Context, Ego Centric Voting and Support for the Conservative Party at the 1997 General Election in England and Wales," *Environment and Planning A*, vol. 32, no. 4, April, 673–694.

Johnston, R. J., Jones, K., Propper, C., Sarker, R., Burgess, S. and Bolster, A. (2005b) "A Missing Level in the Analysis of British Voting Behaviour: The Household as Context as Shown by Analyses of a 1992–1997 Longitudinal Survey," *Electoral Studies*, vol. 24, no. 2, June, 201–225.

Johnston, R. J., Manley, D. and Jones, K. (2016) "Spatial Polarisation of Presidential Voting in the United States, 1992–2012: The 'Big Sort' Revisited," *Annals of the Association of American Geographers*, vol. 106, no. 5, July, 1047–1062.

Johnston, R. J., Pattie, C. J., Pemberton, H. and Wickham-Jones, M. (2016a) " 'If You've Got Friends and Neighbours': Constituency Voting Patterns for the UK Labour Party Leader in 2010," *Journal of Elections, Public Opinion and Parties*, vol. 26, no. 1, January, 58–77.

Johnston, R. J., Pattie, C. J., Scully, R. M. and Cutts, D. J. (2016b) "Constituency Campaigning and Canvassing for Support at the 2011 National Assembly of Wales Election," *Politics*, vol. 36, no. 1, February, 49–62.

Johnston, R. J., Propper, C., Burgess, S., Sarker, R., Bolster, A. and Jones, K. (2005c) "Spatial Scale and the Neighbourhood Effect: Multinomial Models of Voting at Two Recent British General Elections," *British Journal of Political Science*, vol. 35, no. 3, July, 487–514.

Johnston, R. J., Propper, C., Sarker, R., Jones, K., Bolster, A. and Burgess, S. (2005a) "Neighbourhood Social Capital and Neighbourhood Effects," *Environment and Planning A*, vol. 37, no. 8, August, 1443–1461.

Jones, K., Johnston, R. J. and Pattie, C. J. (1992) "People, Places and Regions: Exploring the Use of Multi-Level Models in the Analysis of Electoral Data," *British Journal of Political Science*, vol. 22, no. 3, July, 343–380.

Key, V. O. (1949) *Southern Politics in State and Nation*, New York: Alfred A. Knopf.

MacAllister, I., Johnston, R. J., Pattie, C. J., Tunstall, H., Dorling, D. and Rossiter, D. J. (2001) "Class Dealignment and the Neighbourhood Effect: Miller Revisited," *British Journal of Political Science*, vol. 31, no. 1, January, 41–60.

McClurg, S. (2006) "The Electoral Relevance of Political Talk: Examining Disagreement and Expertise Effects in Social Networks on Political Participation," *American Journal of Political Science*, vol. 50, no. 3, July, 737–754.

Miller, W. L. (1977) *Electoral Dynamics in Britain Since 1918*, London: Macmillan.

Morris, C. (2012) *Parliamentary Elections, Representation and the Law*, Oxford: Hart Publishing.

Mutz, D. C. (2006) *Hearing the Other Side: Deliberative Versus Participatory Democracy*, Cambridge: Cambridge University Press.

Mutz, D. C. and Mondak, J. J. (2006) "The Workplace as a Context for Cross-Cutting Political Discourse," *Journal of Politics*, vol. 68, no. 1, February, 140–155.

Parker, A. J. (1982) "The "Friends and Neighbours" Voting Effect in Galway West Constituency," *Political Geography Quarterly*, vol. 1, no. 3, July, 243–262.

Pattie, C. J. and Johnston, R. J. (2000) "'People Who Talk Together Vote Together': An Exploration of the Neighborhood Effect in Great Britain," *Annals of the Association of American Geographers*, vol. 90, no. 1, March, 41–66.

Pattie, C. J. and Johnston, R. J. (2014) "The Impact of the Scandal on the 2010 General Election Results," in vanHeerde-Hudson, J. (ed.) *The Political Costs of the 2009 British MPs' Expenses Scandal*, Basingstoke: Palgrave-Macmillan: 98–110.

Pattie, C. J., Dorling, D. and Johnston, R. J. (1995) "A Debt-Owning Democracy: The Political Impact of Housing Market Recession at the British General Election of 1992," *Urban Studies*, vol. 32, no. 8, August, 1293–1315.

Pattie, C. J., Whitworth, A. and Johnston, R. J. (2015) "Does Campaign Contact Influence Individuals' Vote Choices? An Alternative Approach," *European Political Science*, vol. 14, no. 3, September, 279–297.

Speaker's Conference on Parliamentary Representation (2010) *Final Report*, London: The Stationery Office.

Tingsten, H. (1937) *Political Behaviour*, London: P. S. King.

Walks, R. A. (2004) "Place of Residence, Party Preferences, and Political Attitudes in Canadian Cities and Suburbs," *Journal of Urban Affairs*, vol. 26, no. 3, August, 269–295.

Walks, R. A. (2006) "The Causes of City-Suburban Political Polarization? A Canadian Case Study," *Annals of the Association of American Geographers*, vol. 96, no. 2, June, 390–414.

Walks, R. A. (2007) "The Boundaries of Suburban Discontent? Urban Definitions and Neighbourhood Political Effects," *The Canadian Geographer*, vol. 51, no. 2, September, 160–185.

Weng, L-C. D. (2015) "Contextual Effects on Individual Voting Behaviour: The Case of Taiwan," *Asian Journal of Political Science*, vol. 23, no. 3, September, 321–345.

Williams, R. (1998) *Political Scandals in the USA*, Edinburgh: Keele University Press.

Wood, D. and Norton, P. (1992) "Do Candidates Matter? Constituency-Specific Vote Changes for Incumbent MPs, 1984–1987," *Political Studies*, vol. 40, no. 2, June, 227–238.

Wright, G. C. Jr. (1977) "Contextual Models of Electoral Behavior: The Southern Wallace Vote," *American Political Science Review*, vol. 71, no. 2, June, 497–508.

Zuckerman, A., Dasovic, J. and Fitzgerald, J. (2007) *Partisan Families: The Social Logic of Bounded Partisanship in Germany and Britain*, Cambridge: Cambridge University Press.

21

VOTING BEHAVIOR IN REFERENDUMS

Michael Marsh

Most of the research into voting behavior is carried out in the context of elections for parliaments and, particularly in the US, of an executive. These elections tend to focus on parties, and to a variable extent on individuals who will assume responsibility for policy making. However, in many countries voters are also provided on occasion with the chance to vote directly on policy options through a referendum. These have long been common in Switzerland, where citizens can initiate such votes, and in Italy, and have also been common in some US cities and states, but have been less common in most democracies. Major constitutional changes and questions of sovereignty have often been put to a referendum, as have moral issues. The establishment, and particularly the enlargement of the EU, seems boosted to the referendum industry as states have provided opportunities to the electorate to vote on initial membership, on treaty change and even, in Greenland and the UK, on whether or not to remain a member. Several European countries have also held votes on changes to laws, or constitutional provisions on moral issues like divorce and abortion and same-sex marriage, but we have also seen votes on matters as diverse as a new flag, a new electoral system, water privatization or cuts in judges' pay. The question addressed in this chapter is how far what we know about voting behavior from looking at elections generalizes to voting behavior in referendums.

What decides elections?

We can start by considering some of the more widespread findings about parliamentary and presidential elections. Probably the most basic one concerns party loyalties. Critically, voters do not start to make their choice with a blank slate. As studies from the 1950s and onwards showed, voters tend to have partisan loyalties, and these influence vote choice both directly and indirectly, by influencing the selection of and interpretation of information about the election. There are disputes about the stability of these loyalties and certainly there are questions about how they develop in new party systems, but these loyalties are a factor that cannot be ignored. For some, party leaders are becoming as important, if not more important, than the parties themselves, with loyalties to parties weakened by a disliked leader, or attractive leader for some other party. (A strong case is made in Clarke, Kornberg and Stewart 2004. An alternative view is taken by Curtice and Holmberg 2005.) However, when we move on to think about referendums, whether the important factor is the leader or the party is perhaps secondary to the fact that a "party" and its leader may be recommending a yes or no vote.

The second general set of findings about elections focuses on issues. There have been two broad interpretations of how voters and parties think about issues in elections. The first, and most obvious, is that on any issue a voter has a position, and that the party whose stance is closest to that position is most likely to be chosen. One problem here is that of course there are lots of issues and the closest party on one issue might not be the closest on another. This is commonly dealt with by just taking the most important issues, or by dealing with issues in much broader terms, summarizing them in terms of liberal–conservative or left–right. Both approaches make it easier for the analyst, but also recognize the challenge for any voter in developing a position across multiple issues and finding out where each party stands. Much of the research on voting behavior has demonstrated that voters do not have the knowledge to assess parties issue by issue, but something like "left–right" can help by reducing the amount of detailed information that a voter needs to make a sensible decision, and arguably the decision they would make with full information (the most comprehensive discussion of this can be found in Lupia and McCubbins 1998).

A rather different way to look at issues is to recognize that on most of the topics that dominate political debate voters are in broad agreement, and parties do not differ. Peace, security, economic prosperity are what Donald Stokes (1963) called "valence issues," and voters will pick the party considered most competent to deliver these. Voters arguably do not need a lot of information to judge competence in areas that impinge on them directly. V. O. Key (1966) suggested a voter simply needed to know was he better off than at the last election to judge economic competence, and there is a wealth of research linking voters' judgments about the economy to support for incumbent parties (a good review is Lewis-Beck and Stegmaier 2000).

Whether we consider issues in terms of position or valence it is possible that the same party would not "win" on all issues. A party strong on economic prosperity might be beaten by another on security; a party with a position close to a voter on health might be beaten by another on education policy. Hence there is an incentive for parties to fight the election on the issues that are most favorable to them. This is not something they can control, given the existence of other parties with other agendas, but we can recognize that the election agenda will favor some parties over others.

Campaigns could be important whether elections are about parties or issues – and of course they are about both of these. In general, campaigns give parties an opportunity to mobilize support on the basis of existing loyalties. To the extent that issues matter, they should matter more – and in predictable ways – following a campaign which raises voter awareness. Gelman and King (1993) suggested that campaigns made voting more predictable, as voters were more likely to vote in ways that we would expect them to, given past loyalties, social background and general political attitudes. Arguably, the deep rooted determinants of electoral behavior are now much less influential in most countries as party attachment wanes (Dalton and Wattenberg 2003) and social structure becomes less important (Franklin, Mackie and Valen 2009), something that should allow for campaigns to become more important.

All parties do their best to mobilize those they expect to support them, and ensure such people go out and vote. It is always possible that when turnout is not universal some parties are hurt more than others by the failure of their supporters to vote, with the suggestion in some research that parties of the left, who rely on less educated, poorer and perhaps younger voters, suffer a systematic disadvantage (Pacek and Radcliff 1995). This has been rejected by other findings (Fisher 2007; Bernhagen and Marsh 2007). But even if there are not systematic differences over time and place, turnout can still matter in any election, particularly if it falls far short of 100 percent.

These broad approaches are important in explaining voting behavior in elections. We will now turn to look at each of them in the context of voting choice in a referendum to assess how useful each approach is. We might expect that since a referendum is about an issue rather than selecting a person or party to govern, the "issue" itself would be of primary importance and the relevance of party, and incumbency, questionable. We might also expect campaigns to be of considerable importance as referendums – and in particular referendums on a particular issue – are typically unusual events, in contrast to regular elections. As turnout is often much lower than in general elections at least, there is ample opportunity for differential turnout to be significant.

The referendum experience: practice and research

Before exploring the reasons why people vote as they do in referendums, we should first summarize the extent and nature of referendums in democracies (for general accounts, see Butler and Ranney 1994; Gallagher and Ulieri 1996; LeDuc 2003). There are broadly two kinds of votes. The first, and this is the nature of referendums in most countries that have them, is a vote called by parliament. The results may or may not be binding, but the key is that the vote is a consequence of a decision, usually by the government, that a particular policy is to be followed. In most cases, the policy requires a constitutional change and it is this that necessitates a referendum. Referendums have been most common across Europe on constitutional matters, with membership of the European Union and on issues of public morality such as divorce and abortion in Catholic countries common reasons for constitutional change, but they remain relatively rare events, much less common than elections in all but very few countries: Ireland stands out with three dozen votes and Australia has held two dozen. This first type of referendum can also be subdivided, according to whether or not it is necessary. The UK referendums on the EU in 1975 and 2016 were not required, but were wholly political decisions, whereas those in Ireland are required to make changes in a constitution that is particularly specific and anachronistic on many issues (a referendum was needed to restrict the provision of bail conditions for those facing criminal charges, and another – perhaps very many – would be needed to remove sexist language in that constitution, written as it was in a traditional Catholic society in the 1930s). Referendums may also be binding or not, but typically they can only be non-binding in circumstances when they are not formally required.

The second type of referendum is one called by the public, or at least a section of it. This is the Swiss experience, where there have been hundreds of such votes, and there is also a provision for this in Italy, which has seen more than fifty such votes since the mid-1970s to reject (or not) pieces of new legislation.[1] It is also common at the local level across the US in some states, and in the UK local referendums can be forced by a petition on issues such as directly electing a mayor.

The variations in the rules governing referendums are potentially important. As the study of voting developed, researchers were able to use a comparative approach to demonstrate a degree of conditionality in behavior. Different electoral rules and different types of party system, for instance, had an impact on the weight of different factors on vote choice. The same, it has been argued, can be true of referendums, with the required and binding ones providing different incentives for voters than do non-required and non-binding ones, as will be discussed below.

Studies of electoral behavior are now based on very extensive post-election surveys, supplemented increasingly by more surveys through the campaign and beyond, but academic studies of referendums typically have been more limited. While the comparative study of voting behavior is now well developed, properly comparative studies of referendums are much less so, although this literature has been growing, prompted not least by the fact that several countries have sometimes held referendums of EU treaty change at about the same time (the pioneer here was Pierce, Valen and Listhaug 1983; subsequently Franklin, Marsh and McLaren 1994 on Maastricht referendums, Glencross and Trechsel 2011 and Hobolt and Brouard 2010 on the European Constitutional Treaty, and Hug 2002, Hobolt 2005, 2007 and Petithomme 2011 on EU referendums more generally, while Svensson 2002 and Marsh 2015 provide comparative studies of several referendums within the same country).

The referendum experience: parties

Much of the research does find that party matters in referendum voting, and often matters a great deal. There are a number of reasons why party loyalties can become very significant factors. The first is that the vote is prompted by a government, and this typically identifies the government party (or parties) with the position of supporting a position in the vote. This brings in a government vs. opposition dimension, allowing the possibility of embarrassing or weakening the government by defeating the referendum. The second is that the issue conflict in the referendum may be reflected in the party system, so it would be natural for (some) opposition parties to campaign against proposals by the government.

However, it is not at all unusual to find that the issue conflict is not one that underlies the party system, and in those circumstances it might be expected either that a party is divided on the position to take, or that a party takes a back-seat. In each of these cases, party loyalties will not be mobilized effectively and so partisanship will not be such a strong factor in the vote. It may be more difficult for a governing party that has initiated a vote to do this. This is not to say that supporters of a government party will always be more likely to support that party's position than those of any other party, but it does suggest that governing parties will normally do a better job of maximizing potential support among its own supporters for its position, other things being equal. A good illustration of this is support in recent referendums on EU Treaty change in Ireland. There was a Fianna Fail (FF) led government in place for four of the last five such votes, and a Fine Gael (FG) led government in place for the most recent one. Expert opinion would see FG as slightly more pro-European than FF, although both are center-right parties that have always actively supported Ireland's membership.[2] In the four referendums where FF led the government, FF voters were more likely to vote "yes" than those of FG. In the most recent vote in 2012, FG voters were more inclined to vote "yes" than those of FF (Marsh 2015). A study of one of the Norwegian and British votes on EU membership suggested that, when parties were divided, so were their followers (Pierce, Valen and Listhaug 1983). Government office is a good incentive to minimize division. But it would be wrong to think that government party voters are always more likely to support their party's position since that is not the case. Of course in the 2016 "Brexit" referendum in the UK, divisions in the ruling party prompted the referendum in the first place, and so ensured that "party" would not be a unifying factor for Conservative voters.

It was argued by Franklin, Marsh and McLaren (1994; see also Franklin, van der Eijk and Marsh 1995) that referendum voting could become little more than a vote on the popularity of the government. The argument drew on interpretations of European Parliament elections as "second-order" votes (Reif and Schmitt 1980). Although the European Parliament might have a different function and issue agenda to a national parliament, the second-order argument is that voters will pay little attention to that but use the vote as a "referendum" on the current government of the country (similar arguments have been made about sub-national elections). An important condition here must be how salient to voters are the issues raised by the referendum. The "second-order" argument requires voters to have little interest in the ostensible issue per se. As we will see below, there is ample evidence that issues can and do matter in referendums, including those on EU-related matters. Even so, most research on EU referendums have found evidence of an – admittedly sometimes small – anti-government effect where those dissatisfied with the current administration are more likely, other things being equal, to reject the government's proposal.

It is not uncommon in referendums for parties on both sides (or neither) to cede some of the work to non-party or cross-party campaign organizations. In some countries, such structures to promote the yes or no side are essentially a requirement for funding and media access, but they also provide an opportunity for both sides to remove some of the partisan edge from the debate. This can be useful for the government parties. Commenting on the "success" of Ireland's second referendum on the Lisbon Treaty *The Irish Times* noted the important role of civil society activists "whose arguments made it possible to disconnect the treaty as an issue in the minds of voters from the performance of the government" (quoted in Laffin 2015). Indeed, in this referendum, government popularity was not a significant factor at all, despite its remarkably low rating in the wake of the public bailout of Ireland's banks (Marsh 2015).

There is some evidence that the importance of parties and government status can be conditional on the type of referendum. Hug and Sciarini (2000; see also Hug 2002) find from their study of fourteen referendums on the EU across Europe that government supporters will be mobilized more effectively when the referendum is not required and when the outcome is binding, arguing that in such circumstances the vote is essentially one of support for the government (the "Brexit" referendum provided a notable exception to this, for reasons already given). In contrast, where the decision to hold a vote is not really the choice of the government and, in particular, where the result is not binding, voters are freer to follow their issue preferences.

In many referendums, parties are relatively uninvolved as the impetus for the vote comes from outside the party system. The Italian case is interesting as such votes need a quorum in order to defeat legislation, and while one party may be critical in gathering the signatures necessary to provoke the vote, others – particular parties in government – may do as little as possible so as to suppress turnout and so defeat the proposed abrogation (Ulieri 2002).

The referendum experience: issues

Parties matter but issues often matter more is a general theme of referendum voting research. What is most interesting here is what is meant by "issues" in this context, and how the campaign frames the vote in terms of an issue or issues. If issues are important, how are issues related to the vote? If general elections are commonly fought on "valence" issues, what about referendums? Do they revolve around the decision of what will best ensure the "good life," or is there more room for "positions" to matter, as voters can be expected to have very different attitudes to some of the questions that come up in referendums? Certainly some research has looked at issues in these positional terms, explaining choice in a referendum in terms of attitudes to what might be thought of as the broader issue (some examples are discussed below). In the case of EU-related votes, this means attitudes to European integration. The EU as an issue is not necessarily aligned with the major underlying dimensions of party politics. In most countries, there is a strong economic left–right dimension, often reinforced by a religious–secular one. Europe does not fit naturally into that. Although there was a tendency in some countries in earlier years for the left to be more skeptical about a union based on a free market, currently opposition to the EU is stronger on both the left and right margins of party systems and support is greater in the center, including center-right and center-left. This makes the task of assessing the pros and cons of EU-related referendums more difficult for voters.

However, Danish research has consistently argued that attitudes to the EU are fairly stable and do predict votes in EU-related referendums. This applies to votes on the Maastricht Treaty as well as to those on things like the Euro, where the conditionality of their support led Danes to vote to stay out of the common currency. Svensson (2002: 748) argues strongly that the Danish experience shows how "consistent values may be developed on a salient issue and may become the basis for voting behavior in one or more referendums."

A positional approach has been taken by Hobolt (2007). She treats each voter as having an "ideal point" with regard to an issue, one that can be compared with the status quo, and the position that would hold if the referendum change were approved. Hence, a voter would have to decide whether the referendum would bring policy closer to her ideal than the status quo. The problem with such an approach, as with positional voting in elections, is identifying the underlying issue dimension. This may be easier when the issue dimension is well structured and relatively stable within a country, but is more problematic when it is not.

The way in which the subject of the referendum is framed can be crucial (de Vreese and Semetko 2004; see also Dekavella 2016 on how the referendum on Scottish independence was framed in the media). Just as with elections, yes and no sides will seek to place the vote on a terrain which is favorable to their own side. Issues still matter in this situation, and they may be positional, but the issues may differ across groups. For instance, in votes on the European Treaty in the Netherlands, those concerned about "identity threats" voted no (de Vreese and Boomgaarden 2007); in various treaty referendums in Ireland, those worried about "neutrality" voted no (Marsh 2015; Garry, Marsh and Sinnott 2005). It may be that the issue is in fact not affected by the referendum, but the important point is that some people are persuaded that an issue matters in a particular vote. Atikcan (2015) shows how pro-change campaigners in rerun referendums sought to focus their efforts better so as to ensure the campaign would be fought on more favorable grounds.

On some votes, the question of what best ensures economic prosperity can come to the fore, as in most elections. As in elections, each side generally seeks to argue that its recommendation provides the best path. This is more of a valence issue, which comes down to the voter's trust in the advice of one side rather than another. In elections, voters can be seen to be influenced by recent economic conditions; that is, people may judge economic competence by recent economic circumstances. This is harder to generalize to a referendum. Arguably, the economy feeds into government satisfaction, and as discussed above, this is a common influence, but it could also be that bad conditions also influence the way voters think about the possible change that a referendum could bring, making them more fearful, or feeling they have little to lose (for a discussion and some evidence, see Sattler and Urpelainen 2012).

The referendum experience: knowledge

There is a substantial literature on how much voters know when it comes to elections, but in any one country the level of knowledge cannot be expected to vary hugely from election to election. However, in the case of referendums huge variation can be expected, as the salience of the topic, and the attention of parties, media and civic organizations is far from constant. It has been argued that in lower salience referendums voters are more inclined to take their cues from parties, with "second order" considerations more to the fore (Hobolt 2005, 2007).

Referendums always involve some change. Most commonly this is a change to the constitution to enable new legislation, but in all cases there is the expectation of some change to the status quo. A common argument amongst campaigners against such change to voters unsure of the merits of the proposal is to vote "no" (i.e., for the status quo) if you don't know, and there is evidence that those who feel they do not know enough are inclined to follow this advice. The onus is on those campaigning for a "yes" to demonstrate that the future will be better than the status quo. Bowler and Donovan (1998) find that the least informed are inclined to reject proposal for change and this is also being found in many other studies (see, for example, Nadeau, Martin and Blais 1999; Clarke, Kornberg and Stewart 2004; Whiteley et al. 2012; Schuck and de Vreese 2008; and see also Morisi 2016).

The referendum experience: campaign effects

If election campaigns tend to result in making vote choice more predictable, referendum campaigns can be far less clear in their consequences. Hobolt's argument (2007) that strong campaigns reduce "second-order" effects does not always lead to predictability, even if a strong campaign increases issue voting, because campaigns may frame the debate in unexpected ways (see also Dvořák 2013). LeDuc argues on the basis of a broad comparative study that opinion changes most substantially in cases when "there is little partisan, issue or ideological basis on which voters might tend to form an opinion easily" (LeDuc 2003: 207). Campaigns in these cases involve opinion formation. In contrast, those cases when "the nature of the issue itself or the circumstances of the referendum generate strong cues based on partisanship, ideology or pre-existing opinions" show least evidence of instability (LeDuc 2003: 208). LeDuc describes a third case which should resemble the second type, but where the campaign successfully shifted the bases of decision making. A good illustration is an Australian vote in 1999 on removing the British monarch as head of state, which was lost when the "yes" side divided over the nature of the replacement, whether a president would be elected or appointed. This third type is itself unpredictable. Several votes on EU treaties across Europe were expected to pass on the basis that public opinion favored the EU, as did the major parties, but in the course of the campaign opinion moved against a "yes" vote, for change, as "no" campaigns moved the bases of decision. Hobolt and Brouard (2010) shows how French concerns focused on threats to the "social model" by EU liberalism, while Dutch concerns involved threats to identity (see also Lubbers 2008).

Certainly, polls far in advance of the vote can be very poor guides indeed, and even polls a few weeks before the vote can be very wide of the mark, as the public in many cases have yet to engage with the debate. On the basis of a systematic study of polls in advance of a wide range of referendums in Europe (outside Switzerland) Fisher found clear evidence of a "status quo" effect, with support for change tending to decline over the course of a campaign (Fisher 2016).

The referendum experience: turnout effects

Turnout does vary a lot in referendums, and is often very low, but can vary very significantly from referendum to referendum. Butler and Ranney (1994) observed that turnout is typically less than in a general election. For instance, in Ireland, which has had thirty-nine referendums since 1937, turnout has varied from a low of 29 percent on University Representation in the Upper House, changes to adoption laws and changes to Bail provisions, to a high of 76 percent, adopting the new constitution in 1937, and 68 percent on accession to the EU in 1972. While half of all votes attracted a turnout of between 43 and 62 percent, a quarter were below 42 percent and only a quarter above 62 percent (general election turnout in the same period averages 72 percent, with a low of 63 percent). In the US, proposals tend to be placed on the ballot along with the choices in a variety of elections. Magleby (1984: 90–95) observes that more voters participate in candidate choice than indicate support or opposition to propositions.

This increases the chances differential turnout can matter to the result. Nevertheless, as LeDuc (2003: 172) points out, referendum turnout can be as high or higher than in an election on some occasions.

Individual determinants of turnout in referendums are broadly the same as in elections. That is, we expect older, more educated, more politically interested and wealthier electors to vote. Partisanship, and the activities of parties, can serve to reduce the impact of these individual level factors, but parties typically are less involved in getting out the vote in referendum campaigns. The intensity of the campaign and the familiarity of the subject are two factors highlighted by Kriesi (2005) as contributing to participation rates. He argues on the basis of Swiss evidence that high intensity campaigns in themselves do little to alter the participation differential between aware and unaware citizens, whereas votes on familiar topics see a smaller differential. Kriesi's work notwithstanding (see also Lutz 2007), there has been little systematic work on the impact of lower turnout on referendum outcomes. One argument is that low turnout favors those against change, on the basis that those against something new are more committed, but equally plausible is that proponents of change are more committed. (Of course in referendums where turnout has to be above a threshold for it to have any effect, abstention might well be favored by those against the proposal. A recent example was the referendum in Hungary on migrant quotas. Rejection of the proposal [which was EU policy] was almost universal but only 44 percent voted so the result was invalid.) There was evidence that low turnout did help those in the first Irish vote on the Nice Treaty who were opposed to it. There was a significant increase in turnout in the second vote and this went overwhelming to the "yes" side (Sinnott 2003) but the same effect was far less striking in the two votes on Lisbon, where the increase in the pro-Treaty vote was not down to higher turnout (Sinnott and Elkink 2010). Certainly there is no good evidence from the Irish case to indicate that differential turnout always helps the side opposed to change. Another expectation is that low turnout might benefit the position favored by the right – just as some argue left-wing parties are disadvantaged by low turnout. Lutz (2007) – studying the extensive Swiss experience – found low turnout in fact tended to hurt the right-wing position, but argued that a more informed electorate tended to be more left-wing, so if voters became more informed and so more motivated to vote, the bias might not be so clear. The referendum of Scottish independence in 2014 was notable for the very high level of turnout, over 84 percent, compared with below 70 percent in most recent general elections, but there is no evidence that this boosted the vote for the status quo. "No" voters were in any case more prevalent in those groups where turnout would normally be higher: older, more middle class and living in more affluent areas (Curtice 2014).

Conclusions

This chapter has summarized much of the work done in recent years on voting in referendums. While there is far less written on this topic than has been produced on elections, the body of work has been growing rapidly, not least because referendums have become rather more common in recent times. While referendums are ostensibly about particular policy issues or decisions and so differ from elections, in which people are voted in to office and make policy and take decisions across a very wide range of matters, there are some broad themes which run across research both referendums and elections. The role of parties and their leaders in providing a basis for the voter to make their referendum choice, just as this plays an important role in most elections, is one such theme. A second is the place of issues in such votes; and as in elections, research on referendums finds that not everyone views the same issues as important, and shows that for some voters the issue may not be connected directly to the immediate vote. As in elections, the way in which the vote is framed is important. Because referendums are much more irregular than elections, and even when they are common, the topics may vary hugely, campaigns are typically much more important than they are in elections, as more people decide, and decide in unpredictable ways, during the last few weeks and days before the vote. One conclusion then is that what we know about elections generalizes to referendums in as much as the processes underlying decisions are similar but the context can be important, the actors can be different and the weight given to certain factors can be very different. While these themes do run across the growing body of work on voting behavior in referendums, there is also considerable diversity across these studies. In part this is because the study designs, the measures used and the theoretical approaches adopted vary considerably. While election studies have become relatively institutionalized in many countries, allowing both cross-time and cross-country comparisons, referendums are still treated for the most part as one-off events and most of the surveys used to study referendums are quite separate from the more normal election studies. Of course the referendums themselves differ enormously, in terms of topics, the role of parties and other actors in campaigns, and the institutional basis of the vote, but until such variables can be built into particular studies, we are not able to assess properly quite how important that variation is to explaining differences in results obtained by different studies. Just as much of what we are coming to know about electoral behavior shows that institutional context is often a critical conditioning factor, so with referendums, conditionality is perhaps even more important and future research should be designed with this in mind if it is to properly develop our understanding of voter choice in referendums.

Notes

1 Italy also provides for constitutional referendums, triggered by proposed changes to the constitution. Unlike the popular referendums in Italy, these are not subject to a quorum.
2 Using the Chapel Hill series of expert surveys, this author's analysis shows Fine Gael averages 6.5 and Fianna Fail 5.8 on a 10-point pro-EU scale. On the expert surveys, see Bakker et al. (2015). On Ireland, see also Benoit (2009).

References

Atikcan, E. Ö. (2015) "The Puzzle of Double Referendums in the European Union," *Journal of Common Market Studies*, vol. 53, no. 5, September, 937–956.

Bakker, R., de Vries, C., Edwards, E., Hooge, L., Jolly, S., Marks, G., Polk, J., Rovny, J., Steenbergen, M. and Vachudova, M. A. (2015) "Measuring Party Positions in Europe: The Chapel Hill Expert Survey Trend File, 1999–2010," *Party Politics*, vol. 21, no. 1, January, 143–152.

Benoit, K. (2009) "Irish Political Parties and Policy Stances on European Integration," *Irish Political Studies*, vol. 24, no. 4, December, 447–466.

Bernhagen, P. and Marsh, M. (2007) "The Partisan Effects of Low Turnout: Analyzing Vote Abstention as a Missing Data Problem," *Electoral Studies*, vol. 26, no. 3, September, 401–413.

Bowler, S. and Donovan, T. (1998) "Two Cheers for Direct Democracy," *Representation*, vol. 35, no. 4, Winter, 247–254.

Butler, D. and Ranney, A. (eds.) (1994) *Referendums Around the World*, London: Macmillan.

Clarke, H. D., Kornberg, A. and Stewart, M. (2004) "Referendum Voting as Political Choice: The Case of Quebec," *British Journal of Political Science*, vol. 34, no. 2, April, 345–355.

Curtice, J. (2014) "So Who Voted Yes and Who Voted No?," Available online: http://blog.whatscotland-thinks.org/2014/09/voted-yes-voted/, [accessed February 20, 2017].

Curtice, J., and Holmberg, S. (2005) "Leaders," in Thomassen, J. (ed.) *The European Voter: A Comparative Study of Modern Democracies*, Oxford: Oxford University Press: 125–166.

Dalton, R. and Wattenberg, M. (eds.) (2003) *Parties Without Partisans: Political Changes in Advanced Industrial Societies*, Oxford: Oxford University Press.

De Vreese, C. H. and Boomgaarden, H. G. (2007) "Immigration, Identity, Economy and the Government: Understanding Variations in Explanations for Outcomes in EU-Related Referendums," in de Vreese, C. H. (ed.) *The Dynamics of Referendum Campaigns: An International Perspective*, Basingstoke: Palgrave Macmillan: 186–205.

De Vreese, C. H. and Semetko, H. A. (2004) *Political Campaigning in Referendums: Framing the Referendum Issue*, Abingdon: Routledge.

Dekavella, M. (2016) "Framing Referendum Campaigns: The 2014 Scottish Independence Referendum in the Press," *Media, Culture and Society*, vol. 28, no. 6, September, 793–810.

Dvořák, T. (2013) "Referendum Campaigns, Framing and Uncertainty," *Journal of Elections, Public Opinion and Parties*, vol. 23, no. 4, November, 367–386.

Fisher, S. D. (2007) "(Change in) Turnout and (Change in) the Left Share of the Vote," *Electoral Studies*, vol. 26, no. 3, September, 598–611.

Fisher, S. (2016) "Do People Tend to Vote Against Change in Referendums?," Available online: https://constitution-unit.com/2016/06/22/do-people-tend-to-vote-against-change-in-referendums/, [accessed June 17, 2017].

Franklin, M., van der Eijk, C. and Marsh, M. (1995) "Referendum Outcomes and Trust in Government: Public support for Europe in the Wake of Maastricht," *West European Politics*, vol. 18, no. 3, 101–117.

Franklin, M., Mackie, T. T. and Valen, H. (eds.) (2009) *Electoral Change: Responses to evolving Social and Attitudinal Structures in Western Countries*, Colchester: ECPR Press.

Franklin, M., Marsh, M. and McLaren, L. (1994) "Uncorking the Bottle: Popular Opposition to European Unification in the Wake of Maastricht," *Journal of Common Market Studies*, vol. 32, no. 4, December, 455–472.

Gallagher, M. and Ulieri, P. V. (eds.) (1996) *The Referendum Experience in Europe*, London: Macmillan.

Garry, J., Marsh, M. and Sinnott, R. (2005) "'Second-Order' Versus 'Issue Voting' Effects in EU Referendums: Evidence from the Irish Nice Treaty Referendums," *European Union Politics*, vol. 6, no. 2, June, 201–221.

Gelman, A and King, G. (1993) "Why Are American Presidential Election Campaign Polls So Variable When Votes Are So Predictable?," *British Journal of Political Science*, vol. 23, no. 4, October, 409–451.

Glencross, A. and Trechsel, A. (2011) "First or Second Order Referendums? Understanding the Votes on the EU Constitutional Treaty in Four EU Member States," *West European Politics*, vol. 34, no. 4, July, 755–772.

Hobolt, S. (2005) "When Europe Matters: The Impact of Political Information on Voting Behaviour in EU Referendums," *Journal of Elections, Public Opinion and Parties*, vol. 15, no. 1, February, 85–109.

Hobolt, S. B. (2007) "Campaign Information and Voting Behaviour," in de Vreese, C. H. (ed.) *The Dynamics of Referendum Campaigns: An International Perspective*, Basingstoke: Palgrave Macmillan: 84–116.

Hobolt, S. B. and Brouard, S. (2010) "Contesting the European Union? Why the Dutch and the French Rejected the European Constitution," *Political Research Quarterly*, vol. 64, no. 2, June, 309–322.

Hug, S. (2002) *Voices of Europe: Citizens, Referendums and European Integration*, Lanham: Rowan and Littlefield.

Hug, S. and Sciarini, P. (2000) "Referendums on European Integration: Do Institutions Matter in the Voter's Decision," *Comparative Political Studies*, vol. 33, no. 1, February, 3–36.

Key, V. O. (1966) *The Responsible Electorate: Rationality in Presidential Voting 1936–60*, Cambridge, Harvard University Press.

Kriesi, H. P. (2005) "The Participation in Swiss Direct-Democratic Votes," in de Vreese, C. H. (ed.) *The Dynamics of Referendum Campaigns: An International Perspective*, Basingstoke: Palgrave Macmillan: 117–141.

Laffin, B. (2015) "Confronting Europe: The Irish Referendums on Lisbon," in Elkink, J. A. and Farrell, D. M. (eds.) *The Act of Voting: Identities, Institutions and Localities*, London: Routledge: 116–134.

LeDuc, L. (2003) *The Politics of Direct Democracy: Referendums in Global Perspective*, Toronto: University of Toronto Press.

Lewis-Beck, M. and Stegmaier, M. (2000) "Economic Determinants of Electoral Outcomes," *Annual Review Political Science*, vol. 3, June, 183–219.

Lubbers, M. (2008) "Regarding the Dutch 'Nee' to the European Constitution: A Test of the Identity, Utilitarian and Political Approaches to Voting 'No'," *European Union Politics*, vol. 9, no. 1, March, 59–86.

Lupia, A. and McCubbins, M. (1998) *The Democratic Dilemma: Can Citizens Learn What They Need to Know?*, Cambridge: Cambridge University Press.

Lutz, G. (2007) "Low Turnout in Direct Democracy," *Electoral Studies*, vol. 26, no. 3, September, 624–332.

Magleby, D. (1984) *Direct Legislation: Voting on Ballot Propositions in the United States*, London: Johns Hopkins.

Marsh, M. (2015) "Voting on Europe, Again and Again: Stability and Change in the Irish Experience with EU Referendums," *Electoral Studies*, vol. 38, June, 170–182.

Morisi, D. (2016) "Voting Under Uncertainty: The Effect of Information in the Scottish Independence Referendum," *Journal of Elections, Public Opinion and Parties*, vol. 26, no. 3, 354–372.

Nadeau, R., Martin, P. and Blais, A. (1999) "Attitude Towards Risk-Taking and Individual Choice in the Quebec Referendum on Sovereignty," *British Journal of Political Science*, vol. 29, no. 3, July, 523–539.

Petithomme, M. (2011) "Awakening the Sleeping Giant? The Displacement of the Partisan Cleavage and Change in Government-Opposition Dynamics in EU Referendums," *Perspectives on European Politics and Society*, vol. 12, no. 1, April, 89–110.

Pacek, A. and Radcliff, B. (1995) "Turnout and the Vote for Left-of-Centre Parties: A Cross-National Analysis," *British Journal of Political Science*, vol. 25, no. 1, January, 137–43.

Pierce, R., Valen, H. and Listhaug, O. (1983) "Referendum Voting Behavior: The Norwegian and British Referenda in Membership in the European Community," *American Journal of Political Science*, vol. 2, no. 1, February, 43–63.

Reif, K. and Schmitt, H. (1980) "Nine Second-Order National Elections – A Conceptual Framework for the Analysis of European Election Results," *European Journal of Political Research*, vol. 8, no. 1, March, 3–44.

Sattler, T. and Urpelainen, J. (2012) "Explaining Public Support for International Integration: How Do National Conditions and Treaty Characteristics Interact with Individual Beliefs?" *Journal of Politics*, vol. 74, no. 4, October, 1108–1124.

Schuck, A. and de Vreese, C. H. (2008) "The Dutch No to the EU Constitution: Assessing the Role of EU Skepticism and the Campaign," *Journal of Elections, Public Opinion and Parties*, vol. 18, no. 1, January, 101–128.

Sinnott, R. (2003) *Attitudes and Behaviour of the Irish Electorate in the Second Referendum on the Nice Treaty*, Report for the European Commission Representation in Ireland, Institute for the Study of Social Change, University College Dublin.

Sinnott, R. and Elkink, J. A. (2010) *Attitudes and Behaviour in the Second Referendum on the Treaty of Lisbon*, Dublin: Geary Institute and School of Politics and International Relations.

Stokes, D. E. (1963) "Spatial Models of Party Competition," *American Political Science Review*, vol. 57, no. 2, June, 368–377.

Svensson, P. (2002) "Five Danish Referendums on the European Community and European Union: A Critical Assessment of the Franklin Thesis," *European Journal of Political Research*, vol. 41, no. 6, October, 733–750.

Ulieri, P. V. (2002) "On Referendum Voting in Italy: YES, NO or Non–Vote? How Italian Parties Learned to Control Referendums," *European Journal of Political Research*, vol. 41, no. 6, October, 863–883.

Whiteley, P., Clarke, H. D., Sanders, D. and Stewart, M. C. (2012) "Britain Says NO: Voting in the AV Ballot Referendum," *Parliamentary Affairs*, vol. 65, no. 2, November, 301–322.

22

NETWORKS, CONTEXTS, AND THE PROCESS OF POLITICAL INFLUENCE[1]

Robert Huckfeldt, Matthew T. Pietryka and John B. Ryan

A significant body of evidence demonstrates that voters are politically interdependent. They talk, they quarrel, they display yard signs and bumper stickers, and at times they persuade one another to adopt new and different opinions regarding parties, issues, and candidates. The modern origins of this research date to the pre-survey era (Tingsten 1932; Key 1949), but the dawn of survey research led to some signal accomplishments in locating the behavior of voters within a variety of spatially defined social and political contexts.

The Columbia University sociologists (Lazarsfeld, Berelson, and Gaudet 1948; Berelson, Lazarsfeld, and McPhee 1954; McPhee 1963) provided compelling accounts of the importance of locally defined communities for political communication and choice. Butler and Stokes (1969) demonstrated the role of British constituencies as arenas for social influence and persuasion. While the Michigan voting studies have been criticized for an individualistic and atomized account of citizens in politics, Miller (1954), Converse (1964), and Miller and Stokes (1963) made substantial contributions to our understanding of the relationship between spatial location and the behavior of individual citizens. Finally, the intellectual origins of the literatures on context and politics owe a particularly significant debt to the path-breaking work of influential European social scientists (e.g., Tingsten 1932; Dogan and Rokkan 1974; Cox 1969; Johnston 1986; Johnston and Pattie 2006; Pattie, Johnston, and Fieldhouse 1995; Pappi 2015; and others).

Scholars often attribute the importance of spatially defined contexts to only vaguely defined patterns of social interaction operating within these contexts, thus giving rise to skepticism regarding the actual underlying mechanisms of influence. Correctly or incorrectly, the modern age is frequently believed to liberate social interaction from spatial constraint. The automobile, the telephone, and the internet are all given credit for removing spatially defined boundaries on association and communication. Thus the question naturally arises, how do counties, precincts, neighborhoods, municipalities, and constituencies produce these effects on social interaction?

Why contexts matter: the implications for social networks

Specifying the mechanisms that translate social contexts into a source of influence for individual citizens has progressed over time. Some of the earliest work stipulated a political effect that was mediated through social loyalties. A particularly compelling example is found in Langton and

Rapoport's (1975) work on support for Allende in Santiago, Chile. Santiago residents who lived among the working class were more likely to identify as working class and to support Allende. The question thus becomes, what are the mechanisms and processes through which social loyalties are affected? Indeed, the source of the effect on social loyalties is also likely to be the source for effects on political loyalties, opinions, preferences, and attitudes.

The research on mechanisms for translating political and social contexts into a source of individual influence took a new turn in the late 1970s as work emerged on the role of social networks in affecting individual behavior (Laumann 1973; Granovetter 1973; Burt 1978; McPherson, Smith-Lovin, and Cook 2001). The social network mechanism suggests that social contexts, conceived as the composition of various locally defined populations, have consequences for the political configuration of social networks (Fieldhouse et al. 2014). For example, individuals who reside in environments populated by supporters of Democratic candidates are likely to demonstrate enduring patterns of interaction with individuals who support Democrats. Moreover, it gave rise to a literature that tied together networks and contexts with individual-level political behavior (Johnston 1986; Huckfeldt and Sprague 1995; Huckfeldt, Johnson, and Sprague 2004; Johnston 1999; Fieldhouse, Lessard-Phillips, and Edmonds 2016).

In contrast, an individualistic explanation for social homophily within networks is that birds of a feather do *indeed* flock together, and people typically select associates who, for example, share their own political inclinations. The logical implication is that politics would thus become a context-free zone that is wholly dependent on a priori political preference. That is, political preference might dictate social interaction, rather than social interaction affecting politics (McPherson, Smith-Lovin, and Cook 2001).

At the same time, the work of McPherson and Smith-Lovin (1987) also points to the importance of structurally induced homophily. That is, context and social structure impose the boundaries of supply on associational choice. You may be a Christian Democrat who prefers talking politics with other Christian Democrats, but if you move to a locale with few Christian Democrats, you may end up in political conversation with a friendly coworker who shares your passion for football but whose political preferences tack toward the Social Democrats. Thus the arrows run both ways: people have associational preferences, but their preferences are multidimensional, and their social interaction choices are limited by locally defined availability (Huckfeldt 1983; Huckfeldt and Sprague 1988).

This is the underlying substantive logic of a model that places contextual constraints on the process of network formation (Huckfeldt 1983; Huckfeldt and Sprague 1995). It is not that people do not have associational preferences based on politics, but rather that the opportunity to exercise these preferences is limited by the locally imposed constraints of work, neighborhood, and other contextual boundaries. Hence the relationships among networks, contexts, and associational preference are understood in terms of a stochastic process that is constrained by supply (Huckfeldt and Sprague 1995). Indeed, other research shows that there are even national-level constraints on network formation. Supporters of minor parties and candidates in Germany, the United States, and Japan during the early 1990s were likely to be imbedded in political discussion networks with higher levels of political disagreement (Huckfeldt, Ikeda, and Pappi 2005).

Citizenship in contexts and networks

The importance of social networks and social contexts for the exercise of citizenship has produced an avalanche of important questions and issues with respect to democratic politics. Beginning perhaps with Rousseau's early lament (1994, 1762) that the success of democracy depends on fully informed citizens acting in social isolation, a cascade of research issues have arisen, many of which relate to underlying processes of influence. Is Rousseau's concern warranted? Are we at the mercy of electorates with collective judgments that are undermined by interdependence – by a process in which social contagion drives voters to embrace the cause or candidate of the moment, with little capacity for carefully reasoned individual scrutiny and judgment?

Serious concern regarding the civic capacity of modern democratic electorates is not a new development in the systematic study of political behavior (Michels 1911; Ortega y Gasset 1930; Schumpeter 1942), and contemporary reservations arose in the context of the first modern election studies. Both the Columbia and Michigan election studies revealed individual voters who were often poorly equipped to exercise political judgment (Berelson, Lazarsfeld, and McPhee 1954; Converse 1964). In contrast to the problem of the poorly informed, Lodge and Taber (2013) address the stubborn intransigence of the *well* informed. Rather than responding to new information in a thoughtful manner, the well informed are more likely to be emotionally committed to their viewpoints and judgments. Their preferences are non-negotiable as a consequence of their ability to rationalize in the face of new information that conflicts with previously held beliefs.

Issues such as these push the literature on contexts and networks toward a more complete specification of the political influence process as it occurs among individual citizens (Fieldhouse and Cutts 2012). Are democratic citizens the political dupes of their more knowledgeable peers? Are they capable of forming judgments that endure in time, regardless of socially communicated messages to the contrary? Questions such as these are best addressed with a second model of process – a model that takes into account deliberative judgment within the context of social communication among citizens.

Experts and activists in everyday life

Several streams of work focus on the social transmission of information from politically biased sources (Huckfeldt and Sprague 1995; Huckfeldt, Johnson, and Sprague, 2004). This work shows that individuals are likely to rely on others for guidance, and the individuals most likely to provide that guidance are the "experts" and "activists" who populate the corridors of everyday life (Ahn, Huckfeldt, and Ryan 2014) – individuals who are, in fact, more interested and more knowledgeable about politics. Indeed, we see that survey respondents are more likely to report conversation with their well informed and politically engaged associates, regardless of whether they hold agreeable political views (Huckfeldt 2001; Ryan 2010). Hence such a process can be seen as propagating the biased views of Lodge and Taber's highly motivated citizens.

We employ a model of Bayesian decision-making to consider political communication among citizens within this particular context. Bayesian updating is typically translated to suggest that voters form an opinion based on their own devices, but then continue to revise and update their opinion in a more or less objective response to new incoming information (Bullock 2009; Gerber and Green 1998; Bartels 2002). The problem is that, to the extent citizens invoke the bias of their own prior beliefs as well as the biased beliefs of others within their social networks, one might question whether they are capable of updating to take account of new information that conflicts with their own pre-existent beliefs in any sort of objective way.

We begin by addressing the problem in the hypothetical context of a voter's judgment regarding a candidate based on an informant's report regarding the candidate's trustworthiness. In formal terms, the Bayes theorem says that:

$$P(A\mid B) = \frac{P(B\mid A)P(A)}{P(B)} = P(B\mid A) \times \frac{P(A)}{P(B)} \tag{1}$$

where:

A = an individual believes that a particular candidate is honest.

B = an informant alleges that the candidate is honest.

$P(A)$ = the base rate or the prior: the probability that the individual believes the candidate is honest, absent the informant's report.

$P(A|B)$ = the conditional probability that the individual believes the candidate is honest, given the informant's report.

$P(B)$ = the probability that the informant would report that the candidate is honest.

$P(B|A)$ = the likelihood function, or the probability that the informant's report would allege the candidate is honest, given that the candidate is honest.

The likelihood function is particularly important, effectively indexing the individual's assessment regarding the informant's judgment – a "best guess regarding the probability distribution from which the evidence is drawn" (Bullock 2009). In this context, the likelihood provides the expected probability that the informant's report converges with the individual's own prior belief, and for these purposes it is helpful to re-express the likelihood function in its definitional form as:

$$P(B|A) = \frac{P(A \text{ and } B)}{P(A)} = \frac{P(A \cap B)}{P(A)}$$

Hence the likelihood simply indexes the probability of agreement between the individual's prior and the informant's report, relative to the individual's prior. If the likelihood function is large, it suggests the individual will be more likely to trust the informant's report. In the context of Equation 1, a larger likelihood function weights the individual's prior judgment more heavily in estimating the posterior judgment.

In contrast, as the likelihood function approaches zero in Equation 1, the individual becomes more likely to reject the informant's report and the $P(A|B)$ converges on zero. At one extreme, the new information simply confirms what the individual already believed. At the opposite extreme, when the likelihood approaches zero, the individual rejects the new information, and $P(A|B)$ converges on zero.

Does Bayesian updating imply an objective analysis of incoming information? To the contrary, Equation 1 suggests that the key to the influence of new information is a function of whether the recipient trusts the message, where "trust" is anchored in an expectation that the individual and the informant share priors with the same or similar probability distributions. This lack of trust in new information from a suspect source closely resembles Lodge and Taber's (2013) supremely self-confident rationalizing voter!

While the likelihood function hardly qualifies as an objective screening device, within this narrowly defined context it may make sense for individuals to take information from others who share their general preferences (see Downs 1957; Ahn, Huckfeldt, and Ryan 2014). The important point is that the Bayes theorem does not require that individuals give equal weight to messages anchored in viewpoints that diverge from their own.

Other readers may question whether the report of an informant actually qualifies as information, inasmuch as it is mediated by another individual's subjective viewpoint. The problem is that virtually all information is mediated. Even the most objective news reports are mediated by editors, writers, and the current supply of newsworthy items (Boydstun 2013). The important point is that a Bayesian analysis of incoming information employs a credibility filter that is contingent on a shared probability distribution for the prior beliefs of the producers and recipients of political information. In short, the Bayesian model does not assume that voters base their updates on a random sample of the available data. To the contrary, the sample is weighted in favor of information that comes from a trusted source with shared preference distributions.

The update as a weighted summation

In this context, the Bayes theorem and its likelihood function do not theoretically presuppose a great deal, and it might even reasonably appear that Equation 1 and its rearrangement are simply accounting equations. As Bullock demonstrates, much of the value (and perhaps the controversy) of applying Bayes' theorem to the beliefs of voters and their response to new information arises if we are willing to assume that the probability distributions are normally distributed.

In the following discussion, we assume that a candidate's honesty is an inherent underlying characteristic of the particular candidate that is fixed in time (see Bullock 2009) – once a crook always a crook! At the same time, we assume that the basic underlying characteristic will manifest itself in a range of behaviors and reports of such behaviors that demonstrate a normal distribution around a central tendency. That is, even the most crooked political boss sometimes *did* pass out turkeys and hods of coal at Christmas, and even a president who stole his first Senate election might have possessed an honest and sincerely altruistic motive in supporting the twentieth century's most significant civil rights legislation (Caro 1982, 1990). On this basis it can be shown (Bullock 2009: 1111; Lee 2004: 34–37) that:

$$\text{belief}_1 \mid x_1 = \text{belief}_0 \left(\tau_0 / (\tau_0 + \tau_x) \right) + x_1 \left(\tau_x / (\tau_0 + \tau_x) \right) \tag{2}$$

where:

$\text{belief}_1 \mid x_1 =$ the individual's view regarding the candidate's honesty at time 1, given the informant's communicated view regarding the candidate's honesty at time 1.

$\text{belief}_0 =$ the individual's prior judgment, at time 0.

$\tau_0 =$ the precision of the prior belief $= 1/\sigma_0^2$, where σ_0^2 is the variance around the prior.

$\tau_x =$ the precision of the news report $= 1/\sigma_x^2$, where σ_x^2 is the variance around the news report.

Thus the updated belief is simply a sum of the weighted prior belief plus the weighted new information – in this instance the news report. The weights are the relative precision of each component, with precision measured as the inverse of the variance.

This form of the Bayesian expectation is intuitively appealing. It says that people rely on their priors more heavily when these prior judgments are more precise – less variant. They depend on the incoming stream of information more heavily when it repeatedly confirms the same message, thereby converging on a common signal.

Some individuals, lacking well-anchored views, are likely to believe everything they read or hear. If this is the case, it means the likelihood function is small, and the updated judgment will rely heavily on the news report. Alternatively, some individuals with particularly strong attitudes blame the messenger when a message contradicts their prior judgments. Indeed, hearing a message from a persistently adversarial news outlet (Fox News for some and MSNBC for others) may generate pre-conscious negative responses to the message.

At the same time, the Bayesian expectation leaves two questions unanswered regarding the implications for judgment and behavior. First, how do individuals arrive at these weights on prior judgments and new information? Second, how much political information is purposefully acquired and evaluated. Finally, how much information and guidance is an incidental byproduct of generalized patterns of social interaction. Much of the resistance to Bayesian reasoning in political science has been motivated by disbelief regarding the capacity of voters to incorporate Bayesian decision-making strategies in a self-conscious manner. That is, do we *really* think that the same voters whom Converse (1964) discovered in his classic work – the voters who hold inconsistent views, are incapable of thinking about politics in systematically ideological terms, and demonstrate low levels of knowledge and awareness – are capable of employing the Bayesian logic of Equation 1? Perhaps not!

To the contrary, many voters might, in fact, be *unintentional* Bayesians. Without ever hearing of Bayes or wrapping their heads around conditional probabilities and likelihood functions, they arrive at decisions that *appear* to be Bayesian because they recognize, or at least form *inherently subjective judgments* regarding, the levels of variance both in their own priors as well as in the stream of new information they confront. Several hypotheses arise, drawing on the form of the Bayesian logic portrayed in Equation 2 as well as studies in conformity theory, motivated reasoning, and social network effects on individual behavior.

Bayes, Asch, and conformity

The Asch conformity experiments (1955, 1963) are frequently seen as compelling evidence regarding the malleability of individual perception, the strong pressures that produce conformity within social groups, and the incapacities of individuals to sustain their own independent judgments. In the Asch experiments, individual subjects participate as one of eight subjects in what they believe to be a group experiment. Unknown to the one true subject, the other seven participants are confederates in a hoax. The group is shown two cards – the first has one straight line and the second has three straight lines of different lengths. Each individual is asked, in turn, to identify the line on the second card that is the same length as the line on the first card (Asch 1955).

In some instances, all the bogus subjects identify the wrong line. In this context, subjects conform to the incorrect judgment of the other subjects nearly one-third of the time. Approximately three-fourths of the subjects conformed at least once, and thus approximately one-fourth never conformed.

What are we to make of these results? A cognitive dissonance interpretation is that individuals form judgments to reduce dissonance. In the world of politics and political communication, one might expect that individuals adopt the political views of their surrounding associates in an effort to reduce the discrepancy between their own beliefs and the beliefs of others. The experiments have often been seen as a powerful demonstration of conformity effects because, after all, if individuals can be persuaded to deny their own sensory perceptions, it would seem they might be persuaded to believe almost anything! Indeed, carried to its extreme, the logic suggests that one might be able to persuade almost anyone of almost anything, and hence we should not be surprised to see very high levels of political homogeneity within small social groups.

Ross and his colleagues (1976) call this interpretation into question. According to their account, the particular nature of the Asch experiments made conformity pressures especially compelling. When fellow "subjects" in the Asch experiments inexplicably and unexpectedly adopt a position that runs contrary to the true subject's perception of the obvious reality, the individual confronts a substantial quandary. Thus the power of the Asch experiments is anchored in an attribution effect – there was no obvious way to attribute a cause for the mistaken consensus. What possible explanation could account for the other subjects' unanimous but mistaken judgments? Indeed, it is the lack of variance in the false subjects' judgments that is so particularly powerful. When just one of the seven bogus subjects diverged from the group's false judgment by consistently providing a correct report, majority opinion was effectively nullified. Can these results be interpreted within the Bayesian framework of Equation 2?

The true subjects' priors are based on their own sensory perceptions regarding the length of the lines. We would expect this prior to have low variance, assuming that individuals are generally able to trust their own judgments in discriminating something as straightforward as the length of lines on a piece of paper. Thus, it requires unanimity in the incoming information stream, for a variance of zero, to overturn the prior, and even then the prior is not always overturned. In short, it is possible to understand the Asch experiment, with its dramatic example of group conformity effects, within the context of Bayesian updating. Hence it is possible to comprehend the power of conformity effects with reference to the variance attached to an incoming information stream, but what of the variance attached to prior judgments?

Bayes and motivated reasoning

In the context of politics and political information, motivated reasoning reflects the resistance and unwillingness of individuals to take political experience and political information at face value. People do not engage in an objective search for the truth when confronting new political events and new political information. To the contrary, they process new information and new experience within the context of their own political views, the most important of which are anchored in deeply held emotions and attitudes that have been reinforced over time. This tendency often means that they resist the information streams produced through print and electronic media, as well as through social communication, based on pre-conscious responses to political stimuli that they find repugnant or objectionable. Rather than being the objective evaluators of new information, they are the biased evaluators of the information streams they encounter based on their own particular preferences and viewpoints (Kunda 1990).

Who are the most likely to engage in motivated reasoning? In general, motivated reasoning is more likely among the most sophisticated – those who are more attentive, better informed, and hence more committed to their own viewpoints (Lodge and Taber 2013). Indeed, we would expect that a reasonable updating process would consider new information in the context of old information. That is, indeed, the primary democratic value typically cited in support of a well-informed citizenry. One reason to educate the citizenry in a democratic political system is to ensure that voters are not swept along by fads, movements, and ephemeral causes. At the same time, carried to its extreme, motivated reasoning produces real problems for democratic politics.

Anti-democratic as well as democratic values carry the potential to generate motivated reasoning. Moreover, the sophisticated members of all tribes are susceptible: liberals and conservatives, radicals and reactionaries, Democrats and Republicans. All share the same human instinct – the more they know, the more confident they become in their own judgment, and the less likely they are to entertain new information. Indeed, as they become truly confident, their response to contrary arguments is likely to be anchored in a physiological rather than a reasoned response – patterns of association in long-term memory that might short circuit a deliberative response (Fazio 1995; Huckfeldt et al. 1998, 1999).

Is political polarization the ultimate result? We are persuaded by Bullock's argument that there is nothing in Bayes' theorem to suggest that either polarization or convergence is a necessary outcome of an updating process that reflects the weights placed on priors and new information. Indeed, our argument is that it is not the updating process or the priors that necessarily dictate the outcome of the process, but rather the nature of the individuals' subjective levels of confidence, both in their own priors as well as in the incoming stream of new information to which they are exposed. The question remains: do subjective levels of confidence reflect the objective reality, which in this instance is the level of precision in priors and information streams?

In order for this to be a meaningful question, we must demonstrate that people do, in fact, have the opportunity to confront political stimuli that conflict with their own prior judgments. Indeed, many analysts have argued that people's judgments are never threatened by disagreeable information and viewpoints. In Bayesian terms, people never budge from their priors because they are located in political environments and exposed to information streams that simply reinforce whatever viewpoints they hold (Tam Cho, Gimpel, and Hui 2013; Bishop 2008).

Voters and social communication in a national election

Information streams come in a variety of forms with varying content conveyed through various channels: newspapers, television, and social communication through a wide variety of media – personal conversations at work and over the dinner table; yard signs and bumper stickers on neighborhood lawns and cars; and even interactions with strangers wearing political lapel pins. The political content of these information streams is particularly important, and for illustrative purposes we focus our attention on the social communication that occurs through small groups.

Each respondent to the post-election survey of the 2000 National Election Study (NES) was asked the first names of the people with whom they discussed "government, elections, and politics." After providing these names, they were asked to make a judgment regarding the presidential candidates for whom each of these discussants voted. Hence we have the opportunity to address the respondents' presidential candidate preferences within the context of their perceptions regarding the preferences of their primary political discussants.

Several concerns quite naturally arise regarding the capacity of individuals to make accurate judgments regarding the preferences of others. One possibility is that a false consensus effect might be produced (Fabrigar and Krosnick 1995) in which individuals assume or perceive that associates agree with their own preferences when, in fact, these associates hold divergent views regarding the presidential candidates. Other analyses, from elections in 1984, 1992, and 1996, using a battery of questions very similar to that employed in the 2000 NES (Huckfeldt and Sprague 1995; Huckfeldt et al. 1995; Huckfeldt, Johnson, and Sprague 2004), show that a false consensus effect does in fact exist. Unlike the 2000 NES, these other studies included a snowball component in which the associates of the main respondent were identified as well, thereby making it possible to verify the respondents' perceptions regarding the political preferences of their discussants.

Several properties of the false consensus effect are important. First, it is generated as much by the preferences held by others in the ego's environment as it is by the particular preference of the particular alter. In other words, there is a tendency for individuals to generalize based on their own preferences as well as the preferences of others when discerning the preferences held by a particular associate.

Second, this false consensus bias does not swamp the signal being transmitted, and individuals are generally quite accurate in perceiving the preferences held by others in their political communication networks. Hence we can say that people are communicating real information in real relationships.

Based on the 2000 NES data, Table 22.1 shows the level of diversity within the respondents' political communication networks (Huckfeldt, Johnson, and Sprague 2004). First, there is a tendency toward homophily – Bush voters are less likely to have Gore supporters in their networks, and Gore voters are less likely to have Bush supporters in their networks. At the same time, less than half of the Bush voters report being located in homogeneous Bush networks,

Table 22.1 Level of diversity within political communication networks for the respondents to the 2000 National Election Study; weighted data

	Gore	Neither	Bush
A Percent of network voting for Gore by respondent's vote (unweighted N = 1147)			
None (0%)	14.2%	58.2%	64.3%
Some	44.3%	29.3%	28.5%
All (100%)	41.5%	12.5%	7.2%
Weighted N =	436	268	399
B Percent of network voting for Bush by respondent's vote (unweighted N = 1147)			
None (0%)	63.2%	46.7%	12.6%
Some	32.3%	36.2%	39.9%
All (100%)	4.5%	17.0%	47.5%
Weighted N =	436	268	399

Source: 2000 National Election Study.

Note
Unit of analysis is respondent; weighted data.

and less than half of the Gore voters report being located in homogeneous Gore networks. Additionally, more than one-third of Gore voters had a Bush supporter in their network, and more than one-third of Bush voters had a Gore supporter in their network.

In short, many voters confront a significant level of variance in the political messages they encounter within communication networks, but others encounter a uniform stream of information. Indeed, by virtue of the fact that they are able to provide a generally accurate account regarding the preferences of their associates, they are by definition registering their own awareness regarding these levels of variance.

A question naturally arises: if information is influential, how does disagreement survive within these networks. First, it is important to establish that these networks are not typically constructed as hermeneutically sealed primary groups. To the contrary, some of our friends are not typically the friends of our other friends, and this fact carries important consequences in a number of contexts (Granovetter 1973).

In the current context, it means that Andreas may be a Social Democrat and his friend Bernd may be a Christian Democrat. At the same time, the other friends of Andreas may share his Social Democratic loyalties, and Bernd's other friends may be Christian Democrats. In short, disagreement and disagreeing associates are likely to be the manageable exception rather than the rule. At the same time, Table 22.1 and Huckfeldt, Johnson, and Sprague (2004) show that it is not a rare exception, and it carries important consequences for the social flow of political information, as well as for "socially sustained disagreement" (117ff.). People are imbedded in social environments that emit political signals, but the signals are not uniformly heterogeneous. Many individuals confront a non-constant stream of signals, and individuals tend to recognize the variance within their own social contexts.

Second, political scientists have employed the seven-point party identification battery in interviews with voters for nearly 70 years. A primary virtue of this battery is that it captures the extremity (and implicitly the variance) of an individual's prior partisan judgment regarding candidates and issues. In short, the Equation 2 rendering of Bayesian updating would seem to be a reasonable match to the task that voters address in elections, based on the measures that political scientists have developed to address the problem.

Some of these voters are strong partisans in correspondingly strong partisan contexts – their priors and the stream of information they experience have low levels of variance and point in similar directions. Others have weak priors and are located in networks that send conflicting political messages with high levels of variance. In short, one size does not fit all, but a theoretic construct based on Bayesian updating does not necessarily constitute a dramatic departure from what political psychologists and political behavior scholars have been asserting for quite some time. It is possible to introduce a similar Bayesian logic into a dynamic experimental framework for assessing communication and influence among individuals (Huckfeldt, Pietryka, and Reilly 2014).

Conclusion: social contexts and unintentional Bayesians

Without ever intending to do so, people often act as Bayesian decision-makers. They are likely to make explicit or implicit judgments relative to the precision of their own judgments, as well as to precision of the incoming information – the quality and heterogeneity of the information being offered by newspapers, television, and radio, as well as by other individuals. At the same time, their judgments regarding precision are open to criticism. That is, there is potentially a great deal of variance and perhaps bias in their estimates regarding the quality of their own judgments as well in their estimates regarding the variance in the stream of information upon which they are relying to formulate priors and reach judgments regarding relevant information.

The discussion of citizens as Bayesian decision-makers is too often contingent on an excessively self-conscious model of decision-making. People making everyday decisions – such as their presidential election vote – are unlikely to consider contingent probabilities and likelihoods in arriving at a course of action. They do, however, arrive at implicit assumptions and pre-conscious assessments regarding the reliability of their own subjective attitudes toward the candidates, as well as the pre-conscious judgments regarding the reliability of the new information they are obtaining from the media, from the candidates, and from other voters (Huckfeldt 2007). Indeed, we have seen that the likelihood function is directly related to the ability and willingness of individuals to filter incoming messages based on their own opinions and expectations. In this context, these unintentional Bayesians employ many of the devices typically identified with rationalizing voters.

The same logic and analytic framework helps to explain the status and role of opinion leaders in democratic politics. Two qualities give rise to opinion leadership: the opinion leader's confidence in her own beliefs and opinions, as well as an increased frequency of communication with others about politics (Ahn, Huckfeldt, and Ryan 2014). This increased frequency of communication arises for two reasons. First, people are reassuringly accurate not only in recognizing the political viewpoints of their associates, but also in recognizing their associates' levels of political expertise (Huckfeldt and Sprague 1995; Huckfeldt 2001). Second, those who invest more heavily in political information become more confident in their own opinions as well as becoming more likely to share their opinions with others. Indeed, this investment leads to a preconscious commitment to their own views, frequently making it difficult for them to stay quiet in the collective deliberations of democratic politics!

Finally, in terms of social communication in politics, the most influential new information often arrives via the backdoor through interactions predicated on purposes unrelated to politics. Daily encounters in the family, the workplace, and the neighborhood are unlikely to be carefully screened on the basis of political viewpoints. Thus politically heterogeneous views carry the potential to slip in under the radar with important consequences not only for an individual's political views, but also for their assessments regarding the distribution of opinions in their locally defined environments (Ahn, Huckfeldt, and Ryan 2014; Huckfeldt and Sprague 1995: Chapter 8).

Note

1 The authors are grateful for the very helpful comments of Prof. John Bullock.

References

Ahn, T. K., Huckfeldt, R., and Ryan, J. B. (2014) *Experts, Activists, and Democratic Politics: Are Electorates Self-Educating?*, New York: Cambridge University Press.

Asch, S. E. (1955) "Opinions and Social Pressure," *Scientific American*, vol. 193, no. 5, November, 31–35.

Asch, S. E. (1963) "Effects of Group Pressure Upon the Modification and Distortion of Judgments," in Guetzkow, H. (ed.) *Groups, Leadership and Men: Research in Human Relations*, New York: Russell and Russell: 177–190.

Bartels, L. M. (2002) "Beyond the Running Tally: Partisan Bias in Political Perceptions," *Political Behavior*, vol. 24, no. 2, June, 117–150.

Berelson, B. R., Lazarsfeld, P. F., and McPhee, W. N. (1954) *Voting: A Study of Opinion Formation in a Presidential Election*, Chicago: University of Chicago Press.

Bishop, B. (2008) *The Big Sort: Why the Clustering of Like-Minded America is Tearing Us Apart*, New York: Houghton-Mifflin.

Boydstun, A. E. (2013) *Making the News*, Chicago: University of Chicago Press.

Bullock, J. G. (2009) "Partisan Bias and the Bayesian Ideal in the Study of Public Opinion," *Journal of Politics*, vol. 71, no. 3, July, 1109–1124.

Burt, R. S. (1978) "Cohesion Versus Structural Equivalence as a Basis for Network Subgroups," *Sociological Methodology and Research*, vol. 7, no. 2, November, 189–212.

Butler, D. and Stokes, D. E. (1969) *Political Change in Britain*, London: Macmillan.

Caro, R. (1982) *The Path to Power*, New York: Knopf.

Caro, R. (1990) *Means of Ascent*, New York: Knopf.

Converse, P. E. (1964) "The Nature of Belief Systems in Mass Publics," in Apter, D. E. (ed.) *Ideology and Discontent*, New York: Free Press: 206–261.

Cox, K. R. (1969) "The Voting Decision in a Spatial Context," *Progress in Geography*, vol. 1, no. 1, 81–117.

Dogan, M. and Rokkan, S. (eds.) (1974) *Social Ecology*, Cambridge, MA: MIT Press.

Downs, A. (1957) *An Economic Theory of Democracy*, New York: Harper and Row.

Fabrigar, L. and Krosnick, J. A. (1995) "Attitude Importance and the False Consensus Effect," *Personality and Social Psychology Bulletin*, vol. 21, no. 5, May, 468–479.

Fazio, R. H. (1995) "Attitudes as Object-Evaluation Associations: Determinants, Consequences, and Correlates of Attitude Accessibility," in Petty, R. E. and Krosnick, J. A. (eds.) *Attitude Strength: Antecedents and Consequences*, Hillsdale: Erlbaum: 247–282.

Fieldhouse, E., and Cutts, D. (2012) "The Companion Effect: Household and Local Context and the Turnout of Young People," *Journal of Politics*, vol. 74, no. 3, July, 856–869.

Fieldhouse, E., Cutts, D., John, P., and Widdop, P. (2014) "When Context Matters: Assessing Geographical Heterogeneity of Get-Out-The-Vote Treatment Effects Using a Population Based Field Experiment," *Political Behavior*, vol. 36, no. 1, March, 77–97.

Fieldhouse, E., Lessard-Phillips, L., and Edmonds, B. (2016) "Cascade or Echo chamber? A Complex Agent-Based Simulation of Voter Turnout," *Party Politics*, vol. 22, no. 1, March, 241–256.

Gerber, A. and Green, D. P. (1998) "Rational Learning and Partisan Attitudes," *American Journal of Political Science*, vol. 42, no. 3, July, 794–818.

Granovetter, M. (1973) "The Strength of Weak Ties," *American Journal of Sociology*, vol. 78, no. 6, May, 1360–1380.

Huckfeldt, R. (1983) "Social Contexts, Social Networks, and Urban Neighborhoods: Environmental Constraints on Friendship Choice," *American Journal of Sociology*, vol. 89, no. 3, November, 651–669.

Huckfeldt, R. (2001) "The Social Communication of Political Expertise," *American Journal of Political Science*, vol. 45, no. 2, April, 425–438.

Huckfeldt, R. (2007) "Unanimity, Discord, and the Communication of Public Opinion," *American Journal of Political Science*, vol. 51, no. 4, October, 978–995.

Huckfeldt, R. and Sprague, J. (1988) "Choice, Social Structure, and Political Information: The Informational Coercion of Minorities," *American Journal of Political Science*, vol. 32, no. 2, May, 467–482.

Huckfeldt, R. and Sprague, J. (1995) *Citizens, Politics, and Social Communication: Information and Influence in an Election Campaign*, New York: Cambridge University Press.

Huckfeldt, R., Beck, P. A., Dalton, R. J., and Levine, J. (1995) "Political Environments, Cohesive Social Groups, and the Communication of Public Opinion," *American Journal of Political Science*, vol. 39, no. 4, November, 1025–1054.

Huckfeldt, R., Ikeda, K., and Pappi, F. U. (2005) "Patterns of Disagreement in Democratic Politics: Comparing Germany, Japan, and the United States," *American Journal of Political Science*, vol. 49, no. 3, July, 497–514.

Huckfeldt, R., Johnson, P. E., and Sprague, J. (2004) *Political Disagreement: The Survival of Diverse Opinions within Communication Networks*, New York: Cambridge University Press.

Huckfeldt, R., Levine, J., Morgan, W., and Sprague, J. (1998) "Election Campaigns, Social Communication, and the Accessibility of Discussant Preference," *Political Behavior*, vol. 20, no. 4, December, 263–294.

Huckfeldt, R., Levine, J., Morgan, W., and Sprague, J. (1999) "Accessibility and the Political Utility of Partisan and Ideological Orientations," *American Journal of Political Science*, vol. 43, no. 3, July, 888–911.

Huckfeldt, R., Pietryka, M. T., and Reilly, J. (2014) "Noise, Bias, and Expertise in Political Communication Networks," *Social Networks*, vol. 36, no. 1, January, 110–121.

Johnston, R. (1986) "Places and Votes: The Role of Location in the Creation of Political Attitudes," *Urban Geography*, vol. 7, no. 2, March, 103–117.

Johnston, R. (1999) "Conversation and Electoral Change in British Elections, 1992–1997," *Electoral Studies*, vol. 20, no. 1, March, 17–40.

Johnston, R. and Pattie, C. (2006) *Putting Voters in their Place: Geography and Elections in Great Britain*, Oxford: Oxford University Press.

Key, V. O., Jr. (1949) *Southern Politics in State and Nation*, New York: Vintage Books.

Kunda, Z. (1990) "The Case for Motivated Reasoning," *Psychological Bulletin*, vol. 108, no. 3, November, 480–498.

Langton, K. P. and Rapoport, R. (1975) "Social Structure, Social Context, and Partisan Mobilization: Urban Workers in Chile," *Comparative Political Studies*, vol. 8, no. 3, October, 318–344.

Laumann, E. O. (1973) *Bonds of Pluralism: The Forms and Substance of Urban Social Networks*, New York: Wiley.

Lazarsfeld, P. F., Berelson, B., and Gaudet, H. (1948) *The People's Choice: How the Voter Makes up his Mind in a Presidential Campaign*, New York: Columbia University Press.

Lee, P. M. (2004) *Bayesian Statistics: An Introduction*, 3rd Edition, London: Arnold.

Lodge, M. and Taber, C. A. (2013) *The Rationalizing Voter*, New York: Cambridge University Press.

McPhee, W. N. (1963) *Formal Theories of Mass Behavior*, New York: Free Press.

McPherson, J. M. and Smith-Lovin, L. (1987) "Homophily in Voluntary Organizations: Status Distance and the Composition of Face-to-Face Groups," *American Sociological Review*, vol. 52, no. 3, June, 370–379.

McPherson, J. M., Smith-Lovin, L., and Cook, J. M. (2001) "Birds of a Feather: Homophily in Social Networks," *Annual Review of Sociology*, vol. 27, August, 415–444.

Michels, R. (1911) *Political Parties: A Sociological Study of the Oligarchical Tendencies of Modern Democracy*, New York: Hearst's International Library.

Miller, W. E. (1956) "One-Party Politics and the Voter Revisited," *American Political Science Review*, vol. 50, 707–725.

Miller, W. E. and Stokes, D. E. (1963) "Constituency Influence in Congress," *American Political Science Review*, vol. 57, no. 1, March, 45–56.

Ortega y Gasset, J. (1930) *Revolt of the Masses*, New York: Norton.

Pappi, F. U. (2016) *Die Politikpräferenzen der Wähler und die Wahrnehmung von Parteipositionen als Bedingungen für den Parteienwettbewerb um Wählerstimmen*, Mannheim: Mannheimer Zentrum für Europäische Sozialforschung.

Pattie, C. J., Johnston, R. J., and Fieldhouse, E. (1995) "Winning the Local Vote: The Effectiveness of Constituency Campaign Spending in Great Britain, 1983–1992," *American Political Science Review*, vol. 89, no. 4, December, 969–986.

Ross, L., Bierbrauer, G., and Hoffman, S. (1976) "The Role of Attribution Processes in Conformity and Dissent: Revisiting the Asch Situation," *American Psychologist*, vol. 3, no. 2, February, 148–157.

Rousseau, J-J. (1994) *The Social Contract or the Principles of Political Right*, New York: Oxford University Press. (Original work published 1762.)

Ryan, J. B. (2010) "The Effects of Network Expertise and Biases on Vote Choice," *Political Communication*, vol. 27, no. 1, January, 44–58.

Schumpeter, J. A. (1942) *Capitalism, Socialism, and Democracy*, New York: Harper and Row.

Tam Cho, W. K., Gimpel, J. G., and Hui, I. S. (2013) "Voter Migration and the Geographic Sorting of the American Electorate," *Annals of the Association of American Geographers*, vol. 103, no. 4, 856–870.

Tingsten, H. (1963) *Political Behavior: Studies in Election Statistics*, translated by V. Hammarling, Totowa, NJ: Bedminster. (Originally published in 1937.)

23

PERSUASION AND MOBILIZATION EFFORTS BY PARTIES AND CANDIDATES

Justin Fisher

Introduction

At the heart of any discussion about persuasion and mobilization efforts by parties and candidates is the extent to which campaigns have any significant electoral impact at all. A perusal of the literature on voting behavior and turnout in this volume, for example, could lead one to the conclusion that campaigns are, in fact, little more than a ritual with negligible impact on the outcome of an election. This might seem a bizarre claim – after all, parties and candidates expend a great deal of time, energy and money on campaigning. If they had so little effect, why would they bother? Yet, in any examination of campaign effects, we must first ask two questions: *why might campaigns (not) matter?* And, *will campaigns always be equally (in)effective?*

Holbrook (1996) neatly summarizes key points that are pertinent to the first question. He outlines a series of scenarios where efforts in persuasion and mobilization may or may not be seen as being electorally significant. First, drawing on work going back to Campbell et al.'s *The American Voter*, long-term influences on voting behavior such as partisan identification and socio-demographic effects suggest that campaigning may be less significant. While there may be short-term effects, many voters are likely to behave in accordance with existing predispositions (Holbrook 1996: 6–7). Second, from a different perspective and drawing on V. O. Key's (1966) important work, party performance may be said to be the deciding factor. Here, voters' interpretations of incumbent performance and challenger potential are the deciding factors rather than the self-promotion in campaigns (Holbrook 1996: 8). Third, economic interpretations (which may be related to party performance) may be said to drive electoral popularity. Moreover, as Fiorina (1981) argues, it may be such judgments over time which contribute to the formation of a partisan identification – a form of brand loyalty derived from satisfactory product performance rather than emotional attachment. Finally, there is the principal argument often cited against campaign effects and inspired originally by Lazerfield, Berelson and Gaudet's seminal study (1944: 102–104) – namely that few voters change their minds as a result of campaigns. Rather, that reinforcement is the most likely outcome. Consequently, it is argued that this suggests the relative unimportance of campaigns. Of course, none of these arguments say that campaigns have no effect, rather that their impact will frequently be negligible in terms of electoral impact.

On the other side of the coin, there is a series of arguments that suggest campaigning may be (potentially) effective. First and foremost, we need to challenge the assumption that a lack of change in voting behavior is evidence of the ineffectiveness of campaigns. There is no good reason why a voter's change of mind should be conceived as being any more significant than the reinforcement of both committed and wavering supporters. The down-playing of reinforcement makes no logical sense. To be sure, voter switch may be easier to measure, but the cementing of voter choice is just as significant and, indeed, is more likely to occur. Fundamentally, reinforcement is just as significant as change. Second, while long-term factors such as partisan identification and socio-demographic effects may well limit some of the potential for campaign effects, there is clear evidence in many countries that the intensity of voters' partisan attachments has declined significantly (see, for example, Crewe and Denver 1985; Dalton 2002a). Equally, the impact of socio-demographic factors is weaker, leading in many cases to greater electoral volatility (Pederson 1979; Crewe and Denver 1985; Dalton 2002b; Dalton, Wattenburg and McAllister 2002). Under such conditions, the potential for campaign effects is much greater.

Third, and relatedly, there is some evidence that voter indecision has increased (Holbrook 1996: 12–13; McAllister 2002: 23–27). In Britain, for example, while some may have reservations about the survey question capturing when voters decided how to vote, there has been a clear and consistent increase over time in voters deciding their vote closer to polling day (see Figure 23.1). This also presents greater potential for campaign effects. Fourth, while voters may indeed make electoral judgments on the basis of performance which are ostensibly exogenous to campaigning, there is an argument to be made that long-term party campaigning will act to some degree as a preference shaper of voter judgments. In other words, voters' assessments of party and candidate performance may be endogenous where campaigning occurs over the long term, rather than only in the period immediately before elections.

Overall, therefore, it appears there are good reasons to suggest that campaigns have the potential to deliver electoral impact. The question then becomes an empirical one as to whether they do in fact make any difference to outcomes and, more specifically, under what circumstances these effects are most likely to occur? This latter question is one that has gained increasing attention from those analyzing the persuasion and mobilization efforts by parties and candidates (Cox and Thies 2000; Fisher, Cutts and Fieldhouse, 2011a; Farrell and Schmitt-Beck, 2002).

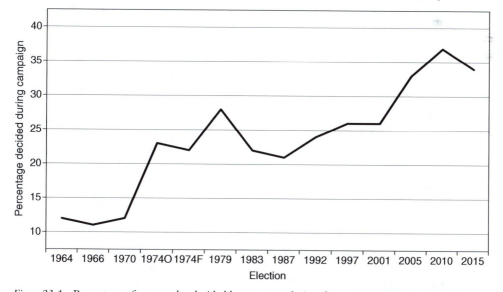

Figure 23.1 Percentage of voters who decided how to vote during the campaign in Britain, 1964–2015

Source: British Election Study

Which campaigns?

When thinking about electoral campaigns, a distinction is usually drawn between national and local (district or constituency) campaigns. Reference is frequently (and still) made to the "ground" and "air" wars: the latter being the national campaigns fought through television, the national press and, increasingly, the internet and social media (see Ward, Gibson and Cantijoch in this volume); the former being the work conducted by activists at the local (district or constituency) level. The distinction between the two levels has never been completely neat and has become increasingly open to challenge (Fisher and Denver 2008). Notwithstanding this blurring of boundaries, it is clear from only a cursory look at the literature that national campaigns have historically been the primary focus of academic attention, especially since the onset of the tele-visual age from the 1950s onwards. Butler and Rose (1960: 120), for example, in their study of the 1959 British general election concluded that "...if all constituency campaigning were abandoned, the national outcome would probably be little altered." Writing ten years later, Dennis Kavanagh (1970: 79) similarly dismissed local efforts as inconsequential, asserting that the main value of the constituency campaign is that it "gives the members something to do. ... It is, for many, the only time they help apart from voting and paying dues." As this chapter makes clear, however, these conclusions about the marginal impact and even death of district-level campaigning have proven to be highly exaggerated.

Demonstrating electoral effects of campaigns at the national level has always presented significant methodological challenges. For example, when is it accurate to say that a campaign has started? What counts as campaign spending and what is "routine"? How do you capture the effects of non-party or non-candidate campaigns – so called "third party" activity? One attempt to tackle some of these questions can be seen in the work of Fisher (1999). In particular, he sought to address the problem of defining a campaign starting point by studying the impact of annual party expenditure on poll ratings over a thirty-five year period. This meant that party popularity was measured on an annual basis rather than just at the time of elections. Furthermore, the use of a more continuous measure of party popularity reduced the bias caused by the omitted effects of "third party" activity, since such efforts would be occurring almost entirely in election years. The results were interesting in that they showed that national campaigns, as captured by annual party expenditure, delivered very little in terms of consistent or sizeable electoral payoffs.

Separate to the problems of accurately measuring the electoral impact of national campaigns, there has been a growing questioning of the assumption that campaign effects are confined to the national level. Indeed, Fisher (2015) has gone so far as to suggest that the national campaign may now be effectively subsumed into district-level activities. Consequently, attention has shifted to measuring the persuasion and mobilization attempts by parties and candidates, and their effects at lower levels of aggregation – districts or constituencies. This switch has also been accompanied by an increasing variation in the range and level of methodological sophistication among the analyses conducted.

Election spending

The most common approach taken to understanding the drivers and consequences of campaigning at the district level has involved the study of election spending by candidates and parties (in part, due to data availability). Gary Jacobson (1978, 1980, 1990) was a pioneer in this regard, using data from US congressional elections to examine whether money was a significant factor in determining the electoral fortunes of candidates. While he hypothesized that spending would matter, his key insight was that it would be of greater significance for challengers than for incumbents. This was based on the logic that *ceteris paribus*, voters will choose to support those candidates about whom they have the most information. Since incumbents can use their office to publicize themselves, they require less publicity – and therefore less funding – during an election campaign. Moreover, incumbents will be likely to spend less if they feel that their re-election is reasonably assured. Conversely a challenger, who has not enjoyed the benefits of incumbent publicity, will have greater need for campaign finance (Jacobson 1980: 36–37). As a result, money spent by challengers should have a greater electoral impact than that spent by incumbents.

While empirical analysis has largely supported his arguments, Jacobson's work has been subject to some criticism. Green and Krasno (1988), for example, contended that incumbent spending was more significant than Jacobson claimed and that challenger spending less so, and subject to diminishing returns. Gerber (1998: 402) also suggested that, while incumbents are likely to be better known and have an information advantage, challengers may also spend money to address new issues that are not on the established political agenda. As a consequence, challengers have the advantage, in theory, of coming to be seen as the champions of a particular cause. On more methodological grounds, Cox and Thies (2000: 41) have claimed that Jacobson's findings about the lower impact of incumbent spending may be due to omitted variable bias.

Notwithstanding these criticisms, Jacobson's main conclusion that candidates' efforts to persuade voters (indicated by their levels of campaign spending) has an electoral payoff has been borne out by further research in the US and other democratic contexts (Benoit and Marsh 2003; Carty and Eagles 1999; Forrest, Johnston and Pattie 1999; Johnston and Pattie 1995; Maddens et al. 2006; Palda and Palda 1998; Pattie, Johnston and Fieldhouse 1995). A key finding from this latter body of work has been that challenger spending has its most beneficial effect in elections that use single member districts rather than proportional representation systems (Sudulich, Wall and Farrell 2013: 771).

Overall, the use of election spending as a measure for campaign intensity has provided some highly compelling findings. However, despite the generally supportive findings, the use of campaign expenditure as a measure of campaign strength is nevertheless potentially problematic. First, as Fisher (1999) observes, the relationship between spending and electoral payoffs depends on an assumption that different candidates or parties will spend with equal degrees of skill. This, of course, can be subject to empirical testing, but suffice to say the assumption that X dollars will buy Y votes is not a robust one. Second, the focus on activity which incurs cost ignores that which does not. Fisher et al. (2014) show, for example, that free campaigning may deliver more in the way of electoral payoffs than candidate spending, and thus a less financially endowed candidate may be able to offset her disadvantage by engaging in more "free" campaigning. As a consequence, while a useful indicator of campaign strength, it is clear that a sole focus on spending is likely to fail to capture a significant amount of non-monetary but highly influential campaign activity.

Measuring district-level campaign effects

Notwithstanding the concerns about the use of campaign spending, a significant comparative literature has developed since the early work of Jacobson, suggesting that campaigning efforts by political parties and candidates impact positively, in terms of both mobilization and turnout (Gerber and Green 2000; Karp, Banducci and Bowler 2007; Hillygus 2005; Marsh 2004, Carty and Eagles 1999). The UK case has been particularly prominent (Clarke et al. 2004, 2009;

Whiteley and Seyd 1994; Whiteley et al. 2013; Pattie, Johnston and Fieldhouse 1995; Denver and Hands 1997; Denver et al. 2003; Fieldhouse and Cutts 2009; Fisher, Cutts and Fieldhouse 2011a; Johnston and Pattie 2014).

Overall, the approaches employed in the comparative literature can be broadly divided into two types: those that rely on individual-level survey data and those relying on aggregate-level indicators of campaign strength (such as campaign spending). In addition, there are also isolated examples that use experimental methods (see, for example, Gerber and Green 2000). Those studies employing individual-level data typically use national or cross-nation election study data and specifically measures of self-reported campaign contact by candidates and parties (see, for example, Karp, Banducci and Bowler 2007; Clarke et al. 2004, 2009; Whiteley et al. 2013). They then examine the extent to which this contact has affected voter decision-making. These approaches have generally indicated that more contacts can deliver positive effects – especially amongst voters who are undecided closer to polling day (Clarke et al. 2004, 2009; Whiteley et al. 2013; Fisher, Cutts and Fieldhouse 2011a).

These individual-level analyses suffer, however, from three significant drawbacks. First, they rely on respondent recall. While respondents may well remember a personal encounter with a candidate or party worker, they are far less likely to accurately recall the number of leaflets they received or how often they were contacted through social media. Leaflets, it is often argued, are as likely (maybe more likely) to go the way of the unsolicited pizza advertisement as they are to be read by voters. Equally, social media sites contain a vast amount of peripheral information which is likely to reduce the accuracy of contact recalled by respondents online. The second problem that studies using individual survey data face is that, for the purposes of measurement, respondents will almost certainly be unable to ascertain the origin of the communication they receive. To be sure, they can tell which party is being promoted, but unless they are familiar with the intricacies of electoral law, will be unaware of whether communication came from the district campaign or the national one. This is, obviously, only a problem for political scientists – not the (potential) voter. However, it illustrates very neatly the ongoing methodological difficulties associated with isolating the effects of campaign activity within a district. The third problem use of these data present is a practical one. To capture the variety of different means of voter contact for all parties running in elections requires a considerable amount of survey space, which is not always available. The 2015 British Election Study, for example, featured more questions than ever before on campaign contacts. Yet, there was still insufficient space to capture some of the main ways voter contact can occur through online channels.

To address some of these problems, scholars have turned to forms of aggregate data that tap into the extent of local party effort and party members' levels of activism. This approach has been particularly prevalent in the UK, first in an important series of studies by Seyd and Whiteley (1992, 1994), making use of party membership survey data to examine the impact of local activism, during and outside of election periods, on parties' electoral fortunes. The authors found that for both Labour and Conservative parties, higher levels of activism had a positive impact on their party's share of the constituency vote. Their analysis thus complemented and enhanced the earlier work of Johnston and Pattie which had focused on expenditure by capturing the impact of pre-campaign and also campaign activity that incurred no cost. Like previous studies, however, it also faced a number of key limitations. First, like expenditure, party activism was a proxy rather than direct measure of actual campaign intensity. Second, given it was an off-shoot of a larger project on party members, the data did not cover all constituencies – particularly in the study of Conservative members (Denver and Hands 1997: 243–245). Finally, as later work revealed, a significant proportion of the labor undertaken in district-level campaigns is typically done by activists who are not themselves party members (Fisher, Fieldhouse and Cutts 2014).

It thus again missed a significant part of the campaign effort that was happening locally. Despite these shortcomings, the analyses using party member data were important in reinforcing the notion that campaigning mattered and could deliver electoral payoffs.

A second approach was pioneered by Denver and Hands (1997) in their study of the 1992 British general election. To capture a fuller picture of campaign intensity, the authors surveyed the individuals responsible for running campaigns at the district level. In the British context, this was the candidates' electoral agent. Denver and Hands devised a set of questions, which captured more than just members' campaign activities and those things that cost money. Rather, the survey captured a range of important factors which contribute to varying levels of campaign intensity: preparation, organization, manpower, use of computers, use of telephones, polling day activity, use of direct mail, level of doorstep canvassing and leafleting. These data had several advantages over the previous types used, the most important of these being that they provided a direct rather than proxy measure of campaign intensity. In addition, the survey captured campaign effort that incurred costs, and those that were delivered for free. Finally, it covered more districts than the study of members.

This approach is, of course, not entirely bias or error free. First, like the studies based on national election survey data, the analyses are based on self-reported responses to a questionnaire. This raises the strong possibility of inflated claims in respect of activity levels. This complaint, however, should be considered against the considerable variance in the levels of campaign intensity that is evident in basic frequency reports from the surveys. Thus, if respondents are inflating their effort by 10 percent, while this may affect the absolute values reported, it does not necessarily affect the relative differences observed between campaigns. Certainly, repeated comparisons between the distribution of campaign effort reported by agents and candidate spending indicate the data are robust. Second, and again similarly to all survey-based methods, there is a missing data problem due to non-response. This has made some analyses that rely on responses for all parties in a given district more challenging, though approaches such as those employed by Fieldhouse and Cutts (2009), which have combined survey and spending data, have helped to alleviate the problem of missing data to a degree.

In step with the findings from previous studies by Johnston and Pattie and Seyd and Whiteley, Denver and Hands showed that more intense constituency campaigning did deliver electoral payoffs. However, they also showed that the effects were not uniform. What was critical was the effective targeting of campaigns. For campaigns to have electoral impact they needed to occur in districts where candidates and parties were either seeking to take a seat or defend it from a realistic challenge. More specifically, it was revealed that both Labour and Liberal Democrat campaigns yielded payoffs, while those run by Conservatives did not. This difference was due primarily to the fact that the latter's strongest campaigns took place in those seats that it held comfortably. The Denver and Hands methodology has been refined over the years to reflect new developments in campaigning (see Fisher, Cutts and Fieldhouse 2011a). Its central finding remains, however. Campaigning at the district level can produce electoral payoffs, but those payoffs will be greater if efforts are properly targeted where they are needed most.

While the study of local level campaigning is most developed in the British case, it is nevertheless striking how the findings are replicated across other countries. Both single country and comparative studies, using a variety of approaches, have reported similar findings, despite variations in electoral systems (see, for example, André and Depauw 2016; Gschwend and Zittel 2015; Karp, Banducci and Bowler 2007; Marsh 2004; Sudulich, Wall and Farrell 2013). The broad universality of results across electoral systems is important, since we might expect targeting to occur mostly in majoritarian systems with single member districts (where the winner takes all in an individual district), rather than more proportional ones (where the relationship between votes and seats may be less dependent on electoral geography). Karp, Banducci and Bowler (2007) and Viñuela, Jurado and Riera (2015), however, demonstrate this is not the case. In line with the expectations of Karp, Banducci and Bowler (2007: 92), parties "expend greater effort on mobilizing voters when the expected benefits of turning out voters are greatest, relative to cost."

Thus far, we have shown that a variety of different methodological approaches applied across a range of different countries support the view that campaigning matters. In general, it seems that well-targeted, more intensive campaigning leads to a stronger electoral performance. In addition to affecting vote choice, there is also evidence to suggest that campaigning can boost turnout. Karp, Banducci and Bowler (2007), for example, in a large N comparative study using survey data find that campaigning does mobilize voters, while Fisher et al. (2016a) and Trumm and Sudulich (2016) show that the same holds in more detailed studies of the British general election of 2010. All three studies, however, also show that there is variation in terms of effects. Karp, Banducci and Bowler (2007) find that campaigning in candidate-based systems is more likely to mobilize voters than in party-based systems – a result they attribute to the fact that levels of party contact in safe seats in countries with single member districts are still higher than in those of countries using proportional representation. Thus, although there does appear to be greater scope for targeting seats in majoritarian systems, this does not necessarily mean that voters in non-target seats are neglected (Trumm and Sudulich 2016: 6). Fisher et al. (2016a) find that campaign effects on turnout vary by party in Britain, with campaigns of less popular parties having the least impact and, in some seats, actually appearing to diminish turnout.

The importance of context

The preceding review makes clear the importance of comparative studies in developing the literature on campaign effects, both across space and time. Essentially this work has provided very convincing evidence to show that any effects are variable and contingent on a range of exogenous factors. While this may seem to be an obvious point, in truth, most studies have failed to progress beyond answering the initial question of *whether campaigns have electoral effects*. Much less attention has been given to the second but equally important question of *whether campaigns are equally effective and under what circumstances*. This latter issue is now fast becoming one of the important new puzzles to occupy those analyzing campaign effects.

Fisher, Cutts and Fieldhouse (2011a), for example, have argued that the effectiveness of a campaign is dependent on four key elements that are exogenous to the campaign effort: the closeness of the election, the likelihood of the election producing significant change, the effectiveness of the targeting that occurs and the level of clarity on the objectives a party has in any election. The first of these elements – the closeness of the election – is likely to increase the impact of the campaign given that voters are more primed or cued to receive party messages. The effects of competitiveness are, however, also moderated by parties' popularity – where parties are not unusually popular or unpopular at the national level – popularity equilibrium within the parties' usual range of support (Fisher, Cutts and Fieldhouse 2011a: 818). If parties are unusually unpopular, the impact of their campaigns is less likely to be decisive since voters will be less receptive to their messages. For more popular parties, the campaign has a more negligible impact since voters typically will already have decided to vote for them. Research using experimental methods has certainly supported the idea that campaign interventions are affected by the level of popularity of the party (Niven 2001; Hillygus 2005; Arceneaux and Nickerson 2009; Fieldhouse et al. 2014). Similarly, in terms of turnout, Karp, Banducci and Bowler (2007: 95–96) have shown that parties in a non-competitive position find it difficult to persuade potential voters to go to the polls. The rationale being that mobilizing in support of such a party is perceived as making very little difference to the outcome.

The second key element linked by Fisher, Cutts and Fieldhouse (2011a) to an effective campaign is the likelihood that the election will lead to a change in the current political status quo. Anticipation of a change of government provides added momentum to the campaign, and particularly for that of the challenger, building a so-called bandwagon effect (Bartels 1988). The logic is that the momentum of challengers where electoral change is likely makes voters more receptive to their message. The third factor they see as increasing the impact of campaigns relates to the extent and type of targeting that takes place. While in general more targeting might be expected to yield stronger electoral benefits, given that resources are finite, logic would suggest that parties targeting a large number of seats would enjoy smaller electoral returns since resources would be diluted, thereby lowering the intensity of individual campaigns. Conversely, targeting fewer seats should produce greater electoral payoffs as the intensity will be better concentrated in those seats that matter most. As with the first factor, however, party popularity – or again unpopularity – is likely to moderate these expectations. Where there is a party that is particularly unpopular, parties that are more popular are likely to see greater dividends in targeting larger numbers of seats. Despite their resources being more diluted and producing a less intense individual campaign, voters will be less receptive to the unpopular parties' campaigning.

The final condition these authors see as boosting campaign effectiveness, independent of level of the effort being made follows on from, and links to, the previous factor. Where the campaign has a strong central management that can efficiently coordinate and direct district efforts then it is better able to set and deliver on its targeting objectives and thus run a more successful campaign. If parties have clear objectives (such as winning a small majority or denying another party a majority, rather than just trying to win as many seats as possible), the electoral benefits are likely to be greater. These second two points are important, because the negative effects of national-level party unpopularity can be countered to a degree if campaigns have clear goals and are appropriately targeted. These four elements are summarized in Table 23.1.

What types of campaigning matter?

As well as understanding the external circumstances under which a campaign is most likely to be effective, it is also important to consider the type of campaign activity that is being undertaken. As we have seen, those studies that focus on a particular activity or set of behaviors, using surrogate measures such as spending or local party member activism, are unlikely to capture the full range of techniques that parties and candidates employ to persuade and mobilize voters. This type of differentiation requires starting with a broader and more abstract classificatory schema.

Drawing upon the developmental narratives and frameworks set out by Norris (2002) and Farrell and Webb (2002), we can identify three broad types of campaigning strategies: traditional,

Table 23.1 Exogenous factors influencing likely effectiveness of constituency campaigns

	More effective campaigns	*Less effective campaigns*
Closeness of election	Popularity equilibrium	Unpopular party(ies)
Significant change likely	Challenger(s)	Incumbent
High numbers of targeted seats	Unpopular party(ies)	Popularity equilibrium
Central management	Clear objectives	Unclear objectives

Source: Fisher, Cutts and Fieldhouse (2011a).

modern and e-campaigning.[1] Traditional campaigns are seen as being characteristic of the early years of competitive elections. They are labor intensive and typically include activities such as leafleting, doorstep canvassing and "last minute" polling day activity to ensure voters make it to the polls. By way of contrast, "modern campaigning" reflects the incorporation of technology into campaigns through the use of computers, specialist campaign software, direct mail and the use of telephones to both canvass voters and remind them to vote. A third and more recent development refers to the integration of email, internet and social media into campaign communication and the associated increasing specificity and personalized quality of that contact (see Ward, Gibson and Cantijoch in this volume).

Differentiating campaigns in this way is important for two principal reasons. First, it helps us understand how campaigning styles have developed over time, and reminds us that they will continue to do so. This particularly applies in respect of the adoption of technology, where developments are often rapidly superseded by newer or alternative technologies. As a consequence, it makes little sense to assume that what is used in past campaigns will automatically be used in subsequent ones. Second, we can extend the analysis to look at voters' responses to each campaigning mode and how far they are likely to have an effect on their decision to turn out and also on whom to support.

To date, the findings about the electoral effects of the broad categories of traditional, modern and e-campaigning have shown some differences across types. Of course, in the "real world" no candidate or party campaign is exclusively traditional, modern or electronic, just as no campaign is either based solely on spending or free work. Furthermore, if a candidate or a party engages in intense traditional campaigning, it is likely that they will also engage in intense modern campaigning, too. It is thus almost impossible to completely isolate the effects of any particular approach. Nonetheless, some convincing attempts to try to measure the relative effects of engaging in more or less traditional, modern or electronic campaigning has been undertaken. The results show that voters do respond to all three types of *stimuli*, with positive responses becoming more common as an approach becomes entrenched. The findings with regard to e-campaigning are mixed, with some studies reporting a significant boost to candidate support if they engage in such activity (D'Alessio 1997; Gibson and McAllister 2011; Sudulich and Wall 2010), whereas others have struggled to find much in the way of positive electoral effects (Fisher, Cutts and Fieldhouse 2011b; Fisher et al. 2016b; Hansen and Kosiara-Pederson 2014). By way of contrast, the findings for the effectiveness of traditional campaigning methods in securing votes are subject to no such debate (Sudulich and Wall 2011; Fisher et al. 2014; Fisher et al. 2016b). Voters may respond to many cues, but respond best to human contact.

Finally, it is worth saying something about diversification of methods used and campaign effectiveness. While few, if any, campaigns rely exclusively on one type of activity, the range of methods that are used varies considerably. Sudulich and Wall (2011) examined the extent to which a greater diversification of methods paid off electorally for candidates in the Irish general election of 2007. Analyzing candidate spending returns they found a positive electoral impact of diversification when it was accompanied by a significant monetary investment. Candidates with lower budgets were found to be more successful if they diversified less and focused instead on doing a few things well rather than several things poorly (Sudulich and Wall 2011: 98). This matters, because it shows that there is no "one size fits all" in respect to campaign effects. Campaigns are more or less electorally effective depending on context, just as diverse campaigns are more or less successful depending upon the level of available resources.

Conclusions

The decline in the intensity of group and voter attachment to parties has created significant potential for campaign effects. In this chapter, we have shown how a range of studies, conducted in different electoral settings and using different types of data, have supported the idea that campaigns are now filling the gap that those more fixed forces once occupied. At the district level in particular, it has been shown that campaigning can increase turnout and deliver electoral payoffs for particular parties. Given this well-established finding, attention is now switching to looking at differential campaign effects and identifying the circumstances under which campaigns are more or less effective.

At the party or candidate level this seems to come down – in part – to one's status as a challenger or incumbent. Overall or general popularity, however, also matters. It is much more difficult for a party to campaign effectively if that party is already unpopular since voters will be less receptive to any messages they send. Equally, highly popular parties or candidates will also have less effective campaigns, since voters are already likely to plan on voting for them. At the macro level then, the wider political and institutional context matters. Campaigns do not take place in a vacuum. The electoral environment and the degree to which campaigns are properly coordinated and planned are key variables in determining the likelihood of delivering payoffs. Campaign efforts matter; but they don't matter equally all of the time.

Finally, we have made the point that campaigns are multi-faceted and operate across different levels and in different modes. A contemporary campaign will use cutting-edge technology alongside old-fashioned personal contact – indeed increasingly they may try to integrate the two together, blurring the boundaries and creating new hybrid forms of voter mobilization. However, it remains worth stressing that the mere existence of a new approach does not guarantee it will be electorally successful. Voters take time to become accustomed to new forms of contact and not all are successful in the longer term. Certainly one method that has stood the test of time is that of human contact. Indeed, such is the continuing importance of human contact that it makes less sense to speak of campaigns following an inevitable linear path of evolution, and more sense to say that, whatever happens, human contact forms the most important part of campaigns. Rather, it is the supporting cast of technology that evolves.

Note

1 The frameworks set out by Norris (2002) and Farrell and Webb (2002) were originally developed to capture developments in national-level campaigning. Fisher and Denver (2008) develop these frameworks to better reflect developments in district-level campaigning.

References

André, A. and Depauw, S. (2016) "The Electoral Impact of Grassroots Activity in the 2012 Local Elections in Flanders," *Acta Politica*, vol. 51, no. 2, April, 131–352.

Arceneaux, K. and Nickerson, D. W. (2009) "Who is Mobilized to Vote? A Re-Analysis of Eleven Randomized Field Experiments," *American Journal of Political Science*, vol. 53, no. 1, January, 1–16.

Bartels, L. M. (1988) *Presidential Primaries and the Dynamics of Public Choice*, Princeton: Princeton University Press.

Benoit, K. and Marsh, M. (2003) "For a Few Euros More: Campaign Spending Effects in the Irish Local Elections of 1999," *Party Politics*, vol. 9, no. 5, September, 561–582.

Butler, D. E. and Rose, R. (1960) *The British General Election of 1959*, London: MacMillan.

Carty, K. R. and Eagles, D. M. (1999) "Do Local Campaigns Matter? Campaign Spending, the Local Canvass and Party Support in Canada," *Electoral Studies*, vol. 18, no. 1, March, 69–87.

Clarke, H. D., Sanders, D., Stewart, M. C. and Whiteley, P. (2004) *Political Choice in Britain*, Oxford: Oxford University Press.

Clarke, H. D., Sanders, D., Stewart, M. C. and Whiteley, P. F. (2009) *Performance Politics and the British Voter*, Cambridge: Cambridge University Press.

Cox, G. W. and Thies, M. F. (2000) "How Much Does Money Matter? Buying Votes in Japan, 1967–1990," *Comparative Political Studies*, vol. 33, no. 1, February, 37–57.

Crewe, I. and Denver, D. (1985) (eds.) *Electoral Change in Western Democracies*, Basingstoke: Croom Helm.

D'Alessio, D. W. (1997) "Use of the Web in the 1996 US Election," *Electoral Studies*, vol. 16, no. 4, December, 489–501.

Dalton, R. (2002a) "The Decline of Party Identifications," in Dalton, R. and Wattenburg, M. (eds.) *Parties Without Partisans: Political Change in Advanced Industrial Democracies*, Oxford: Oxford University Press: 19–36.

Dalton, R., (2002b) "Political Cleavages, Issues and Electoral Change," in LeDuc, L., Niemi, R. G. and Norris, P. (eds.) *Comparing Democracies 2*, London: Sage: 189–209.

Dalton, R., Wattenburg, M. and McAllister, I. (2002) "The Consequences of Partisan Dealignment," in Dalton, R. and Wattenburg, M. (eds.) *Parties Without Partisans: Political Change in Advanced Industrial Democracies*, Oxford: Oxford University Press: 64–76.

Denver, D. and Hands, G. (1997) *Modern Constituency Electioneering: Local Campaigning at the 1992 General Election*, London: Frank Cass.

Denver, D., Hands, G., Fisher, J. and MacAllister, I. (2003) "Constituency Campaigning in Britain 1992–2001: Centralisation and Modernisation," *Party Politics*, vol. 9, no. 5, September, 541–559.

Farrell, D. M. and Schmitt-Beck, R. (2002) *Do Political Campaigns Matter?* London: Routledge.

Farrell, D. M. and Webb, P. (2002) "Political Parties as Campaign Organisations," in Dalton, R. J. and Wattenburg, M. (eds.) *Parties without Partisans: Political Change in Advanced Industrial Democracies*, Oxford: Oxford University Press: 102–128.

Fieldhouse, E. and Cutts, D. (2009) "The Effectiveness of Local Party Campaigns in 2005: Combining Evidence from Campaign Spending and Agent Survey Data," *British Journal of Political Science*, vol. 39, no. 2, April, 367–388.

Fieldhouse, E., Cutts, D., John, P. and Widdop, P. (2014) "When Context Matters: Assessing Geographical Heterogeneity of Get-Out-The-Vote Treatment Effects Using a Population Based Field Experiment," *Political Behavior*, vol. 36, no. 1, March, 77–97.

Fiorina, M. (1981) *Retrospective Voting in American National Elections*, New Haven: Yale University Press.

Fisher, J. (1999) "Party Expenditure and Electoral Prospects: A National Level Analysis of Britain," *Electoral Studies*, vol. 18, no. 4, December, 519–532.

Fisher, J. (2015) "Party Finance: The Death of the National Campaign?," *Parliamentary Affairs*, vol. 68, Supplement 1, 133–153.

Fisher, J. and Denver, D. (2008) "From Foot-Slogging to Call Centres and Direct Mail: A Framework for Analysing the Development of District-Level Campaigning," *European Journal of Political Research*, vol. 47, no. 6, October, 794–826.

Fisher, J., Cutts, D. and Fieldhouse, E. (2011a) "The Electoral Effectiveness of Constituency Campaigning in the 2010 British General Election: The 'Triumph' of Labour," *Electoral Studies*, vol. 30, no. 4, December, 816–828.

Fisher, J., Cutts, D. and Fieldhouse, E. (2011b) "Constituency Campaigning in 2010," in Wring, D. (eds.) *Political Communication in Britain: TV Debates, the Media and the Election*, Basingstoke: Palgrave: 198–217.

Fisher, J., Cutts, D., Fieldhouse, E. and Rotweiller, B. (2016b) "The Evolution of District-Level Campaigning in Britain: The Resilience of Traditional Campaigning?," Paper presented at the 2016 Annual Conference of the American Political Science Association, Philadelphia, September 1–4.

Fisher, J., Fieldhouse, E. and Cutts, D. (2014) "Members are Not the Only Fruit: Volunteer Activity in British Political Parties at the 2010 General Election," *The British Journal of Politics and International Relations*, vol. 16, no. 1, February, 75–95.

Fisher, J., Fieldhouse, E., Cutts, D., Johnston, R. and Pattie, C. (2016a) "Is All Campaigning Equally Positive? The Impact of District Level Campaigning on Voter Turnout at the 2010 British General Election," *Party Politics*, vol. 22, no. 2, March, 215–226.

Fisher, J., Johnston, R., Cutts, D., Pattie, C. and Fieldhouse, E. (2014) "You Get What You (Don't) Pay For: The Impact of Volunteer Labour and Candidate Spending at the 2010 British General Election," *Parliamentary Affairs*, vol. 67, no. 4, October, 804–824.

Forrest, J., Johnston, R. and Pattie, C. (1999) "The Effectiveness of Constituency Campaign Spending in Australian State Elections During Times of Electoral Volatility: The New South Wales Case, 1988–95," *Environment and Planning*, vol. 31, no. 6, June, 1119–1128.

Gerber, A. (1998) "Estimating the Effect of Campaign Spending on Senate Election Outcomes Using Instrumental Variables," *American Political Science Review*, vol. 92, no. 2, June, 401–412.

Gerber, A. S. and Green, D. P. (2000) "The Effects of Personal Canvassing, Telephone Calls, and Direct Mail on Voter Turnout: A Field Experiment," *American Political Science Review*, vol. 94, no. 3, September, 653–664.

Gibson, R. K. and McAllister, I. (2011) "Do Online Election Campaigns Win Votes? The 2007 Australian 'YouTube' Election," *Political Communication*, vol. 28, no. 2, April, 227–244.

Green, D. P. and Krasno, J. S. (1988) "Salvation for the Spendthrift Incumbent: Reestimating the Effects of Campaign Spending in House Elections," *American Journal of Political Science*, vol. 32, no. 4, November, 884–907.

Gschwend, T. and Zittel, T. (2015) "Do Constituency Candidates Matter in German Federal Elections? The Personal Vote as an Interactive Process," *Electoral Studies*, vol. 39, September, 338–349.

Hansen, K. M. and Kosiara-Pedersen, K. (2014) "Cyber-Campaigning in Denmark: Application and Effects of Candidate Campaigning," *Journal of Information Technology and Politics*, vol. 11, no. 2, February, 206–219.

Hillygus, D. S. (2005) "Campaign Effects and the Dynamics of Turnout Intention in Election 2000," *Journal of Politics*, vol. 66, no. 1, February, 50–68.

Holbrook, T. M. (1996) *Do Campaigns Matter?*, London: Sage.

Jacobson, G. (1978) "The Effects of Campaign Spending in Congressional Elections," *American Political Science Review*, vol. 72, no. 2, June, 469–491.

Jacobson, G. C. (1980) *Money in Congressional Elections*, New Haven, Yale University Press.

Jacobson, G. C. (1990) "The Effects of Campaign Spending in House Elections: New Evidence for Old Arguments," *American Journal of Political Science*, vol. 34, no. 2, May, 334–362.

Johnston, R. and Pattie, C. (1995) "The Impact of Spending on Party Constituency Campaigns in Recent British General Elections," *Party Politics*, vol. 1, no. 2, April, 261–273.

Johnston, R. J. and Pattie, C. J. (2014) *Money and Electoral Politics: Local Parties and Funding at General Elections*, Bristol: The Policy Press.

Karp, J. A., Banducci, S. and Bowler, S. (2007) "Getting Out the Vote: Party Mobilization in a Comparative Context," *British Journal of Political Science*, vol. 38, no. 1, January, 91–112.

Kavanagh, D. (1970) *Constituency Electioneering in Britain*, London: Longmans Green & Co.

Key, V. O. (1966) *The Responsible Electorate*, Cambridge, MA: Belknap.

Lazerfield, P., Berelson, B. and Gaudet, H. (1944) *The People's Choice*, New York: Duell, Sloane & Pearce.

Maddens, B., Wauters, B., Noppe, J. and Fiers, S. (2006) "Effects of Campaign Spending in an Open List PR System: The 2003 Legislative Elections in Flanders/Belgium," *West European Politics*, vol. 29, no. 1, January, 161–168.

Marsh, M. (2004) "None of that Post-Modern Stuff Around Here: Grassroots Campaigning in the 2002 Irish General Election," *British Elections and Parties Review*, vol. 14, 245–267.

McAllister, I. (2002) "Calculating or Capricious? The New Politics of Late Deciding Voters," in Farrell, D. M and Schmitt-Beck, R. (eds.) *Do Political Campaigns Matter?*, London: Routledge: 22–40.

Niven, D. (2001) "The Limits of Mobilization: Turnout Evidence from State House Primaries," *Political Behavior*, vol. 23, no. 4, December, 335–350.

Norris, P. (2002) "Campaign Communications," in LeDuc, L., Niemi, R. G. and Norris, P. (eds.) *Comparing Democracies 2*, London: Sage: 127–147.

Palda, F. and Palda, K. (1998) "The Impact of Campaign Expenditures on Political Competition in the French Legislative Elections of 1993," *Public Choice*, vol. 94, no. 1, January, 157–174.

Pattie, C. J., Johnston, R. J. and Fieldhouse, E. A. (1995) "Winning the Local Vote: The Effectiveness of Constituency Campaign Spending in Great Britain, 1983–1992," *American Political Science Review*, vol. 89, no. 4, December, 969–983.

Pederson, M. N. (1979) "The Dynamics of European Party Systems: Changing Patterns of Electoral Volatility," *European Journal of Political Research*, vol. 7, no. 1, March, 1–27.

Seyd, P. and Whiteley, P. (1992) *Labour's Grass Roots*, Oxford: Clarendon Press.

Sudulich, M. L. and Wall, M. (2010) " 'Every Little Helps': Cyber-Campaigning in the 2007 Irish General Election," *Journal of Information Technology and Politics*, vol. 7, no. 4, 340–355.

Sudulich, L. and Wall, M. (2011) "How Do Candidates Spend Their Money? Objects of Campaign Spending and the Effectiveness of Diversification," *Electoral Studies*, vol. 30, no. 1, March, 91–101.

Sudulich, L., Wall, M. and Farrell, D. M. (2013) "Why Both Campaigning? Campaign Effectiveness in the 2009 European Parliament Elections," *Electoral Studies*, vol. 32, no. 4, December, 768–778.

Trumm, S. and Sudulich, L. (2016) "What Does It Take to Make it to the Polling Station? The Effects of Campaign Activities on Electoral Participation," *Party Politics*, available online: http://journals.sagepub.com/doi/abs/10.1177/1354068816647209.

Viñuela, E. G., Jurado, I. and Riera, P. (2015) *Allocating Campaign Effort in Proportional Systems: Evidence from Spanish General Elections*, Unpublished Manuscript, Universidad Complutense de Madrid.

Whiteley, P. and Seyd, P. (1994) "Local Party Campaigning and Electoral Mobilization in Britain," *Journal of Politics*, vol. 56, no. 1, February, 242–251.

Whiteley, P., Clarke, H. D., Sanders, D. and Stewart, M. C. (2013) *Affluence, Austerity and Electoral Change in Britain*, Cambridge: Cambridge University Press.

24

CAMPAIGN STRATEGIES, MEDIA, AND VOTERS

The fourth era of political communication

Holli A. Semetko and Hubert Tworzecki

A number of interrelated developments have transformed election campaigns and, taken together, have ushered in a new, fourth, era in political communication. Advancing technology and the new uses to which it is put in campaigns and elections is a key feature of this fourth era, which can be distinguished from the influential three-era framework of political communication of the late 1990s and early 2000s (Farrell, 1996; Farrell and Webb, 2000; Norris, 2000; Schmitt-Beck and Farrell, 2002). The fourth era began to take shape with the rapid growth of social media from the mid-2000s.

From the perspective of advancing technology and the new uses to which it is put in campaigns and elections, three major developments distinguish the fourth era of political communication from the previous eras. One development is the rise of "big data": a massive increase in the volume of electronically stored information about individuals, households and geographical units such as postal code zones, along with the hardware, tools and analytical techniques for deploying this information in campaign settings. A second major development is the turn toward news consumption via social media, which on the one hand has had a profoundly democratizing effect in that it gave an unprecedentedly large number of people a means of joining in national political discourse, but on the other hand – and, paradoxically, with ominous consequences for democracy – it has diminished the fact-checking and gate-keeping roles once played by political and media elites, giving free and very visible reign to falsehood, incivility and outright hate speech. An important related development is the impact of big data analytics on news flows, and the realization by key actors that these news flows can be gamed, including by what Howard (2012) calls "computational propaganda," meaning automated "bots" and other algorithms that can catapult a message into a heralded "viral" or "trending" status that then feeds traditional news agendas. The third major development is "globalization" of campaigning, not only in the sense of growing similarity of strategies and techniques used throughout the world and across a wide range of economic, cultural and political contexts, but also in the sense of growing trans-national circulation of money, personnel, know-how and other campaign resources. While in the past this had usually meant Western (especially American) influence spreading to other countries, now-adays it can also mean the expertise and resources of non-democratic states being deployed in the West. An especially prominent example was Russia's use of hackers during the 2016 US pres-idential election, a development described by the head of the National Security Agency as a "conscious effort by a nation-state to achieve a specific effect" (The Wall Street Journal, 2016).

The opportunities and challenges for candidates and parties on the campaign trail in this fourth era of political communication can be found in more countries, and among more political parties, than ever before. This is not only because of the global spread of technology to lower-income countries, but also because of the growth in the number of countries holding multi-party election campaigns, which now includes many states governed by what political scientists describe as "competitive authoritarian" regimes (Levitsky and Way, 2010).

Our discussion of the fourth era in political communication includes examples from recent campaigns in higher-income democracies in North America and Europe, India, a lower-income country with a rapidly growing economy, and Russia as an example of a competitive authoritarian regime. Across each of these contexts, the evidence points to growing sophistication among campaign strategists worldwide in the use of online tools for gathering voter data, managing campaign resources, mobilizing voters, rapidly generating new (mis)information and enhancing the effectiveness of political communication.

The eras of political campaigning

Periodizations that refer to several distinct "eras" of political campaigning began to appear in the literature around twenty years ago. Farrell (1996) and, later, Farrell and Webb (2000) and Schmitt-Beck and Farrell (2002) proposed that we ought to think about eras broadly corresponding to the newspaper age, the television age and the (then just emerging) digital age. A similar argument was made by Norris (2000), who identified pre-modern, modern and post-modern eras of campaigning and later redefined these as people-intensive, broadcast-based and internet-based eras (Norris, 2005). In all of these frameworks, each era was defined by a combination of factors including the organization of political parties, the nature of social and partisan alignments, the available technology of communication, the prevailing techniques of coordination, mobilization and feedback-gathering, as well as factors such as campaign costs, duration, staffing patterns and so forth.

In the case of the United states, the first era, spanning about a century and ending around 1950, relied on partisan printed press and, later, radio broadcasts, combined with "whistle-stop" tours by leaders and mostly decentralized campaigning operations, involving rallies and doorstep canvassing, ran by local activists. During the second era, from the 1950s to mid-1980s, parties and candidates relied heavily on being featured in news programs on network television (which back then was generally speaking non-partisan) for political messaging and campaign communication. The second era was also characterized by more centralization and greater professionalization of campaigns, which in turn entailed longer duration and rising costs. The third era – from the late 1980s to late 1990s – was that of the "permanent campaign," characterized by "narrowcasting" of messages through direct mail and targeted television advertising and a return to decentralization, but with a vastly greater role (compared to the first era) played by professional consultants, pollsters and marketing specialists, all against the backdrop of dealigning electorates and fragmenting audiences as deregulation and new technologies – cable, satellite and early internet – led to a great expansion in the number of media outlets. Timing differences aside, this framework also applies to many other democracies besides the US.

The fourth era represents an evolutionary development and not a revolutionary break with the past. Some aspects – like the fact that campaigns are now heavily professionalized, expensive and pretty much permanent – are not changing. However, a number of features set the fourth era apart from its predecessor. As with the previous transitions, technological innovation is a big part of this evolutionary story, and in the case of the fourth era it involves new campaigning tools, techniques and capabilities opened up by the rise of "big data" technologies on the one hand and the rise of social media as news distribution channels on the other. While it is true that social media have empowered ordinary citizens and made it possible for a much greater diversity of voices to be heard, in combination with big data they have also given campaign professionals the means of identifying potential supporters and bombarding them with messages with far greater precision than ever before, while at the same time giving them greater freedom to play fast and loose with the facts. In this world of "post-truth politics" (Viner, 2016), the line between factual information and opinion is increasingly blurred, and the recipients of campaign messages, ensconced in "information bubbles" courtesy of individually-tailored news feeds delivered to them by social media platforms, are not likely to encounter either authoritative corrections to deliberately spread falsehoods, or indeed any other information inconsistent with their tastes, sensibilities and political commitments.

And, last but by no means least, what makes the fourth era distinct is that political campaigning techniques have gone global in a way that was not the case in the past. In contrast to previous decades, these days almost all countries – even those run by strongman dictators – hold elections that superficially look the same as in democracies, use many of the same technologies of communication and mobilization, and sometimes are even managed by the very same professional advisors who also work in democracies. However, far from representing a de facto capitulation of authoritarianism to democratic norms, the fourth era has also been characterized by increasingly widespread use of manipulation and misinformation techniques in campaigning originally developed in authoritarian settings. This development stands in sharp contrast to past eras during which observers noticed – in the alleged worldwide "Americanization" of campaign techniques (Plasser, 2000) – that know-how was spreading in one direction only.

Political campaigns and big data

We begin with a look at one set of consequences of technological change for political campaigning, namely the rapidly falling costs of digital storage, along with the development of hardware and software capable of analyzing vast quantities of information about individuals, households and geographical units such as electoral districts or postal code zones. Of course, various forms of mass-scale data collection and processing have existed for decades, and arguably can be traced all the way back to the use of paper punch cards in the 1890 US census. But data storage remained limited and expensive well into the modern era, and even during the 1970s and 1980s the mainframe computers of that period had to make do with reel-to-reel tape drives that could hold only about 200 megabytes per tape. In practical terms, this meant that, although some experimentation with new campaigning tools such as computer databases of donors, voters or volunteers began back in the 1970s, it was only about twenty years ago when large-scale deployment of these new technologies became both economically and technologically viable.

Moves toward the use of "big data" in election campaigns began in the 1990s, first in the United States, then in other industrial democracies, and finally in other parts of the world. The United States was a frontrunner in these efforts for a number of reasons. Under US election laws, candidates and parties must overwhelmingly rely on private rather than public financing, which has meant that the demands of fundraising have been among the major drivers of technological innovation, closely followed by the ever-present need to maximize the efficiency of GOTV (get-out-the-vote) efforts across large geographical areas with relatively low population densities. In the mid-1990s, both major US parties began to put together national databases of potential supporters by compiling information from voter registration files, census records, membership lists of issue advocacy organizations (NRA, AARP and so forth), supplementing it with commercially-available data on income, assets and even shopping habits from credit-reporting agencies. The Help America Vote Act (HAVA), passed by Congress in 2002, and requiring states to maintain computerized, state-wide voter registration lists (which are considered public records and are made available to campaigns), helped to speed these efforts along. In the event, the Republican Party's project called Voter Vault was ready by 2002. The Democrats' big data initiatives were called Demzilla and DataMart, and were first used in the 2004 presidential election (Gertner, 2004). In 2008 and 2012, the Democrats contracted with Catalist, a company that served the Obama campaign and most of the party's campaigns at various levels, along with affiliated organizations and interest groups. Catalist maintains a continually updated national database of voters, in which each voter is listed with more than 700 predicted characteristics. The targeting database is most actively used by competitive campaigns across House, Senate and gubernatorial races for large-scale canvassing operations (Hersh, 2015). Catalist also partners with NGP-VAN (Voter Activation Network), which gathers the data to provide an easily accessible portal for campaign strategists. Last but not least, the past several years have seen the entry into this market of private firms that sell individual-level data as a commercial product. Some of these firms (e.g., Nationbuilder) are non-partisan and make their services available to anyone, from national political campaigns to local community activists. Others, like Cambridge Analytica (CA), which in 2016 was retained by the Trump campaign and the Brexit "leave" campaign, specialize in targeting only one side of the political spectrum. According to press reports, CA claims to have: "as many as 3,000 to 5,000 data points on each of us, be it voting histories or full-spectrum demographics – age, income, debt, hobbies, criminal histories, purchase histories, religious leanings, health concerns, gun ownership, car ownership, homeownership – from consumer-data giants," and in the 2016 US presidential campaign used these data to produce "microtargeted" Facebook ads, such as those intended to depress turnout in selected areas, such as in "Miami's Little Haiti neighborhood with messages about the Clinton Foundation's troubles in Haiti..." (Funk, 2016).

Despite these technological advances, well into the 2000s many American campaigns for national or high-level state office continued to be run in a fairly traditional mold by professional consultants skeptical of (or not trained in) quantitative, data-driven approaches. In any case, the avalanche of data that was becoming available at the time could not be fully exploited because the necessary "predictive analytics" algorithms aimed at identifying the most persuadable voters had not yet been developed or tested (Nickerson and Rogers, 2014). Indeed, it was not until 2008 when Barack Obama's presidential campaign fully utilized data-driven strategies to engage citizens (Stromer-Galley, 2014). Yet, as Hersh (2015) reveals, these first data-driven campaigns were far more successful at mobilizing existing supporters than at persuading new or undecided voters. And as Rasmus Kleis Nielsen (2012) demonstrates, grassroots door-to-door canvassing and fundraising continued to be very important in Barack Obama's 2008 and 2012 campaigns.

Similar technological advances have been taking place in campaigns in other countries. For example, the Conservative Party in Britain purchased the Voter Vault software from the Republicans and used it for planning campaign activities during the 2005 general election. At roughly the same time, the Labour Party and the Liberal Democrats created their own, in-house data/software products (Foster, 2010). Comparable efforts have been under way for over a decade in Canada, with the Liberals, Conservatives and the NDP all starting to develop voter databases in the mid-2000s. In India's 2014 national election, in contrast to the incumbent center-left Indian National Congress (INC) Party that campaigned largely as in past elections in terms of their use of social media, which was not part of their strategy, the opposition center-right Bharatiya Janata Party (BJP) announced in 2013 that it had identified 160 constituencies ripe for a digital strategy.

The BJP's new digital campaign cell implemented that strategy supported by online donations, many from Indians living abroad, and made social media another layer of strategic messaging beyond the traditional advertising and campaigning budget. The BJP not only won in these digital constituencies, the party also came into office with an unprecedented absolute majority of seats.

As is often the case with rapidly advancing technologies, the development of safeguards against potential misuse – including appropriate standards for data security, voter privacy, transparency about what data are gathered and how they are used – has lagged behind. At the time of writing, the story of how state-sponsored Russian hackers breached the Democratic Party's voter databases for the presumed purpose of meddling in the 2016 US presidential election is front-page news (Lichtblau, 2016), having incidentally revealed not only the weakness of existing regulatory frameworks for keeping this kind of information safe but also the problematic cybersecurity infrastructure. Such legislation as does currently exist in this area has been crafted with little publicity by politicians and, rather unsurprisingly, tends to reflect their priorities. As Hersh (2015) argues, US politicians are particularly interested in enhancing their micro-targeting capabilities by designing legislation to build better databases for future campaigns. Indeed in one of the rapid post-election assessments on the most recent 2015 Canadian election, Steve Patten (2015, p. 15) points out that party databases are not governed by Canada's privacy laws, and argues that:

> data-driven micro-targeting shifts the focus of partisan campaigns from the work of public persuasion and the building of a national consensus toward what could be described as manipulative exercises in private persuasion ... [and therefore is] not making a positive contribution to Canadian democracy.

The social media revolution

The internet and social media in particular have also transformed political campaigning in recent years. It is of course true that in some versions of the three-era framework, such as in Norris (2005), the third era was recast as the era of the internet. However, at the time – the first half of the first decade of the twenty-first century, prior to the rise of social media as a mass phenomenon – online campaign communications mostly involved broadcast-style "one-to-many" message flows from media outlets and party/candidate websites to audiences of news consumers. What has changed since then – and what warrants the claim that a new, fourth era of campaigning is at hand – is the rising importance of social media platforms (Facebook, Twitter and their counterparts in other countries) as content delivery mechanisms for political news and information. Crucially, these mechanisms have empowered, albeit in different ways, both the political and media elites and the general public.

For the elites – and this is where the "big data" and social media aspects of the story meet – the change is mostly about the "analytics": the ability to gain precise knowledge of what content people actually like to consume, and to deliver more of the same in an individually-tailored manner. As one internet media company CEO put it in a widely-quoted phrase, the key thing to keep in mind about this brave new world of communication is "not the immediacy of it, or the low costs, but the measurability" (Petre, 2015). For media companies, measurability – knowing exactly who clicks on what content, and linking it to information about his or her income, place of residence and so on – is important because it helps to increase market share in targeted demographic groups, which in turn helps to sell advertising. For politicians and campaign professionals, measurability is important because it generates instant feedback and lets them fine-tune their messages and deliver them with unprecedented precision to the kinds of voters (e.g., "undecideds" in competitive districts) whose support will matter the most on polling day.

As for the general public, compared to past eras, social media platforms now provide vastly greater opportunities for individuals and groups to participate in a broad range of political activities. Today's national election campaigns feature a diversity of voices and opinions unimaginable two decades ago, and can be experienced in a more immediate, participatory sense by anyone with an internet connection. Furthermore, social media platforms have transformed election campaigns by lessening the perceived distance between politicians and their constituents by allowing citizens to correspond with prominent political figures directly (e.g. via Twitter), publicly and in near real time. Yet another consequence has been the way in which campaign communication environments have been transformed by the near-total disappearance of barriers to entry into the world of broadly-defined political journalism, so that nowadays almost literally anyone – regardless of background, formal education or knowledge of politics – can contribute to national discussion of broadly-defined public affairs in ways that range from recording a YouTube video, to writing a blog entry, to "sharing" somebody else's post with one's Facebook friends.

However, although the social media revolution has produced tangible benefits for both elites and ordinary citizens, its overall impact could ultimately prove deleterious to everyone and, indeed, to the well-being of democracy itself. There is growing evidence that the kind of information people consume online is increasingly a function of what appears in their personal news feeds, because it is either shared with them by their friends or is generated automatically by algorithms that push "trending" stories. This model of communication leads to two kinds of problems: first, it can give rapid and widespread visibility to outright falsehoods – such as the story that Pope Francis endorsed Donald Trump's candidacy, which was shared almost a million times on Facebook (Isaac, 2016) – planted either as pranks, as a way to make money from page clicks (Silverman and Alexander, 2016) or as part of a deliberate misinformation strategy by domestic or foreign political actors. And second, it makes this misinformation difficult to correct because, as Sunstein (2001) predicted at the turn of the twenty-first century, personalized news means that people can live in "echo chambers" or "information bubbles" that effectively cut them off from unwelcome facts and disagreeable opinions. These developments have been linked (Pew Research Center, 2016) to a polarization of attitudes, the hollowing out of the political center and the rise of radical populist parties and movements, oftentimes with a deeply illiberal bent, all of which set politics of the fourth era apart from the bland, accommodative centrism that prevailed in many advanced democracies through the 1990s and early 2000s. The changes are so profound that we are only now beginning to recognize their cumulative impact. As President Obama said in conversation with the journalist David Remnick:

> The new media ecosystem "means everything is true and nothing is true ... And the capacity to disseminate misinformation, wild conspiracy theories, to paint the opposition in wildly negative light without any rebuttal ... make it very difficult to have a common conversation."
>
> (Remnick, 2016)

To be sure, the actual magnitude and impact of these effects is hotly debated by political scientists and communication scholars. There is much that we do not know, since much of the available evidence is anecdotal in nature, as exemplified by this widely circulated post-Brexit referendum comment by the British internet activist Tom Steinberg:

> I am actively searching through Facebook for people celebrating the Brexit leave victory, but the filter bubble is SO strong ... that I can't find anyone who is happy despite the fact that over half the country is clearly jubilant today.
>
> *(Quoted in Viner, 2016)*

Of course, proving these kinds of claims empirically on nationally-representative samples is another matter, and plenty of work remains to be done in this regard. It may well be that the information bubble effect (both online and with traditional media) is limited to the most politically-engaged segment of the population (Prior, 2013), but then this is the segment that is the most motivated and ultimately the most influential in deciding election outcomes.

While developments in the US and UK provide examples of Facebook's echo chamber effect, India now follows the US as the number two country in the world with the most Facebook users (n.a., Top 10). As internet access becomes more readily available in rural India, it remains an open question as to whether the country will also experience the echo chamber phenomenon. A decade after India's 2004 national election, when internet access was patchy even though many parties had websites (Tekwani and Shetty, 2007), access in major cities had increased significantly. A massive digital divide still remains between urban and rural, with rural areas often lacking electricity. Despite this, most have access to TV and viewers learned in 2013 that a smartphone was not necessary to be on Facebook from a popular ad campaign cosponsored with Airtel, clips from which can be found on YouTube. Facebook's presence in India was already highly visible in the month prior to the official launch of the 2014 national election, when the company purchased India's most popular messaging service WhatsApp for $19 billion. In the spring 2014 national election campaign, traditional media quoted top party spokespersons appearing on unprecedented Facebook town halls to take questions from users in what was described as the country's first internet election. BJP leader Narendra Modi, himself an avid Twitter user, often crowdsourced his speech topics on Twitter as he was flying into one of his five campaign stops a day (Price, 2015), and Mr. Modi also appeared in 100 cities simultaneously by delivering a speech in a 3D hologram. A study of campaign engagement in 2014 in three major cities (Delhi, Bengaluru and Mumbai) found that sharing information face-to-face and electronically (defined to include cell phones with SMS as well as email and social media) were both significant influences on political engagement with each of the three main parties' campaigns (Neyazi et al., 2016). The example of India is also relevant to countries in the Global South, such as Brazil and Indonesia, that now follow the US and India as numbers three and four on the list of countries with the most Facebook users. Although internet use remains too underdeveloped for the Facebook echo chamber effect in the Brexit referendum to impact electoral thinking across India, it nevertheless remains important to consider the echo chamber hypothesis in urban areas where rates of internet access are much higher.

But it is not just an echo chamber effect that might be at work. Another unintended consequence of the social media revolution for political campaigning is that the line between facts and opinion has become increasingly blurred. Of course politicians have always attempted to cherry-pick and interpret factual information about economic conditions, crime rates, foreign relations and so on in a manner beneficial to themselves. However, in communication environments dominated by traditional media outlets, especially those with strong norms of impartiality and journalistic professionalism (Hallin and Mancini, 2004), there was a stronger likelihood that filtering and gatekeeping institutions, such as the front pages of major newspapers, would help to maintain a kind of baseline knowledge of "how things are going" in the country, and that politicians would face consequences for speaking blatant untruths. So one of the great paradoxes of the social media revolution is, while more people than ever before have been empowered to have their voices heard, the resulting "unmooring" of political discussion from a common version of the facts has made democratic debate more difficult. This problem exists in all of the aforementioned countries, but is especially evident in weaker democracies and hybrid regimes, where impartial traditional media outlets have either never existed or have been forced to toe the government line.

Global diffusion

Although much of the literature on changes in campaign technologies and strategies inevitably focuses on advanced industrial democracies, it is important not to lose sight of the fact that when we discuss the fourth era of political campaigning, we are considering a truly global phenomenon and, indeed, an increasingly global industry with a pool of ideas, techniques and human talent employed across a wide range of political regime types. There are three main reasons for this. First, in the past quarter-century the worldwide mix of political regimes has changed significantly in the direction of greater competitiveness. Until the 1990s, the so-called "closed" authoritarianisms (i.e., those that suppressed all political competition) constituted the plurality (around 45 percent) of all political regimes, followed by democracies (at around 38 percent). Today, democracies are the most common type (around 55 percent), followed by so-called "competitive-" or "electoral-authoritarian" regimes that make up around 30 percent of the total (Miller, 2015; Wahman et al., 2013; Cheibub et al., 2010). Although political science has struggled to define competitive authoritarianisms with precision, these are sometimes described as political regimes in which, even though the "rules of the game" may be rigged in favor of the incumbents, political competition is real enough that on election night "the incumbents are forced to sweat" (Levitsky and Way, 2010, p. 12). By extension, elections in these hybrid regimes are no mere smokescreens or empty rituals, but meaningful (if deeply flawed) contests for a share of political power.

Indeed, political science scholarship increasingly sees elections as an integral component of non-democratic rule. Most such regimes – even those of a decidedly hardline, non-competitive variety – hold elections of one sort or another. A number of reasons for why they do so have been suggested, including as a mechanism for the distribution of benefits to elites and favored groups in society, for coopting potential opposition, for collecting information (both about the public's mood and about the competence of the regime's own cadres), for demonstrating strength and invincibility and for generating the appearance of popular legitimacy both domestically and internationally (Gandhi and Lust-Okar, 2009). It could be argued that, after the fall of communism and the decline of comprehensive ideological alternatives to democracy, more and more authoritarian rulers have resigned themselves to institutionalizing electoral competition at least in theory, even as they continued to subvert it in practice.

Second, the world has become interconnected to such an extent that pulling up the proverbial drawbridge is no longer an option even for non-democracies. Today, North Korean-style economic, cultural and ideational isolation is an aberration, but not too long ago it was the reality in many authoritarian regimes, including in the bulk of countries of the Soviet bloc. As an illustrative example, it is worth recalling that in the early 1980s the Soviet authorities simply dismantled much of the international telecommunications infrastructure, literally digging up telephone cables to eliminate direct dialing calls to the United States and other countries (United Press International, 1982). In 2016, such a cutoff would be regarded as economically suicidal, which suggests that today's authoritarian and hybrid regimes are caught in a classic "dictator's dilemma" of trying to balance their natural inclination to control information against the demands of participation in the global economy (Wintrobe, 2007).

And third, in this increasingly interconnected world, it made less and less sense for candidates and parties in different countries to reinvent the proverbial wheel when it came to political campaigning. Scholars have long wondered whether post-authoritarian countries, especially the so-called "third wave" democratizers in Southern and Eastern Europe, Latin America and South-East Asia, would follow in the footsteps of older democracies or trace their own distinct paths. Of course an exact retracing was never on the cards given vast differences between the West in the last years of the nineteenth century and the new democracies a century later in everything from the character of social cleavages to the presence of new communication technologies. Nonetheless, it was not beyond the realm of possibility that, when it came to election campaigns, these new democracies would draw on their own traditions and cultural repertories. In the event, borrowing of campaign techniques from more advanced democracies was common-place, and this tendency has only become stronger during the fourth era as rapid expansion and falling costs of online technologies have placed the same kinds of tools and techniques within reach of campaign professionals everywhere.

Nowadays, however, the borrowing also takes place in the other direction as well, with techniques that originated in competitive authoritarian settings eventually finding their way into election campaigns in democracies. A good case in point is provided by Russia, whose propagandists have in recent years developed a wide range of so-called "political technologies," meaning tools ranging from deliberately polluting the information environment with fake news, to promoting conspiracy theories, to flooding social media with relentless negativity spread by automated or human "trolls," to more old-fashioned techniques of pressuring journalists and media companies such as the "carrot of corruption in conjunction with the stick of 'compromat' (compromising materials)" (Greene, 2014). A number of these techniques were then picked up by candidates and parties contesting elections in other countries in the post-Soviet space, including Georgia, Ukraine and Estonia, then made an appearance in elections in Hungary, the Czech Republic, Poland and the rest of Eastern Europe, eventually spreading to the West and making a very visible appearance with the "post-truth" approach to campaigning in the 2016 Brexit referendum and the US presidential election of the same year.

Conclusions

It is worth remembering that it was only 2004 when Facebook was launched in a Harvard dorm room. In less than a decade, Facebook has come to define the pinnacle of success for every large and small social media platform around the world today. Campaigns have changed dramatically with the growth of the internet and social media, shifting from primarily top-down models of party and media influence to include many significant online citizen-driven episodes that may indeed influence party strategies and electoral outcomes. In campaigns from the Americas to Asia, young people appear to be driving social media use and therefore social change, but the world's "competitive authoritarian regimes" are also increasingly skilled in the use of this technology to forestall challenges to their rule.

The fourth era of political communication began to take shape with the growth of social media in the first decade of this century. In this chapter, we discussed the three major developments that set apart the fourth era of political communication from the previous three in terms of political campaigning: the rise of big data, changing communication flows with the growing use of social media and the globalization of campaigning technology and techniques. We provided evidence on these developments from democracies such as the UK, Canada, India and the US as well as Russia, an example of a competitive authoritarian regime. Elections in competitive authoritarian regimes account for most of the steep rise in the number of elections around the world and are therefore of great interest to political scientists and political consultants.

For better or worse – and in this case, definitely for the worse – campaigning today is a global industry in which techniques shown to be effective in one country spread to others. Political *dramaturgiia* is no longer just a Russian phenomenon. Campaigns consciously and unashamedly "unmoored from the facts" – aided by "personal information snowflake" patterns of news consumption via social media, and abetted by party-aligned newspapers and TV outlets – could be observed in recent years as far and wide as in the 2015 Polish parliamentary elections (Tworzecki and Markowski, 2015), the 2016 Brexit referendum (Viner, 2016) and the 2016 US presidential election (Belluz, 2016). Understanding these developments and their long-term consequences represents a major future challenge for political science.

As technology and publicly-available data combine to provide increasingly sophisticated micro-targeting algorithms, observers in some countries such as Canada are calling for legislation to protect voters' privacy and rights to information about what political parties know about them. In other countries such as India, and elsewhere in the Global South, rural voters await the arrival of reliable electricity and internet access.

Campaigns have not yet been able to custom tailor social media messages to the sensibilities of individual recipients, yet this sort of capability may not be too far off in the future. We may not know now what new opportunities will be delivered by artificial intelligence (AI) for campaigning in 2020, but we can expect that those who utilize AI effectively will be more successful than those who do not. We anticipate that efforts to persuade politically by algorithm and automation will grow substantially in both democracies and competitive authoritarian regimes in future campaigns, with far-reaching implications for both political theory and political practice.

References

Belluz, J. (2016) "Why Is Politics Filled With So Many Pants-On-Fire Lies These Days?" [Online]. Vox. com. Available: www.vox.com/2016/6/28/12046126/brexit-donald-trump-facts-politics [accessed June 28, 2016].

Cheibub, J. A., Gandhi, J., and Vreeland, J. R. (2010) "Democracy and Dictatorship Revisited," *Public Choice*, vol. 143, no. 2, April, 67–101.

Farrell, D. M. (1996) "Campaign Strategies and Tactics," in Leduc, L., Niemi, R. G., and Norris, P. (eds.) *Comparing Democracies: Elections and Voting in Global Perspective*, Thousand Oaks, CA: Sage Periodicals Press: 160–183.

Farrell, D. M. and Webb, P. (2000) "Political Parties as Campaign Organizations," in Dalton, R. J. and Wattenberg, M. P. (eds.) *Parties without Partisans: Political Change in Advanced Industrial Democracies*, Oxford: Oxford University Press: 102–128.

Foster, S. (2010) *Political Communication*, Edinburgh: Edinburgh University Press.

Funk, M. (2016) "The Secret Agenda of a Facebook Quiz" [Online]. Available: www.nytimes.com/2016/11/20/opinion/the-secret-agenda-of-a-facebook-quiz.html?_r=0 [accessed January 13, 2017].

Gandhi, J. and Lust-Okar, E. (2009) "Elections Under Authoritarianism," *Annual Review of Political Science*, vol. 12, June, 403–422.

Gertner, J. (2004) "The Very, Very Personal Is the Political," *New York Times Magazine*, February 15, p. 43.

Greene, J. (2014) *Russian Responses to NATO and EU Enlargement and Outreach*, Chatham House Briefing Paper.

Hallin, D. C. and Mancini, P. (2004) *Comparing Media Systems: Three Models of Media and Politics*, Cambridge: Cambridge University Press.

Hersh, E. D. (2015) *Hacking the Electorate: How Campaigns Perceive Voters*, Cambridge: Cambridge University Press.

Howard, P. (2012) "Computational Propaganda Project" [Online]. Available: http://philhoward.org/projects/computational/ [accessed September 25, 2016].

Isaac, M. (2016) "Facebook, in Cross Hairs After Election, Is Said to Question Its Influence" [Online]. Available: www.nytimes.com/2016/11/14/technology/facebook-is-said-to-question-its-influence-in-election.html [accessed November 15, 2016].

Levitsky, S. and Way, L. A. (2010) *Competitive Authoritarianism: Hybrid Regimes After the Cold War*, Cambridge: Cambridge University Press.

Lichtblau, E. (2016) "Computer Systems Used by Clinton Campaign Are Said to Be Hacked, Apparently by Russians," *New York Times*, July 29, p.A1.

Miller, M. K. (2015) "Electoral Authoritarianism and Human Development," *Comparative Political Studies*, vol. 48, no. 12, October, 1526–1562.

Neyazi, T. A., Kumar, A., and Semetko, H. A. (2016) "Campaigns, Digital Media, and Mobilization in India," *The International Journal of Press/Politics*, vol. 21, no. 3, July, 398–416.

Nickerson, D. W. and Rogers, T. (2014) "Political Campaigns and Big Data," *Journal of Economic Perspectives*, vol. 28, no. 2, Spring, 51–74.

Nielsen, R. K. (2012) *Ground Wars: Personalized Communication in Political Campaigns*, Princeton: Princeton University Press.

Norris, P. (2000) *A Virtuous Circle: Political Communications in Postindustrial Societies*, Cambridge: Cambridge University Press.

Norris, P. (2005) *Developments in Party Communications*, Washington, DC: National Democratic Institute for International Affairs (NDI).

Patten, S. (2015) "Data-Driven Microtargeting in the 2015 General Election" [Online]. Vancouver, BC: UBC Press. Available: www.ubcpress.ca/CanadianElectionAnalysis2015 [accessed August 1, 2016].

Petre, C. (2015) "The Traffic Factories: Metrics at Chartbeat, Gawker Media, and The New York Times" [Online]. Columbia Journalism School: Tow Center for Digital Journalism. Available: http://towcenter.org/research/traffic-factories/ [accessed June 20, 2017].

Pew Research Center (2016) "The Political Environment on Social Media" [Online]. Available: www.pewinternet.org/2016/10/25/the-political-environment-on-social-media/ [accessed November 15, 2016].

Plasser, F. (2000) "American Campaign Techniques Worldwide," *Press/Politics*, vol. 5, no. 4, September, 33–54.

Price, L. (2015) *The Modi Effect: Inside Narendra Modi's Campaign to Transform India*, London: Hodder & Stoughton.

Prior, M. (2013) "Media and Political Polarization," *Annual Review of Political Science*, vol. 16, May, 101–127.

Remnick, D. (2016) "Obama Reckons with a Trump Presidency," *The New Yorker*, November 28.

Schmitt-Beck, R. and Farrell, D. M. (2002) "Studying Political Campaigns and Their Effects," in Farrell, D. M. and Schmitt-Beck, R. (eds.) *Do Political Campaigns Matter? Campaigns Effects in Elections and Referendums*, London and New York: Routledge: 1–21.

Silverman, C. and Alexander, L. (2016) "How Teens in the Balkans Are Duping Trump Supporters With Fake News" [Online]. Available: www.buzzfeed.com/craigsilverman/how-macedonia-became-a-global-hub-for-pro-trump-misinfo [accessed November 15, 2016].

Stromer-Galley, J. (2014) *Presidential Campaigning in The Internet Age*, Oxford, UK: Oxford University Press.

Sunstein, C. R. (2001) *Republic.com*, Princeton: Princeton University Press.

Tekwani, S. and Shetty, K. (2007) "Two Indias: The Role of the Internet in the 2004 Elections," in Kluver, R., Jankowski, N., Foot, K., and Schneider, S. M. (eds.) *The Internet and National Elections: A Comparative Study of Web Campaigning*, London: Routledge: 150–162.

The Wall Street Journal (2016) "A Conscious Effort by a Nation-State to Attempt to Achieve a Specific Effect," NSA chief on WikiLeaks [Online]. Available: https://twitter.com/WSJ/status/798647324687929344 [accessed November 15, 2016].

Top 10 Most Facebook User Country in the World [Online]. Available: http://worldknowing.com/top-10-most-facebook-user-country-in-the-world/ [accessed September 20, 2016].

Tworzecki, H. and Markowski, R. (2015) "Did Poland Just Vote in an Authoritarian Government?" [Online]. Available: www.washingtonpost.com/blogs/monkey-cage/wp/2015/02/26/russian-and-ukrainian-tv-viewers-live-on-different-planets/ [accessed July 30, 2016].

United Press International (1982) "The Soviet Union Intends to Cut its Telephone Connections" [Online]. Available: www.upi.com/Archives/1982/06/29/The-Soviet-Union-intends-to-cut-its-telephone-connections/6195394171200/ [accessed June 15, 2016].

Viner, K. (2016) "How Technology Disrupted the Truth" [Online]. Available: www.theguardian.com/media/2016/jul/12/how-technology-disrupted-the-truth?CMP=share_btn_tw [accessed July 31, 2016].

Wahman, M., Teorell, J., and Hadenius, A. (2013) "Authoritarian Regime Types Revisited: Updated Data in Comparative Perspective," *Contemporary Politics*, vol. 19, no. 1, 19–34.

Wintrobe, R. (2007) "Dictatorship: Analytical Approaches," in Boix, C. and Stokes, S. C. (eds.) *Oxford Handbook of Comparative Politics*, Oxford, UK: Oxford University Press: 363–394.

25

THE ROLE OF MASS MEDIA IN SHAPING PUBLIC OPINION AND VOTER BEHAVIOR

Susan Banducci[1]

Introduction

A necessary condition for democracy to function properly is that information is available that allows citizens to make decisions and behave in a manner that maintains accountability and popular sovereignty (Key 1966). Most theories of democracy share a minimal condition that citizens are informed about the candidates or policy proposals presented to them (see, for example, Dryzek 2000; Schumpeter 1950). Delli Carpini and Keeter (1996: 8) write that "Political information is to democratic politics what money is to economics: it is the currency of citizenship." Despite competition from social media, the traditional mass media (television and newspapers) play a privileged role in informing citizens through their provision of news and current affairs programming. Contemporary developments in media and political structures, such as the expansion of commercial broadcasting and weakening of political parties and social ties, further elevate the supply of quality information as an indicator of the strength of electoral democracy. As the dominant source of political information for citizens, there seems to be little question that the media matter as providers of information in politics in general and in elections in particular. But another aspect to this relationship is whether media influence political attitudes and behavior, and here researchers have been hard pressed to build a conclusive body of evidence that demonstrates media effects.

For decades, researchers viewed the media as having a minimal effect on opinion and behavior (Berelson, Lazarsfeld and McPhee 1954; Klapper 1960; Patterson and McClure 1976). The not so minimal effects of the media extolled by earlier researchers suggested that all information was distilled through a partisan lens and any new information simply served to reinforce existing predispositions (Lazarsfeld, Berelson and Gaudet 1968). Since then some have argued that expecting opinion to change or the media to persuade audiences to leave behind predispositions may be setting the bar too high for media effects. The suggestion was that the media could have a range of effects beyond opinion change such as reinforcing predispositions or crystalizing "fundamentals" (Sigelman and Buell 2004), priming issues to alter the basis on which political evaluations are made (Iyengar, Peters and Kinder 1982; McCombs and Shaw 1972; Stevens et al. 2011) and mobilization (Prior 2005). Furthermore, effects can extend beyond election campaigns (Prior 2007). Applying new methods and opening up the range of effects to extend beyond preference formation, these scholars have suggested that the media can be influential and have begun to explore the conditions under which the media are more or less influential.

Since the breakthrough in agenda setting and priming research, there has not been a consensus on the role of the media in shaping opinion, with Bartels (1993: 267) referring to our state of knowledge as "one of the most notable embarrassments of modern social science." More recently, there has been a debate as to whether we are seeing an "ushering in of a new era of minimal effects" (Bennett and Iyengar 2008) due to increased polarization amongst the electorate and changes in the media environment that allow for increased selectivity. Some have even suggested that the discipline of "media effects" research as a paradigm is in crisis (Lang 2013). Still others defend the state of research and accept that findings will be conditional (Holbert, Garrett and Gleason 2010). Given that political communications research crosses a number of disciplines from psychology, communications and political behavior it may not be surprising that there is no consensus on either the state of the discipline or the state of research findings.

After decades of research, the record of empirical research is still mixed. For example, in the area of the media and learning (i.e., political knowledge), some studies report positive effects for the mass media while others report null or even negative effects (Becker and Whitney 1980; Craig, Kane and Gainous 2005; Eveland 2004; Mondak 1995a; Robinson and Davis 1990). This mixed record of evidence extends into new areas of research. While initially thought to democratize access to information, there is conflicting evidence on how use of the internet influences public opinion (de Zúñiga, Copeland and Bimber 2014; Sudulich et al. 2014). Additionally, recent research has focused on how Web 2.0 technology, which allows users to interact with information in new ways – sharing, producing and selecting – and as with other lines of research the conclusions about the direction and size of effect varies (Bode 2016; de Zúñiga, Copeland and Bimber 2014).

While the record of empirical evidence is mixed, it is clear the media environment is changing as audiences are capable of selecting media sources and stories, and sharing these stories within their online networks. The transition to a Web 2.0 environment was preceded by other shifts in audience engagement with news and the structure of news media environments. Probably one of the most salient audience trends is the decline in newspaper readership. A range of studies have indicated a decline in newspaper readership, through reported news consumption habits that have been mirrored by declining circulation figures, in the US (Bogart 1989) and Europe (Curtice 1997). The decline in readership in Europe reflects a cohort effect with newer generations not developing a newspaper habit (Lauf 2001). Alongside the decline in newspaper readership, the privileged position of the news media as a trusted source of political information is on the decline in the US most markedly (Dautrich and Hartley 1999; Ladd 2011) but in other countries as well (Tsfati and Ariely 2014). Trust in media is important as it conditions the influence of media as well as reflecting general levels of trust in political institutions.

Given these changes, political communication has an outstanding need for new theories and methods able to capture the ongoing shift from mass media communication to *mass self-communication* (Castells 2007). These theories and methods should reflect a fundamental change in the media landscape, with increasing complexity in the flows of information (between social and traditional media, and within social media), new patterns of audience exposure (socially mediated and selective) and alternate modes of content production (e.g., user-generated content) (Valkenburg and Peter 2013). These new modes of exposure and content production have led to diversity of empirical findings and models. For example, the increased ability of political actors to target messages via data-driven techniques (Bennett and Manheim 2006) or the use of computer algorithms to direct users to specific content (Hindman 2009; Pariser 2011) means that the model of information flows could be reduced to a "one-step flow" or to "filter bubbles." On the other hand, the ability to share messages and content through social media platforms could reinforce the role of the opinion influencer in the two-step flow model (Messing and Westwood 2014).

Despite the lack of consensus over the direction and size of effects from traditional media sources and the introduction of new forms of communication, there have been advances in terms of conceptualizing the nature of media influence (Bennett and Iyengar 2008; Iyengar and Simon 2000) and the methods used to study them. This chapter reviews work that addresses new approaches to studying media effects that move beyond reinforcement effects to focus on knowledge, learning as well as re-examining valence and priming effects. In terms of methodological advances, I focus on three areas of innovation in research designs. First, cross-national and comparative media effects studies have allowed researchers to investigate how media system characteristics, such as public funding, that structure the supply of information interact with individual news consumption habits. Second, using computer-aided content analysis and machine learning techniques, researchers are now able to analyze a much larger corpus of news information. Given the amount of information available online and the enormous amount of text, computer-aided content analyses has also opened up new sources of data and new possibilities for examining media effects. Third, experiments, the gold standard for examining media effects, have moved out of the lab and into the field and online. This has allowed researchers to make generalizations from research settings that are closer to the real world in which news exposure happens. I start by examining methodological challenges and then move to discuss new findings. I conclude with a discussion and recent empirical findings that attempt to account for media exposure in a dynamic, interconnected online media environment, where there are many sources of content, many channels by which content can be delivered, and where the user exercises unprecedented levels of choice in the media they consume.

Methodological challenges in studying media effects

There seems to be little question that the media matter in politics in general and in elections in particular. Despite what seems to be this accepted truism, researchers have been hard pressed to demonstrate without question that media influence political attitudes and behaviors. Of the situation, Mondak wrote:

> what seems perfectly obvious at face value does not always lend itself to ready empirical confirmation. If media truly are a nearly all-pervasive force, then we are left with a variable that does not vary. Largely for precisely this reason, researchers have struggled to demonstrate the existence of media effects on political behaviour.
>
> *(Mondak 1995a: 15)*

In media effects research the driving question is whether exposure to media content causes changes in behavior and/or attitudes. In its simplest formulation, as media effects researchers we want to know whether watching or reading a particular news story, viewing a particular campaign advertisement or being exposed to a string of media messages will alter how citizens perceive political candidates or leaders, their levels of political knowledge and understanding, the salience of issues in political choices or whether citizens are engaged in the campaign. The first step in determining media effects is to examine whether exposure to a message is accompanied by any observed change in behavior or attitudes. For example, we might expect that citizens more likely to report seeing advertisements for party A are more likely to vote for party A. If a correlation or covariation is observed in our data, the underlying causal mechanism could be one of media effects – seeing the campaign advert has caused citizens to be more likely to support party A. However, the underlying causal mechanism can also be one of self-selection where partisan supporters are more likely to view and pay attention to ads from their own party or even spurious where a third factor, such as the viability of the party, is actually causing both the number of advertisements and the support for the party.

Within political communications research, the most appropriate technique to establish media effects, ruling out self-selection and a spurious relationship, is to employ experiments. In an experiment, manipulation of the media content and the intervention with the designated groups allows the researcher to control how and to what messages the experimental groups are exposed. Controlling for observable as well as unobservable factors is achieved through random assignment. Therefore, through controlling when and to what subjects are exposed, researchers can be fairly certain that observed changes in attitudes or reported behaviors can be attributed to the treatment or differences in exposure to media content. Experiments have been very successful in demonstrating consistent and strong media effects starting with the landmark studies (Iyengar, Peters and Kinder 1982; McCombs and Shaw 1972). When experiments are not available, the conclusions about media effects are more tenuous and require careful design consideration. As many have noted, in survey-based research it is difficult to sort out cause and effect. Many measures that are used of exposure (such as days spent reading a newspaper) are highly correlated with the political variables of interest such as political interest and probability of voting or becoming engaged in the campaign. Furthermore, surveys, or observational work, measure reported exposure and cannot control what other messages respondents might be exposed to nor can they account for them in a model. Furthermore, most observational studies do not take into account the actual message to which respondents have been exposed.

Norris and co-authors ran a series of media effects experiments in Britain during the 1997 and 2001 general elections (Norris 1999; Norris and Sanders 2003; Sanders and Norris 2005). The general design of the experiments worked as such: subjects were exposed to a 30-minute compilation of television news items drawn from broadcasts aired on the main channels' major news programs in the months before the general election. There were several different treatments, including examinations of agenda setting, learning and valence – 10 minutes of stories about taxation, jobs, health, pensions, Europe or overseas aid in the middle of 20 minutes of neutral stories. The findings are consistent with previous research demonstrating a modest role for the media in influencing attitudes. For example, there were minimal effects on agenda setting where only of foreign affairs news, about the EU or overseas aid, altered perceptions of the importance of the issue (Norris 1999) and party election broadcasts showed no direct effects on attitudes (Sanders and Norris 2005).

In general, outside these experimental studies, studies can be grouped according to whether measures of media content are included. Some studies analyze reported media exposure while others provide an explicit link between exposure and the content to which respondents are exposed. Many studies on negative advertising and the effects of television on political attitudes and behavior fall into the first category of analyzing reported exposure (Brians and Wattenberg 1996; Dilliplane 2011; Eveland Jr and Scheufele 2000; Zhao and Chaffee 1995). These studies measure consumption and then enter days viewing or reported exposure to advertising, for example, as independent variables but do not include measures of media content. This design is the one most often used in survey-based political communications research (Barabas and Jerit 2009). In addition to yielding conflicting results (for example, see debate on the mobilizing impact of negative advertising), relying on consumption measures alone is to base the demonstration of media effects on measures that are flawed in many respects (Bartels 1993; Dilliplane,

Goldman and Mutz 2013; Price and Zaller 1993; Prior 2009, 2013). In addition to lacking a measure of the actual content, because these consumption measures are highly correlated with the dependent variables of interest such as political interest, knowledge and engagement, it is difficult to sort out cause and effect in cross-sectional research.

There is a smaller category of studies linking media content to survey data (Curran et al. 2009; Jerit, Barabas and Bolsen 2006; Nicholson 2003; Price and Czilli 1996; Stevens et al. 2011). For example Jerit, Barabas and Bolsen (2006) link aggregate indicators of the saliency of an issue in the news to public opinion polls to estimate the impact of the information environment on political knowledge. The study is explicit in linking the media content but uses only an aggregate indicator allowing it to vary across surveys rather than by individual news consumption patterns in terms of both frequency and outlets. Therefore, the results indicate an effect of the general news environment on knowledge and as such do not approximate media effects as demonstrated in an experimental setting. In another study, Barabas and Jerit (2009) improve measurably on the design by comparing within subjects, demonstrating that a single individual exposed to different levels of information about two different topics will have different levels of information about the topics.

Building on this latter group of studies, there has been a growing recognition that, while experiments remain the gold standard for establishing media effects, they cannot reflect the multitude of sources of information and how individuals interact with these in the real world. Therefore, the type of design that incorporates various levels of exposure and variations in media content, either in a within subject design or a between subject design, increasingly becomes the norm for observational studies of media effects. Automated text analysis has made it less costly to analyze a large corpus of media content and this development encourages linking measures of media exposure to survey measures of content in order to better reflect media exposure in the real world. Cross-national studies, using both automated and human coding, of media effects are able to capture variations in media content across media systems which are important drivers of the supply of messages. Finally, there are a growing number of field experiments aiming to capture how public opinion can be influenced by media messages.

Advances in computer-aided text analysis

Given the importance of understanding the content of media messages in political communication, it is unsurprising that considerable effort has been made to understand the ways in which news coverage shapes elections. Large media content analyses have become fixtures in campaign and election studies in individual countries, such as Austria (Eberl et al. 2015), Britain (see, for example, Deacon and Wring 2016), Germany (Rattinger et al. 2015) and for Europe overall (Banducci et al. 2014). While these efforts have been instrumental in our understanding of the relationship between news media and elections, large content analyses come with an equally large cost. Thousands of hours of coding at an enormous cost are required to produce these data, presenting serious challenges for researchers interested in the relationship between media and political behavior. However, advances in machine learning can help human coders and researchers to understand media coverage and their effects across a vast body of material. The goal is not to replace human coders, but to focus attention on which tasks may be safely assigned to a computer and which tasks cannot.

Computer-aided coding of texts has been used successfully for over 10 years (Grimmer and Stewart 2013; Laver, Benoit and Garry 2003) and has aided advances in our theoretical and empirical understanding of phenomena from party policy positions (Benoit, Laver and Mikhaylov 2009) to open-ended survey responses (Roberts et al. 2014). However, the coding of media texts does present some additional challenges. While texts are easily digitized for analysis, radio and television broadcasts must first be transcribed, and this is an expensive task. There are differences across media in the structure of a news story, reporting style and language, which need to be taken into account when applying any supervised or unsupervised classification. These considerations are particularly important when considering the reliability and validity of automated coding (Soroka 2014). That said, there has been great progress in automated coding that has allowed for new insights into the negativity of news (Soroka, Young and Balmas 2015) and news framing (Burscher et al. 2014). In turn, these content measures can then be linked to survey-based measures of exposure and political behavior to assess the impact of the media across the entire range of outlets.

Cross-national media effects studies

There is a growing body of cross-national media effects research that accounts for the mediating and conditioning role of media systems in political communication research (see, for example, Curran et al. 2009, 2014; De Vreese and Boomgaarden 2006). These studies have suggested two mechanisms by which characteristics of media systems might influence the level of citizen political knowledge. First, factors such as greater investment in public service broadcasting may increase the amount of quality information available to citizens and produce a better informed citizenry (Curran et al. 2009). Second, the media landscape (i.e., alternatives for news information), influenced by commercialization or a partisan press, can alter the news consumption patterns of citizens and influence exposure and attention to news information. For example, in more commercialized markets, citizens have more entertainment options and are thus more inclined to opt out of news gathering, leading to a decrease in political knowledge (Prior 2005, 2007).

Hallin and Mancini (2004) give us a framework that identifies and codifies a set of dimensions by which media systems can be compared and allows us to develop media system indicators that potentially influence the amount and quality of news information. Prior's (2005, 2007) "conditional political learning" model demonstrates additional links between the media system and political knowledge by showing that acquisition of political information is dependent on the availability of choices (i.e., competition with news) combined with preferences for news versus entertainment. The advent of broadcast news in the 1950s and 1960s in America served to increase turnout (and knowledge), while the proliferation of choices via entertainment only channels in the 1980s and 1990s has had the opposite effect. Increasingly, these linkages, as specified by Hallin and Mancini, and Prior, are taken into account in cross-national media studies (Banducci, Giebler and Kritzinger 2017; De Vreese and Boomgaarden 2006; Soroka et al. 2013). Not only can cross-national media studies capture variations in media systems but cross-national studies linking media content and survey data allow for variation in content.

One of the most fruitful areas of cross-national media effects research has been examining the effect of media on political engagement and knowledge. Aalberg, Van Aelst and Curran (2010) show public service media systems have greater levels of political information. However, the patterns are not consistent, with important variation across countries with similar media systems. Therefore, while aspects of the media system do seem to be related to the amount of electorally relevant information, the relationship is not consistent enough that spending can be used as a proxy for the amount of information in the environment, for example. To date, however, there is no large-scale cross-national study of the amount of political or electoral information available to voters, as measured with content analysis, and the decision to vote. Some studies show that viewing public broadcasting increases levels of political information and engagement (Aarts and

Semetko 2003; Norris 2000). A more recent study shows that public service television devotes more time to public affairs than commercial media systems and that in countries where the public service model is dominant there tends to be a smaller knowledge gap (Curran et al. 2009).

Using field experiments to examine media effects

Field experiments avoid the trade-offs between experiments (causal inference) and observational studies (generalizability) by random assignment to treatment in the field, or in natural settings (Gerber and Green 2012). In one experiment (Gerber, Karlan and Bergan 2009), non-newspaper subscribers are randomly assigned to the treatment (receive a copy of a Washington DC based newspaper) or control group. Those assigned to the *Washington Post*, a left-leaning paper, were significantly more likely to vote for the Democratic Party, but no effect was observed for the *Washington Times*, a right-leaning newspaper. Those who received a newspaper were also 2.8 percentage points more likely to vote than those who did not receive a newspaper subscription. However, this significant effect was for the next election rather than the most immediate election to the treatment. In other studies, localities holding mayoral elections were randomly assigned to receive get-out-the-vote radio spots which altered the competitiveness of the contests (Panagopoulos and Green 2008) and approximately $2 million of television and radio advertising deployed experimentally in a gubernatorial campaign, which showed that televised ads have strong but short-lived effects on voting preferences (Gerber et al. 2011).

Naturally-occurring experiments or quasi-experiments – where comparable groups exist but only one receives a treatment and there is no random assignment to these groups – have also been used to examine media effects. One of the best known of these is Mondak's (1995b) study of the consequences of a newspaper strike in Pittsburgh that meant residents did not have a daily newspaper during most of the 1992 campaign period prior to a vote for president, the Senate and the House. He compared Pittsburgh voters to those in a similar city, Cleveland, which did not experience a strike. He found no difference in information-seeking behavior, but found that citizens of Pittsburgh based their decisions on different sorts of information and were not as knowledgeable about candidates down the ballot (House candidates). Another natural or quasi-experiment that has been exploited for studying the influence of the media is the switching of party endorsements in the UK's partisan press. In 1997, The *Sun* newspaper switched support from the Conservative Party and endorsed Tony Blair of the Labour Party. Then, in 2009–10, it switched support back again to the Conservatives. Studies examining this endorsement switch find that approximately 8.6 percent of voters altered their party identification in line with newspaper endorsements (Ladd and Lenz 2009) and that a switch in endorsements can significantly increase party support (Reeves, McKee and Stuckler 2016). Still others claim that the partisan press in Britain and their endorsements have little influence on electoral choices (Curtice 1997).

These experiments, whether field or lab based, are not free from challenges. Researchers are increasingly recognizing that even natural experiments have drawbacks (Sekhon and Titiunik 2012). Experiments allow us to distinguish between causal and selection effects but do not allow for generalizations across contexts and may exaggerate the effects of information (Barabas and Jerit 2010). Furthermore, experimental settings tend not to accurately reflect how citizens encounter or engage with news media content in the real world. In the time since Bartels' criticism and Mondak's observation, researchers have developed methods for estimating media effects with cross-section data in order to take advantage of the strength of these data – capturing people as they naturally encounter political information. First, media effects researchers have employed sample matching (Barabas 2004; Ladd and Lenz 2009; Levendusky

2011) – a technique based on the logic of experimentation that allows the creation of two equivalent groups similar on characteristics except the "treatment" variable – for example, high media use vs. low media use (see, for example, Dehejia and Wahba 1999). Second, news media content that can be linked to survey data measuring exposure to specific sources is increasingly available to researchers and is advantageous in capturing variation in the information environment (see, for example, Barabas and Jerit 2010; Stevens et al. 2011; Stevens and Karp 2012).

Media effects studies and the changing information environment

The changing media landscape (declining newspaper readership and trust, increasing use of social media) begs the questions of where voters are obtaining their information. Social media has become a fundamental tool for voters gathering news stories (Bode 2016; Boulianne 2015) and for candidates connecting to audiences (Aldrich et al. 2015). The structural characteristics of the new media environment allow for information on demand, via internet and mobile devices, and are interactive, allowing feedback and creative participation (Castells 2007, 2009). Within this environment, public affairs/political news information constitutes a large amount of the content circulated in social media (Kwak et al. 2010). In the UK, tweets are increasingly used as sources by journalists with social media profiles, often driving the news agenda (Broersma and Graham 2013). These changes mean that the traditional media no longer play a gatekeeping function (Shoemaker, Vos and Reese 2009), and their influence on mass and elite political opinions and behavior has arguably weakened. Second, traditional models of flows of campaign communication, from elites to opinion leaders to the masses, may no longer be relevant in an age in which social media can provide a platform for opinion leaders (and the masses) to produce information. Political parties and leaders rely heavily on the internet and social media to communicate directly with their supporters and party activists (Lilleker and Jackson 2010). However, empirical evidence on the impact of online campaigning and new media on voters' attitudes and behavior is far from conclusive, and scholars have been cautious in drawing causal inferences (Bimber and Davis 2003; Quintelier and Vissers 2008). Indeed, recent evidence points to the continued primary impact of traditional forms of campaign mobilization on turnout and no impact of e-campaigning (e.g., social media or e-mail) on political behavior (i.e., turnout) (Fisher et al. 2016).

The advent of Web 2.0 – the second generation of the world wide web that allows users to interact, collaborate, create and share information online, in virtual communities – has radically changed the media environment and the types of content the public is exposed to, as well as the exposure process itself. Individuals are faced with a wider range of options (from social and traditional media), new patterns of exposure (socially mediated and selective) and alternate modes of content production (e.g., user-generated content) (Valkenburg and Peter 2013). Networks shape how citizens receive and interpret information and, in turn, these networks are constructed by individuals (Huckfeldt and Sprague 1987, 1995; McClurg 2006). Within these networks, the influence of the media was conceptualized as uni-directional with information flowing from the source to the individual (Beck et al. 2002) and methodologically the issue had been devising a method to determine whether individuals construct networks of opinions similar to their own or whether the information received from the network influences individual opinion (Fowler et al. 2011). Yet analysis of embedded hyperlinks in blogs reveals the underlying social network architecture linking bloggers (Adamic and Glance 2005; Elgesem, Steskal and Diakopoulos 2015); bloggers tend to link their own posts to posts by other bloggers that they read.

Outside of the question of media exposure, research on media effects raises many potential avenues to explore but an equal number of challenges. Studies on social media and political behavior fall into three categories. First, there are studies examining how social media (e.g., Twitter, Facebook) alter political behavior and attitudes. A second group of studies uses social media data to estimate variables of interest (e.g., Google searches indicating salience of issues or public opinion). Third, a related group of studies focuses on political or media actors using social media to mobilize, persuade or inform supporters and/or citizens. Each of these types of studies poses interesting challenges that are linked to the data itself as well as in developing research designs that can capture the influence on public opinion. From the first group, one of the most convincing studies to date on social media effects demonstrates that social pressure can mobilize Facebook users to vote (Bond et al. 2012). With the help of the social media site, 611,000 users (1 percent) received an "informational message" at the top of their news feeds, which encouraged them to vote, provided a link to information on local polling places and included a clickable "I voted" button and a counter of Facebook users who had clicked it. A large group of 60 million users (98 percent) received a "social message," which included the same elements but also showed the profile pictures of up to six randomly selected Facebook friends who had clicked the "I voted" button. The remaining 1 percent of users were assigned to a control group that received no message. Those who got the informational message voted at the same rate as those who saw no message at all. But those who saw the social message were 2 percent more likely to click the "I voted" button and 0.4 percent more likely to vote. Social pressure, therefore, can explain how social media works to mobilize users.

Conclusions

There is no question that news media are an important source of political information for citizens. The challenge has been understanding how and under what conditions this information will influence the behavior and attitudes of individuals. As a review of past research on this question, this chapter has addressed two related themes on developments in political communications. First, how have changes in the media environment shaped our understanding of the types and conditions of media effects? We understand that media effects may be small in real-world empirical studies but this likely reflects the reality that citizens receive political information from a range of sources, politics tends not to be held prominently in the day-to-day thoughts and activities of most people and media information seeking tends to reflect already established interests and predispositions. Second, while emerging technologies and social media have led us to reconsider media effects, the same technologies have led us to develop and apply innovative methodologies for studying media effects. These new methods have allowed researchers, for example, to analyze larger bodies of news text than previously imagined.

In terms of methodological approaches, laboratory and field experiments have been useful in illustrating the impact of the media with controlled treatments. Their strength is precisely in isolating the effect of a news media treatment from other rival explanations. On the one hand, despite having the shortcomings outlined in the above chapter, the greatest strength of observational media effects research is that it attempts to examine people in real-world settings and in the way in which they would usually encounter political information. When Bartels described the body of research on media effects as "one of the most notable embarrassments of modern social science" (Bartels 1993), he attributed this state of affairs primarily to a combination of measurement error and the absence of longitudinal research designs capable of detecting media effects. Increasingly, panel studies and repeated cross-sectional studies are being used to study media effects. This development alongside the use of improved exposure measures as well as linking surveys to media content have yielded promising results about the nature of media effects.

These improvements in the research designs for studying media effects have also incorporated new technologies. These new technologies have allowed the study of large bodies of media text but also mean that citizens are being exposed to information in new ways. Indeed, a report from the OECD Global Science Forum attributes social scientists' inability to anticipate the political movements such as the Arab Spring to a failure to understand "the new ways in which humans communicate" (OECD 2013: 6–7). At the same time, the report calls for advances in tools that allow researchers to link online/open data to traditional data sources (such as surveys) to understand the human condition. These efforts are now being undertaken.

This chapter has focused mainly on understanding how media influence attitudes and behavior and the methods used to assess these influences. However, there is also a need to understand the drivers of news media coverage. Less well understood is how media systems and the polity shape the amount of politically relevant news. Given that television and newspapers produce the information, transitions evident in media systems, such as the move from public service to regulated commercial systems and the decline in newspaper readership, are likely to impact on the information available and may have consequences for the accountability function of electoral processes. Recent research has demonstrated both that the news alternatives available to voters influence political knowledge by altering news consumption patterns (Prior 2007) and that the rules and institutions governing news coverage affect political participation (Baek 2009). Both findings suggest an important role of media system characteristics in understanding the relationship between news and political attitudes and behavior. The comparative studies by Curran, Aalberg and others are an important step in this direction.

Note

1 This work was supported by the Economic and Social Research Council grants ES/M010775/1 and ES/K004395/1.

References

Aalberg, T., Van Aelst, P. and Curran, J. (2010) "Media Systems and the Political Information Environment: A Cross-National Comparison," *The International Journal of Press/Politics*, vol. 15, no. 3, July, 255–271.

Aarts, K. and Semetko, H. A. (2003) "The Divided Electorate: Media Use and Political Involvement," *Journal of Politics*, vol. 65, no. 3, August, 759–784.

Adamic, L. A. and Glance, N. (2005) "The Political Blogosphere and the 2004 U.S. Election: Divided They Blog," in *Proceedings of the 3rd International Workshop on Link Discovery*, New York, NY, USA: ACM: 36–43.

Aldrich, J. H., Gibson, R. K., Cantijoch, M. and Konitzer, T. (2015) "Getting Out the Vote in the Social Media Era: Are Digital Tools Changing the Extent, Nature and Impact of Party Contacting in Elections?," *Party Politics*, vol. 22, no. 2, March, 165–178.

Baek, M. (2009) "A Comparative Analysis of Political Communication Systems and Voter Turnout," *American Journal of Political Science*, vol. 53, no. 2, April, 376–393.

Banducci, S., De Vreese, C. H., Semetko, H. A., Boomgarden, H. G., Luhiste, M., Peter, J., Schuck, A. and Xezonakis, G. (2014) "European Parliament Election Study, Longitudinal Media Study 1999, 2004, 2009," GESIS Data Archive, available online: http://dx.doi.org/10.4232/1.5178.

Banducci, S., Giebler, H. and Kritzinger, S. (2017) "Knowing More from Less: How the Information Environment Increases Knowledge of Party Positions," *British Journal of Political Science*, vol. 47, no. 3, July, 571–588.

Barabas, J. (2004) "How Deliberation Affects Policy Opinions," *American Political Science Review*, vol. 98, no. 4, November, 687–701.

Barabas, J., and Jerit, J. (2009) "Estimating the Causal Effects of Media Coverage on Policy-Specific Knowledge," *American Journal of Political Science*, vol. 53, no. 1, January, 73–89.

Barabas, J. and Jerit, J. (2010) "Are Survey Experiments Externally Valid?" *American Political Science Review*, vol. 104, no. 2, May, 226–242.

Bartels, L. M. (1993) "Messages Received: The Political Impact of Media Exposure," *American Political Science Review*, vol. 87, no. 2, June, 267–285.

Beck, P. A., Dalton, R. J., Greene, S. and Huckfeldt, R. (2002) "The Social Calculus of Voting: Interpersonal, Media, and Organizational Influences on Presidential Choices," *American Political Science Review*, vol. 96, no. 1, March, 57–73.

Becker, L. B. and Whitney, D. C. (1980) "Effects of Media Dependencies Audience Assessment of Government," *Communication Research*, vol. 7, no. 1, January, 95–120.

Bennett, W. L. and Iyengar, S. (2008) "A New Era of Minimal Effects? The Changing Foundations of Political Communication," *Journal of Communication*, vol. 58, no. 4, December, 707–731.

Bennett, W. L. and Manheim, J. B. (2006) "The One-Step Flow of Communication," *The ANNALS of the American Academy of Political and Social Science*, vol. 608, no. 1, November, 213–232.

Benoit, K., Laver, M. and Mikhaylov, S. (2009) "Treating Words as Data with Error: Uncertainty in Text Statements of Policy Positions," *American Journal of Political Science*, vol. 53, no. 2, April, 495–513.

Berelson, B. R., Lazarsfeld, P. F. and McPhee, W. N. (1954) *Voting: A Study of Opinion Formation in a Presidential Election*, Chicago: University of Chicago Press.

Bimber, B. and Davis, R. (2003) *Campaigning Online: The Internet in US Elections*, Oxford: Oxford University Press.

Bode, L. (2016) "Political News in the News Feed: Learning Politics from Social Media," *Mass Communication and Society*, vol. 19, no. 1, May, 24–48.

Bogart, L. (1989) *Press and Public: Who Reads What, When, Where, and Why in American Newspapers*, Hove: Psychology Press.

Bond, R. M., Fariss, C. J., Jones, J. J., Kramer, A. D., Marlow, C., Settle, J. E. and Fowler, J. H. (2012) "A 61-Million-Person Experiment in Social Influence and Political Mobilization," *Nature*, vol. 489, no. 7415, September, 295–298.

Boulianne, S. (2015) "Social Media Use and Participation: A Meta-Analysis of Current Research," *Information, Communication and Society*, vol. 18, no. 5, May, 524–538.

Brians, C. L. and Wattenberg, M. P. (1996) "Campaign Issue Knowledge and Salience: Comparing Reception from TV Commercials, TV News and Newspapers," *American Journal of Political Science*, vol. 40, no. 1, February, 172–193.

Broersma, M. and Graham, T. (2013) "Twitter as a News Source: How Dutch and British Newspapers Used Tweets in Their News Coverage, 2007–2011," *Journalism Practice*, vol. 7, no. 4, August, 446–464.

Burscher, B., Odijk, D., Vliegenthart, R., De Rijke, M. and De Vreese, C. H. (2014) "Teaching the Computer to Code Frames in News: Comparing Two Supervised Machine Learning Approaches to Frame Analysis," *Communication Methods and Measures*, vol. 8, no. 3, July, 190–206.

Castells, M. (2007) "Communication, Power and Counter-Power in the Network Society," *International Journal of Communication*, vol. 1, no. 1, 238–266.

Castells, M. (2009) *Communication Power*, Oxford: Oxford University Press.

Craig, S. C., Kane, J. G. and Gainous, J. (2005) "Issue-Related Learning in a Gubernatorial Campaign: A Panel Study," *Political Communication*, vol. 22, no. 4, December, 483–503.

Curran, J., Coen, S., Soroka, S., Aalberg, T., Hayashi, K., Hichy, Z., Iyengar, S., Jones, P., Mazzoleni, G., Papathanassopolous, S., Rhee, J. W., Rojas, H. Rowe, D. and Tiffen, R. (2014) "Reconsidering 'Virtuous Circle' and 'Media Malaise' Theories of the Media: An 11-Nation Study," *Journalism*, vol. 15, no. 7, October, 815–833.

Curran, J., Iyengar, S., Lund, A. B. and Salovaara-Moring, I. (2009) "Media System, Public Knowledge and Democracy: A Comparative Study," *European Journal of Communication*, vol. 24, no. 1, March, 5–26.

Curtice, J. (1997) "Is the Sun Shining on Tony Blair? The Electoral Influence of British Newspapers," *The Harvard International Journal of Press/Politics*, vol. 2, no. 2, March, 9–26.

Dautrich, K. and Hartley, T. H. (1999) *How the News Media Fail American Voters: Causes, Consequences, and Remedies*, New York: Columbia University Press.

De Vreese, C. H. and Boomgaarden, H. (2006) "News, Political Knowledge and Participation: The Differential Effects of News Media Exposure on Political Knowledge and Participation," *Acta Politica*, vol. 41, no. 4, December, 317–341.

de Zúñiga, H. G., Copeland, L. and Bimber, B. (2014) "Political Consumerism: Civic Engagement and the Social Media Connection," *New Media and Society*, vol. 16, no. 3, May, 488–506.

Deacon, D. and Wring, D. (2016) "The UK Independence Party, Populism and the British News Media: Competition, Collaboration or Containment?" *European Journal of Communication*, vol. 31, no. 2, April, 169–184.

Dehejia, R. H. and Wahba, S. (1999) "Causal Effects in Nonexperimental Studies: Reevaluating the Evaluation of Training Programs," *Journal of the American Statistical Association*, vol. 94, no. 448, December, 1053–1062.

Delli Carpini, M. X. and Keeter, S. (1996) *What Americans Don't Know About Politics and Why It Matters*, New Haven: Yale University Press.

Dilliplane, S. (2011) "All the News You Want to Hear: The Impact of Partisan News Exposure on Political Participation," *Public Opinion Quarterly*, vol. 75, no. 2, Summer, 287–316.

Dilliplane, S., Goldman, S. K. and Mutz, D. C. (2013) "Televised Exposure to Politics: New Measures for a Fragmented Media Environment," *American Journal of Political Science*, vol. 57, no. 1, January, 236–248.

Dryzek, J. S. (2000) *Deliberative Democracy and Beyond: Liberals, Critics, Contestations*, Oxford: Oxford University Press.

Eberl, J. M., Vonburn, R., Haselmayer, M., Jacobu, C., Kleinen-von Konigslo, K., Schonbach, K. and Boomgarden, H. (2015) "AUTNES Manual Content Analysis of the Media Coverage 2013," GESIS Data Archive, available online: http://dx.doi.org/10.4232/1.12565.

Elgesem, D., Steskal, L. and Diakopoulos, N. (2015) "Structure and Content of the Discourse on Climate Change in the Blogosphere: The Big Picture," *Environmental Communication*, vol. 9, no. 2, 169–188.

Eveland, W. P. (2004) "The Effect of Political Discussion in Producing Informed Citizens: The Roles of Information, Motivation, and Elaboration," *Political Communication*, vol. 21, no. 2, June, 177–193.

Eveland Jr, W. P. and Scheufele, D. A. (2000) "Connecting News Media Use with Gaps in Knowledge and Participation," *Political Communication*, vol. 17, no. 3, July, 215–237.

Fisher, J., Fieldhouse, E., Johnston, R., Pattie, C. and Cutts, D. (2016) "Is All Campaigning Equally Positive? The Impact of District Level Campaigning on Voter Turnout at the 2010 British General Election," *Party Politics*, vol. 22, no. 2, March, 215–226.

Fowler, J. H., Heaney, M. T., Nickerson, D. W., Padgett, J. F. and Sinclair, B. (2011) "Causality in Political Networks," *American Politics Research*, vol. 39, no. 2, March, 437–480.

Gerber, A. S. and Green, D. P. (2012) *Field Experiments: Design, Analysis, and Interpretation*, London: W. W. Norton.

Gerber, A. S., Gimpel, J. G., Green, D. P. and Shaw, D. R. (2011) "How Large and Long-Lasting are the Persuasive Effects of Televised Campaign Ads? Results from a Randomized Field Experiment," *American Political Science Review*, vol. 105, no. 1, February, 135–150.

Gerber, A. S., Karlan, D. and Bergan, D. (2009) "Does the Media Matter? A Field Experiment Measuring the Effect of Newspapers on Voting Behavior and Political Opinions," *American Economic Journal: Applied Economics*, vol. 1, no. 2, April, 35–52.

Grimmer, J. and Stewart, B. M. (2013) "Text as Data: The Promise and Pitfalls of Automatic Content Analysis Methods for Political Texts," *Political Analysis*, vol. 21, no. 3, Summer, 267–297.

Hallin, D. C. and Mancini, P. (2004) *Comparing Media Systems: Three Models of Media and Politics*, Cambridge: Cambridge University Press.

Hindman, D. B. (2009) "Mass Media Flow and Differential Distribution of Politically Disputed Beliefs: The Belief Gap Hypothesis," *Journalism and Mass Communication Quarterly*, vol. 86, no. 4, December, 790–808.

Holbert, R. L., Garrett, R. K. and Gleason, L. S. (2010) "A New Era of Minimal Effects? A Response to Bennett and Iyengar," *Journal of Communication*, vol. 60, no. 1, March, 15–34.

Huckfeldt, R. and Sprague, J. (1987) "Networks in Context: The Social Flow of Political Information," *American Political Science Review*, vol. 81, no. 4, December, 1197–1216.

Huckfeldt, R. R. and Sprague, J. (1995) *Citizens, Politics and Social Communication: Information and Influence in an Election Campaign*, Cambridge: Cambridge University Press.

Iyengar, S. and Simon, A. F. (2000) "New Perspectives and Evidence on Political Communication and Campaign Effects," *Annual Review of Psychology*, vol. 51, February, 149–169.

Iyengar, S., Peters, M. D. and Kinder, D. R. (1982) "Experimental Demonstrations of the "Not-So-Minimal" Consequences of Television News Programs," *American Political Science Review*, vol. 76, no. 4, December, 848–858.

Jerit, J., Barabas, J. and Bolsen, T. (2006) "Citizens, Knowledge, and the Information Environment," *American Journal of Political Science*, vol. 50, no. 2, April, 266–282.

Key, V. O. (1966) *The Responsible Electorate*, Cambridge: Belknap Press.

Klapper, J. T. (1960) *The Effects of Mass Communication*, New York: Free Press.

Kwak, H., Lee, C., Park, H. and Moon, S. (2010) "What is Twitter, a Social Network or a News Media?," *Proceedings of the 19th International Conference on World Wide Web*, 591–600, available online: http://dl.acm.org/citation.cfm?id=1772751.

Ladd, J. M. (2011) *Why Americans Hate the Media and How It Matters*, Princeton: Princeton University Press.

Ladd, J. M. and Lenz, G. S. (2009) "Exploiting a Rare Communication Shift to Document the Persuasive Power of the News Media," *American Journal of Political Science*, vol. 53, no. 2, April, 394–410.

Lang, A. (2013) "Discipline in Crisis? The Shifting Paradigm of Mass Communication Research," *Communication Theory*, vol. 23, no. 1, February, 10–24.

Lauf, E. (2001) "Research Note: The Vanishing Young Reader Sociodemographic Determinants of Newspaper Use as a Source of Political Information in Europe, 1980–98," *European Journal of Communication*, vol. 16, no. 2, June, 233–243.

Laver, M., Benoit, K. and Garry, J. (2003) "Extracting Policy Positions from Political Texts Using Words as Data," *American Political Science Review*, vol. 97, no. 2, May, 311–331.

Lazarsfeld, P. F., Berelson, B. and Gaudet, H. (1968) *The People's Choice: How the Voter Makes Up His Mind in a Presidential Campaign*, 3rd Edition, New York: Columbia University Press.

Levendusky, M. S. (2011) "Rethinking the Role of Political Information," *Public Opinion Quarterly*, vol. 75, no. 1, Spring, 42–64.

Lilleker, D. G. and Jackson, N. A. (2010) "Towards a More Participatory Style of Election Campaigning: The Impact of Web 2.0 on the UK 2010 General Election," *Policy and Internet*, vol. 2, no. 3, August, 69–98.

McClurg, S. D. (2006) "The Electoral Relevance of Political Talk: Examining Disagreement and Expertise Effects in Social Networks on Political Participation," *American Journal of Political Science*, vol. 50, no. 3, July, 737–754.

McCombs, M. E. and Shaw, D. L. (1972) "The Agenda-Setting Function of Mass Media," *Public Opinion Quarterly*, vol. 36, no. 2, Summer, 176–187.

Messing, S. and Westwood, S. J. (2014) "Selective Exposure in the Age of Social Media: Endorsements Trump Partisan Source Affiliation When Selecting News Online," *Communication Research*, vol. 41, no. 8, December, 1042–1063.

Mondak, J. J. (1995a) "Media Exposure and Political Discussion in US Elections," *Journal of Politics*, vol. 57, no. 1, February, 62–85.

Mondak, J. J. (1995b) *Nothing to Read: Newspapers and Elections in a Social Experiment*, Ann Arbor: University of Michigan Press.

Nicholson, S. P. (2003) "The Political Environment and Ballot Proposition Awareness," *American Journal of Political Science*, vol. 47, no. 3, July, 403–410.

Norris, P. (1999) *On Message: Communicating the Campaign*, London: Sage.

Norris, P. (2000) *A Virtuous Circle: Political Communications in Postindustrial Societies*, Cambridge: Cambridge University Press.

Norris, P. and Sanders, D. (2003) "Message or Medium? Campaign Learning During the 2001 British General Election," *Political Communication*, vol. 20, no. 3, 233–262.

OECD (2013) *New Data for Understanding the Human Condition: International Perspectives*, available online: www.oecd.org/sti/sci-tech/new-data-for-understanding-the-human-condition.htm, [accessed August 2, 2016].

Panagopoulos, C. and Green, D. P. (2008) "Field Experiments Testing the Impact of Radio Advertisements on Electoral Competition," *American Journal of Political Science*, vol. 52, no. 1, January, 156–168.

Pariser, E. (2011) *The Filter Bubble: What the Internet is Hiding from You*, London: Penguin.

Patterson, T. E. and McClure, R. D. (1976) "Television and the Less-Interested Voter: The Costs of an Informed Electorate," *The ANNALS of the American Academy of Political and Social Science*, vol. 425, no. 1, May, 88–97.

Price, V. and Czilli, E. J. (1996) "Modeling Patterns of News Recognition and Recall," *Journal of Communication*, vol. 46, no. 2, June, 55–78.

Price, V. and Zaller, J. (1993) "Who Gets the News? Alternative Measures of News Reception and Their Implications for Research," *Public Opinion Quarterly*, vol. 57, no. 2, Summer, 133–164.

Prior, M. (2005) "News vs. Entertainment: How Increasing Media Choice Widens Gaps in Political Knowledge and Turnout," *American Journal of Political Science*, vol. 49, no. 3, July, 577–592.

Prior, M. (2007) *Post-Broadcast Democracy: How Media Choice Increases Inequality in Political Involvement and Polarizes Elections*, Cambridge: Cambridge University Press.

Prior, M. (2009) "Improving Media Effects Research Through Better Measurement of News Exposure," *Journal of Politics*, vol. 71, no. 3, July, 893–908.

Prior, M. (2013) "The Challenge of Measuring Media Exposure: Reply to Dilliplane, Goldman, and Mutz," *Political Communication*, vol. 30, no. 4, October, 620–634.

Quintelier, E., and Vissers, S. (2008) "The Effect of Internet Use on Political Participation an Analysis of Survey Results for 16-Year-Olds in Belgium," *Social Science Computer Review*, vol. 26, no. 4, Winter, 411–427.

Rattinger, H., Roßteutscher, S., Schmitt-Beck, R., Weßels, B. and Wolf, C. (2015) "Campaign Media Content Analysis, Print Media (GLES 2013)," GESIS Data Archive, available online: http://dx.doi.org/10.4232/1.12293.

Reeves, A., McKee, M. and Stuckler, D. (2016) "'It's The Sun Wot Won It': Evidence of Media Influence on Political Attitudes and Voting from a UK Quasi-Natural Experiment," *Social Science Research*, vol. 56, March, 44–57.

Roberts, M. E., Stewart, B. M., Tingley, D., Lucas, C., Leder-Luis, J., Gadarian, S. K., Albertson, B. and Rand, D. G. (2014) "Structural Topic Models for Open-Ended Survey Responses," *American Journal of Political Science*, vol. 58, no. 4, October, 1064–1082.

Robinson, J. P. and Davis, D. K. (1990) "Television News and the Informed Public: An Information-Processing Approach," *Journal of Communication*, vol. 40, no. 3, September, 106–119.

Sanders, D. and Norris, P. (2005) "The Impact of Political Advertising in the 2001 UK General Election," *Political Research Quarterly*, vol. 58, no. 4, December, 525–536.

Schumpeter, J. A. (1950) *Capitalism, Socialism, and Democracy*, 3rd Edition, New York: Harper.

Sekhon, J. S. and Titiunik, R. (2012) "When Natural Experiments Are Neither Natural nor Experiments," *American Political Science Review*, vol. 106, no. 1, February, 35–57.

Shoemaker, P. J., Vos, T. P. and Reese, S. D. (2009) "Journalists as Gatekeepers," in Wahl-Jorgensen, K. and Hanitzsch, T. (eds.) *The Handbook of Journalism Studies*, New York: Routledge: 73–87.

Sigelman, L. and Buell, E. H. (2004) "Avoidance or Engagement? Issue Convergence in US Presidential Campaigns, 1960–2000," *American Journal of Political Science*, vol. 48, no. 4, October, 650–661.

Soroka, S. N. (2014) "Reliability and Validity in Automated Content Analysis," in Hart, R. P. (ed.) *Communication and Language Analysis in the Corporate World*, Hershey: Informational Science Reference: 352–363.

Soroka, S. N., Andrew, B., Aalberg, T., Iyengar, S., Curran, J., Coen, S., Hayashi, K., Jones, P., Mazzoleni, G., Woong Rhee, J., Rowe, D. and Tiffen, R. (2013) "Auntie Knows Best? Public Broadcasters and Current Affairs Knowledge," *British Journal of Political Science*, vol. 43, no. 4, October, 719–739.

Soroka, S., Young, L. and Balmas, M. (2015) "Bad News or Mad News? Sentiment Scoring of Negativity, Fear, and Anger in News Content," *The ANNALS of the American Academy of Political and Social Science*, vol. 659, no. 1, May, 108–121.

Stevens, D. and Karp, J. A. (2012) "Leadership Traits and Media Influence in Britain," *Political Studies*, vol. 60, no. 4, December, 787–808.

Stevens, D., Banducci, S., Karp, J. and Vowles, J. (2011) "Priming Time for Blair? Media Priming, Iraq, and Leadership Evaluations in Britain," *Electoral Studies*, vol. 30, no. 3, September, 546–560.

Sudulich, L., Wall, M., Gibson, R., Cantijoch, M. and Ward, S. (2014) "Introduction: The Importance of Method in the Study of the 'Political Internet'," in Cantijoch, M., Gibson, R. and Ward, S. (eds.) *Analyzing Social Media Data and Web Networks*, New York: Springer: 1–21.

Tsfati, Y. and Ariely, G. (2014) "Individual and Contextual Correlates of Trust in Media Across 44 Countries," *Communication Research*, vol. 41, no. 6, August, 760–782.

Valkenburg, P. M. and Peter, J. (2013) "Five Challenges for the Future of Media-Effects Research," *International Journal of Communication*, vol. 7, December, 197–215.

Zhao, X. and Chaffee, S. H. (1995) "Campaign Advertisements Versus Television News as Sources of Political Issue Information," *Public Opinion Quarterly*, vol. 59, no. 1, Spring, 41–65.

26

DIGITAL CAMPAIGNING

Stephen Ward, Rachel Gibson and Marta Cantijoch

Introduction

It is now over 20 years since political parties began to move online and fight elections using new internet technologies, although in most established democracies it took another decade, or more, before internet access spread to the majority of voters. Much of the initial research tracked the adaptation of parties, and to a lesser extent voters, to the internet. In particular, research was dominated by supply-side web content analyses examining how parties were using the technology (what if anything was new?), and how they compared with one another (who gained, if anyone?). On the demand side of the equation, there was a much more restricted field of quantitative studies of voter attitudes and behaviors online. Much of the initial research spent time looking for uniform effect patterns – notably, whether the internet provided any boost to political engagement. The empirical results of the early years were often underwhelming, although it is arguable whether: expectations of "internet effects" were too high; researchers were asking the right questions; and they were looking in the right places. However, as the internet has matured, with a second wave of social media technologies (so-called Web 2.0), scholars have both revisited earlier questions and also increasingly expanded their range of methods and tools. Furthermore, the era of big data has provided a new stimulus to study and as the internet has become embedded into everyday life, research has arguably moved away from its focus on the technology toward more socially structured approaches.

The purpose of this chapter, therefore, is to provide an overview of the development of research in the online party campaign sphere focusing on three main aspects: how technologies fit into the evolution of campaigning over time and whether they have introduced new characteristics and a new style to election campaigns; how voters have responded to the growth of the internet and social media and whether it has changed the way voters engage with parties and campaigns; and, finally, what difference, if any, the internet has made to party competition and supposed decline of parties (have there been winners and losers in the internet era?).

The evolution of campaign style: data-driven and citizen-led campaigns

A series of articles in the late 1990s and early 2000s discussed the evolution of election campaigning over the course of the last century (Blumler and Kavanagh 1999; Norris 2001; Farrell and Webb 2000). Commonly, they identified three campaign stages tied to changes in the social and political environment, party organizations and the media–communication nexus. Whilst none of these articles argued that technology was the only driver to party behavior, changes in media–communication environment are a clear thread in all of the models. In most advanced liberal democracies, it was argued that parties by the 1990s had moved (or were in the process of moving) toward a third age of campaigning – what Norris refers to as the post-modern era. This was stimulated most notably by the rise of new media technologies and the fragmentation of the media environment. Campaigns had become permanent, increasingly professionalized and marketized and with a renewed emphasis on localizing and personalizing national messages. Parties and candidates used stylized packaging and sharp marketing techniques, where their efforts were focused on discovering what the voter wants and shaping and targeting their policies (products) to meet these demands (Norris 2000; Bowers-Brown and Gunter 2002; Lees-Marshment 2005). This marked a significant shift from the previous modern campaign era that centered on parties bringing their message to the people particularly via the electronic media, especially television, with a focus on the national – often presidentialized – campaign. The new era also heralded a more mixed approach with a return to more localized campaigning.

Whilst some scholars were busy looking for evidence of this shift to the third era of postmodern campaigns, others had already begun to announce a fourth era of political communication built around internet communication. As Blumler explains: "Its crux must be the ever-expanding diffusion and utilization of Internet facilities – including their continual innovative evolution – throughout society, among all institutions with political goals and with politically relevant concerns and among many individual citizens" (Blumler 2013: n.p.). The apparently distinctive feature of the new era is the end to the pyramidal model of political communication where audience members, most of the time, were simply receivers of institutionally originated communications. Blumler also goes on to note that the internet has meant that previously interpersonal communication has become public; that it is now easier than ever before to communicate horizontally peer-to-peer, creating a potentially vibrant civic sphere. However, the vertical communication axis between citizens and politicians remains problematic, leaving a potentially lopsided democracy. Yet, how far this really represents a distinctively new stage is open to question. As Blumler himself notes, many of the features of the fourth age represent intensified third age characteristics, such as: the abundance of communication and information; centrifugal diversification leading to a mushrooming of civic associations; and non-party voices and medialization. Rather than a distinctive fourth stage, therefore, perhaps it would be better viewed as a halfway house – stage 3.5 perhaps?

Whilst new media technologies are, therefore, seen as central to models of the third/fourth campaign era, attention has focused more specifically on three supposedly critical features of twenty-first century campaigns: electronic targeting; interactive communication; and a decentralization of organizational control (Ward, Gibson and Lusoli 2008; Ward 2008; Lilleker and Vedel 2013):

- Targeting: computer technologies, databases and social media all enhanced the ability of parties/candidates to gather more data on the electorate, identify key swing voters (Bowers-Brown 2002) and target their campaign messages to particular groups or even personalize communication to individuals (narrowcasting).
- Decentralization: web tools were also seen as promoting a degree of decentralization by providing candidates, local parties and even individual supporters or activists with low-cost platforms for message dissemination (Norris 2000; Gibson and Ward 2003). The creation of these multiple communication channels theoretically made it more difficult for parties to

monitor and control information flows thus creating more opportunities for localization, personalization and message diversity, potentially fragmenting national party campaigns.

- Interactivity: perhaps what excited the most attention amongst democratic scholars was the interactive elements of new technologies (Hacker and van Dijk 2000; Shane 2004). In theory, the extent to which the public can become engaged with, and involved in, the campaign can be increased through internet technologies. Parties/candidates can now provide numerous opportunities via websites, blogs, email and social media to draw in the public and engage them in dialogue, changing the nature of campaigns from top-down events to more horizontal and conversational interactions (Ward, Gibson and Lusoli 2003).

Evidence to support such shifts in campaigning is, however, more mixed. It is arguable that, in terms of targeting, these were trends that had begun to be noted pre-internet (Denver and Hands 1997). Additionally, with regard to interactivity, repeated studies have consistently indicated parties'/candidates' reluctance to engage in interactivity or dialogue with voters (Stromer-Galley 2000; Gibson and Ward 2009; Jackson and Lilleker 2009). Content analysis of party websites almost uniformly found that parties largely used them for information provision rather than to stimulate interaction, and opportunities to participate online were often limited (Newell 2001; Strandberg 2006; Ward 2005). Often websites were simply seen as static electronic brochures (Gibson 2012). Similarly, interviews with party communication strategists revealed a marked reluctance to develop interactivity, especially in the context of election campaigns (Stromer-Galley 2000a; Ward 2005) for fear of opening oneself up to abuse and also losing control of the agenda to one's opponents. Even the arrival of social media platforms was greeted cautiously with relatively slow uptake by candidates/parties across many democracies (Southern and Ward 2011). Where candidates established a social media presence, critics often accused them of remaining in old-fashioned broadcast mode (Williamson 2010).

The question of whether internet technologies are to some extent decentralizing election campaigns is an intriguing one. Early research in the UK and the Netherlands stressed that computer technologies provide a further potential for centralization since party headquarters, leadership and campaign bureaucracies are often best placed to use the technology available (Nixon and Johansson 1999; Smith 1998, 2000). More directly, new groups of campaign professionals dedicated to web technologies (web designers, e-pollsters, e-campaign managers) were developing centered around party headquarters. Moreover, the growth of centralized database technologies targeting voters in key constituencies could further empower national party HQ to coordinate and direct campaigns (again trends identified in the pre-internet era). As time has progressed, however, it is clear that candidates and activists below the national level have increasingly adopted technologies – particularly social media platforms – and are in some instances using them to further personalize campaigning and establish media profiles (Southern and Ward 2011; Southern 2015). However, there is still debate as to how far this really individualizes or diversifies campaigns. Evidence from both the UK and Australia initially suggested a sort of top-down, centrally coordinated, localism (Gibson, Lusoli and Ward 2008), whereby candidates either replicated uniform web brochures or used social media to amplify (retweeted) centrally driven campaign messages. Again, such observations are not unique to the internet age. They reflect similar behavior by parties in respect of central oversight of candidates' leaflets (see, for example, Denver et al. 2002).

In sum, much of the supposed distinctiveness of digital campaigns is, more accurately, intensification and acceleration of some pre-existing trends (notably around targeting, personalization and organization). However, digital era campaigns do seem to have produced two distinct strands of campaigning: on the one hand, a private, data-driven, top-down approach using online data-gathering and marketing aimed at identifying and mobilizing small groups of swing voters. Arguably, this is more of a continuation of the post-war model of centralized, professionalized, command and control electioneering. The second strand (characterized, in particular, by Obama's 2008 campaign) suggests a more novel approach of a more public citizen-initiated campaign model whereby parties/candidates make extensive use of new social media tools (blogs and social network sites) to outsource core campaign tasks (e.g., fundraising, canvassing) to ordinary supporters (Vacarri 2010; Norquay 2008; Bimber 2014). The web-based nature of citizen-initiated campaign actions means that, as well as bringing more citizen input and direction into the campaign management process itself, it also has the potential to bring more citizens as a whole into the electoral and political arena by increasing voter contact opportunities (Gibson 2012). Further empirical research is needed to understand the dynamics, contradictions and likely success of these two distinct approaches.

Internet "effects": mobilizing and polarizing?

In the myriad of studies concerning internet effects, two debates have tended to dominate the field: first, could the internet change the nature and patterns of engagement between parties and voters, especially in an era of dealignment and protest where parties need to work hard to build and maintain support? Second, to what extent is the internet responsible for intensifying political polarization and hardening inter-party animus with potentially damaging effects for representative democracy?

The mobilization debate

There was considerable hope at the outset that the internet might offer at least a partial solution to declining turnouts and increasing dissatisfaction with politics and parties. Acres of newsprint and academic work have been devoted to the normative benefits of technology and how it might be harnessed to drive political engagement (see, for example, Barber 1998; Coleman 1999; Shane 2004; Dahlgren 2009). The case for technology providing mobilization boosts and enhancing participation rests on a combination of:

- Lowering the costs of engagement: whilst traditional participation in parties often involved a high degree of commitment it also limited who could connect. One suggestion was that participation could be widened, since the internet lowered the barriers to mobilization (Bonchek 1995; Bimber 1998; Gibson et al. 2003). Essentially, connecting with political parties could be done at a time of the citizen's choosing from the comfort of their own homes. Thus for those time-poor or housebound, for example, virtual tools could enhance their ability to engage more regularly.
- Increased informational stimuli: traditional political science already identified benefits of information stimuli to voter mobilization (Norris 2001; Bimber 1999). The suggestion was, therefore, that the internet would increase these stimuli by providing easy access to vast amounts of information and data.
- Enhanced ability to network: the importance of ties and solidarity have long been recognized in political science in terms of building supporter and activist bases (Castells 2001). Connections and peer networks have been important in developing shared beliefs and commitment to political organizations. Internet technologies provided an additional opportunity to develop such ties in a virtual context. Hence, online search engines make it easier

to identify like-minded individuals, share ideas and build solidarity that might deepen supporters' commitment to a candidate or party.

- Self-expression and creativity: the interactive nature of technology and users' relative control have led some to suggest that the internet is more stimulating and creative and provides a greater sense of enjoyment and expression than traditional methods of engagement, thus indirectly increasing users' efficacy (Chadwick 2009; Vaccari et al. 2015).
- Enhanced ability to target: whilst individuals can find others of similar political beliefs, the internet also enables parties to target such individuals more effectively and to keep them engaged even without a widespread activist base on the ground. Internet data gathering tools allow parties to identify potential sympathizers and to direct their marketing more efficiently to these people. Once links are formed, participation and engagement can be maintained and deepened through regular online contacts, invites and information to develop a thicker level of engagement (Lusoli and Ward 2004; Etzioni and Etzioni 1997).
- Generational boost: within all the above elements, it was also noted that there was an increased opportunity for a generational shift, since younger voters (often the least likely to participate in formal politics) were the ones most likely to engage extensively with internet technologies (Livingstone, Bober and Helsper 2005; Coleman 2005; Bennett 2008; Vromen 2007; Bakker and de Vreese 2011).

Skeptics, however, pointed out that the basis of any mobilization effects were mainly built on technologically determinist approaches but largely neglected political and social factors that shaped voters predilection to participate or engage with parties (Davis 1999; Bimber and Davis 2003). Consequently, a number of scholars indicated that the most likely impact of internet technologies was the reinforcement of existing patterns of engagement since political interest was unlikely to be changed by technology alone. In essence, those most likely to engage politically online were voters with a pre-existing political interest. Essentially, therefore, internet technologies preached to the converted (Norris 2001).

In testing these ideas, much of the early survey work, especially during campaigns, did seem to support the reinforcement concept, although data were often limited and patchy outside the US. Surveys indicated that there was relatively low direct engagement with party online campaigns and, where it did occur, the profile of participants was similar to traditional patterns of engagement – that is, it was those with high levels of political interest, partisanship and civic skills, though there was evidence of a more youthful audience (Koc-Michalska and Vedel 2009; Rainie and Smith 2008). One explanation for this familiar pattern was the focus of participatory studies. Graham and co-authors have suggested that to get a fully rounded picture of engagement in the internet era there is a need to move beyond formal political sites or to go where people are, rather than where we would like them to be (Graham et al. 2016).

If evidence of broad direct effects was limited, several researchers did raise other intriguing possibilities, including gains in political knowledge, discussion and efficacy via online methods (Xenos and Moy 2007; Lupia and Philpot 2005; Vacarri et al. 2015). One interesting example directly related to election campaigning found evidence of potential two-step flows and indirect effects in relation to internet mobilization (Norris and Curtice 2008). The smaller group of political engaged and interested were further engaged by online tools but were then also more likely to converse with relatively inattentive citizens through traditional offline mechanisms, producing the possibility of indirect participation boosts.

Analyses of the deepening of engagement and stimulation of activism within parties have also often seemed relatively limited. The most popular forms of online activity did not differ that much from traditional participation, with information gathering and low-commitment activities, such as donating and signing petitions, consistently amongst the most common. Though, as Gibson and Cantijoch (2013) have noted, it is possible that the internet is blurring high- and low-intensity participation. The argument here being that what were previously seen as passive acts of engagement, such as accessing news and information in the offline environment, have become more demanding and pro-active tasks in the online world. Keeping up with digital news typically involves seeking out sources and pulling them toward you rather than consuming prepared news programming that is pushed out through regular media channels.

Further research in both the US and the UK suggested that, whilst it might be possible to mobilize party/candidate supporters online, it is difficult to maintain engagement and party membership through online methods alone – that is, they required further face-to-face contact to boost engagement (Lusoli and Ward 2004), otherwise many dropped out. In the UK, this pattern of low-commitment activity and possible short-term engagement seems to have been maintained in the social media era. Poletti, Bale and Webb's recent work on the Labour Party's new membership base has found that recent joiners were "more likely to be clicktivists and slacktivists rather than activists" (2016: np) – engaging online, but much less likely to be committed to traditional activist behaviors, such as attending meetings, canvassing and leafleting. In short, therefore, whilst one can find high-profile examples of online mobilization (notably Obama's 2008 campaign), the difficulty for parties is to maintain supporters beyond short campaigns and deepen their engagement within party structures.

The overall picture of online mobilization is perhaps best summed up by Boulianne's (2009) large-scale, meta-analysis of over 50 studies of online participation that demonstrated modest positive effects. Thus, whilst the internet may not have radically transformed who engages with parties, it has undoubtedly added to the way that we do politics and in turn this may eventually recalibrate our expectations of parties and politicians.

Polarization and intensification

The second major area of the effects literature is one concerning the intensification of political attitudes leading to balkanization. Donald Trump's US presidential victory along with the UK's EU referendum campaign in 2016 prompted renewed interest in the issue of growing polarization amongst voters. Media commentators have drawn attention to a coarsening of political debate, increasingly outlandish political claims and the rise of abuse and fake news. The finger was often pointed at social media and the so-called echo chambers that it creates for intensifying partisan negativity. Fears have been expressed that social media is driving voters into increasingly partisan and even extremist positions. Yet, none of these fears are necessarily new. In part, it replicates earlier longstanding concerns or debates surrounding the effects of the partisan bias of the print media in terms of agenda setting, priming, framing and cuing (Gunther 1998; Graber 1988). Additionally, even before the internet reached much beyond an elite audience, Nicholas Negroponte (1995) was already referring to the notion of "the Daily Me," where people would receive increasingly personalized news feeds. The notion of the Daily Me was subsequently expanded by Cass Sunstein (2001), who warned that the increasing choice and personalization of news raised the possibility of electoral balkanization where audiences largely consumed media which reinforced their existing prejudices but did little to foster deliberation in debate across ideological or social divides.

The notion that the internet exacerbates polarization amongst voters is based on a number of factors: first, that the internet and social media have significantly increased the amount of partisan sources of information available to the electorate. The lowering of costs of producing news and circulating means that potentially anyone with a mobile or tablet can create news sources and stories. Moreover, information and news produced online was not necessarily subject to the same professional journalistic standards as mainstream media or, particularly, public service broadcasting. Hence, the internet could be seen primarily as fora for emotion and opinion-based statements. Second, increasingly, voters consume content on the basis of selective exposure – that is, they are drawn to material that backs up pre-existing beliefs or coincides with their pre-existing interests. The increasing levels of media choice mean that people can more easily access news and current affairs but also screen out information deemed as uninteresting, irrelevant or disagreeable (Prior 2007). Third, this selective exposure is then supported by, and intertwined with, people's online networks and filters. In part, this reflects automated filter bubbles. For example, platforms such as Facebook automatically promote posts that fit with our declared interests and views. Additionally, the argument behind polarization suggests that our networks are largely homogenous, with like-minded people communicating with one another – the birds of a feather flock together argument (McPherson, Smith-Lovin and Cook 2001). The import-ance of these networks is strengthened by research that indicates that we are much more likely to pay attention to messages from friends, family and close colleagues (Sunstein 2006). Hence, Twitter, in particular, is often seen as an echo chamber where people of similar political out-looks spread or replicate each other's messages but are rarely challenged by alternative view-points or voices. The apparent long-term impact of increased exposure to like-minded views is the adoption of more extreme positions (Mutz and Martin 2001). Fourth, some psychological studies have indicated that not only are the networks similar but we are more susceptible and pay more attention to material and information we like or that we agree with and conversely are more likely to discount or delete material which does not fit with our belief patterns (Colle-oni, Rozza and Arvidsson 2014). This filtering is then heightened by the anonymity of some elements of technology. This reduces social and psychological inhibitions and cues, thus stimu-lating individuals to express more extreme views and/or indulge in abuse of opponents in ways that they would not in the offline world (Joinson 2007).

Whilst intuitively these arguments make logical sense, the research evidence on voter polari-zation and social media consumption is far from clear-cut. At the outset, it is worth remember-ing that polarization trends in the US were identified well before the internet came along. Authors such as Prior (2013) argue that it was the development of cable news especially that was more significant in changing patterns of partisan news consumption. Furthermore, various researchers have reminded us of the continued importance of mainstream media in elections. Whilst internet sources may have grown dramatically in importance over the past decade, televi-sion and familiar mainstream media (MSM) sources that have moved online remain important players in terms of news consumption (Nielson and Schroder 2014; Meijer and Kormelink 2015). Indeed, in countries with a strong public service broadcast tradition, trust in these relat-ively non-partisan sources remains high (Brevini 2013). Even in the US, it is argued that the bulk of voters remain wedded to mainly middle-of-the-road media sources (Prior 2013).

Yet, Lelkes, Sood and Iyengar (2015), in their broad study of impact of access to broadband media, have contended that there is a link to increasing polarization in the US. This is because access to internet broadband has led to both increased supply and demand for partisan program-ming and, more specifically, increasing exposure to imbalanced partisan rhetoric and sources for audiences. They argue that even small changes in media choice can impact significantly on preferences and attitudes. Furthermore, when changes in media consumption develop over longer periods of time then effects can be cumulative.

Whilst there is plenty of support for the notion of homophily in online networks, there is still disagreement about both its extent and its impact. Early research on the US blogosphere indicated intense degrees of clustering between either liberal or republican bloggers (Adamic and Glance 2005; Hargittai, Gallo and Kane 2008). In terms of social media networks (especially Twitter and Facebook), a range of reports have found high levels of ideological and social clustering (Halberstam and Knight 2016; Huber and Malhotra 2016; Lee et al. 2014). Nevertheless, there are still some analyses that have pointed to a more diverse nature in social media networks (Gentzkow and Shapiro 2011). In particular, it has been suggested that people may have wider networks online than they do in real life. Although many of the links are relatively weak, they are still important in providing diversity to people's sources of information. Consequently, there is evidence that citizens are more likely to be accidentally exposed to information on social media than in Web 1.0 or even via MSM since both these require a greater degree of selection (Gil de Zúñiga and Valenzuela 2011). Indeed, Barberá's (2015) comparative study of Germany, Spain and the US actually refutes the popular wisdom and goes as far as to suggest that social media is reducing polarization.

One common line of thought on polarization is that its greatest impact is on the more politically committed. The majority of the electorate pays far less attention or, indeed, screens it out. Thus, Prior (2013) finds evidence of polarization mainly amongst the relatively small core activist groups. However, such activist partisan groups are likely to have more impact on overall conduct and debate in campaigns since they are the most engaged. So it could be that these groups drive the agenda toward more extreme positions, whilst the majority electorate become increasingly disillusioned and detached.

At the time of writing, there is renewed concern over internet driven polarization following acrimonious campaigns in the US presidential race, referendum campaigns in the UK and Italy (Brookings Institute 2016; Duggan and Smith 2016; McCutcheon 2016) and the rise of the populist right in Europe more generally (Habermas 2016; Engesser et al. 2016). Two themes in particular have emerged; first, much popular attention has centered on the rise and impact of the spread of fake news via social media (Guardian 2016), especially in the US presidential race. A US Buzzfeed news analysis (2016) reported that the large partisan Facebook news sites were regularly producing false news stories about opponents. This is not simply a US problem; recent elections in Europe have likewise seen false claims spread virally and rapidly. For example, the 2016 Austrian presidential election saw websites spread rumors that the Independent-Green backed candidate was suffering from dementia. Similarly, in the 2016 French primary, rumors were spread of false links between one leading center-right candidate (Alain Juppé) and the Muslim brotherhood (Guardian 2016). Second, related to this rise in fake news is the apparent growth of automated political propaganda generated by bots (Forelle et al. 2015). Research calculated that, as US election day approached, bot messaging was increasing significantly. In addition, the vast majority of bots (85 percent) were producing partisan messages and pro-Trump bots were considerably more prevalent than Clinton ones (Kollanyi, Howard and Woolley 2016).

In summarizing the debate around political polarization and the internet, there is widespread agreement that the internet may have exacerbated rather than started the problem. However, it is also not clear how far polarization has spread amongst electorates, especially outside the US. More nuanced readings of data suggest that polarization is more likely to occur amongst the already politically partisan. What is clear though is that debates about social media and polarization are likely to increase in the wake of the rise of populism across liberal democracies.

Party competition: who benefits?

One early line of thought was that political parties generally would be losers in the internet era (Rheingold 1993; Negroponte 1995; Morris 2000). In particular, much interest was generated in ideas of direct forms of democracy with electronic technology stimulating the growth of electronic voting and referendums, and the ability of individual citizens to participate in politics bypassing collective organizations (Rash 1997; Morris 2000). Alternatively, some argued that, whilst all organizations might gain from new technologies, the real winners were likely to be the more flexible, less hierarchical, protest networks (Bimber 1998; Castells 2019; Bennett and Segerberg 2013). It is no coincidence that much of this enthusiasm for direct plebiscitary democracy emerged in the US where the internet achieved significant penetration rates earlier than elsewhere but perhaps more importantly political culture individualized and was less party-centered than European democracies. However, in many established democracies, politicians and mainstream parties were concerned that the internet might further erode their support base (see Blears 2008).

Twenty years on and clearly parties have not disappeared. Indeed, the internet has been seen as crucial to the rise of some candidates and parties. For instance, the success of the Five Star Movement in Italy has been attributed, in part, to its online organization (Mosca, Vaccari and Valeriani 2013), whilst in the UK the rise of Jeremy Corbyn to the leadership of the Labour Party has also been partially attributed to the harnessing of social media to significantly increase the party membership base (Bale 2016). Thus parties per se are not necessarily threatened by internet technologies but nevertheless mainstream political parties have undoubtedly been challenged by demands for more direct methods of participation and the often disruptive nature of social media (Margetts et al. 2015). It is, therefore, worth considering two decades after the emergence of the internet whether there have been any distinct patterns in terms of party adaption to the net and whether there have been any real winners or losers?

Equalization and normalization: leveling the communication playing field?

The dominant question of many studies of party campaigns online has been the notion of equalization of party competition online and whether minor and outsider parties were likely to be the main beneficiaries of the technology. The idea of equalization or the leveling of the communication playing field rests on a combination of elements (Corrado and Firestone 1996; Rash 1997; Gibson and Ward 1998; Gibson, Römmele and Ward 2003; Lilleker and Vedel 2013): first, that internet technologies have weakened the power of so-called mainstream media, especially the power of newspapers as gatekeepers and controllers of the political agenda. In the old world of television, radio and newspapers, there was limited space for political coverage and editors/journalists primarily determined who had access to that space and what would be of interest to their publics. The virtual sphere is largely without editorial control and therefore has been viewed as a more open space. Hence, political parties that were squeezed out of MSM could establish a platform and presence much more easily online. Interrelated to this notion of a more open space, is the idea that the internet lowers cost of campaigning. Whilst older media forms required a considerable outlay of resources and expertise, the suggestion was that, with minimal levels of skills and technology, outsider and minor parties/candidates could establish a campaign platform to sit alongside their mainstream rivals. In short, therefore, the internet allowed them greater access to get their message across to voters. In allowing these minor parties presence and access, it also potentially provided an additional benefit – that of amplification. By establishing themselves online, relatively minor parties could appear larger and more credible online than they were in reality (Ackland and Gibson 2013).

The benefit of the internet was not simply to minor party organizations themselves, but also to their supporters and activists. The interactive nature of the internet allowed supporters to find one another and to build networks of support even across large geographical areas. Whereas distance had hampered the building of activism in the pre-internet world, the virtual sphere collapsed many of these barriers (Gillan 2009).

The idea of equalization has also been supported from time to time by the emergence of high-profile campaigns by outsider candidates. One of the first to attract attention was the Independent Jesse Ventura's 1998 success in the Minnesota Gubernatorial race. This, in part, was attributed to his ability to build email networks almost from scratch and encourage online donations (Stromer-Galley 2000b); although it is worth remembering that Ventura already had a high media profile as a former wrestler and radio talk show host. Similarly, Howard Dean's ultimately failed bid for the Democratic presidential nomination in 2004 garnered considerable media attention for its innovative use of blogs, meet-ups and online mobilization. The Dean campaign was seen as a template of how a little known outsider with limited resources could build a national campaign from scratch using the internet (Trippi 2004). Obama's triumph in the Democratic primary in 2007/8 overcoming the initial favorite, Hillary Clinton, was also seen as evidence of how innovative web campaigning could help organize campaigns and build virtual momentum (Pollard, Chesebro and Studinski 2009; Vaccari 2010). Nor were such outsider examples necessarily limited to the US. The success of South Korean challenger candidate Roh Moo-Hyun in the 2002 presidential race was seen as the result of his ability to mobilize younger Koreans via internet tools (Hague and Uhm 2003). In recent years, the Italian Five Star Movement (5SM) has been seen as another exemplar of outsider success built on online platforms. The movement party was popularized initially via its founder's blog site and latterly by social media organization (Tronconi 2015; Hartleb 2013). Yet, whilst organizationally 5SM benefited from new technologies, its political successes stemmed more from the collapse in confidence in the Italian political establishment (Fella and Ruzza 2013).

These high-profile examples largely remain the exceptions though. The idea of equalization or leveling has been regularly challenged by the concept of normalization, arguing that internet campaigns should not be seen as divorced from the traditional world of politics. Indeed, normalizers such as Margolis and Resnick (2000) claimed that mainstream parties would come to dominate cyberspace as they did traditional campaign space, particularly as the internet became more and more commercialized. Running sophisticated online campaigns, it was argued, still required significant resources and skills, notably as the web design become more professionalized. Moreover, as Bimber and Davis (2003) noted, the traditional media still remained important as voters still primarily relied on television for news and current affairs and the MSM also tend to shape the agenda of online discussion rather than vice-versa. Additionally, Hindman, Tsioutsiouliklis and Johnson (2003) pointed out that, given many voters used search engines to find information, the playing field could be significantly influenced by search engine rankings, which were often significantly skewed toward already influential players. Thus, overall, the expectation of normalizers was that online party competition would increasingly come to resemble the offline world.

Examining the empirical studies conducted over the past two decades in a range of democracies provides a fairly consistent story in relation to party online competition. The so-called Web 1.0 era almost uniformly suggested a generalized pattern of normalization (see Table 26.1). Only a few early studies prior to 2007 suggested equalization. For example, Gibson and Ward's (1998: 22) report on the 1997 UK general election concluded that: "far from leaving the minor parties in the dust the internet appears to be doing more to equalize exposure of parties' ideas to the electorate compared to other media."

The vast majority of the analyses, though, concluded that the larger parties ran the richest websites in terms of their functionality (depth of information provided, opportunities to engage and resource gathering) but also used their pre-existing resource advantages to drive traffic to their sites. Yet, underlying the broad picture of normalization was an acceptance that some minor parties could at least establish a website presence more effectively on the internet. Moreover, in isolation, the virtual sphere was at least more level than MSM. With this in mind, Ward (2005, 2008) argued that rather than leveling the communication playing field, the internet had widened it allowing more parties or candidates to survive politically but not necessarily thrive electorally. Political system factors, such as electoral thresholds or non-proportional electoral systems, often still mitigated against translating such online presence into electoral success.

Nonetheless, moves toward normalization did not necessarily represent a steady evolution. There is evidence from some studies of an ebb and flow pattern in competition – notably, that major parties were more likely to dominate in election campaigns whilst minor counterparts were more successful outside election periods (Gibson and Ward 2009; Lilleker and Vedel 2013). The rise of social media has subsequently seen a renewed interest in re-examining the dominance of normalization (Gueoguieva 2008; Kalnes 2009; Strandberg 2009). Social media, it was suggested, provided an even lower cost platform than increasingly costly and professionalized websites and a greater ability to organize and motivate supporters for minor parties. Empirically, there are some indications here that, whilst normalization still predominates, there is greater degree of hope for some of the smaller parties. Early Web 2.0 studies in Finland (Strandberg 2009) and Norway (Kalnes 2009) both found that minor parties had, at least, an established presence. However, Gibson and McAllister (2015), in their longitudinal study of Australia, went even further. They found that, compared to their major counterparts, Green Party candidates were not only more likely to adopt new media but also received an electoral boost (in vote terms) for doing so.

Beyond normalization?

Studies have also indicated though that, whilst generalized normalization seems to predominate, the concept of normalization needs refining beyond simply the size of a party. For example, two minor party families have repeatedly been highlighted in empirical work as outperforming their counterparts – the Greens and the far right. Incentives for using internet technologies are seen as one persistent explanation for this pattern. In the case of Green parties, beyond the cost/resources incentives outlined above, their core audience is seen as heavy internet users (for example, students or public-sector, university-educated workers), providing additional stimuli for technology use. Moreover, some studies indicate an ideological element, with the internet facilitating organizational models of operation favored by Green parties – that is, decentralized, less hierarchical and network based (Voerman and Ward 2000). There may also be an ideological component to far right activity online, with many groups viewing the traditional media as part of a corrupt liberal establishment that seeks to lock them out of political discussion (Copsey 2003). However, there may be more practical reasons why far right groups have consistently used online technologies to mobilize – secrecy and anonymity. Whilst far right sympathizers may be reluctant to admit their preference in real-world situations, online they can find support for their views and are potentially emboldened to then act (Whine 2000; Copsey 2003; Lilleker and Jackson 2011).

Whilst much of the focus of party competition online has been on adaptation and use of the internet, the second part of the equalization equation – whether this makes any electoral difference – is much less prominent in research. The assumption, often based on interviews with party campaign strategists, is that the internet has made limited difference to electoral performance. As early as 1997, D'Alessio found a positive and significant effect of having a website on US congressional candidates' vote. A positive relationship was also detected between candidates' online campaign presence and electoral support by Gibson and McAllister (2006, 2015) in

Table 26.1 Party competition studies

Author	Publication date	Country	Competition	Notes
Voerman	1998	Netherlands	Normalization	
Margolis et al.	1996 and 1999	US	Normalization	
Gibson and Ward	1998	UK	No clear trend	
Gibson and Ward	2000a	UK	No clear trend	Possible ebb and flow between elections and peace time
Gibson and Ward	2000b	UK (EU elections)	Equalization	
Gibson, Newell and Ward	2000	Italy	Normalization	
Newell	2001	Italy	Normalization	Minimal distinction between parties
Gibson and Ward	2002	Australia	Normalization	
Cunha et al.	2003	Italy, Spain, Portugal, Greece	Normalization	
Tkach-Kawasaki	2003	Japan	Normalization	
March	2004	Russia	Normalization	
Lusoli	2005	EU elections	Normalization	
Conway and Dorner	2004	New Zealand	Normalization	
Hara and Jo	2007	South Korea and US	Didn't fit either	
Schweitzer	2005 and 2008	Germany	Normalization	
Small	2008	Canada	Normalization	
Latimer	2008	US	Normalization	Sub presidential study
Jackson and Lilleker	2009	UK (EU elections)	Weak normalization, possible ebb and flow	

Author	Year	Location	Finding	Study type
Ward	2011	British Columbia	Normalization	Over-time study
Vergeer and Hermans	2013	Netherlands	No clear pattern	
Klinger	2013	Switzerland	Normalization	Social media study
Xu	2011	Singapore	Equalization on presence but not on outcome	Social media study
Sudulich	2013	Ireland, UK, Italy, Spain	Normalization	Over-time study
Gomez and Muhamed	2010	Singapore, Malaysia	No clear fit, lean towards normalization	
Hinz	2014	Germany	Equalization (party) Normalization (candidate)	Social media study
Lorenzo-Rodriguez	2014	Spain and Italy	Variable but social media looks more promising for equalization	Over-time study
Hansen and Pedersen	2014	Denmark	No fit	
Koc-Michalska et al.	2016	Poland, Germany, UK, France	Normalization	Web 2.0 study
Ridout et al.	2015	US (Senate)	Normalization	YouTube study
Samuel-Azran, Yarchi and Wolfsfeld	2015	Israel	Equalization	Social media study
Southern	2015	UK	Normalization (adoption) but social media shows signs of equalization	
Koc-Michalska et al.	2016	UK, Poland, France, Germany	Normalization	Over-time study
Gibson and McAllister	2015	Australia	Variable – normalization Web 1.0 era, more balanced social media era	Over-time study
Guðmundsson	2016	Iceland	Normalization	
Tan, Tng and Yeo	2016	Singapore	Normalization	Social media study

Australia between 2001 and 2010. Similar results were reported by Sudulich and Wall (2010) in Irish parliamentary elections. In seeking to account for the positive findings Gibson and McAllister (2011: 240) speculated that it might be seen as "a proxy for a degree of candidate professionalism and competence not captured by the standard Australian Candidate Study measures" but required further investigation. Other studies, however, have not observed much in the way of positive electoral effects (Fisher, Cutts and Fieldhouse 2011; Fisher et al. 2016; Hansen and Pederson 2014).

Although work on normalization/equalization has now covered a large range of democracies research has tended to consist of electoral snapshots of individual campaigns and there is far less comparative or longitudinal work. As a result, authors such as Anstead and Chadwick (2008) have argued that the importance of the systemic political and media environment in explaining party and voter activity online is underplayed. Hence, in comparing the US and the UK they pointed to five key variables (degree of systemic institutional pluralism; organization of membership; candidate recruitment and selection; campaign finance; and the "old" campaign communication environment) as offering a framework to shaping difference in internet campaigning cross-nationally. Rigorously testing out the influence of such systemic factors still remains to be conducted.

Conclusions

Looking back on 20 years of digital campaigning, the early hopes of radical internet-driven transformation provided a framework that was not altogether helpful in terms of developing our understanding of the relationship between the internet and politics. Indeed, the empirically generated backlash of limited effects studies has then arguably understated the extent of change as the internet has become embedded into political life. Democratic theorists and commentators spent much time initially focusing on the creation of virtual public spheres and notions of electronic democracy. However, the focus of parties and campaigns has often been driven by more prosaic concerns, particularly how to maximize their message in an increasingly noisy and competitive communication environment. In academic terms, it took some time before internet research was grounded in, and related to, existing knowledge/theory of campaigns, media and communication effects, party organization and political participation. However, there is growing realization that our older definitions and models of what constitute politics or political participation are being blurred and expanded by internet technologies.

The three broad areas we have assessed here exhibited similar patterns of initial hype, followed by a search for grand uniform effects, before settling into examination of more nuanced social theory-led approaches. Hence, whilst the internet may not have equalized competition, there is evidence that it does challenge elites and has created new uncertainties for politicians. The world of social media politics seems to have exacerbated earlier trends toward personalized, populist and oppositional style politics, although it remains to be seen whether it can maintain long-term constructive activism or support effective party governance. Similarly, the internet may not have radically reshaped who participates (in campaigns), but it has changed the nature of campaigns and how we participate. It has been a hugely beneficial tool for the political activist and politically interested, which can help stimulate overall mobilization. However, there is increasing evidence that, in some circumstances, social media may well be furthering polarizing attitudes and creating participation divides. The risk is that increasingly hostile and heated campaigns are fought out amongst the politically committed but are largely divorced from, and disillusion, the bulk of the less politically engaged.

References

Ackland, R. and Gibson, R. (2013) "Hyperlinks and Networked Communication: A Comparative Study of Political Parties Online," *International Journal of Social Research Methodology*, vol. 16, no. 3, 231–244.

Adamic, L. A. and Glance, N. (2005) "The Political Blogosphere and the 2004 U.S. Election: Divided They Blog," Paper presented at the 2005 International Workshop on Link Discovery, Chicago, August 21–25.

Anstead, N. and Chadwick, A. (2008) "Parties, Election Campaigning, and the Internet: Toward a Comparative Institutional Approach," in Chadwick, A. and Howard, P. (eds.) *The Handbook of Internet Politics*, London: Routledge: 56–71.

Bakker, T. P. and de Vreese, C. H. (2011) "Good News for the Future? Youth's Internet Use and Political Participation," *Communication Research*, vol. 38, no. 4, August, 1–20.

Bale, T. (2016) "Jezza's Bezzas: Labour's New Members," *The Huffington Post*, June 28th 2016, available online: www.huffingtonpost.co.uk/tim-bale/jeremy-corbyn-labour-membership_b_10713634.html, [accessed December 19, 2016].

Barber, B. R. (1998) "Three Scenarios for the Future of Technology and Strong Democracy," *Political Science Quarterly*, vol. 113, no. 4, Winter, 573–589.

Barberá, P. (2015) "How Social Media Reduces Mass Political Polarization: Evidence from Germany, Spain, and the U.S.," Paper presented at the 2015 Annual Meeting of the American Political Science Association, San Francisco, September 3–6.

Bennett, W. L. (2008) *Civic Life Online: Learning How Digital Media Can Engage Youth*, Cambridge, MA: MIT Press.

Bennett, W. L. and Segerberg, A. (2013) *The Logic of Connective Action: Digital Media and the Personalization of Contentious Politics*, Cambridge: Cambridge University Press.

Bimber, B. (1998) "The Internet and Political Transformation: Populism, Community and Accelerated Pluralism," *Polity*, vol. 31, no. 1, Autumn, 133–160.

Bimber, B. (1999) "The Internet and Citizen Communication with Government: Does the Medium Matter?," *Political Communication*, vol. 16, no. 4, October, 409–429.

Bimber, B. (2014) "Digital Media in the Obama Campaigns of 2008 and 2012: Adaptation to the Personalized Political Communication Environment," *Journal of Information Technology and Politics*, vol. 11, no. 2, 130–150.

Bimber, B. and Davis, R. (2003) *Campaigning Online: The Internet and US Elections*, Oxford: Oxford University Press.

Blears, H. (2008) "Tackling Political Disengagement," Speech to Hansard Society, November 5, 2008, available online: https://revitalisingpolitics.files.wordpress.com [accessed December 17, 2016].

Blumler, J. (2013) "The Fourth Age of Political Communication." Available online: www.fgpk.de/en/2013/gastbeitrag-von-jay-g-blumler-the-fourth-age-of-political-communication-2/ [accessed December 20, 2016].

Blumler, J. and Kavanagh, D. (1999) "The Third Age of Communication: Influences and Features," *Political Communication*, vol. 16, no. 3, July, 209–230.

Bonchek, M. (1995) "Grassroots in Cyberspace: Recruiting Members on the Internet or Do Computer Networks Facilitate Collective Action? A Transaction Cost Approach," Paper presented at the 1995 Annual Meeting of the Midwest Political Science Association, Chicago, April 6–8.

Boulianne, S. (2009) "Does Internet Use Affect Engagement? A Meta-Analysis of Research," *Political Communication*, vol. 26, no. 2, April, 193–211.

Bowers-Brown, J. and Gunter, B. (2002) "Political Parties' Use of the Web During the 2001 General Election," *Aslib Proceedings*, vol. 54, no. 3, 166–176.

Brevini, B. (2013) *Public Service Broadcasting Online: A Comparative Policy Study of PSB 2.0*, Basingstoke: Palgrave.

Brookings Institute (2016) "Brexit: The First Major Casualty of Digital Democracy," June 29, 2016, available online: www.brookings.edu/blog/order-from-chaos/2016/06/29/brexit-the-first-major-casualty-of-digital-democracy/ [accessed December 20, 2016].

Buzzfeed (2016) "This Analysis Shows How Fake Election News Stories Outperformed Real News On Facebook," November 16, 2016, available online: www.buzzfeed.com/craigsilverman/viral-fake-election-news-outperformed-real-news-on-facebook?utm_term=.pk5YEKwQE#.gkvMevyxe [accessed December 18, 2016].

Castells, M. (2001) *The Internet Galaxy*, Oxford: Oxford University Press.

Castells, M. (2009) *Communication Power*, Oxford: Oxford University Press.

Chadwick, A. (2009) "Web 2.0: New Challenges for the Study of E-Democracy in an Era of Informational Exuberance," *I/S: Journal of Law and Policy for the Information Society*, vol. 5, no. 1, 9–41.

Coleman, S. (1999) "Can the New Media Invigorate Democracy?" *The Political Quarterly*, vol. 70, no. 1, January, 16–22.

Coleman, S. (2005) "New Mediation and Direct Representation: Reconceptualizing Representation in the Digital Age," *New Media and Society*, vol. 7, no. 2, April, 177–198.

Colleoni, E., Rozza, A. and Arvidsson, A. (2014) "Echo Chamber or Public Sphere? Predicting Political Orientation and Measuring Political Homophily in Twitter Using Big Data," *Journal of Communication*, vol. 64, no. 2, April, 317–332.

Conway, M. and Dorner, D. (2004) "An Evaluation of New Zealand Political Party Websites," *Information Research*, vol. 9, no. 4, July.

Copsey, N. (2003) "Extremism on the Net: The Extreme Right and the Value of the Internet," in Gibson, R. K., Nixon, P. and Ward, S. J. (eds.) *Political Parties and the Internet: Net Gain?* London: Routledge: 218–233.

Corrado, A. and Firestone, C. (1996) *Elections in Cyberspace: Toward a New Era in American Politics*, Washington, DC: Aspen Institute.

Cunha, C., Martin, I., Newell, J. and Ramiro, L. (2003) "Southern European Parties and Party Systems, and the New ICTs," in Gibson, R. K., Nixon, P. and Ward, S. J. (eds.) *Political Parties and the Internet: Net Gain?* London: Routledge: 70–97.

D'Alessio, D. W. (1997) "Use of the Web in the 1996 US Election," *Electoral Studies*, vol. 16, no. 4, December, 489–501.

Dahlgren, P. (2009) *Media and Political Engagement: Citizens, Communication and Democracy*, Cambridge: Cambridge University Press.

Davis, R. (1999) *The Web of Politics*, Oxford: Oxford University Press.

Denver, D. and Hands, G. (1997) *Modern Constituency Electioneering: Local Campaigning at the 1992 General Election*, London: Frank Cass.

Denver, D., Hands, G., Fisher, J. and MacAllister, I. (2002) "Constituency Campaigning in 2001: The Effectiveness of Targeting," in Bartle, J., Mortimore, R. and Atkinson, S. (eds.) *Political Communications: The General Election Campaign of 2001*, London: Frank Cass: 159–180.

Duggan, M. and Smith, A. (2016) *The Political Environment on Social Media*, Washington, DC: Pew Research Center, available online: www.pewinternet.org/2016/10/25/the-political-environment-on-social-media/ [accessed December 20, 2016].

Engesser, S., Ernst, N., Esser, F. and Büchel, F. (2016) "Populism and Social Media: How Politicians Spread a Fragmented Ideology," *Information, Communication and Society*, available online: www.tandfonline.com/doi/abs/10.1080/1369118X.2016.1207697 [accessed December 20, 2016].

Etzioni, A. and Etzioni, O. (1997) "Communities: Virtual vs. Real," *Science*, vol. 277, no. 5324, July, 295.

Farrell, D. and Webb, P. (2000) "Political Parties as Campaign Organizations," in Dalton, R. and Wattenberg, M. (eds.) *Parties Without Partisans: Political Change in Advanced Industrial Democracies*, Oxford: Oxford University Press: 102–128.

Fella, S. and Ruzza, C. (2013) "Populism and the Fall of the Centre-Right in Italy: The End of the Berlusconi Model or a New Beginning?," *Journal of Contemporary European Studies*, vol. 21, no. 1, March, 38–52.

Fisher, J., Cutts, D. and Fieldhouse, E. (2011) "Constituency Campaigning in 2010," in Wring, D. (ed.) *Political Communication in Britain: TV Debates, the Media and the Election*, Basingstoke: Palgrave: 198–217.

Fisher, J., Fieldhouse, E., Cutts, D., Johnston, R. and Pattie, C. (2016) "Is All Campaigning Equally Positive? The Impact of District Level Campaigning on Voter Turnout at the 2010 British General Election," *Party Politics*, vol. 22, no. 2, March, 215–226.

Forelle, M. C., Howard, P. N., Monroy-Hernández, A. and Savage, S. (2015) "Political Bots and the Manipulation of Public Opinion in Venezuela." Available online: https://arxiv.org/ftp/arxiv/papers/1507/1507.07109.pdf [accessed July 17, 2017].

Gentzkow, M. and Shapiro, J. M. (2011) "Ideological Segregation Online and Offline," *Quarterly Journal of Economics*, vol. 126, no. 4, November, 1799–1839.

Gibson, R. K. (2012) "From Brochureware to 'MyBo': An Overview of Online Elections and Campaigning," *Politics*, vol. 32, no. 2, June, 77–84.

Gibson, R. K. (2013) "Party Change, Social Media and the Rise of 'Citizen-Initiated' Campaigning," *Party Politics*, vol. 21, no. 2, March, 183–197.

Gibson, R. K. and Cantijoch, M. (2013) "Conceptualizing and Measuring Participation in the Age of the Internet: Is Online Political Engagement Really Different to Offline?," *Journal of Politics*, vol. 75, no. 3, July, 701–716.

Gibson, R. K. and McAllister, I. (2006) "Does Cyber-Campaigning Win Votes? Online Communication in the 2004 Australian Election," *Journal of Elections, Public Opinion and Parties*, vol. 16, no. 3, October, 243–263.

Gibson, R. K. and McAllister, I. (2011) "Do Online Election Campaigns Win Voters? The 2007 Australian 'YouTube' Election," *Political Communication*, vol. 28, no. 2, April, 227–244.

Gibson, R. K. and McAllister, I. (2015) "Normalizing or Equalizing Party Competition? Assessing the Impact of the Web on Election Campaigning," *Political Studies*, vol. 63, no. 3, August, 529–547.

Gibson, R. K. and Ward, S. J. (1998) "UK Political Parties and the Internet – 'Politics as Usual' in the New Media?," *Harvard International Journal of Press/Politics*, vol. 3, no. 3, June, 14–38.

Gibson, R. K. and Ward, S. J. (2000a) "New Media, Same Impact? British Party Activity in Cyberspace," in Gibson, R. and Ward, S. (eds.) *Reinvigorating Government? British Politics and the Internet*, Aldershot, UK: Ashgate: 107–128.

Gibson, R. K. and Ward, S. J. (2000b) "An Outsider's Medium? The European Elections and UK Party Competition on the Internet," in Cowley, P., Denver, D., Russell, A. and Harrison, L. (eds.) *British Parties and Elections Review*, vol. 10, London: Frank Cass: 173–191.

Gibson, R. K. and Ward, S. J. (2002) "Virtual Campaigning: Australian Parties and the Impact of the Internet," *Australian Journal of Political Science*, vol. 37, no. 1, March, 99–129.

Gibson, R. K. and Ward, S. J. (2003) "Online and On Message? Candidates' Websites in the 2001 General Election," *British Journal of Politics and International Relations*, vol. 5, no. 2, May, 188–205.

Gibson, R. K. and Ward, S. J. (2009) "Parties in the Digital Age: A Review Article," *Representation*, vol. 45, no. 1, April, 87–100.

Gibson, R. K., Lusoli, W. and Ward, S. J. (2008) "Nationalizing and Normalizing the Local? A Comparative Analysis of Online Candidate Campaigning in Australia and Britain," *Journal of Information Technology and Politics*, vol. 4, no. 4, 15–30.

Gibson, R. K., Margolis, M., Resnick, D. and Ward, S. J. (2003) "Election Campaigning on the WWW in the US and UK: A Comparative Analysis," *Party Politics*, vol. 9, no. 1, January, 47–76.

Gibson, R. K., Newell, J. L. and Ward, S. J. (2000) "New Parties, New Media: Italian Party Politics and the Internet," *South European Society and Politics*, vol. 5, no. 1, Summer, 123–136.

Gil de Zúñiga, H. and Valenzuela, S. (2011) "The Mediating Path to a Stronger Citizenship: Online and Offline Networks, Weak Ties, and Civic Engagement," *Communication Research*, vol. 38, no. 3, June, 397–421.

Gillan, K. (2009) "The UK Anti-War Movement Online: Uses and Limitations of Internet Technologies for Contemporary Activism," *Information, Communication, and Society*, vol. 12, no. 1, February, 25–43.

Gomez, J., and Muhamad, R. (2010) "New Media and Electoral Democracy: Online Opposition in Malaysia and Singapore," Paper presented at the 2010 Workshop "Malaysia and Singapore – Media, Law, Social Commentary, Politics," Melbourne, June 10–11.

Graber, D. A. (1988) *Processing the News: How People Tame the Information Tide*, 2nd Edition, New York: Longman.

Graham, T., Jackson, D. and Wright, S. (2016). "'We need to get together and make ourselves heard': Everyday online spaces as incubators of political action." *Information, Communication & Society*, vol. 19, no. 10, 1373–1389.

Guardian (2016) "Facebook's Failure: Did Fake News and Polarized Politics get Trump Elected?" November 10, 2016, available online: www.theguardian.com/technology/2016/nov/10/facebook-fake-news-election-conspiracy-theories [accessed December 20, 2016].

Gueorguieva, V. (2008) "Voters, MySpace and YouTube: The Impact of Alternative Communication Channels on the 2006 Election Cycle and Beyond," *Social Science Computer Review*, vol. 26, no. 3, Autumn, 288–300.

Gunther, A. C. (1998) "The Persuasive Press Inference: Effects of Mass Media on Perceived Public Opinion," *Communication Research*, vol. 25, no. 5, 486–504.

Guðmundsson, B. (2016) "New Media-Opportunity for New and Small Parties? Political Communication before the Parliamentary Elections in Iceland in 2013," Stjórnmál og Stjórnsýsla, vol. 12, no. 1, Spring, 47–66.

Habermas, J. (2016) "How to Pull the Ground from under Right Wing Populism." Available online: www.socialeurope.eu/2016/11/democratic-polarisation-pull-ground-right-wing-populism/ [accessed December 19, 2016].

Hacker, K. L. and van Dijk, J. (2000) *Digital Democracy: Issues of Theory and Practice*, London: Sage.

Hague, R. and Uhm, S-Y. (2003) "Online Groups and Offline Parties," in Gibson, R. K., Nixon, P. and Ward, S. J. (eds.) *Political Parties and the Internet: Net Gain?* London: Routledge: 195–217.

Halberstam, Y. and Knight, B. (2016) "Homophily, Group Size, and the Diffusion of Political Information in Social Networks: Evidence from Twitter," *Journal of Public Economics*, vol. 143, November, 73–88.

Hansen, K. and Pedersen, K. (2014) "Cyber-Campaigning in Denmark: Application and Effects of Candidate Campaigning," *Journal of Information Technology and Politics*, vol. 11, no. 2, May, 206–219.

Hara, N. and Jo, Y. (2007) "Internet Politics: A Comparative Analysis of U.S. and South Korea Presidential Campaigns," *First Monday*, vol. 12, no. 9, September.

Hargittai, E., Gallo, J. and Kane, M. (2008) "Cross-Ideological Discussions Among Conservative and Liberal Bloggers," *Public Choice*, vol. 134, no. 1, January, 67–86.

Hartleb, F. (2013) "Anti-Elitist Cyber Parties?," *Journal of Public Affairs*, vol. 13, no. 4, November, 355–369.

Hindman, M., Tsioutsiouliklis, K. and Johnson, J. A. (2003) "'Googlearchy': How a Few Heavily-Linked Sites Dominate Politics on the Web," Paper presented at the 2003 Annual Meeting of the Midwest Political Science Association, Chicago, April 3–6.

Hinz, K. (2014) "Campaigning on Facebook and Twitter: Information Provision of Candidates in the Social Web during Germany's Federal Election Campaign 2013," Paper presented at the 2014 ECPR Graduate Student Conference, Innsbruck, July 3–5.

Huber, G. A. and Malhotra, N. (2016) "Political Homophily in Social Relationships: Evidence from Online Dating Behavior," *Journal of Politics*, vol. 79, no. 1, January, 269–283.

Jackson, N. and Lilleker, D. (2009) "Building an Architecture of Participation? Political Parties and Web2.0 in Britain," *Journal of Information Technology and Politics*, vol. 6, no. 4, 232–250.

Joinson, A. (ed.) (2007) *Oxford Handbook of Internet Psychology*, Oxford: Oxford University Press.

Kalnes, O. (2009) "Norwegian Parties and Web 2.0," *Journal of Information Technology and Politics*, vol. 6, no. 4, 251–266.

Klinger, U. (2013) "Mastering the Art of Social Media," *Information, Communication and Society*, vol. 16, no. 5, June, 717–736.

Koc-Michalska, K. and Vedel, T. (2009) "The Internet and French Political Communication in the Aftermath of the 2007 Presidential Election," Paper presented at the 2009 ECPR General Conference, Potsdam, September 10–12.

Koc-Michalska, K., Lilleker, D. G., Smith, A. and Weissmann, D. (2016) "The Normalization of Online Campaigning in the Web.2.0 Era," *European Journal of Communication*, vol. 31, no. 3, June, 331–350.

Kollanyi, B., Howard, P. N. and Woolley, S. C. (2016) *Bots and Automation over Twitter During the U.S. Election*, Oxford: Project on Computational Propaganda. Available online: http://politicalbots.org/wp-content/uploads/2016/11/Data-Memo-US-Election.pdf [accessed December 18, 2016].

Latimer, C. P. (2008) "Utilizing the Internet as a Campaign Tool: The Relationship Between Incumbency, Political Party Affiliation, Election Outcomes, and the Quality of Campaign Web Sites in the United States," *Journal of Information Technology and Politics*, vol. 4, no. 3, 81–95.

Lee, J. K., Choi, J., Kim, C. and Kim, Y. (2014) "Social Media, Network Heterogeneity, and Opinion Polarization," *Journal of Communication*, vol. 64, no. 4, August, 702–722.

Lees-Marshment, J. (2005) *Political Marketing and British Political Parties*, 2nd Edition, Manchester: Manchester University Press.

Lelkes, Y., Sood, G. and Iyengar, S. (2015) "The Hostile Audience: The Effect of Access to Broadband Internet on Partisan Affect," *American Journal of Political Science*, vol. 61, no. 1, January, 5–20.

Lilleker, D. and Jackson, N. (eds.) (2011) *Political Campaigning, Elections and the Internet: Comparing the US, UK, France and Germany*, Abingdon: Routledge.

Lilleker, D. and Vedel, T. (2013) "The Internet in Campaigns and Elections," in Dutton, W. (ed.) *Oxford Handbook of Internet Studies*, Oxford: Oxford University Press: 401–420.

Livingstone, S., Bober, M. and Helsper, E. J. (2005) "Active Participation or Just More Information? Young People's Take-Up of Opportunities to Act and Interact on the Internet," *Information, Communication and Society*, vol. 8, no. 3, September, 287–314.

Lorenzo-Rodriguez, J. (2014) "Political Parties Online: What Do They Offer? A Longitudinal Analysis of Italian and Spanish Cases," Paper presented at the 2014 Annual Meeting of the Midwest Political Science Association, Chicago, April 3–6.

Lupia, A. and Philpot, T. (2005) "Views from Inside the Net: How Websites Affect Young Adults' Political Interest," *Journal of Politics*, vol. 67, no. 4, November, 1122–1142.

Lusoli, W. (2005a) "The Internet and the European Parliament Elections: Theoretical Perspectives, Empirical Investigations and Proposals for Research," *Information Polity*, vol. 10, no. 4, December, 153–163.

Lusoli, W. (2005b) "A Second-Order Medium? The Internet as a Source of Electoral Information in 25 European Countries," *Information Polity*, vol. 10, no. 4, December, 247–265.

Lusoli, W. and Ward, S. J. (2004) "Digital Rank-And-File: Party Activists' Perceptions and Use of the Internet," *The British Journal of Politics and International Relations*, vol. 6, no. 4, November, 453–470.

March, L. (2004) "Russian Parties and the Political Internet," *Europe-Asia Studies*, vol. 56, no. 3, May, 369–400.

Margetts, H., John, P., Hale, S. and Yasseri, T. (2015) *Political Turbulence: How Social Media Shape Collective Action*, Princeton: Princeton University Press.

Margolis, M. and Resnick, D. (2000) *Politics as Usual: The Cyberspace Revolution*, vol. 6, Thousand Oaks, CA: Sage Publications.

Margolis, M., Resnick, D. and Tu, C.-C. (1996) "Campaigning on the Internet: Parties and Candidates on the World Wide Web in the 1996 Primary Season," *The Harvard International Journal of Press/Politics*, vol. 2, no. 1, 59–78.

Margolis, M., Resnick, D. and Wolfe, J. D. (1999) "Party Competition on the Internet in the United States and Britain," *The Harvard International Journal of Press/Politics*, vol. 4, no. 4, 24–47.

McCutcheon, C. (2016) "Populism and Party Politics," *CQ Researcher*, vol. 26, 721–744.

McPherson, M., Smith-Lovin, L. and Cook, J. M. (2001) "Birds of a Feather: Homophily in Social Networks," *Annual Review of Sociology*, vol. 27, August, 415–444.

Meijer, I. and Kormelink, T. G. (2015) "Checking, Sharing, Clicking and Linking: Changing Patterns of News Use Between 2004 and 2014," *Digital Journalism*, vol. 3, no. 5, 664–679.

Morris, D. (2000) *Vote.com*, Los Angeles: Renaissance Books.

Mosca, L., Vaccari, C. and Valeriani, A. (2015) "An Internet Fuelled Party? The Movemento 5 Stelle and the Web," in Tronconi, F. (ed.) *Beppe Grillo's Five Star Movement: Organization, Communication and Ideology*, London: Routledge: 127–151.

Mutz, D. C. and Martin, P. S. (2001) "Facilitating Communication Across Lines of Political Difference: The Role of Mass Media," *American Political Science Review*, vol. 95, no. 1, March, 97–114.

Negroponte, N. (1995) *Being Digital*, New York: Alfred A. Knopf.

Newell, J. L. (2001) "Italian Political Parties on the Web," *Harvard International Journal of Press Politics*, vol. 6, no. 4, September, 60–87.

Nielson, R. K. and Schroder, K. C. (2014) "The Relative Importance of Social Media for Accessing, Finding, and Engaging with News," *Digital Journalism*, vol. 2, no. 4, 472–489.

Nixon, P. and Johansson, H. (1999) "Transparency Through Technology: The Internet and Political Parties," in Hague, B. and Loader, B. (eds.) *Digital Democracy: Discourse and Democracy in the Information Age*, London: Routledge: 135–153.

Norquay, G. (2008) "Organizing without Organization: The Obama Networking Revolution," *Policy Options*, October, 58–61.

Norris, P. (2000) *A Virtuous Circle: Political Communication in Postindustrial Societies*, Cambridge: Cambridge University Press.

Norris, P. (2001) *Digital Divide: Civic Engagement, Information Poverty, and the Internet*, Cambridge: Cambridge University Press.

Norris, P. and Curtice, J. (2008) "Getting the Message Out: A Two-Step Model of the Role of the Internet in Campaign Communication Flows during the 2005 British General Election," *The Journal of Information Technology and Politics*, vol. 4, no. 4, 3–13.

Poletti, M., Bale, T. and Webb, P. (2016) "Explaining the Pro-Corbyn Surge in Labour Membership," *LSE British Politics and Policy Blog*, November 16, 2016, available online: http://blogs.lse.ac.uk/politicsandpolicy/explaining-the-pro-corbyn-surge-in-labours-membership/ [accessed December 20, 2016].

Pollard, T. D., Chesebro, J. and Studinski, D. P. (2009) "The Role of the Internet in Presidential Campaigns," *Communication Studies*, vol. 60, no. 5, October, 574–588.

Prior, M. (2007) *Post-Broadcast Democracy: How Media Choice Increases Inequality in Political Involvement and Polarizes Elections*, Cambridge: Cambridge University Press.

Prior, M. (2013) "Media and Political Polarization," *Annual Review of Political Science*, vol. 16, May, 101–127.

Rainie, L. and Smith, A. (2008) "The Internet and the 2008 Election," Washington, DC: Pew Research Center. Available online: www.pewinternet.org/2008/06/15/the-internet-and-the-2008-election/ [accessed December 20, 2016].

Rash, W. (1997) *Politics on the Nets: Wiring the Political Process*, New York: W. H. Freeman.

Rheingold, H. (1993) *The Virtual Community: Homesteading on the Electronic Frontier*, Reading, MA: Addison-Wesley.

Ridout, T. N., Fowler, E. F., Branstetter, J. and Borah, P. (2015) "Politics as Usual? When and Why Traditional Actors Often Dominate YouTube Campaigning," *Journal of Information Technology and Politics*, vol. 12, no. 3, 237–251.

Samuel-Azran, T., Yarchi, M. and Wolfsfeld, G. (2015) "Equalization versus Normalization: Facebook and the 2013 Israeli Elections," *Social Media and Society*, available online: http://journals.sagepub.com/doi/abs/10.1177/2056305115605861 [accessed December 19, 2016].

Schweizer, E. (2005) "Election Campaigning Online: German Party Websites in the 2002 National Elections," *European Journal of Communication*, vol. 20, no. 3, 327–351.

Schweitzer, E. (2008) "Innovation or Normalization in E-campaigning?: A Longitudinal Content and Structural Analysis of German Party Websites in the 2002 and 2005 National Elections," *European Journal of Communication*, vol. 23, no. 4, December, 449–470.

Shane, P. M. (2004) *Democracy Online: The Prospects for Political Renewal Through the Internet*, London: Routledge.

Small, T. A. (2008) "Equal Access, Unequal Success: Major and Minor Canadian Parties on the Net," *Party Politics*, vol. 14, no. 1, January, 51–70.

Smith, C. (1998) "Political Parties in the Information Age: From Mass Party to Leadership Organization," in Snellen, I. and van de Donk, W. (eds.) *Handbook on Public Administration in the Information Age*, Amsterdam: IoS Press: 175–189.

Smith, C. (2000) "British Political Parties in the Information Age: Continuity and Change in the Information Age," in Hoff, J., Horrocks, I. and Tops, P. (eds.) *Democratic Governance and New Technology*, London: Routledge: 71–86.

Southern, R. (2015) "Is Web 2.0 Providing a Voice for Outsiders? A Comparison of Personal Web Site and Social Media Use by Candidates at the 2010 UK General Election," *Journal of Information Technology and Politics*, vol. 12, no. 1, 1–17.

Southern, R. and Ward, S. J. (2011) "Below the Radar? Online Campaigning at the Local Level in the 2010 Election," in Wring, D. (ed.) *Political Communication in Britain: The Leader Debates, the Campaign and the Media in the 2010 General Election*, Basingstoke: Palgrave: 218–240.

Strandberg, K. (2006) *Parties, Candidates and Citizens On-Line – Studies of Politics on the Internet*, Åbo: Åbo Akademi University Press.

Strandberg, K. (2009) "Online Campaigning: An Opening for the Outsiders? An Analysis of Finnish Parliamentary Candidates' Websites in the 2003 Election Campaign," *New Media and Society*, vol. 11, no. 5, August, 835–854.

Stromer-Galley, J. (2000a) "Online Interaction and Why Candidates Avoid It," *Journal of Communication*, vol. 50, no. 4, December, 111–132.

Stromer-Galley, J. (2000b) "Democratizing Democracy: Strong Democracy, US Political Campaigns and the Internet," *Democratization*, vol. 7, no. 1, March, 36–58.

Sudulich, M. L. (2013) "Do Ethos, Ideology, Country and Electoral Strength Make a Difference in Cyberspace?," in Nixon, P. G., Rawal, R. and Mercea, D. (eds.) *Politics and the Internet in Comparative Context: Views from the Cloud*, Abingdon: Routledge: 75–94.

Sudulich, M. L. and Wall, M. (2010) "Every Little Helps: Cyber Campaigning in the 2007 Irish General Election," *Journal of Information Technology and Politics*, vol. 7, no. 4, 340–355.

Sunstein, C. R. (2001) *Republic.com*, Princeton: Princeton University Press.

Sunstein, C. R. (2006) *Republic.com*, 2nd Edition, Princeton: Princeton University Press.

Tan, T. H., Tng, Y. H. and Yeo, A. (2016) "Normalization versus Equalization Effects of the Internet for Political Parties: Singapore's General Election 2015 as a Case Study," Paper presented at the 2016 E-Democracy and Open Government Conference, Budapest, May 18–20.

Tkach-Kawasaki, L. (2003) "Politics@Japan: Party Competition on the Internet in Japan," *Party Politics*, vol. 9, no. 1, January, 105–123.

Trippi, J. (2004) *The Revolution Will Not Be Televised: Democracy, the Internet, and the Overthrow of Everything*, New York: Regan Books.

Tronconi, F. (ed.) (2015) *Beppe Grillo's Five Star Movement: Organisation, Communication and Ideology*, Farnham, Surrey, UK: Ashgate.

Vaccari, C. (2010) "Technology Is a Commodity: The Internet in the 2008 United States Presidential Election," *Journal of Information Technology and Politics*, vol. 7, no. 4, 318–339.

Vaccari, C. Valeriani, A., Barberá, P., Bonneau, R., Jost, J. T., Nagler, J. and Tucker, J. A. (2015) "Political Expression and Action on Social Media: Exploring the Relationship Between Lower- and Higher-Threshold Political Activities Among Twitter Users in Italy," *Journal of Computer-Mediated Communication*, vol. 20, no. 2, March, 221–239.

Vergeer, M. and Hermans, L. (2013) "Campaigning on Twitter: Microblogging and Online Social Networking as Campaign Tools in the 2010 General Elections in the Netherlands," *Journal of Computer-Mediated Communication*, vol. 18, no. 4, July, 399–419.

Voerman, G. (1998) "Dutch Political Parties and the Internet," *ESPN News*, vol. 1, no. 10, Autumn.

Voerman, G. and Ward, S. J. (2000) "New Media and New Politics: Green Parties Intra Party Democracy and the Internet," in Voerman, G. and Lucardie, P. (eds.) *Jaerbook Documentatiecentrum Nederlandse Politieke Partijen 1999*, Groningen: University of Groningen: 192–215.

Vromen, A. (2007) "Australian Young People's Participatory Practices and Internet Use," *Information, Communication and Society*, vol. 10, no. 1, February, 48–68.

Ward, I. (2011) "Does the Internet Encourage Small Parties? A Case Study of the Minutiae of BC Politics, 1996–2009," *Australian Journal of Political Science*, vol. 46, no. 2, June, 229–242.

Ward, S. J. (2005) "The Internet, E-Democracy and the Election: Virtually Irrelevant?," in Geddes, A. and Tonge. J. (eds.) *Britain Decides: The UK General Election 2005*, London: Palgrave: 210–225.

Ward, S. J. (2008) "Parties and Election Campaigning Online: A New Era?," in Davis, R., Owen, D., Taras, D. and Ward, S. J. (eds.) *Making a Difference? Internet Campaigning in Comparative Perspective*, Lanham: Lexington Books: 1–15.

Ward, S. J., Gibson, R. K. and Lusoli, W. (2003) "Online Participation and Mobilization in Britain: Hype, Hope and Reality," *Parliamentary Affairs*, vol. 56, no. 4, October, 652–668.

Ward, S. J., Gibson, R. K. and Lusoli, W. (2008) "Not Quite Normal? Parties and the 2005 UK Online Election Campaign," in Davis, R., Owen, D., Taras, D. and Ward, S. J. (eds.) *Making a Difference? Internet Campaigning in Comparative Perspective*, Lanham: Lexington Books: 133–160.

Whine, M. (2000) "Far Right Extremists on the Internet," in Douglas, T. and Loader, B. D. (eds.) *Cybercrime: Law Enforcement, Security and Surveillance in the Information Age*, New York: Routledge: 234–250.

Williamson, A. (2010) *Digital Citizens and Democratic Participation*, London: Hansard Society.

Xenos, M. and Moy, P. (2007) "Direct and Differential Effects of the Internet on Political and Civic Engagement," *Journal of Communication*, vol. 57, no. 4, December, 704–718.

Xiaoge, Xu (2011) "Singapore General Election 2011 on Twitter: Equalized or Normalized?" Available online: www.academia.edu/1851004/Singapore_General_Election_2011_on_Twitter_Equalized_or_Normalized [accessed July 17, 2017].

PART V

The nature of public opinion

27

ATTITUDES, VALUES AND BELIEF SYSTEMS

Oddbjørn Knutsen

Introduction

The topic of this chapter comprises three concepts that are central within public opinion research, namely attitudes, values and belief systems. The chapter starts with examining how these concepts are defined within social science in general, and then within political science more specifically. The section on belief systems focuses on a major debate within public opinion research – that concerning people's democratic competence.

Attitudes

The attitude concept

Much of the theoretical framework and conceptualization of attitudes has been developed within social psychology.[1] In general, an attitude is an expression of favor or disfavor toward a person, place, thing or event (the attitude object). Eagly and Chaiken (1993: Chapter 1) define, for example, an attitude as "a psychological tendency that is expressed by evaluating a particular entity with some degree of favor or disfavor." *Psychological tendency* refers to a state that is internal to the individual. *Evaluating* refers to all classes of evaluative response, whether overt or covert, cognitive, effective or behavioral. This psychological tendency can be regarded as a type of bias that *predisposes* the individual toward evaluative responses that are positive or negative. An attitude develops on the basis of *evaluative responding*: An individual does not have an attitude until he or she responds to an entity on an affective, cognitive or behavioral basis.

Attitude is one of many hypothetical constructs that are not directly observable, but can be inferred from observable responses. Attitudes are one of numerous implicit states or dispositions that psychologists have constructed to explain why people react in certain ways in the presence of certain stimuli.

Multi-component models of attitudes are the most influential. A classic tripartite view is that an attitude contains cognitive, affective and behavioral components:

- The *cognitive component* contains thoughts or ideas that people have about the attitude object. These thoughts are sometimes conceptualized as beliefs which are understood to be associations or linkages that people establish between the attitude object and various attributes.

- The *affective component* consists of feelings, moods, emotions and sympathetic nervous system activity that people experience in relation to the attitude object.
- The *behavioral component* is a predisposition to action under appropriate conditions. It is also referred to as the *conation element* or an individual's *action tendencies* towards the object. It is also argued that attitudes can be derived from past behavior.

The assumption that attitudes have three different components and that attitudes are formed through cognitive, affective and behavioral processes has been advanced in numerous discussions of attitudes. This approach raises a question about the consistency or empirical validity of these components.

Another theoretical view is that the three components described above are distinct entities, which may or may not be related, depending on the particular situation. This viewpoint has been strongly advocated by Fishbein and Ajzen (1975). In their theory, the term "attitude" is reserved for the affective component. The cognitive dimension is labeled as beliefs, and is defined as a person's subjective probability that an object has a particular characteristic. This is often referred to as the one-dimensional view of attitudes.

Milton Rokeach (1968: Chapter 5) has a somewhat different conceptualization of attitudes. His definition is perhaps more relevant for social and political attitudes. He defines an attitude as "a relatively enduring organization" of beliefs around an object or situation predisposing one to respond in some preferential manner. A belief is defined as any simple proposition, conscious or unconscious, inferred from what a person says or does, capable of being preceded by the phrase "I believe that...:" In this conceptualization:

1 *An attitude is relatively enduring*. Some predispositions are momentary and, as such, are not called attitudes. The concept of attitude is typically reserved for more enduring, persistent organizations of predispositions.

2 *An attitude is an organization of beliefs*. Rokeach differentiated between three types of beliefs: (a) descriptive beliefs which describe the object of the beliefs as true or false, correct or incorrect, (b) evaluative beliefs which evaluate the object as good or bad, and (c) prescriptive beliefs which advocate a certain course of action or a certain state of existence as being desirable or undesirable.

3 All beliefs are *predispositions to action*. An attitude is thus a set of interrelated predispositions to action organized around an object or situation. Each belief within an attitude organization is conceived as having the three components that are emphasized in other approaches (cognitive, affective and behavioral).

4 They are *organized around an object or a situation*. Attitude objects are considered as static objects of regard, concrete or abstract, such as a person, group, an institution or issue. A situation is a dynamic event of activity around which a person organizes a set of related beliefs about how to behave.

5 They involve a *set of interrelated predispositions to respond*, meaning that attitudes are not single predispositions but sets of interrelated predispositions.

6 *A preferential response* implies that the response can be either affective or evaluative or both. It is not assumed that there is a one-to-one relationship between affect and evaluation.

Political attitudes

Political attitudes are defined more broadly in political science than in social psychology. Based on Rokeach's (1968) definition of attitudes, we can define a political attitude in the following way: Political attitudes are relatively enduring organizations of beliefs around political objects or situations which predispose individuals to respond in some preferential manner.

The most immediate political objects are political actors, institutions and political issues. Therefore, various levels of political trust and support are central political attitudes, from orientations to politicians and political parties, to political institutions and evaluation of regime performance (Norris 2011: Chapter 2).[2]

Political issues are probably the most studied political attitudes. In some ways, the literature does not always differentiate clearly between issues (attitudes) and values regarding the dimensions, antecedents and behavioral consequences. Much of what is written about political values is thus relevant for studies of political issues. The dimensions of political issues and values are therefore addressed together under the "Values" section below.

There are, however, considerable measurement equivalence problems (Ariely and Davidov 2012) when examining political attitudes over time and cross-nationally. These problems are caused by the fact that attitudes address objects and situations: these may change over time even though there is no real change in basic orientation. In politics, "situations" can reflect unfolding political events, the current state of a given policy area, the political debate about where to move from the present state, the specific behavior of politicians that draws attention, and so on.

Values

The value concept

The concept of values is used in many of the social sciences. Values are considered to be a basic aspect of individuals' belief systems and central in the culture of a given social group and in a given country. Several definitions of "values" have been influential. For the anthropologist Clyde Kluckhohn (1951), a value is a conception of that which is desirable and which influences the selection of available modes, means and ends of action. Central to this definition is the notion "a conception of the desirable." A desire is a wish or a preference, while the term "desirable" goes beyond a wish or a want by including considerations of moral content.

For Milton Rokeach (1973: Chapter 1), a "value is an enduring belief that a specific mode of conduct or end-state of existence is preferable to opposite or converse modes of conduct or end-states of existence." Rokeach's definition includes elements that can be used as a point of departure for discussing several dimensions of the value concept. Rokeach indicated that there are two types of values: terminal (end-state of existence) and instrumental (mode of conduct) values. Rokeach also differentiated between personal and social values. People have values they want to emphasize in their own lives (self-centered) but also values they would emphasize in their social environment (societal-centered). This differentiation can be expanded to different domains where we can talk about family values, work values, bureaucratic values, political values, and others.

For Rokeach, a value is a basic and relatively stable element in a person's belief system. A value is a *prescriptive belief* wherein some means or end of action are judged to be desirable or undesirable. Values are sometimes contrasted with attitudes. A value is considered to be a basic (prescriptive) belief that often influences a specific attitude together with other beliefs.

Building on Rokeach and others, Shalom Schwartz (2007) identifies formal characteristics that are the defining features of basic human values.

Values are beliefs:

a   about desirable end-states or behaviors (modes of conduct),
b   which transcend specific situations or actions,

c   that guide selection or evaluation of behavior and events,

d   are ordered by relative importance to form a value system,

e   where the relative importance of values guides attitudes and behavior.

Other researchers such as Jan van Deth and Elinor Scarbrough (1995) consider the relationship between values and attitudes as reciprocal, which, at the individual level, provides opportunities for the modification and adaption of values. These scholars use the notion *"value orientation"* for constellations of attitudes that can be patterned in some empirical way and are theoretically interpreted in a meaningful way. This implies that value orientations can be studied by data that comprise indicators that can be attitudes.

Culture can be considered as the rich complex of meanings, beliefs, symbols, norms and values prevalent among people in a society. Cultural differences can be studied along many dimensions. Given that values are central elements in individuals' belief systems, the values that are emphasized in a society may be a very central feature of culture. The same applies to political values in relation to political culture.

Political values

A point of departure for conceptualizing the notion of political values is the distinction made by Rokeach (1973: 7–8) between personal and social (terminal) values. Values may be self-centered or society-centered, intra-personal or inter-personal in focus. Some values may relate to the individual's own life, while others relate to society or even the political sphere. These latter values can then be considered as political values.

Terminal political values can be considered as end-states that individuals would like to see characterizing society as a whole and see implemented through the political system. Instrumental political values are modes of conduct that are considered legitimate (or illegitimate) in influencing political decisions – for example, various types of political participation (Knutsen 2011). Inspired by Rokeach and Schwartz and others, Goren, Federico and Kittelson (2009: 805) define "core political values" as abstract normative beliefs about desirable end-states or modes of conduct that operate in the political realm. These political values are quite stable and guide preferences on short-term political controversies and issues of the day. Similarly, McCann (1997: 565) defines a citizen's core political values as consisting of overarching normative principles about government, citizenship and (American) society. These principles and assumptions facilitate positions taking on more concrete domains by serving as general focal points in the otherwise confusing environment. Kinder (1998: 808) used the notions of "principles" and "values" interchangeably, indicating that the former is used more frequently within political science while "values" are used more frequently within social psychology. His definition of political principles and values is that they transcend particular objects and specific situations; they are relatively abstract and durable claims about virtue and the good society. Furthermore, these principles and values are motivating and lead to particular positions being taken on political issues and help people to evaluate and make judgments.

Political value and attitude dimensions

The number of political issues and value dimensions depends on how many items are included in dimensional analyses such as factor analyses. As a rule, there should be at least three indicators for tapping a theoretically meaningful dimension. When this rule is followed, the issue or value structure is multidimensional. Some of the dimensions that have been focused upon in the literature are reviewed below.

Christian values focus on the importance of Christian morals and principles in society and politics, and on traditional moral guidelines in school and society in general. Secularization is often understood as a process whereby mundane reality is less interpreted from a supernatural perspective, and secular values are based on more modern norms of morality where the individual wants to determine for him- or herself without the guidelines of the church (Halman and Moor 1994; Norris and Inglehart 2004).

The most important political value orientations that emerged in the Industrial Revolution were economic left–right values. These value orientations are economic in nature, and refer in particular to the role of government in creating more economic equality in society versus the need for economic incentives and efficiency. These values include workers' control and state regulation of the economy versus private enterprise, private property and the market economy (Knutsen 1995).

The moral value dimension and economic left–right values are often referred to as "Old Politics" because they capture the essence of the traditional lines of conflict in industrial society. In contrast, "New Politics" refers to value conflicts emerging from post-industrial society. The most well-known new political value dimension is that of the materialist/post-materialist value orientations. These value orientations were originally formulated by Inglehart (1977, 1990), who argued that new post-materialist values are deeply rooted and stand in opposition to more traditional materialist values. Materialist values emphasize economic and physical security such as economic stability and growth, law and order, and strong defense. Post-materialist values emphasize self-expression, subjective well-being and the quality of life.

New Politics values can, however, be conceptualized along three different dimensions: The value conflict between *environmental versus economic growth values* is firmly rooted in the public mind, and in many West European countries conflicts over environmental values seem to be the most manifest expression of the "New Politics" conflict (Dalton 2009).

In a series of articles, Scott Flanagan emphasized that *a libertarian/authoritarian* dimension is the central New Politics dimension (Inglehart and Flanagan 1987; Flanagan and Lee 2003). The libertarian/authoritarian value orientations are also central components in Herbert Kitschelt's (1994, 1995) works.

The third set of New Politics orientation is related to immigration and immigrants. This has become a major policy area in Europe with different views among the mass publics. Comparative research has shown that these orientations are closely related to and reflect basic values and beliefs about different conceptions of national identity, ethnicity and multiculturalism (Hainmueller and Hiscox 2007: 429–434).

A final dimension is the relationship between national and supranational orientations. This dimension is particularly related to attitudes toward European integration. It also includes various orientations toward economic and political globalization versus emphasis on national sovereignty and identity (Marks and Steenbergen 2004).

Inglehart's broader value dimensions

Inglehart has broadened his study of value dimensions by emphasizing that his materialist/post-materialist dimension is only one component of a much larger value syndrome, and by including an additional dimension (Inglehart and Welzel 2005). In an alternative approach to conceptualizing and analyzing value orientations in a long-term perspective, a two-dimensional value structure is emphasized: one dimension based on traditional versus secular–rational values; the other based on survival versus self-expression/well-being values. These two dimensions are associated with the structural changes occurring in the transition from pre-industrial to industrial society, and from industrial to post-industrial society, respectively.

Political value change

Inglehart incorporates most explicitly the issue of cultural change in his work. He identifies a "silent revolution" in which a gradual value change takes place along the materialist/ post-materialist dimension. As older and more materialist generations die, they are continuously replaced by younger, less materialist generations. Inglehart's theory is based on two hypotheses: The *scarcity hypothesis* implies that short-term effects may induce all cohorts to emphasize post-materialist values when economic conditions are good and materialist values when economic conditions decline. The cohort differences are explained by differences in economic and physical security during the formative years of the various cohorts. This *socialization hypothesis* predicts a watershed between the post-war and the pre-war cohorts in value priorities because they have such different experiences in their formative years regarding economic security (economic scarcity versus economic prosperity) and physical security (war versus absence of war).[3]

Empirical research has shown a fairly consistent decline in religiosity in rich, advanced industrial countries. The most important aspects of secularization at the individual level are the decline in both religious beliefs and church religiosity. In other parts of the world, religiosity has been much more stable. Overall, the world is becoming more religious even though the advanced industrial countries in the West have become considerably more secular (Norris and Inglehart 2004).

Belief systems

Definitions of belief systems

Beliefs, attitudes and values do not exist in isolation but are connected with many other beliefs in an organized system. According to Rokeach (1968:123), a belief system "represents the total universe of a person's beliefs about the physical world, the social world, and the self. It is conceived to be organized along several dimensions." Converse (1964) defined a belief system in a more narrow sense:

> as a configuration of ideas and attitudes in which the elements are bound together by some form of constraint or functional interdependence. In the static case, given initial knowledge, "constraint" meant the success in predicting that if an individual holds a specified attitude – that he holds certain further ideas and attitudes.
>
> *(Converse 1964: 207)*

The belief system debate

A main controversy in the debate about ideology and belief systems commenced with the findings in *The American Voter* (Campbell et al. 1960), and in particular Converse's article "The Nature of Belief Systems in Mass Publics" (1964). Converse's theses are still by many considered to be the strongest argument in the field. At the heart of the debate is the question of whether citizens are qualified to understand and have a coherent and stable set of political attitudes and beliefs.

Converse studied three aspects of belief systems:

* constraints (correlations) among political attitudes and values,
* stability of political attitudes at the individual level,
* levels of political/ideological conceptualization.

Although Converse (1964: 207) originally avoided ideology for "belief system," the notion of ideology is frequently used for more sophisticated belief systems; in fact the higher level of conceptualization is designated "ideological" (see also the section on "ideology and belief systems" below).

First, Converse's approaches and empirical findings are presented, then some other works that challenge or support Converse's views. Each topic (constraint, stability and conceptualization) is examined separately. Within the review of constraint a brief review of constraint between issue dimensions and party choice is also presented.

Converse's approach

Constraint

Converse (1964: 227–231) compared the correlations between economic left–right issues and foreign policy issues in the mass publics and the political elite (congressional candidates) and found much higher correlations among the elite. He also focused upon other aspects of constraint in a more broad-based context:

- The correlation between political issues and party choice was also much higher among the elites (Converse 1964: 229).
- The impact of social structural variables like social class and religious denomination on party choice is much larger among those with a higher level of political conceptualization (see below) than among those with a low level of conceptualization (Converse 1964: 231–235).
- The mass public had, however, a high degree of constraint with regard to different attitudes toward a group they liked or disliked. Such attitude objects have a higher centrality in the belief systems of the mass than of the elites. In such cases it is not the general principle that is included in the question that is important, but the positive or negative attitude toward the given social group. Various mass attitudes toward concrete objects (social groups) might then be expected to be highly constrained and also stable over time among the mass public.

Attitude stability: the black and white model

Converse studied stability in political issue attitudes over time using panel data from 1956, 1958 and 1960 (Converse 1964: 238–245). He anticipated a low degree of stability in particular for more abstract and remote attitude items while attitudes toward bounded and visible groups like Negroes and Catholics would be more stable. This is exactly what he found. There is one group of individuals who have a well crystallized and stable attitude pattern, and a larger group where the response sequence over time is statistically random. He explains the pattern by what he calls *a black and white model* comprising polar opposites regarding belief system stability. The model does not specify the proportion of the population falling into either category. These expectations are to a large degree confirmed by his empirical analyses, although he allows for a "third force" which he leaves open to the possibility of real attitude change over time. This third force is, however, small compared to the two other groups.

Based on the findings regarding the lack of stability in political attitudes, Converse formulated the notion of *non-attitudes*. Large portions of the population (and voters) do not have real attitudes on specific issues.

Levels of political conceptualization

These aspects of the mass public's political belief systems were measured by open-ended questions resulting in lengthy materials which measured the respondents' evaluation of the political scene in the respondents' own words. The original measure of levels of conceptualization in Campbell et al. (1960) and Converse (1964) was based on eight open-ended questions relating to American political parties and presidential candidates. The respondents were classified into theoretically meaningful categories which tapped a hierarchy of political or ideological differentiation. There were two dimensions of levels of conceptualization. *An active use of ideological dimensions of judgment* was based on questions about what the respondents liked and disliked of the two presidential candidates and the two major American political parties. Here, a differentiation was made between those who focused on ideological arguments, group interests, important issues of the time, and those who were not able to mention any issue content.

In order to measure *recognition of ideological dimensions of judgment*, the respondents were first asked which of the American parties (Democrats or Republicans) is most conservative and liberal and then why they think so. Five different levels of recognition were identified.

Converse's main view

According to Converse, "ideological thinking" is a central aspect of political sophistication. This is, for example, expressed in this way:

> At the same time, moving from top to bottom of this information dimension, the character of the objects central in a belief system undergoes systematic change. These objects shift from the remote, generic, and abstract to the increasingly simple, concrete, or "close to home." Where potential political objects are concerned, this progression tends to be from abstract, "ideological" principles to the more obviously recognizable social groupings or charismatic leaders, and finally to such objects of immediate experience as family, job, and immediate associates.
>
> *(Converse 1964: 213)*

The results of Converse's surveys and analysis cast doubt on many of these assumptions by revealing the apparent lack of understanding of ideology or even differentiation between the two political parties on the liberal–conservative continuum. Most people fall, for example, into the lower levels of conceptualization, giving rise to concerns as to whether voters are competent to make the decisions they are called upon to make in a democratic polity (see Bølstad in this volume).

The controversy[4]

Constraint

Later analyses, based on a variety of techniques designed to cleanse the data of measurement error, have challenged Converse's conclusions. Studies using such methods report very high levels of "true" attitude stability and substantial (as much as 50 percent) random error in the raw data. Similarly, upwardly adjusted attitudinal consistency coefficients have led to much more favorable comparisons between the mass public and Converse's elite sample of congressional candidates (see, for example, Achen 1975; Judd and Milburn 1980).

Another aspect of constraint concerns the dimensionality of the political attitudes. The issue of multidimensional attitude structure raises the question of how the pattern differs between individuals with higher and lower level of political sophistication. Is the attitude structure more unidimensional among those with a higher level of sophistication or are the various dimensions more strongly expressed among this group? This issue is examined, but not solved, in various contributions to the literature on the topic (see Marcus, Tabb and Sullivan 1974; Peffley and Hurwitz 1985). The critical argument regarding Converse's approach is that his inability to find evidence of ideological constraint may be due to his use of correlation coefficients – a statistic which can measure response consistency only on a single liberal–conservative dimension.

Goren (2013: Chapter 3) differentiates between issue attitudes and attitudes toward policy principles. Policy principles reference more abstract ideas than issue preferences. Core principles stand above the issue attitude and are quite similar to political values as defined in the previous section. Goren analyzes constraint among several policy preferences that measure central policy principles, and finds that politically unsophisticated, moderately sophisticated and highly sophisticated individuals hold real attitudes toward central policy principles. He finds that the highly sophisticated do not systematically rely more on these principles to constrain their policy preferences than do the unsophisticated (Goren 2004; 2013: Chapter 5).

Converse (1974, 1980) has challenged the validity of "corrected" correlations, arguing that measurement error is a product of both the questions used in a survey and the competence of the respondents. Several efforts to verify or reject this proposition have been made, but this issue remains controversial (see also Erikson, this volume).

Stability over time, non-attitudes

Achen (1975) identified two possible sources of weak correlation coefficients among citizens' political survey responses: (1) the instability of a voter's political attitudes, and (2) the low reliability of opinion survey questions (measurement errors). A statistical model designed to separate these two sources of response instability was developed and applied to Converse's data. The survey questions suffered from fairly weak reliabilities. When the correlations among attitudes were corrected for this unreliability, the result was a sharply increased estimate of the stability and coherence of voters' political thinking (see also Judd and Mulburn 1980).

Hill and Kriesi (2001) examined a Swiss panel that had been asked several questions about environmental pollution four different times during a two-year period (1993–95). The authors used a probability model in order to differentiate between those who had stable attitudes (called opinion holders) across the various waves, those who were vacillating changers and those who were durable changers. Their conclusion was that the portion that held stable opinions was larger than in Converse's data, but there were also large proportions of vacillating changers with unstable opinions. The group of durable changers was small.

Inglehart (1985) analyzed items designed by Rokeach and Inglehart to tap basic value priorities. These items showed modest individual-level stability, together with remarkably high aggregate stability structured in ways that could not occur if random responses were the prevailing pattern. Materialist/postmaterialist values showed, for example, large differences between birth cohorts. These aggregated results are skewed to result from random answering and cannot be attributed to methods effects. While random response to given items does play an important role, it is much less widespread than Converse's black and white model implies, and does not generally reflect an absence of relevant preferences.

The use of various statistical programs to control for measurement errors in the belief system debate has been challenged. Measurement error varies according to political knowledge and education, as Feldman (1989) has shown, and a significant part of measurement error might be caused by the survey instruments, which are interpreted differently among people with different levels of political knowledge (Norpoth and Lodge 1985). When these aspects of measurement error are controlled for by the statistical programs, important aspects of differences between belief systems in the mass public are hidden.

Issues, political principles and party choice

Converse found a much stronger correlation between political issues and party choice among the elite than among the mass public. In the following, some different findings regarding this aspect of the debate will be reviewed.

The sophistication–interaction hypothesis implies that the correlation and effect of attitudes and values on party choice will vary significantly between people at different sophistication levels. Goren (2013: Chapter 8) argues that the nature of policy principles is such that reliance on these speaks well for the political competence of all voters, independent of political sophistication. His analyses of the determinants of the presidential vote based on US election studies shows that policy principles have large effects on the presidential vote, but very few interaction effects with political sophistication are significant. However, several studies of issue voting (specific or more broad) have shown considerable and significant differences in the impact of political issues on voting. MacDonald, Rabinowitz and Listhaug (1995) compare the impact of several issues on evaluation of parties in Norway and the United States and of presidential candidates in the United States based on election studies in the two countries. When controlling for demographic variables in both models, the explanatory power varies considerably between the sophistication levels for nearly all parties and presidential candidates. Other comparative research has also shown that issue and value-based voting varies strongly with levels of political sophistication (Lachat 2008).

Level of conceptualization

The original study of ideological conceptualization was based on the 1956 election study. Longitudinal studies have shown that ideological thinking became considerably more prevalent during the 1964 election and has remained largely stable since then (Lewis-Beck et al. 2008: 293). The most pronounced critic of the level of conceptualization approach has been Smith (1980, 1981), who questioned the fundamental reliability and validity of the levels of conceptualization, on methodological and conceptual grounds. He documented that changes in the levels which occurred across two and four-year periods were so large that the measure possessed an unacceptably low level of reliability. He also questioned whether the open-ended questions measured that which was intended and therefore claimed that their validity was low. This view has been countered by several scholars. Hagner and Pierce (1982) analyzed the criterion validity of the open-ended response variables, and showed that the conceptualization levels differentiate fairly stably across time between various social background variables (e.g., education), psychological involvement and political participation, political knowledge, political efficacy, etc. Cassel (1984) also examined the validity and reliability of the levels. She concluded – as had Hagner and Pierce – that the validity was good and that the levels of conceptualization indexes used in previous studies measured ideological sophistication and not merely campaign rhetoric.

Comparative works on belief systems

There are a few comparative works on the issues of constraint and political attitude stability. In an influential comparative work based on surveys of Sweden and the United States, Granberg and Holmberg (1988) concluded that there was more constraint among attitudes, more stability of attitudes over time and more evidence of issue voting in Sweden (see also Niemi and Westholm 1984). The level of conceptualization research was followed up by comparative data and analyses in the Political Action project in the works of Klingemann (1979). Klingemann relied to a large degree on Converse's framework. Five countries were included in the study: Austria, Britain, Germany, the Netherlands and the United States. With regard to the active use of an ideological mode of thoughts, between 34 and 36 percent in the Netherlands and Germany were classified as ideologues, and 20–21 percent in Austria, Britain and the United States. Klingemann also examined ideological recognition and understanding and found – as did Converse – that the proportions classified as ideologues were considerably larger than those with an active use of ideology. Ideological recognition and understanding was most frequently found in Germany (56 percent), the Netherlands (48 percent), Austria (39 percent), the United States and Britain (both 33–34 percent).

Ideology and belief systems

The "end of ideology" debate that commenced following the publication of Daniel Bell's work *The End of Ideology* (Bell 1960) penetrated mainstream political science in several ways. It drew attention to the need for defining the term, and was central in the rejection of the "isms" that was part of a drive toward a rational and empirical discipline (Knight 2006: 622). Below three different ways of approaching ideology after the end of ideology debate are briefly reviewed.

Sartori (1969) coupled an ideological belief system or an ideological mentality to a "closed" cognitive structure that he defined as a state of dogmatic impermeability concerning both evidence and arguments. The opposite was a pragmatic mentality that was identified as an "open" cognitive structure[5] where cognitive openness was defined as a state of mental permeability. He also associated ideology with a rationalistic process, coding and contrasting this with empirical process coding. Ideologies were central for elites in obtaining political mobilization and for maximizing the possibility of mass manipulation.

By contrast, for Converse, ideology – or the ability of individuals to think ideologically – was defined in such a way that ideology became entangled with political sophistication. Although Converse (1964: 207) originally avoided ideology for "belief system," the notion of ideology is frequently used for more sophisticated belief systems; in fact the higher level of conceptualization is designated "ideological." It is evident from Converse's work that he considered ideology and political sophistication as more or less synonymous, and that an ideological belief system was characterized by (a) a high level of constraint, (b) stable political attitudes, and (c) an "ideological" level of recognition and active use of ideological concepts.

Another common way of using the ideology concept in studies of mass belief systems is to consider the various political values and attitude dimensions which were outlined in the section on values above, as *ideological dimensions*, and the poles as representing various ideologies without including level of sophistication in the definition.

Conclusion

The conceptualization of attitudes and values, and the differences between these concepts, are central within public opinion research. As has been shown, it is frequently difficult in practice to maintain this differentiation. Many items which were intended to tap political values use the notions "more" or "less," and thereby resemble attitude items by taking the existing situation as a point of departure, although they are formulated as general policy orientations. The political value and attitude structure is multidimensional, not one or two-dimensional, when a larger number of items are examined.

Most of the contributions in the debate concerning citizens' democratic competence were published before 2000 as the above review confirms. There are also important contributions from after 2000. The review has indicated some unresolved issues in the debate and also emphasized that advanced statistical methods have proven to be somewhat problematic – at least for some scholars – in solving the basic issues in the debate.

Notes

1 This review of the general attitude concept is based on Ajzen (2005), Eagly and Chaiken (1993), Fishbein and Ajzen (1975), Oskamp and Schultz (2005) and Rokeach (1968).
2 The more general regime support levels, approval or core regime principles and values, and national identities, are closer to political values than to attitudes.
3 An alternative hypothesis would be that new values become inculcated rather as a consequence of new political choices than as a cause. See van der Brug and Franklin (in this volume) and Evans and Northmore-Ball (in this volume).
4 A thorough review of works on these topics by Campbell et al. (1960) and Converse (1964) and the American debate can be found in Lewis-Beck et al. (2008: Chapters 8–10). See also Critical Review's 2006 (vol. 18) special issue on "Democratic Competence" based on the debate of Converse's view. Other works where Converse elaborates his views are found in Converse (1970, 2000, 2006).
5 Sartori based his differentiation between open and closed mind on Rokeach's (1960) well-known work.

References

Achen, C. H. (1975) "Mass Political Attitudes and the Survey Response," *American Political Science Review*, vol. 69, no. 4, December, 1218–1231.

Ajzen, I. (2005) *Attitudes, Personality and Behaviour*, 2nd Edition, Maidenhead: Open University Press.

Ariely, G. and Davidov, E. (2012) "Assessment of Measurement Equivalence with Cross-National and Longitudinal Surveys in Political Science," *European Political Science*, vol. 11, no. 3, September, 363–377.

Bell, D. (1960) *The End of Ideology: On the Exhaustion of Political Ideas in the Fifties*, Glencoe: Free Press.

Campbell, A., Converse, P. E., Miller, W. E. and Stokes, D. E. (1960) *The American Voter*, New York: John Wiley and Sons.

Cassel, C. A. (1984) "Issues in Measurement: The 'Levels of Conceptualization' Index of Ideological Sophistication," *American Journal of Political Science*, vol. 28, no. 2, May, 418–429.

Converse, P. E. (1964) "The Nature of Belief Systems in Mass Publics," in Apter, D. E. (ed.) *Ideology and Discontent*, New York: Free Press: 206–261.

Converse, P. E. (1970) "Attitudes and Non-Attitudes: Continuation of a Dialogue," in Tufte, E. R. (ed.) *Quantitative Analysis of Social Problems*, Reading, MA: Addison-Wesley: 168–189.

Converse, P. E. (1974) "Comments: The Status of Nonattitudes," *American Political Science Review*, vol. 68, no. 2, June, 650–660.

Converse, P. E. (1980) "Comment: Rejoiner to Judd and Milburn," *American Sociological Review*, vol. 45, no. 4, 644–646.

Converse, P. E. (2000) "Assessing the Capacity of Mass Electorate," *Annual Review of Political Science*, vol. 3, no. 1, June, 331–353.

Converse, P. E. (2006) "Democratic Theory and Electoral Reality," *Critical Review*, vol. 18, no. 3, Winter, 297–329.

Dalton, R. J. (2009) "Economic, Environmentalism and Party Alignments: A Note on Partisan Change in Advanced Industrial Democracies," *European Journal of Political Research*, vol. 48, no. 2, March, 161–175.

Deth, J. W. van and Scarbrough, E. (1995) "The Concept of Values," in van Deth, J. W. and Scarbrough, E. (eds.) *The Impact of Values*, Oxford: Oxford University Press: 21–47.

Eagly, A. H. and Chaiken, S. (1993) *The Psychology of Attitudes*, Fort Worth: Harcourt Brace Johanovich.

Feldman, S. (1989) "Measuring Issue Preferences: The Problem of Response Instability," *Political Analysis*, vol. 1, January, 25–60.

Fishbein, M. and Ajzen, I. (1975) *Belief, Attitude, Intention, and Behavior: An Introduction to Theory and Research*, Reading, MA: Addison-Wesley.

Flanagan, S. C. and Lee, A–R. (2003) "The New Politics, Culture Wars, and the Authoritarian-Libertarian Value Change in Advanced Industrial Democracies," *Comparative Political Studies*, vol. 36, no. 3, April, 235–270.

Goren, P. (2004) "Political Sophistication and Policy Reasoning: A Reconsideration," *American Journal of Political Science*, vol. 48, no. 3, July, 462–478.

Goren, P. (2013) *On Voter Competence*, Oxford: Oxford University Press.

Goren, P., Federico, C. H. and Kittelson, M. C. (2009) "Source Cues, Partisan Identities, and Political Value Expression," *American Journal of Political Science*, vol. 53, no. 4, October, 805–820.

Granberg, D. and Holmberg, S. (1988) *The Political System Matters: Social Psychology and Voting Behavior in Sweden and the United States*, Cambridge: Cambridge University Press.

Hagner, P. R. and Pierce, J. C. (1982) "Correlative Characteristics of the Conceptualization in the American Public 1956–1976," *Journal of Politics*, vol. 44, no. 3, August, 779–807.

Hainmueller, J. and Hiscox, M. J. (2007) "Educated Preferences: Explaining Attitudes Towards Immigration in Europe," *International Organisation*, vol. 61, no. 2, April, 399–442.

Halman, L. and de Moor, R. (1994) "Religion, Churches and Moral Values," in Ester, P., Halman, L. and de Moor, R. (eds.) *The Individualizing Society: Value Change in Europe and North America*, Tilburg: Tilburg University Press: 37–65.

Hill, J. L. and Kriesi, H. (2001) "An Extension and Test of Converse's 'Black-and-White' Model of Response Stability," *American Political Science Review*, vol. 95, no. 2, June, 397–413.

Inglehart, R. (1977) *The Silent Revolution – Changing Values and Political Styles Among Western Publics*, Princeton: Princeton University Press.

Inglehart, R. (1985) "Aggregate Stability and Individual Level Flux in Mass Belief Systems: The Level of Analysis Paradox," *American Political Science Review*, vol. 79, no. 1, March, 97–116.

Inglehart, R. (1990) *Cultural Shift in Advanced Industrial Society*, Princeton: Princeton University Press.

Inglehart, R. and Flanagan, S. C. (1987) "Value Changes in Industrial Societies," *American Political Science Review*, vol. 81, no. 4, December, 1289–1319.

Inglehart, R. and Welzel, C. (2005) *Modernization, Culture Change, and Democracy: The Human Development Sequence*, Cambridge: Cambridge University Press.

Judd, C. M. and Milburn, M. A. (1980) "The Structure of Attitude Systems in the General Public: Comparisons of a Structural Equation Model," *American Sociological Review*, vol. 45, no. 4, August, 627–643.

Kinder, D. R. (1998) "Opinion and Action in the Realm of Politics," in Gilbert, D. T., Fiske, S. T. and Lindzey, G. (eds.) *The Handbook of Social Psychology*, 4th Edition, New York: McGraw-Hill: 778–867.

Kitschelt, H. (1994) *The Transformation of European Social Democracy*, Cambridge: Cambridge University Press.

Kitschelt, H. (1995) *The Radical Right in Western Europe: A Comparative Analysis*, Ann Arbor: The University of Michigan Press.

Klingemann, H.-D. (1979) "Measuring Ideological Conceptualizations," in Barnes, S. H. and Kaase, M. (eds.) *Political Action: Mass Participation in Five Western Democracies*, London: Sage: 215–254.

Kluckhohn, C. (1951) "Values and Value Orientations in the Theory of Action: An Exploration in Definition and Classification," in Parsons, T. and Shils, E. (eds.) *Towards a General Theory of Action*, Cambridge, MA: Harvard University Press: 388–433.

Knight, K. (2006) "Transformations of the Concept of Ideology in the Twentieth Century," *American Political Science Review*, vol. 100, no. 4, November, 619–626.

Knutsen, O. (1995) "Left–Right Materialist Value Orientations," in van Deth, J. W. and Scarbrough, E. (eds.) *The Impact of Values*, Oxford: Oxford University Press: 160–196.

Knutsen, O. (2011) "Values," in Badie, B., Berg-Schlosser, D. and Morlino, L. (eds.) *International Encyclopedia of Political Science*, Volume 8, Los Angeles: Sage: 2691–2697.

Lachat, R. (2008) "The Impact of Party Polarization of Ideological Voting," *Electoral Studies*, vol. 27, no. 4, December, 687–698.

Lewis-Beck, M. S., Jacoby, W. G., Norpoth, H. and Weisberg, H. (2008) *The American Voter Revisited*, Ann Arbor: The University of Michigan Press.

MacDonald, S. E., Rabinowitz, G. and Listhaug, O. (1995) "Political Sophistication and Models of Issue Voting," *British Journal of Political Science*, vol. 25, no. 4, October, 453–483.

Marcus, G., Tabb, D. and Sullivan, J. L. (1974) "The Application of Individual Differences Scaling to the Measurement of Political Ideologies," *American Journal of Political Science*, vol. 18, no. 2, May, 405–420.

Marks, G. and Steenbergen, M. R. (eds.) (2004) *European Integration and Political Conflict*, Cambridge: Cambridge University Press.

McCann, J. A. (1997) "Electoral Choices and Core Value Change: The 1992 Presidential Campaign," *American Journal of Political Science*, vol. 41, no. 2, April, 564–583.

Niemi, R. G. and Westholm, A. (1984) "Issues, Parties and Attitudinal Stability: A Comparative Study of Sweden and the United States," *Electoral Studies*, vol. 3, no. 1, April, 65–83.

Norpoth, H. and Lodge, M. (1985) "The Difference Between Attitudes and Nonattitudes in the Mass Publics: Just Measurements?," *American Journal of Political Science*, vol. 29, no. 2, May, 291–307.

Norris, P. (2011) *Democratic Deficit: Critical Citizens Revisited*, Cambridge: Cambridge University Press.

Norris, P. and Inglehart, R. (2004) *Sacred and Secular: Religion and Politics Worldwide*, Cambridge, MA: Cambridge University Press.

Oskamp, S. and Schultz, P. W. (2005) *Attitudes and Opinions*, 3rd Edition, Manhwa: Lawrence Erlbaum Associates.

Peffley, M. A., and Hurwitz, J. (1985) "A Hierarchical Model of Attitude Constraint," *American Journal of Political Science*, vol. 29, no. 4, November, 871–890.

Rokeach, M. (1960) *The Open and Closed Mind: Investigations into the Nature of Belief Systems and Personality Systems*, New York: Basic Books.

Rokeach, M. (1968) *Beliefs, Attitudes and Values: A Theory of Organization and Change*, San Francisco: Jossey-Bass.

Rokeach, M. (1973) *The Nature of Human Values*, London: The Free Press.

Sartori, G. (1969) "Politics, Ideology and Belief Systems," *American Political Science Review*, vol. 63, no. 2, June, 398–411.

Schwartz, S. H. (2007) "Value Orientations: Measurement, Antecedents and Consequences Across Nations," in Jowell, R., Roberts, C., Fitzgerald, R. and Eva, G. (eds.) *Measuring Attitudes Cross-Nationally: Lessons from the European Social Survey*, Los Angeles: Sage: 161–193.

Smith, E. R. A. N. (1980) "The Levels of Conceptualization: False Measures of Ideological Sophistication," *American Political Science Review*, vol. 74, no. 3, September, 685–696.

Smith, E. R. A. N. (1981) "Reply to Abramson, Nie, Verba and Petrocik," *American Political Science Review*, vol. 75, no. 1, March, 152–155.

28

THE STABILITY OF POLITICAL ATTITUDES

Robert S. Erikson

How swayable is public opinion? Can people be easily influenced by the latest political argument they hear? Or do they usually hold firm? In the political science literature, one can trace two very different lines of argument.

On the one hand, it is well-known that answers to survey questions can be influenced by subtle aspects of how the question is framed (Druckman 2004) and how the question is exactly worded (Aldrich and McGraw 2011). With online survey experiments, researchers can manipulate responses with small variations in the presentation of political statements (Mutz 2011). From such facts, one might think that people routinely shift their opinions and will change again in response to the next political argument they learn. The depiction is a public that is open-minded, perhaps even to a fault.

On the other hand, consider the growing evidence that our political views are captive to our hardwired political predispositions. Especially in terms of partisanship and ideology, one's political views are conditioned by one's early political environment or perhaps one's personality characteristics (Gerber et al. 2011) or genetic makeup (Alford, Funk and Hibbing 2005). When attitudes can be traced to one's permanent traits or even one's genes, they obviously are resistant to change.

So how open are citizens to political persuasion? Both interpretations presented above are correct. People do have political predispositions that influence their political responses and these predispositions rarely change. Yet at the same time, citizens are malleable in the short term as their responses to survey questions are sensitive to the stimuli that affect them at the moment. The distinction is that short-term influences have a short-half life. For predicting people's political views in the future, their current long-term disposition is the most important. In terms of today's survey response, the challenge is to separate the long-term component from the short-term influences.

Philip Converse's nonattitude model

For a general discussion of the stability of political attitudes, the place to start is the influential essay on "The Nature of Belief Systems in the Mass Public" by Philip E. Converse (1964), one of the four authors of the classic 1960 book on US elections, *The American Voter* (Campbell et al. 1960). Converse's essay examined survey data from the American National Election Study

(ANES) panel of citizens who were interviewed over the three election campaigns of 1956, 1958, and 1960. His analysis painted a dismal picture for those expecting a rational, active citizenry. Perhaps his most alarming finding was that while people changed their response to a question when asked more than once, their shifts of response followed a pattern as if they were generally responding randomly. The view quickly spread in the world of public opinion analysis that many people who answer questions by public opinion researchers are making up answers on the spot, and perhaps had no real opinions at all.

After analyzing turnover patterns from the 1950s panel, Converse (1964) proposed that virtually all respondents who change their position over time hold no true convictions but instead express random responses or "nonattitudes." The compelling evidence for infrequent true change is that response instability varies little with the time between surveys. Whether the two surveys were conducted two years apart or four years apart mattered little. Each comparison yielded about the same amount of response turnover. If people were actually changing their minds, observed opinions would be more stable over the briefer time interval.

If the nonattitude thesis is correct, most observed response change is random error, as if changers are simply flipping coins. Just as coins can be flipped heads one time and tails the next, they can also be flipped consistently heads or tails both times. Thus a further implication of the nonattitudes thesis is that many consistent responses are random responses that appear stable only by chance. On one notorious issue from the 1950s panel, the abstract "power and housing" question (whether "the government should leave things like electric power and housing for private businessmen to handle"), Converse reached a startling conclusion (1964: 293). He estimated that less than 20 percent of the adult public held meaningful attitudes on this issue even though about two-thirds ventured a viewpoint on the matter when asked in a survey.

Consider the stylized example where the pattern of responses over three waves of a survey show the following pattern, where responses are either liberal (L) or conservative (C) (Table 28.1).

At first glance, this pattern might suggest that many respondents were truly changing their views, just as we might imagine how open-minded and attentive citizens would behave. However, notice that people who switch responses from "liberal" to "conservative" or from "conservative" to "liberal" between waves 1 and 2 are equally likely at wave 3 to switch once again as they are to maintain their wave 2 position. This pattern is exactly what would be expected if respondents were flipping coins. Coin-flippers would be equally divided into eight equally probable categories based on their three flips over three interviews. Given that the coin-flippers are found equally in the six groups where the respondent changed their reported opinion (as if flipping coins as heads, heads, tails, for instance), another 10 percent would be coin-flippers within the 20 percent who respond liberal three times and another 10 percent within the

Table 28.1 Turnover of opinion responses over three survey waves: a hypothetical example

Wave 1	Wave 2	Wave 3	Proportion with this pattern (%)
Liberal	Liberal	Liberal	20
Liberal	Liberal	Conservative	10
Liberal	Conservative	Liberal	10
Liberal	Conservative	Conservative	10
Conservative	Liberal	Liberal	10
Conservative	Liberal	Conservative	10
Conservative	Conservative	Liberal	10
Conservative	Conservative	Conservative	20

20 percent who respond conservative three times. So by this interpretation, only 10 percent are true liberals and another 10 percent are true conservatives. The implication would be that few people hold meaningful positions but those who do are steadfast in their beliefs.[1]

Many have found the implications of Converse's nonattitudes explanation quite disturbing. In a democracy, public officials presumably respond to the policy preferences of the public, enacting these preferences into law. But if people generally lack coherent preferences or don't even hold preferences at all, why should elected officials heed their views? Indeed, if survey responses are largely nonattitudes, why should anyone take public opinion polls seriously? Fortunately, there are ways to avoid such a pessimistic assessment.

The "measurement error" explanation

An obvious implication of the nonattitudes explanation is that the seemingly random element to survey responses is the fault of the respondents themselves, as if their lack of political sophistication is to blame. People have not thought about the political question or they do not prefer to engage, but they would prefer the interviewer to not see them as politically ignorant. So they just make something up as their answer. If so, the assumption is that when people give unstable responses to opinion questions the reason is a lack of the political sophistication necessary to form crystallized opinions.

In fact, contrary to this prediction of nonattitude theory, response instability varies little if at all with measures of political sophistication or political knowledge (Achen 1975; Erikson 1979; Feldman 1989). The disturbing level of instability found for surveys of the general public is also found for subsamples representing the sophisticated and informed. If even politically sophisticated individuals respond with a seeming random component, what is to blame? It probably is not a lack of capability on the part of those being interviewed.

For this reason, a measurement error explanation has been proposed to account for response error (Achen 1975; Erikson 1979). This explanation does not challenge the evidence that most response instability represents error rather than true change. However, by the measurement error explanation, the "blame" for the response instability is placed not so much on the capabilities of the respondents as on the survey questions themselves. Even the best survey questions produce some instability from respondents who hold weak or ambivalent attitudes about policy issues. Some inherent limitations in the survey enterprise make measuring attitudes an imprecise task. These include ambiguities in question wording, single-item indicators, the problem of investigator-defined responses to closed-ended questions that may not be congruent with the way respondents think about issues, and the problem of respondents having to give immediate answers to perhaps 100 or more questions with virtually no opportunity for reflection or considered judgment. Thus it is the inherent limitations of the survey method that mostly explain response instability, not the inherent limitations of the respondent.

An explanation based on response probability

John Zaller and Stanley Feldman offer a "theory of the survey response" that provides a more general explanation for response instability and incorporates the findings of both the nonattitudes and the measurement approaches (Zaller and Feldman 1992; Zaller 1992). From this perspective, respondents do not hold fixed, stable attitudes on many issues, but they *do* have propensities to respond one way or another. The answer they give, however, depends on the considerations that come to mind when a question is asked. A consideration is simply anything that affects how someone decides on a political issue, one way or another. For example, when one is asked for an opinion on universal health insurance, considerations may include higher taxes, sick people unable to get medical care, and government bureaucracies. The actual survey response depends on the considerations that are accessible when the question is asked. Assuming the considerations listed were of equal importance, the respondent would oppose universal health insurance as two considerations point in that direction versus one that points to support.

But the considerations that come to mind at one point in time may not be the same as at another. Usually, for our hypothetical respondent, the considerations that come to mind induce opposition to universal health care. But perhaps she recently saw a TV news story about a hardworking man paid poverty-level wages who could not afford medical treatment for his bedridden wife. When asked the universal health care question, that consideration may be at the top of the head and induce support for universal health care. But the news story will eventually be forgotten, and considerations that induce opposition will again predominate. Thus, for many issues, responses are probabilistic. There is a propensity to come down on one side of an issue, but the probability is something greater than zero and less than 1.0.

Even though the opinions expressed on an issue may vary, the underlying attitudes that give rise to them may be quite stable. Suppose our hypothetical individual has a 70 percent probability of choosing the conservative response on national health insurance, and further assume that this places her at the eightieth percentile of conservatism on the issue (the respondent is more conservative than 80 percent of citizens). Within a period of two to four years, our respondent should still be near the same eightieth percentile. Stimuli in the environment might cause minor variations in probabilistic responses – for example, a liberal national mood swing might lower everybody's probability of a conservative response. But our hypothetical respondent would still be more conservative than 80 percent of citizens.

We are left with a paradox. On the one hand, *latent* attitudes would tend to be stable over time as described above. On the other hand, any particular survey response would be problematical. Given this dilemma, how can we improve the measurement of political opinion? One solution is to ask multiple questions of respondents on similar issues and record their average response. When using multiple items to measure a general attitude, such as one's degree of support for government to help people, response stability increases significantly, suggesting that our supposition about latent attitudes is correct (Ansolabehere, Rodden and Synder 2008).

An example: opinion on diplomacy versus use of force, 2004

A useful example for illustration is a question the National Election Survey asked its respondents in Fall 2004, both during the Bush vs. Kerry presidential campaign and after in a post-election panel wave. This was at the height of the controversial Iraq War. The question is as follows:

> Some people believe the United States should solve international problems by using diplomacy and other forms of international pressure and use military force only if absolutely necessary. Suppose we put such people at "1" on this scale.
>
> Others believe diplomacy and pressure often fail and the US must be ready to use military force. Suppose we put them at number 7.
>
> And of course others fall in positions in-between, at points 2, 3, 4, 5, and 6. Where would you place YOURSELF on this scale, or haven't you thought much about this?

Here, we collapse the responses as pro-diplomacy (1, 2, or 3), in-between (4) or pro-force (5, 6, or 7). Table 28.2 shows the 3×3 grid of responses on the two questions. Even with the forewarning of our previous discussion, the degree to which responses are inconsistent might

Table 28.2 Response turnover on diplomacy vs. use of force in international affairs, Fall 2004

Wave 2 (November or December)	Wave 1 (September or October)		
	Diplomacy	In-between	Force
Diplomacy	27.8	8.1	3.8
In-between	5.1	8.8	7.8
Force	5.9	9.2	23.9

Data source: American National Election Study.

Note

N = 901(weighted). Cell entries are percentages of those offering an opinion in both waves.

surprise. A full 25 percent of respondents declined to offer an opinion in at least one of the two waves, indicating that they could not engage in the debate on diplomacy versus force. But of the remaining 75 percent who chose a position on the 1–7 scale both times, barely half (52 percent) took a consistently "liberal" position favoring diplomacy (1, 2 or 3) or a consistently "conservative" pro-force position (5, 6 or 7) in both survey waves. Thirty-eight percent took the middle route of parking at the "4" middle position at least once, while 10 percent seemingly switched sides from wave 1 to wave 2. How should we interpret this result?

One temptation is to see this table as evidence of the public's incapability of offering a rational judgment on foreign policy. Perhaps people do not really hold meaningful viewpoints on matters of war and peace and are just not capable of responding well to complicated questions of diplomacy and the use of force.

But there is another aspect to the response inconsistency that should be considered. The question asks the public to choose from two competing actions (diplomacy and force) where the appropriate answer can depend on the circumstances. The question has no context to guide the respondent. A respondent might think "well, diplomacy is good if it works, but sometimes our government must resort to a threat of force." The question asks the respondent to decide which consideration the government should weight more heavily. It is plausible that many survey respondents shift from one survey to the next in the weight they assign to diplomacy and force, depending on which considerations pop into their head at the moment.

Does Table 28.2 show the residue of random responding or are the gradations of opinion response generally meaningful? An important clue is whether different levels of consistency can be found as a function of the respondent's level of information. The ANES rates respondents on an information scale whereby they are asked to identify the jobs held by four individuals – the US Vice President, the Prime Minister of the United Kingdom, the Chief Justice of the United States, and the Speaker of the US House. For instance, 2004 respondents were given the name "Dick Cheney." If the respondent said he was the Vice President, that was coded as the correct answer. Let us identify the 2004 respondents as "informed" if they could correctly identify at least three of the four individuals, and "uninformed" if they could identify no more than one (those in the middle with two correct identifications are set aside).

Table 28.3 compares the response turnover by the high- and low-information voters. Let us focus again on the percentage who are consistently liberal (pro-diplomacy) or consistently conservative (pro-force). Although the low-information voters are less consistent, the differential is modest – 49 percent consistent among low-information voters versus 59 percent consistent among high-information voters. Even among highly-informed voters, a question about diplomacy versus force can generate very wobbly answers.

Table 28.3 Response turnover on diplomacy vs. force, by information of respondent

Wave 2	Wave 1		
	Diplomacy	*In-between*	*Force*
Low-information respondents			
Diplomacy	27.9	6.7	2.1
In-between	9.0	10.2	9.5
Force	9.8	9.0	20.9
High-information respondents			
Diplomacy	30.9	6.9	3.8
In-between	2.9	10.8	5.5
Force	3.7	7.6	28.0

The next question is, do these wobbly answers have much predictive power? We obtain a positive answer by assessing how well these wobbly answers predict support for President Bush in 2004 at the height of the Iraq War. It turns out that diplomacy-vs.-force attitudes are among the strongest predictors of voting for President Bush or John Kerry, particularly when the diplomacy-vs.-force responses for the two survey responses are combined. The pattern is shown in Figure 28.1. Note that it is not just the extreme positions on diplomacy-vs.-force matter. The various gradations of the average position on the diplomacy-vs.-force seven-point scale matter for predicting the vote. These wobbly answers are good predictors of how Americans voted in 2004. The results would be even crisper if somehow we could measure latent opinion on diplomacy-vs.-force perfectly.

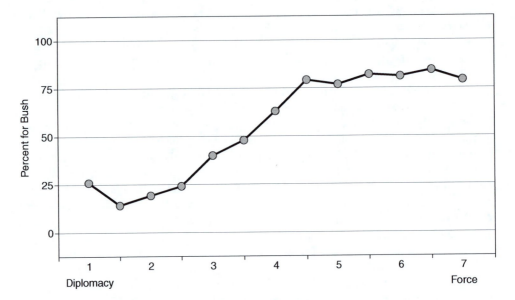

Figure 28.1   Bush percentage of two-party vote in 2004 as a function of the respondent's mean position on the diplomacy versus force scale

Data source: 2004 American National Election Study.

Modeling opinion over time

How much do political opinions change over time? We define the over-time correlation as the correlation between a specific attitude as measured for one point in time and the same attitude as measured for the same individuals at a different time. To separate the over-time correlation of observed opinions (measured with error) and the over-time correlation of latent opinion (unobserved, no error) requires at least three readings of opinion with the time intervals between times 1 and 2 being roughly equal to that between times 2 and 3. By applying a set of reasonable assumptions, the degree of stability of latent opinion depends on the degree to which the correlation between observed readings of opinion decays as a function of the length of time between readings.

Consider two possible extremes. First, suppose the over-time correlation is constant no matter how much time lapses between readings. If so, all observed change in reported opinion would be attributed to measurement error, as if the latent attitude remains constant (as in our discussion of Converse's "power and housing" example). At the other extreme, suppose the correlation between observations decays exponentially with the time interval between readings: the correlation at times 1 and 3 were to equal the product of the correlation between observations at times 1 and 2 and the correlation between observations at times 2 and 3. Then the attribution would be that latent opinion equals observed opinion without error. The truth would be somewhere in between.

Much of the modeling of opinion over time has been performed on US party identification, a 1–7 scale from "Strong Democrat" (1) to "Strong Republican" (7).[2] Changes in latent party identification are infrequent. For political attitudes in general, the observed over-time correlation decays only slightly as a function of the time between measurements. This makes sense only if, over many years, people's latent attitudes change little. Shifts from one survey to the next represent mainly short-term response shifts with only slight movement in terms of latent attitudes or dispositions.

Examples

As examples, let us consider the over-time correlations for three political attitudes. Two are the standard political items of party identification and ideological identification, each on a seven-point scale. The third is the respondent's position on the standard ANES policy question of whether the government should guarantee jobs and a good standard of living.

For this exercise we use three waves of a panel survey with respondents answering at three points in time. Using three time points allows us to not only observe the actual correlations but also estimate the correlations among the latent values of the attitudes (as discussed above). Further, Table 28.4 shows the results for two panel surveys. One is an ANES panel for the years 1992, 1994, and 1996. The other is the Jennings-Niemi Political Socialization Study (Jennings and Niemi 1982), in which the same respondents were interviewed as adults in 1973, 1982, and 1997 − a 24-year range (respondents had first been interviewed when high-school seniors in 1965).

Consider first the observed correlations in the top panels of Table 28.4. One sees three patterns in the correlations of attitudes over the three-waves. First, the correlations are largest for party identification and smallest for the jobs question, with ideological identification in between. This is consistent with our earlier discussion. Second, compared to waves 1 to 2 or waves 2 to 3, the over-time correlations tend to be smaller between waves 1 and 3, although not by as much as one might think. The slight decay of the correlations with the time gap indicates some slow change in latent attitudes. A third pattern is that the correlations are smaller, as we would expect, for the longer time gaps in the Political Socialization Survey than over the four years of the ANES study. Over nearly a quarter century, people do change, even in terms of their latent opinion.

The bottom panels of Table 28.4 show the estimated correlations among the latent attitudes, using the Wiley and Wiley (1970) methodology. For the short span of two or four years, the estimated over-time correlations are high – trending into the 0.90s and in a few cases even exceed their natural ceiling of 1.00 (the exact estimates are only approximations). The lesson is that, over a span of a few years, people's underlying latent attitudes rarely change. Shifts in observed responses are mere short-term variation of no lasting consequence.

For the Political Socialization Panel spanning 24 years, the latent correlations are smaller than over four years, which we would expect. Latent political attitudes do shift or erode over time. Still, attitudes of young adults in 1973 did generally carry over into middle age in 1997. This is especially true for ideological identification, where the 0.73 implied 24-year over-time correlation suggests that slightly more than half the variance in latent ideology at about age 49 could be explained by ideological tendency at about age 25.[3] Similar findings can be found from other data and other studies (Alwin, Cohen and Newcomb 1991).

Vote choice: an exception

If survey responses to attitudinal questions are a function of both long-term and short-term forces, one might think that this model applies to vote choice in presidential elections. Even over the short term, voters are not as much influenced as we might think by campaign messages, a phenomenon that can suggest perhaps the absence of thinking (Achen and Bartels 2016). But voters do predictably choose based on their long-standing partisan and ideological beliefs. (Ansolabehere, Rodden and Snyder 2008).

At least in presidential elections, most voters make an early choice and stick to it throughout the campaign – influenced by their long-standing partisan and ideological predispositions, plus their group interests and idiosyncratic factors. Once decided, they are not easily swayed to

Table 28.4 Over-time correlations from two panels, observed and estimated for the latent variable

Observed over-time correlations	*1992–1994*	*1994–1996*	*1992–1996*	*1973–1982*	*1982–1997*	*1973–1997*
Party identification	0.80	0.87	0.79	0.65	0.65	0.47
Ideological identification	0.73	0.79	0.73	0.45	0.58	0.44
Guaranteed jobs and standard of living	0.58	0.49	0.46	0.35	0.40	0.24
Latent variables over-time correlations						
Party identification	0.91	0.91	0.99	0.74	0.72	0.53
Ideological identification	0.91	1.01★	0.92	0.76	0.96	0.73
Guaranteed jobs and standard of living	0.79	1.09★	0.86	0.56	0.75	0.41

Notes
Latent variable correlations are estimated using the Wiley and Wiley (1970) method. Starred (★) estimates exceed the maximum value of 1.00. *N*s for the 1990s survey are 407 (ideology), 497 (jobs), and 584 (party identification). *N*s for the Socialization survey are 728 (ideology), 793 (jobs), and 892 (party identification).

change their mind. Where casual survey evidence suggests that voters are swayed by candidate policy stances, it is more likely that their vote choice influenced their stance on the issue than the other way around (Lenz 2012). Over the many election campaigns where the American National Election Studies asked people for their vote choice pre-election and then asked how they voted, 95 percent of those who offered a choice both times were consistent in their pre-election preference and eventual vote choice (Erikson and Wlezien 2012).

Macro-level opinion change

So far we have been discussing opinion change at the micro-level of individual citizens. We often are interested in opinion change by the public as a whole. The question then arises that if people have such stable latent attitudes, how can we account for polls that show people collectively changing their mind? The answer is that small shifts at the micro-level can appear major on the macro-level canvas (Erikson, MacKuen and Stimson 2002). When public opinion collectively moves (say, conservative to liberal – or vice versa – on some policy question), it generally makes sense (Page and Shapiro 1992). Moreover, when the ideological tone of public opinion shifts in a liberal or conservative direction it is often in response to government policy or economic performance (Erikson, MacKuen and Stimson 2002). At the macro-level, partisanship (or "macropartisanship") moves in response to government performance (Erikson, MacKuen and Stimson 1998). These shifts can be traced to small collective changes in latent attitudes as people modify their political predispositions to fit changing circumstances in the political environment.

Summary and conclusions

Public opinion can be analyzed in terms of short-term responses as measured by survey researchers. Or it can be treated as a set of stable political predispositions (latent attitudes, not directly measurable) that are like people's personal mean positions or set points. People can be moved off their set-points by persuasive arguments, yet these short-term effects do not last long.

People's political predispositions are essentially stable, especially in the short run of a few years. Over the long haul, they also change in response to fresh political conditions, but perhaps less than we think. If adults' core political attitudes are essentially stable, then where do they come from? An implication is that to understand why we are the way we are, we need to know more about people's earliest political experiences (Stoker and Bass 2011). In recent years, researchers have been particularly interested in political ideology – what separates liberals from conservatives (Jost 2009; Hetherington and Weiler 2009; Haidt 2013). The current research frontier is on the role of personality traits and even our genetic programing that we inherit at birth. Stay tuned.

Appendix

This section offers a more formal analysis of opinion responses over time. Here, we consider opinion not as simply taking sides but rather as a continuous interval-level variable that is measured on a scale such as the ANES' seven-point scales for issue positions, ideological identification, and party identification.

Figure 28.2 presents a causal model of the opinion responses for one attitude over three waves of a panel.[4] The key statistical assumption is that latent opinion evolves as an AR1

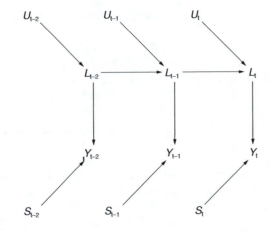

Figure 28.2 Wiley–Wiley causal model of a variable over three survey waves. Y = observed value,
L = long-term or latent value, S = short-term value (error), and U = input to L

process, meaning that its value at time t is a function of its value at time $t-1$ t but independent of latent opinion at earlier time $t-2$. In other words, if we know latent opinion at one time ($t-1$ in the model) earlier history does not matter. This AR1 assumption provides the leverage for modeling latent opinion over time.

A second assumption is that survey responses to the same question at different points in time are connected only via the continuity of latent opinion. A survey response at time t is a function of latent opinion L at time t plus a deviation from latent opinion we will call S, for short-term response. S can represent a short-term response to immediate stimuli (Zaller's top-of-the-head response) or it could be simple measurement error. The crucial assumption is that S_t is unrelated to S_{t-1}.

Armed with these assumptions, we can employ the statistical procedure known as two-stage least squares to estimate the effect of latent opinion at time $t-1$ (L_{t-1}) on latent opinion at time t (L_t) without worrying about contamination from the short-term factor S. Here, a third measurement of opinion at $t-2$ is needed. One predicts observed opinion Y at $t-1$ from observed opinion Y at $t-2$ and uses this prediction of Y_{t-1} as the "instrument" to predict Y at time t. The assumption for 2SLS to work is that the only connection between Y_{t-2} and Y_t is via Y_{t-1}, which is the AR1 assumption. The outcome of this statistical manipulation is an estimate of the coefficient predicting Y_t from Y_{t-1}. With a further bit of manipulation and the assumption of constant variance for S, the short-term or error variance (Wiley and Wiley, 1970), it is possible to estimate the variance of S_t (the short-term forces), and u_t, the variance of the shock to Y_t unaccounted for by Y_{t-1}.

Notes

1 The stylized example is simplified for ease of exposition in that the coin being flipped is unbiased with equal chances of heads and tails. In many examples of response turnover, the division is not close to 50–50, which requires the coin-flipping example to involve a biased coin, e.g., if opinion is 60–40 liberal to conservative, the coin-flipping analogy could be a coin that comes up heads 60 percent of the time and tails 40 percent of the time. In the real-world example of the "power and housing" question, the opinions expressed were more conservative (pro-private industry) than liberal. The allowance of the equivalent of a biased coin does not affect the generality of the argument.
2 See especially Green and Palmquist (1994) and Green, Palmquist and Schickler (2002).

3 From the AR1 assumption, the implied latent value correlation from time 1 to time 3 must equal the time 1 – time 2 correlation × the time 2 – time 3 correlation.

4 For convenience, assume that variables in the model are de-meaned – that is, they are measured as deviations from their means.

References

Achen, C. H. (1975) "Mass Political Attitudes and the Survey Response," *American Political Science Review*, vol. 69, no. 4, December, 1218–1231.

Achen, C. H. and Bartels, L. M. (2016) *Democracy for Realists: Why Elections Do Not Produce Responsive Government*, Princeton: Princeton University Press.

Aldrich, J. H. and McGraw, K. H. (eds.) (2011) *Improving Public Opinion Surveys: Interdisciplinary Innovation and the American National Election Studies*, Princeton: Princeton University Press.

Alford, J. R., Funk, C. L., and Hibbing, J. R. (2005) "Are Political Orientations Genetically Transmitted?," *American Political Science Review*, vol. 99, no. 2, May, 153–169.

Alwin, D. F., Cohen, R. L., and Newcomb, T. M. (1991) *Political Attitudes over the Life Span*, Madison: University of Wisconsin Press.

Ansolabehere, S., Rodden, J., and Synder, J. M. Jr. (2008) "The Strength of Issues: Using Multiple Measures to Gauge Preference Stability, Ideological Constraint, and Issue Voting," *American Political Science Review*, vol. 102, no. 2, May, 215–232.

Campbell, A., Converse, P. E., Miller, W. E., and Stokes, D. E. (1960) *The American Voter*, New York: Wiley.

Converse, P. E. (1964) "The Nature of Belief Systems in Mass Publics," in Apter, D. (ed.) *Ideology and Discontent*, New York: Free Press: 206–261.

Druckman, J. N. (2004) "Political Preference Formation: Competition, Deliberation, and the (Ir)relevance of Framing Effects," *American Political Science Review*, vol. 98, no. 4, November, 671–686.

Erikson, R. S. (1979) "The SRC Panel Data and Mass Attitudes," *British Journal of Political Science*, vol. 9, no. 1, January, 89–114.

Erikson, R. S. and Wlezien, C. (2012) *The Timeline of Presidential Elections: How Campaigns Do (and Do Not) Matter*, Chicago: University of Chicago Press.

Erikson, R. S., MacKuen, M. B., and Stimson, J. A. (1998) "What Moves Macropartisanship? A Reply to Green, Palmquist, and Schickler," *American Political Science Review*, vol. 92, no. 4, December, 901–912.

Erikson, R. S., MacKuen, M. B., and Stimson, J. A. (2002) *The Macro Polity*, New York: Cambridge University Press.

Feldman, S. (1989) "Measuring Issue Preferences: The Problem of Response Instability," *Political Analysis*, vol. 1, no. 1, January, 25–60.

Gerber, A. S., Huber, G. A., Doherty, D., Dowling, C. M., and Ha, S. E. (2011) "Personality and Political Attitudes: Relationships Across Issue Domains and Political Contexts," *American Political Science Review*, vol. 104, no. 1, February, 111–133.

Green, D. and Palmquist, B. (1994) "How Stable is Party Identification," *Political Behavior*, vol. 16, no. 4, May, 437–464.

Green, D., Palmquist, B., and Schickler, E. (2002) *Partisan Hearts and Minds: Political Parties and the Social Identities of the Voters*, New Haven: Yale University Press.

Haidt, J. (2013) *The Righteous Mind: Why Good People Are Divided by Politics and Religion*, New York: Pantheon.

Hetherington, M. J. and Weiler, J. D. (2009) *Authoritarianism and Polarization in American Politics*, Cambridge: Cambridge University Press.

Jennings, M. K. and Niemi, R. G. (1982) *Generations and Politics*, Princeton: Princeton University Press.

Jost, J. T. (2009) "Elective Affinities: On the Psychological Bases of Left-Right Differences," *Psychological Inquiry*, vol. 20, no. 3, April, 129–141.

Lenz, G. (2012) *Follow the Leader?: How Voters Respond to Politicians' Policies and Performance*, Chicago: University of Chicago Press.

Mutz, D. (2011) *Population Based Survey Experiments*, Princeton: Princeton University Press.

Page, B. I. and Shapiro, R. Y. (1992) *The Rational Public*, Chicago: University of Chicago Press.

Stoker, L. and Bass, J. (2011) "Political Socialization: Ongoing Questions and New Directions," in Shapiro, R. Y. ad Jacobs, L. (eds.) *The Handbook of American Public Opinion and the Media*, Oxford: Oxford University Press: 453–470.

Wiley, D. E. and Wiley, J. A. (1970) "The Estimation of Measurement Error in Panel Data," *American Sociological Review*, vol. 35, no. 1, February, 112–117.

Zaller, J. (1992) *The Nature and Origins of Mass Opinion*, Cambridge: Cambridge University Press.

Zaller, J. and Feldman, S. (1992) "A Simple Theory of the Survey Response: Answering Questions and Revealing Preferences," *American Journal of Political Science*, vol. 36, no. 3, August, 579–616.

29

POLITICAL KNOWLEDGE

Measurement, misinformation and turnout

Jennifer vanHeerde-Hudson

Introduction

This chapter examines a key dimension of public attitudes – political knowledge – its measurement and impact on policy preferences and turnout. Specific attention is given to the role of misinformation – that is, confidently held, but factually incorrect beliefs – and whether misinformation can be corrected. In so doing it casts a wide net over a volume of literature on knowledge and political participation, with an emphasis on the former. Throughout the chapter, attention is given to methodology and measurement, showing how experimental political science in particular, has reshaped the way we approach the study of political knowledge.

In the first part of this chapter, I focus on political knowledge – citizens' factual beliefs about political processes, actors and institutions. I provide a brief review of two "schools" of thought on political knowledge – what I term "traditionalists" and "revisionists" – and how these approaches have influenced the measurement of political knowledge. I show how measurement issues are at the core of some of the more robust findings in the literature and illustrate this with an in-depth look at the literature on the gender gap in political knowledge.

I then turn to a key development in the literature on political knowledge, Kuklinksi et al.'s (2000) concept of misinformation, confidently held, but factually incorrect beliefs. The literature has convincingly demonstrated the consequences of misinformation on policy preferences and vote choice; however, studies of correcting misinformation are fewer in number and with limited evidence of success. The second part of this chapter looks at the consequences of political information for one form of political participation, turnout.

Political knowledge: measurement, misinformation and corrections

The study of political knowledge has occupied scholars of political behavior for nearly a century. Understanding political knowledge helps to answer one of the fundamental questions of democratic politics: can citizens participate in political life and what do they need to know in order to do so? Political knowledge has been defined in a variety of ways, commonly as "the range of factual information about politics that is stored in long-term memory" (Delli Carpini and Keeter 1996: 10), and alternatively as, "a measure of a citizen's ability to provide correct answers to a specific set of fact-based questions" (Boudreau and Lupia 2013: 171). Both definitions highlight the centrality of "objective facts" in measuring and understanding citizens' political knowledge which has long been taken as given, but has recently come under scrutiny (Shapiro and Bloch Elkon 2008; Gaines et al. 2007). But these two definitions do more than frame the concept; they illustrate an underlying tension or difference in approach to understanding the concept of political knowledge, which has played out in the literature. Two "schools of thought" have developed, what I term "traditionalists" and "revisionists" (see Table 29.1).

The traditionalist school dates back to the early and mid-twentieth century. Within this approach, the idea that "information matters" was a widely accepted norm: citizens need to be politically knowledgeable to execute their democratic duties. The normative thrust of this approach was firmly linked to Berelson, Lazarsfeld and McPhee, who wrote:

> The democratic citizen is expected to be well-informed about political affairs. He is supposed to know what the issues are, what their history is, what the relevant facts are, what alternatives are proposed, what the party stands for, what the likely consequences are. By such standards, the voter falls short.
>
> *(1954: 308)*

Despite rejecting this view as too demanding a set of expectations for the modern citizen (Kuklinski et al. 2000), it nevertheless became an anchor for a generation of research on political knowledge (Campbell et al. 1960; Converse 1964; Delli Carpini and Keeter 1993). The *key* finding to emerge from this literature was the ignorance of the average (American) voter.[1]

Nowhere was the ignorance of the average American more laid bare than in Delli Carpini and Keeter's (1996) *What Americans Know about Politics and Why It Matters*, which resurrected scholarly interest in political knowledge and its relationship to political behavior. It also illustrated the normative thrust of the traditional school: political knowledge matters because it helps to inform preferences and behavior based on cognitive, rather than simply emotional or affective engagement. "Political information," they argued "is to democratic politics what money is to economics: it is the currency of citizenship" (Delli Carpini and Keeter 1996: 8).

Drawing on thousands of historical survey questions on political figures, institutions, processes, policies and politics – among their many valuable findings – three warrant detailing briefly. They too, find more evidence documenting Americans as a nation of "know-nothings": just over half of respondents could answer four (or more) of ten knowledge items correctly. Second, knowledge was unevenly distributed among the public – with white, educated, older males at the top end of the scale. Third, low and uneven knowledge matters for political participation, particularly turnout. Those with higher levels of political knowledge are more likely to turn out to vote, and have a greater sense of efficacy and interest in politics. Consequently, how politicians view and respond to public opinion may be skewed toward the politically knowledgeable at the expense of the less informed.

The traditionalist approach stands in contrast to the "revisionist" school in understanding how citizens participate in political life and what they need to know in order to do so. Table 29.1 draws out the key distinctions between the two approaches. Here, scholars have taken a less critical view of the average citizen: few citizens pay close attention to politics, they have different interests in and appetites for political information (Popkin 1991; Sniderman, Brody and Tetlock 1991). That few citizens meet the standards of democratic citizenship is less worrying for revisionists because citizens can use heuristics or shortcuts available to them (e.g., partisan or elite cues) to help inform preferences (Lupia and McCubbins 1998). How citizens process available information is of more importance than the absolute level of knowledge they have (Bartels 1996).

Table 29.1 Two schools of thought on political knowledge

	Traditionalists	Revisionists
Normative position	Citizens should be factually informed	Low levels of political knowledge are not worrisome for democratic government or responsiveness
Argument	Citizens should be well-informed; facts are important	Citizens use heuristics or shortcuts to overcome lack of knowledge
Citizens have	Knowledge; facts are used to inform judgments and policy preferences	Rationality; can process information by reasoning
Key works	Berelson, Lazarsfeld and McPhee (1954); Converse (1964); Delli-Carpini and Keeter (1996); Althaus (1998)	Popkin (1991); Page and Shapiro (1992); Sniderman, Brody and Tetlock (1991); Lupia and McCubbins (1998)
Does public opinion reflect public's interests/preferences?	No – political knowledge is not evenly distributed among the public but concentrated in the better educated and politically interested	Yes – errors are random so aggregating opinion cancels out opposing preferences
Criticism/weakness	Even the well-informed fall short of normative expectations; "facts" can be interpreted differently	Cues are not neutral; subject to framing

At the individual level, shortcuts allow citizens to arrive at "true" preferences even if they start from low levels of knowledge. Rational and "reasoning" citizens simply make use of the information available to them. Moreover, revisionists worry less about the unequal distribution of knowledge in the population and its consequences for meaningful public opinion, because the process of aggregating (uninformed) individual preferences produces meaningful collective preferences. Any errors in preference formation at the individual level are assumed to be random and therefore cancel each other out in the aggregate (Bartels 1996).

A key question arising then is how would collective preferences change – if at all – if citizens were fully informed? Are low knowledge levels consequential for collective public opinion? The evidence suggests there are indeed consequences of poorly informed publics. Althaus (1998) asks, is there evidence of an "information effect" or "bias in the shape of collective opinion caused by the low levels *and* [emphasis added] uneven social distribution of political knowledge in a population" (1998: 545). Using data from the American National Election Study (ANES), he simulates fully-informed preferences in four policy issue areas: fiscal, foreign policy, social policy and operative. He finds real and sizeable changes – roughly 7 percent on average – in collective policy preferences between the simulated fully-informed and actual knowledge levels. One consequence of an uneven distribution of knowledge is that the US public looks more conservative on some issues and more progressive on others.

Using simulated data from the ANES as well as an experimental design, Gilens (2001) compares the macro policy preferences of fully-informed respondents with and without policy-specific information. Using both statistical imputation of preferences and an experimental design to help tease out whether the manipulation of information affects preferences, Gilens shows that policy-specific information matters. Respondents who perform well on general political knowledge items, fall short on policy-specific knowledge, which affects their preferences to a greater extent than general political information. In other words "what separates actual political preferences from hypothetical 'enlightened preferences' is due to ignorance of specific policy-relevant facts, not a lack of general political knowledge or the cognitive skills or orientations that measures of general political information reflect" (Gilens 2001: 380). He also shows that policy-specific information has a stronger influence on those with high levels of political knowledge. For those who "don't know much," the addition of policy-specific information does not shift their preferences much; but for those who "know a lot" already, the addition of policy-specific information has a substantial effect on the preferences.

Shifting focus to vote choice in US Presidential elections from 1972–92, Bartels' (1996) evidence finds little support for the revisionist claim that at the micro-level uninformed voters can use heuristics accurately, and at the macro-level errors in preference formation cancel each other out. Moreover, the deviations are not random but directed. Substantively, he claims that "the deviations [from fully informed voting] display two clear and politically consequential patterns: relatively uninformed voters are more likely, other things being equal, to support incumbents and Democrats" (Bartels 1996: 218).

Taken together these studies do not provide sufficient evidence to reject revisionists' claims, although they do challenge them. In the section below, I show how the study of "misinformation" and attempts to correct it have changed the course of study on political knowledge. But questions remain as to how robust these findings are for different political contexts. Notwithstanding Gilens' (2001) experimental approach, future work could adopt experimental designs to better tease out the mechanisms by which individual preferences do/do not reflect collective ones. Future work exploring the impact of information on preferences in other contexts would also help to determine the robustness of these findings: how do these processes work in contexts with better/worse information environments, in different types of political systems or in emerging democracies?

Measuring political knowledge

Political knowledge has become, as Mondak (2001: 238) notes, "a cornerstone construct in research on political behavior"; however, measuring political knowledge remains subject to debate. In this section, I outline debates around content, construct and item validity and how this has shaped the political knowledge research agenda going forward.

What does it mean for a citizen to be politically knowledgeable? Barber (1973) argued that "citizens need to know what government *is* and *does*" (cited in Delli Carpini and Keeter 1996: 63); in other words, to be politically knowledgeable was to know general "facts" of political life.[2] Historically, this has meant being able to answer questions on political institutions; for example, the number of Supreme Court justices or which party controls the lower chamber or about political people; for example, identifying the Chancellor of the Exchequer in Britain, Charles de Gaulle or Ruth Bader Ginsburg. More recent measures have attempted to move away from people and institutions to include both domestic and international policy and politics and social and political history, but the emphasis on knowing "the facts" has persisted.

Correct answers to fact-based knowledge items are then summed and the resulting knowledge scales used, most commonly, as predictors of political behavior. This approach was exemplified by work by Delli Carpini and Keeter (1993), who argued that knowledge was a uni-dimensional concept and can be measured with a handful of items with relative accuracy. Using five items from the large battery in the US National Election Study, they show that "carefully chosen items can measure political knowledge with an acceptable level of reliability and validity" (Delli Carpini and Keeter 1993: 1202).

There are three critiques of the traditional summative knowledge scales approach that, with some variation, has become the standard for measuring political knowledge. The first challenge relates to content and construct validity; a second relates to item validity; and a third challenge comes from experimental approaches which show the limitations of survey response in observational data.

How (content) valid are knowledge scales or do they measure what they intend to? In other words, do fact-based measures of political knowledge capture citizens' ability to understand the broad tenets and workings of the political system, the choices on offer and the potential outcomes of each choice? Lupia's (2006) critique asserts that a form of elitism underpins standard measures of political knowledge and does little to help citizens translate or make use of information in determining their preferences. He argues that it remains unclear how factual information about the number of legislators helps them to make choices among candidates, parties or policies.

The construct validity of standard knowledge scales has also been challenged. First, traditional knowledge scales may measure other properties than factual knowledge. Mondak (1999) shows evidence that traditional knowledge scales also measure underlying personality traits: self-confidence, competitiveness and propensity to take risks. Second, the distribution of "Don't know" and incorrect items, which are usually collapsed into a single category, are substantively different. Survey respondents who offer incorrect responses may have partial information – they are not inattentive to politics – but may be missing key bits of information or have confused information in answering the item. But incorrect responses have historically been treated the same as "Don't know" responses, introducing imprecision in measurement.

"Don't know" response options have been the subject of much study. Mondak's (1999: 79) contribution was to advise scholars to "discourage 'Don't knows,' provide them randomly to help account for guessing, or test experimentally so the consequences of encouraging and discouraging DKs could be assessed in head-to-head tests." Miller and Orr's (2008) experimental analysis of encouraging, discouraging and omitting "Don't knows" has led them to recommend removing the DK option from knowledge items altogether. They show that eliminating the DK option "yielded higher estimates of knowledge, both on a per-item and aggregate basis for political and general knowledge" (Miller and Orr 2008: 775). Because DK options conceal information, they reveal less about citizens' political knowledge.

Finally, Boudreau and Lupia (2013) show how manipulating the survey context undermines the validity of fact-based knowledge measures, which are affected by:

> question wording, variation in respondents' incentives to think before answering, whether respondents feel threatened by unusual aspects of survey interview contexts and personality variations the make some respondents unwilling to give correct answers to survey interviewers even when they are knowledgeable about the subject matter.
>
> *(Boudreau and Lupia 2013: 173)*

For example, Prior (2014) has shown that simply adding visuals to equivalent knowledge items increases the number of correct items.

Prior and Lupia (2008) find that existing measures may underestimate citizens' political knowledge because they neither incentivize respondents to perform well, nor do they helpfully differentiate between quick recall and political learning, the latter of which is deemed fundamental to citizens' ability to acquire political information and use it to inform their preferences. Their study experimented with financial incentives for answering questions correctly and time. Respondents were randomly allocated to one of four groups: a control group where respondents had one minute to answer each of the 14 knowledge questions; a group where respondents had one minute to answer each question and were incentivized $1 for each correct answer; a group with 24 hours to answer all questions; and a final group with 24 hours to answer all questions and the $1 incentive for each correct answer.

The results showed that, compared with the control group, simply incentivizing respondents a small amount of money resulted in an average 11 percent increase in the number of items answered correctly. And importantly, there were differential effects for demographic sub-groups. "Among respondents who report being moderately interested in politics, the monetary incentive increased correct answers by 32%. Men, white Americans, and those between 35–59 years of age also improved their performance disproportionately ..." (Prior and Lupia 2008: 175). And similar to the financial incentives, allowing respondents to take extra time to complete the knowledge items resulted in an 18 percent increase in the number correct compared to the control group, and 24 percent for the group with extra time and financial incentives. And here too there were heterogeneous effects: women performed better with extra time. Prior and Lupia show that the gender gap in political knowledge – which I take up in the next section – is exacerbated by traditional measures of political knowledge because women do "not carry as much political information in declarative memory as men, but when given an opportunity to employ their procedural memory their scores increased more on average than those of men" (Prior and Lupia 2008: 177).

What these studies and others like them show is that small but important changes in survey measurement and context produce significant changes in the profile of citizens' political knowledge. While the evidence and the received wisdom has been that citizens fail to live up to the standard of "informed democratic citizenship," recent work has shown citizens to be more knowledgeable or have different motivations, incentives or means to becoming politically informed. However, it is not just by experimental methods that our understanding of political knowledge has been advanced. Recent work by Barabas et al. (2014) has shown political knowledge questions to have two key dimensions, a temporal dimension (i.e., when a fact was established) and a topical dimension (i.e., whether information is general or policy-specific). Their framework shows how the questions used to measure knowledge affect observed levels. They show that the mechanisms of becoming informed "operate differently across types of knowledge questions" (Barabas et al. 2014: 851),[3] which has particular implications for gender differences in political knowledge, to which we now turn.

Mind the gender gap? Differences in men's and women's political knowledge

One of the more robust findings in the literature is evidence of a gendered dimension to political knowledge: on balance, men perform better than women on knowledge items in surveys (Delli Carpini and Keeter 1996; Burns, Schlozman and Verba 2001; Kenski and Jamieson 2000; Mondak and Anderson 2004; Lizotte and Sidman 2009). The standard survey items that ask respondents to identify political leaders, the roles and functions of government or the relative positions of candidates and parties on issues show sizeable and meaningful differences in men's and women's knowledge of politics (Dolan 2011).

However, the robustness of the gender gap finding has been called into question on two fronts, both relating to measurement. Kenski and Jamieson (2000), and more explicitly, Mondak and Anderson (2004), first raised the alarm on differences between men's and women's political knowledge, arguing that the gap was a result of question format, hypothesizing that men were less likely to opt for "Don't know" response options than women, effectively inflating the chances of getting items correct and widening the gap between men and women on these items.

They show that women are more likely to use the "Don't know" option, even when they know as much (or more than men) and, second, removing the "Don't know" option reduces the gender gap by approximately 50 percent. The gap still persists, but its magnitude is significantly smaller than once thought. These findings are supported by Lizotte and Sidman (2009), who identify women's risk aversion as the mechanism for being more likely to tick "Don't know," and more recently by Ferrin, Fraile and Garcia-Albacete (2015). Using survey experiments, they show that question format – that is, open vs. closed-ended items – do not help explain the gap in political knowledge, but even where treatments do discourage the use of "Don't know" options, women are more likely than men to say they don't know.

A second critique comes from feminist scholars who have argued that traditional knowledge items capture masculine dimensions of knowledge or, that women and men may know about different things. The notion of domain-specific knowledge was first raised by Delli Carpini and Keeter (1996), who found that differences in political knowledge disappear when the knowledge being tested was gender related – that is, on issues relevant to women's lives and experiences. The importance of testing domain-specific items was taken up by Sanbonmatsu (2003), who demonstrated the link between types of political knowledge and policy preference, showing that different types of knowledge help shape preferences. Sanbonmatsu (2003) tested the hypothesis that knowledge about the level of women's representation in the US explains support for electing more women to Congress. She found that men were more accurate in their estimates of the percentage of women in the House. Women, however, were more likely to overestimate the percentage of women representatives, which made them less likely to support increasing women's representation. The consequence, she notes, is that the "gender gap in gender-related political knowledge has consequences for the ability of women to further their group interests" (Sanbonmatsu 2003: 368).

Using data from a Canadian telephone survey, Stolle and Gidengil's (2010) study explicitly takes up the feminist critique of traditional political knowledge items, by asking respondents questions where experience of government services and provisions and their daily lives intersect – public services and welfare policies. They find evidence that this more "practical" type of knowledge of politics offsets or reverses the gender gap. Importantly, however, they show that while the more expansive measure of knowledge reduced the gap between men and women, it also showed wider gaps in knowledge among women, particularly for low-income, immigrant and older women. Similarly, they make the point that this type of knowledge has political consequences: "the more women know about these matters (benefits and services), the more likely they are to vote for a party of the left, and the less likely they are to be attracted to a party of the right" (Stolle and Gidengil 2010: 103). Dolan (2011), comparing the traditional items to "gender-relevant" items, found that gender differences in knowledge do not emerge when taking into account measures that are "women friendly." Like previous studies, she finds significant differences between women and men when modeling drivers of traditional political knowledge items; however, these differences disappear when modeling knowledge of gender-relevant items.

What about the misinformed?

A key development in the literature on political knowledge is the introduction of "misinformation," which moved scholarly focus from a binary distinction between the politically informed vs. the uninformed, to a third category – *the misinformed* (Kuklinksi et al. 2000).

> To be *informed* means, first, that people have factual beliefs and second, that the beliefs be accurate. If people do not hold factual beliefs at all, they are merely *uninformed*.

They are, with respect to the particular matter, in the dark. But if they firmly hold beliefs that happen to be wrong, they are *misinformed* – not just in the dark, but wrongheaded.

(Kuklinski et al. 2000: 792–793)

Their work spawned two decades of research relating to three questions. First, if knowledge matters for policy preferences and outcomes, what happens if the public is misinformed? Second, what happens if people hold policy preferences, they would have not otherwise, if they were better informed? And third, can misinformation or misperceptions be corrected? I take up each of these questions and their findings in turn below.

The argument for a well-informed citizenry is that information or factual beliefs are prerequisites determining policy preferences. If facts are not readily available or citizens cannot use them in informing their preferences, a deficit in democratic functions exists. But the question for Kuklinski et al. (2000) is what happens when misinformed citizens – people who confidently hold incorrect beliefs – use them to form their policy preferences? Their experimental findings show a majority of respondents hold mistaken beliefs on welfare in the US, and those with the most inaccurate views were also the most confident in their beliefs. Importantly, the most confidently "wrongheaded" were also the strongest partisans.

But does giving respondents correct information matter for their policy preferences? Kuklinski et al. (2000) test this in two ways, first in a "soft test" by comparing a group that received the facts on welfare and a group that didn't. The evidence suggests the facts didn't change individual respondents' policy preferences, including strong partisans. A second, "hard test" shows what they call the "limits of resistance" to the facts. Respondents were asked to estimate how much was spent on welfare and how much they prefer to be spent; half were then told how much was spent on welfare. For the group given the facts, neither their initial estimate nor their preferred spending levels mattered on their policy position, but both mattered for the group who didn't get the facts. They conclude that explicit corrections of information can inform policy preferences, but the effects may not be long-lasting (Kuklinski et al. 2000: 805).

More recently, scholars have taken up the question of whether it is possible to correct misperceptions and the lasting effects thereof (see Table 29.2). Nyhan and Reifler's (2010) analysis moved the debate forward in two ways. First, they examined the effectiveness of corrections in news stories – a more natural and "less authoritative" manner – and second, by measuring the impact of the correction on the factual belief itself, rather than on policy preferences. Using an experimental design they test for corrections across three policy domains: weapons of mass destruction in Iraq, tax cuts and stem cell research. Their findings help to illustrate why misperceptions persist and are difficult to correct. First, they show that corrections vary depending on the respondent's degree of ideological commitment – that is, corrections are more likely to change misperceptions where respondents are less partisan. Similar to Kuklinski et al. (2000), they find that corrections do not change misperceptions for the most ideologically committed (i.e., strong partisans), and can in some cases strengthen incorrect factual beliefs. The persistence or "backfire" effect of corrections has also been demonstrated for the politically knowledgeable (Nyhan, Reifler and Ubel 2013).

As shown in Table 29.2, there is limited evidence that corrections work. Research from experimental psychologists looking at the effectiveness of corrections offers insights into the perseverance of misperceptions. Johnson and Seifert (1994) show that misinformation can influence judgments and perceptions regardless of whether the correction was given early or later in a sequence of information. They argue that belief perseverance or the tendency to hold onto one's beliefs despite conflicting or contradictory information limits the effectiveness of correcting misinformation. However, the news is not all bad. They also find evidence that

Table 29.2 Key studies on correcting misperceptions

Research	Question	Outcome	Data/method	Do corrections work?	Going forward
Kuklinski et al. (2000)	How does misinformation affect policy preferences?	Preferences on welfare policy	Telephone survey experiment	Mixed – receiving factual information doesn't work; need to "hit them between the eyes" with relevant facts	Preferences are hard to shift; use of heuristics may be problematic
Nyhan and Reifler (2010)	Can misperceptions be corrected? (Policy domains: Iraq, WMD and tax cuts)	Respondents' factual beliefs	University students survey experiment using mock-up newspaper articles	No – ideology moderates responses to corrections, strongest partisans report a "backfire effect" where corrections can increase misperceptions	Investigate misperceptions in view of "motivated reasoning"
Nyhan, Reifler and Ubel (2013)	Does aggressive fact checking to correct for misperceptions work? (Affordable Care Act [ACA], death panels)	Policy views on ACA	Opt-in internet panel; survey experiment	Yes – for respondents who had unfavorable views of ACA and Sarah Palin or who had favorable views of Palin, but low knowledge; corrections fail for highly knowledgeable Palin supporters	Difficulty in correcting misperceptions for motivated, knowledgeable respondents
Lawrence and Sides (2014)	What are the consequences of innumeracy in estimating racial composition of US, median income, unemployment and poverty?	Respondents' attitudes towards public policies	Survey experiment	No – for any of the policy domains examined	What are the conditions under which corrections work? What are citizens' motivations for incorporating facts or new information?

rather than just negating previously held views and information, offering an alternative explanation – that is, engaging with the belief and showing another possible alternative – helps to reduce the effect of misperceptions.

Research on misperceptions and corrections has not yet "bottomed out." There is much more to be done to better understand why some citizens, particularly the politically interested, knowledgeable and ideologically committed, are more immune to corrections. More work needs to be done to understand Nyhan and Reifler's "backfire" effect. This body of research is all the more timely in the current political climate where evidence of a more polarized and divisive politics is emerging. It also suggests a "dark side" to partisanship – or more committed partisanship – than has previously been identified. Finally, and with reference to the 2016 US presidential election contests, more research is needed to understand the interplay between misinformation and corrections, in the context of digital information environments.

The impact of political knowledge on political participation: a brief look at turnout

In this section, I look at political knowledge as a correlate or predictor of turnout. Similar to section one, this review is motivated by a similar question: do more knowledgeable voters turn out more than their less knowledgeable counterparts? If so, what consequences are there for this disparity? It also looks at the methods used in examining links between knowledge and turnout, highlighting how, with few exceptions, studies that rely on observational data remain plagued by problems of endogeneity and potentially spurious correlations.

What evidence is there for a link between political knowledge and turnout?[4] Political knowledge sits within the resource model of voting, which posits that resources help citizens make sense of complex processes or unfamiliar choices (Brady, Verba and Schlozman 1995). In terms of vote choice, citizens with more knowledge are better able to choose from among the range of politicians, parties or policies that best reflect their preferences. As political knowledge is not randomly distributed, individual-level differences in this resource can produce unequal turnout for citizens with varying levels of knowledge.[5]

What, then, are the consequences of the inequalities in turnout? Howe's (2006) study of Canada and the Netherlands shows that, while knowledge levels have fallen in both countries, particularly among the youngest cohorts, there are differential effects on turnout. In Canada, the decline in knowledge has negatively affected turnout, but the same is not true in the Netherlands. Howe attributes this to differences in civic literacy in the two countries, arguing that the same erosion in civic literacy in Canada has not taken place in the Netherlands. Consequently, broader cultural differences may help to explain these divergent findings.

Combining both individual and institutional level factors, Fisher et al. (2008) examine how the proportionality of the electoral system and knowledge affect turnout. They show that citizens with low-level knowledge are less likely to turn out under plurality rule elections; a robust finding controlling for a range of individual and macro-level variables. Finally, Wells et al. (2009) examine how voters' values and political knowledge affect their understanding of facts related to an initiative. They show differential relationships among political sophisticates.

> For high-sophisticates or respondents who knew something about endorsements around the initiative, attitudes towards government regulation are predicted by one's views of the facts related to the initiative. But for low sophisticates, their values did not distort their views of initiative-related facts.
>
> *(Wells et al. 2009: 965)*

Can the media be effective in moderating the relationship between knowledge and turnout and does the source of information matter? Prior (2005) shows how increased choice of media outlet widens gaps in both political knowledge and turnout. His analysis shows that, as media choices proliferate, citizens can become more selective in where they receive news. For the less motivated who wish to avoid political news altogether, this is rather easy to do. Citizens with access to the internet and who prefer news are more knowledgeable and more likely to turn out. But there is also evidence to indicate that, with wider access to media outlets, those who have preferences for entertainment over news are less knowledgeable and less likely to turn out. In short, the increasing diversity in the media environment isn't a panacea to the political ignorance problem because citizens can select in, and out, of political news.

Lassen (2005) also takes up the question of whether better-informed citizens are more likely to turn out. Exploiting a natural experiment in Denmark, four of fifteen districts were selected for a decentralization experiment whereby a majority of services formerly handled at the municipal level were devolved to the district. He finds a causal effect for being informed on the likelihood to vote in the referendum. However, a potential weakness of Lassen's study is his use of a subjective measure of being informed – that is, whether respondents thought the referendum went "well, medium-well, or bad." If respondents indicated yes to any of these options, they were considered "informed," otherwise they were considered not to have an opinion. While there is some evidence that subjective and objective measures of knowledge are correlated, other research has cast doubt on the use of subjective measures.

Studies like Lassen (2005) go some way to addressing the issue of causal identification in studies of knowledge and turnout. Most studies have relied on observational data, reporting correlations rather than identified causal effects. As he notes: "The problem is that information acquisition is endogenous and, therefore, that both the decision to vote and the decision to obtain an education or become informed about political issues can be caused by some third, unobservable factor" (Lassen 2005: 104).

There are fewer examples of experimental approaches in studying the relationship between information and turnout, but a useful example is Larcinese's (2007) instrumental variables approach. Using data from the 1997 British general election, he "instruments political knowledge by using various measures of the information supply to which voters have been exogenously exposed" (Larcinese 2007: 391). Larcinese's analysis usefully differentiates education and information on turnout, the former not a significant predictor, the latter significant across different model specifications controlling for a range of observed factors. Moreover, he finds significant effect sizes: voters with the highest level of knowledge are roughly one-third more likely to turn out than voters at the lowest level.

Conclusion

This chapter shows that, while political knowledge has long been considered a prerequisite for healthy democratic politics, most empirical studies show low levels of political knowledge, with negative consequences for individual and collective policy preferences and political participation. It has also considered the limits of fact-based measures of political knowledge. First, they can be weak on content validity: knowledge of people and institutions captures only a small proportion of what we might consider to be politically relevant knowledge and they are gendered. Second, knowledge items may be measuring other constructs, such as personality or appetite for risk. Third, experimental approaches show the limitations of survey response in observational data.

Acknowledging these limitations is not a call for fact-based approaches to be abandoned – quite the contrary. Moving forward, there are two additional challenges for scholars interested in political knowledge and its relationship to political behavior. The first relates to content validity and whether fact-based measures remain the best way to measure political knowledge in twenty-first century politics. Do fact-based measures of political knowledge remain fit for purpose? Lupia (2006) posed a similar challenge many years ago, arguing that a form of elitism underpinned the dominant approach. Do current measures conceal more than they reveal about citizens' ability to form preferences, make informed policy choices and understand the political process? Are there alternative measures of political knowledge that may yield more insight, for example, measuring political experience or more practical forms of knowledge (see Stolle and Gidengil 2010) as a companion to a fact-based approach?

Second and related, what role is there for fact-based measures of knowledge given widespread misinformation in political life and discourse? What are the implications for political life when we cannot agree or choose not to agree on the facts? Recent events, such as the rise of Donald Trump in US politics and the UK referendum on membership in the European Union, or "Brexit," have led many a commentator to make the claim politics is now post-fact or post-truth. In other words, if political discourse and debate has largely abandoned the use of evidence and mutually agreed "facts," do current measures of political knowledge help us understand political behavior better? The prevalence and impact of "misinformation" or firmly held but incorrect beliefs will undoubtedly be important in understanding the policy preferences and behavior of citizens and electorates going forward.

Notes

1 See Bartels (1996). Much of the evidence here is limited to the US context but political ignorance is well-documented in other democratic contexts – for example, Grönlund and Milner (2006).
2 See Gilens (2001), who documents the importance of policy-specific knowledge. Delli Carpini and Keeter acknowledge in their 1993 article the idea of issue specialists or citizens with domain-specific knowledge and that this may not be highly correlated with general political knowledge.
3 Barabas et al. (2014: 851) find that the gender gap is robust: "the shrinking of the knowledge gap between men and women on gender-relevant topics is invariant to differences across the questions."
4 There is a separate and substantial literature (see, for example, Franklin 2004 and Blais 2006) that examines aggregate level predictors or turnout: institutional arrangements (e.g., nature of the electoral system – specifically proportional v. majoritarian systems, unicameralism, voting rules and compulsory voting); socio-demographic factors (e.g., education, age, economic growth); and party systems.
5 Education is another resource that is highly correlated with political participation (Brady, Verba and Schlozman 1995), and a separate and substantial literature has documented the relationship between knowledge and turnout at the individual level (Leighley and Nagler 2014). Although highly correlated, education and political knowledge are separate constructs. Education reduces the costs of acquiring political information; consequently, better-educated voters are more likely to be more knowledgeable. As shown above, citizens have to have access to and make use of information that is available to them. Education facilitates that process, but it does not determine it.

References

Althaus, S. (1998) "Information Effects in Collective Preferences," *American Political Science Review*, vol. 92, no. 3, September, 545–558.
Barabas, J., Jerit, J., Pollock, W. and Rainey, C. (2014) "The Question(s) of Political Knowledge," *American Political Science Review*, vol. 108, no. 4, November, 840–855.
Bartels, L. (1996) "Uninformed Votes: Information Effects in Presidential Elections," *American Journal of Political Science*, vol. 40, no. 1, February, 194–230.
Berelson, B., Lazarsfeld, P. and McPhee, W. (1954) *Voting: A Study of Opinion Formation in a Presidential Campaign*, Chicago: Chicago University Press.
Blais, A. (2006) "What Affects Voter Turnout?" *Annual Review of Political Science*, vol. 9, June, 111–125.

Boudreau, C. and Lupia, A. (2013) "Political Knowledge," in Druckman, J., Green, D., Kuklinski, J. and Lupia, A. (eds.) *Handbook of Experimental Political Science*, New York: Cambridge University Press: 171–186.

Brady, H., Verba, S. and Schlozman, K. (1995) "Beyond SES: A Resource Model of Political Participation," *American Political Science Review*, vol. 89, no. 2, June, 271–294.

Burns, N., Schlozman, K. and Verba, S. (2001) *The Private Roots of Public Action*, Cambridge: Harvard University Press.

Campbell, A., Converse, P., Miller, W. and Stokes, D. (1960) *The American Voter*, New York: Free Press.

Converse, P. (1964) "The Nature of Belief Systems in Mass Publics," in Apter, D (ed.) *Ideology and Discontent*, New York: Free Press: 206–261.

Delli Carpini, M. X. and Keeter, S. (1993) "Measuring Political Knowledge: Putting First Things First," *American Journal of Political Science*, vol. 37, no. 4, November, 1179–1206.

Delli Carpini, M. X. and Keeter, S. (1996) *What Americans Know About Politics and Why It Matters*, New Haven: Yale University Press.

Dolan, K. (2011) "Do Women and Men Know Different Things? Measuring Gender Differences in Political Knowledge," *Journal of Politics*, vol. 73, no. 1, January, 97–107.

Ferrin, M., Fraile, M. and Garcia-Albacete, G. (2017) "The Gender Gap in Political Knowledge: Is It All About Guessing? An Experimental Approach," *International Journal of Public Opinion Research*, vol. 29, no. 1, Spring, 111–132.

Fisher, S., Hobolt, S., Lessard-Phillips, L. and Curtice, J. (2008) "Disengaging Voters: Do Plurality Systems Discourage the Less Knowledgeable from Voting?," *Electoral Studies*, vol. 27, no. 1, March, 89–104.

Franklin, M. (2004) *Voter Turnout and the Dynamics of Electoral Competition in Established Democracies Since 1945*, Cambridge: Cambridge University Press.

Gaines, B., Kuklinski, J., Quirk, P., Peyton, B. and Verkuilen, J. (2007) "Same Facts, Different Interpretations: Partisan Motivation and Opinion on Iraq," *Journal of Politics*, vol. 69, no. 4, November, 957–974.

Gilens, M. (2001) "Political Ignorance and Collective Policy Preferences," *American Political Science Review*, vol. 95, no. 2, June, 379–393.

Grönlund, K. and Milner, H. (2006) "The Determinants of Political Knowledge in Comparative Perspective," *Scandinavian Political Studies*, vol. 29, no. 4, December, 386–406.

Howe, P. (2006) "Political Knowledge and Electoral Participation in the Netherlands: Comparisons with the Canadian Case," *International Political Science Review*, vol. 27, no. 2, April, 137–166.

Johnson, H. and Seifert, C. (1994) "Sources of the Continued Influence Effect: When Misinformation in Memory Affects Later Inferences," *Journal of Experimental Psychology: Learning, Memory and Cognition*, vol. 20, no. 6, November, 1420–1436.

Kenski, K. and Jamieson, K. (2000) "The Gender Gap in Political Knowledge: Are Women Less Knowledgeable Than Men About Politics?," in Jamieson, K. (ed.) *Everything You Need to Know About Politics ... And Why You Are Wrong*, New York: Basic Books: 83–89.

Kuklinski, J. H., Quirk, P. J., Jerit, J., Schweider, D. and Rich, R. F. (2000) "Misinformation and the Currency of Democratic Citizenship," *Journal of Politics*, vol. 62, no. 3, August, 790–816.

Larcinese, V. (2007) "Does Political Knowledge Increase Turnout? Evidence from the 1997 British General Election," *Public Choice*, vol. 131, no, 3, June, 387–411.

Lassen, D. (2005) "The Effect of Information on Voter Turnout: Evidence from a Natural Experiment," *American Journal of Political Science*, vol. 49, no. 1, January, 103–118.

Lawrence, E. and Sides, J. (2014) "The Consequences of Political Innumeracy," *Research & Politics*, July–September, 1–8.

Leighley, J. and Nagler, J. (2014) *Who Votes Now? Demographics, Issues, Inequality and Turnout in the United States*, Princeton: Princeton University Press.

Lizotte, M. and Sidman, A. (2009) "Explaining the Gender Gap in Political Knowledge," *Politics and Gender*, vol. 5, no. 2, June, 127–152.

Lupia, A. (2006) "How Elitism Undermines the Study of Voter Competence," *Critical Review*, vol. 18, no. 3, October, 217–232.

Lupia, A. and McCubbins. M. (1998) *The Democratic Dilemma: Can Citizens Learn What They Need to Know?*, Cambridge: Cambridge University Press.

Miller, M. and Orr, S. (2008) "Experimenting with a 'Third Way' in Political Knowledge Estimation," *Public Opinion Quarterly*, vol. 72, no. 4, Winter, 768–780.

Mondak, J. (1999) "Reconsidering the Measurement of Political Knowledge," *Political Analysis*, vol. 8, no. 1, January, 57–82.

Mondak, J. (2001) "Developing Valid Knowledge Scales," *American Journal of Political Science*, vol. 45, no. 1, January, 224–238.

Mondak, J. and Anderson, M. (2004) "The Knowledge Gap: A Reexamination of Gender-Based Differences in Political Knowledge," *Journal of Politics*, vol. 66, no. 2, May, 492–512.

Nyhan, B. and Reifler, J. (2010) "When Corrections Fail: The Persistence of Political Misperceptions," *Political Behavior*, vol. 32, no. 2, June, 303–330.

Nyhan, B., Reifler, J. and Ubel, P. (2013) "The Hazards of Correcting Myths about Health Care Reform," *Medical Care*, vol. 51, no. 2, February, 127–132.

Page, B. and Shapiro, R. (1992) *The Rational Public: Fifty Years of Trends in Americans' Policy Preferences*, Chicago: University of Chicago Press.

Popkin, S. (1991) *The Reasoning Voter: Communication and Persuasion in Presidential Campaigns*, Chicago: Chicago University Press.

Prior, M. (2005) "News vs. Entertainment: How Increasing Media Choice Widens Gaps in Political Knowledge and Turnout," *American Journal of Political Science*, vol. 49, no. 3, July, 577–592.

Prior, M. (2014) "Visual Political Knowledge: A Different Road to Competence?," *Journal of Politics*, vol. 76, no. 1, January, 41–57.

Prior, M. and Lupia, A. (2008) "Money, Time, and Political Knowledge: Distinguishing Quick Recall and Political Learning Skills," *American Journal of Political Science*, vol. 52, no. 1, January, 169–183.

Sanbonmatsu, K. (2003) "Gender-Related Political Knowledge and the Descriptive Representation of Women," *Political Behavior*, vol. 25, no. 4, December, 367–388.

Shapiro, R. and Bloch-Elkon, Y. (2008) "Do the Facts Speak for Themselves? Partisan Disagreement as a Challenge to Democratic Competence," *Critical Review*, vol. 20, no. 1–2, September, 115–139.

Sniderman, P., Brody, R. and Tetlock, P. (1991) *Reasoning and Choice: Explorations in Political Psychology*, New York: Cambridge University Press.

Stolle, D. and Gidengil, E. (2010) "What Do Women Really Know? A Gendered Analysis of Varieties of Political Knowledge," *Perspectives on Politics*, vol. 8, no. 1, March, 93–109.

Wells, C., Reedy, J., Gastil, J. and Lee, C. (2009) "Information Distortion and Voting Choices: The Origins and Effects of Factual Beliefs in Initiative Elections," *Political Psychology*, vol. 30, no. 6, December, 956–969.

30

IS THERE A RATIONAL PUBLIC?

Jørgen Bølstad

Popular notions of democracy assume that citizens have policy preferences that can and should be reflected in public policy. Elections provide citizens with the opportunity to select representatives with whom they agree, and opinion polls track the mood of the public, providing additional information for those who are elected. This system thus demands quite a lot on the part of the citizens, who are ultimately supposed to be in charge. If the average citizen were completely uninformed and uninterested in politics and public policy, a fundamental condition for democracy as a form of government would appear to be missing. Justifying the privileged status of public opinion as a guide for public policy would indeed be hard under such circumstances.

Yet existing scholarship is divided on whether this very basic condition of well-functioning democracy is fulfilled. A number of scholars working in this area can be identified as either optimists or pessimists, and their lines of work follow long traditions in democratic theory. The idea that the will of the people should be the ultimate guide for public policy is found, for example, in the works of Enlightenment thinkers, such as Rousseau (1997 [1762]). Two centuries later, Dahl stated "a key characteristic of democracy is the continuing responsiveness of the government to the preferences of its citizens, considered as political equals" (Dahl 1971: 1). Yet Dahl was also doubtful about the prospects of achieving full-fledged democracy, noting that existing practices fell short of his ideals. Still more pessimistic, Schumpeter "had a low estimation of the political and intellectual capacities of the average citizen" (Held 1996: 180), and famously argued "democracy does not mean and cannot mean that the people actually rule in any obvious sense of the terms 'people' and 'rule'" (Schumpeter 1976: 284).

Current scholarship is more carefully empirical, yet different authors still provide strikingly different pictures of the capacities of average citizens and their ability to influence public policy. Echoing Schumpeter, Achen and Bartels (2016) argue that popular notions of government responsiveness to public preferences – what they refer to as "the folk theory" of democracy – "has been severely undercut by a growing body of scientific evidence presenting a different and considerably darker view of democratic politics" (Achen and Bartels 2016: 1). Their argument stands in notable contrast to two other literatures. The first explores the ways in which even a scarcely informed electorate can reach reasonable decisions (Lupia 1994; Lupia and McCubbins 1998; Popkin 1991). The second strand, which is further discussed in Wlezien's contribution to this volume (Chapter 32), demonstrates that governments indeed often are responsive to public opinion (see, for example, Erikson, MacKuen and Stimson 2002).

This chapter presents an overview and discussion of how these strands of literature fit together. The chapter starts with a discussion of the political sophistication of individual citizens and moves on to the question of whether the citizenry as a collective is able to act as a rational guide for public policy.

The bad news

In an ideal world, all citizens would read the news every day, have stable and coherent political views, yet be open to deliberation and adjust their views when faced with new information or better arguments. They would carefully develop informed opinions and vote accordingly. But this is, of course, quite unrealistic. In fact, the earliest studies of (American) voter behavior painted a dismal picture of the political sophistication of ordinary citizens (Campbell et al. 1960; Converse 2006 [1964]). While the most educated and informed members of the public showed some understanding of the liberal–conservative spectrum, the majority of voters appeared not to engage in such abstract thinking (Converse 2006 [1964]). In the former group, ideology served to "constrain" voter's opinions, in the sense that their position on one issue would help predict their position on other issues. Among the majority, however, positions appeared non-ideological and many voters seemed to answer completely at random. When interviewed repeatedly at a two-year interval, "only about thirteen people out of twenty manage to locate themselves even on the same side of the controversy in successive interrogations, when ten out of twenty could have done so by chance alone" (Converse 2006 [1964]: 45).[1]

Another troubling observation was that party attachments appeared to explain vote choices far better than other variables, including ideological ones (Campbell et al. 1960). Party identification appeared to act as an "unmoved mover," placed early in the "funnel of causality." Thought to be formed early in life, based on the influence of parents, family members, and others, party identification was presented as "an attachment widely held through the American electorate with substantial influence on political cognitions, attitudes, and behavior" (Campbell et al. 1960: 146).[2] Rather than choosing the party that best fit their policy preferences and ideological positions, many voters seemed to first form a party attachment, and then adapt their perceptions and opinions to fit this attachment.[3] Accordingly, partisanship has been presented as a key factor determining how individuals react to new political information (Zaller 1992; Bartels 2002). Overall, the findings discussed above have held up quite well, and they form some of the key arguments reiterated by Achen and Bartels (2016).[4]

Following the work of Campbell et al. (1960), a number of authors have argued that voters rationalize party preferences either by perceiving their party's position to be closer to their own than it truly is, or by altering their own position, moving it closer to their party (Brody and Page 1972; Markus and Converse 1979; Conover and Feldman 1982). The implication is that the extent of true policy-based "spatial voting" will be (even) lower than estimates based on naïve recursive models would suggest. Yet, it is worth noting that taking the position of the party – often referred to as "persuasion" – may be a rational approach for a low-information voter. It may indeed serve as a useful heuristic of the kind discussed in the next section. In line with this notion, Carsey and Layman (2006) argue that voters are more likely to be persuaded by their party on issues they do not find important, whereas they would be more likely to reduce their support for the party when they disagree on important issues.[5] This puts such behavior in a more slightly favorable light, although the combination of partisan voting and rationalization in general appears problematic from a democratic perspective.

Another line of work has focused specifically on political knowledge. In their seminal study, Delli Carpini and Keeter (1996) confirm that American voters generally know very little about politics and that the level of knowledge has remained fairly stable, despite rising levels of education and increasing access to information (see also Prior 2007). As Delli Carpini and Keeter focus on the US (just like much of the relevant literature, as well as this chapter), a key question is whether Americans are particularly uninformed about politics. Yet this does not seem to be the case to any large extent (Delli Carpini 2005; Grönlund and Milner 2006). A more important point is that knowledge tends to be more equally distributed in more egalitarian societies. For example, individual levels of knowledge are much more dependent on education in the US than in countries with smaller income differences (Grönlund and Milner 2006). Accordingly, Delli Carpini and Keeter (1996) find considerable inequalities in knowledge, with older, richer, white men having the most. This matters because those with more knowledge are "more likely to participate in politics, more likely to have meaningful, stable attitudes on issues, better able to link their interests with their attitudes, [and] more likely to choose candidates who are consistent with their own attitudes" (Delli Carpini and Keeter 1996: 272).

Cues and heuristics

While findings such as those above may seem to leave little hope for a well-functioning democratic process, other authors have pointed out that it may not be necessary for voters to be fully informed. In fact, people never have full information about anything, and yet they often manage to get through their lives just fine. It appears that bounded rationality often works satisfactory. The idea that voters in the absence of complete information use shortcuts to assess the utility they would get from seeing a particular party in office was discussed already in Downs' (1957) *An Economic Theory of Democracy*, and later work has elaborated on this idea. Relying on a theory of low-information rationality, Popkin (1991) argues that voters are able to assess candidates based on the limited pieces of information they gain through their daily lives. They learn about the economy from the way it impacts them as well as the way it is reported in the media; they notice which opinion leaders they agree with and learn to trust their opinions; and they discuss new information with the people around them as a way to develop their opinions.

According to Popkin (1991), voters use several types of heuristics. One example is comparing a candidate to a stereotype of how a class of people acts. They may compare the limited information they have about a candidate to how a person who "does the right thing" would act or to what "a good president" should be like. Such considerations may be based on a politician's voting records, but personal information tends to be more important, as such information is more suited to constructing narratives about the candidates. In fact, voters may put more emphasis on how "presidential" a candidate looks than on their actual political track record. Furthermore, voters let media framing influence their assessments: The media help determine which issues are considered more or less important, and which aspect of an issue, such as the state of the economy, is given priority.

Popkin (1991) also notes that people use information in a way akin to a "drunkard's search." This metaphor refers to a drunk looking for his lost keys under the streetlight, even though that is not where they were lost. It is simply where there is light. Similarly, voters are likely to focus on easily available and accessible information, conducting one-dimensional assessments, relying on single traits, symbols, or events. They may focus more on traits like sincerity or competence than issue positions. Another interesting point is that people dislike uncertainty and will be more confident in their assessments when they can use heuristics. They will also be more certain (or over-confident) when all information points in the same direction or when probabilities are close to zero or one, as more intermediate probabilities are harder to understand and work with.

Partly drawing on Popkin, Lupia and McCubbins (1998) make a similar argument. In particular, they argue that reasoned choice does not require full information, but ability to predict the consequences of available choices – which they refer to as knowledge. They note that people disregard most of the information they could acquire, and rely on a very limited set of information. They further view representation as a principal-agent problem, where voters (as principals) must trust representatives (agents), because it is too costly for the former to monitor every move the latter makes. This problem can be reduced by the presence of a "speaker" that takes on the task of monitoring and assessing the agents. Potential speakers include, for instance, commentators, other politicians, or friends.

In line with a lot of earlier work, Lupia and McCubbins note that people learn both from personal experience and from others. A key point, however, is that such learning is active, and that people choose which sources to rely on – that is, from whom they learn. The authors "define persuasion as one person's successful attempt to change the beliefs of another," and argue "[i]n settings where reasoned choice requires learning from others, persuasion is a necessary condition for reasoned choice" (Lupia and McCubbins 1998: 40). The question is when speakers are persuasive, and the authors argue this is the case when speakers have interests in common with the voter and appear to be knowledgeable about the topic – traits that the voter can gain information about and assess over time. Furthermore, institutions can clarify the incentives of different speakers, and thus facilitate the decision on whom to trust. In sum, the argument is that advice from others can help voters reach reasoned decisions in the absence of relevant information.

The shortcomings of shortcuts

While heuristic approaches have been presented as a potential solution for voters to overcome their lack of information, they are unfortunately not without problems. As Achen and Bartels (2016) note, the notions of bounded rationality and heuristics were introduced by psychologists who reexamined economic behavior. Ironically, one of their main interests was to examine the potentially irrational and adverse effects heuristics can have (see, for example, Kahneman, Slovic and Tversky 1982). If we consider the ideal that voters elect representatives who will produce policies and outcomes in line with their preferences, it is clear that many heuristics may lead people astray also in the political arena. Notably, most of the limited information involved in the behaviors discussed by Popkin (1991) is unrelated to policy. Assessing a candidate based on whether he or she appears "presidential" or seems to be a person "who does the right thing" will only work if voters with different policy preferences define these notions differently and candidates who fit their stereotypes also share their preferences. Unfortunately, this appears unlikely. It seems more likely that voters who rely on such heuristics will make superficial, if not irrational, choices.

The argument of Lupia and McCubbins (1998) requires that there are reliable observers or "speakers" that voters can trust to do the more careful monitoring and assessment for them. Furthermore, the voters need to identify those speakers that will help them make the right choice, which itself can be a demanding task. As Lupia and McCubbins note, relying on the advice of others not only offers an opportunity for enlightenment, but also a risk of being deceived, in the sense that "the testimony we hear reduces our ability to predict accurately the consequences of our actions" (Lupia and McCubbins 1998: 8). The authors argue that voters reduce this risk by taking the advice of actors they perceive to be knowledgeable and trustworthy, which in turn requires an accurate assessment of these two characteristics. They argue speakers are more trustworthy when they face penalties for lying (e.g., reputational loss), and that they can demonstrate their trustworthiness by sending costly signals. The problem is that this model may already put too great demands on the voters, in terms of acquiring and processing relevant information. After all, the voters who could use reliable advice the most are the ones with the least information in the first place (cf., for example, Delli Carpini and Keeter 1996). A study by Lau and Redlawsk (2001) even suggests that, while reliance on heuristics can improve the accuracy of votes cast by political experts, it *decreases* the probability of a correct vote by low information voters.

The "miracle of aggregation"

Another line of work suggesting that the public can make reasonable choices despite widespread ignorance is based on the "miracle of aggregation" (a term coined by Converse 1990). While aggregation simply refers to the process of gathering items, in this context we typically mean the construction of summary measures of individual data – for example, estimating average popular opinion by taking the mean of a sample's survey responses. Or, for that matter, letting the electoral system translate individual votes into a distribution of parliamentary seats, or the selection of a presidential candidate – the key inputs to the political system are nearly always aggregated in some sense.

The "miraculous" feature of this process is that random noise cancels out. Consider a typical survey question, such as "how much responsibility do you think governments should have to ensure sufficient child care services for working parents?" This question can be found in the European Social Survey, and the answer categories range from (0) "Not governments' responsibility at all" to (10) "Entirely governments' responsibility." Now, assume each citizen has a hypothetical opinion that they would be able to state after gathering sufficient information and contemplating the issue thoroughly. We could then define the mean of those opinions as the "true" public opinion on the issue. Let us also assume that most people lack sufficient time and information, which introduces an error in their response. If those errors are distributed randomly (and independently), with a mean of zero, the consequences would be fairly limited. Any particular response would most likely be an inaccurate reflection of a given respondent's views, but the mean of the responses would still be a good estimate of the average public opinion, as the errors sum to zero and thus cancel each other out.[6] All we need is a sufficiently large sample to minimize the impact of particular errors. Fortunately, both survey research and elections typically involve large samples.

Moving from the individual to the aggregate level may thus serve to remove noise and crystallize the underlying signal from the public. This can be particularly useful for identifying changes in public opinion over time. An example of pioneering work in this area is Stimson's *Public Opinion in America* (Stimson 1991), which pieced together an extensive set of data from different surveys. Focusing on policy issues (rather than valence issues and symbols), Stimson finds that the survey responses generally can be mapped onto the liberal–conservative dimension. Furthermore, he finds long-term trends in aggregate opinion – representing what he refers to as the public policy mood. This mood behaves largely as observers of American politics would expect. For example, "popular culture … holds the 1960s to have been a time of great liberalism, the 1980s equally conservative," which is what the data show – with the exception that "the preference measure is ahead of cultural expectations" (Stimson 2004: 89).

Another key contribution relying on aggregation is *The Rational Public* by Page and Shapiro (1992). The authors argue that the American public is predominantly rational, in the sense that it "as a collectivity, holds a number of real, stable, and sensible opinions about public policy, and that these opinions develop and change in a reasonable fashion, responding to changing circumstances and to new information" (Page and Shapiro 1992: 1). On most of the issues examined by the authors, aggregate public opinion showed no significant change, and most of the identified changes could be explained by such factors as external events, new information, and generational replacement. According to the authors, these features of public opinion imply that the public "has the capacity to govern" (Page and Shapiro 1992: 383).

Indeed, the shift in focus to aggregate public opinion has triggered a comprehensive literature on the public's capacity to govern. In line with the notion that the public behaves rationally, Wlezien (1995) develops a model of "the public as thermostat," suggesting that public calls for "more" of a certain policy should weaken as "more" of this policy is delivered. Such a negative response has indeed been found in a number of settings (Franklin and Wlezien 1997; Soroka and Wlezien 2004, 2005, 2010).[7] Furthermore, building on the notion of a policy mood, Stimson, Mackuen, and Erikson (1995) develop a model of "dynamic representation," where calls for more of a certain policy are followed by increases in such policy. This type of responsiveness has also been found in a number of settings (Erikson, MacKuen, and Stimson 2002; Soroka and Wlezien 2010; Bølstad 2015; Hakhverdian 2010). Overall, this literature seemingly attests to the public's ability to respond rationally to changes in public policy, as well as its ability to shape public policy according to its wishes.[8]

The weakness of aggregation

Unfortunately, aggregation is not quite the miraculous cure it might seem either. Its limited promise bears in it what we might call "the weakness of aggregation": Aggregation will crystallize *any* signal, whether it is relevant or not. It will only cancel out random noise, while all systematic influences are incorporated in the aggregate measure. Alas, a situation in which all noise is random is extremely unlikely – some surely will be, but a lot of it will not.[9] As the literature on heuristics may illustrate, voters are likely to sometimes be swayed by *the same* irrelevant or erroneous considerations. If a great number of voters decide to vote for the candidate who appears to be "a good guy" or looks the most "presidential," their aggregate vote may not be very representative of their policy preferences.

The aggregate signal may also appear irrational in other ways. For instance, a key theory in the vast literature on voting behavior is that voters punish incumbents for bad economic conditions and reward them for good ones, which may seem like a rational choice for voters who value economic growth and stability.[10] However, as Achen and Bartels (2016: Chapter 6) note, voters tend to be *myopic*, focusing almost exclusively on the last quarter preceding the election, while ignoring the rest of the term. Such behavior gives incumbents an incentive to stimulate the economy before elections (Nordhaus 1975), but it turns out to be a very poor basis for selecting candidates with superior economic competence. Achen and Bartels (2016: 168) find "no support for the notion that retrospective voters can reliably recognize and reward competent economic management." Instead, a close election may hinge on whether the incumbent is lucky with the state of the economy during the campaign. According to Achen and Bartels (2016: 176), "the voters toss a coin."

Perhaps more troubling, voters appear to reward and punish incumbents for events that are blatantly out of their control. In the summer of 1916, for example, a string of unprecedented shark attacks led to four deaths and one injury along the Jersey shore, which in turn caused economic losses for nearby resorts. Examining the presidential election in November that year, Achen and Bartels (2016: Chapter 5) estimate a substantial loss for incumbent president Woodrow Wilson in the most affected communities. In a more general analysis, they further argue that voters hold incumbent governments accountable for droughts and floods, even if "the government could not possibly have prevented the problem" (Achen and Bartels 2016: 135). A potential counterargument is that voters hold governments accountable for their disappointing responses to the natural disasters, rather than the disasters themselves, but this would imply that American voters almost invariably find the responses disappointing – even those that are above average. This would seem to suggest that voters have unrealistically high expectations, while also failing to incentivize their governments by rewarding those that perform better. In the words of Achen and Bartels, voters engage in "blind retrospection."[11]

A final issue is that aggregated opinions and votes may systematically misrepresent the opinions of groups with lower levels of political information and participation. At first glance, the literature on dynamic representation suggests that public policy over time will stay reasonably close to public opinion on salient issues. Furthermore, the parallelism found in public opinion trends among different segments of the population (Soroka and Wlezien 2008; Page and Shapiro 1992; Erikson, MacKuen, and Stimson 2002) might seem to limit the scope for inequalities in representation. Unfortunately, the resulting equilibrium level of public policy may still be biased if not all voters are equally informed and making their voices heard. That is, if a certain segment of the population is less likely to answer surveys accurately, or to vote in accordance with their preferences, this segment may fail to influence public policy to the extent others do. While Soroka and Wlezien (2008) argue that preference similarities across different groups limit the scope for such inequalities, others such as Gilens (2009) disagree. There is a sizeable literature arguing that public policy tends to reflect the preferences of the highest income groups (Bartels 2009; Gilens 2005, 2012), and that opinion polls and election outcomes would look different if the whole electorate were better informed (Bartels 1996; Delli Carpini and Keeter 1996; Althaus 1998; Lau and Redlawsk 2006).

Conclusion

The existing literature offers strikingly different images of the public's ability to serve as a rational guide for public policy. What most observers agree upon is that citizens generally hold very limited information about their nation's politics and policies. "[T]he 'average' citizen is woefully uninformed about political institutions and processes, substantive policies and socio-economic conditions, and important political actors such as elected officials and political parties" (Delli Carpini 2005: 28). It seems most citizens simply do not have the time or motivation to obtain such information. The question is whether and to what extent this matters for democratic governance. Unfortunately, while heuristics may help low-information voters reach *a* choice, there is no guarantee that this will be a *good* one – there is even evidence suggesting that heuristics may lead such voters to worse decisions.

Furthermore, while aggregation cancels out random noise, crystallizing a signal from the public, this signal is not necessarily a meaningful and rational one. In this regard, there is a striking contrast between the pessimistic views of Achen and Bartels (2016) and the optimistic views of Erikson, MacKuen, and Stimson (2002) and Soroka and Wlezien (2010). When we consider opinions on specific issues, it seems reasonable that these respond "thermostatically" to policy change, as uninformed voters may largely produce random noise, while the informed may respond rationally. Such behavior attests to the public's ability to provide useful aggregate input to the political system. Yet when we turn to votes, there are a number of other systematic, but essentially irrelevant influences that also come into play – such as superficial candidate evaluations with no connection to actual policy positions, or penalties for random natural disasters and external economic shocks.

Interestingly, while Erikson, MacKuen, and Stimson (2002) find the public policy mood to have a strong influence on election outcomes (offering an important way for this mood to influence public policy), Achen and Bartels (2016) leave the public mood out of their models, noting that most forecasters do the same (including Erikson and Wlezien 2012). Erikson, MacKuen, and Stimson (2002) also find covariation between their political and economic variables, and suggest such relationships may be part of the larger macro political system. As analyses in this area often rely on relatively few observations, such covariation may pose a notable challenge to proper identification of causal effects. A key task for future research may thus be to further examine these relationships with a view to better distinguish between correlation and causation. Another key task (and ongoing effort) is to expand the geographical reach of this debate, including, for instance, countries with proportional electoral systems.

Another interesting question is *why* the electorate appears uninformed. Downs (1957) posited that a single vote plays such a small role in the overall election result that many voters will remain rationally ignorant. One might even hypothesize that low engagement with politics signals a general satisfaction with the current state of affairs, allowing more personal preoccupations to take priority. The attractive promise of the dynamic representation model of Erikson, MacKuen, and Stimson (2002) is that a sufficiently dissatisfied public can make its voice heard and change public policy – that is, the policy mood serves as an error-correction mechanism. It could be that the public takes a hands-off approach to politics because things are going reasonably well. The only trouble with this interpretation is that the least privileged voters tend to have the least information (Delli Carpini and Keeter 1996), suggesting that low engagement is the result of hardship rather than privilege. There is thus a risk that the least well off are continuously under-represented while being dissatisfied with public policy.

The general picture emerging from the literature is one in which a small part of the electorate is reasonably well-informed and responding rationally to new information, while a majority is considerably less informed and dependent on cues and heuristics that at best help them make good decisions, and at worst may lead to very bad ones.[12] It is thus hard to avoid the conclusion that the typical citizen's low level of information leaves the political system very vulnerable. The aggregate behavior of the public appears to be quite predictable, but not necessarily rational, as it often hinges on circumstances not controlled by those up for election – such as short-term fluctuations in the economy. One might say the public is boundedly rational, at best. Fortunately, this may also suffice, as it appears to be the case that the public – despite its faults – often gets policies that are broadly in line with what it wants.

Notes

1 However, as Erikson discusses in his contribution to this volume, such tests may underestimate the degree of latent opinion stability. See also Inglehart (1985).

2 For early critiques, see, for example, Key (1966), Fiorina (1981), or Franklin and Jackson (1983).

3 The mechanism typically held to be driving such behavior is cognitive dissonance (Festinger 1957), which has also been used to explain other aspects of attitudinal change (e.g., Bølstad, Dinas, and Riera 2013).

4 More generally, Achen and Bartels (2016) argue group membership and identity are key factors that have received too little attention in electoral research. This is in line with recent studies, such as Bølstad and Dinas (forthcoming), who find in-group biases in spatial voting.

5 See Hutchings and Jefferson's contribution to this volume for a more detailed discussion of partisanship.

6 Note that this example ignores any effect of dealing with a bounded scale. Especially if the true population mean were close to 0 or 10, the errors might pull the aggregate estimate away from the closest bound and toward the center.

7 This pattern has also been found to influence election outcomes (Erikson, MacKuen, and Stimson 2002), but it is not clear whether such "thermostatic voting" – effectively punishing incumbents for implementing their programs – is rational on part of the electorate (Bølstad 2012).

8 This literature is discussed in more detail by Wlezien, in Chapter 32 of this volume.

9 "Random" here means distributed independently with a mean of zero.

10 Although subjective assessments of the economy are often endogenous to political affiliations (van der Eijk et al. 2007).

11 It should be noted, however, that Bechtel and Hainmueller (2011), examining the 2002 Elbe flooding in Germany, find a seven-percentage-point gain for the incumbent party in the affected areas, following a massive policy response.

12 Note that the parallelism in mood trends reported by Erikson, MacKuen, and Stimson (2002) and others does not deny this point. Parallelism only requires that there are some citizens (possibly a minority) within each examined subgroup that change their opinions in the same direction.

References

Achen, C. H. and Bartels, L. M. (2016) *Democracy for Realists: Why Elections Do Not Produce Responsive Government*, Princeton: Princeton University Press.

Althaus, S. L. (1998) "Information Effects in Collective Preferences," *The American Political Science Review*, vol. 92, no. 3, September, 545–558.

Bartels, L. M. (1996) "Uninformed Votes: Information Effects in Presidential Elections," *American Journal of Political Science*, vol. 40, no. 1, February, 194–230.

Bartels, L. M. (2002) "Beyond the Running Tally: Partisan Bias in Political Perceptions," *Political Behavior*, vol. 24, no. 2, June, 117–150.

Bartels, L. M. (2009) "Economic Inequality and Political Representation," in Jacobs, L. and King, D. (eds.) *The Unsustainable American State*, Oxford: Oxford University Press: 167–196.

Bechtel, M. M. and Hainmueller, J. (2011) "How Lasting Is Voter Gratitude? An Analysis of the Short-and Long-Term Electoral Returns to Beneficial Policy," *American Journal of Political Science*, vol. 55, no. 4, October, 852–868.

Bølstad, J. (2012) "Thermostatic Voting: Presidential Elections in Light of New Policy Data," *PS: Political Science and Politics*, vol. 45, no. 1, January, 44–50.

Bølstad, J. (2015) "Dynamics Of European Integration: Public Opinion in the Core and Periphery," *European Union Politics*, vol. 16, no. 1, March, 23–44.

Bølstad, J. and Dinas, E. (forthcoming) "A Categorization Theory of Spatial Voting: How the Center Divides the Political Space," *British Journal of Political Science*, available online: www.cambridge.org/core/journals/british-journal-of-political-science/article/a-categorization-theory-of-spatial-voting-how-the-center-divides-the-political-space/7B2CE3674B6CCA0400FC41FCBC78819A.

Bølstad, J., Dinas, E., and Riera, P. (2013) "Tactical Voting and Party Preferences: A Test of Cognitive Dissonance Theory," *Political Behavior*, vol. 35, no. 3, September, 429–452.

Brody, R. A. and Page, B. I. (1972) "Comment: The Assessment of Policy Voting," *American Political Science Review*, vol. 66, no. 2, June, 450–458.

Campbell, A., Converse, P. E., Miller, W. E., and Stokes, D. E. (1960) *The American Voter*, New York: Wiley.

Carsey, T. M. and Layman, G. C. (2006) "Changing Sides or Changing Minds? Party Identification and Policy Preferences in the American Electorate," *American Journal of Political Science*, vol. 50, no. 2, April, 464–477.

Conover, P. J. and Feldman, S. (1982) "Projection and the Perception of Candidates' Issue Positions," *The Western Political Quarterly*, vol. 35, no. 2, June, 228–244.

Converse, P. E. (1990) "Popular Representation and the Distribution of Information," in Ferejohn, J. A. and Kuklinski, H. (eds.) *Information and Democratic Processes*, Urbana: University of Illinois Press: 369–388.

Converse, P. E. (2006) [1964] "The Nature of Belief Systems in Mass Publics," *Critical Review*, vol. 18, no. 3, Winter, 1–74.

Dahl, R. A. (1971) *Polyarchy: Participation and Opposition*, New Haven: Yale University Press.

Delli Carpini, M. X. (2005) "An Overview of the State of Citizens' Knowledge About Politics," in McKinney, M. S., Kaid, L. L., Bystrom, D. G. and Carlin, D. B. (eds.) *Communicating Politics: Engaging the Public in Democratic Life*, New York: Peter Lang: 27–40.

Delli Carpini, M. X. and Keeter, S. (1996) *What Americans Don't Know About Politics and Why It Matters*, New Haven: Yale University Press.

Downs, A. (1957) *An Economic Theory of Democracy*, New York: Harper and Row.

Eijk, C. van der, Franklin, M., Demant, F., and van der Brug, W. (2007) "The Endogenous Economy: 'Real' Economic Conditions, Subjective Economic Evaluations and Government Support," *Acta Politica*, vol. 42, no. 1, April, 1–22.

Erikson, R. S. and Wlezien, C. (2012) "The Objective and Subjective Economy and the Presidential Vote," *PS: Political Science and Politics*, vol. 45, no. 4, October, 620–624.

Erikson, R. S., MacKuen, M. B., and Stimson, J. A. (2002) *The Macro Polity*, Cambridge: Cambridge University Press.

Festinger, L. (1957) *A Theory of Cognitive Dissonance*, Evanston: Row, Peterson.

Fiorina, M. P. (1981) *Retrospective Voting in American National Elections*, New Haven: Yale University Press.

Franklin, C. H. and Jackson, J. E. (1983) "The Dynamics of Party Identification," *American Political Science Review*, vol. 77, no. 4, December, 957–973.

Franklin, M. N. and Wlezien, C. (1997) "The Responsive Public: Issue Salience, Policy Change, and Preferences for European Integration," *Journal of Theoretical Politics*, vol. 9, no. 3, July, 347–363.

Gilens, M. (2005) "Inequality and Democratic Responsiveness," *Public Opinion Quarterly*, vol. 69, no. 5, January, 778–796.

Gilens, M. (2009) "Preference Gaps and Inequality in Representation," *PS: Political Science and Politics*, vol. 42, no. 2, April, 335–341.

Gilens, M. (2012) *Affluence and Influence: Economic Inequality and Political Power in America*, Princeton: Princeton University Press.

Grönlund, K. and Milner, H. (2006) "The Determinants of Political Knowledge in Comparative Perspective," *Scandinavian Political Studies*, vol. 29, no. 4, December, 386–406.

Hakhverdian, A. (2010) "Political Representation and its Mechanisms: A Dynamic Left-Right Approach for the United Kingdom, 1976–2006," *British Journal of Political Science*, vol. 40, no. 4, October, 835–856.

Held, D. (1996) *Models of Democracy*, 2nd Edition, Boston: Polity Press.

Inglehart, R. (1985) "Aggregate Stability and Individual-Level Flux in Mass Belief Systems: The Level of Analysis Paradox," *The American Political Science Review*, vol. 79, no. 1, March, 97–116.

Kahneman, D., Slovic, P., and Tversky, A. (eds.) (1982) *Judgment Under Uncertainty: Heuristics and Biases*, Cambridge: Cambridge University Press.

Key, V. O. (1966) *The Responsible Electorate*, New York: Vintage.

Lau, R. R. and Redlawsk, D. P. (2006) *How Voters Decide: Information Processing in Election Campaigns*, Cambridge: Cambridge University Press.

Lau, R. R., and Redlawsk, D. P. (2001) "Advantages and Disadvantages of Cognitive Heuristics in Political Decision Making," *American Journal of Political Science*, vol. 45, no. 4, October, 951–971.

Lupia, A. (1994) "Shortcuts Versus Encyclopedias: Information and Voting Behavior in California Insurance Reform Elections," *American Political Science Review*, vol. 88, no. 1, March, 63–76.

Lupia, A. and McCubbins, M. D. (1998) *The Democratic Dilemma: Can Citizens Learn What They Need to Know?* Cambridge: Cambridge University Press.

Markus, G. B. and Converse, P. E. (1979) "A Dynamic Simultaneous Equation Model of Electoral Choice," *American Political Science Review*, vol. 73, no. 4, December, 1055–1070.

Nordhaus, W. D. (1975) "The Political Business Cycle," *The Review of Economic Studies*, vol. 42, no. 2, April, 169–190.

Page, B. I. and Shapiro, R. Y. (1992) *The Rational Public: Fifty Years of Trends in Americans' Policy Preferences*, Chicago: University of Chicago Press.

Popkin, S. L. (1991) *The Reasoning Voter: Communication and Persuasion in Presidential Campaigns*, Chicago: University of Chicago Press.

Prior, M. (2007) *Post-Broadcast Democracy: How Media Choice Increases Inequality in Political Involvement and Polarizes Elections*, Cambridge: Cambridge University Press.

Rousseau, J-J. (1997) [1762] *Rousseau: "The Social Contract" and Other Later Political Writings*, Cambridge: Cambridge University Press.

Schumpeter, J. A. (1976) *Capitalism, Socialism, and Democracy*, 5th Edition, London: Allen and Unwin.

Soroka, S. N. and Wlezien, C. (2004) "Opinion Representation and Policy Feedback: Canada in Comparative Perspective," *Canadian Journal of Political Science*, vol. 37, no. 3, September, 531–559.

Soroka, S. N. and Wlezien, C. (2005) "Opinion–Policy Dynamics: Public Preferences and Public Expenditure in the United Kingdom," *British Journal of Political Science*, vol. 35, no. 4, October, 665–689.

Soroka, S. N. and Wlezien, C. (2008) "On the Limits to Inequality in Representation," *PS: Political Science and Politics*, vol. 41, no. 2, April, 319–327.

Soroka, S. N. and Wlezien, C. (2010) *Degrees of Democracy: Politics, Public Opinion, and Policy*, Cambridge: Cambridge University Press.

Stimson, J. A. (1991) *Public Opinion in America. Moods, Cycles, and Swings*, Boulder: Westview Press.

Stimson, J. A. (2004) *Tides of Consent: How Public Opinions Shapes American Politics*, Cambridge: Cambridge University Press.

Stimson, J. A., Mackuen, M. B., and Erikson, R. S. (1995) "Dynamic Representation," *American Political Science Review*, vol. 89, no. 3, September, 543–565.

Wlezien, C. (1995) "The Public as Thermostat: Dynamics of Preferences for Spending," *American Journal of Political Science*, vol. 39, no. 4, November, 981–1000.

Zaller, J. R. (1992) *The Nature and Origins of Mass Opinion*, Cambridge: Cambridge University Press.

31

THE GEOMETRY OF PARTY COMPETITION

Parties and voters in the issue space

Lorenzo De Sio

Introduction: policy issues and the curse of dimensionality

The idea of party competition lies at the heart of even minimal definitions of democracy (Sartori 1976: 63; Schumpeter 1942). Indeed, as we show in this chapter, the geometry of that competition plays a critical role in determining whether democratic politics proves possible in practice. For such competition to function effectively, a necessary starting point is that voters and parties have a common language, one that allows the former to identify which of the latter are most congruent with their ideas and make their choice accordingly. This common language typically centers on the identification of continua or dimensions of conflict (Downs 1957),[1] with the left–right divide being the most widely recognized of these (Fuchs and Klingemann 1989). Of course, given the wide range of issues over which political conflict occurs, the reality is a more complex and multidimensional issue space. Multidimensionality as defined here is premised on the understanding that the dimensions in question are largely, if not wholly, unrelated to each other. The position of a voter or party on one issue does not help in predicting their position on another issue. The resultant issue space thus becomes considerably complex (Enelow and Hinich 1984).

Such complexity of course affects voter decision-making and inspired one of the most widely known problems addressed in democratic theory – the paradox of voting. First identified by Condorcet (1785) and then generalized by Arrow (1951) as the impossibility theorem, the core of the paradox is that rational (i.e., transitive) individual preference rankings of more than two policy alternatives, when aggregated according to majority rule, may lead to irrational (i.e., intransitive) and unstable collective preference rankings. While Arrow ultimately concluded that a stable preference ranking was incompatible with democratic rules, Black (1948) persisted to reveal that the paradox originated in the multidimensionality of the issue space. When individual preferences align on a single dimension, he argued, the paradox dissolves and a Condorcet-winner alternative emerges.[2] Majority rule under such conditions can produce a single outcome – the position espoused by the median voter – that beats all alternatives. Democracy in effect now becomes possible.

This more singular understanding of party competition anchored many of the theoretical debates and empirical approaches to understanding developments in party systems over several decades following the Second World War. Its resilience has come under increasing challenge, however, in the face of the new parties and new issue dimensions that emerged in more recent decades. Such developments have required adoption of a more innovative and flexible framework that can accommodate the growing spatial complexity of political conflict. In particular, we need a new approach that can combine conceptual speculation with a workable empirical model permitting systematic analysis and theory testing. In the final section of the chapter, we outline the "issue yield" theory as one of the more promising attempts to fill this gap.

The evolving geometry of Western European party systems: conflict in a uni-dimensional space

According to the classic work of Lipset and Rokkan (1967), modern democratic states emerged in West European countries after a process of consolidation and reduction in the lines of political conflict. Indeed such was the level of consolidation that occurred, the period from the 1920s until the 1970s were widely seen as dominated by a small set of social cleavages that coalesced ultimately around the class divide. This singularity was further reflected in a consistent model of electoral competition that emerged over time in many of these countries whereby government switched hands between two main parties (or party blocs).[3] These historical developments appeared increasingly compatible with the assumption of uni-dimensionality in political conflict that was a cornerstone of Downs' (1957) highly influential work *An Economic Theory of Democracy*. Under such an assumption, both voters and parties agree on the absorption of a multiplicity of issues into one single dimension – the left–right dimension. This then allows for a "proper" theory of democracy to emerge whereby rational voters facing two vote-seeking dominant parties (or blocs) will produce a Condorcet-winning Nash equilibrium, corresponding to the position espoused by the median voter.

Despite the limitations of Downs' median voter theorem in terms of its restriction to a one-dimensional space, it did prove a formidable step in the development of a general theory of political equilibrium. Furthermore, in practical terms, its ability to show that representative democracy could produce a political equilibrium that represented the will of the people was important, in an age where liberal democracy was clearly not the only viable model of political regime. Within political science, the Downsian framework continued to be widely used as a tool for understanding the behavior of parties and voters in the decades that followed. Indeed its influence can be traced, somewhat paradoxically, to the development of one of the main theoretical approaches for understanding parties' emphases on multiple policy issues – salience theory (Robertson 1976; Budge and Farlie 1983). According to this logic, parties engage in political competition by adopting a *selective emphasis* strategy. This means that rather than taking explicit positions on most issues, they focus disproportionately on a particular subset that can act as a proxy for their overall political platform. This history of attention to, and credibility for, certain issues means that parties become in effect the "owners" of those issues and the main beneficiaries of a rise in their salience. The link back to Downsian theory is not immediately apparent but becomes more so when we realize that the practice of selective emphasis is in effect a means for parties to signal to the electorate their location on a broader continuum of ideological conflict.[4] A common example of this type of signaling can be seen in parties' position-taking vis à vis economic policy and particularly the classic tax and welfare trade-off. Social-democratic parties focus almost exclusively on the desirability of welfare provisions while avoiding the necessary implication of higher taxes. Conservative parties, by contrast, advertise tax cuts and hide the implied reduction of welfare. Here we see how a selective issue emphasis serves as a means for parties to communicate their position in broader left–right terms.

Such was the success and appeal of salience theory as a means of interpreting parties' policy positions that it led to the founding of one of the flagship studies of post-war comparative politics – the Manifesto Project. By measuring the variation in the emphasis given by parties to specific policies during election campaigns it became possible to track their spatial location across the left–right continuum over time (Budge 2015). These cumulative data could then provide a means for assessing the capacity of the party system to successfully represent the views of the *median voter*, and thus ultimately its capacity to produce desirable democratic outcomes, in line with Downsian theory.

The preceding accounts take a largely consensual and functional view of the institutions and actors necessary to democratic, legitimate decision-making. A limited range of parties arrayed across a single dimension of conflict essentially makes a political equilibrium possible, thereby justifying the preservation of such procedures and competition patterns. A party which emerges to focus on new non-aligned issues could thus potentially be regarded as a threat given that it would reduce the chances for political equilibrium and ultimately the efficient functioning of a democratic system. As one might imagine, however, an alternative perspective on issues and party competition has subsequently emerged that accommodates a more multidimensional and conflictual political reality. According to this viewpoint, political conflict and resolution is better understood as a series of temporary equilibria or settlements that are likely to change again in the future, as the balance of power changes between actors. According to such a perspective, a party engaging in mobilizing around new disruptive issues can be seen as the rational exploitation of strategic tools by actors that are losing in the current equilibrium.

Breaking the game: multidimensionality and the rise of issue voting

The idea that a multiplicity of issues could be seen as a strategic resource, especially for parties attempting to escape an unfavorable competition context, presented a clear challenge to the Downsian state of political equilibrium. The earliest systematic articulation of this idea emerged in Stokes' seminal work on valence politics (Stokes 1963). Inspired by the successful Eisenhower campaign of 1952, Stokes identified a critical turning point in the election when the Republican nominee turned disadvantage into a landslide victory. This pivoted on the realization by the Eisenhower campaign that voters were not tied to the left–right distinction and that victory in fact lay in "exploiting relatively new and transitory political attitudes" across a wide range of non-partisan issues such as Korea, corruption and communism on which the candidate had significant credibility (Stokes 1963: 372). The key insight of Stokes' work relevant to discussion here[5] is that a party facing an unfavorable equilibrium would emphasize alternative issues in order to shift the attention of the public. This was important in that it introduced to the literature the idea of issue emphasis as a strategic resource.

Rather surprisingly, this understanding of issues as strategic tools for party competition lay dormant for a long period of time. Riker's introduction of heresthetics constituted the first attempt to develop it theoretically to understand political outcomes (Riker 1986). According to Riker, the intransitivity-related disequilibria produced by multidimensionality – while detrimental to democracy in the long term – should realistically be seen as a resource for political actors to escape an unfavorable equilibrium. Or stated in more practical and individual terms, "For a person who expects to lose on some decision, the fundamental heresthetical device is to divide the majority with a new alternative, one the person prefers to the alternative previously expected to win" (Riker 1986: 1). This strategy captures entirely the Eisenhower logic of 1952. According to Riker, a heresthetic strategy deliberately exploits multidimensionality in order to successfully subvert what – under uni-dimensionality – would be considered as a stable Nash equilibrium.

As well as more effectively capturing the complexity of political competition in a liberal democracy, the new approach can be seen as taking an alternative and rather less idealized view of citizen decision-making. In rejecting the idea of a political equilibrium, it follows that voters do not formulate electoral choices primarily on stable ideological criteria but are influenced by more transient issues. While such an assumption arguably resonated among the US electorate as early as the 1950s, it was some decades before it was regarded as applying to the voters of West European nations. As the frozen cleavages identified by Lipset and Rokkan (1967) underpinning the party systems of the region began to unfreeze, however, the relevance of valence politics and theories of issue voting assumed an increasingly important role for scholars of electoral behavior.

From issue voting to issue politics

Although scholars remain divided over the key drivers of the decline in cleavage politics (Evans and Tilley 2012), general agreement exists that from the 1970s onward most West European countries have seen a decrease in the importance of the social determinants of vote choice and a corresponding growth in levels of electoral volatility and issue voting (Franklin, Mackie and Valen 1992; Mair 2002; Knutsen 2004; Thomassen 2005; Aardal and van Wijnen 2005). A comparative interpretation of this process has framed it in terms of changes in the political context of party choice. In particular, Thomassen (2005) has related the two key competing drivers of cleavage decline – party dealignment and individualization of vote choice – to the increasing innovation in party strategy and push toward a catch-all, ideology-lite orientation. Recent empirical research has shown support for the idea of decreasing ideological differentiation between parties (Adams, de Vries and Leiter 2012; Adams, Green and Milazzo 2012; Hellwig 2014).[6] In such a context, issues acquire more importance not only in voters' decision processes, but also in party strategy. If ideological differentiation loses its distinctive ability, it is not surprising that parties will attempt to identify new dimensions of competition.

A first possibility is of course to shift the focus toward valence issues. Manin's (1997) theory of audience democracy corresponds well to such a strategy. Here party competition hinges largely on the credibility of political actors to achieve shared goals for the polity as a whole.[7] A wide range of empirical studies have supported the idea of such a shift, demonstrating how party competition has moved toward issue emphasis and competence rather than positionally-based conflict (Nadeau et al. 2001; Blais et al. 2004; van der Brug 2004; Clarke et al. 2004, 2009; Bellucci 2006; Bélanger and Meguid 2008; Duch and Stevenson 2008; Green and Hobolt 2008; Sanders et al. 2011).[8]

A second possibility, more in tune with Riker's understanding of heresthetics, is that parties can seek to selectively focus on specific positional issues. While such a response is in theory open to all parties, it is likely to be particularly appealing to those parties for whom a valence strategy is unrealistic if not impossible – that is, the smaller, more radical players who lack government experience and/or have little chance of entering government. Again empirical evidence has served to confirm the validity of this approach. Green-Pedersen (2007), for example, has documented a continuous decline in the left–right content of election manifestos as parties take on a wider variety of policy issues. At the same time, we have seen the rise of a range of smaller parties mobilized around key issues such as the environment (O'Neill 1997; Mair 2001; Talshir 2002), immigration (Betz 1994; Kitschelt 1995; Hainsworth 2000), and more recently EU integration (de Vries and Hobolt 2012). Indeed such has been the proliferation of these new actors that the new labels of "niche" (Meguid 2005, 2008; Adams et al. 2006; Ezrow 2008) and "challenger" (de Vries and Hobolt 2012) parties have now been added to the lexicon of party types.[9]

The growth in importance of issues in structuring party competition and vote choice means that it is now more accurate to talk about issue politics in general rather than specific instances of issue voting. As this review has shown, there have been considerable advances on theoretical grounds with regard to understanding how and why parties manipulate issue emphasis for electoral gain. In addition, the empirical literature has clearly demonstrated the value and importance of an issue-oriented party strategy. What is needed now, however, is to develop a new framework that can trace back the dynamics of *strategic issue selection* – that is, the logical step that precedes the selective issue emphasis by parties in a multidimensional space. Furthermore, it should be one that is potentially applicable across all issues and all parties, rather than reserved to a specific subset. We move now in our final section to outline one of the most promising candidates in this regard – issue yield theory.

Issue yield theory

Issue yield theory is an adaptation of Downsian logic and centers on four key assumptions:

a   Party strategy is driven by vote maximization.
b   Voters evaluate parties in Downsian terms – that is, voter–party proximity calculations.
c   Contrary to Downs, however, change in a party's issue position is more difficult and costly than a change in issue emphasis.
d   The importance that voters assign to issues varies and is sensitive to priming effects – that is, the emphasis placed on issues by parties.

Should these assumptions be met, then parties are incentivized to pursue a strategic issue emphasis strategy. That is, they will seek to focus on a limited number of favorable issues which they prime in the minds of voters as the core criteria to rely on in making their party choice.

The challenge that parties face in adopting this approach, therefore, is to identify their most favorable issues. The issue yield model stipulates that such issues are those that meet the two following conditions: first, the policy attracts the lowest amount of internal division possible and, second, the policy is widely supported in the electorate at large – that is, beyond the current support base. This combination of low risk and high opportunity both minimizes the potential for loss of existing support and expands the opportunity to gain new voters. The combination can be expressed in numerical terms through an issue yield index (constructed from public opinion data on policy and party support) that ranges – for each party-issue combination – from −1 (worst issues) to +1 (best issues).[10] Policies that provide the best combination of these two desirable properties – that is, a united party base and the potential to reach out to a larger electorate – have the highest issue yields. In theoretical terms, those with the highest issue yield can be regarded as forming a new type of "bridge" policy, so named because they create a bridge between current and new voters. Bridge policies essentially unify current voters by staying in line with the party ideology, while extending its appeal to new voters.[11]

While such issues can be articulated in theory, the key question of course is whether they exist in practice. Empirical research on EU countries and also the US (De Sio 2010; De Sio, De Angelis and Emanuele 2016; De Sio and Weber 2014; Weber and De Sio 2016) has consistently shown that almost all parties rely on a set of high-yield bridge issues where the party position is almost unanimously supported within the party and also widely shared outside the party. Such a combination makes the issue a powerful resource for gaining new voters. Examples range from financial market reform for the US Democratic Party (support of 92 percent within the party and 77 percent at large, with a yield of 0.88) and opposition to tighter gun control for the US

Republican Party (84 percent within the party, 56 percent at large, yield = 0.78), to more restrictive laws on immigration for the Italian Northern League (95 percent within-party, 78 percent at large, yield = 0.95) and finally reduction of income inequality for the Italian PD (91 percent within-party, 84 percent at large, yield = 0.85).[12] While each issue presents a different risk–opportunity combination for each party, it is clear that any party enjoys at least a small number of high yield issues. The inevitable theoretical expectation is that parties will disproportionately focus on making these high-yield bridge policies salient in voters' minds during election campaigns in order to gain electoral advantage.[13]

This last point has also been consistently supported by empirical research, which has tested a number of causal implications of the issue yield model. In particular, scholars have shown the yield index to work at the individual level in predicting issue preference among supporters of different parties (De Sio 2010). It has also worked at the party level, explaining issue emphasis in campaign platforms in EU countries and the US (De Sio and Weber 2014; Weber and De Sio 2016), and the dynamics of issue of competition over EU integration after the economic crisis (De Sio, Franklin and Weber 2016). Perhaps most innovatively, a subsequent analysis of the Italian case has shown how issue yield predicts the content of parties' and their leaders' official Twitter feeds during the campaign (De Sio, De Angelis and Emanuele 2016). Significantly, all of these studies have found no interaction effects for party size.[14] As such, it would seem to offer a highly resilient and effective new approach to understanding the complexities of issue selection by political parties in a multidimensional environment and thus an important step toward filling the theoretical gap outlined earlier.

Viewed in historical context, the issue yield model appears to fit more within the Rikerian than Downsian tradition of understanding party competition. There is no attempt to demonstrate the presence of equilibria. The emphasis is instead upon how the disequilibria resulting from conflict in a multidimensional space can be used to subvert an existing equilibrium.[15] This should not be seen as supporting a view that parties pursue short-sighted, short-term strategies. On the contrary, party strategy is very firmly anchored in the past in that the existing party base provides the final reference point for choosing which policies can be exploited and which cannot. The model thus predicts an incremental evolution of party platforms and support base over time rather than swift change.[16]

Concluding remarks

The idea that the political issue space has become increasingly multidimensional and conflictual over the past few decades appears to be widely accepted among parties and election scholars. One consequence of this process is that models of party competition based on a reduction in the dimensionality of the issue space, in order to achieve efficient and legitimate decision-making, have come under increasing pressure. In their place, more flexible theories have emerged that see the growing multiplicity of issues as a resource for disadvantaged actors to use in a bid to escape an unfavorable equilibrium. One of the strongest contenders in this regard, we have argued, is issue yield theory, which presents a more general explanatory framework of party behavior in this new era of issue politics and increasing specificity of vote choice. In terms of its longer term applicability, it is clear that if current trends continue and even intensify then we would expect the issue yield model to increase in value as a means of accounting for party policy choices. Should the current state of volatility subside, however, in favor of a resurgence of the type of stable voter–party alignments associated with past cleavages, we do not expect issue yield's relevance to entirely fade from view. Parties will continue to face strategic challenges on whether and how to integrate different issues into their platforms. Which of these two scenarios is most likely to occur, however, is the task of other chapters in this volume to address.

Notes

1 This spatial representation of politics does not require any market analogy.

2 Black's result was then incorporated into the second edition (1963) of Arrow's *Social Choice and Individual Values* (Grofman 2004).

3 An additional source of tension toward a one-dimensional scheme is also clear from the structure of alliances and coalitions reconstructed in detail by Lipset and Rokkan (1967: 37), where it clearly appears that actors defined by different cleavages tend to coalesce in supporting (or opposing) the nationalizing elite group. In this regard, it is the very mechanism of majority rule that pushes political conflict toward a one-dimensional scheme (see, for example, Duverger 1964). Also, the reduction of the complexity of the issue space to a very low number of dimensions might be considered an inevitable development of the party system in order to present voters with more manageable cognitive tasks (Jackman and Sniderman 2002; Sniderman and Bullock 2004). The special relevance of the left–right dimension among Western European voters might be indeed confirmed by their enduring ability to place themselves on the left–right continuum (Knutsen 1995, 1997) despite the repeated claims of its death (Giddens 1994).

4 And one that allows researchers to conveniently measure such location.

5 While we extract this aspect of Stokes' work to develop the key point of interest in this chapter, it should be noted that the main contribution of the article in question was the introduction of the valence politics framework. See, for example, Keith Dowding's chapter in this volume for further discussion of valence theory.

6 Hellwig (2014) argues that the importance of the left–right dimension has decreased as a result of a clear perception (shared by elites and voters) of a narrowing of the credible range of possible policies on the economic issues that constitute the core of the left/right divide.

7 Also, Manin's original formulation (visibly inspired from François Mitterrand's first mandate) explicitly related audience democracy to the presence of an international context with a high level of interdependence (thus limiting the available spectrum of policies, especially on the economy), and where the protection of shared national interests becomes crucial.

8 In fact, a large part of the economic voting literature, with special regard to retrospective voting (Fiorina 1981), can be considered as adopting a valence framework (Stokes 1992: 156). On valence vs. positional perspectives in economic voting, see e.g., Lewis–Beck and Nadeau (2011).

9 Although the operational definition of a niche party is far from uncontroversial, and it can be claimed that the niche attribute might be more appropriate for the party platform than for the party itself (Wagner 2011).

10 Calculated according to a non-linear formula derived through geometric reasoning (see De Sio and Weber 2014). If: p is the percentage of respondents supporting a party; i the percentage approving a policy statement; f the percentage jointly supporting the party and approving the statement; then issue yield is expressed by $\dfrac{f - ip}{p(1-p)} + \dfrac{i-p}{1-p}$.

11 Such policies, enjoying a high level of popular support, can be considered quasi-valence issues (De Sio and Weber 2014), albeit without the volatility of credibility reputations that make "pure" valence issues somehow risky.

12 Sources: CCES 2010 for the US, CISE (Italian Centre for Electoral Studies, 2014) for Italy.

13 Of course parties cannot be expected to use tools such as issue yield in their campaign calculations (although issue yield might perhaps be used as a tool for testing the potential of new issues); simply, the issue yield model attempts to systematize a typical intuitive reasoning that can be expected from party strategists. Also, in multi-party systems parties can be expected to consider additional concerns, i.e., whether an issue with a high yield might have a higher yield for another party, so that emphasizing it would in fact advantage a competitor. In this case a party might perhaps emphasize another issue – even with a lower yield – where it can claim some sort of yield "monopoly." Various approaches have been proposed to model such a strategy (De Sio and Weber 2014; De Sio, De Angelis and Emanuele 2016).

14 Despite its size insensitivity, the issue yield model does carry an expectation that smaller parties will have stronger incentives to pursue issue politics compared to their larger counterparts. One of the key resources offered by a high yield issue is the ability to expand beyond the current support base. Thus in statistical terms there will be a larger number of such issues for parties sitting on 10 percent of the vote compared with those gaining a 35 percent vote share.

15 This resonates with the recent success of many "anti-establishment" parties in challenging the electoral primacy of mainstream parties, by relying on new issues.

16 This process resonates with the integration of "new politics" issues by mainstream leftist parties during the 1980s. Another example is the impact of post-crisis measures (with a drop in EU integration support), which impacted very asymmetrically pro- and anti-EU parties, resulting in important new opportunities for anti-EU parties (De Sio, Franklin and Weber 2016).

References

Aardal, B. and van Wijnen, P. (2005) "Issue Voting," in Thomassen, J. (ed.) *The European Voter*, Oxford: Oxford University Press: 192–212.

Adams, J., Clark, M., Ezrow, L. and Glasgow, G. (2006) "Are Niche Parties Fundamentally Different from Mainstream Parties? The Causes and the Electoral Consequences of Western European Parties' Policy Shifts, 1976–1998," *American Journal of Political Science*, vol. 50, no. 3, July, 513–529.

Adams, J., de Vries, C. E. and Leiter, D. (2012) "Subconstituency Reactions to Elite Depolarization in the Netherlands: An Analysis of the Dutch Public's Policy Beliefs and Partisan Loyalties, 1986–98," *British Journal of Political Science*, vol. 42, no. 1, January, 81–105.

Adams, J., Green, J. and Milazzo, C. (2012) "Who Moves? Elite and Mass-Level Depolarization in Britain, 1987–2001," *Electoral Studies*, vol. 31, no. 4, December, 643–655.

Arrow, K. J. (1951) *Social Choice and Individual Values*, New York: Wiley.

Bélanger, É. and Meguid, B. M. (2008) "Issue Salience, Issue Ownership, and Issue-Based Vote Choice," *Electoral Studies*, vol. 27, no. 3, September, 477–491.

Bellucci, P. (2006) "Tracing the Cognitive and Affective Roots of 'Party Competence': Italy and Britain, 2001," *Electoral Studies*, vol. 25, no. 3, September, 548–569.

Betz, H-G. (1994) *Radical Right Wing Populism in Western Europe*, New York: St. Martin's Press.

Black, D. (1948) "On the Rationale of Group Decision-Making," *The Journal of Political Economy*, vol. 56, no. 1, February, 23–34.

Blais, A., Turgeon, M., Gidengil, E., Nevitte, N. and Nadeau, R. (2004) "Which Matters Most? Comparing the Impact of Issues and the Economy in American, British and Canadian Elections," *British Journal of Political Science*, vol. 34, no. 3, July, 555–563.

Brug, W. van der (2004) "Issue Ownership and Party Choice," *Electoral Studies*, vol. 23, no. 2, June, 209–233.

Budge, I. and Farlie, D. J. (1983) *Explaining and Predicting Elections: Issue Effects and Party Strategies in Twenty-Three Democracies*, London: Allen & Unwin.

Budge, I. (2015) "Issue Emphases, Saliency Theory and Issue Ownership: A Historical and Conceptual Analysis," *West European Politics*, vol. 38, no. 4, July, 761–777.

Clarke, H. D., Sanders, D., Stewart, M. C. and Whiteley, P. F. (2004) *Political Choice in Britain*, New York: Oxford University Press.

Clarke, H. D., Sanders, D., Stewart, M. C. and Whiteley, P. F. (2009) *Performance Politics and the British Voter*, 1st Edition, Cambridge: Cambridge University Press.

Condorcet, M. J. A. N. (1785) *Essai sur L'application de L'analyse à la Probabilité des Décisions Rendues à la Pluralité des Voix*, Paris: Imprimerie royale.

De Sio, L. (2010) "Beyond 'Position' and 'Valence': A Unified Framework for the Analysis of Political Issues," Working Paper, European University Institute, available online: http://cadmus.eui.eu/handle/1814/14814, [accessed September 4, 2013].

De Sio, L., De Angelis, A. and Emanuele, V. (2016) "Issue Yield and Strategic Party Communication on Twitter: A Case Study," Paper presented at the 2016 Annual Conference of the Midwest Political Science Association, Chicago, April 7–10.

De Sio, L., Franklin, M. N. and Weber, T. (2016) "The Risks and Opportunities of Europe: How Issue Yield Explains (Non-)Reactions to the Financial Crisis," *Electoral Studies*, vol. 44, December, 483–491.

De Sio, L. and Weber, T. (2014) "Issue Yield: A Model of Party Strategy in Multidimensional Space," *American Political Science Review*, vol. 108, no. 4, November, 870–885.

de Vries, C. E. and Hobolt, S. B. (2012) "When Dimensions Collide: The Electoral Success of Issue Entrepreneurs," *European Union Politics*, vol. 13, no. 2, June, 246–268.

Downs, A. (1957) *An Economic Theory of Democracy*, New York: Harper.

Duch, R. M. and Stevenson, R. T. (2008) *The Economic Vote: How Political and Economic Institutions Condition Election Results*, Cambridge: Cambridge University Press.

Duverger, M. (1964) *Political Parties*, London: Methuen.

Enelow, J. M. and Hinich, M. J. (1984) *The Spatial Theory of Voting: An Introduction*, Cambridge: Cambridge University Press.

Evans, G. and Tilley, J. (2012) "How Parties Shape Class Politics: Explaining the Decline of the Class Basis of Party Support," *British Journal of Political Science*, vol. 42, no. 1, January, 137–161.

Ezrow, L. (2008) "Research Note: On the Inverse Relationship between Votes and Proximity for Niche Parties," *European Journal of Political Research*, vol. 47, no. 2, March, 206–220.

Fiorina, M. P. (1981) *Retrospective Voting in American National Elections*, New Haven: Yale University Press.

Franklin, M. N., Mackie, T. T. and Valen, H. (1992) *Electoral Change*, Cambridge: Cambridge University Press.

Fuchs, D. and Klingemann, H-D. (1989) "The Left–Right Schema," in Jennings, M. K. and van Deth, J. W. (eds.) *Continuities in Political Action*, Berlin: de Gruyter: 203–234.

Giddens, A. (1994) *Beyond Left and Right*, Cambridge: Polity Press.

Green, J., and Hobolt, S. B. (2008) "Owning the Issue Agenda: Party Strategies and Vote Choices in British Elections," *Electoral Studies*, vol. 27, no. 3, September, 460–476.

Green-Pedersen, C. (2007) "The Growing Importance of Issue Competition: The Changing Nature of Party Competition in Western Europe," *Political Studies*, vol. 55, no. 3, October, 607–628.

Grofman, B. (2004) "Downs and Two-Party Convergence," *Annual Review of Political Science*, vol. 7, June, 25–46.

Hainsworth, P. (2000) *The Politics of the Extreme Right: From the Margins to the Mainstream*, London: Pinter.

Hellwig, T. (2014) "The Structure of Issue Voting in Postindustrial Democracies," *The Sociological Quarterly*, vol. 55, no. 4, Autumn, 596–624.

Jackman, S. and Sniderman, P. M. (2002) "The Institutional Organization of Choice Spaces: A Political Conception of Political Psychology," in Monroe, K. R. (ed.) *Political Psychology*, Mahwah: Lawrence Erlbaum: 209–224.

Kitschelt, H. (1995) *The Radical Right in Western Europe: A Comparative Analysis*, Ann Arbor: University of Michigan Press.

Knutsen, O. (1995) "Value Orientations, Political Conflicts and Left–Right Identification: A Comparative Study," *European Journal of Political Research*, vol. 28, no. 1, July, 63–93.

Knutsen, O. (1997) "The Partisan and the Value-Based Component of Left–Right Self-Placement: A Comparative Study," *International Political Science Review*, vol. 18, no. 2, April, 191–225.

Knutsen, O. (2004) *Social Structure and Party Choice in Western Europe*, Basingstoke: Palgrave Macmillan.

Lewis-Beck, M. S. and Nadeau, R. (2011) "Economic Voting Theory: Testing New Dimensions," *Electoral Studies*, vol. 30, no. 2, June, 288–294.

Lipset, S. M. and Rokkan, S. (1967) "Cleavage Structures, Party Systems, and Voter Alignments: An Introduction," in Lipset, S. M. and Rokkan, S. (eds.) *Party Systems and Voter Alignments: Cross-National Perspectives*, New York: Free Press: 1–64.

Mair, P. (2002) "In the Aggregate: Mass Electoral Behaviour in Western Europe, 1950–2000," in Keman, H. (ed.) *Comparative Democratic Politics: A Guide to Contemporary Theory and Research*, London: SAGE Publications: 122–140.

Mair, P. (2001) "The Green Challenge and Political Competition: How Typical Is the German Experience?," *German Politics*, vol. 10, no. 2, August, 99–116.

Manin, B. (1997) *The Principles of Representative Government*, Cambridge: Cambridge University Press.

Meguid, B. M. (2005) "Competition Between Unequals: The Role of Mainstream Party Strategy in Niche Party Success," *American Political Science Review*, vol. 99, no. 3, August, 347–359.

Meguid, B. M. (2008) *Party Competition between Unequals*, Cambridge: Cambridge University Press.

Nadeau, R., Blais, A., Gidengil, E. and Nevitte, N. (2001) "Perceptions of Party Competence in the 1997 Election," in Thornburn, H. G. and Whitehorn, A. (eds.) *Party Politics in Canada*, 8th Edition, Toronto: Prentice Hall: 413–430.

O'Neill, M. (1997) *Green Parties and Political Change in Contemporary Europe: New Politics, Old Predicaments*, Aldershot: Ashgate.

Riker, W. H. (1986) *The Art of Political Manipulation*, New Haven: Yale University Press.

Robertson, D. B. (1976) *A Theory of Party Competition*, New York: J. Wiley.

Sanders, D., Clarke, H. D., Stewart, M. C. and Whiteley, P. (2011) "Downs, Stokes and the Dynamics of Electoral Choice," *British Journal of Political Science*, vol. 41, no. 2, April, 287–314.

Sartori, G. (1976) *Parties and Party Systems*, Cambridge: Cambridge University Press.

Schumpeter, J. A. (1942) *Capitalism, Socialism, and Democracy*, London: Harper and Brothers.

Sniderman, P. M. and Bullock, J. (2004) "A Consistency Theory of Public Opinion and Political Choice: The Hypothesis of Menu Dependence," in Saris, W. and Sniderman, P. M. (eds.) *Studies in Public Opinion: Attitudes, Nonattitudes, Measurement Error, and Change*, Princeton: Princeton University Press: 337–357.

Stokes, D. (1992) "Valence Politics," in Kavanagh, D. (ed.) *Electoral Politics*, Oxford: Clarendon Press: 141–164.

Stokes, D. E. (1963) "Spatial Models of Party Competition," *American Political Science Review*, vol. 57, no. 2, June, 368–377.

Talshir, G. (2002) *The Political Ideology of Green Parties: From the Politics of Nature to Redefining the Nature of Politics*, New York: Palgrave.

Thomassen, J. (2005) *The European Voter: A Comparative Study of Modern Democracies*, Oxford: Oxford University Press.

Wagner, M. (2011) "Defining and Measuring Niche Parties," *Party Politics*, vol. 18, no. 6, November, 845–864.

Weber, T. and De Sio, L. (2016) "Party Agendas, Issue Yield and Political Inequality," Paper presented to the 2016 EPSA Annual Conference, Brussels, June 23–25.

32

THE THERMOSTATIC MODEL

The public, policy and politics[1]

Christopher Wlezien

Democratic accountability and control require that people are reasonably well-informed about what policymakers do. Consider that an uninformed public is unable to hold policymakers accountable. Policymakers would have little incentive to represent what the public wants in policy – there would be no real benefit for doing so and no real cost for not doing so. An uninformed public, being unaware of what policymakers have already done, also is unable to guide policy. Policymakers thus would have little basis for representing the public even if they wanted to – expressed public preferences would contain little meaningful information about what the public wants. We clearly need an informed public; effective democracy depends on it.

Political scientists have posited that such a public would behave like a thermostat (Wlezien 1995, 2004; Soroka and Wlezien 2010). Imagine a situation in which the public prefers more policy than currently is in place and sends a signal to adjust policy accordingly, that is, to provide "more." Further imagine that policymakers respond, and provide more but not too much more; the new policy position would more closely correspond to the public's preferred level. Now, if the public is indeed responsive to what policymakers do, then it would not favor as much more policy. It might still favor more, on balance, but not as substantially as in the prior period. In effect, following the thermostatic metaphor, a departure from the favored policy temperature – which itself can change – produces a signal to adjust policy accordingly and, once sufficiently adjusted, the signal stops.

This conception of the public (and policymakers' behavior) has deep roots in political science, particularly Easton's (1965) depiction of a political system and Deutsch's (1963) models of "control." It still may seem far too stylized given the traditional view of public opinion (Campbell et al. 1960; Converse 1964; Kinder 1983; even Key 1961). It is even more demanding than Page and Shapiro's (1992) fairly sophisticated characterization in their now-classic book, *The Rational Public*, in which they depicted a public whose preferences remained fairly stable over the short run but changed over time in understandable ways.[2] Other work has supported Page and Shapiro's view, highlighting the importance of heuristics to compensate for information shortfalls (Ferejohn and Kuklinski 1990; Sniderman, Brody and Tetlock 1991; Lupia 1994; Lau and Redlawsk 2006). More recent research has directly tested thermostatic public responsiveness and policy representation as well, and found evidence of both, as we will see below (for a summary, see Wlezien and Soroka 2016).

This chapter examines the thermostatic model and its applicability. First, it provides a basic formal representation of the model, focusing on public responsiveness to policy and policy responsiveness to public opinion. Second, it presents the empirical literature examining whether and under what conditions the model works, highlighting the characteristics of issues and political institutions. Third, it explores implications for politics, particularly election outcomes but also judgments of the broader political system. We will see that the simple thermostatic model is quite powerful; while it does not work everywhere or equally well even where it does work, the model helps us understand much of policymaking and politics in representative democracies.

The thermostatic model

The thermostatic model of opinion and policy consists of two equations, one for public responsiveness to policy and the other for policy representation of opinion.

The public responsiveness equation

The model implies that the public's preference for "more" policy – its relative preference, R – represents the difference between the public's preferred level of policy ($P\star$) and the level it actually gets (P):

$$R_t = P_t^* - P_t \tag{1}$$

where t represents time. Thus, as the preferred level of policy *or* policy itself changes, the relative preference signal changes accordingly. Notice that, unlike the thermostat that governs the heating (and/or air conditioning) units in our homes, which sends a dichotomous signal, R captures both direction and magnitude.

This equation is straightforward in theory, less so in practice. Most importantly, we rarely observe $P\star$. Survey organizations typically do not ask people how much policy they want. Instead, these organizations ask about relative preferences, whether we are spending "too little," whether spending should "be increased," or whether we should "do more." This, presumably, is how people think about most policies. (Imagine asking people how much health or education spending they want.) The public preference, however defined, also is necessarily relative. In one sense, this is quite convenient, as we can actually measure the thermostatic signal the public sends to policy makers – to test the model, we need a measure of relative preferences, after all.

Because we do not directly measure the public's preferred level of policy ($P\star$), and because all of the variables would have different metrics, we need to rewrite the model of R as follows:

$$R_t = a_0 + \beta_1 P_t + \beta_2 O_t + e_t \tag{2}$$

where a and e_t represent the intercept and the error term respectively, and O designates a variety of "other," exogenous determinants of R. The public's preferences for defense spending may be driven by perceived security threats, for instance; preferences for welfare policy may be conditioned by concerns about economic security. Note that these variables, O, should not be viewed as control variables, but as instruments for $P\star$. That is, in lieu of having measures of preferred levels of policy, these are factors that we think are associated with $P\star$. The most critical part of equation 2 is the coefficient of feedback, β_1. If people respond thermostatically, β_1 will be negative.

Negative feedback of policy on preferences is the fundamental feature of the thermostatic model. It is what distinguishes a reasonably informed public – one that knows something about what policymakers actually do – from an uninformed public. Observing it means that the signal that the public sends to policymakers contains useful information. And it makes possible effective accountability and control, as the public is in a position to reward or punish the incumbent government for its actions. The public may not respond thermostatically to policy change, of course, and it even may be that policy feeds back positively on preferences – an increase in spending could lead people to want more spending in that domain. We do not gainsay these possibilities, which should be settled empirically, and the proof actually is in the empirical pudding of equation 2. There is nothing that requires β_1 to be negative, after all.[3]

Although we have thus far characterized public responsiveness across time, an identical model applies across spatial contexts as well, whether across countries, across states or provinces within countries, or across counties, cities and even school districts within states. We have reason to think that the preferred level of education policy differs across contexts, say, states in the US. We know that the level of policy also differs. If the thermostatic model applies, the public's relative preference would reflect the difference between the two across states j:

$$R_j = P_j^* - P_j \tag{3}$$

Here, the preference for more (or less) policy in each state will depend on whether and to what extent the public's preferred level is greater than policy itself in the different states.

The policy representation equation

Now, let us turn to the policy representation equation. If there is representation, *changes* in policy (P) will be associated with *levels* of the public's relative preference (R), which register support for policy change. We can express this expectation as follows:

$$\Delta P_t = a_0 + \gamma_1 R_{t-1} + \gamma_2 G_{t-1} + u_t, \tag{4}$$

where a_1 and u_t represent the intercept and the error term, respectively, and G the partisan control of government. (Of course, other variables can be added to the model.) Notice that equation 4 actually captures both indirect and direct representation of public opinion. The former – representation through elections and the partisan control of government – is reflected in the coefficient γ_2; the latter – policy adjustment to changing preferences – is captured by γ_1.[4]

The coefficient γ_1 is of special importance, as it provides evidence of policy responsiveness. It is important to recognize that a positive coefficient does not mean that politicians literally respond to changing public preferences, as it may be that they and the public both respond to something else – for example, changes in the need for more spending. All we can say for sure is that γ_1 captures policy responsiveness in a statistical sense – the extent to which policy change is systematically related to public preferences, other things being equal. This is significant, as we want to know whether public policy follows public preferences.

Evidence of responsiveness also does not mean that public preferences and policy actually are congruent (Achen 1978). It may be that there is a bias in representation, where policy correlates with opinion, but is consistently more (or less) conservative than people would like. Even if there is no bias, it may be that responsiveness is weak, and does not fully reflect preferences. For there to be congruence, we would need to observe not only a positive relationship between opinion and policy, but an actual match. That is, we would need to know that policy equals opinion, at least that the two are not significantly different in the usual statistical sense.[5] To make this determination, we need measures of opinion that tap the public's preferred level of policy *and* which are on the same scale as policy. That this is not easily accomplished makes it difficult to directly observe congruence between the public's preferred levels of policy and the actual policy level.[6]

Finally, it is worth noting that modeling the change in policy in year t as a function of preferences in year $t - 1$ is not meant to imply that responsiveness is lagged, but to reflect the reality of decision making on fiscal matters, the subject of many empirical tests of the thermostatic model. That is, the model captures responsiveness to opinion when most budgetary decisions are made. The specification of opinion effects on policy differs from that for the effects of policy on opinion, which are at time t, as per equation 1. This makes clear that the influences of each on the other are not simultaneous, but play out over time.[7] The coefficients also are expected to be oppositely-signed, where opinion has a positive effect on policy and policy has a negative effect on opinion. As such, the effect in one direction cannot explain the effect in the other.

The model in practice

So far we have described a theoretical model. But does it work in practice? Under what conditions? As noted earlier, there is a good amount of research on the subject, which initially focused on the United States but increasingly has turned to other countries. Let us consider what we have learned, focusing first on public responsiveness to policy and then policy representation.

Thermostatic public responsiveness

The original statement of the thermostatic model focused on dynamics of spending preferences (Wlezien 1995), and much of the ensuing research has as well. This is not surprising given that we have had regular surveys, at least in the US, that ask about support for more (less) spending in different domains. The question typically asks "Are we spending too much, too little or about the right amount on [the military, armaments and defense]?"[8] Spending is recurring as well and fairly easy to measure. (We need measures of both relative preferences for policy and policy itself to test the thermostatic model, after all.) Recall from equations 1 and 2 that it also is important to measure the public's underlying preferred levels of policy, at least indirectly. Wlezien's analysis of eight spending domains incorporated certain instruments and found that aspects of security – economic for social domains and national for defense – were particularly important.

Most importantly, Wlezien's results revealed thermostatic responsiveness. That is, when spending increases (decreases), the public's support for more spending decreases (increases), other things being equal. This was and is important. That the pattern of responsiveness varied across domains also is important. In some domains, especially defense and welfare, there was clear evidence of public responsiveness and it is very specific, where the public responds to spending within each of the separate domains. In other areas, namely, the remaining social spending domains, specific thermostatic responsiveness was not evident. Further analysis demonstrated that preferences in these areas are thermostatic but in a more general way, to spending in the set of social domains taken together, not separately. In yet other areas, it was not clear whether there is any thermostatic responsiveness whatsoever. The findings comport with research on the electoral salience of different issues (see Asher 1992; Abramowitz 1994). The influence of salience on public responsiveness is expected. Issues people care about are ones on which they are likely to have meaningful opinions that structure party support and candidate evaluation. Candidates are likely to take positions on the issue and it is likely to form the subject of political debate, and people are more likely to pay attention to politicians' behavior, as reflected in news media reporting or as communicated in other ways.[9]

Soroka and Wlezien brought the analysis to other countries in which similar spending preference questions were asked, specifically Canada (2004) and the UK (2005). This research also revealed thermostatic public responsiveness, particularly in the latter country. Their subsequent (2010) book on *Degrees of Democracy* explicitly incorporated characteristics of issues and political institutions into the theoretical model and empirical analysis. They demonstrated that issue importance significantly enhanced thermostatic public responsiveness and that the federal nature of a domain – that is, the degree to which spending happens at multiple levels of government – dampened it. A high level of mixing makes responsibility less clear to citizens, though there are other possible mechanisms at work (see Wlezien and Soroka 2011).

Other scholars have examined thermostatic responsiveness in particular domains over time. There is research in the US on the dynamics of racial policy (Kellstedt 2003) and recent innovations in health care, namely, the Affordable Care Act (Morgan and Kang 2015). Research on asylum applications and public support for asylum in the UK also finds negative feedback (Jennings 2009). We see the pattern with defense spending preferences in a set of different countries (Eichenberg and Stoll 2003) and in support for European unification across countries (Franklin and Wlezien 1997).

Some research studies relationships in particular domains across contexts at particular points in time, not over time. Much of this research concentrates on the US states, for which there is a good amount of data. Goggin and Wlezien's (1993) study of abortion policy and opinion was the first of these, though there also is work on the environment (Johnson, Brace and Arceneaux 2005) as well as education and welfare (Pacheco 2013). All of this research finds negative feedback of policy on public preferences.

Other scholars have focused on general patterns of preferences across issues, most notably Erikson, MacKuen and Stimson's (2002) examination of policy "mood" that forms part of their classic *Macro Polity* treatise. For their analysis, Erikson, MacKuen and Stimson rely on Stimson's (1991) measure of policy sentiment that captures the common flow of public opinion in various policy domains, in effect, the parallelism in those preferences. They find strong evidence of thermostatic public responsiveness to legislation.[10] This also is true in other countries, including the UK (Bartle, Delleplaine and Stimson 2011) and there is evidence across a range of countries (Wlezien and Soroka 2012).

It thus is clear that thermostatic responsiveness is evident on numerous issues and across contexts. The relationship varies across issues to be sure, as discussed, and the public importance of issues matters as does their federal quality. (The latter also has implications for differences across contexts, e.g., countries, as well.) What may be most striking is that responsiveness tends to hold across subgroups of the public, perhaps most importantly, education levels. People with less than a high school education in the US are almost as responsive as those who have been to college (Soroka and Wlezien 2010). Much the same is true for differences in income and party identification. This is not entirely surprising given Page and Shapiro's (1992) analysis of parallel publics, discussed above.[11]

That there is thermostatic public responsiveness is important. It means that the public somehow receives information about policy and uses it, at least in certain salient policy domains and contexts. Surely the information the public receives is mediated, as few people have budgets on their coffee tables or desktops, but the mechanism is unclear. We do know that only basic information is required; that is, people need only recognize that spending on, say, health, has gone up, ideally whether it has increased by a little or a lot (Soroka and Wlezien 2010).[12] And there is reason to think that such information is available in mass media reporting and that people can fairly easily draw basic inferences from this coverage, at least in certain areas (Neuner, Soroka and Wlezien 2015). That said, determining what information is transmitted about the policy activities of government in different domains requires more research.

Policy representation

Thermostatic public responsiveness indicates that the preference signals the public sends to policymakers in some policy domains are meaningful. This is important to be sure, but we also want to know whether policymakers follow those signals. Indeed, we are interested in public opinion largely because we want to know whether it matters for what policymakers do. Not surprisingly, the research on policy representation is voluminous, much larger than for public responsiveness. Much of the work focuses on representatives' voting behavior and their positions, which we will eschew here; thankfully, there are useful summaries (see, for example, Burstein 2003; Shapiro 2011; Wlezien and Soroka 2016). Instead we focus on policy, and especially, but not exclusively, work in the thermostatic tradition (this complements the discussion of public responsiveness).

As for public responsiveness, some of the research on policy representation has focused on broad policy aggregates. Erikson, MacKuen and Stimson's (2002) examination stands out. In addition to analyzing the positions of institutional actors in the US – the president, Congress and the Supreme Court – they examined "significant enactments," building on David Mayhew's (1991) novel data set. Erikson, MacKuen and Stimson found that the number of liberal-conservative enactments closely followed trends in Stimson's measure of public mood, introduced in the discussion of public responsiveness. Public opinion is not the only thing that matters for policy in their analysis, and party control of the White House and Congress also play powerful roles.

Some research examines broad macro-representation in other countries. Most notable is Wlezien and Soroka's (2012) analysis of domestic spending, which reveals a general pattern of representation that varies across countries. In another cross-national analysis, Hobolt and Klemmensen (2008) examine the relationship between the public's issue priorities and public expenditure, and find a strong representational relationship that also varies across countries. Other work focuses specifically on government policy priorities, and this finds a correspondence between what the public cares about and government policy activities (Hobolt and Klemmensen 2005; Hakhverdian 2010; Bevan and Jennings 2014; also see Baumgartner and Jones 2005).

Numerous studies concentrate on specific issues. Hartley and Russett (1992) show that public opinion influences defense spending in the US. Wlezien (1996) confirms this finding and explores the dynamic interplay of thermostatic public responsiveness and representation. In other work, he shows that the representation relationship varies across US spending domains and the pattern is largely symmetrical to what we observe for public responsiveness (2004). There is a growing comparative literature as well. Eichenberg and Stoll (2003) find that defense spending follows opinion in the US and four European countries. In conjunction with their studies of opinion, Soroka and Wlezien examine representation in Canada (2004) and the UK (2005), and then for the US, Canada and UK taken together (Soroka and Wlezien 2010). They find that spending follows opinion in most domains but the relationship varies quite a lot.

Some of this work highlights the role of political institutions, both electoral and governmental (especially see Soroka and Wlezien 2010 and Hobolt and Klemmensen 2008). First, as regards electoral systems, scholars posit that proportionality dampens government responsiveness to public opinion between elections. This expectation contrasts with research that focuses on representation after elections (Powell 2000), where coalition governments are predicted to better represent the median voter. The thinking in the recent work is that coalition governments cannot as effectively respond to changing opinion in between elections, and for a variety of reasons (Wlezien and Soroka 2015).[13] Second, as regards government institutions, the research suggests that horizontal division of powers across legislative and executive branches enhances policy responsiveness to opinion. The idea here is that a balance of powers affords less policy independence and more "error correction," that is, where one branch can check the misrepresentational tendencies of the other (see Soroka and Wlezien 2010). There is support for both expectations in broad comparative analysis (Wlezien and Soroka 2012).[14]

All of this research highlights that there is representation, at least in certain policy domains and institutional contexts. This is of obvious importance. But what is not clear from this work is who gets represented. Is it the preferences of the median citizen? Or are others better represented? There now is much work in this exploding area of research. Gilens' (2012) powerful book examines the responsiveness of numerous policies to the preferences of different income groups. He demonstrates that policy change is responsive to the preferences of high-income citizens and less to the opinions of people with incomes in the middle and not at all to those at the bottom of the distribution.

Scholars continue to debate the issue. Soroka and Wlezien (2008) emphasize that unequal representation really matters when preferences differ and then show that this typically is not the case across income groups, at least for politically important spending domains; perhaps most importantly, the gaps they do detect are primarily between the poor on the one hand and the middle and upper classes on the other.[15] In a very prominent article, Gilens and Page (2014) assess the influence of rich and middle income preferences and conclude that economic elites completely dominate American politics. They conclude: "When a majority of citizens disagrees with economic elites or with organized interests, they generally lose" (576). Enns (2015) challenges this result, and shows that even where rich and middle income preferences differ, it would not make a difference whether policymakers represented one group or the other. Branham, Soroka and Wlezien (2017) further demonstrate that, even when the rich and middle do disagree, both groups do almost equally as well.[16] Clearly there is more research to be done, both in the US and in other countries.

Implications for elections and politics

We have seen that the thermostatic model works under some conditions, and that issues and institutions matter. There is evidence of both public responsiveness to policy and policy representation of opinion. In theory, this has implications for politics and political systems. To begin with, as discussed above, it provides the basis for electoral accountability.[17] It also has potential consequences for public evaluations of democracy and the broader political system, which scholars are only beginning to consider.

There has been surprisingly little work on the electoral implications. What research there is mostly focuses on broad macro-representation and has concentrated on US elections, particularly for the presidency. Erikson, MacKuen and Stimson (2002) provide an indirect test. They show that the general public mood toward policy influences presidential elections in an expected way; that is, the more (less) liberal the mood, the greater (lesser) the vote for the Democratic candidate. Given that mood responds thermostatically to policy, discussed above, the result implies that the degree of representation matters for elections. Bølstad (2012) targets direct evidence and to that end includes the net number of liberal-conservative laws in his analysis of the presidential vote. The results support what he refers to as "thermostatic voting," whereby the greater (lesser) the net liberal laws, the lesser (greater) the support for the Democratic candidate. Wlezien (2017) further demonstrates that the tendency accounts for a substantial portion of the cost of ruling effect in US presidential elections. To be absolutely clear, policy liberalism under presidents from different parties diverges over time as their tenure in the White House increases, and the degree to which it does negatively impacts electoral support for the party of the president.

There is little research on other countries, though Bartle, Delleplaine and Stimson (2011) show that policy mood influences the UK vote, which, like Erikson, MacKuen and Stimson's (2002) analysis of the US, implies thermostatic voting. A promising theoretical development is "issue yield" theory, where political parties stress policies that promise the highest vote yield, which depends on the importance of the issue and the degree to which demands are met (De Sio and Weber 2014; De Sio, Franklin and Weber 2016). Since yield declines as votes are harvested, parties must move on to the next promising issue once public demand has been satisfied. Issue yield theory may therefore prove able to incorporate the thermostatic model within a broader framework that additionally provides guidance to parties (this volume, Chapter 31).

There has been even less work on the consequences of policy representation. Very recent work by Mayne and Hakhverdian (2017) considers whether and how representation influences satisfaction with democracy and reveals an effect. They find evidence that people care about what the authors call "egocentric" congruence – the match between individuals' own preferences and the positions of elected officials. There is less support for broader "sociotropic" congruence – the correspondence between majoritarian public preferences and officials' positions. This is not surprising given traditional conceptualizations and models of policy voting, which embed individuals' personal preferences.

Other recent research on support for government responsiveness indicates similar egocentric effects. Bowler (2017) finds that individuals' preferences for government representation of the public reflects their own support of the government, where those who are close to the governing parties – that is, people who voted for them – are less in favor of majoritarian responsiveness. Rossett, Giger and Bernauer (2017) demonstrate further that people's responsiveness preferences depend on whether they stand to gain from such representation. This research is powerfully suggestive, though it really only begins to scratch the surface of public preferences for representation and their consequences.

Conclusion

A large body of research tests the thermostatic model and that research makes clear that the model works. We see that the public responds to policy. We also see that policymakers represent – effectively respond to – public preferences. The model does not work in all policy domains to be sure; indeed, it may not work in most domains. Even where it does, the model does not work equally well. Characteristics of issues matter and political context does as well. These causes also appear to have consequences, as representation impacts election outcomes and satisfaction with democracy itself.

What we do not know is exactly how well the thermostatic model works. While we have evidence of both public and policy responsiveness, we cannot determine whether the public ultimately gets what it wants – whether there is congruence. As discussed above, this is difficult to assess, particularly in areas where we cannot directly measure how much policy people want, frequently because people simply do not know. (It also is true where we have measures of absolute support for particular policies.) It thus may be that policymakers are not representing the public writ large, but a particular, privileged segment. It still may be that the average citizen often gets what it wants, but only because preferences of different groups in society often are quite similar. The problem is that we just cannot tell, at least not yet. That remains a subject for future research.

Notes

1 I thank Mark Franklin for making me write this chapter.
2 Indeed, Page and Shapiro demonstrated that different subgroups of the public responded in strikingly similar ways, what they referred to as "parallel publics."
3 In practice, the parameter is the net effect of positive and negative feedback. If positive feedback is dominant, then it will overwhelm negative feedback and β_1 will be positive; if negative feedback is dominant, as we expect to generally be the case, then β_1 will be negative.
4 Technically, indirect representation reflects both γ_2 and the coefficient relating relative preferences (R) and the partisan composition of government (G).
5 We also can depict this formally, following Achen (1978):

$$P = a + BP^* + e,$$

where the units can be temporal, spatial or else policy types. If there is congruence, the coefficient (B) for opinion would be a perfect "1.0" and the intercept (a) would equal "0," i.e., there would be no bias. If B is greater than 0 and less than 1, there still would be responsiveness; it just would not perfectly match preferences.
6 It is possible to match support for specific policies and policy adoption, and some scholars (Lax and Phillips 2012) have done this for various issues in the American states.
7 The effects are different as well, one between levels of policy and opinion and the other between levels of opinion and changes in policy.
8 Surveys ask about a wide range of categories, including welfare, health, education, the environment, big cities, crime and foreign aid, among others.
9 Politicians, meanwhile, are likely to pay attention to public opinion on the issue – it is in their self-interest to do so, after all. There are many different and clear expressions of this conception of importance. In issue domains that are not important, conversely, people are not likely to pay attention to politicians' behavior, and politicians are by implication expected to pay less attention to public opinion in these areas. This reflects a now classic perspective (see, for example, Geer 1996).
10 Other work (Ura 2014) indicates that mood responds to judicial action, and in complex ways, with negative feedback in the short run and positive feedback over longer stretches of time.
11 Also see Enns and Kellstedt (2010) and Enns and Wlezien (2011).
12 That said, Ellis and Faricy (2011) demonstrate that the public responds very differently to direct spending on social programs and the indirect spending from tax expenditures.
13 The friction that characterizes coalition governments, particular diverse ones, is a leading suspect, but electoral incentives may matter as well.
14 Other research has elaborated the empirical effects of electoral systems (Soroka and Wlezien 2015).
15 Also see Enns and Wlezien (2011).
16 Of course, this is not to say that the rich do not matter more than they should.
17 Also see Franklin, Soroka and Wlezien (2014).

References

Abramowitz, A. I. (1994) "Issue Evolution Reconsidered: Racial Attitudes and Partisanship in the U.S. Electorate," *American Journal of Political Science*, vol. 38, no. 1, February, 1–24.

Achen, C. (1978) "Measuring Representation," *American Journal of Political Science*, vol. 22, no. 3, August, 475–510.

Asher, H. B. (1992) *Presidential Elections and American Politics*, Pacific Grove, California: Brooks/Cole.

Bartle, J., Delleplaine, S. and Stimson, J. (2011) "The Moving Centre: Preferences for Government Activity in Britain, 1950–2005," *British Journal of Political Science*, vol. 41, no. 2, April, 259–285.

Baumgartner, F. and Jones, B. (2005) *The Politics of Attention: How Government Prioritizes Problems*, Chicago: University of Chicago Press.

Bevan, S. and Jennings, W. (2014) "Representation, Agendas and Institutions," *European Journal of Political Research*, vol. 53, no. 1, February, 37–56.

Bølstad, J. (2012) "Thermostatic Voting: Presidential Elections in Light of New Policy Data," *PS: Political Science and Politics*, vol. 45, no. 1, January, 44–50.

Bowler, S. (2017) "Trustees, Delegates, and Responsiveness in Comparative Perspective," *Comparative Political Studies*, vol. 50, no. 6, May, 766–793.

Branham, A., Soroka, S. and Wlezien, C. (2017) "When do the Rich Win?," *Political Science Quarterly*, vol. 132, no. 1, Spring, 43–62.

Burstein, P. (2003) "The Impact of Public Opinion on Public Policy: A Review and an Agenda," *Political Research Quarterly*, vol. 56, no. 1, March, 29–40.

Campbell, A., Converse, P. E., Miller, W. E. and Stokes, D. E. (1960) *The American Voter*, Chicago: University of Chicago Press.

Converse, P. E. (1964) "The Nature of Belief Systems in Mass Publics," in Apter, D. (ed.) *Ideology and Discontent*, New York: Free Press: 206–261.

De Sio, L. and Weber, T. (2014) "Issue Yield: A Model of Party Strategy in Multidimensional Space," *American Political Science Review*, vol. 108, no. 4, November, 870–885.

De Sio, L., Franklin, M. N. and Weber, T. (2016) "The Risks and Opportunities of Europe: How Issue Yield Explains Reactions to the Financial Crisis," *Electoral Studies*, vol. 44, December, 484–491.

Deutsch, K. W. (1963) *Nerves of Government*, New York: The Free Press.

Easton, D. (1965) *A Framework for Political Analysis*, Englewood Cliffs: Prentice-Hall.

Eichenberg, R. and Stoll, R. (2003) "Representing Defense: Democratic Control of the Defense Budget in the United States and Western Europe," *Journal of Conflict Resolution*, vol. 47, no. 4, August, 399–423.

Ellis, C. and Faricy, C. (2011) "Social Policy and Public Opinion: How the Ideological Direction of Spending Influences Public Mood," *Journal of Politics*, vol. 73, no. 4, October, 1095–1110.

Enns, P. (2015) "Relative Policy Support and Coincidental Representation," *Perspectives on Politics*, vol. 13, no. 4, December, 1053–1064.

Enns, P. and Kellstedt, P. (2010) "Policy Mood and Political Sophistication: Why Everyone Moves Mood," *British Journal of Political Science*, vol. 38, no. 3, July, 433–454.

Enns, P. and Wlezien, C. (eds.) (2011) *Who Gets Represented?*, New York: Russell Sage Foundation.

Erikson, R. S., MacKuen, M. B. and Stimson, J. A. (2002) *The Macro Polity*, Cambridge: Cambridge University Press.

Ferejohn, J. A. and Kuklinski, J. H. (eds.) (1990) *Information and Democratic Processes*, Urbana: University of Illinois Press.

Franklin, M. and Wlezien, C. (1997) "The Responsive Public: Issue Salience, Policy Change, and Preferences for European Unification," *Journal of Theoretical Politics*, vol. 9, no. 3, July, 347–363.

Franklin, M., Soroka, S. and Wlezien, C. (2014) "Elections," in Bovens, M., Goodin, R. and Schillemans, T. (eds.) *Oxford Handbook of Public Accountability*, Oxford: Oxford University Press: 389–404.

Geer, J. G. (1996) *From Tea Leaves to Opinion Polls: A Theory of Democratic Leadership*, New York: Columbia University Press.

Gilens, M. (2012) *Affluence and Influence*, Princeton: Princeton University Press.

Gilens, M. and Page, B. (2014) "Testing Theories of American Politics: Elites, Interest Groups and Average Citizens," *Perspectives on Politics*, vol. 12, no. 3, September, 564–581.

Goggin, M. and Wlezien, C. (1993) "Abortion Opinion and Policy in the American States," in Goggin, M. (ed.) *Understanding the New Politics of Abortion*, Newbury Park: Sage: 190–202.

Hartley, T. and Russett, B. (1992) "Public Opinion and the Common Defence: Who Governs Military Spending in the United States?," *American Political Science Review*, vol. 86, no. 4, December, 905–915.

Hakhverdian, A. (2010) "Political Representation and Its Mechanisms: A Dynamic Left-Right Approach for the United Kingdom, 1976–2006," *British Journal of Political Science*, vol. 40, no. 4, October, 835–856.

Hobolt, S. B. and Klemmensen, R. (2005) "Responsive Government? Public Opinion and Policy Preferences in Britain and Denmark?," *Political Studies*, vol. 53, no. 2, June, 379–402.

Hobolt, S. B. and Klemmensen, R. (2008) "Government Responsiveness and Political Competition in Comparative Perspective," *Comparative Political Studies*, vol. 41, no. 3, March, 309–337.

Jennings, W. (2009) "The Public Thermostat, Political Responsiveness and Error Correction: Border Control and Asylum in Britain, 1994–2007," *British Journal of Political Science*, vol. 39, no. 4, October, 847–870.

Johnson, M., Brace, P. and Arceneaux, K. (2005) "Public Opinion and Dynamic Representation in the American States: The Case of Environmental Attitudes," *Social Science Quarterly*, vol. 86, no. 1, March, 87–108.

Kellstedt, P. (2003) *The Mass Media and the Dynamics of American Racial Policy Attitudes*, Cambridge: Cambridge University Press.

Key, V. O. (1961) *Public Opinion and American Democracy*, New York: Knopf.

Kinder, D. E. (1983) "Diversity and Complexity in American Public Opinion," in Finifter, A. (ed.) *Political Science: The State of the Discipline*, Washington, DC: American Political Science Association: 389–425.

Lau, R. R. and Redlawsk, D. P. (2006) *How Voters Decide: Information Processing During Election Campaigns*, Cambridge: Cambridge University Press.

Lax, J. R. and Phillips, J. H. (2012) "The Democratic Deficit in the States," *American Journal of Political Science*, vol. 56, no. 1, January, 148–166.

Lupia, A. (1994) "The Effect of Information on Voting Behavior and Electoral Outcomes: An Experimental Study of Direct Legislation," *Public Choice*, vol. 78, no. 1, January, 65–86.

Mayhew, D. R. (1991) *Divided We Govern*, New Haven: Yale University Press.

Mayne, Q. and Hakhverdian, M. (2017) "Ideological Congruence and Citizen Satisfaction: Evidence from 25 Advanced Democracies," *Comparative Political Studies*, vol. 50, no. 6, May, 822–849.

Morgan, S. L. and Kang, M. (2015) "A New Conservative Cold Front? Democrat and Republican Responsiveness to the Passage of the Affordable Care Act," *Sociological Science*, vol. 2, September, 502–526.

Neuner, F., Soroka, S. and Wlezien, C. (2015) "The Clues in the News: Unpacking Thermostatic Responsiveness to Policy," Paper presented at the Toronto Political Behaviour Workshop, Montreal, November 6–7.

Pacheco, J. (2013) "The Thermostatic Model of Responsiveness in the American States," *State Politics and Policy Quarterly*, vol. 13, no. 3, September, 306–332.

Page, B. I. and Shapiro, R. Y. (1992) *The Rational Public: Fifty Years of Trends in Americans' Policy Preferences*, Chicago: University of Chicago Press.

Powell, G. B. (2000) *Elections as Instruments of Democracy: Majoritarian and Proportional Views*, New Haven: Yale University Press.

Rossett, J., Giger, N. and Bernauer, J. (2017) "I the People: Self Interest and Demand for Government Responsiveness," *Comparative Political Studies*, vol. 50, no. 6, May, 794–821.

Shapiro, R. Y. (2011) "Public Opinion and American Democracy," *Public Opinion Quarterly*, vol. 75, no. 5, December, 982–1017.

Sniderman, P. M., Brody, R. A. and Tetlock, P. (1991) *Reasoning and Choice: Explorations in Political Psychology*, Cambridge: Cambridge University Press.

Soroka, S. N. and Wlezien, C. (2004) "Opinion Representation and Policy Feedback: Canada in Comparative Perspective," *Canadian Journal of Political Science*, vol. 37, no. 3, September, 531–560.

Soroka, S. N. and Wlezien, C. (2005) "Opinion–Policy Dynamics: Public Preferences and Public Expenditure in the United Kingdom," *British Journal of Political Science*, vol. 35, no. 4, October, 665–689.

Soroka, S. N. and Wlezien, C. (2008) "On the Limits to Inequality in Representation," *Political Science and Politics*, vol. 41, no. 2, April, 319–327.

Soroka, S. N. and Wlezien, C. (2010) *Degrees of Democracy: Politics, Public Opinion and Policy*, Cambridge: Cambridge University Press.

Soroka, S. N. and Wlezien, C. (2015) "The Majoritarian and Proportional Visions and Democratic Responsiveness," *Electoral Studies*, vol. 40, December, 539–547.

Stimson, J. A. (1991) *Public Opinion in America: Moods, Cycles, and Swings*, Boulder, Colo.: Westview Press.

Ura, J. (2014) "Backlash and Legitimation: Macro Political Responses to Supreme Court Decisions," *American Journal of Political Science*, vol. 59, no. 1, January, 110–126.

Wlezien, C. (1995) "The Public as Thermostat: Dynamics of Preferences for Spending," *American Journal of Political Science*, vol. 39, no. 4, November, 981–1000.

Wlezien, C. (1996) "Dynamics of Representation: The Case of US Spending on Defense," *British Journal of Political Science*, vol. 26, no. 1, January, 81–103.

Wlezien, C. (2004) "Patterns of Representation: Dynamics of Public Preferences and Policy," *Journal of Politics*, vol. 66, no. 1, February, 1–24.

Wlezien, C. (2017) "Policy (Mis)Representation and the Cost of Ruling: US Presidential Elections in Comparative Perspective," *Comparative Political Studies*, vol. 50, no. 6, May, 711–738.

Wlezien, C. and Soroka, S. (2011) "Federalism and Public Responsiveness to Policy," *Publius*, vol. 41, no. 1, Winter, 31–52.

Wlezien, C. and Soroka, S. (2012) "Political Institutions and the Opinion-Policy Link," *West European Politics*, vol. 35, no. 6, October, 1407–1432.

Wlezien, C. and Soroka, S. (2015) "Electoral Systems and Opinion Representation," *Representation*, vol. 51, no. 3, 273–285.

Wlezien, C. and Soroka, S. (2016) "Public Opinion and Public Policy," in Dalton, R. (ed.) *Oxford Research Encyclopedia in Politics: Behavior*, Oxford: Oxford University Press. Online: http://politics.oxfordre.com/view/10.1093/acrefore/9780190228637.001.0001/acrefore-9780190228637-e-74.

33

REGIME SUPPORT

Pedro C. Magalhães

Introduction

What do citizens think about the political regimes they live under and how do they view other conceivable ways of organizing the polity? How do we explain changes or continuity in these attitudes and what consequences do they hold for the functioning and stability of the political system? These are all questions that have been posed with increasing frequency by comparative researchers since the publication of Almond and Verba's (1963) pioneering work *The Civic Culture* in the early 1960s. While the conclusions that have been reached have differed across time and space, scholars have been largely united in their choice of methodology, with most relying on large-scale survey data to measure and test their core concepts. The release of Eurobarometer data from 1970 onward in particular prompted a rush of interest in comparing citizen attitudes toward their governing institutions. A decade later, both the European Values Study and the World Value Survey (EVS/WVS) began, alongside a range of other resources, providing further impetus to development of this literature.[1] In this chapter we provide an overview of the work that these initiatives fostered, with specific reference to understanding cross-national patterns in popular support for political regimes. We begin by defining the central object of study – that is, regime support. We then profile the main research questions that have been investigated in relation to regime support across countries, and the empirical findings that have been produced. We move on to discuss the measurement problems that such research has faced and evaluate how well these challenges have been overcome. Finally, we focus on outlining the main questions that remain for this line of research to address.

The theoretical importance of regime support

Support, according to Easton, a pioneer in the study of political systems, is "an attitude by which a person orients himself to an object either favorably or unfavorably, positively or negatively" (Easton 1975: 436). The focus of this chapter is on those studies that have examined support for a particular type of object – the political regime – which again, following Easton's thinking, we define as "the so-called rules of the game […], the constitutional principles […] governing the way in which resolutions of differences of claims are to take place" (Easton 1957: 392). To further distinguish the concept of interest, Easton helpfully contrasted it with two other major objects or components of the system – first, the wider *political community* and, second, the more specific actors that constituted the *political authorities*. While the former comprises the entire set of actors – understood as a collective – within a given system, the latter refers to the specific personnel that make up the government. In profiling studies of regime support, therefore, we are not including analyses of trends in identification with the nation-state or "in-group or we-group feeling" that characterizes support for the political community (Easton 1957: 392). Nor are we interested in work that centers on measuring changes in support for the political authorities – that is, "those who are responsible for the day-to-day actions taken in the name of a political system" (Easton 1975: 437).

There are several compelling reasons for narrowing the lens to examine orientations to the political regime rather than focusing on these other dimensions of public support. Perhaps the most compelling of these is the lack of attention they have received in the literature to date, relative to their overall contribution to the functioning of the polity. Easton himself expressed concerns about the extent to which empirical research on political support has been dominated by a focus on the "allocative aspects" of political systems – that is, those dealing with the relationships among the leaders, the policies, and the led, rather than more fundamental concerns about deeper attachments to the polity. As he notes, while the former studies are important, discontent with governments and their policies is "not always, or even usually, the signal for basic political change" (Easton 1975: 436).

By contrast, regime support, as the inter-war period revealed, is critical to understanding the survival of democracies. According to Seymour Martin Lipset (1959), it is when regimes face "crises of effectiveness, such as depressions or lost wars" that their "legitimacy" or capacity to "engender and maintain the belief that existing political institutions are the most appropriate or proper ones for the society" becomes crucial for understanding their chances of survival (1959: 86). Along the same lines, Linz saw regime legitimacy – the belief "that these political institutions are the best to govern the country in which they live; that they are better than the alternatives; and that they deserve obedience" – as central to the fate of democracies in the aftermath of the Great Depression, protecting those where legitimacy was high (Linz 2001: 92, see also Linz 1976).

Beyond the challenges of defining regime support and specifying its theoretical and substantive political importance, there is also the task of measuring it, and demonstrating its relevance empirically. Difficulties in this respect abound and are often noted in the literature: "there are doubts about the efficiency of empirical research when trying to isolate the different types of support, as public sentiments can blend adjacent orientations and indicators of public support frequently overlap between levels" (Torcal and Moncagatta 2011: 2565). How have these doubts been dealt with? In the section that follows, we address this question.

Discontent is not the same as (il)legitimacy

The new impetus to undertake empirical study of regime support was inspired by three key post-war developments. The first was the already mentioned expansion in the availability of comparative survey data. The second was the growing concern with the "legitimacy crisis" that Western democracies were seen to be experiencing during the 1970s (Habermas 1976) and its attitudinal manifestation in increasing rates of citizen "dissatisfaction with and lack of confidence in the functioning of the institutions of democratic government" (Crozier, Huntington, and Watanuki 1975: 158–159). Finally, there was the so-called "third wave of democratization" which raised questions about the extent to which newer democracies enjoyed the kind of popular support that would favor their survival (Huntington 1991).

As new sources of comparative data became available, the question of whether the West was facing a "crisis of democracy" became easier to answer. By the mid-1990s, analysis of Eurobarometer data for the *Beliefs in Government* project had shown that such fears were largely ungrounded. The major conclusion reached was that "there is no pervasive or general trend toward decreasing satisfaction with the way democracy works in the member states of the European Union," and the same applied to confidence in institutions (Kaase and Newton 1995: 61; see also Fuchs, Guidorossi, and Svensson 1995; Listhaug and Wiberg 1995).

Even more optimistically, subsequent empirical work conducted in the late 1990s by Montero, Gunther, and Torcal on the newly democratized case of Spain (1997) revealed that even if negative trends on these indicators had been in evidence, this did not spell disaster for democracy. Instead these authors showed convincingly that while levels of "satisfaction with the way Spanish democracy works" had fluctuated widely over time, in line with evaluations of the political and economic situation, a large and stable majority of citizens still agreed with the notion that "democracy is the best system for a country like ours" (Montero, Gunther, and Torcal 1997). In addition, factor analysis of individual survey responses revealed that while the items measuring opinions of democratic performance loaded strongly on a "political discontent" factor, a preference for "democracy" as the best system available, as well as other more abstract measures of regime level support, constituted an independent factor.[2] Analysis by Klingemann (1999), using *World Values Survey* (WVS) data from 38 countries, confirmed this split in citizens' political outlook, concluding that citizens do appear to separate support for "democracy" as a regime and their satisfaction with how the regime is currently performing or the level of confidence they place in the regime's institutions (1999: 37).[3]

Closer analysis of the underlying correlates and drivers of "political discontent" as compared with more overt preference for democracy as a regime have helped to tease out these differences in attitudinal orientations. For example, "satisfaction with the way democracy works" appears in many comparative studies to be driven by economic outcomes, objective or perceived (Quaranta and Martini 2016). These motives are further enhanced under conditions of low economic development (Rohrschneider and Loveless 2010) and where lines of governing responsibility are clear (Criado and Herreros 2007). In addition, partisanship is important, with positive orientations increasing when one's party is in power, and particularly so in majoritarian political systems (Anderson and Guillory 1997). More generally, the quality of governance in the country also plays a role (Wagner, Schneider, and Halla 2009; Linde 2012) with perceptions of low procedural fairness in particular found to be significant in determining levels of dissatisfaction (Magalhães 2016).

By contrast, accounting for variance on the extent to which individuals in different contexts are likely to see democracy as intrinsically preferable to other regime types has proven more difficult. Much less variance is typically explained by similar explanatory models and some contradictory results have emerged. At the individual level, education, income, postmaterial values, and social trust are generally found to be the strongest predictors of positive attitudes toward democratic government. At the macro level, economic development and a longer history of liberal democracy appear to be among the most consistent correlates (see Dalton 2004; Zmerli and Newton 2008; Huang, Chang, and Chu 2008; Staton and Reenock 2008; Norris 2011). These findings are returned to below when we turn to unpack thorny questions of causality and endogeneity in the formation of regime preferences. The main point emerging from this discussion, however, is that negative orientations toward democracy are not necessarily linked to feelings of discontent with regime performance or with the political authorities. Furthermore, it is possible to distinguish empirically, and not just conceptually or theoretically, between citizens' perceptions of democratic legitimacy and their feelings of political discontent.

Deepening our understanding of "regime support"

The findings from this growing body of empirical literature helped move scholarly opinion toward a more positive view of support for democracy globally. "By the mid-1990s democracy has come to be widely regarded as the ideal form of government in the countries where we have evidence in Western and Eastern Europe, North and South America, and Asia" (Norris 1999: 17; see also Chapter 18 by Norris in this volume). Such optimism was not universally shared, however. In particular, Mishler and Rose (2001) argued against what they saw as the "idealist approach" that characterized these studies, whereby it was assumed that citizens knew what democracy meant and how it ought to work. This, they argued was a problematic assumption, especially in those countries where experience with actual democratic governance was absent or limited (Mishler and Rose 2001). Norris herself shared some of these concerns, noting that "abstract approval of the broad ideals and principles of democracy may be rooted in shallow support for particular aspects, like tolerance of dissenting views or minority rights." Such distinctions meant that it was important "to go much further to deepen our analysis of what people understand by the principles and values of democracy" (Norris 1999: 17). The research that ensued in response to this challenge can be seen as having taken three main directions.

Refining measures of democratic support

The first line of enquiry focused primarily on methodological issues and sought to refine existing measures and indicators of democratic support. Looking at EVS and WVS data from the late 1990s that extended to around 80 percent of the world's population, Inglehart (2003: 52) noted that, "in the median country, fully 92 percent of those interviewed gave a positive account of democracy." And yet, "when one probes deeper, one finds disturbing evidence that mass support is not nearly as solid" (2003: 52). For example, majorities in several of these same countries endorsed the notion that "a strong leader [...] does not have to bother with elections or parliament." To address the apparent contradiction, Inglehart proposed a more balanced multi-item index to measure regime support – the "Democracy/Autocracy" index. This essentially involved subtracting the level of support for non-democratic forms of governance from the levels of support for democracy.

Use of the new adjusted measure of support, with some variation, has been adopted in subsequent studies. The change has led to distinctly more negative conclusions being drawn, particularly among the more recently democratized states. In a study of those countries included in the Afrobarometer, "recalculating the proportions that both say democracy is preferable and reject all three authoritarian alternatives reveals that only a minority (48 percent) can be labeled as 'committed democrats.'" Such a finding "warrants a sober assessment of the depth of democratic legitimacy in Africa" (Mattes and Bratton 2007: 194). Analysis of Asia Barometer data by Chu et al. (2008) has concluded that "most East Asian democracies do not enjoy deep legitimation" (28), and studies of the Latino Barometer data have found that "opponents of authoritarian rule [...] constitute a small minority of less than one-quarter" (Shin 2007: 274). Among the newer democracies of Europe, a similar story emerges, with "relative support for democracy" being found to be "ten times higher in Germany than in Bulgaria and more than four times higher in non-English-speaking protestant Western Europe than in post-communist Eastern Europe" (Dalton and Shin 2014: 108). Overall, therefore, it seems that "in the eyes of global citizenries, democracy is yet to become the final achievement of history" (Dalton and Shin 2014: 108).

While use of these more refined measures helped to update and modify contemporary understanding of the extent of support that democratic systems enjoyed worldwide, it did not lead to any re-specification of its correlates. If anything, the new measures helped to reinforce the relevance of existing explanatory variables, with solid democratic support appearing to be most strongly prevalent among richer and older democracies (Dalton and Shin 2014: 98). At the individual level, the known effects of education and income are also reemphasized (de Jonge 2016). On the other hand, as Inglehart and Welzel (2005) show, the "democratic-autocracy" index was a much stronger predictor of whether a country was likely to be democratic than simpler measures of support for democracy. Therefore, our understanding of regime support seems to have improved with these refined measures. First, they seem to have helped correcting for the large overstatement of support for democracy that resulted from employing more simplistic measures. Second, their correlates emerged much more clearly than before (de Jonge 2016).

There remain, however, a number of causes for concern. These are primarily methodological and center on the robustness and validity of the "democracy-autocracy index" for cross-national research. In particular, items measuring support for democracy were found to lack equivalence across countries and recommendations against their inclusion in the index issued (Ariely and Davidov 2011). In addition, the "rejection of autocracy" items failed to load on the main construct in around one out of four countries examined. Finally, even for those cases where the items did load, partial scalar invariance cannot be established, making the widespread practice of comparing mean values across countries unadvisable (Ariely and Davidov 2011: 279).

Focusing on regime principles

Given the problems associated with soliciting overt preferences for "democracy" as a measure of support, several alternative methods have been proposed. One widely adopted approach has been to avoid the inclusion of any survey questions that refer directly to the regime "type" altogether. Instead, items tapping support for regime *principles* are used. Here, the focus turns primarily to the endorsement of democratic norms and practices by citizens, rather than to overt preferences for abstract regime types.

Schedler and Sarsfield (2007), for example, used cluster analysis to segment the Mexican electorate into groups based on their orientation to liberal values such as freedom of organization and expression and political equality. Their findings revealed that only one of the groups (corresponding to about 14 percent of the sample) displayed consistent support for liberal values. All other respondents were classified as "non-democrats" or to have inconsistent attitudes whereby they supported democracy in the abstract but exhibited low tolerance for dissenting views and discriminatory attitudes to minorities. Carlin and Singer (2011) extended this analysis by examining support for "polyarchy" across 12 Latin American democracies. Polyarchy was defined using a multi-item indicator that tapped opposition to censorship, support for the participation of those who oppose the regime, support for limits to executive authority, and rejection of the admissibility of suspending the legislature and the Supreme Court. The findings supported those of Schedler and Sarsfield in that only 18 percent of citizens were identified as consistent supporters of "polyarchy," while most presented "a mixed profile" (2011: 1510).

Comparative work by Booth and Seligson (2009) measuring support for principles of democratic participation also found surprisingly modest levels of endorsement, with countries scoring an average of 68 on a scale of 0 to 100. In line with the findings of other studies, it was those nations with a longer democratic history that proved most supportive. Furthermore, at the individual level, education, political knowledge, media exposure, and social trust were all associated with a greater commitment to democracy participatory principles (Booth and Seligson 2009: 121–124).

The move to focus on regime principles, therefore, ultimately helped to underscore the growing impression that global preferences for "democracy" were not as deeply rooted as scholars had previously thought to be the case. Instead such preferences were seen as essentially coexisting alongside a range of less liberal views which questioned the importance of dissent and the exercise of political freedoms, particularly among ethnic minorities, as well as the value of political participation itself.

The meanings of democracy

A third approach to improving our understanding of the nature of regime support has been to explore where the disjuncture between overt preferences and deeper attitudes stems from. This has shifted the focus of enquiry onto more psychological and interpretive factors in a bid to understand the meaning assigned by people to the very concept of "democracy." The results obtained in these studies, as one might expect, depend to a significant degree on how the questions are asked. When an open-ended format is used, we see a predominantly liberal understanding emerging (Fuchs and Roller 2006; Camp 2001). As one set of authors neatly summarized it, "When people say that democracy is the best form of government, they are thinking in terms of the freedom and liberty it provides" (Dalton, Shin, and Jou 2007: 10).

However, a significant minority of citizens also associate a more specific set of socioeconomic outcomes with democracy, such as "jobs for all," universal access to education, income equality, or the elimination of poverty. Moreover, the weight given to these "goods" varies by country (Bratton, Mattes, and Gyimah-Boadi 2005; Dalton, Shin, and Jou 2007; de Regt 2013). While this multitude of meanings can emerge in response to open-ended questions, (Canache 2012), such variations are more evident when we move to closed-ended items. The WVS, for example, has measured popular understandings of "democracy" across a range of dimensions since 2005. This has included support for the "procedural" elements of democracy – that is, legal protections of civil rights, gender equality, and the operation of free elections. It has also covered the pursuit of more substantive goals or outcomes, such as income redistribution, prosperity, and law and order.

While the procedural understanding has proven to be "the most widespread and popular interpretation across all types of societies," the more substantive and instrumental interpretations are in fact only slightly less common among Western European publics, according to Norris (2011). More recent evidence from a study using data from the European Social Survey (ESS) lends further support to the idea that citizens harbor an expansive and multifaceted definition of democracy. In addition to an adherence to classic liberal democratic principles, many Europeans also see ideals of direct democracy and social justice as key components of any well-functioning democracy. As the authors conclude, "The European's vision of democracy is […] not limited to the liberal democratic model. […] Their views of democracy often include substantive elements, above all the idea that the government should protect its citizens against poverty" (Kriesi and Morlino 2016: 309).

As well as identifying the differing understandings of democracy, scholars have also been interested in what drives them. Explanations centering on advances in human development appear to be of particular relevance in this regard. Welzel (2011), for example, has shown that economic and cognitive resources are significantly and positively correlated with stronger endorsements of autonomy, freedom of choice, and emancipation, which in turn align most closely to a procedural understanding of democracy.[4] However, the notion of a "developmental universalism" (Welzel 2011: 1), whereby an emancipatory logic emerges across cultures as human capital expands, has been challenged by other scholars who argue that the effects of the political and institutional context needs to be considered. Work by Ceka and Magalhães (2016), for instance, has found that systems with a longer experience of democracy and also of direct democracy mechanisms do see a positive association between individuals' socioeconomic status and endorsement for both liberal and direct democracy views. However, in countries with the opposite features, the opposite occurs. Those of higher socioeconomic status are more likely to espouse views about democracy that conform to the status quo – that is, the existing institutions of a country (Ceka and Magalhães 2016: 110). A similar emphasis on the importance of political context in determining individuals' outlook on democracy is also present in Franklin and Riera's (2016) analysis of European societies. Here they show how historically defined cohorts of individuals – socialized during or after the prevalence of "cleavage politics" in each country – tend to adhere to different views about what democratic representation should mean.

Challenges

Overall, therefore, some agreement does appear to have been reached within the literature over the nature of regime support in general, and the state of support for democratic regime types more specifically. First, it would seem that Easton was correct about the need to distinguish between attitudes toward specific actors within a polity and attachment to more abstract rules of governance. It seems that citizens are indeed able to express support or discontent for political authorities while also holding "respect for the offices themselves, for the way in which they are ordered, and for the community of which they are a part" (Easton 1975: 437). Second, it is also clear that we should not assume that those who express an overt preference for democracy as a regime type automatically hold negative views of other regime types. Support for democracy does not preclude support for rival systems that are distinctly non-democratic. Nor is it the case that those expressing support for democracy in the abstract are necessarily strong proponents of basic liberal democratic principles, or even understand "democracy" as a concept at all, let alone according to the classic liberal procedural definition.

However, despite having reached something of a substantive consensus on key aspects of regime support, a number of challenges and concerns do still remain for the literature to address. Below we focus on two of these in more detail. The first centers on measurement issues and the second on problems of causal modeling, and particularly how to distinguish between the causes and consequences of regime support.

Measurement

The ability of researchers to introduce new levels and sub-domains to the concept of "regime support" has not been matched by their ability to devise reliable and valid measurements for all of them. For example, the sub-division of Easton's "regime support" into support for regime principles, performance, and institutions (Norris 1999: 11), or the notion that each of those levels should be seen as having "diffuse" and "specific," or "affective" and "evaluative" components (Torcal and Moncagatta 2011: 2565; Dalton 2004: 23), while acceptable readings of past theoretical work, have been difficult to validate empirically. Even the validity of one of the most widely used survey items to measure support for democracy – whether an individual is "satisfied with how democracy works" – is contested (Canache, Mondak, and Seligson 2001; Linde and Eckman 2003; but see Quaranta 2017 for a recent validation).[5]

This lack of consensus over issues of measurement has resulted in varying and even contradictory conclusions being reached regarding trends in the nature and level of regime support over time. One of the core areas of debate has centered on the growth of a group of critical but engaged citizens, identified initially by Klingemann as "dissatisfied democrats." Even in introducing the concept, however, Klingemann was quick to acknowledge the problems it raised for measurement and operationalization, noting that "change over time ... is difficult to assess" (1999: 49). Thus, for some scholars, the evidence clearly indicates that "citizens have grown more distant from political parties, more critical of political elites and political institutions, and less positive about government" (Dalton 2004: 45–46). For others, the picture is much more blurred in that "overall fluctuations over time usually prove far more common than straightforward linear or uniform downward trends" (Norris 2011: 82).

While measurement issues may not be the only cause of these contrasting diagnoses of current democratic conditions, certainly a stronger consensus and consistency in the core variables used would contribute greatly to moving the literature forward. In particular, some agreement on the use of multi-item indicators, as well on avoiding those items known to be problematic, would constitute important first steps in this direction (Booth and Seligson 2009). Some recent diagnostics of new "trends" in democratic support still seem to stem from excessive reliance in single-item indicators and "overt" preferences (see Foa and Munck 2016). More investigation of the cross-national equivalence of regime support measures should also be undertaken, rather than simply assumed (Ariely and Davidov 2011; Davidov et al. 2014). Finally, most measures of "regime support" in comparative survey research have centered on popular feelings about democracy. Gauging the support for autocratic regimes has been largely dismissed given their reliance on coercion, co-optation, and performance (economic or otherwise) for their survival (Haggard and Kaufman 1995; Geddes 1999). Where such perceptions are measured they are usually regarded simply as an additional indicator of democratic support, or more accurately, lack thereof. However, it is entirely possible that support for these regimes represents a deeper and more positive endorsement of them on ideological, religious, nationalistic, or traditional or charismatic grounds (Gerschewski 2013: 20). It is thus a future challenge for the literature to develop new measures that better capture support for non-democratic regimes.[6] In setting such a goal, it is of course important that we keep in mind the challenges that any cross-national fieldwork presents to consistency and reliability of data collection, particularly so when that includes non-democracies (Romero 2004).

Causes and consequences

Investigation of the factors associated with support for democracy at the macro level has thus far identified two main correlates – the length of time a country has lived under democratic rule and its level of economic prosperity. These relationships are mirrored to a degree at the micro level, in that citizens with greater material and cognitive resources exhibit a stronger commitment to democratic rules and principles. The extent to which causation can be inferred from these associations, however, and the precise mechanism through which it occurs, is a topic of ongoing debate.

In essence, the argument centers around the age-old "chicken and egg" dilemma that has dominated the study of the structure and performance of democratic institutions *writ large*. Are institutions simply reflective of the political culture within which they exist or do they have an independent capacity to inflict change on that society? The debate gained fresh impetus from the late 1980s onward through works that sought to resolve the dilemma through comparative empirical analysis. In the context of regime support studies, the debate essentially coalesced into opposition between those who saw "emancipative values" and human development as the key drivers behind citizen preferences for democracy (Inglehart 1988) and those who prioritized "institutional learning" and the importance of regime performance as the main generator of such support (Muller and Seligson 1994).

Despite the strenuous claims put forward on both sides, the empirical evidence has remained somewhat inconclusive. While the human development thesis does appear to be consistently supported by cross-sectional analyses, the application of more complex longitudinal models and data has indicated a negligible impact of values over time, or at best suggested a pattern of reverse causation (Hadenius and Teorell 2005; Dahlum and Knutsen 2017; for responses, see Welzel and Inglehart 2006; Welzel, Inglehart, and Kruse 2017). Furthermore, new questions have arisen about the long-standing Eastonian belief in the orthogonality of political discontent and perceived regime legitimacy. According to this widely accepted logic, citizen dissatisfaction with the outer workings of government does not necessarily indicate something is rotten at the heart of the regime and that it is in danger of imminent collapse. What happens, however, when this discontent persists over time? When does persistent dissatisfaction with a government's economic and/or political performance become corrosive of regime legitimacy? Easton himself noted the potential for "...spill-over effects from evaluations of a series of outputs and of performance over a long-period of time" (Easton 1975: 446). Given the growing evidence showing that regime support can be affected by performance-related factors such as government effectiveness (Magalhães 2014), economic evaluations (Singh and Carlin 2014), or incumbent approval (de Jonge 2016), it would seem that the causal pendulum may now be swinging in support of the institutional learning perspective.

We should perhaps not be entirely surprised that so many questions still remain unanswered within this literature. Comparative survey research is a relatively new and resource-intensive endeavor. Repeated measures of political attitudes have become more common in cross-national surveys but still trail some way behind traditional socioeconomic and behavioral indicators in the prominence and priority ascribed to them. Furthermore, even if more survey measures are adopted, one of course still faces the intrinsic limitations of this type of observational data, particularly for drawing causal inferences. The experimental or quasi-experimental approaches that are now emerging in the field thus present a particularly exciting new mode of enquiry to deal precisely with this problem (Bloom and Arikan 2013; Alkon and Wang 2016). More generally, however, a resolution of these controversies cannot lie solely with empirical or methodological developments, it must involve theoretical advances. In a nutshell, rather than seeing the main challenge for future research as the ability to nail down or prove which is the core driver of citizen perceptions – values, learning, or performance – researchers should instead view the process in a much more joined-up manner, with the primary aim being to map and model the interactive and mutually reinforcing dynamics between these forces in the creation of citizens' political attitudes (Besley and Persson 2016).

Notes

1 For analyses of these developments and available resources, see, for example, Heath, Fisher, and Smith (2005), Kittilson (2007), and Norris (2009).

2 For an earlier work confirming the multidimensional nature of support (for community, regime, and authorities), see Kornberg and Clarke (1992).

3 See also Gunther, Montero, and Torcal (2007), using Comparative National Elections Project (CNEP) data, and Belluci and Memoli (2012), using European Values Study (EVS) data.

4 See also Welzel (2013) and Norris (2011). Ariely (2015), however, notes that the factor solution separating procedural, instrumental, illiberal, and social views, which emerged with the pooled dataset, does not emerge in many countries. Only in the procedural dimension emerges a "common conception of the procedures of democracy that enables cross-national comparison" (Ariely 2015: 622).

5 Although it is suggestive to see that many of the correlates of satisfaction of democracy that emerge in the literature – economy, ideology, partisanship, corruption – are exactly the same as those of trust in institutions, and in fact, of government approval and even voting for the incumbent.

6 Several works on "Asian values" have come closest to addressing this problem. See, for example, Park and Shin (2006).

References

Alkon, M. and Wang, E. H. (2016) "Pollution and Regime Support: Quasi-Experimental Evidence from Beijing," Available at SSRN: http://ssrn.com/abstract=2757858.

Almond, G. A. and Verba, S. (1963) *The Civic Culture: Political Attitudes and Democracy in Five Nations*, Princeton: Princeton University Press.

Anderson, C. J. and Guillory, C. A. (1997) "Political Institutions and Satisfaction with Democracy: A Cross-National Analysis of Consensus and Majoritarian Systems," *American Political Science Review*, vol. 91, no. 1, March, 66–81.

Ariely, G. (2015) "Democracy-Assessment in Cross-National Surveys: A Critical Examination of How People Evaluate Their Regime," *Social Indicators Research*, vol. 121, no. 3, April, 621–635.

Ariely, G. and Davidov, E. (2011) "Can We Rate Public Support for Democracy in a Comparable Way? Cross-National Equivalence of Democratic Attitudes in the World Value Survey," *Social Indicators Research*, vol. 104, no. 2, November, 271–286.

Bellucci, P. and Memoli, V. (2012) "The Determinants of Democracy Satisfaction in Europe," in Sanders, D., Magalhães, P. C., and Tóka, G. (eds.) *Citizens and the European Polity: Mass Attitudes Towards the European and National Polities*, Oxford: Oxford University Press: 9–39.

Besley, T. and Persson, T. (2016) "Democratic Values and Institutions," Unpublished Manuscript, London School of Economics.

Bloom, P. B. N. and Arikan, G. (2013) "Priming Religious Belief and Religious Social Behavior Affects Support for Democracy," *International Journal of Public Opinion Research*, vol. 25, no. 3, Autumn, 368–382.

Booth, J. A. and Seligson, M. A. (2009) *The Legitimacy Puzzle in Latin America: Political Support and Democracy in Eight Nations*, New York: Cambridge University Press.

Bratton, M., Mattes, R. B., and Gyimah-Boadi, E. (2005) *Public Opinion, Democracy, and Market Reform in Africa*, New York: Cambridge University Press.

Camp, R. A. (2001) *Citizen Views of Democracy in Latin America*, Pittsburgh: University of Pittsburgh Press.

Canache, D. (2012) "Citizens' Conceptualizations of Democracy Structural Complexity, Substantive Content, and Political Significance," *Comparative Political Studies*, vol. 45, no. 9, September, 1132–1158.

Canache, D., Mondak, J. J., and Seligson, M. A. (2001) "Meaning and Measurement in Cross-National Research on Satisfaction with Democracy," *Public Opinion Quarterly*, vol. 65, no. 4, Winter, 506–528.

Carlin, R. E. and Singer, M. M. (2011) "Support for Polyarchy in the Americas," *Comparative Political Studies*, vol. 44, no. 1, November, 1500–1526.

Ceka, B. and Magalhães, P. C. (2016) "How People Understand Democracy: A Social Dominance Approach," in Ferrín, M. and Kriesi, H. (eds.) *How Europeans View and Evaluate Democracy*, Oxford: Oxford University Press: 90–110.

Chu, Y. H., Diamond, L., Nathan, A. J., and Shin, D. C. (2008) "Comparative Perspectives on Democratic Legitimacy in East Asia," in Chu, Y. H., Diamond, L., Nathan, A. J., and Shin, D. C. (eds.) *How East Asians View Democracy*, New York: Columbia University Press: 1–38.

Criado, H. and Herreros, F. (2007) "Political Support Taking into Account the Institutional Context," *Comparative Political Studies*, vol. 40, no. 12, December, 1511–1532.

Crozier, M., Huntington, S. P., and Watanuki, J. (1975) *The Crisis of Democracy: Report on the Governability of Democracies to the Trilateral Commission*, New York: New York University Press.

Dahlum, S. and Knutsen, C. H. (2017) "Democracy by Demand? Reinvestigating the Effect of Self-Expression Values on Political Regime Type," *British Journal of Political Science*, vol. 47, no. 2, April, 437–461.

Dalton, R. J. (2004) *Democratic Challenges, Democratic Choices: The Erosion of Political Support in Advanced Industrial Democracies*, Oxford: Oxford University Press.

Dalton, R. J. and Shin, D. C. (2014) "Reassessing the Civic Culture Model," in Dalton, R. J. and Welzel, C. (eds.) *The Civic Culture Transformed: From Allegiant to Assertive Citizens*, New York: Cambridge University Press: 91–115.

Dalton, R. J., Shin, D. C., and Jou, W. (2007) *Popular Conceptions of the Meaning of Democracy: Democratic Understanding in Unlikely Places*, UC Irvine: Center for the Study of Democracy, available online: http://escholarship.org/uc/item/2j74b860.

Davidov, E., Meuleman, B., Cieciuch, J., Schmidt, P., and Billiet, J. (2014) "Measurement Equivalence in Cross-National Research," *Annual Review of Sociology*, vol. 40, July, 55–75.

de Jonge, C. P. K. (2016) "Should Researchers Abandon Questions About 'Democracy'? Evidence from Latin America," *Public Opinion Quarterly*, vol. 80, no. 3, Autumn, 694–716.

de Regt, S. (2013) "Arabs Want Democracy, but What Kind?," *Advances in Applied Sociology*, vol. 3, no. 1, March, 37–46.

Easton, D. (1957) "An Approach to the Analysis of Political Systems," *World Politics*, vol. 9, no. 3, April, 383–400.

Easton, D. (1975) "A Re-Assessment of the Concept of Political Support," *British Journal of Political Science*, vol. 5, no. 4, October, 435–457.

Foa, R. S. and Mounk, Y. (2016) "The Democratic Disconnect," *Journal of Democracy*, vol. 27, no. 3, July, 5–17.

Franklin, M. N. and Riera, P. (2016) "Types of Liberal Democracy and Generational Shifts: How Citizens' Views of Democracy Differ Across Generational Cohorts," in Ferrín, M. and Kriesi, H. (eds.) *How Europeans View and Evaluate Democracy*, Oxford: Oxford University Press: 111–129.

Fuchs, D. and Roller, E. (2006) "Learned Democracy? Support of Democracy in Central and Eastern Europe," *International Journal of Sociology*, vol. 36, no. 3, Autumn, 70–96.

Fuchs, D., Guidorossi, G., and Svensson, P. (1995) "Support for the Democratic System," in Klingemann, H-D. and Fuchs, D. (eds.) *Citizens and the State*, Oxford: Oxford University Press: 323–353.

Geddes, B. (1999) "What Do We Know About Democratization After Twenty Years?," *Annual Review of Political Science*, vol. 2, June, 115–144.

Gerschewski, J. (2013) "The Three Pillars of Stability: Legitimation, Repression, and Co-Optation in Autocratic Regimes," *Democratization*, vol. 20, no. 1, January, 13–38.

Gunther, R., Montero, J. R., and Torcal, M. (2007) "Democracy and Intermediation: Some Attitudinal and Behavioural Dimensions," in Gunther, R., Montero, J. R., and Puhle, H-J. (eds.) *Democracy, Intermediation, and Voting in Four Continents*, Oxford: Oxford University Press: 29–73.

Habermas. J. (1976) *Legitimation Crisis*, London: Heinemann.

Hadenius, A. and Teorell, J. (2005) "Cultural and Economic Prerequisites of Democracy: Reassessing Recent Evidence," *Studies in Comparative International Development*, vol. 39, no. 4, December, 87–106.

Haggard, S. and Kaufman, R. R. (1995) *The Political Economy of Democratic Transitions*, Princeton: Princeton University Press.

Heath, A., Fisher, S., and Smith, S. (2005) "The Globalization of Public Opinion Research," *Annual Review of Political Science*, vol. 8, June, 297–333.

Huang, M. H., Chang, Y. T., and Chu, Y. H. (2008) "Identifying Sources of Democratic Legitimacy: A Multilevel Analysis," *Electoral Studies*, vol. 27, no. 1, March, 45–62.

Huntington, S. P. (1991) *The Third Wave: Democratization in the Late Twentieth Century*, Norman: University of Oklahoma Press.

Inglehart, R. (1988) "The Renaissance of Political Culture," *American Political Science Review*, vol. 82, no. 4, December, 1203–1230.

Inglehart, R. (2003) "How Solid is Mass Support for Democracy – And How Can We Measure It?," *Political Science and Politics*, vol. 36, no. 1, January, 51–57.

Inglehart, R. and Welzel, C. (2005) *Modernization, Cultural Change, and Democracy: The Human Development Sequence*, New York: Cambridge University Press.

Kaase, M. and Newton, K. (1995) *Beliefs in Government*, Oxford: Oxford University Press.

Kittilson, M. (2007) "Research Resources in Comparative Political Behavior," in Dalton, R. J. and Klingemann, H-D. (eds.) *The Oxford Handbook of Political Behavior*, Oxford: Oxford University Press: 865–894.

Klingemann, H-D. (1999) "Mapping Political Support in the 1990s: A Global Analysis," in Norris, P. (ed.) *Critical Citizens: Global Support for Democratic Government*, Oxford: Oxford University Press: 31–56.

Kornberg, A. and Clarke, H. D. (1992) *Citizens and Community: Political Support in a Representative Democracy*, New York: Cambridge University Press.

Kriesi, H. and Morlino, L. (2016) "Conclusion: What Have We Learnt, and Where Do We Go from Here?," in Ferrín, M. and Kriesi, H. (eds.) *How Europeans View and Evaluate Democracy*, Oxford: Oxford University Press: 307–326.

Linde, J. (2012) "Why Feed the Hand That Bites You? Perceptions of Procedural Fairness and System Support in Post-Communist Democracies," *European Journal of Political Research*, vol. 51, no. 3, May, 410–434.

Linde, J. and Ekman, J. (2003) "Satisfaction with Democracy: A Note on a Frequently Used Indicator in Comparative Politics," *European Journal of Political Research*, vol. 42, no. 3, May, 391–408.

Linz, J. J. (1976) *The Breakdown of Democratic Regimes: Crisis, Breakdown, and Reequilibration*, Baltimore: Johns Hopkins University Press.

Linz, J. J. (2001) "Some Thoughts on Democracy and Public Opinion Research," in Katz, E. and Warshel, Y. (eds.) *Election Studies: What's Their Use*, Boulder: Westview Press: 83–110.

Lipset, S. M. (1959) "Some Social Requisites of Democracy: Economic Development and Political Legitimacy," *American Political Science Review*, vol. 53, no. 1, March, 69–105.

Listhaug, O. and Wiberg, M. (1995) "Confidence in Political and Private Institutions," in Klingemann, H-D. and Fuchs, D. (eds.) *Citizens and the State*, Oxford: Oxford University Press: 298–322.

Magalhães, P. C. (2014) "Government Effectiveness and Support for Democracy," *European Journal of Political Research*, vol. 53, no. 1, February, 77–97.

Magalhães, P. C. (2016) "Economic Evaluations, Procedural Fairness, and Satisfaction with Democracy," *Political Research Quarterly*, vol. 69, no. 3, September, 522–534.

Mattes, R. and Bratton, M. (2007) "Learning About Democracy in Africa: Awareness, Performance, and Experience," *American Journal of Political Science*, vol. 51, no. 1, January, 192–217.

Mishler, W. and Rose, R. (2001) "Political Support for Incomplete Democracies: Realist vs. Idealist Theories and Measures," *International Political Science Review*, vol. 22, no. 4, October, 303–320.

Montero, J. R., Gunther, R., and Torcal, M. (1997) "Democracy in Spain: Legitimacy, Discontent, and Disaffection," *Studies in Comparative International Development*, vol. 32, no. 3, September, 124–160.

Muller, E. N. and Seligson, M. A. (1994) "Civic Culture and Democracy: The Question of Causal Relationships," *American Political Science Review*, vol. 88, no. 3, September, 635–652.

Norris, P. (1999) "Introduction: The Growth of Critical Citizens?," in Norris, P. (ed.) *Critical Citizens: Global Support for Democratic Government*, Oxford: Oxford University Press: 1–27.

Norris, P. (2009) "The Globalization of Comparative Public Opinion Research," in Landman, T. and Robinson, N. (eds.) *The SAGE Handbook of Comparative Politics*, London: Sage Publications: 522–539.

Norris, P. (2011) *Democratic Deficit: Critical Citizens Revisited*, New York: Cambridge University Press.

Park, C. M. and Shin, D. C. (2006) "Do Asian Values Deter Popular Support for Democracy in South Korea?," *Asian Survey*, vol. 46, no. 3, June, 341–361.

Quaranta, M. (2017) "How Citizens Evaluate Democracy: An Assessment Using the European Social Survey," *European Political Science Review*, available online: https://doi.org/10.1017/S1755773917000054.

Quaranta, M. and Martini, S. (2016) "Does the Economy Really Matter for Satisfaction with Democracy? Longitudinal and Cross-Country Evidence from the European Union," *Electoral Studies*, vol. 42, June, 164–174.

Rohrschneider, R. and Loveless, M. (2010) "Macro Salience: How Economic and Political Contexts Mediate Popular Evaluations of the Democracy Deficit in the European Union," *Journal of Politics*, vol. 72, no. 4, October, 1029–1045.

Romero, V. F. (2004) "Developing Countries," in Greer, J. G. (ed.) *Public Opinion and Polling Around the World: A Historical Encyclopedia*, Volume 1, Santa Barbara: ABC-Clio: 485–490.

Schedler, A. and Sarsfield, R. (2007) "Democrats with Adjectives: Linking Direct and Indirect Measures of Democratic Support," *European Journal of Political Research*, vol. 46, no. 5, August, 637–659.

Shin, D. C. (2007) "Democratization: Perspectives from Global Citizenries," in Dalton, R. J. and Klingemann, H-D. (eds.) *The Oxford Handbook of Political Behavior*, Oxford: Oxford University Press: 259–282.

Singh, S. P. and Carlin, R. E. (2014) "Happy Medium, Happy Citizens: Presidential Power and Democratic Regime Support," *Political Research Quarterly*, vol. 68, no. 1, March, 3–17.

Staton, J. K. and Reenock, C. (2008) "Substitutable Protections: Credible Commitment Devices and Socioeconomic Insulation," *Political Research Quarterly*, vol. 63, no. 1, March, 115–128.

Torcal, M. and Moncagatta, P. (2011) "Political Support," in Badie, B., Berg-Schlosser, D. and Morlino, L. (eds.) *International Encyclopedia of Political Science*, Thousand Oaks: Sage: 2563–2566.

Wagner, A. F., Schneider, F., and Halla, M. (2009) "The Quality of Institutions and Satisfaction with Democracy in Western Europe – A Panel Analysis," *European Journal of Political Economy*, vol. 25, no. 1, March, 30–41.

Welzel, C. (2011) "The Asian Values Thesis Revisited: Evidence from the World Values Surveys," *Japanese Journal of Political Science*, vol. 12, no. 1, April, 1–31.

Welzel, C. (2013) *Freedom Rising*, New York: Cambridge University Press.

Welzel, C. and Inglehart, R. (2006) "Emancipative Values and Democracy: Response to Hadenius and Teorell," *Studies in Comparative International Development*, vol. 41, no. 3, September, 74–94.

Welzel, C., Inglehart, R., and Kruse, S. (2017) "Pitfalls in the Study of Democratization: Testing the Emancipatory Theory of Democracy," *British Journal of Political Science*, vol. 47, no. 2, April, 463–472.

Zmerli, S. and Newton, K. (2008) "Social Trust and Attitudes Toward Democracy," *Public Opinion Quarterly*, vol. 72, no. 4, Winter, 706–724.

34

GENERATIONAL REPLACEMENT

Engine of electoral change

Wouter van der Brug and Mark N. Franklin

Introduction

Generational replacement is one of the most important drivers of social and political change. This is because values and voting habits are acquired early in life and then remain relatively stable over time. The older people become, the more they tend to get "set in their ways" (Franklin 2004) and the less likely they are to change their habits, basic values and attitudes. Political events thus exert the strongest impact on the youngest voters who are not yet "set in their ways." To the extent that political attitudes and behavioral habits are acquired early in life during the most "formative years,"[1] and remain stable afterwards, generational replacement is the main driver of change. It works a bit like a diesel engine. It has a slow start, but continues to run for a long time.

To be clear, the habits we are talking about are not immutable. Having a "habit of voting" does not mean that one will turn out to vote at every election, and being a "habitual party supporter" does not mean that one will invariably support that party. Rather these habits provide a "home base" to which people generally return after any defection from behavior that conforms to the habit concerned.

In order to study the impact of generational replacement, one has to disentangle three types of effects, which all contribute to change over time: (1) life-cycle effects, which are changes that take place as a result of growing older, (2) cohort effects, which are stable differences between generations, and (3) period effects, which are social developments and events that potentially exert an effect on all generations and age groups (though perhaps not equally). While social scientists have long been aware of the importance of generational replacement as a driver of social change, most political scientists tend to ignore it because for several reasons it is notoriously difficult to study. The first is the fact that life-cycle effects, period effects and birth cohort effects are so highly interconnected that they are (statistically) difficult to disentangle. The year in which one was born follows logically from the combination of the year in which a survey was conducted and the age of the respondent.[2] So the only way to statistically disentangle the three effects is to estimate them while making one or more restrictions to the model – for instance, by assuming a linear effect of age and/or by clustering groups of respondents into larger "birth cohorts."

The second (albeit related) problem is a data issue. Ideally one would want panel data spanning several decades to study the stability and change of behaviors and attitudes at the individual level. A few such long-running panels exist (e.g., the British and German Household Surveys) but these contain few questions of interest to political scientists. Moreover, these long-running panels pose additional challenges, such as panel attrition. Finally, in such a dataset both the youngest and the oldest voters, those of greatest interest in any study of generational replacement, are not present in all waves.[3]

Because of these problems, scholars usually resort to studies at a more aggregated level, commonly known as cohort-level analyses, which compare aggregate statistics, such as the proportion of respondents with certain characteristics, across different birth cohorts at different moments in time. If the samples are randomly selected and sufficiently large, the assumption is that the subsample of each birth cohort is a representative sample of that generation. So, if a specific birth cohort were to systematically differ from other birth cohorts, controlling for year and age, this would be indicative of a generation effect. These designs require long time series but not panel data, and are thus the most common way to study life-cycle and generation effects. Generations are either defined by historical events that delimit or characterize their formative years (e.g., "the baby boom generation") or by systematically defined birth cohorts (e.g., born in the 1930s, 1940s, etc.). We focus on the second but mention the first in contexts where other scholars have done so.

The purpose of this contribution is to provide an overview of research on electoral change, with a specific focus on generational replacement. Because of a dearth of studies that take a generational approach to explaining partisanship decline, we include some original research on this topic. We begin with an inventory of the broader field of socialization research, how generations are distinguished and which are the "formative years" before turning to the main dependent variables in electoral research, turnout on the one hand and party support on the other.

Political socialization/learning

One of the most influential studies in electoral research, *The American Voter* (Campbell et al. 1960), introduced the concept of "Party Identification" (see Chapters 2 and 12 in this volume). The authors of *The American Voter* assumed that many voters would learn from their parents the values and partisan orientations that would characterize their adult lives – especially the link between social identity and partisanship. Jennings and Niemi (1968) presented convincing evidence in support of this notion, by means of surveys among young people and their parents (see also Jennings and Markus 1984; Jennings 2007). To the extent that people derive their political orientations through parental socialization, they would enter adulthood with established partisan loyalties. In such a world we would not expect there to be much political change. Each generation would have the same basic attitudes as the generations before them. So differences between generations would be small and election outcomes would be stable. This was indeed largely the case in the post-World War II period until the 1960s in most countries, with limited electoral volatility and remarkable stability of party systems, to the extent that these were characterized as "frozen" (Lipset and Rokkan 1967).

Yet, the political protests in the 1960s suggested that a large divide had emerged between the values and political orientations of the generation of post-war baby-boomers and their parents, which inspired new academic interest in the formation of political orientations and in the role of political events therein (for an overview, see Jennings 2007).

An important contribution came from Inglehart (1984), who argued that a widespread value shift was taking place, largely due to generational replacement, with members of the post-war generation prioritizing new concerns, which he called post-materialist values (see Knutsen in this volume). Yet, these shifts do not take place overnight, so he argues. Older generations who grew up in times of economic scarcity and who experienced World War II were more likely to give priority to material values, even after decades of peace and economic growth. A complete transformation of values would have to wait on the complete replacement of contemporary electorates with voters holding post-material values. Though challenging the parental socialization thesis, these findings strongly support the "formative years" hypothesis, which holds that pre- or early adult experiences carry more weight in people's values than events that occur later in life. It is not entirely clear though which exactly are the "formative years." Most political scientists tend to see the years of adolescence and early adulthood as the period in life that is most "formative." Yet, habits of partisanship (for those who did not "inherit" these) evidently can develop later – perhaps considerably later.[4]

While scholars do not deny that parents still play an important role in the socialization of young children and adolescents, Inglehart made it clear that the post-war generations did not simply "inherit" parental values and loyalties. Instead the dominant pattern found in contemporary research is that such values and loyalties are to a large extent acquired during young adulthood, when attitudes and behaviors are influenced by many from outside the home, such as friends, teachers and the media. Rather than being socialized into certain beliefs *before* entering the electorate, many citizens now learn their political orientations *after* having entered the electorate; and behavioral habits (in terms of turnout and party choice) arise from repeated behavioral affirmations (see Dinas 2014 and this volume; Bølstad, Dinas and Riera 2013).[5] So there seems to have been a reduction in the importance of parental socialization occurring with generations entering the electorates of their countries after the mid-1960s, with implications for learning processes.

The era of frozen party systems – when most voters supported the party (or parties) of their family's most salient social identity (generally religion, class or race/ethnicity) – did indeed come to an end in the period concerned, with the United States at the forefront in the 1950s and Italy bringing up the rear in the 1990s (Alford 1963; Franklin, Mackie and Valen 2009).[6] Given a lower rate of inherited partisanship, most young voters now spend their first adult decades acquiring one, as we will demonstrate below. So while older voters today are mostly tied to a particular party as "home base," in much the same ways as in earlier generations, younger voters are much freer to acquire a new partisanship (Gomez 2013), often overriding whatever socialization they may have received from their parents.

We now shift attention to the role of generational change in election outcomes, and focus on the two main dependent variables: turnout and party support.

Turnout and generations

The "engine of generational replacement" is particularly clear in the evolution of long-term change in electoral turnout, which has declined almost everywhere among advanced industrial democracies in recent years. To some extent, this decline is closely linked to the unfreezing of party systems mentioned above. People who are strong supporters of a party tend to vote for that party (Heath 2007), so the decline of partisanship especially among younger voters that occurred in the last quarter of the twentieth century was necessarily associated with a decline in the turnout of those young voters, yielding an overall decline in turnout that was quite marked in some countries, depending on the extent to which party systems moved into a state of flux. The importance of generational change is, however, more easily seen when it comes to institutional changes, such as the abolition of compulsory voting, the lowering of the voting age or the enfranchisement of women.

Figure 34.1 is adapted from Franklin (2004, Figure 3.4). The solid line shows precisely the long-term expectation for turnout evolution following a reform such as the abolition of compulsory voting. For such a reform, we expect an initial drop as all those whose habit of voting

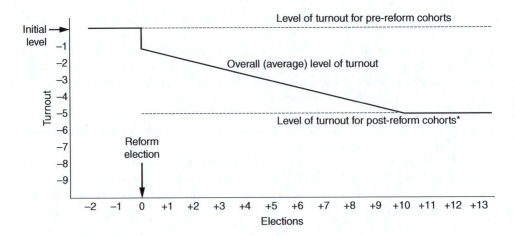

Figure 34.1 Expected evolution of turnout after the abolition of compulsory voting

Note
* These levels might be different in different countries.

is not yet established adjust their turnout to the new situation. This fall is then amplified over time as new cohorts of voters enter the electorate with a level of turnout suited to the new situation. On this graph, two dashed lines show turnout among established voters, unaffected by the change in election law, and among new voters once they become habituated to voting at the new level. The slope that we see occurs because the voters with one level of turnout are being replaced by voters with the other level of turnout. The figure is drawn on the overly simplistic assumption that, beyond the reform election itself (which sees some recently adult voters shifting to the new level), there are no other factors affecting aggregate level turnout. Franklin (2004) demonstrates that the expectation illustrated in Figure 34.1 is largely fulfilled over the countries he was studying.

As a real-world illustration, Figure 34.2 shows the match found in practice between the expected evolution of turnout depicted in Figure 34.1 and the actual evolution of turnout when

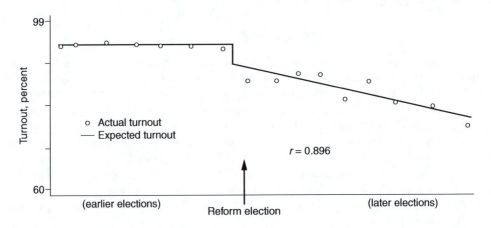

Figure 34.2 Expected compared with actual evolution of turnout after the abolition of compulsory voting (average of turnout in the Netherlands and Italy)

Source: IDEA turnout data: Italy 1972 to 2008; Netherlands 1948–2002.

we average the turnout seen in the only two countries among (then) established democracies that did abolish compulsory voting during the last half of the twentieth century. As can be seen, there is a good match between the actual turnout, averaged across successive elections before and after a reform occurring at very different times in each country, with turnout expected on the basis of generational replacement (for independent confirmation of the generational basis of Italian turnout decline, see Scervini and Segatti 2012). Prototypical expectations, also fulfilled, for other sorts of electoral reform are shown in Franklin (2004, Figures 3.2 and 3.3) – expectations applying to previously disenfranchised groups, such as 18–21 year olds along with women and immigrants.

Party support and generational change

Partisanship

The unfreezing of party systems referred to above has resulted in lower overall levels of partisanship (because so many younger voters have not yet acquired one) and higher levels of volatility as younger voters give support to new party offerings, perhaps voting for different parties in successive elections. Nevertheless, this malleability is curtailed as many voters eventually settle down to stable support for a single party, though not necessarily the same party as supported by their parents. Given the link between successive reaffirmations of vote choice and habitual behavior documented in Dinas (in this volume), there should be a relationship between partisanship and age: older voters should be more likely to be partisans, although such age differences may not always have been present.

Figure 34.3 shows clearly for a representative group of West European countries that it is quite unlikely for "new voters" in their early 20s and born after the 1950s to report feeling close to a party. Yet, as they grow older, this likelihood increases and there is much less difference between cohorts in the proportion of partisans among those 40 years old and more. The cohort born in the 1950s is the only exception. Apparently this cohort was born into circumstances that came close to matching those of earlier cohorts but then experienced a major period effect while not yet habituated to their initial circumstances, causing them to be transformed from behaving like older cohorts to behaving like younger cohorts, and apparently exemplifying for partisanship the "step" shown for turnout at the reform election in Figure 34.1. Seemingly, before that step was taken, partisanship was largely the result of parental transmission; after that step it had to be learned (we will address the nature of the step later in this section).[7]

Figure 34.4 shows essentially the same pattern for the United States (the wider confidence intervals are due to the smaller N), though with the period effect associated with the step we just referred to evidently occurring 20 years earlier (see also Alford 1963; Franklin, Mackie and Valen 2009). As in Europe, the patterns in the US suggest that at one time partisanship was passed from parent to child but that, starting in the 1960s, new cohorts began to enter the electorate with much lower partisanship, as reported by Nie, Verba and Petrocik (1979). Although Nie's study came too early to detect the fact that partisanship then increases with age among the younger US cohorts just as it does in Europe. So both in Europe and in the US there are more weak partisans today than used to be the case because young adults have lower partisanship than used to be the case. We observe the highest degrees of partisanship among the oldest cohorts, both in the US and in Europe (top three lines of both graphs). Cohorts already in the electorate but not well-established (born during the 1950s in Europe; during the 1930s in the United States) lose a degree of partisanship before recovering.[8] Later cohorts enter their electorates with ever-lower partisanship scores but nevertheless eventually acquire a degree of partisanship similar

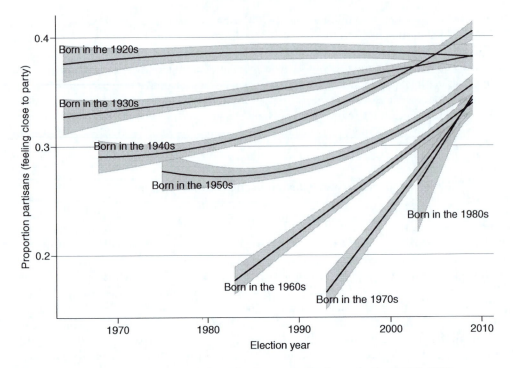

Figure 34.3 Proportion of Europeans feeling "close" to a party by electoral cohort, 1970–2010

Source: National election studies for a diverse group of European countries (Britain, Germany, Norway, Spain and Sweden), chosen as exemplars with long-running election studies of clear partisanship decline. Shaded areas are 95 percent confidence intervals.

to their elders. These are big cohort differences. The idea that change in partisanship has a major generational component was strongly present in Nie, Verba and Petrocik (1979), but more recent literature on partisanship decline, tends to overlook these generational differences.

As well as showing very distinct differences between the US and Europe in terms of the timing of partisanship decline our graphs also show differences in the overall strength of partisanship. In the US, the proportion of strong partisans is never less than about 50 percent and appears to rise to some 70 percent among older cohorts. In Europe, the percentage of those feeling close to a party can be little more than 10 percent among the youngest cohorts, rising to only about 40 percent among older cohorts. To some extent, this difference reflects differences in question wording and calibration, but it has also been well-established that party identification as a concept does not travel well from the United States to Europe (Holmberg 2007). In the Netherlands, and also in other multi-party systems, party identification seems rather to be a consequence of party support than a cause (see, for example, Thomassen 1976). Nevertheless, in both the US and in Europe the extent of partisanship remains an excellent indicator of the likelihood that people will (not) switch between parties, as well as of the likelihood that they will vote.

One cannot peruse Figures 34.3 and 34.4 without asking what it was that produced the sea change in the partisanship of post–World War II cohorts when young. Inglehart's theory (see above) does not answer this question because it does not address the mechanical impediment of previously inherited partisanship. The decline of cleavage politics (Franklin 2009) was about breaking a link between party choice and "inherited" social characteristics (mainly class and

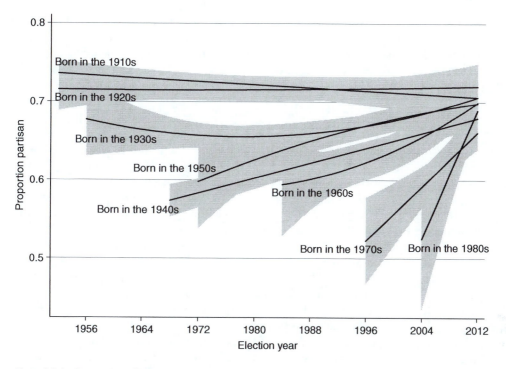

Figure 34.4   Proportion of US strong partisans by electoral cohort, 1952–2012

Source: American National Election Studies, 1952–2012, cumulative file. Shaded areas are 95 percent confidence intervals.

religion) that new voters shared with their parents.[9] The broken link showed itself partly in younger voters supporting a party other than the one associated with their social group and partly in their support for new parties not clearly associated with any social groups. Evidently this presumably tentative association between young voters and parties comes with the possibility that these young voters will not only support a party different from the one their parents supported but will also switch between parties, "trying out" one party after another until they settle on a party that they continue to support. Gomez (2013) documents the far higher volatility among younger than among older voters, which is evidently a concomitant of lack of partisanship. With the lower power of social cleavages to determine party choice the link to parental partisanship is also broken,[10] though over time any new basis for party choice may acquire inter-generational continuity and hence lower levels of volatility.

It should be possible to determine whether this volatility is cause or consequence of low partisanship (and whether the direction of causality is the same in Europe as in the US) but this topic is far beyond the remit of a handbook chapter (see Bowler, this volume, for more). We note, however, that if volatility is indeed the cause then, in the absence of renewed major volatility, overall partisanship should recover over time (as it has in recent years in the US). Of course major volatility can always return, as it has in the 2010s in many European countries, and the volatility approach to understanding the evolving cohort differences in levels of partisanship would lead us to expect a renewed drop in partisanship as a consequence.

Confirmation that partisanship is enhanced by behavioral consistency in party choice (Dinas, in this volume) explains the clear existence of a life-cycle effect among those reaching voting age in the contemporary period. The formation of party attachments has thus come to be a self-reinforcing mechanism, just like the mechanism we observed for turnout. At all events, it is clear that the oldest generations are least likely to change their longstanding party preferences and that any patterns of long-term change in party support are most likely to be observed among the youngest cohorts. This observation has strong implications for realignment processes.

Realignments of party systems

The word "realignment" describes large and longstanding changes in the character of a party system, often a change in the identity of the party holding a dominant position and usually of the policies implemented by the resulting government. How realignments come about has been a major concern in political science research for many years, but the sea change we described earlier introduced a discontinuity in the nature of such realignments. In the days of frozen party systems, realignments were cataclysmic events, but this is evidently not so true of the modern era. Today, realignments are more generally incremental than cataclysmic.

Given that people as they age get set in their ways, so that they develop certain behavioral regularities in terms of turnout and party support, we would assume that the set of considerations underlying party choice would also become stable over time. So someone who, based on religious values and beliefs, acquired a preference for a Christian Democratic Party during her most formative years will be unlikely to change this way of looking at the party system when she is 80 years old. Yet, a new voter, who is still learning her way around the party system and the main differences among the parties, is more likely to base her choice on issues that are currently most salient (see Knutsen in this volume). So realignments should have a strong generational component. Our literature search found this to be a very under-studied topic.

The massive European literature on realignment has focused traditionally on the decline of religious and class voting; a process that is visible across Western Europe in the last quarter of the twentieth century, but which began at different times in different countries (see, for example, Franklin 2009) and the few studies that looked at cohort differences in the factors determining the vote have confirmed that "cleavage voting," in terms of social class or religion, is most prominent among the oldest cohorts, which entered their electorates before the 1970s (see, for example, Franklin 2009; van der Brug 2010). But these studies do not include the most recent cohorts.

Evidently, in the contemporary era following the decline of cleavage politics, the engine of generational replacement can readily account for long-term change in party systems. The unfreezing of party systems opened up opportunities for new parties to compete for political support – especially green parties and far-right parties (Franklin and Rüdig 1995; van der Brug and van Spanje 2009). To the extent that young voters adopted habits of voting for such new parties, those parties will have tended to gain support over time as young voters aged and became "set" in their support for the parties concerned. To the extent that previously dominant parties failed to replace their supporters because of this movement toward new parties, established parties will in the same way have lost support. Such changes, once they engage the motor of generational replacement, become both progressive and enduring.

In the United States, Carmines and Stimson (1981, 1986, 1989) showed that electorates contain quite enough younger voters, lacking enduring party attachments, to account for relatively rapid change. They describe long-term change in party support in a manner that follows closely the logic set out above for long-term change in turnout, though it employs a different vocabulary. The "reform election" of turnout theory becomes a "critical moment" in issue evolution. Most such moments concern temporary defections of partisans who later return to their long-term party orientations. A few such moments, however, have more permanent effects "driven by normal population replacement" (1986: 902). The picture drawn for turnout in Figures 34.1 and 34.2 above is echoed in Meffert, Norpoth and Ruhil (2001), who explicitly build on Carmines and Stimson's logic and whose Figure 2 (Meffert, Norpoth and Ruhil 2001: 959) shows the same sharp drop followed by long-term reinforcement as shown in our Figures 34.1 and 34.2. However, Meffert, Norpoth and Ruhil make no direct reference to generational replacement as an engine of change, and we found this to be typical. Osborne, Sears and Valentino (2011) show that the oldest cohorts in the South were most resistant to the region-wide realignment of support from Democrats to Republicans, while at the same time they were most conservative in terms of their value orientations; but the generational implications are not addressed (see also Miller 1991; Abramowitz and Saunders 1998; Valentino and Sears 2005; Lewis-Beck et al. 2008). The arguments of Carmines and Stimson appear never to have been called into question but, though they are often referenced, neither are they used as building blocks for developing models of change based on generational replacement.

Few scholars, either in the US or elsewhere, recognize realignment processes as currently understood to differ in any important way from the processes that existed in the era of frozen cleavages, though Carmines and Stimson (1986: 902) observe that "[T]he critical moment is ... large enough to be noticeable, but considerably less dramatic than the critical election of traditional realignment theory." They do not address the question why this is so, but our earlier distinction between traditional partisan inheritance and contemporary partisan learning makes it clear that before the 1960s the US political world was distinctively different, just as was the European political world before the 1980s. And the classic first attempt at making sense of long-term change in US politics, found in Campbell et al. (1960), was written about that earlier world. In addressing the American "New Deal" realignment of the 1930s, these authors focus on new voters as engines of change and stress that it likely took more than one election to accomplish the realignment (Campbell et al. 1990: 525). Twenty years later, Andersen (1979a, 1979b) re-analyzed *The American Voter* data employed by Campbell et al. in order to reconstruct the 1930s electorate on the basis of recall of first vote. She showed how the huge increase in the size of the 1930s electorate due to late nineteenth century immigration could have supplied the votes needed to fuel the New Deal realignment without the need for massive conversion of existing voters.[11]

In Europe, the importance of new voters has been underlined by the evident role of successive enlargements of European electorates that happened with successive franchise extensions occurring in the late nineteenth and early twentieth centuries and repeatedly led to new party formation; and Franklin and Ladner (1995) demonstrated how the British realigning election of 1945, which saw the achievement of majority status by the British Labour Party, was fueled almost exclusively by generational replacement, using the same methodology as Andersen's (1979) reconstruction. Because there was no election in Britain between 1935 and 1945, the distinction between a realigning election and a realigning era is not relevant in the British case, which thus produces findings that can less readily be contested than the corresponding US findings (see note 11).

Carmines and Stimson (1981) repeatedly stress that generational replacement is a constant fact of life but does not become an engine of change in party support unless fueled by an important (generally emotionally charged) issue (see, for example, Carmines and Stimson 1981: 109). In the US, such issues have focused primarily on race, abortion and the role of the government in the economy. In Europe, they have also focused on the role of government and, more recently, on environmental and immigration concerns. When citizens base their party choice on different considerations than before, the relationships between parties and voters change, new conflict lines structure party competition, which in turn change the opportunities for the formation of governing coalitions in continental European countries and for a switch between dominant parties in the US and UK. Stimson and Carmines, along with other scholars studying change in US party systems, stress the role of party elites in fueling issue change, with voters falling into line behind new party positions. In Europe, we have seen such developments as well (Mrs. Thatcher's conservative revolution in Britain had widespread repercussions across other European countries). However, in Europe new parties are often the agents pushing new issues onto the political agenda, and thus driving realignment.

In sum, realignments of party systems occur mainly due to supply-side changes in what policies are on offer rather than to citizens changing their bases of party support (such changes may also be involved in the decline of cleavage politics described earlier, as proposed in Evans and Northmore-Ball, this volume); though the role of changing voter norms and concerns in providing opportunities for entrepreneurial initiatives should not be ignored (cf. Dalton 2015). At least some issues (those often seen as being part of the "socio-cultural dimension" such as immigration and European integration) are more important to young voters than to voters of earlier generations (Walczak, van der Brug and de Vries 2012), a finding confirmed by Wagner and Kritzinger (2012).

The role of left–right self-placement in relation to the left–right locations of parties is crucial in Europe, but research on generational differences in the effect of left–right location on the vote is scarce. Van der Brug (2010) found that left–right distances exert the strongest effect on party preferences for the generation socialized in the 1970s/1980s. A complicating factor is that new issues become part of the left–right dimension when these become politicized (see, for example, Kitschelt 2004; van der Brug and van Spanje 2009). Consequently, the meaning of the terms left and right change gradually over time. De Vries, Hakhverdian and Lancee (2013) demonstrated that, since the 1990s, left–right positions of Dutch voters have become gradually more correlated with attitudes toward immigration. Rekker (2016) showed that there is a clear generational pattern underneath this. In the older cohorts, secular-religious issues are most strongly correlated with left–right. In the middle-aged cohorts, a relatively strong correlation is found between left–right and civil liberties, while in the youngest cohorts, the correlation with attitudes toward immigration is relatively strong. It thus seems that new voters learn to orient themselves toward the party system through the lens of left–right locations. Yet, the issues that they associate with left and right are particularly the issues that are most salient to voters during their "formative years." It is likely that the same process occurs in the US in regard to the liberal–conservative dimension there, as suggested by Carmines and Stimson (1986). However, the evidence for this account of electoral realignments is still sketchy.

Conclusions and new avenues

In order to understand electoral change, or social change more generally, we need to be aware of the fact that the youngest cohorts of voters are the most likely to be affected by new developments and events, while the oldest cohorts are most resistant to change. Even though most electoral scholars are aware of this, there is no widely accepted methodology for incorporating processes of generational replacement into accounts of realignment processes.

Our contribution has focused on cohort differences in relation to three topics in electoral research: turnout, partisanship and the determinants of party support. As far as we can see, two areas require more research. The first is the matter of generational differences in the causal relationship between partisanship and party choice. Since the publication of *the American Voter* (Campbell et al. 1960), electoral researchers have assumed partisanship to be a stable political orientation that is acquired early in life and that structures party choice thereafter. However, the descriptive patterns that we have shown seem to clearly indicate that partisanship in the contemporary era only develops somewhat later, opening an opportunity for new behavioral norms such as those highlighted by Dalton (2015).

A second topic that requires (further) research is the extent to which different generations base their party choice on different sets of considerations. Evidence from Europe suggests that socio-cultural issues are more important determinants of the vote for younger than for older cohorts. Also, left–right orientations are more strongly correlated with socio-cultural issues among younger than older citizens. While this suggests that realignment involves not the arrival of a different dimension than left–right but rather the evolution of left–right itself as it acquires a new meaning, the evidence is a bit thin. In the US, there has been more work on the role of specific issues, but the role of generational replacement in bringing new issues to bear on party choice, though repeatedly affirmed, has been studied no more extensively than in Europe.

Notes

1 These are often known as "impressionable years."
2 Attempts to do so carry various risks that make it hard to unambiguously attribute effects to each component of the APC (age–period–cohort) framework. See contributions of Neundorf and Niemi (2014) for discussion.
3 Thus a panel study with waves fielded annually from 1970 to 1990 would contain no-one in the 1990 wave who reached voting age before 1970 (so no-one under 38 years old in 1990, 37 years old in 1989, and so on) and no-one who died before 1990 (so almost no-one over the age of 60 in 1970, 61 in 1971, and so on).
4 Developmental psychologists argue that basic orientations are already formed during (pre-) adolescent years (see, for example, Sapiro 2004; Campbell 2008; Hooghe 2004; Hooghe and Wilkenfeld 2008; Torney-Purta, Barber and Richardson 2004). However, for research on electoral processes, understanding the exact origins of such attitudes seems less urgent, which is why we do not dwell on this line of research.
5 A sea-change of this kind invalidates the expectations expressed by, for example, Wattenberg (2015) that behavioral patterns should be found to be the same in different eras, an important test for his contrary thesis.
6 The fact that party systems started to unfreeze a decade earlier than the decline of partisanship suggests that, if the connection was causal, cleavage decline caused lower partisanship (perhaps by way of increased volatility), but this must be the subject of future research.
7 When we break out the data for Britain, we see a renewed decline in partisanship in the youngest cohorts starting in the mid-1990s, perhaps a precursor of effects that will be seen in other countries as the volatility that accompanies anti-EU attitudes spreads across Europe, especially in the aftermath of the Great Recession. See below for more discussion on this point.
8 Van der Eijk and Franklin (2009), who show cohorts delineated by first election rather than by birth decade, also show such a fall and recovery for US cohorts born between 1935 and 1947 and entering the US electorate between 1956 and 1968 (Figure 7.1, page 181).
9 This approach does not fully answer the question either, though see van der Eijk et al. (2009) for a discussion of this point. But it gets closer to the mechanics involved, raising the question (discussed more fully below) whether post-material (or any other) values result from new party preferences rather than causing them.
10 Much controversy surrounds the question of whether and to what extent links between parties and social groups declined in the last third of the twentieth century (see Evans and Northmore-Ball in this volume). By focusing on the unfreezing of party systems rather than on the extent of class and religious voting we hope to bypass that controversy.
11 Andersen's conclusions were contested in a widely cited re-analysis of 1930s survey data (Erikson and Tedin 1981) but those data did not come from a random sample, and the conversions observed in those data may not have been enduring and may not have fueled the realignment. A still later reconstruction, based on the same and other 1930s data weighted to correct for sampling bias (Campbell 1985),

reaffirmed Andersen's findings based on 1950s recall data. However, US literature to this day (see, for example, Meffert, Norpoth and Ruhil 2001; Carmines and Wagner 2006; Campbell and Trilling 2014) tends to avoid addressing the role of newly eligible voters in fueling the evolution of party preferences, as already stated. However, these works often mention in passing the role of younger voters in being especially susceptible to new influences.

References

Abramowitz, A. I. and Saunders, K. L. (1998) "Ideological Realignment in the U.S. Electorate," *Journal of Politics*, vol. 60, no. 3, August, 634–652.

Alford, R. (1963) *Party and Society: The Anglo-American Democracies*, Chicago: Rand McNally.

Andersen, K. (1979a) "Generation, Partisan Shift, and Realignment: A Glance Back to the New Deal," in Nie, N. H., Verba, S. and Petrocik, J. R. (eds.) *The Changing American Voter*, 2nd Edition, Cambridge, MA: Harvard University Press: 74–95.

Andersen, K. (1979b) *The Creation of a Democratic Majority, 1928–1936*, Chicago: University of Chicago Press.

Bølstad, J., Dinas, E. and Riera, P. (2013) "Tactical Voting and Party Preferences: A Test of Cognitive Dissonance Theory," *Political Behavior*, vol. 35, no. 3, September, 429–452.

Brug, W. van der (2010) "Structural and Ideological Voting in Age Cohorts," *West European Politics*, vol. 33, no. 3, May, 586–607.

Brug, W. van der and Spanje, J. van (2009) "Immigration, Europe and the 'New' Cultural Dimension," *European Journal of Political Research*, vol. 48, no. 3, May, 309–334.

Campbell, A., Converse, P. E., Miller, W. E. and Stokes, D. E. (1960) *The American Voter*, New York: John Wiley and Sons.

Campbell, B. A. and Trilling, R. J. (2014) *Realignment in American Politics: Toward a Theory*, Austin: University of Texas Press.

Campbell, D. E. (2008) "Voice in the Classroom: How an Open Classroom Climate Fosters Political Engagement Among Adolescents," *Political Behavior*, vol. 30, no. 4, December, 437–454.

Campbell, J. E. (1985) "Sources of the New Deal Realignment: The Contributions of Conversion and Mobilization to Partisan Change," *The Western Political Quarterly*, vol. 38, no. 3, September, 357–376.

Carmines, E. G. and Stimson, J. A. (1981) "Issue Evolution, Population Replacement, and Normal Partisan Change," *American Political Science Review*, vol. 75, no. 1, March, 107–118.

Carmines, E. G. and Stimson, J. A. (1986) "On the Structure and Sequence of Issue Evolution," *American Political Science Review*, vol. 80, no. 3, September, 901–920.

Carmines, E. G. and Stimson, J. A. (1989) *Issue Evolution: Race and the Transformation of American Politics*, Princeton: Princeton University Press.

Carmines, E. G. and Wagner, M. W. (2006) "Political Issues and Party Alignments: Assessing the Issue Evolution Perspective," *Annual Review of Political Science*, vol. 9, June, 67–81.

Dalton, R. J. (2015) *The Good Citizen: How a Younger Generation is Reshaping American Politics*, Washington, DC: CQ Press.

Dinas, E. (2014) "Does Choice Bring Loyalty? Electoral Participation and the Development of Party Identification," *American Journal of Political Science*, vol. 58, no. 2, April, 449–465.

Eijk, C. van der and Franklin, M. (2009) *Elections and Voters*, London: Palgrave Macmillan.

Eijk, C., van der, Franklin, M., Mackie, T. and Valen, H. (2009) "Cleavages, Conflict Resolution and Democracy," in Franklin, M., Mackie, T. and Valen, H. (eds.) *Electoral Change: Responses to Evolving Social and Attitudinal Structures in Western Countries*, 2nd Edition, Cambridge: Cambridge University Press: 403–426.

Erikson, R. S. and Tedin, K. L. (1981) "The 1928–1936 Partisan Realignment: The Case for the Conversion Hypothesis," *American Political Science Review*, vol. 75, no. 4, December, 951–962.

Franklin, M. (2004) *Voter Turnout and the Dynamics of Electoral Competition in Established Democracies Since 1945*, New York: Cambridge University Press.

Franklin, M. (2009) "The Decline of Cleavage Politics," in Franklin, M., Mackie, T. and Valen, H. (eds.) *Electoral Change: Responses to Evolving Social and Attitudinal Structures in Western Countries*, 2nd Edition, Cambridge: Cambridge University Press: 381–402.

Franklin, M. and Ladner, M. (1995) "The Undoing of Winston Churchill: Mobilization and Conversion in the 1945 Realignment of British Voters," *British Journal of Political Science*, vol. 25, no. 4, October, 429–452.

Franklin, M. and Rüdig, W. (1995) "On the Durability of Green Politics: Evidence from the 1989 European Election Study," *Comparative Political Studies*, vol. 28, no. 3, October, 409–439.

Franklin, M., Mackie, T. and Valen, H. (eds.) (2009) *Electoral Change: Responses to Evolving Social and Attitudinal Structures in Western Countries*, 2nd Edition, Cambridge: Cambridge University Press.

Gomez, R. (2013) "All That You Can (Not) Leave Behind: Habituation and Vote Loyalty in the Netherlands," *Journal of Elections, Public Opinion and Parties*, vol. 23, no. 2, 134–153.

Heath, O. (2007) "Explaining Turnout Decline in Britain, 1964–2005: Party Identification and the Political Context," *Political Behavior*, vol. 29, no. 4, December, 493–516.

Holmberg, S. (2007) "Partisanship Reconsidered," in Dalton, R. J. and Klingemann, H-D. (eds.) *The Oxford Handbook of Political Behavior*, Oxford: Oxford University Press: 557–570.

Hooghe, M. (2004) "Political Socialization and the Future of Politics," *Acta Politica*, vol. 39, no. 4, December, 331–341.

Hooghe, M. and Wilkenfeld, B. (2008) "The Stability of Political Attitudes and Behaviors across Adolescence and Early Adulthood: A Comparison of Survey Data on Adolescents and Young Adults in Eight Countries," *Journal of Youth Adolescence*, vol. 37, no. 2, February, 155–167.

Inglehart, R. (1984) "The Changing Structure of Political Cleavages in Western Society," in Dalton, R. J., Flanagan, S. C. and Beck, P. A. (eds.) *Electoral Change in Advanced Industrial Democracies: Realignment or Dealignment?* Princeton: Princeton University Press: 25–69.

Jennings, M. K. (2007) "Political Socialization," in Dalton, R. J. and Klingemann, H-D. (eds.) *The Oxford Handbook of Political Behavior*, Oxford: Oxford University Press: 29–44.

Jennings, M. K. and Markus, G. B. (1984) "Partisan Orientations Over the Long Haul: Results from the Three-Wave Political Socialization Panel Study," *American Political Science Review*, vol. 78, no. 4, December, 1000–1018.

Jennings, M. K. and Niemi, R. G. (1968) "The Transmission of Political Values from Parent to Child," *American Political Science Review*, vol. 62, no. 1, March, 169–184.

Kitschelt, H. (2004) *Diversification and Reconfiguration of Party Systems in Postindustrial Democracies*, Bonn: Friedrich Ebert Stiftung.

Lewis-Beck, M. S., Jacoby, W. G., Norpoth, H. and Weisberg, H. F. (2008) *The American Voter Revisited*, Ann Arbor: University of Michigan Press.

Lipset, S. M. and Rokkan, S. (1967) (eds.) *Party Systems and Voter Alignments: Cross-National Perspectives*, Volume 7, New York: Free Press.

Meffert, M. F., Norpoth, H. and Ruhil, A. V. (2001) "Realignment and Macropartisanship," *American Political Science Review*, vol. 95, no. 4, December, 953–962.

Miller, W. E. (1991) "Party Identification, Realignment, and Party Voting: Back to the Basics," *The American Political Science Review*, vol. 85, no. 2, June, 557–568.

Neundorf, A. and Niemi, R. G. (2014) "Beyond Political Socialization: New Approaches to Age, Period, Cohort Analysis," *Electoral Studies*, vol. 33, March, 1–6.

Nie, N. H., Verba, S. and Petrocik, J. R. (1979), *The Changing American Voter*, 2nd Edition, Cambridge, MA: Harvard University Press.

Osborne, D., Sears, D. O. and Valentino, N. A. (2011) "The End of the Solidly Democratic South: The Impressionable Years Hypothesis," *Political Psychology*, vol. 32, no. 1, February, 81–108.

Rekker, R. (2016) "The Lasting Impact of Adolescence on Left–Right Identification: Cohort Replacement and Intracohort Change in Associations with Issue Attitudes," *Electoral Studies*, vol. 44, December, 120–131.

Sapiro, V. (2004), "Not Your Parents' Political Socialization: Introduction for a New Generation," *Annual Review of Political Science*, vol. 7, June, 1–23.

Scervini, F. and Segatti, P. (2012) "Education, Inequality and Electoral Participation," *Research in Social Stratification and Mobility*, vol. 30, no. 4, December, 403–413.

Thomassen, J. (1976) "Party Identification as a Cross-National Concept: Its Meaning in the Netherlands," in Budge, I., Crewe, I. and Farlie, D. (eds.) *Party Identification and Beyond: Representations of Voting and Party Competition*, London: John Wiley: 263–266.

Torney-Purta, J., Barber, C. H. and Richardson, W. K. (2004) "Trust in Government-Related Institutions and Political Engagement Among Adolescents in Six Countries," *Acta Politica*, vol. 39, no. 4, December, 380–406.

Valentino, N. A. and Sears, D. O. (2005) "Old Times There are Not Forgotten: Race and Partisan Realignment in the Contemporary South," *American Journal of Political Science*, vol. 49, no. 3, July, 672–688.

Vries, C.E. de Hakhverdian, A. and Lancee, B. (2013) "The Dynamics of Voters' Left/Right Identification: The Role of Economic and Cultural Attitudes," *Political Science Research and Methods*, vol. 1, no. 2, December, 223–238.

Wagner, M. and S. Kritzinger (2012) "Ideological Dimensions and Vote Choice: Age Group Differences in Austria," *Electoral Studies*, vol. 31, no. 2, June, 285–296.

Walczak, A., van der Brug, W. and de Vries, C. (2012) "Long- and Short-Term Determinants of Party Preferences: Inter-Generational Differences in Western and East Central Europe," *Electoral Studies*, vol. 31, no. 2, June, 273–284.

Wattenberg, M. P. (2015) *Is Voting for Young People?*, New York: Routledge.

PART VI

Methodological challenges and new developments

35

SELECTING THE DEPENDENT VARIABLE IN ELECTORAL STUDIES: CHOICE OR PREFERENCE?

Cees van der Eijk

One of the central questions in electoral research concerns the understanding of individual behavior that, in the aggregate, produces election outcomes. This chapter focuses on that aspect of this behavior that involves electoral support for parties or candidates, while only cursorily touching upon the electoral participation aspect. The apparent simplicity of the notion of party support does not encourage conceptual reflection on the phenomenon under study, which can be referred to in terms of either *choice* (between parties or candidates) or *preference*. These two terms are very frequently treated as synonyms. Yet, there are good reasons to keep them conceptually distinct, and doing so has practical consequences for the way they are studied.

In Downs' (1957) seminal theory of the electoral interactions between electoral entrepreneurs and voters, he conceptualizes *choice* as resulting from a comparison of *preferences* (which he refers to as "utilities"). He postulates that voters have preferences for each of the options from which, under most electoral systems, they can choose only one; implying that the process that results in choice consists of two stages. In a first stage, individuals assess their preference for each choice-option; the process that generates these preferences can be summarized in a preference function (sometimes also referred to as a utility function). In the second stage, a decision rule determines the choice on the basis of these preferences (this is usually seen as selecting the option that has the highest preference). It has to be emphasized that Downsian utilities refer to variables whose values can range from low to high, which is somewhat different from ordinary parlance where the term "preference" is often synonymous with "preferred," referring only to high values on such a variable ("my preference is for the Liberals"). In spite of the fact that Downs' contribution has been of immense influence on electoral studies over a considerable period of time, this conceptual distinction between preferences and choice, and the practical implications of that distinction, has been widely overlooked. This is evident from the content of election surveys, which invariably include questions about electoral choice, but not always (actually, quite often not) about electoral preferences.

Elections constrain the expression of voters' electoral preferences. Most electoral systems allow only a single option to be chosen. Systems that allow the ranking of parties, such as the alternative vote (AV) or the single transferable vote (STV), impose other constraints – for example, by preventing more than one party from being ranked first (respectively, second etc.) in preference order on the ballot. Because of such constraints, choice reflects only a single aspect of the underlying preferences, namely which of the preferences was highest. Choice does thus not reflect other aspects of the underlying preferences, such as the strength of preference for the chosen option (ranging from "least-repugnant" to "best-that-can-be"), or how much better the chosen option is compared to other ones (ranging from "no-noticeable-difference" to a "wide chasm"). The only inference about preferences that can therefore be made from choices is the relative preference of one of the options (the one that is chosen) versus all other ones. These limitations have long been recognized by scholars such as Converse (1974: 742–743), Sartori (1976: 338–339) and Powell (2000: 160), who all emphasize that the constrained character of the ballot (and of survey questions about choice) do not provide a suitable basis for the observation and analysis of citizens' preferences regarding the options from which they can choose.

To overcome these limitations, so-called "non-ipsative" measures of electoral preferences have been developed which are increasingly more often included in election survey studies. The term "ipsative" refers to constraints imposed on the expression of preferences, such as "choose only one," that generate dependencies in the observed preferences for the various options (under the "choose only one" constraint, the observation that party A is chosen implies that all other parties are not chosen). Choices thus tell us little about the underlying "non-ipsative" preferences. To avoid unnecessary jargon, such non-ipsative preferences for parties will be referred to in this chapter as *multiple party preferences*. Survey questions about multiple party preferences ask respondents to report the strength of their preference for each (or for the most important) of the parties available. There are various ways in which these strengths of preferences can be solicited. The simplest form is by way of a dichotomy between "preferred" and "non-preferred" parties, as in a "pick any that apply" task. More nuances of strength can be expressed when some kind of rating scale is employed (e.g., when asking for scores between 0, which reflects not preferred at all, and 10, which reflects very strongly preferred).[1] Since the 1990s, such measures have spawned a variety of innovations in the study of support for political parties along with related phenomena of electoral participation, electoral competition and the comparative analyses of elections and electoral behavior.

Varieties of multiple party preferences

Multiple party preference data are available in many contemporary election studies, and exist predominantly in a few "flavors" which differ regarding what it is about parties that is preferred to a greater or lesser degree. The oldest is the so-called "feeling thermometer" used in the American National Election Studies (ANES). Respondents are requested to indicate on a scale from 0 to 100 how "warm or favorable" (respectively, how "cold or unfavorable") they feel for each of the parties about which they are being questioned, with the midpoint (50) as a neutral point ("no feeling at all"). This is a long-running question in the ANES, and has also been included in election surveys in other countries, although more rarely as a long-running question. A second form in which multiple party preferences are asked is the so-called "likes-dislikes" question that has become a recurring element in the data collected as part of the Comparative Study of Electoral Systems (CSES) and therefore also of all national election studies in which the CSES is incorporated. This question asks respondents to indicate (usually on a scale of 0 to 10) how strongly they "like" or "dislike" each of the parties for which the question is asked. The third popular form in which multiple preferences are asked was first introduced in 1982 in the Dutch Parliamentary Election Study (DPES) where it has been a recurring question ever since. This question has been included in a growing number of national election studies as well as in the European Parliament Election Studies (EES) where it has become one of the core questions asked in all studies since 1989. This question, which has become known as the "propensity to vote" question (PTV), asks respondents to indicate (usually on a scale from 0 to 10) "how likely it is that you will ever vote for" each of the parties for which the question is asked. A more recent way of eliciting multiple party preferences derives from the so-called "consideration set" approaches that focus not on all parties on offer, but only those that voters "consider" to vote for (cf. Wilson 2008; Oskarson et al. 2016). Some surveys contain questions about parties respondents consider voting for (which is a straightforward and dichotomous "pick any that applies" task for respondents). As yet the development and validation of such questions is still in its infancy.[2]

The main difference between these various existing kinds of multiple preference measures lies in what the respondents are asked to express. The feeling thermometer and likes-dislikes questions most clearly seem to focus on affect, while the PTV and "which parties do you consider" questions focus more directly on electoral preferences of the kind conceptualized by Downs (1957). Some surveys have asked two, or even three, of these kinds of questions to the same respondents, which makes it possible to compare responses in terms of the extent to which they match actual party choice. After all, in Downs' view, the party yielding the highest preference should be the one chosen, which implies that a relatively simple test of construct validity consists of assessing the extent to which respondents' choices accord with their highest preferences. Such comparisons (based on Dutch, Irish and British national election study data) yield the following conclusions. The proportion of respondents who choose the party to which they give the highest preference is highest for the PTV questions, somewhat lower for the likes-dislikes and much lower for the feeling thermometer. For the PTVs, this concordance between most-preferred party and party voted for is generally far in excess of 80 percent, often even in excess of 90 percent.[3] In terms of construct validity, this means that feeling "warm" or "cold" is evidently something else than electoral preference, although as an indicator of affect it may well be one of the drivers thereof. These, and other validating analyses, indicate PTVs as the most valid indicators for Downsian electoral preferences, with likes-dislikes as a somewhat weaker but acceptable alternative (Tillie 1995; van der Eijk et al. 2006; van der Eijk and Marsh 2011).

Choice or preferences: when to focus on which?

Analysts interested in electoral support for parties sometimes have a decision to make about the kind of variable on which to focus: choice, or multiple preferences. If datasets include, for the political systems and elections that they are interested in, information on multiple preferences as well as choice, which of these should they focus on, and why? The answer to this question is mainly dependent on the research problem that they want to address and, to some extent, also on the kind of political system that they study.

The substantive questions that analysts may want to pursue with respect to parties' electoral support can be distinguished into *party-specific* questions on the one hand, and *systemic* or *generic* questions on the other hand. Party-specific questions focus on the factors and conditions that drive electoral choice for a given party, such as "what is the association between religious affiliation and voting for the CDU/CSU" (in Germany), or "does the working class still support the Labour Party" (in Britain), or "to what extent do Democrats depend on the support of Latinos" (in the USA)? Such questions are not only of interest to political analysts, but also to journalists, politicians and interested citizens. The second kind of question, which we refer to here as "generic," focuses on the structure of the process that underlies choices. Such questions are of the kind "what drives party choices *in general*: religion, class or ethnicity?" Or, "what is more important for party choice *in general*: party characteristics or leader characteristics?" Or, "under which conditions do issues of the day trump long-term ideological orientations?" In such research questions, we refer to "a party," a generic entity, rather than to "Party A," a specific party.

These different kinds of research interests – party-specific and generic questions – generally require different analytical strategies, and possibly different kinds of data, except in the specific (and exceptional) context of elections in which only two parties or candidates compete. In an election between only two contenders, both kinds of questions can be answered by a single binary logistic regression of electoral choice on attitudes, orientations and group membership of voters. This is because any given factor that benefits one of the parties harms the other party to the same degree. But in a multi-party context this does not hold. A multinomial logit analysis will in principle address party-specific questions via party-specific coefficients of contrasts between each party and a reference party. But the plethora of coefficients generated by such analyses will not provide a straightforward answer to generic research questions. This is because a factor that benefits one of the parties may at the same time benefit some of the other parties as well, while hurting yet other ones, and not all of this can be expressed in a single coefficient. One common approach to deal with this problem is by applying some kind of discrete-choice modeling, amongst which conditional logit analysis is probably the most popular variety. This approach has a number of advantages. Owing to the "long" or "stacked" data format used in such analyses it becomes possible to incorporate party characteristics (e.g., party size) as variables explaining party preferences, which is not possible in multinomial logistic analysis (cf. Alvarez and Nagler 1998). On the other hand, it is difficult in conditional logit analysis to incorporate respondent characteristics that for the same respondent do obviously not vary across parties. This leads often to hybrids of conditional logit and multinomial logistic models, which become increasingly more cumbersome as the number of choice options increases and which still contain (in their multinomial parts) party-specific coefficients that defy unequivocal expression of their importance in the choice process. An additional problem of conditional logit is the presence of unobserved heterogeneity, as parties are only distinguished in terms of "chosen" (category 1, assigned to only one party) and "not chosen" (category 0, assigned to all other parties), with the "0" category plausibly being heterogeneous in terms of electoral preference. It is particularly here – when addressing generic research questions in multi-party contexts – that multiple party preferences become a useful approach (as elaborated below).

If one has available empirical information about multiple preferences as well as about electoral choice, and one studies a multi-party context, then one should consider focusing on multiple preferences when interested in generic questions. Party-specific questions can then generally be well addressed by focusing on electoral choice, although even there multiple preferences may add relevant detail. In a two-party context, generic and party-specific questions can both be largely addressed by a focus on electoral choice, although here, too, analyses of multiple preferences may add useful detail.[4]

Analyzing multiple party preferences

Multiple preference questions provide a separate variable for each of the parties for which the question is asked. These can be used in at least two different ways when studying the bases of electoral support: separately (which addresses party-specific questions) or jointly (which addresses generic questions).

Analyzing multiple preferences separately – for each, or for some, or conceivably for only one of the parties for which they have been asked – is particularly useful for addressing party-specific, descriptive and politically relevant questions about the electoral relationships between various individual characteristics (including group memberships) and political parties. In particular, these preference variables provide detail that cannot be obtained from traditional kinds of analyses that describe from which groups the various parties obtain votes. By tracing the strength of support for a party in a variety of segments of the population (defined by their demographic, socio-economic, residential or media-usage characteristics, or by their ideological orientations or involvement with particular issues), these analyses can depict differences in intensity of preferences for various parties. Such analyses can also usefully illuminate the competitive structure of party support, by identifying groups where a political party may gain additional votes (because that party is highly favored even if not actually voted for), or where the votes it gets are under threat of defection to other parties (for which support is almost as great even if not realized in terms of votes). Such information is of obvious relevance for the market segmentation and resource allocation strategies that are part of modern election campaigning. Moreover, multiple preferences also help alleviate the common problem of small numbers of observations that analysts of the electoral basis of small parties encounter. In a well-designed sample of (say) 1000 respondents, only some 50 respondents will have chosen or intend to choose a party that obtains, for example, 5 percent of the vote. Such small numbers severely limit how detailed the analysis can be of the support base of small parties. When using multiple preferences, however, all respondents in the sample are asked to express their electoral preference for the party in question, thus providing a much larger basis for analysis. Moreover, because the responses contain more variance (ranging from no preference to very strong preferences), they also provide a more productive basis for exploring correlates and possible drivers of electoral preferences. These advantages are even greater because when respondents provide multiple preferences they are not hindered by indecision about choice between several parties (which often leads to "don't know" responses to a choice question), or by non-voting (which leads to an "inapplicable" coding for a choice question). Although largest for small parties, these advantages also apply to larger ones.[5] Given these advantages, it is little wonder that multiple preferences are increasingly used for the analysis of electoral support of individual parties, both by practitioners involved in the running and management of campaigns and by academic analysts (cf. van der Brug et al. 2000, 2009; Mellon and Evans 2016; Vezzoni and Mancosu 2016).

Yet, party-specific analyses have clear limitations when trying to answer more general questions about the overall importance of factors driving electoral preferences and choice, irrespective of whether they are based on choices or on multiple preferences. Does class outweigh religion in determining party support? Do leader evaluations become more important over time? Is left/right ideology less important in newly established democracies? Party-specific analyses of support or choice cannot answer such questions as they yield a different result for each party. This problem becomes even more pressing when one realizes that coefficients from separate regression analyses of multiple preferences for different parties are incomparable because of distributional differences. How important are, for example, ideological orientations for voters' electoral preferences? When analyzing multiple preferences separately, the answer to this question will be clear, but different for each party. Consider, for example, the correlation between multiple preferences for parties on the one hand and respondents' left/right positions on the other. For a right-wing party, the relationship is likely to be strongly positive (being right-wing resulting in stronger preferences for a right-wing party). For a left-wing party, the relationship is likely to be strongly negative, while the relationship might appear to be close to zero for a centrist party (only because the relationship is non-linear). To solve this problem, a form of analysis is required that considers the multiple preferences for all parties jointly. Such a procedure is also required to avoid another problem inherent in analyzing electoral preferences separately for each of the parties: the omission of explanatory variables that only vary between parties, but that are constant for each party separately.[6] Party size or parties' government/opposition status are such factors which are often hypothesized to matter in voters' preferences, but which cannot be assessed on the basis of separate, party-specific analyses.

Analyzing electoral preferences for all parties jointly can be done by shifting the unit of analysis from the respondent to the response: a respondent's stated preference for a particular party (this yields a "long" or "stacked" data structure in which every respondent is represented by as many records as there are parties for which preferences have been asked). This is analogous to how conditional logit analysis structures data, with the party voted for coded "1" and all other parties coded "0." The main difference is that with conditional logit analysis this variable is constrained (only one preference is non-zero) and dichotomous. Multiple preferences such as likes-dislikes and PTVs are empirically much richer and more informative, reflecting more gradations both in absolute levels of preference and in the degree to which one party may be preferred to other ones.[7] The stacked structure of the data requires that many explanatory variables have to be defined in terms of relationships between the individual and party in question; thus, in order to assess the importance of left/right ideology in a stacked data arrangement, the relevant variable is not respondents' left/right *position* (as it would be in a "wide" data arrangement where each of the multiple preferences is a separate variable) but instead the left/right *distance* between the respondent and each of the parties in question. For some kinds of variables, this is relatively easy to do (at least if the necessary data are available), but for other variables, such as demographics or attitudes, the relationship or "affinity" between respondents and parties has to be constructed in the form of synthetic variables (De Sio and Franklin 2011). Procedures to accomplish this exist[8] and, when applied, provide the possibility to analyze all multiple preferences jointly as a single, generic variable (i.e., preference for a party). This in turn allows explanatory analyses of this generic variable that can incorporate the following different kinds of explanatory variables:

- *Individual-specific variables*, which are characteristics of respondents. The values of these variables vary between individuals for each party, but not between parties for each individual. Examples include demographics, attitudes, etc. Coefficients for these variables reflect the effect of voter characteristics on preferences for all parties;
- *Party-specific variables*, which are characteristics of parties. The values of these variables vary between parties for each individual, but not between individuals for each party. Examples are parties' size, government status, etc. Coefficients for these variables reflect the effect on preferences of party characteristics that are the same for all respondents;
- *Individual-party affinities*, which are characteristics of respondent-party dyads. The values of these variables vary between parties for each individual, and also between individuals for each party. Examples are distances in ideological or issue dimensions or sympathy scores for the leaders of parties, but also synthetic affinities that express how attractive each of the parties is for a respondent given their demographic characteristics, attitudes, etc. (see note 8). Coefficients for these variables reflect the effect on preferences of party-respondent distance or affinity;
- Interactions between these kinds of variables.

Preference scores for multiple parties can, when structured in the stacked form, thus be analyzed in the following general form:

$$PP_{ij} = a + \sum_{k=1}^{k} b_k R_{ik} + \sum_{m=1}^{m} b_m P_{jm} + \sum_{q=1}^{q} b_q D_{ijq}[+ \text{ possible interactions}] + e_{ij} \qquad [1]$$

where PP represents party preferences, one for each combination of respondents (i) and parties (j), R_{ik} represents respondents' scores on k different individual characteristics; P_{jm} represents parties' scores on each of *m* different party characteristics; and D_{ijq} represents the scores of all $i \times j$ respondent–party dyads on *q* different dyadic characteristics.[9] This approach is a straightforward application of Przeworski and Teune's (1970) recommendation to climb the ladder of abstraction by replacing specific (non-comparable) phenomena by more general (and hence more comparable) ones, and to replace proper names by theoretically relevant characteristics.

Use of multiple preferences in comparative research

Analyses of multiple party preferences in the generic form described above do not lead to conclusions about specific parties, but instead to conclusions about party preferences in general, and the factors that generate higher or lower preferences. This is of particular interest for comparative electoral studies because this generic perspective on party preferences provides a solution to the endemic problems caused by the fact that party systems are qualitatively different in different countries (and sometimes also at different moments in a single country). Traditionally, comparisons between political systems of choices or preferences for political parties have resorted to one of several solutions to this problem, none of which was quite satisfactory. One solution consists of replacing parties by party families which are supposed to be more comparable across countries than are the individual parties.[10] This poses additional problems, such as what typology of party families to use; and how to classify parties in such a typology (particularly parties that do not easily fit within any of the families, such as, for example, Sinn Féin in Ireland). A second traditional approach to the incomparability of party systems is to distinguish the parties on the basis of some dichotomy: government versus opposition, or left versus right, or working class vs. others,[11] and so forth. In this approach, too, the assumption is that the dichotomous distinction is more comparable between political systems than the separate parties are. This approach often creates the same problem of where to place particular parties, and almost always creates a problem of unobserved heterogeneity in one or even in both of the categories distinguished. A third way that has traditionally been used to deal with the incomparability of party systems consists of characterizing parties by their location on a single dimension (for instance, left/right) that is supposed to be of dominant importance in all countries to be compared. This solution reduces the problem of arbitrary classification, but makes the implausible assumption that other characteristics of parties are irrelevant for voters' preferences.[12]

The generic perspective on party preferences discussed above solves these problems. It does not ask who is, or is not, attracted to a particular party, or to the parties of a particular party family, or to, for example, left parties, but instead it asks "what makes a party attractive to a citizen?" and it answers that question in a form (reflected in the equation at the end of the previous section) that is equally applicable to all parties and all citizens in all political systems under consideration. Survey data containing multiple preferences from different political systems can thus be pooled in a single analysis in which respondents' preferences for political parties (in stacked form) constitute the dependent variable and with the same kinds of variables distinguished in equation 1 as independents.[13] Such a data structure is obviously hierarchical in character, necessitating a multi-level analysis with responses (to the party preference questions) as level 1 units, respondents as level 2 units, parties cross-classified as a different set of level 2 units, and political systems as level 3 units.

Some of the first wide-ranging applications of this approach are Oppenhuis (1995) and van der Eijk and Franklin (1996), which both used 1989 and 1994 European Parliament Election Study data.

Additional analytical uses of multiple party preferences

Multiple party preferences are powerful instruments in the analysis of electoral support for political parties. However, they are also important as the empirical basis for other phenomena in the realm of electoral research, most notably electoral participation and electoral competition and the quality of electoral supply. Without going into great detail, this section summarizes these kinds of uses.

Multiple party preferences and electoral participation

It should come as no surprise that preferences for parties are highly predictive of whether or not citizens go to the polls. If none of the parties on offer engenders enthusiasm (as expressed in responses to multiple preference questions), there is little reward in voting. For a respondent to vote, at least one party should be sufficiently highly preferred.[14] What is "sufficiently high" cannot be determined on the basis of first principles, but has to be assessed empirically, and may differ for different kinds of respondents and different contexts. Irrespective of the kind of preference scores used, levels of turnout increase monotonically with the magnitude of the highest preference score. Yet the relationship is distinctly not linear. Drop-off of turnout rates occurs particularly when (on a PTV scale from 0 to 10) the highest preference drops below 7, while values below 5 correspond to almost total abstention. Interestingly, multiple preferences allow detailed assessment of the importance of two often hypothesized conditions of non-voting: alienation and indifference, particularly in multi-party systems.[15] Analyses based on CSES data (using the likes-dislikes measure of preferences) demonstrate that alienation is a very potent force driving electoral abstentions, while effects of indifference are much weaker (Falk Pedersen, Dassonneville and Hooghe 2014; Aarts and Wessels 2005).

Multiple party preferences, electoral competition and the quality of electoral supply

Survey questions about multiple party preferences provide a basis for measuring and analyzing party competition or the quality of the electoral supply side, by deriving from these multiple preferences a variety of other measures pertaining to individuals, parties, sets of parties and of entire party systems.

For individual respondents, their responses to multiple preference questions can be used to operationalize alienation from the party system and indifference toward the choices on offer, as noted above in the discussion of electoral participation. Another measure that can be derived from preferences for different parties is the magnitude of the difference (the "gap") between highest and next highest preference. For some respondents, the two most preferred parties are tied (making the gap zero), for some it is small, and for others it is large(r). This measure has been found to be strongly related to party-switching: those with a small gap have a much higher likelihood of switching than those with a larger gap. This measure is therefore particularly useful for managers of political campaigns who aim to identify those who are subject to intense electoral competition and who may therefore easily change their actual choice within a relatively short period such as, for example, during an election campaign.[16] In academic usage the likely switchers are of particular interest in counterfactual analyses, focusing on how election outcomes would change if certain conditions were to be different (cf. van der Brug et al. 2007: 137–169).

At the level of political parties the set of multiple preference scores can be used to derive plausible estimates of the vote share that they maximally could obtain, and thus also of the complementary share of the electorate that, for all practical purposes, is beyond their reach. Such potential vote shares are unrealistic in the sense that they can only be obtained if, simultaneously, all relevant conditions favor the party in question and at the same time undermine its competitors. They are nevertheless important for political practitioners as evidence-based criteria of what is and what is not possible regarding electoral performance under given competitive circumstances.[17] A party's potential vote share is often considerably larger than its actual or predicted magnitude because of electoral competition, which manifests itself in the overlap of these potential vote shares across multiple parties. These overlaps are generated by respondents who have relatively high preferences for several parties at the same time. Such multiple high preferences (i.e., small "gaps" between preferences for the most preferred parties) are in European countries extremely common.[18] The extent of overlap between parties' potential vote shares can easily be calculated and reflects the effective electoral competition between them.[19] These competitive relationships can be assessed for a party vis-à-vis any other party (or set of other parties), or for groups of parties vis-à-vis each other (e.g., the "left" parties versus the "right" parties), and all of these can easily be visualized in Venn-like diagrams. Further refinements consist of distinguishing for each party the competitive risks (potential vote switching away from the party in question by those who do or intend to vote for it) and the competitive opportunities (vote switching toward a party by those who do or intend to vote for another party). These various kinds of competitive relationships can be further specified by identifying the demographic or attitudinal profiles of the groups involved. From an academic perspective, analyses such as these are particularly important to analyze the factors underlying changing patterns of electoral competition and their consequences for electoral outcomes. Van der Eijk and Elkink (2017), for example, identify how generational replacement and cohort effects contributed to the dramatic Irish parliamentary election outcome of 2011 in which the incumbent Fianna Fáil lost almost 60 percent of its vote share.[20]

At yet a higher level of aggregation, entire political systems or party systems can be characterized in terms of degree and structure of electoral competition, by using various kinds of aggregations of the individual- or party-level characteristics discussed above. Alienation from the party system can be defined at the individual level, but aggregation leads to the measurement of party systems in terms of the degree of alienation that they engender among its citizens, or (when perceived from the opposite perspective) the quality of electoral supply. It then becomes a contextual variable that itself can be used as the phenomenon to be explained (what explains variations in alienation between countries?) or as an independent variable (what are the consequences of such variations between countries?).

Concluding remarks

Empirical data on multiple party *preferences*, in addition to data on electoral *choice*, provide large and important benefits to analysts of elections, electoral behavior and electoral competition. One of the most important of these is the possibility to model the relationships between voters and parties very flexibly in a generic way. For the study of multi-party systems, multiple preferences are indispensable to address such questions, while even for two-party systems they will provide useful added insights. As discussed, the advantages over more traditional discrete choice models include a reduced reliance on (sometimes heroic) assumptions,[21] the avoidance of unaccounted-for heterogeneity, and the straightforward possibility of pooling data from multiple political systems (with their qualitatively different party systems) in a single model. The advantages of multiple preference questions for party-specific and descriptive research interests include the enormous increase in the number of relevant observations which allow more detailed comparisons between subgroups such as cohorts than would be possible if only information on choice would be available. Moreover, empirical information on preferences is more detailed than the coarse black-and-white of choice distinctions. Both aspects provide more statistical power than any analysis based on choice. The advantages of multiple preference questions for the study of electoral competition lie not only in the detail of relevant information, but particularly in the possibility they provide for comparing the competitive situations in which different parties find themselves at the point in time at which the questions are asked.

Moreover, multiple preferences yield, much more than choice, relevant information for non-academic stakeholders in electoral research: parties, politicians, campaign managers and interested citizens.

These advantages come, of course, at the price of a greater pressure on questionnaire space than if one were to only ask about *choice*. Yet, in all instances where questions about multiple preferences were included in surveys, the investment has paid off handsomely. If, therefore, one overarching and compelling conclusion can be drawn from this chapter, it is that surveys about electoral behavior and support for parties should include questions about multiple party preferences.

Compared to analyses of survey data about choice, which now rely on accumulated experience of some 50 to 75 years (depending on the country one looks at), experiences with analyses of multiple preferences are still relatively limited. For many countries, the inclusion of such questions in election surveys is a recent departure or one that has not yet occurred. But the analysis of multiple preferences is certainly not in its infancy, and it can be expected that the passage of time will propel important innovations with respect to data collection, statistical and analytical procedures, and theoretical insights. In the next edition of this handbook, this chapter should reflect such progress.

Notes

1 Much more refined is magnitude estimation of strength of preferences, which yields interval-level measurement, and which is useful to calibrate the ordinal information obtained from rating scales (for an example, see Tillie 1995).

2 The consideration set approach does not necessarily require dedicated survey questions and can be based on the other multiple preference questions discussed above (cf. Bochsler and Sciarini 2010).

3 The Irish National Election Study (INES) of 2002 is the only large-scale study in which these three kinds of multiple measures were all included. The concordance between multiple preferences and choice was 87 percent for PTV, 83 percent for likes-dislikes and 65 percent for the thermometer question (cf. Van der Eijk and Marsh 2011). The same rank order of performance has been found in large-scale studies that incorporated two of these three kinds of questions.

4 In two-party contests multiple preferences allow more incisive analyses of electoral participation and of electoral competition, as described later in this chapter.

5 In many multi-party systems, a vote share of some 30 percent is sufficient to make a party one of the "large" ones. Depending upon registration procedures this may represent a considerably smaller segment of the voting-age population, as illustrated by the British Conservative Party, which polled almost 37 percent of the votes in 2015 but was supported by only 24 percent of the voting-age population. As a consequence, numbers of respondents having voted for a "large" party in a representative sample may be disappointingly limited.

6 These same issues are equally problematic when analyzing choices in a multinomial logistic analysis.

7 Moreover, multiple preferences avoid the problem of unobserved heterogeneity in conditional logit analysis that was already mentioned earlier and which generally leads to biased estimates; this advantage is mostly lost, however, when only focusing on the most strongly preferred parties, as is done in the consideration set approach, as that approach restricts the variance of the dependent variable.

8 Several approaches to the construction of such synthetic affinity variables exist. One is the so-called "y-hat" procedure (cf. van der Eijk and Franklin 1996: Chapter 20; van der Eijk et al. 2006); another

procedure is based on the application of Joint Correspondence Analysis (cf. Franklin and Weber 2014). Yet another, widely used by sociologists, compares individual characteristics with the average for all supporters of each given party, producing a "quasi-distance" measure that is comparable across parties.

9 As the data structure is clustered, a multi-level specification of this model is necessary if the residuals display significant intra-class correlation; for examples, see Franklin and Renko (2013).

10 Examples of the reduction of party systems to a set of party families include Marks et al. (2002), Ennser (2012) and Knutsen (2013).

11 Reducing a party system to a dichotomy is commonplace in much of the literature on economic voting, using the distinction between government and opposition parties (cf. Andersen 1995; Lewis-Beck and Paldam 2000); for a critique of this approach, see van der Brug et al. (2007: 9–15). Such a reduction on the basis of a different dichotomy was also used by Franklin et al. (1992, 2009), who use a binary distinction between "left" and "right" parties. Yet another binary distinction underlies well-known indices of class-voting (cf. Alford 1962), and many analyses of particular kinds of parties, such as extreme right parties (cf. van der Brug et al. 2000).

12 Examples of the reduction of party systems to a single dimension include Dalton (2008), and, in dichotomized form, Franklin et al. (1992, 2009).

13 Obviously, for these situations, equation 1 has to be extended, at least in principle, with a class of independent variables pertaining to the political system and, possibly, interactions thereof in order to take account of any system-specific deviations from a common pattern of effects.

14 This implies the need in many analyses of a new variable created as the maximum of the responses to the party preference questions.

15 Alienation would be reflected inversely in the magnitude of the highest preference, and indifference would be reflected in ties between preference scores for different parties.

16 Respondents who claim to be "undecided" are not, as is often thought, necessarily tied in their party preferences. If we ask undecided voters about their preferences for different parties, we often find many of them with a party that is well ahead of all others in terms of preferences. "Undecided" then indicates that the respondent has not yet focused on the decision that they need to make.

17 The following episode illustrates this. In the mid-1980s, Dutch opinion polls showed that one of the political parties in the country would lose virtually all of its parliamentary seats at the next election. This led to a grassroots appeal for its leader to be replaced by a charismatic predecessor. Before taking action, the latter wanted to know whether there was any realistic hope of success. An analysis of multiple preferences revealed that the party's realistic potential electorate was far from negligible, which persuaded the former leader to again take charge of the party, and within weeks the party had regained in the polls its former strength (a situation that continued until the next parliamentary election). This was only possible because for many voters their preferences for this party were high, but just shy of being their first (highest) preference. The change of leadership increased their preference for the party by just a little, but sufficiently for it to become their highest preference.

18 Kroh et al. (2007) estimate that in 1999 more than 40 percent of citizens across the EU countries have a gap of no more than 1 (on a PTV-scale of 0–10) between their two most preferred parties.

19 Competition is here conceptualized in terms of openness on the demand side, referred to by Bartolini (2002) as availability. This emphasizes not the outcome of competition, but the range of counterfactual outcomes that can ensue from it, a perspective also emphasized by Elkins (1974).

20 These authors also provide a set of formal equations for the definition of these, and yet other, such relationships.

21 This is elaborated in more detail in van der Eijk et al. (2006).

References

Aarts, K. and Wessels, B. (2005) "Electoral Turnout," in Thomassen, J. (ed.) *The European Voter: A Comparative Study of Modern Democracies*, Oxford: Oxford University Press: 64–83.

Alford, R. (1962) "A Suggested Index of the Association of Social Class and Voting," *Public Opinion Quarterly*, vol. 26, no.3, Fall, 417–425.

Alvarez, R. M. and Nagler, J. (1998) "When Politics and Models Collide: Estimating Models of Multiparty Elections," *American Journal of Political Science*, vol. 42, no. 1, January, 55–96.

Andersen, C. (1995) *Blaming the Government: Citizens and the Economy in Five European Democracies*, Armonk: M. E. Sharpe.

Bartolini, S. (2002) "Electoral and Party Competition: Analytical Dimensions and Empirical Problems," in Gunther, R., Montero, J. R. and Linz, J. (eds.) *Political Parties – Old Concepts and New Challenges*, Oxford, Oxford University Press: 84–110.

Bochsler, D. and Sciarini, P. (2010) "So Close but So Far: Voting Propensity and Party Choice for Left-Wing Parties," *Swiss Political Science Review*, vol. 16, no. 3, Autumn, 373–402.

Brug, W. van der, Eijk, C. van der and Franklin, M. (2007) *The Economy and the Vote – Economic Conditions and Elections in Fifteen Countries*, Cambridge: Cambridge University Press.

Brug, W. van der, Fennema, M. and Tillie, J. (2000) "Anti-Immigrant Parties in Europe: Ideological or Protest Vote?," *European Journal of Political Research*, vol. 37, no. 1, January, 77–102.

Brug, W. van der, Hobolt, S. and de Vreese, C. (2009) "Religion and Party Choice in Europe," *West European Politics*, vol. 32, no. 6, November, 1266–1283.

Converse, P. E. (1974) "Some Priority Variables in Comparative Electoral Research," in Rose, R. (ed.) *Electoral Behavior: A Comparative Handbook*, New York: The Free Press: 727–745.

Dalton, R. J. (2008) "The Quantity and the Quality of Party Systems: Party System Polarization, Its Measurement, and Its Consequences," *Comparative Political Studies*, vol. 41, no. 7, February, 899–920.

De Sio, L. and Franklin, M. (2011) "Generic Variable Analysis: Climbing the Ladder of Generality with Social Science Data," Paper presented at the 2011 European Conference on Comparative Electoral Research, Sofia, December 1–3.

Downs, A. (1957) *An Economic Theory of Democracy*, New York: Harper and Row.

Eijk, C. van der, Brug, W. van der, Kroh, M. and Franklin, M. (2006) "Rethinking the Dependent Variable in Voting Behaviour – On the Measurement and Analysis of Electoral Utilities," *Electoral Studies*, vol. 25, no. 3, September, 424–447.

Eijk, C. van der and Elkink, J. A. (2017) "How Generational Replacement Undermined the Electoral Resilience of Fianna Fáil," in Marsh, M., Farrell, D. M. and McElroy, G. (eds.) *A Conservative Revolution? Electoral Change in 21st Century Ireland*, Oxford: Oxford University Press: 102–122.

Eijk, C. van der and Franklin, M. (eds.) (1996) *Choosing Europe? The European Electorate and National Politics in the Face of Union*, Ann Arbor: The University of Michigan Press.

Eijk, C. van der and Marsh, M. (2011) "Comparing Non-Ipsative Measures of Party Support," Paper presented at the 2011 European Conference on Comparative Electoral Research, Sofia, December 1–3.

Elkins, D. E. (1974) "The Measurement of Party Competition," *American Political Science Review*, vol. 68, no. 2, June, 682–700.

Ennser, L. (2012) "The Homogeneity of West European Party Families: The Radical Right in Comparative Perspective," *Party Politics*, vol. 18, no. 2, February, 151–171.

Falk Pedersen, E., Dassonneville, R. and Hooghe, M. (2014) "The Effect of Alienation and Indifference Toward the Party System on Voter Turnout, A Comparative Analysis," Paper presented at the 2014 Belgian-Dutch Political Science Conference, Maastricht, June 12–13.

Franklin, M. and Renko, M (2013) "Studying Party Choice," in Bruter, M. and Lodge, M. (eds.) *Political Science Research Methods in Action*, Basingstoke: Palgrave Macmillan: 93–118.

Franklin, M. and Weber, T. (2014) *A Structuring Theory of Electoral Politics*, Unpublished Manuscript, available online: www.trincoll.edu/~MarkFranklin/Structuring_UBC_w_appendix.pdf.

Franklin, M., Mackie, T. and Valen, H. (eds.) (1992) *Electoral Change: Responses to Evolving Social and Attitudinal Structures in Western Countries*, New York: Cambridge University Press.

Franklin, M., Mackie, T. and Valen, H. (eds.) (2009) *Electoral Change: Responses to Evolving Social and Attitudinal Structures in Western Countries*, Colchester: ECPR Press.

Knutsen, O. (2013) "Party Choice," in Keil, S. I. and Gabriel, O. W. (eds.) *Society and Democracy in Europe*, London: Routledge, 244–269.

Kroh, M., van der Brug, W. and van der Eijk, C. (2007) "Prospects for Electoral Change," in van der Brug and van der Eijk (eds.) *European Elections and Domestic Politics – Lessons from the Past and Scenarios for the Future*, Notre Dame: University of Notre Dame Press: 236–253.

Lewis-Beck, M. and Paldam, M. (2000) "Economic Voting: An Introduction," *Electoral Studies*, vol. 19, no. 2–3, June, 113–122.

Marks, G., Wilson, C. J. and Ray, L. (2002) "National Political Parties and European Integration," *American Journal of Political Science*, vol. 46, no. 3, July, 585–594.

Mellon, J. and Evans, G. (2016) "Class, Electoral Geography and the Future of UKIP: Labour's Secret Weapon?," *Parliamentary Affairs*, vol. 69, no. 2, April, 492–498.

Oppenhuis, E. V. (1995) *Voting Behavior in Europe: A Comparative Analysis of Electoral Participation and Party Choice*, Amsterdam: Het Spinhuis.

Oskarson, M., Oscarsson, H. and Boije, E. (2016) "Consideration and Choice: Analyzing Party Choice in the Swedish European Election 2014," *Scandinavian Political Studies*, vol. 39, no. 3, September, 242–263.

Powell, G. B. (2000) *Elections as Instruments of Democracy*, New Haven: Yale University Press.

Przeworski, A. and Teune, H. (1970) *The Logic of Comparative Social Inquiry*, New York: Wiley-Interscience.

Sartori, G. (1976) *Parties and Party Systems: A Framework for Analysis*, Cambridge: Cambridge University Press.

Tillie, J. (1995) *Party Utility and Voting Behavior*, Amsterdam, Het Spinhuis.

Vezzoni, C. and Mancosu, M. (2016) "Diffusion Processes and Discussion Networks: An Analysis of the Propensity to Vote for the 5 Star Movement in the 2013 Italian Election," *Journal of Elections, Public Opinion and Parties*, vol. 26, no. 1, February, 1–21.

Wilson, C. J. (2008) "Consideration Sets and Political Choices: A Heterogeneous Model of Vote Choice and Sub-National Party Strength," *Political Behavior*, vol. 30, no. 2, June, 161–183.

36

THE QUEST FOR REPRESENTATIVE SURVEY SAMPLES

Laura Stoker and Andrew McCall

Survey research is in the midst of an era of extraordinary new developments and challenges. People have increasingly moved away from having landline telephones to having mobile phones or no phone at all, which poses new challenges for all aspects of telephone surveying. Response rates continue to deteriorate for face-to-face (FTF) and – especially – telephone surveys. Web-based surveying is booming, with platforms proliferating and the use of nonprobability samples on the rise.

An enormous literature on survey methods has arisen in response to these and other developments. The searchable, online bibliography created by Websm.org (www.websm.org/), which compiles materials on survey methods, contains nearly 5,000 entries from the past ten years alone. Efforts to generalize about developments in the field are hindered by the vastness of this literature and by the fact that technological, social, and political conditions bearing on survey research are rapidly changing and variable across nations. It is often not clear whether findings from studies carried out a decade ago still apply to today, nor whether findings from studies of one country are germane to another.

This chapter considers developments related to the quest for representative survey samples. We begin by discussing the decline in survey response rates, which has prompted new thinking about how response rates relate to sample bias, how to design a survey so as to minimize sample bias, what to use in lieu of the response rate as an index of the representativeness of a survey, and how to construct an optimal weighting scheme. We then briefly review the evolution of thinking about the value of nonprobability survey samples and conclude by drawing attention to two issues worthy of further research.

Declining response rates and their consequences

Survey response rates have continued their now decades-long pattern of decline. Most studies documenting response rate trends have focused on US-based surveys, but similar trends have been found worldwide (Groves 2011). A recent overview estimates the rate of decline to be three times larger for telephone than for FTF surveys in the US (Tourangeau and Plewes 2013). Whereas the response rates for the FTF American National Election Studies were at or above 70 percent for studies from 1980–1992, they dropped steadily to a low of 49 percent by 2012. The telephone-based US Survey of Consumer Attitudes showed even more dramatic response rate declines, from 72 percent in 1979 (Curtin, Presser, and Singer 2005) to 16 percent in 2013 (Dutwin and Lavrakas 2016). Over a more recent period (1997 to 2012), response rates for a "typical" Pew Research Center (Pew) telephone survey fell from 36 percent to 9 percent, while those for a "high effort" survey dropped from 61 percent to 22 percent (Kohut et al. 2012). The substitution of mobile phones for landlines is partially fueling these trends, as contact and non-response rates are lower for respondents contacted by mobile phones (Kohut et al. 2012). Yet, response rates are dropping for both landline and mobile phone samples (Dutwin and Lavrakas 2015, see also Brick and Williams 2013). Government-sponsored surveys in the US have managed to maintain high response rates, though they too have evidenced modest declines. Panel attrition rates appear to be holding steady (Schoeni et al. 2013).

Alarm over declining response rates has been tempered by research showing that the extent of bias in survey estimates is at best weakly related to the survey response rate. Some studies have followed one or more survey projects over time, examining whether the extent of bias grew as the response rate declined (see, for example, Kohut et al. 2012), while others have compared contemporaneous surveys to see if the extent of bias in a given survey can be predicted by its rate of response (see, for example, Groves 2006). In both cases, the answer is essentially no. Still other studies have experimentally varied respondent incentives (see, for example, Martin, Helm-schrott, and Rammstedt 2014) or fieldwork strategies (see, for example, Groves and Peytcheva 2008) and showed that such variations have significant effects on response rates but insignificant effects on sample bias.

Furthermore, evidence is accumulating that the bias is often minimal even when response rates are low, especially if survey estimates are adjusted for non-response through effective weighting techniques (see, for example, Holbrook, Krosnick, and Pfent 2008; Keeter et al. 2000; Kohut et al. 2012). That said, it is also typical to find a large degree of variability across survey measures in the extent of bias that is evident. For example, weighted results from a Pew survey with a 9 percent response rate matched the benchmark Current Population Survey (CPS) data for voter registration, but exceeded the CPS results by 21 percent and 28 percent for the percentage contacting public officials and reporting volunteer work, respectively (Kohut et al. 2012).

To make sense of these findings, researchers have turned to formal models of survey non-response that were initially developed in the mid-1970s (Groves 2006; Bethlehem 2010; Beth-lehem and Biffignandi 2011; Bethlehem, Cobben, and Schouten 2011). Most influential here is the stochastic non-response model, which depicts each potential respondent as having a latent probability, P, of responding to the survey. This model shows that bias in the sample mean of a given variable, Y, is influenced by three factors related to P. First of all, bias increases with the degree of correlation between P and the survey response itself (Y) – that is, with the extent to which people's likelihood of responding to the survey is correlated with the responses they would provide. Bias disappears if this correlation is zero. Otherwise, bias in the sample mean of Y grows as the mean of P declines – that is, as the overall response rate declines – and as the vari-ance of P increases – that is, as the probability of responding becomes more variable within the population one is sampling from. The worst case scenario arises when potential respondents vary dramatically in their propensity to respond, when that propensity to respond is strongly corre-lated with the variable(s) of interest, and when the overall rate of response is low. Figure 36.1 illustrates how the magnitude of the bias depends upon all three factors considered together.[1]

The Y axis in Figure 36.1 is the extent of the bias in the sample mean of Y assuming that the standard deviation (SD) of Y is 20. Y could be thought of as a 0–100 feeling thermometer rating scale, where SDs in the range of 20 points are common. The X axis shows response rates ($\bar{P}$) varying from a low of 10 percent to a high of 95 percent. The four sets of results in the figure

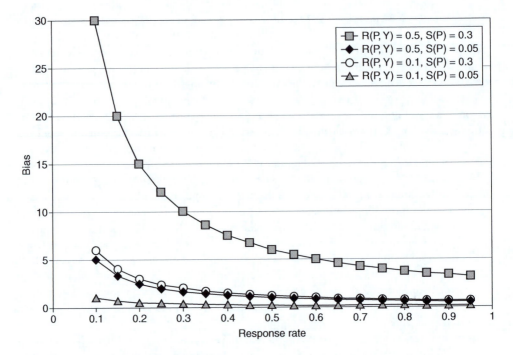

Figure 36.1 Bias in the sample mean as a function of non-response patterns

vary the correlation between Y and the probability of a response, P (either low at 0.10 or high at 0.50), and the SD of P (either low at 0.05 or high at 0.30).[2]

Two main conclusions can be drawn from Figure 36.1. First, bias is much worse when one faces the combination of a high correlation between P and Y and high variation in P. Even if that correlation is high ($R(P, Y) = 0.50$), bias will be minor so long as people do not vary dramatically in their propensity to respond ($S(P) = 0.05$) – even when the response rate is poor. Likewise, even if people vary dramatically in their propensity to respond ($S(P) = 0.30$), bias will be minor so long as the correlation between Y and P is low ($R(P, Y) = 0.10$) – again, even when the response rate is poor. In either of these scenarios, bias only begins to exceed 2 points on the 0–100 scale when the response rate dips below 30 percent. Second, the effect of declining response rates for bias in the estimation of population means is decidedly nonlinear, with the most serious problems arising when response rates become very low. For example, in each of the scenarios the effect on bias as the response rate drops from 30 percent to 10 percent is 3.5 times greater than the effect as the response rate drops from 70 percent to 30 percent.

Importantly, the stochastic non-response model applies just as well to self-selected survey samples as it does to probability survey samples. Although in the former there is no design-based probability of selection, each individual in the population of interest can still be thought of as having a given propensity to participate. Bias in opt-in surveys will be accentuated when those propensities are highly variable, highly correlated with target variables, and the overall rate of response is low. The model can also be elaborated to distinguish between bias that comes from population units being systematically underrepresented within the sample frame ("undercoverage") and bias due to non-response. As discussed by Bethlehem (2010), Callegaro, Manfreda and Vehovar (2015), Groves (2006), and Singer and Ye (2010), among others, these can work in complementary as well as contradictory directions to affect the overall probability of a response and its correlation with target variables. For example, older people are less likely than younger people to have internet access, but response rates among those who do have internet access are higher among the old than the young. This diminishes the extent of bias in web surveys for age and its correlates. On the other hand, bias in socioeconomic status (SES) and its correlates is accentuated by the fact that people with low SES are both less likely to have internet access and to respond to a survey if they do.

It is also worth emphasizing that a high correlation between P and Y will do more than bias sample estimates of population means. It can also affect inferences about associations between variables. When Y refers to a dependent variable, that correlation indexes the degree of what Heckman (1979) and a vast subsequent literature refers to as sample selection bias. Bivariate associations (e.g., correlations, regression coefficients) relating Y to any X will be biased toward zero, and multivariate associations will be biased in effectively unpredictable ways. The survey research literature does make this connection though infrequently and usually then in discussions about weighting (see, for example, Brick 2013; Winship and Radbill 1994). Designers as well as users of survey data need to worry about sample selection bias if they are estimating relationships among variables even if they are unconcerned about the accuracy of the sample means.

At least three developments in the field of survey research have been fueled by the emergence of a clearer understanding of how response rates relate to sample bias – new thinking about how to design the survey so as to minimize sample bias, about what to use in lieu of the response rate as an index of the representativeness of a survey, and about the development of optimal weighting schemes.

Survey researchers have long sought to design surveys so as to optimize the response rate conditional on a budget constraint, thinking that as the response rate increased, so too would the representativeness of the sample. Researchers now realize that efforts to improve response rates can be ineffective or even backfire if they increase the variance of P or increase the correlation of P and Y. Groves and Heeringa (2006: 448–451) describe a study – probably not atypical – in which the procedures used in the last phase of fieldwork led interviewers to focus their efforts on completing interviews with people who were judged to have a high probability of responding. These procedures were a cost-effective way to maximize the response rate that the study could achieve. However, it is likely that such procedures would have increased the variance of P and the correlation of P with any number of Ys, at least when compared to procedures that would have attempted to improve response rates among those with a lower propensity to respond.

Survey researchers are now increasingly aiming to develop fieldwork procedures that follow "adaptive" (Luiten and Schouten 2013; Schouten, Calinescu, and Luiten 2013) and "responsive" (Groves and Heeringa 2006; Särndal 2011) design principles. Adaptive design makes use of data available ahead of time to set forth fieldwork strategies that will enhance representativeness. Responsive design breaks the fieldwork period into phases, using data from earlier phases to select fieldwork procedures for later phases, with the same objective in mind. For example, data from initial fieldwork can yield estimates of P and proxies for Ys, which can be used to determine bias-minimizing procedures for the phases to come. Researchers are also looking anew at procedures developed to increase response rates, such as the use of mixed mode designs (see, for example, Couper 2011; Stern, Bilgen, and Dillman 2014), interviewer incentives (see, for example, Peytchev et al. 2010) and respondent incentives (see, for example, Pforr et al. 2015; Singer and Ye 2013), among others (Kreuter 2013). Research has consistently shown, for example, that respondent incentives increase response rates, with the effects of money greater than those of gifts or lotteries and increasing with the size of the payment, and with the effects of prepaid incentives greater than those of contingent incentives. Now the urgent questions concern whether and which procedures reduce non-response bias: Do incentives have larger effects on those already predisposed to respond? Is non-response bias reduced by providing larger incentives for those predisposed against responding?[3]

Efforts are also underway to develop new measures for indexing the quality or representativeness of a survey sample, which thus far includes R–indicators, H–indicators, and the FMI Index. The R–indicator is the standard deviation of $\hat{P}$, as estimated using data on both non-respondents and respondents for a full set of covariates, while the Partial R–indicator is the same but estimated using only a subset of the covariates (Schlomo, Skinner, and Schouten 2012; Schouten, Cobben, and Bethlehem 2009). The R–indicator is proposed as a measure of overall survey quality, while the Partial R–indicator can be used to determine which covariates are especially relevant to the probability of a response. One problem is that neither R–indicator incorporates data on target variables, Ys, and thus neither considers the extent to which P and Y are correlated. Särndal and Lundström's (2010) H3 is comparable to the R–indicator in that it aims to index the representativeness of a survey, overall, using data on auxiliary variables for respondents and non-respondents but not data on Y. However, their H1 measure is designed to indicate the sample quality for a given target variable, Y, as is the FMI measure developed by Wagner (2012). This is a new and quickly evolving area of research, and before long we will likely see new indices of survey quality that consider P as well as many target variables (Ys).

An additional stream of burgeoning research concerns the optimal weighting scheme to use in order to adjust for sample bias. Using weights will eliminate (reduce) bias if there is no (less) variation in the propensity to respond within each cell of the weighting scheme, which eliminates (reduces) any correlation between P and Y within each cell and in the weighted analysis. Since weighting can and usually will increase standard errors (SEs), it is not helpful to use auxiliary variables for weighting that are uncorrelated with Y. Indeed, the optimal auxiliary variables for weighting will be strongly correlated with both P and Y (Little and Vartivarian 2005). It has become increasingly clear that post-stratification weights based on demographics are inferior to weights using a broader set of auxiliary variables and formed through a two-step procedure: (1) weighting (or adjusting design weights) for non-response, and (2) then adjusting through calibration/raking (Kolenikov 2016; Krueger and West 2014; Rota and Laitila 2015).

The traditional method for developing non-response weights estimates the probability of a response (P) using variables that are available for both respondents and non-respondents. One thrust of the recent survey research literature is the importance of gathering as much information as possible on non-respondents so as to improve the non-response adjustments (Kreuter et al. 2010; Krueger and West 2014; Olson 2013).

A more recently developed and perhaps more promising alternative makes use of gold-standard reference samples – high-quality samples thought to yield accurate population benchmark estimates, like the CPS or the American Community Survey in the US – for non-response weighting. This method estimates P using variables that are common to both samples. Since this "propensity score weighting" method does not require data on non-respondents, it can be used for weighting nonprobability samples. A second virtue is that a potentially much wider set of variables can be utilized when building the non-response model, including attitudinal and behavioral measures in addition to demographics and paradata, though of course the relevant questions must have been asked on each survey. However, there is nothing approaching a consensus as to what questions are essential to include. Studies evaluating the method have differed widely in the variables they incorporate (Berrens et al. 2003; Duffy et al. 2005; Lee 2006; Lee and Valliant 2009; Loosveldt and Sonck 2008; Schonlau et al. 2009). For example, Schonlau et al. (2009) used race, gender, age, income, self-assessed general health, and home ownership, while Berrens et al. (2003) used questions on trust in government, personal efficacy, whether the respondent owned a retirement account, and whether the respondent had read a book, traveled, or participated in a sport recently. As Mick Couper (2013) has argued, building a richer understanding of how survey respondents differ from non-respondents remains one of the most important challenges to be confronted in the decades ahead.

Finally, the data from most major surveys are released along with a single set of survey weights. However, it is clear that a single set of weights will be of limited value in reducing sample bias compared to weights constructed to be optimal for a given Y or set of Ys. Optimal weights would be constructed using non-response covariates strongly related to the $Y(s)$ in question and take into account item non-response as well as unit non-response. Efforts to develop such optimal weights and use them in estimation are underway (Caughey and Wang 2014; Andridge and Little 2011; Särndal and Lundström 2010).

Nonprobability survey samples

Writing in 1999, the prominent American pollster Walter Mitofsky condemned internet polling based on nonprobability samples, stating that "the willingness to discard the use of sampling frames as a means of selecting a sample and then the feeble attempts at manipulating the resulting bias … undermine the credibility of the survey process" (Mitofsky 1999: 26). The current consensus remains skeptical of the value of nonprobability samples for population-based inferences, though puts it less stridently. The oft-quoted 2010 Report on Online Panels from the American Association for Public Opinion Research (AAPOR) concluded:

> Researchers should avoid nonprobability online panels when one of the research objectives is to accurately estimate population values. There currently is no generally accepted theoretical basis from which to claim that survey results using samples from nonprobability online panels are projectable to the general population.
>
> *(AAPOR Standards Committee 2010: 758)*

Similar conclusions are presented in a recent report to the US National Science Foundation (Krosnick et al. 2015) and in an important new volume on internet panel research (Callegaro et al. 2014). Major news organizations in the US, such as the Associated Press and the *New York Times*, generally limit their reporting of surveys to those based on probability samples.[4]

Yet, that consensus is, in certain respects, starting to give way. A first development is signaled by a change in AAPOR's guidelines about efforts to make population-based inferences from self-selected samples. The initial position taken by AAPOR was that any reporting of SEs when working with surveys using self-selected samples was "misleading" and that researchers working with opt-in panels should use the following wording when describing their study: "Because the sample is based on those who initially self-selected for participation [in the panel] rather than a probability sample, no estimates of sampling error can be calculated."[5] However, in 2015 AAPOR revised its Code of Professional Ethics and Practices to allow for the reporting of SEs, "provided that the measures are accompanied by a detailed description of how the underlying model was specified, its assumptions validated and the measure(s) calculated," suggesting a variety of possible methods for estimating SEs, including resampling techniques, Bayesian Credibility Intervals, and Taylor Series Linearization.[6] Although research into the use of these techniques for self-selected samples is just getting started, recent studies have advocated jackknife or bootstrap procedures as optimal for SE estimation with nonprobability samples (Isaksson, Lee, and Sweden 2005; Lee and Valliant 2009; Enderle and Münnich 2014). AAPOR's 2013 Report on the Task Force on Nonprobability Sampling provides much more information on the research and thinking that led to this revision (Baker et al. 2013).[7]

Second, scholars are gaining a better appreciation of the diverse methods that can be used to select and weight respondents from opt-in internet panels and how these bear on sample quality. Many firms allow researchers to design a sample to meet demographic quotas on selected variables, sometimes also constructing weights to remedy remaining imbalances. Other firms use sample matching strategies, which require the use of data from gold-standard reference samples. One variant combines data from online panelists and the reference sample using variables common to both to estimate the propensity to fall into one or the other group, then builds the online survey sample so that its distribution of response propensities matches that of the reference sample (Terhanian and Bremer 2012). A second variant, used by YouGov, seeks to find respondents within the online panels that are best matches to respondents within the reference sample, which is more successful if the pool of online panelists is very large (Rivers 2007; Rivers and Bailey 2009). Either way, weights are constructed using the reference sample and other data on the target population in order to mitigate remaining imbalances. As described earlier, these methods frequently use a rich set of matching/weighting variables, including attitudinal and behavioral measures and paradata in addition to demographic data.

Research is accumulating on how these variations matter to sample representativeness. Studies distributing the same questionnaire to respondents from different online panels demonstrate substantial variation across the panels in how well the results match population benchmarks (Yeager et al. 2011; Gittelman et al. 2015; Kennedy et al. 2016). Quota sampling will yield representativeness on the quota cells and calibration will do so for the calibration variables, but these techniques do not eliminate – or, often, even mitigate – bias on other measures (Malhotra and Krosnick 2007; Yeager et al. 2011). Expanding the set of quota variables does not appear to help (Gittelman et al. 2015). Those within any given quota cell who respond to the survey remain markedly different from those who do not. Sample matching strategies, however, have much more promise, especially when combined with propensity score and calibration weighting (Baker et al. 2013; Rivers 2007; Gittelman et al. 2015; Kennedy et al. 2016; Ansolabehere and Schaffner 2014; Ansolabehere and Rivers 2013; Sanders et al. 2007; Vavreck and Iyengar 2011; Simmons and Bobo 2015). Just how effective, of course, depends on the variables used in the matching/weighting – ideally highly correlated with target variables and the propensity to respond (Little and Vartivarian 2005), while also being exogenous to the phenomena being studied (Kennedy et al. 2016; Rivers 2016).

That is not to say that well-designed and weighted samples drawn from opt-in internet panels are equal in quality to well-designed and weighted probability samples. Studies have typically found more sample bias in opt-in surveys than in surveys conducted FTF, by telephone or over the web with respondents selected using probability methods (see reviews in AAPOR Standards Committee 2010; Callegaro et al. 2014; Fieldhouse and Prosser in this volume). However, few of these studies use opt-in survey samples that were developed and weighted using what we now think to be best practices (Baker et al. 2013). Those that do use best practices show more promising results, but still typically find one or more variables for which the opt-in sample is less accurate (see, for example, Ansolabehere and Schaffer 2014; Simmons and Bobo 2015).[8] Similarly, even the best opt-in surveys have on occasion fared worse than probability-based surveys in predicting electoral outcomes. For example, YouGov underestimated Tory support in the 2015 British elections more so than did the British Election Study, conducted FTF. The main reason, according to YouGov, was that their weighted sample of young people (who tend to vote Labour) were more politically engaged than young people in the electorate overall.[9] Voter turnout in the US also tends to be more inflated in Cooperative Congressional Election Study

(CCES) surveys carried out with YouGov samples than it is in data from ANES surveys based on probability sampling and conducted FTF. Both samples have a greater percentage of validated voters than they should, but the percentage of those falsely claiming to have voted is twice as high in the CCES as it is in the ANES (Ansolabehere and Hersh 2012).[10]

Still, the advantages of using probability-based sampling (plus weighting) instead of sample matching (plus weighting) may disappear when response rates for the former dip into the low double or single digits, as Doug Rivers has long argued (see, for example, Rivers 2009, 2016; see also Baker et al. 2013). An important new study conducted by the Pew Research Center suggests as much (Kennedy et al. 2016). Kennedy et al. solicited nine surveys from eight opt-in panel vendors to compare to surveys of Pew's probability-based panel (ATP), using an identical questionnaire. The ATP response rate was in the 3.4–3.7 percent range. The study compared sample means and multivariate coefficients obtained from the various samples to benchmarks from CPS, examined how well coefficients from the online surveys predicted outcomes in the CPS data, and performed a series of analyses to determine the value added by sample selection vs. sample weighting procedures. In almost every analysis, Sample "I" outperformed ATP and the rest of the opt-in samples, and as Rivers (2016) revealed, Sample I was YouGov. The study judged the YouGov survey superior in its sample selection design as well as in its weighting procedures. At the same time, the study showed that all 10 web surveys reported much more political and, especially, civic engagement than did the CPS after weighting, and tended to be especially inaccurate in depicting the characteristics of sample subgroups including Blacks, Hispanics, and the young. The report concluded that Sample I (YouGov) had developed a "better methodology" that produces "a more representative, more accurate national survey than the competition within the online nonprobability space," while also noting that the ATP performance was "mixed" (p. 5). Although just one study, the Kennedy et al. (2016) report will undoubtedly spur a further conversation on the relative merits of probability-based vs. opt-in web survey samples.

Looking forward

Most of the research on sample quality has focused on how an unrepresentative sample will yield a misleading portrait of the target population writ large, without considering how the inferences regarding subpopulations are affected. Yet, the erosion of response rates and proliferation of nonprobability samples may be affecting our inferences concerning some subgroups more than others. If it is hard to encourage certain groups to participate in surveys – e.g., Blacks or Hispanics, young people, the less educated – then it would not be surprising to find that, among such groups, the people who do participate are especially unlike their non-responding counterparts. Results from the 2012 ANES comparison of web and face-to-face surveys are illustrative. The discrepancy in self-reported 2008 turnout between the web sample (from KnowledgePanel, response rate 2 percent) and the face-to-face sample (response rate 49 percent) was almost five times greater for those with a high school degree or less (14.4 percent) than for those with a college degree or more (2.9 percent), after weighting. The comparable figures for self-reported turnout in 2012 were 9.0 percent vs. −1.5 percent. Without denying the importance of overall sample representativeness, future research should delve more deeply into sample biases affecting our understanding of subgroup differences and how best to alter survey design and weighting procedures to mitigate them.

Little attention has also been given to how bias in survey samples affects interpretation of treatment effects from survey experiments. One prong of the existing research has considered how well results from survey experiments carried out on nonprobability samples compare to benchmarks obtained from population-based survey experiments, which has tended to be reassuring (Berinsky, Huber, and Lenz 2012; Mullinix et al. 2015, also see Barabas and Jerit 2010; Hainmueller, Hangartner, and Yamamoto 2015). Other work examines the question of whether survey-experimental data should be weighted, keeping in mind the fact that the size of the weight is inversely related to the magnitude of the estimated probability of a survey response, $\hat{P}$ (Solon, Haider, and Woodlridge 2015; Levin and Sinclair 2016; see also Cole and Stuart 2010; Hartman et al. 2015; and Stuart et al. 2011, who consider clinical trials not surveys). If a treatment effect is homogeneous or has heterogeneity that is unrelated to P, then the sample average treatment effect (SATE) gives an unbiased estimate of the population average treatment effect (PATE) and a weighted analysis is inadvisable as it will only inflate the SEs. If the treatment effect varies with P and the missing data are ignorable after weights are applied (a heroic assumption), then the weighted analysis will also yield an unbiased estimate of PATE, though not if the treatment effect is estimated while controlling for covariates (Solon, Haider, and Wooldridge 2015). Otherwise, SATE will be a biased estimator of PATE.

The practical advice offered by Solon, Haider, and Woodlridge (2015) is to examine whether the treatment effect is heterogeneous with respect to the weights by analyzing the data with and without weighting, and then to report and discuss both sets of results. It may, however, be more transparent and informative for researchers to simply display and discuss how estimated treatment effects vary with $\hat{P}$. Since P can be estimated for virtually any sample using the propensity score weighting techniques described earlier, even those working with convenience samples should be able to bring this evidence to bear on the generalizability of their results. Levin and Sinclair (2016) and Hartman et al. (2015) go further, proposing techniques for directly estimating the population average treatment effect on the treated (PATT). Levin and Sinclair show how three different techniques for matching treatment and control subjects can be modified to incorporate survey weights. Hartman et al. recommend estimating treatment effects within matched groups of treatment and control subjects, and then estimating PATT by aggregating these effect sizes weighted by the population proportion for each matched set. As this literature develops and starts to affect standards of practice, it should yield a much richer sense of how the quest for representative samples bears on the goal of generalizing sample-based causal inferences.

Notes

1 Bethlehem (2010: 172–173) shows that the bias is approximately $[R(P, Y) \star S(P) \star S(Y)] \div \bar{P}$, the formula used to create Figure 36.1.

2 A SD of 0.05 for P approximates the situation where the distribution is highly skewed (e.g., Beta distribution parameters of 0.2 and 8), while the SD of 0.30 for P approximates the situation where the distribution is uniform or even modestly U-shaped (Beta parameters of 1 and 1, or 0.2 and 0.7).

3 Efforts to reduce non-response bias could also end up increasing measurement error. Recent studies have found that people with a low propensity to respond tend to provide poorer quality data when they do respond, e.g., more item non-response, less consistent responses, more straightlining, and less information in response to open-ended questions (Fricker and Tourangeau 2010; Dahlhamer 2012; Roberts, Allum, and Sturgis 2014).

4 See http://graphics8.nytimes.com/packages/pdf/politics/20110511quick_checklist.pdf for the NYT and http://commonsensej.blogspot.com/2007/11/ap-style-other-recent-updates.html for the AP.

5 www.aapor.org/Education-Resources/For-Researchers/Poll-Survey-FAQ/Opt-In-Surveys-and-Margin-of-Error.aspx.

6 www.aapor.org/getattachment/Education-Resources/For-Researchers/AAPOR_Guidance_Nonprob_Precision_042216.pdf.aspx. See, also, the 2014 joint ESOMAR/WAPOR Guideline on Opinion Polls and Published Surveys, available at http://wapor.org/esomarwapor-guide-to-opinion-polls/.

7 AAPOR still, however, uses the acronym SLOP for "self-selected opinion polls" in the section of their website on "Bad Samples" (www.aapor.org/Education-Resources/For-Researchers/Poll-Survey-FAQ/Bad-Samples.aspx).

8 Mode differences can arise due to differences in sample quality or in response quality. It is often difficult to determine which cause is producing differences. The literature has, however, consistently demonstrated less social desirability bias in web surveys than in those conducted FTF or by telephone, with recent studies also demonstrating that web surveys elicit more negative attitudes (see, for example, Klausch, Hox, and Schouten 2013; Pew 2015; Ye, Fulton, and Tourangeau 2011; Tourangeau and Yan 2007). There is also fairly strong evidence that web surveys elicit more item non-response, speeding, and straightlining (see, for example, Heerwegh and Loosveldt 2008). See Fieldhouse and Prosser (in this volume) for further details.

9 https://yougov.co.uk/news/2015/05/08/general-election-opinion-polls-brief-post-mortem/ and https://yougov.co.uk/news/2015/12/07/analysis-what-went-wrong-our-ge15-polling-and-what/.

10 Since social desirability bias has consistently been found to be lower in self-administered surveys than in FTF surveys, this high rate of misreporting in the CCES is likely tied to sample composition.

References

AAPOR Standards Committee (2010) "AAPOR Report on Online Panels," *Public Opinion Quarterly*, vol. 74, no. 4, Winter, 711–781.

Andridge, R. R. and Little, R. J. (2011) "Proxy Pattern-Mixture Analysis for Survey Nonresponse," *Journal of Official Statistics*, vol. 27, no. 2, June, 153–180.

Ansolabehere, S. and Hersh, E. (2012) "Validation: What Big Data Reveal About Survey Misreporting and the Real Electorate," *Political Analysis*, vol. 20, no. 4, Autumn, 437–459.

Ansolabehere, S. and Rivers, D. (2013) "Cooperative Survey Research," *Annual Review of Political Science*, vol. 16, May, 307–329.

Ansolabehere, S. and Schaffner, B. F. (2014) "Does Survey Mode Still Matter? Findings from a 2010 Multi-Mode Comparison," *Political Analysis*, vol. 22, no. 3, Summer, 285–303.

Baker, R., Brick, J. M., Bates, N. A., Battaglia, M., Couper, M. P., Dever, J. A., Gile, K. J., and Tourangeau, R. (2013) "Summary Report of the AAPOR Task Force on Nonprobability Sampling," *Journal of Survey Statistics and Methodology*, vol. 1, no. 2, November, 90–143.

Barabas, J. and Jerit, J. (2010) "Are Survey Experiments Externally Valid?," *American Political Science Review*, vol. 104, no. 2, May, 226–242.

Berinsky, A. J., Huber, G. A., and Lenz, G. S. (2012) "Evaluating Online Labor Markets for Experimental Research: Amazon.com's Mechanical Turk," *Political Analysis*, vol. 20, no. 3, Summer, 351–368.

Berrens, R. P., Bohara, A. K., Jenkins-Smith, H., Silva, C., and Weimer, D. L. (2003) "The Advent of Internet Surveys for Political Research: A Comparison of Telephone and Internet Samples," *Political Analysis*, vol. 11, no. 1, Winter, 1–22.

Bethlehem, J. (2010) "Selection Bias in Web Surveys," *International Statistical Review*, vol. 78, no. 2, August, 161–188.

Bethlehem, J. and Biffignandi, S. (2011) *Handbook of Web Surveys*, Volume 567, London: John Wiley & Sons.

Bethlehem, J., Cobben, F., and Schouten, B. (2011) *Handbook of Nonresponse in Household Surveys*, Volume 568, London: John Wiley & Sons.

Brick, J. M. (2013) "Unit Nonresponse and Weighting Adjustments: A Critical Review," *Journal of Official Statistics*, vol. 29, no. 3, June, 329–353.

Brick, J. M. and Williams, D. (2013) "Explaining Rising Nonresponse Rates in Cross-Sectional Surveys," *The ANNALS of the American Academy of Political and Social Science*, vol. 645, no. 1, January, 36–59.

Callegaro, M., Baker, R., Bethlehem, J., Goritz, A. S., Krosnick, J. A., and Lavrakas, P. J. (eds.) (2014) *Online Panel Research: A Data Quality Perspective*, Chichester: John Wiley & Sons Ltd.

Callegaro, M., Manfreda, K. L., and Vehovar, V. (2015) *Web Survey Methodology*, Los Angeles: Sage.

Caughey, D. and Wang, M. (2014) "Bayesian Population Interpolation and Lasso-Based Target Selection in Survey Weighting," Paper presented at the 2014 Summer Meeting of the Society for Political Methodology, University of Georgia, July 24–26.

Cole, S. R. and Stuart, E. A. (2010) "Generalizing Evidence from Randomized Clinical Trials to Target Populations: The ACTG 320 Trial," *American Journal of Epidemiology*, vol. 172, no. 1, July, 107–115.

Couper, M. P. (2011) "The Future of Modes of Data Collection," *Public Opinion Quarterly*, vol. 75, no. 5, 889–908.

Couper, M. P. (2013) "Is the Sky Falling? New Technology, Changing Media, and the Future of Surveys," *Survey Research Methods*, vol. 7, no. 3, 145–156.

Curtin, R., Presser, S., and Singer, E. (2005) "Changes in Telephone Survey Nonresponse Over the Past Quarter Century," *Public Opinion Quarterly*, vol. 69, no. 1, Spring, 87–98.

Dahlhamer, J. M. (2012) "The Intersection of Response Propensity and Data Quality in the National Health Interview Survey (NHIS)," Paper presented at the 2012 Joint Statistical Meeting of the American Statistical Association, San Diego, July 28–August 2.

Duffy, B., Smith, K., Terhanian, G., and Bremer, J. (2005) "Comparing Data from Online and Face-To-Face Surveys," *International Journal of Market Research*, vol. 47, no. 6, 615–639.

Dutwin, D. and Lavrakas, P. (2016) "Trends in Telephone Outcomes, 2008–2015," *Survey Practice*, vol. 9, no. 3, 1–9.

Enderle, T. and Münnich, R. (2014) "Accuracy of Estimates in Access Panel Based Surveys," in Engel, U., Jann, B., Lynn, P., Scherpenzeel, A. and Sturgis, P. (eds.) *Improving Survey Methods: Lessons from Recent Research*, Abingdon: Routledge: 250–265.

Fricker, S. and Tourangeau, R. (2010) "Examining the Relationship Between Nonresponse Propensity and Data Quality in Two National Household Surveys," *Public Opinion Quarterly*, vol. 74, no. 5, December, 934–955.

Gittelman, S. H., Thomas, R. K., Lavrakas, P. J., and Lange, V. (2015) "Quota Controls in Survey Research: A Test of Accuracy and Intersource Reliability in Online Samples," *Journal of Advertising Research*, vol. 55, no. 4, December, 368–379.

Groves, R. M. (2006) "Nonresponse Rates and Nonresponse Bias in Household Surveys," *Public Opinion Quarterly*, vol. 70, no. 5, December, 646–675.

Groves, R. M. (2011) "Three Eras of Survey Research," *Public Opinion Quarterly*, vol. 75, no. 5, December, 861–871.

Groves, R. M. and Heeringa, S. G. (2006) "Responsive Design for Household Surveys: Tools for Actively Controlling Survey Errors and Costs," *Journal of the Royal Statistical Society: Series A (Statistics in Society)*, vol. 169, no. 3, July, 439–457.

Groves, R. M. and Peytcheva, E. (2008) "The Impact of Nonresponse Rates on Nonresponse Bias: A Meta-Analysis," *Public Opinion Quarterly*, vol. 72, no. 2, Summer, 167–189.

Hainmueller, J., Hangartner, D., and Yamamoto, T. (2015) "Validating Vignette and Conjoint Survey Experiments Against Real-World Behavior," *Proceedings of the National Academy of Sciences*, vol. 112, no. 8, February, 2395–2400.

Hartman, E., Grieve, R., Ramsahai, R., and Sekhon, J. S. (2015) "From Sample Average Treatment Effect to Population Average Treatment Effect on the Treated: Combining Experimental with Observational Studies to Estimate Population Treatment Effects," *Journal of the Royal Statistical Society: Series A (Statistics in Society)*, vol. 178, no. 3, June, 757–778.

Heckman, J. J. (1979) "Sample Selection Bias as a Specification Error," *Econometrica*, vol. 47, no. 1, January, 153–161.

Heerwegh, D. and Loosveldt, G. (2008) "Face-To-Face Versus Web Surveying in a High-Internet-Coverage Population Differences in Response Quality," *Public Opinion Quarterly*, vol. 72, no. 5, December, 836–846.

Holbrook, A., Krosnick, J. A., and Pfent, A. (2008) "The Causes and Consequences of Response Rates in Surveys by the News Media and Government Contractor Survey Research Firms," in Lepkowski, J. M., Tucker, C., Brick, J. M., deLeeuw, E. D., Japec, L., Lavrakas, P. J., Link, M. W., and Sangster, R. L. (eds.) *Advances in Telephone Survey Methodology*, Hoboken: John Wiley & Sons: 499–528.

Isaksson, A., Lee, S., and Sweden, S. (2005) "Simple Approaches to Estimating the Variance of the Propensity Score Weighted Estimator Applied on Volunteer Panel Web Survey Data – a Comparative Study," *SRMS Proceedings*, 3143–3149.

Keeter, S., Miller, C., Kohut, A., Groves, R. M., and Presser, S. (2000) "Consequences of Reducing Nonresponse in a National Telephone Survey," *Public Opinion Quarterly*, vol. 64, no. 2, Summer, 125–148.

Kennedy, C., Mercer, A., Keeter, S., Hatley, N., McGeeney, K., and Gimenez, A. (2016) *Evaluating Online Nonprobability Surveys*, Washington, DC: Pew Research Center, available online: www.pewresearch.org/2016/05/02/evaluating-online-nonprobability-surveys/ [accessed July 25, 2016].

Klausch, T., Hox, J. J., and Schouten, B. (2013) "Measurement Effects of Survey Mode on the Equivalence of Attitudinal Rating Scale Questions," *Sociological Methods and Research*, vol. 42, no. 3, August, 227–263.

Kohut, A., Keeter, S., Doherty, C., Dimock, M., and Christian, L. (2012) "Assessing the Representativeness of Public Opinion Surveys," Paper presented at the 2012 Annual AAPOR Conference, Orlando, May 17–20.

Kolenikov, S. (2016) "Post-Stratification or Non-Response Adjustment?," *Survey Practice*, vol. 9, no. 3, 1–12.

Kreuter, F. (2013) "Facing the Nonresponse Challenge," *The ANNALS of the American Academy of Political and Social Science*, vol. 645, no. 1, January, 23–35.

Kreuter, F., Olson, K., Wagner, J., Yan, T., Ezzati-Rice, T. M., Casas-Cordero, C., Lemay, M., Peytchev, A., Groves, R. M., and Raghunathan, T. E. (2010) "Using Proxy Measures and Other Correlates of Survey Outcomes to Adjust for Non-Response: Examples from Multiple Surveys," *Journal of the Royal Statistical Society: Series A (Statistics in Society)*, vol. 173, no. 2, April, 389–407.

Krosnick, J. A., Presser, S., Fealing, K. H., Ruggles, S., and Vannette, D. (2015) *The Future of Survey Research: Challenges and Opportunities*, Stanford University: The National Science Foundation Advisory Committee for the Social, Behavioral and Economic Sciences Subcommittee on Advancing SBE Survey Research, available online: www.nsf.gov/sbe/AC_Materials/The_Future_of_Survey_Research. pdf [accessed March 11, 2016].

Krueger, B. S. and West, B. T. (2014) "Assessing the Potential of Paradata and Other Auxiliary Data for Nonresponse Adjustments," *Public Opinion Quarterly*, vol. 78, no. 4, Winter, 795–831.

Lee, S. (2006) "Propensity Score Adjustment as a Weighting Scheme for Volunteer Panel Web Surveys," *Journal of Official Statistics*, vol. 22, no. 2, June, 329–349.

Lee, S. and Valliant, R. (2009) "Estimation for Volunteer Panel Web Surveys Using Propensity Score Adjustment and Calibration Adjustment," *Sociological Methods and Research*, vol. 37, no. 3, February, 319–343.

Levin, I. and Sinclair, B. (2016) "Causal Inference with Complex Survey Designs," in Atkeson, L. R. and Alvarez, M. (eds.) *The Oxford Handbook of Polling and Polling Methods*, Oxford: Oxford University Press, available online: www.oxfordhandbooks.com/view/10.1093/oxfordhb/9780190213299.001.0001/ oxfordhb-9780190213299-e-4.

Little, R. J. and Vartivarian, S. (2005) "Does Weighting for Nonresponse Increase the Variance of Survey Means?," *Survey Methodology*, vol. 31, no. 2, 161–168.

Loosveldt, G. and Sonck, N. (2008) "An Evaluation of the Weighting Procedures for an Online Access Panel Survey," *Survey Research Methods*, vol. 2, no. 2, 93–105.

Luiten, A. and Schouten, B. (2013) "Tailored Fieldwork Design to Increase Representative Household Survey Response: An Experiment in the Survey of Consumer Satisfaction," *Journal of the Royal Statistical Society: Series A (Statistics in Society)*, vol. 176, no. 1, January, 169–189.

Malhotra, N. and Krosnick, J. A. (2007) "The Effect of Survey Mode and Sampling on Inferences About Political Attitudes and Behavior: Comparing the 2000 and 2004 ANES to Internet Surveys with Non-probability Samples," *Political Analysis*, vol. 15, no. 3, Summer, 286–323.

Martin, S., Helmschrott, S., and Rammstedt, B. (2014) "The Use of Respondent Incentives in PIAAC: The Field Test Experiment in Germany," *Methods, Data, Analyses*, vol. 8, no. 2, 223–242.

Mitofsky, W. J. (1999) "Pollsters.com," *Public Perspective*, vol. 10, no. 4, July, 24–26.

Mullinix, K. J., Leeper, T. J., Druckman, J. N., and Freese, J. (2015) "The Generalizability of Survey Experiments," *Journal of Experimental Political Science*, vol. 2, no. 2, January, 109–138.

Olson, K. (2013) "Paradata for Nonresponse Adjustment," *The ANNALS of the American Academy of Political and Social Science*, vol. 645, no. 1, January, 142–170.

Pew Research Center (2015) *From Telephone to the Web: The Challenge of Mode of Interview Effects in Public Opinion Polls*, Washington, DC: Pew Research Center, available online: www.pewresearch. org/2015/05/13/from-telephone-to-the-web-the-challenge-of-mode-of-interview-effects-in-public-opinion-polls/ [accessed July 28, 2016].

Peytchev, A., Riley, S., Rosen, J., Murphy, J., and Lindblad, M. (2010) "Reduction of Nonresponse Bias in Surveys Through Case Prioritization," *Survey Research Methods*, vol. 4, no. 1, 21–29.

Pforr, K., Blohm, M., Blom, A. G., Erdel, B., Felderer, B., Frässdorf, M., Hajek, K., Helmschrott, S., Kleinert, C., Koch, A., and Krieger, U. (2015) "Are Incentive Effects on Response Rates and Nonresponse Bias in Large-Scale, Face-To-Face Surveys Generalizable to Germany? Evidence from Ten Experiments," *Public Opinion Quarterly*, vol. 79, no. 3, Autumn, 740–768.

Rivers, D. (2007) "Sampling for Web Surveys," Paper presented at the 2007 Joint Statistical Meetings, Salt Lake City, July 29–August 2.

Rivers, D. (2009) "Second Thoughts About Internet Surveys," *The Huffington Post*, June 9, 2009, available online: www.huffingtonpost.com/guest-pollster/doug_rivers_b_724621.html.

Rivers, D. (2016) "Pew Research: YouGov Consistently Outperforms Competitors on Accuracy," *YouGov*, May 13, 2016, available online: https://today.yougov.com/news/2016/05/13/pew-research-yougov/.

Rivers, D. and Bailey, D. (2009) "Inference from Matched Samples in the 2008 US National Elections," Paper presented at the 2009 Joint Statistical Meetings, Washington, DC, August 1–6.

Roberts, C., Allum, N., and Sturgis, P. (2014) "Nonresponse and Measurement Error in an Online Panel," in Callegaro, M., Baker, R., Bethlehem, J., Göritz, A. J., Krosnick, J. A., and Lavrakas, P. J. (eds.) *Online Panel Research: A Data Quality Perspective*, London: Wiley: 337–362.

Rota, B. J. and Laitila, T. (2015) "Comparisons of Some Weighting Methods for Nonresponse Adjustment," *Lithuanian Journal of Statistics*, vol. 54, no. 1, 69–83.

Sanders, D., Clarke, H. D., Stewart, M. C., and Whiteley, P. (2007) "Does Mode Matter for Modeling Political Choice? Evidence from the 2005 British Election Study," *Political Analysis*, vol. 15, no. 3, Summer, 257–285.

Särndal, C. E. (2011) "The 2010 Morris Hansen Lecture Dealing with Survey Nonresponse in Data Collection, in Estimation," *Journal of Official Statistics*, vol. 27, no. 1, March, 1–21.

Särndal, C. E. and Lundström, S. (2010) "Design for Estimation: Identifying Auxiliary Vectors to Reduce Nonresponse Bias," *Survey Methodology*, vol. 36, no. 2, 131–144.

Schoeni, R. F., Stafford, F., McGonagle, K. A., and Andreski, P. (2013) "Response Rates in National Panel Surveys," *The ANNALS of the American Academy of Political and Social Science*, vol. 645, no. 1, January, 60–87.

Schonlau, M., Van Soest, A., Kapteyn, A., and Couper, M. (2009) "Selection Bias in Web Surveys and the Use of Propensity Scores," *Sociological Methods and Research*, vol. 37, no. 3, February, 291–318.

Schouten, B., Calinescu, M., and Luiten, A. (2013) "Optimizing Quality of Response Through Adaptive Survey Designs," *Survey Methodology*, vol. 39, no. 1, 29–58.

Schouten, B., Cobben, F., and Bethlehem, J. (2009) "Indicators for the Representativeness of Survey Response," *Survey Methodology*, vol. 35, no. 1, 101–113.

Shlomo, N., Skinner, C. J., and Schouten, B. (2012) "Estimation of an Indicator of the Representativeness of Survey Response," *Journal of Statistical Planning and Inference*, vol. 142, no. 1, January, 201–211.

Simmons, A. D. and Bobo, L. D. (2015) "Can Non-Full-Probability Internet Surveys Yield Useful Data? A Comparison with Full-Probability Face-to-Face Surveys in the Domain of Race and Social Inequality Attitudes," *Sociological Methodology*, vol. 45, no. 1, August, 357–387.

Singer, E. and Ye, C. (2013) "The Use and Effects of Incentives in Surveys," *The ANNALS of the American Academy of Political and Social Science*, vol. 645, no. 1, January, 112–141.

Solon, G., Haider, S. J., and Wooldridge, J. M. (2015) "What are We Weighting for?," *Journal of Human Resources*, vol. 50, no. 2, Spring, 301–316.

Stern, M. J., Bilgen, I., and Dillman, D. A. (2014) "The State of Survey Methodology Challenges, Dilemmas, and New Frontiers in the Era of the Tailored Design," *Field Methods*, vol. 26, no. 3, August, 284–301.

Stuart, E. A., Cole, S. R., Bradshaw, C. P. and Leaf, P. J. (2011) "The Use of Propensity Scores to Assess the Generalizability of Results from Randomized Trials," *Journal of the Royal Statistical Society: Series A (Statistics in Society)*, vol. 174, no. 2, April, 369–386.

Terhanian, G. and Bremer, J. (2012) "A Smarter Way to Select Respondents for Surveys," *International Journal of Market Research*, vol. 54, no. 6, 751–780.

Tourangeau, R. and Plewes, T. J. (eds.) (2013) *Nonresponse in Social Science Surveys: A Research Agenda*, Washington, DC: National Academies Press.

Tourangeau, R. and Yan, T. (2007) "Sensitive Questions in Surveys," *Psychological Bulletin*, vol. 133, no. 5, September, 859–883.

Vavreck, L. and Iyengar, S. (2011) "The Future of Political Communication Research: Online Panels and Experimentation," in Shapiro, R. Y. and Jacobs, L. J. (eds.) *Oxford Handbook of Public Opinion and the Media*, Oxford: Oxford University Press: 156–168

Wagner, J. (2012) "A Comparison of Alternative Indicators for the Risk of Nonresponse Bias," *Public Opinion Quarterly*, vol. 76, no. 3, Autumn, 555–575.

Winship, C. and Radbill, L. (1994) "Sampling Weights and Regression Analysis," *Sociological Methods and Research*, vol. 23, no. 2, November, 230–257.

Ye, C., Fulton, J., and Tourangeau, R. (2011) "More Positive or More Extreme? A Meta-Analysis of Mode Differences in Response Choice," *Public Opinion Quarterly*, vol. 75, no. 2, Summer, 349–365.

Yeager, D. S., Krosnick, J. A., Chang, L., Javitz, H. S., Levendusky, M. S., Simpser, A., and Wang, R. (2011) "Comparing the Accuracy of RDD Telephone Surveys and Internet Surveys Conducted with Probability and Non-Probability Samples," *Public Opinion Quarterly*, vol. 75, no. 4, Winter, 709–747.

37

HORSES FOR COURSES

Using internet surveys for researching public opinion and voting behavior

Edward Fieldhouse and Christopher Prosser

With the rapid growth of the internet and digital technology in recent decades, public opinion and electoral research has undergone a transformation in how data are collected. As in-person surveys based on random probability samples of the population have become increasingly expensive, they have become increasingly rare. Declining response rates for telephone surveys and unresolved questions about the impact of mobile phones on sampling frames have also raised questions about the continued validity of phone samples (Curtin, Presser, and Singer 2005; Lavrakas et al. 2007). At the same time internet-based surveys, which can be delivered at a fraction of the cost in a short time frame, have become widespread. Online panel surveys have become perhaps the predominant way to collect data about political attitudes and behavior.

However, despite a common assumption that internet surveys would eventually make other forms of data collection redundant, the inexorable march of the online panel and the decline of other forms of survey data collection have been hampered by doubts about the accuracy and representativeness of online data.

Funders of research in political science, and customers of public opinion research more generally, have continued to hedge their bets whilst researchers attempt to resolve the on-going debate about whether online surveys can produce data of the same (or better) quality than more traditional methods. Survey research always involves necessary compromise between the quality of the data, the feasibility of contacting respondents, and the cost of doing so (Kish 1987). Internet surveys have a clear advantage in terms of cost – the cost per respondent and speed of data collection is unparalleled in other survey modes. The question for survey researchers is whether the potential risks of internet survey data outweigh these advantages.

In this chapter, we review some of the burgeoning evidence about the quality of internet-based survey methods.[1] There is strong evidence that online surveys enjoy considerable advantages that make them the mode of choice for a number of research purposes, but at the same time other methods – particularly those based on random probability samples – are better suited for making point estimates of population values. In other words, it is not a case of which mode is better, but a case of "horses for courses," meaning that, for the time being at least, online and offline modes of data collection will continue to exist in parallel.

Types of internet survey

Traditional survey modes are often linked to particular sampling methods – face-to-face surveys are usually associated with area sampling, and phone surveys are most often conducted by random digit dialing (RDD) (Tourangeau, Conrad, and Couper 2013). This is not the case for internet surveys, which come in various shapes and sizes, and in terms of assessing the advantages and disadvantages of different modes of data collection, the devil is in the detail.

One important characteristic of most internet surveys is the panel element: whereas it might be feasible to carry out one-off internet surveys amongst a small and known target population, because of the lack of a sampling frame for the population, many internet surveys are based on existing larger *access* panels that are regularly drawn on to complete a variety of different surveys. These access panels are distinct from traditional *longitudinal* panel surveys, which repeatedly measure the attitudes and behaviors of the same respondents. Access panels can themselves be used to create longitudinal panels – for example, the British Election Study Internet Panel (Fieldhouse et al. 2015).

Other forms of internet survey do exist, such as river sampling – where respondents are recruited to take a survey via an advertisement or webpage rather than through an access panel. However, the dominant model of internet survey research is conducted using access panels (AAPOR Standards Committee 2010), and we focus our discussion in this chapter on these.[2] As we discuss below, the panel element of internet samples provides a number of advantages when it comes to researching the dynamics of political attitudes and voter behavior.

The most important characteristic of an internet panel is the method of sampling. There are two main types of samples used in internet survey panels – probability samples and nonprobability (opt-in) samples. Many of the criticisms leveled at internet surveys are aimed at the absence of probability sampling rather than the effects of delivery by internet. When comparing different modes of data collection (for example, telephone and internet), it is important to differentiate between the effects of mode from the effects of sampling. Bias in survey data has two main sources: bias in the sample and bias in the responses. Bias in the sample arises because the sample isn't representative of the target population, which may be due to the way the sample was drawn or to variations in the willingness of different groups to respond to the survey. Response bias, on the other hand, arises because those that do complete the survey may give inaccurate or misleading answers, or may be unable (or unwilling) to answer the questions in the way that was intended by the researcher. Both response and non-response bias are, of course, distinct from (and in addition to) sampling error, which refers to the random sampling variability inherent in any sample data.

Although for practical reasons mode and sampling methods may be related to each other, they can be separated. For example, online panels can be selected by random probability sampling, and in-person surveys can be selected on the basis of nonprobability methods such as quotas. However, in practice, due to the substantial costs of probability sampling over the internet and the potential saving from the removal of all interviewer costs, internet surveys are usually based on nonprobability samples.

Sampling and accuracy

Statistical inference is the idea that one can make generalizations about an entire population from a sample that is drawn from it. This is based on the simple premise that everyone in the population has a non-zero and known chance of being included in the sample.

One of the main threats to inference from internet panel samples is coverage error (Couper 2000). Coverage error is error that arises due to the people that are missing from a sampling frame (and so have a zero probability of being included in the survey) and differences between people covered by the frame and people who are not (Groves 1989). If the sampling frame covers the entire population, or those who are missing from the frame are missing at random, then no coverage error will occur. However, non-internet users are not missing at random from internet surveys. People with internet access and who use the internet regularly are systematically different from those who do not on socio-demographic, attitudinal, and other characteristics (Ragnedda and Muschert 2013; Zickuhr and Smith 2012).

Internet access and use has increased rapidly since the early days of internet survey research. However, there is still a sizeable population without internet access – according to the World Bank, in 2014, 22 percent of the adult population of OECD countries did not have access to the internet. Increasing internet penetration does not mean the risk of coverage error is decreasing. As the population without internet access becomes smaller, differences between people with and without internet access may become more pronounced (Callegaro, Baker et al. 2014).

An additional challenge for internet surveys is that there is no sampling frame of the general population from which to draw a sample, making it impossible to calculate the probability of selection. In-person surveys can sample from fairly complete registers of addresses, and telephone surveys can use random digit dialing, but there are currently no complete registers of e-mail or IP addresses of internet devices (computers, tablets, smartphones, etc.), and there is no clear link between devices and the population unit of interest (i.e., the individual person or voter). Not only are many devices shared (e.g., home computers) but many individuals have multiple devices and others none at all.

To address the lack of sampling frame, some internet panel probability samples are recruited offline using traditional address based or RDD random sampling methods (web probability panels). Coverage errors due to respondents not having internet access are solved by either providing it for them or supplementing the internet survey with additional survey modes (AAPOR Standards Committee 2010). However, this significantly increases the cost of recruiting and maintaining the panel and the dominant form of the internet sample remains the nonprobability based on opt-in panel.

There are many ways in which respondents might be recruited to a nonprobability panel but exactly how respondents are recruited to different panels is often protected as proprietary information (AAPOR Standards Committee 2010). Known methods for recruitment include advertising on websites, target mailing through partner organizations, and recommendation by other panelists. Panelists are usually offered a small incentive for taking part in surveys, generally entries into a prize draw or points which can be redeemed for cash. Examining the reasons people participate in online surveys, Poynter and Comley (2003) find that most (59 percent) respondents say incentives are an important reason, as well as other reasons such as curiosity (42 percent), enjoyment (40 percent), and having their views heard (28 percent).

Once they have developed an access panel, internet survey operators attempt to emulate a population sampling frame by drawing samples from the larger access panel in numbers or quotas for different groups based on the relative size of those groups in the target population. Regardless of its sophistication, no method can transform a nonprobability sample into a probability sample. The goal of all research is to make inferences about phenomena that are unbiased by "disturbing variables" (Kish 1987) that might lead to incorrect conclusions. Probability sampling diminishes the risks of this problem through randomization. Nonprobability samples do not have the benefit of randomization, and if self-selection into a nonprobability panel is related to the variables of interest then there is the substantial risk that inferences will be wrong (Baker et al. 2013). However, as Kish wrote, "Great advances of the most successful sciences … were, and are, achieved without probability sampling … Probability sampling for randomization is not a dogma, but a strategy ..." (1965: 28–29). Nonprobability samples have a long history of use in public opinion research in the form of quota sampling. History has shown that, although quota samples can come up with the right answer some of the time, they can also go drastically wrong (Mosteller et al. 1949; Jowell et al. 1993). Without a theoretic basis, it is impossible to judge how accurate a nonprobability sample will be.

Some scholars have risen to this challenge and have tried to put the use of nonprobability samples on a firmer theoretical footing (Rivers 2007; Terhanian and Bremer 2012). This work draws from case-control methods and uses matching to a control group (Rosenbaum and Rubin 1983) at the sample selection stage and propensity score weighting after sample selection to deal with potential biases in the sample (see Chapter 36 for a more comprehensive examination of these issues).

The most important element of inference with nonprobability samples is whether the self-selection into the sample is "ignorable" (Rivers 2013). Essentially, the opt-in sample (where probability of inclusion is affected by unobserved effects of self-selection, non-response, and non-coverage) can provide an estimate of a variable Y so long as the probability of inclusion is conditionally independent of Y (Rubin 1976). In other words, it is ignorable insofar as it is possible to explain any difference between the survey and the population on Y with a given set of covariates.

Whether self-selection into nonprobability internet panels is ignorable is an empirical question. Research in Britain suggested that nonprobability internet surveys show great promise (Sanders et al. 2004; Sanders et al. 2007; Twyman 2008). However, the early consensus in American studies of internet surveys was that nonprobability panels performed worse than probability surveys of different modes (Malhotra and Krosnick 2007; Chang and Krosnick 2009; Pasek and Krosnick 2010; AAPOR Standards Committee 2010; Yeager et al. 2011). More recent American studies have been more optimistic (Ansolabehere and Schaffner 2014; Kennedy et al. 2016). In the next section, we examine the performance of nonprobability samples in more detail.

Fit for purpose?

It is important to distinguish between two purposes that surveys might have – estimating population values of certain variables and of estimating the relationship between sets of variables. Accurate point estimates *can* be estimated from nonprobability samples (Wang et al. 2015; Kennedy et al. 2016) but that does not mean that they *will* be estimated accurately (see Chapter 36 in this volume). Recent research (Kennedy et al. 2016) has emphasized that certain types of nonprobability panels, particularly those that employ sophisticated matching and propensity score weighting methods, perform much better than other types of panel. The key question is whether those methods can adequately adjust for the effects of selection. The consensus is that if the research goals are point estimates of particular variables in the population the risks of incorrect inferences are substantially lower using probability sampling methods (Baker et al. 2013; Callegaro, Villar et al. 2014).

A perennial problem for surveys of all types is that survey respondents tend to be politically and civically more engaged than the general population, and this is likely to be especially true for opt-in panels (Groves, Presser, and Dipko 2004; Tourangeau, Groves, and Redline 2010; Kennedy et al. 2016). The population distribution of political engagement is essentially unknowable and so if political engagement is a non-ignorable conditioning variable this might present a serious problem. An example of such a problem is demonstrated by Mellon and Prosser (forthcoming) in their examination of the 2015 British polling failure. Mellon and Prosser find that the key explanation for the polling miss was the under sampling of non-voters. The demographics of turnout and party support are correlated – for example, younger people are less likely to vote in general, but more likely to vote Labour when they do vote. When a pool of respondents that does not contain a representative number of non-voters is quota sampled or weighted to look like the population, voters that demographically resemble non-voters (and the parties they support) will be overrepresented in the sample.

Whilst the evidence on the accuracy of point estimates from internet surveys based on non-probability panels is decidedly mixed, many have argued that researchers are often more interested in understanding the relationships between variables, rather than their prevalence in the population. In this respect, the debate is similar to that over the use of convenience samples such as college students in experimental psychology (Mook 1983; Sears 1986). Again the key concern is "ignorability" – there is no basis for assuming the homogeneity of relationships between non-probability samples and the population. In psychology, for instance, there is some evidence that college student samples lead to effect sizes of different magnitude, direction, and significance compared to non-student samples (Peterson 2001). Similarly, a recent comparison of several nonprobability internet samples found that the samples with the least accurate point estimates were also least accurate in terms of relationships between variables (Kennedy et al. 2016).

Comparing probability and nonprobability samples, some studies have found substantial variation in the strength and significance of different coefficients (Malhotra and Krosnick 2007; Pasek and Krosnick 2010) whilst others have found more similar results (Berrens et al. 2003; Sanders et al. 2007; Stephenson and Crête 2011; Ansolabehere and Schaffner 2014; Simmons and Bobo 2015; Bytzek and Bieber 2016; Pasek 2016).

A common finding with internet surveys is higher levels of concurrent and predictive validity on the internet compared to telephone surveys (Chang and Krosnick 2009; Simmons and Bobo 2015; Pasek 2016). For example, Chang and Krosnick (2009) find that vote choice measured in internet surveys was more highly correlated with widely accepted predictors of vote choice, such as government approval and party identification. Whether or not this increased explanatory power is a function of the mode or an artefact of sample composition (Simmons and Bobo 2015) is not clear.

Malhotra and Krosnick (2007) suggest nonprobability samples can be more troublesome for some outcome variables than others. For example, models of turnout are especially problematic as commonly over 90 percent of internet panels (claim to) vote, leaving a very small (and likely unrepresentative) proportion of the sample to explain the differences between voters and non-voters. How important differences in coefficients are is a matter of judgment. Many of the studies which have argued in favor of nonprobability samples find differences in coefficient strength but ultimately argue that you "would make the same policy inference" (Berrens et al. 2003: 20) or reach the same conclusions about different models of vote choice (Sanders et al. 2007).

Even if nonprobability panels can, and often do, result in the same inferences as probability panels, this is not the same thing as saying they *will*. Even studies supporting the use of nonprobability panels contain contradictory results. For example, researchers would reach the opposite conclusions about the effect of gender on turnout depending on whether they used the probability or nonprobability samples reported in Sanders et al. (2007). Although nonprobability samples may be perfectly adequate for many, even most, research purposes, findings from nonprobability samples that contradict theoretical expectations and long-standing trends should be treated with caution.

The use of nonprobability internet samples for research is a rapidly developing area. Increasingly nonprobability samples can, and do, perform just as well as probability samples – and in some cases actually outperform them (Kennedy et al. 2016). The crux of the debate is therefore not whether you can make inferences from nonprobability samples, but about the assumptions that one must make, and whether such assumptions are any less relevant to probability samples with non-response.

Benefits of internet surveys

Despite some of the reservations about the representativeness of (nonprobability) internet samples, delivery of a survey instrument by internet has a number of potential advantages compared to interviewer-based methods of collection. While in-person surveys offer the benefits of personal rapport between interviewer and respondent – encouraging participation, clarifying questions, interpreting responses, and helping reduce item non-response – there are also associated disadvantages. Collection of data by trained interviewers is expensive, particularly with the increasing costs of human labor and travel. Even telephone and mail costs tend to be expensive compared to online completion of surveys (Callegaro, Baker, et al. 2014). But quite apart from costs, online surveys can be fielded very quickly and turnaround times can be kept short as they do not rely on the availability of interviewers. Moreover, respondents can complete the survey at their own convenience, taking breaks when they like, making the experience less demanding. The use of the internet means that complex routing, randomization, and attractive presentation can be used to smooth the survey experience. It also facilitates use of complex visual and audio tools, and the straightforward delivery of survey experiments (Skitka and Sargis 2006). Given the current popularity of experimental methods for making causal inferences, the convenience of being able to implement fairly complex survey experiments (for example, including multimedia) on substantial samples with a panel is an attractive feature of internet surveys (Mutz 2011).

A further advantage of internet surveys is the inherent benefits of a panel design. Whilst in-person survey and telephone surveys can be designed as a panel, the maintenance of the panel element adds to the higher cost compared to internet surveys. When studying political behavior, there are always dangers to causal inference brought about by endogeneity. It is widely accepted that both these problems can be ameliorated, if not eliminated, by a panel design using a range of specialized statistical methods for panel data analysis (Finkel 1995). Internet surveys offer a fast and cost-effective way of delivering repeated measure data for large numbers of citizens and offer a uniquely valuable resource for researchers concerned with understanding within-person change. Just as the representativeness of a sample may be less critical for the relationship between variables than it is for making point estimates, the risks associated with analyzing within-person change are lower still as many unobserved characteristics are constant. For example, if we are interested in factors that affect voters switching from party A to party B, we do not require the sample to be perfectly representative with respect to party support, or even other variables correlated with party support; we only require that factors related to switching are not correlated with the probability of being included in the sample. Because these risks are relatively low compared to the risk of obtaining misleading point estimates, we suggest that the question of which is the better choice (internet versus non-internet) depends on the purpose for which it is needed, as well as the type of sample.

Mode effects

Internet surveys have a great deal in common with other visual and self-administered survey modes (Tourangeau, Conrad, and Couper 2013). A particular concern with all surveys, but particularly self-administered modes is *satisficing* (Krosnick 1991). Satisficing is the use of cognitive shortcuts to reduce required effort to answer survey questions and varies with motivation, ability, and the difficulty of questions. Face-to-face surveys reduce satisficing because interacting with an interviewer in person increases motivation (Holbrook, Green, and Krosnick 2003), whilst internet surveys may be more cognitively demanding because they require respondents to know how to use a computer and answer questions without help from an interviewer (Heerwegh and Loosveldt 2008). Others, however, have argued that visually administered surveys actually reduce the cognitive burden of a survey because respondents do not have to hold information in their working memory (Tourangeau, Conrad, and Couper 2013).

In common with other visually administered surveys, internet surveys are prone to one particular form of satisficing – primacy bias – the tendency for respondents to pick early response options in lists (in contrast to orally administered surveys, which are more likely to suffer recency bias because respondents have to hold information in working memory [Chang and Krosnick 2009]). Primacy bias was originally observed in self-administered paper surveys (Krosnick and Alwin 1987). Evidence from eye-tracking data shows that some respondents in computer-administrated surveys pay more attention to items at the top of a list (Galesic et al. 2008). There is also the possibility of computer-specific primacy effects from certain design options like scrolling answer lists where not all answers are visible at the same time (Couper et al. 2004). However, set against this, internet delivery offers a relatively simple way to randomize the order of response options compared to interviewer-based methods.

Another common concern with internet surveys is *speeding:* the tendency for some respondents to go through a survey as quickly as possible without paying adequate attention to the questions. Tourangeau, Conrad, and Couper (2013) argue that speeding is a problem in any self-administered survey but is associated with internet surveys because it is *detectable.* A recent evaluation of speeding (Greszki, Meyer, and Schoen 2014) found that, although speeding occurs, it does not do so at the high levels some have assumed and is not so prevalent or systematic that it affects estimates.

One form of satisficing that might be of particular concern for some research questions is the tendency for some internet respondents to cheat on knowledge questions. A consistent finding from many studies is that respondents completing surveys online tend to score higher on knowledge questions (Ansolabehere and Schaffner 2014; Fricker et al. 2005; Strabac and Aalberg 2011). These studies have generally concluded that people with internet access are more informed than their offline counterparts. Recent evidence suggests, however, that some respondents cheat on knowledge questions by researching the answers while they take the survey (Clifford and Jerit 2014; Burnett 2016). Despite the dangers of various forms of satisficing, much of the research has demonstrated that overall satisficing is lower in internet surveys than in telephone surveys (Chang and Krosnick 2009).

A widely cited advantage of internet surveys is an improvement in response accuracy for sensitive items. The presence of an interviewer can induce social desirability bias by reducing the sense of privacy (Holbrook, Green, and Krosnick 2003; Tourangeau and Yan 2007; Kreuter, Presser, and Tourangeau 2008; Heerwegh 2009). Mainly this means that interviewees are inclined to hide opinions and behaviors that they perceive to be socially undesirable, or in some sense transgress accepted social norms (Krysan 1998). For example, this might include unwillingness to admit to socially conservative values, such as against immigration or support for extremist parties, and to overestimate socially desirable attributes such as voter turnout. In contrast in internet surveys, respondents can express their socially undesirable opinions in private. For example, Tourangeau, Groves, and Redline (2010) found that self-reported illicit drug use showed consistently higher rates of reporting with self-completion compared to interviewer administration. Chang and Krosnick (2009) find lower levels of socially desirable responding in internet surveys, as measured by the answers provided by white respondents to questions about government programs to support African Americans. Whilst there have been exceptions to this finding (see Ansolabehere and Schaffner 2014), the general consensus is that self-completion internet surveys are likely to have fewer problems of social desirability bias than interviewer-based modes.

Panel conditioning and trained respondents

Internet panelists are often members of multiple panels (Stenbjerre and Laugesen 2005; Vonk, van Ossenbruggen, and Willems 2006) and a small number of panel members account for a large proportion of survey responses (Craig et al. 2013). The effect of repeated participation in survey research can be divided into two types – the effect on respondents' attitudes and behaviors, and the way in which they respond to the survey itself. Sturgis, Allum, and Brunton-Smith (2009) argue that repeatedly administering attitude questions causes respondents to reflect and deliberate on the issues raised by the questions they are asked. The results of this are stronger and more internally consistent attitudes in the later waves of a panel survey. There is also some evidence that being asked about electoral participation might increase the likelihood of actually voting (Greenwald et al. 1987; Granberg and Holmberg 1992).

Most panel conditioning research, however, has examined the effect of survey participation on the survey response process itself. Trained respondents (i.e., those who have taken many surveys) tend to answer surveys more quickly than fresh respondents (Toepoel, Das, and van Soest 2008). This could be in part because trained respondents are used to the question–answering process and learn how to interpret questions but it could also be due to satisficing and trained respondents may not read questions properly and thus make more mistakes. Toepoel, Das, and van Soest (2008) suggest the latter is the case and trained respondents are less likely to notice reverse-worded questions. Other research has found similar results, with a strong correlation between "professional" (those that take a large number of surveys) and inattentive respondents (Vonk, van Ossenbruggen, and Willems 2006). Whether this occurs due to training effects or the type of respondents in non-probability samples is unclear. Chang and Krosnick (2009) find evidence of practice effects for probability internet panel respondents but not for nonprobability panel respondents. Hillygus, Jackson, and Young (2014) suggest that satisficing behavior of professional respondents is not due to panel conditioning but to differences in motivation – professional respondents take surveys because they want compensation rather than because they are interested in the survey topic.

There is also evidence from offline surveys that repeatedly administering questions about sensitive items can lead to more socially desirable reporting (Sharpe and Gilbert 1998; Halpern-Manners and Warren 2012). Sharpe and Gilbert (1998) find that repeated administration of the Beck Depression Inventory leads to more socially desirable responses and Halpern-Manners and Warren (2012) find a similar effect for labor market status. How these effects interact with sensitive item reporting is not yet clear.

Bias from panel conditioning may be exacerbated by differential attrition in panels and varying levels of response to invitations from panel members to specific surveys. For example, panel members who choose to complete political surveys tend to be more interested in politics. This is akin to non-response bias in probability surveys, although response rates in internet surveys are hard to define because of lack of a sampling frame, and there is no agreed way to define response metrics (see Callegaro and DiSogra 2008). Cavallaro (2013) suggests that the problems with attrition – the non-random dropping out of some types of respondents – pose a more serious problem to internet panels than the problem of panel conditioning.

Conclusions

Given the problems we have outlined in this chapter, the reader would be forgiven for thinking that our advice would be to avoid using nonprobability internet panels. This is not our intention and we follow other authors (Farrell and Petersen 2010; Callegaro, Villar et al. 2014) in saying that internet research should not be stigmatized. It is important, however, for users to be aware of the potential pitfalls of particular survey modes and threats to inference that may emerge from internet survey research. A recent report into nonprobability internet panels by the American Association for Public Opinion Research (AAPOR) identified a continuum of the expected accuracy of estimates from nonprobability samples, with the highest risk of false inferences arising from the use of uncontrolled convenience samples but treating the sample as if the respondents were a random sample of the population. The accuracy of estimates is likely to be much higher when using surveys that select respondents and adjust the data for non-ignorable conditioning variables. As the study notes, the challenge for researchers "arises in placing surveys between the two extremes. This is largely uncharted territory for social, opinion, and market research surveys" (Baker et al. 2013: 100).

All survey research is imperfect (Weisberg 2005). The potential problems with internet samples – particularly nonprobability samples – should not be taken to mean that other survey modes are without risks, nor that the problems with internet panels are insurmountable obstacles to inference.

The question for researchers must be what is the aim of their research? An earlier AAPOR report into internet surveys recommended that "researchers should avoid nonprobability online panels when one of the research objectives is to accurately estimate population values" (AAPOR Standards Committee 2010: 758), a conclusion echoed by many others (see, for example, Callegaro, Villar et al. 2014; Simmons and Bobo 2015; Bytzek and Bieber 2016, but see Stoker and McCall in this volume). Although some internet panels have shown great promise and this advice may change in the future, for the time being at least we see no reason to dissent from this view.

For other research purposes, internet panels offer greater potential. Seemingly intractable debates over causal ordering in electoral research mean that cross-sectional surveys are increasingly inadequate to answer research questions (Hillygus 2011). No research is without risk and users of internet surveys should approach internet research with their eyes open, but the potential for low-cost longitudinal panels and embedded survey experiments provides an unparalleled opportunity for researchers to answer important questions about electoral behavior.

Notes

1 For a more detailed look at the potential problems with nonprobability sampling and its similarities with non-response in probability samples, see Chapter 36 in this volume.
2 A further type of internet data collection that is seeing an increasing number of users is what might be termed internet convenience samples – running surveys and experiments on crowdsourced labor platforms such as Amazon Mechanical Turk. We do not discuss this type of data here but many of the same concerns and considerations about data quality in internet panel surveys might equally apply to internet convenience samples (see, for example, Clifford, Jewell, and Waggoner 2015).

References

AAPOR Standards Committee (2010) "AAPOR Report on Online Panels," *Public Opinion Quarterly*, vol. 74, no. 4, Winter, 711–781.

Ansolabehere, S. and Schaffner, B. F. (2014) "Does Survey Mode Still Matter? Findings from a 2010 Multi-Mode Comparison," *Political Analysis*, vol. 22, no. 3, June, 285–303.

Baker, R., Brick, J. M., Bates, N. A., Battaglia, M., Couper, M. P., Dever, J. A., Gile, K. J., and Tourangeau, R. (2013) "Summary Report of the AAPOR Task Force on Non-Probability Sampling," *Journal of Survey Statistics and Methodology*, vol. 1, no. 2, November, 90–143.

Berrens, R. P., Bohara, A. K., Jenkins-Smith, H., Silva, C., and Weimer, D. L. (2003) "The Advent of Internet Surveys for Political Research: A Comparison of Telephone and Internet Samples," *Political Analysis*, vol. 11, no. 1, Winter, 1–22.

Burnett, C. M. (2016) "Exploring the Difference in Participants' Factual Knowledge between Online and in-Person Survey Modes," *Research and Politics*, vol. 3, no. 2, June, 1–7.

Bytzek, E. and Bieber, I. E. (2016) "Does Survey Mode Matter for Studying Electoral Behavior? Evidence from the 2009 German Longitudinal Election Study," *Electoral Studies*, vol. 43, September, 41–51.

Callegaro, M. and DiSogra, C. (2008) "Computing Response Metrics for Online Panels," *Public Opinion Quarterly*, vol. 72, no. 5, December, 1008–1032.

Callegaro, M., Baker, R., Bethlehem, J., Göritz, A. S., Krosnick, J. A., and Lavrakas, P. J. (2014) "Online Panel Research: History, Concepts, Applications and a Look at the Future," in Callegaro, M., Baker, R., Bethlehem, J., Göritz, A. J., Krosnick, J. A., and Lavrakas, P. J. (eds.) *Online Panel Research: A Data Quality Perspective*, London: Wiley: 1–22.

Callegaro, M., Villar, A., Yeager, D. S., and Krosnick, J. A. (2014) "A Critical Review of Studies Investigating the Quality of Data Obtained with Online Panels Based on Probability and Nonprobability Samples," in Callegaro, M., Baker, R., Bethlehem, J., Göritz, A. J., Krosnick, J. A., and Lavrakas, P. J. (eds.) *Online Panel Research: A Data Quality Perspective*, London: Wiley: 23–53.

Cavallaro, K. (2013) "By the Numbers: Theory of Adaptation or Survival of the Fittest?," *Quirks Marketing Research Review*, vol. 27, January, 24–27.

Chang, L. and Krosnick, J. A. (2009) "National Surveys Via Rdd Telephone Interviewing Versus the Internet Comparing Sample Representativeness and Response Quality," *Public Opinion Quarterly*, vol. 73, no. 4, Winter, 641–678.

Clifford, S. and Jerit, J. (2014) "Is There a Cost to Convenience? An Experimental Comparison of Data Quality in Laboratory and Online Studies," *Journal of Experimental Political Science*, vol. 1, no. 2, January, 120–131.

Clifford, S., Jewell, R. M., and Waggoner, P. D. (2015) "Are Samples Drawn from Mechanical Turk Valid for Research on Political Ideology?," *Research and Politics*, vol. 2, no. 4, December, 1–9.

Couper, M. P. (2000) "Web Surveys: A Review of Issues and Approaches," *Public Opinion Quarterly*, vol. 64, no. 4, Winter, 464–494.

Couper, M. P., Tourangeau, R., Conrad, F. G., and Crawford, S. D. (2004) "What They See Is What We Get Response Options for Web Surveys," *Social Science Computer Review*, vol. 22, no. 1, February, 111–127.

Craig, B. M., Hays, R. D., Pickard, A. S., Cella, D., Revicki, D. A., and Reeve, B. B. (2013) "Comparison of US Panel Vendors for Online Surveys," *Journal of Medical Internet Research*, vol. 15, no. 11, November, e260.

Curtin, R., Presser, S., and Singer, E. (2005) "Changes in Telephone Survey Nonresponse over the Past Quarter Century," *Public Opinion Quarterly*, vol. 69, no. 1, Spring, 87–98.

Farrell, D. and Petersen, J. C. (2010) "The Growth of Internet Research Methods and the Reluctant Sociologist," *Sociological Inquiry*, vol. 80, no. 1, February, 114–125.

Fieldhouse, E., Green, J., Evans, G., Schmitt, H., van der Eijk, C., Mellon, J., and Prosser, C. (2015) "British Election Study, 2015: Internet Panel Survey," Available online: www.britishelectionstudy.com/data-objects/panel-study-data/ (doi: 10.15127/1.293723) [accessed June 16, 2017].

Finkel, S. E. (1995) *Causal Analysis with Panel Data*, 1st Edition, Thousand Oaks: Sage Publications.

Fricker, S., Galesic, M., Tourangeau, R., and Yan, T. (2005) "An Experimental Comparison of Web and Telephone Surveys," *Public Opinion Quarterly*, vol. 69, no. 3, Autumn, 370–392.

Galesic, M., Tourangeau, R., Couper, M. P., and Conrad, F. G. (2008) "Eye-Tracking Data New Insights on Response Order Effects and Other Cognitive Shortcuts in Survey Responding," *Public Opinion Quarterly*, vol. 72, no. 5, December, 892–913.

Granberg, D. and Holmberg, S. (1992) "The Hawthorne Effect in Election Studies: The Impact of Survey Participation on Voting," *British Journal of Political Science*, vol. 22, no. 2, April, 240–247.

Greenwald, A. G., Carnot, C. G., Beach, R., and Young, B. (1987) "Increasing Voting Behavior by Asking People If They Expect to Vote," *Journal of Applied Psychology*, vol. 72, no. 2, May, 315–318.

Greszki, R., Meyer, M., and Schoen, H. (2014) "The Impact of Speeding on Data Quality in Nonprobability and Freshly Recruited Probability-Based Online Panels," in Callegaro, M., Baker, R., Bethlehem, J., Göritz, A. J., Krosnick, J. A., and Lavrakas, P. J. (eds.) *Online Panel Research: A Data Quality Perspective*, London: Wiley: 238–262.

Groves, R. M. (1989) *Survey Errors and Survey Costs*, 2nd Edition, New York: Wiley.

Groves, R. M., Presser, S., and Dipko, S. (2004) "The Role of Topic Interest in Survey Participation Decisions," *Public Opinion Quarterly*, vol. 68, no. 1, Spring, 2–31.

Halpern–Manners, A. and Warren, J. R. (2012) "Panel Conditioning in Longitudinal Studies: Evidence from Labor Force Items in the Current Population Survey," *Demography*, vol. 49, no. 4, November, 1499–1519.

Heerwegh, D. (2009) "Mode Differences Between Face-to-Face and Web Surveys: An Experimental Investigation of Data Quality and Social Desirability Effects," *International Journal of Public Opinion Research*, vol. 21, no. 1, Spring, 111–121.

Heerwegh, D. and Loosveldt, G. (2008) "Face-to-Face versus Web Surveying in a High-Internet-Coverage Population Differences in Response Quality," *Public Opinion Quarterly*, vol. 72, no. 5, December, 836–846.

Hillygus, D. S. (2011) "The Evolution of Election Polling in the United States," *Public Opinion Quarterly*, vol. 75, no. 5, December, 962–981.

Hillygus, D. S., Jackson, N., and Young, M. (2014) "Professional Respondents in Nonprobability Online Panels," in Callegaro, M., Baker, R., Bethlehem, J., Göritz, A. J., Krosnick, J. A., and Lavrakas, P. J. (eds.) *Online Panel Research: A Data Quality Perspective*, London: Wiley: 219–237.

Holbrook, A. L., Green, M. C., and Krosnick, J. A. (2003) "Telephone Versus Face-to-Face Interviewing of National Probability Samples with Long Questionnaires: Comparisons of Respondent Satisficing and Social Desirability Response Bias," *Public Opinion Quarterly*, vol. 67, no. 1, Spring, 79–125.

Jowell, R., Hedges, B., Lynn, P., Farrant, G., and Heath, A. (1993) "The 1992 British Election: The Failure of the Polls," *Public Opinion Quarterly*, vol. 57, no. 2, Summer, 238–263.

Kennedy, C., Mercer, A., Keeter, S., Hatley, N., McGeeney, K., and Gimenez, A. (2016) "Evaluating Online Nonprobability Surveys," Pew Research Center, May 2, 2016, available online: www.pewresearch.org/files/2016/04/Nonprobability-report-May-2016-FINAL.pdf [accessed July 18, 2016].

Kish, L. (1965) *Survey Sampling*, 2nd Edition, New York: Wiley-Interscience.

Kish, L. (1987) *Statistical Design for Research*, New York: Wiley.

Kreuter, F., Presser, S., and Tourangeau, R. (2008) "Social Desirability Bias in CATI, IVR, and Web Surveys: The Effects of Mode and Question Sensitivity," *Public Opinion Quarterly*, vol. 72, no. 5, December, 847–865.

Krosnick, J. A. (1991) "Response Strategies for Coping with the Cognitive Demands of Attitude Measures in Surveys," *Applied Cognitive Psychology*, vol. 5, no. 3, June, 213–236.

Krosnick, J. A. and Alwin, D. F. (1987) "An Evaluation of a Cognitive Theory of Response-Order Effects in Survey Measurement," *Public Opinion Quarterly*, vol. 51, no. 2, Summer, 201–219.

Krysan, M. (1998) "Privacy and the Expression of White Racial Attitudes: A Comparison Across Three Contexts," *Public Opinion Quarterly*, vol. 62, no. 4, Winter, 506–544.

Lavrakas, P. J., Shuttles, C. D., Steeh, C., and Fienberg, H. (2007) "The State of Surveying Cell Phone Numbers in the United States 2007 and Beyond," *Public Opinion Quarterly*, vol. 71, no. 5, December, 840–854.

Malhotra, N. and Krosnick, J. A. (2007) "The Effect of Survey Mode and Sampling on Inferences about Political Attitudes and Behavior: Comparing the 2000 and 2004 ANES to Internet Surveys with Non-probability Samples," *Political Analysis*, vol. 15, no. 3, Summer, 286–323.

Mellon, J. and Prosser, C. (forthcoming) "Missing Non-Voters and Misweighted Samples: Explaining the 2015 Great British Polling Miss," *Public Opinion Quarterly*.

Mook, D. G. (1983) "In Defense of External Invalidity," *American Psychologist*, vol. 38, no. 4, 379–387.

Mosteller, F., Hyman, H., McCarthy, P., Marks, E., and Truman, D. (1949) *The Pre-Election Polls of 1948: The Report to the Committee on Analysis of Pre-Election Polls and Forecasts*, New York: Social Science Research Council.

Mutz, D. C. (2011) *Population-Based Survey Experiments*, Princeton: Princeton University Press.

Pasek, J. (2016) "When Will Nonprobability Surveys Mirror Probability Surveys? Considering Types of Inference and Weighting Strategies as Criteria for Correspondence," *International Journal of Public Opinion Research*, vol. 28, no. 2, Summer, 269–291.

Pasek, J. and Krosnick, J. A. (2010) *Measuring Intent to Participate and Participation in the 2010 Census and Their Correlates and Trends: Comparisons of RDD Telephone and Non-Probability Sample Internet Survey Data*, Washington, DC: Statistical Research Division of the US Census Bureau.

Peterson, R. A. (2001) "On the Use of College Students in Social Science Research: Insights from a Second-Order Meta-Analysis," *Journal of Consumer Research*, vol. 28, no. 3, December, 450–461.

Poynter, R. and Comley, P. (2003) "Beyond Online Panels," Technovate: CRM, Internet Research and New Media, 2003 Cannes.

Ragnedda, M. and Muschert, G. W. (eds.) (2013) *The Digital Divide: The Internet and Social Inequality in International Perspective*, Abingdon: Routledge.

Rivers, D. (2007) "Sampling for Web Surveys," Paper presented at the 2007 Joint Statistical Meetings of the American Statistical Association, Salt Lake City, August 1.

Rivers, D. (2013) "Comment," *Journal of Survey Statistics and Methodology*, vol. 1, no. 2, November, 111–117.

Rosenbaum, P. R. and Rubin, D. B. (1983) "The Central Role of the Propensity Score in Observational Studies for Causal Effects," *Biometrika*, vol. 70, no. 1, April, 41–55.

Rubin, D. B. (1976) "Inference and Missing Data," *Biometrika*, vol. 63, no. 3, December, 581–592.

Sanders, D., Clarke, H. D., Stewart, M. C., and Whiteley, P. (2007) "Does Mode Matter for Modeling Political Choice? Evidence From the 2005 British Election Study," *Political Analysis*, vol. 15, no. 3, Autumn, 257–285.

Sanders, D., Clarke, H. D., Stewart, M. C., Whiteley, P., and Twyman, J. (2004) "The 2001 British Election Study Internet Poll," *Journal of Political Marketing*, vol. 3, no. 4, 29–55.

Sears, D. O. (1986) "College Sophomores in the Laboratory: Influences of a Narrow Data Base on Social Psychology's View of Human Nature," *Journal of Personality and Social Psychology*, vol. 51, no. 3, September, 515–530.

Sharpe, J. P. and Gilbert, D. G. (1998) "Effects of Repeated Administration of the Beck Depression Inventory and Other Measures of Negative Mood States," *Personality and Individual Differences*, vol. 24, no. 4, April, 457–463.

Simmons, A. D. and Bobo, L. D. (2015) "Can Non-Full-Probability Internet Surveys Yield Useful Data? A Comparison with Full-Probability Face-to-Face Surveys in the Domain of Race and Social Inequality Attitudes," *Sociological Methodology*, vol. 45, no. 1, August, 357–387.

Skitka, L. J. and Sargis, E. G. (2006) "The Internet as Psychological Laboratory," *Annual Review of Psychology*, vol. 57, 529–555.

Stenbjerre, M. and Laugesen, J. N. (2005) "Conducting Representative Online Research: A Summary of Five Years of Learnings," Paper presented at the 2005 ESOMAR Worldwide Panel Research Conference, Budapest, April 17–19.

Stephenson, L. B. and Crête, J. (2011) "Studying Political Behavior: A Comparison of Internet and Telephone Surveys," *International Journal of Public Opinion Research*, vol. 23, no. 1, Spring, 24–55.

Strabac, Z. and Aalberg, T. (2011) "Measuring Political Knowledge in Telephone and Web Surveys: A Cross-National Comparison," *Social Science Computer Review*, vol. 29, no. 2, May, 175–192.

Sturgis, P., Allum, N., and Brunton-Smith, I. (2009) "Attitudes Over Time: The Psychology of Panel Conditioning," in Lynn, P. (ed.) *Methodology of Longitudinal Surveys*, London: John Wiley & Sons: 113–126.

Terhanian, G. and Bremer, J. (2012) "A Smarter Way to Select Respondents for Surveys?," *International Journal of Market Research*, vol. 54, no. 6, 751–780.

Toepoel, V., Das, M., and van Soest, A. (2008) "Effects of Design in Web Surveys Comparing Trained and Fresh Respondents," *Public Opinion Quarterly*, vol. 72, no. 5, December, 985–1007.

Tourangeau, R. and Yan, T. (2007) "Sensitive Questions in Surveys," *Psychological Bulletin*, vol. 133, no. 5, September, 859–883.

Tourangeau, R., Conrad, F., and Couper, M. (2013) *The Science of Web Surveys*, New York: Oxford University Press.

Tourangeau, R., Groves, R. M., and Redline, C. D. (2010) "Sensitive Topics and Reluctant Respondents Demonstrating a Link between Nonresponse Bias and Measurement Error," *Public Opinion Quarterly*, vol. 74, no. 3, Autumn, 413–432.

Twyman, J. (2008) "Getting It Right: YouGov and Online Survey Research in Britain," *Journal of Elections, Public Opinion and Parties*, vol. 18, no. 4, October, 343–354.

Vonk, T., van Ossenbruggen, R., and Willems, P. (2006) "The Effects of Panel Recruitment and Management on Research Results," ESOMAR World Research Conference, Panel Research 2006, Barcelona.

Wang, W., Rothschild, D., Goel, S., and Gelman, A. (2015) "Forecasting Elections with Non-Representative Polls," *International Journal of Forecasting*, vol. 31, no. 3, September, 980–891.

Weisberg, H. F. (2005) *The Total Survey Error Approach*, Chicago: University of Chicago Press.

Yeager, D. S., Krosnick, J. A., Chang, L-C., Javitz, H. S., Levendusky, M. S., Simpser, A., and Wang, R. (2011) "Comparing the Accuracy of RDD Telephone Surveys and Internet Surveys Conducted with Probability and Non-Probability Samples," *Public Opinion Quarterly*, vol. 75, no. 4, Winter, 709–747.

Zickuhr, K. and Smith, A. (2012) "Digital Differences," Pew Research Center, April 13, 2012, available online: www.pewinternet.org/~/media//Files/Reports/2012/PIP_Digital_differences_041312.pdf [accessed July 19, 2016].

38

THE USE OF AGGREGATE DATA IN THE STUDY OF VOTING BEHAVIOR

Ecological inference, ecological fallacy and other applications

Luana Russo

Introduction

A large part of the most prominent and seminal applied works in the field of voting behavior in political science is based on three major research schools: the School of Columbia, which focuses on the importance of social factors, the School of Michigan, which mainly focuses on party identification, and the rational choice theory, which stresses the importance of rationality, uncertainty and economic voting. The common trait of these three very prominent schools is that their theoretical approach and the applied evidences that they present are based on individual data (Lazarsfeld, Berelson and Gaudet 1944; Campbell et al. 1960; Downs 1957, among others).

After all, voting is an individual act, as individual as the decision-making process connected to it. It only seems self-evident that a large part of the literature on voting and political behavior employs individual data. However, aggregate data are also successfully employed in this field. There are two main reasons to employ aggregate data instead of individual data: first, the latter might not be available/reliable or, second, it might not be the most appropriate in order to answer a given research question which aims to explore a problem from its aggregate perspective.

In the first case, the researcher might want to employ the aggregate data to solve a puzzle at the individual level, whilst in the second he/she aims at exploring the aggregate level per se.

In the first case then, aggregate data are employed to infer individual behavior. This use of the aggregate data is called ecological inference and it is useful when the researcher is interested in the behavior of the individuals but the data are available only at the aggregate level (as for local or comparative electoral politics), unreliable (e.g., racial politics and abstention – areas in which respondents might feel pressured to answer in a certain way due to social desirability), inadequate (e.g., political and electoral geography – due to the unavailability of data sampled at the sub-national level) or unattainable (e.g., history – due to the lack of data) (King 1997). Hence, ecological inference is a mathematical solution to overcome a problem of data limitation – and the most immediate implication of having to deal with a limitation is that the solution is not free of limitations itself. The best way to study individual behavior is obviously to employ individual-level data. Trying to overcome the lack (or the unreliability) of data by using aggregate-level data entails two connected problems: the reliability of the estimates and the *ecological fallacy*, which is the incorrect assumption that the properties of the aggregate must apply to the individuals.

A typical example that fits the second scenario – trying to solve a puzzle that is inherently of aggregate nature – is the study of turnout (Franklin 2004: 16). In fact, the study of turnout from an aggregate perspective is rich in prominent contributions (see Geys 2006 and Blais 2007). A problem may arise when the individual decision of voting and the aggregate nature of turnout are not conceptually separated and the researcher assumes that the relationship found at the individual level can be applied also at the aggregate one (Alker 1969; Welzel and Inglehart 2007) – this is known as the *individualistic fallacy* and it is clearly the mirror image of the ecological fallacy problem.

This chapter aims at offering an overview of what the advantages and the limitations are when a researcher decides to use aggregate data – because those are the only (or the best) data available or because the focus of the analysis is on a concept that is aggregate in nature. Therefore, the chapter is mostly divided into two main parts: first it presents the problem of ecological inference and the related topic of ecological fallacy, it then continues by offering an overview of concepts and measures that are inherently aggregate.

Facing the problem: aggregate data to infer individual behavior

Ecological inference: the problem and an overview of the proposed solutions

The purpose of ecological inference is to infer the behavior of individuals by using aggregate data. The attribute *ecological* originates from the fact that aggregate data are normally issued at a territorial level – that is, from ecological units such as municipalities, constituencies, provinces, regions or countries. The problem is then to obtain an estimate of the behavior of the individuals in a given ecological unit from the information on the aggregate behavior. Table 38.1 shows a practical example from King (1997: 13).

As King (1997: 13) says: "The ecological inference problem involves replacing the question marks in the body of this table with inferences based on information from the marginal." Table 38.1 illustrates the typical ecological problem: for a given territorial area there are data available on (1) how many voters casted a preference for a certain party or did not go to the polls and (2) how many voters of a given ethnic background there are in the area of study. The information that is missing is how many voters for each of the given ethnic background voted, and, if so, for which party. In other words, as Table 38.1 shows, we know the marginal but we do not know how the marginal would be distributed in the cells. Several solutions have been proposed

Table 38.1 The ecological inference problem

Race of voters	Voting decision			Total
	Democrat	Republican	No vote	
Black	?	?	?	55,054
White	?	?	?	25,706
Total	19,896	10,963	49,928	80,760

in order to fill out the cells – and the variety of the solutions itself leads to the bottom of the problem: a fundamental indeterminacy (Duncan and Davis 1953; Tam Cho and Manski 2008; Elff, Gschwend and Johnston 2008). This is due to the fact that the available information is not sufficient to narrow down the feasible set of estimates to an interval that should include the parameter, unless strong assumptions are made. Elff, Gschwend and Johnston (2008) break down the fundamental indeterminacy into two different problems: (1) the modeling indeterminacy – which is linked to the exclusive use of aggregate variables: as long as only aggregate variables are present in the model there will always be multiple solutions (interrelations) to fill out the cells; and (2) the inferential indeterminacy: when a model is adopted, this model will rest on given restrictive assumptions about the population of interest – assumptions that cannot be tested if the only available variables are of aggregate nature. As Elff, Gschwend and Johnston (2008: 73) emphasize: "If the first problem is solved, the second problem is inevitably encountered. If one tries to avoid the second problem, one cannot solve the first one."

Actually, the first problem is mainly due to the will (or the necessity) to obtain point estimates – that is, to fill out the cells in Table 38.1 with one number. In fact, if one follows the Duncan and Davis (1953) approach, no assumptions are needed, but the cells will not be filled out with point estimates but with ranges. In other words, instead of having a single number estimate, one obtains an interval (with a minimum and a maximum bound) which comprises the estimate. The range of the bounds depends on the available data. In certain situations, a bound is sufficient to test a hypothesis and/or to look into a given phenomenon. However, point estimates are often required, and seem to be the most desirable outcome when looking at the flourishing literature that proposes models in order to solve the ecological inference problem.[1]

The key issue when using (or proposing a new) ecological inference model that provides point estimates is how one deals with the assumptions of that model. Each model entails specific assumptions, and the best-case scenario is that the assumptions can be tested. This is, however, rarely possible. Nonetheless, it is always possible to choose a model that is supposedly the best fit for the specific ecological inference problem that needs to be solved. A brief overview of the main logic of the Goodman (1953) and the Freedman et al. (1991) models might help illustrating the matter.

At the basis of the Goodman model (1953) is the "constancy assumption," which holds that the individuals belonging to a given group will behave similarly regardless of the ecological unit examined. It is possible to translate this assumption in a given scenario such as: voters of a particular ethnic origin will vote the same regardless of the neighborhood in which they live. Or: voters of a certain ideological persuasion will vote the same regardless of the municipality/province/region in which they live. Hence, the underlying assumption of this model is that the specific territorial context does not play an important role. In order to show how important these assumptions are in shaping the final model outcome – that is, the point estimates – Freedman et al. (1991) propose a neighborhood model that entails the opposite assumption with respect to the Goodman (1953) model. The neighborhood model adopts a constancy assumption that maintains that voters in the same neighborhood will vote similarly regardless of which particular ethnic group they belong to (or ideological view they hold).

As different assumptions will fit different situations, the variety of models proposed is not surprising. It may be argued that some models seem to be applicable in a wider set of situations than others, but in the end each researcher needs to identify the model that will fit his/her particular needs better.

Ecological fallacy

The previous section discussed how the fundamental indeterminacy that characterizes the possible solutions to the ecological inference problem leads to a multitude of approaches and models. But finding out what model will suit a given study (or a set of data) best is not the only hurdle. There is a widespread skepticism in the academic world about results obtained through ecological inference techniques (and aggregate data in general). This distrustful attitude is due to the fact that these results may be affected by an ecological fallacy.

The discussion on the ecological fallacy originates from the seminal work of Robinson (1950), who observed the inconsistencies between results obtained by performing correlations on individual- and aggregate-level data. Basically, by using the same set of data, Robinson (1950) showed that according to the level of data employed (individual or aggregate) the correlation estimate was different. Goodman (1953) reacted by arguing that if in general Robinson's (1950) argument was correct – and therefore the behavior of the individuals could not be inferred by only using aggregate data – "in very special circumstances the study of regression between ecological variables may be used to make inferences concerning the behavior of individuals" (Goodman 1953: 663). These *special circumstances* consisted of applying this model only when the constancy assumption would hold. This would apply in general to all models: they are intended to produce reliable estimates as long as the assumptions hold. However, the impossibility of empirically testing the assumptions does not provide the assurances that the estimates are free of ecological fallacy.

Welzel and Inglehart (2007: 304) suggest looking at the ecological fallacy debate from a completely new perspective by stating that "the prevailing conception of the ecological fallacy is itself fallacious." They challenge the assumption that in order not to be spurious (and, therefore, reliable) a relation has to appear in the same way both at the individual and at the aggregate level. In order to support their argument, they offer an example based on Weimar Germany, where there was a strong significant correlation between the Nazi vote and unemployment at the regional level. Research (Falter 1991) has shown that when analyzing this relation at the individual level unemployed people were not more likely to vote for Hitler. Do these findings imply that the correlation between unemployment and voting for the Nazis was not valid and therefore non-existent? According to Welzel and Inglehart (2007) this is not the case: considering what is found by using aggregate data as non-valid means plainly overlooking the fact that

> social phenomena, such as unemployment, do not have to influence the behavior of an individual as a *personal* attribute of this individual itself; they can also influence the behavior of an individual as an aggregate attribute of the population in which the individual lives.
>
> *(Welzel and Inglehart 2007: 304–306)*

In other words, being unemployed per se did not increase the *individual* chance to vote for the Nazis, but living in a region with a high unemployment rate did. Hence, both findings – the one at the individual level and the one on the aggregate level – are valid. In the authors' own words: "The fact that many characteristics affect individuals as aggregate attributes of their population, not as their personal attributes, is not an ecological *fallacy* but an ecological *reality*" (Welzel and Inglehart 2007: 306).

The authors take things a step further by arguing that denying the existence of the relation at the aggregate level can be identified as *individualistic fallacy*. The concept of individualistic fallacy was initially proposed by Alker (1969). If ecological fallacy consists in falsely assuming that a relationship found at the aggregate level could be assumed to exist at the individual level, the individualistic fallacy implies just the opposite, with the assumption that a relationship that exists at the individual level would also be found at the aggregate level.

Evidently, Welzel and Inglehart (2007) do not argue that ecological fallacies do not exist, but they warn about two risks: first, assuming that when using aggregate data an ecological fallacy problem would exist *tout court*; second, that if political science is pervaded by skepticism on the use of aggregate data due to the danger of incurring an ecological fallacy problem, the risk of running into an individualistic fallacy problem is widely overlooked.

Data: availability, reliability and feasibility

Considering the difficulties in selecting an appropriate ecological inference model and then trying to avoid ecological fallacy problems when interpreting the results, why is there such a lively debate on ecological inference and why do aggregate data continue to be widely used to infer the behavior of individuals? As mentioned before, there are many instances in which the use of aggregate data is the only or the best alternative to individual data. The most obvious is the unavailability of individual-level data. This might be the case for a comparative study in which the aim is to compare a large number of countries or when one is interested in carrying out a longitudinal (and comparative) study. The existence of large cross-national surveys is a relatively recent phenomenon whilst the chance that data exist at the country (or even local) level for a longer timespan is rather high. Hence, for research that aims to be largely comparative across time and space, aggregate data are often the only viable solution (see, for example, Fornos, Power and Garand 2004).

Lack of survey data can also cause a further problem: a researcher might be interested in studying sub-areas of a country (e.g., macro-areas, regions, provinces, municipalities) but the sample might be conceived to be representative at the national level, hence no reliable result can be obtained for the local level. This has been a serious problem in the advancement of many fields of political science, among which the studies on local voting and political behavior and the discipline of political geography, which had to almost exclusively rely on aggregate data (see, for example, Alford and Lee 1968; Wright 1977; Agnew 1996; Landa, Copeland and Grofman 1995; Shin and Agnew 2002, 2008). The lack of individual-level data at the local level can be ascribed to two connected factors: the large predominance in political science of the compositional approach (i.e., the tradition in which the explanatory role is reserved for the position of the citizen within society and his/her evaluation of the current political-economic situation, as is the case for the three major research schools mentioned in the Introduction) (Johnston and Pattie 2006)[2] and the large cost that a survey that would be representative at a sub-country level would entail.

The other key reason to decide to employ aggregate data alternatively or in addition to survey data is that the latter might pose problems related to their reliability. The reliability of survey data can be compromised by three main factors: technical issues (i.e., sampling errors), memory problems (recalling an electoral preference might be problematic, which poses a problem for studying volatility) and the topic under investigation (a citizen might not be willing to answer certain questions due to social desirability).

In fact, there is a rich literature that employs aggregate data in order to estimate electoral volatility between two elections at a national (see, for example, Agnew 1994; Landa, Copeland and Grofman 1995; Katz and King 1999; De Sio 2008; Russo 2014b) or municipal level (e.g., Landa, Copeland and Grofman 1995; Liu and Vanderleeuw 2001; Forcina, Gnaldi and Bracalente 2012), ticket-splitting (e.g., Johnston and Pattie 2000; Benoit, Laver and Giannetti 2004; Tam Cho and

Gaines 2004; Brunell and Grofman 2009), or in order to cross-validate or compare swing voter estimates obtained by survey data (Russo 2014a). Furthermore, aggregate data can also be employed for election forecasting – this is especially useful in the case of a very volatile electorate, a condition that can easily compromise the reliability of survey estimates, as they are largely based on past data (i.e., the *Seats-Votes model* proposed by Whiteley et al. 2011).

Finally, the topic object of the study might not be suitable to be investigated with survey data due to the insincere answers the study might obtain. This is notoriously the case when investigating turnout (Ansolabehere and Hersh 2012). In fact, it is well documented that surveys tend to overestimate electoral turnout (Selb and Munzert 2013) because of problems of over-representation and misreporting. The over-representation consists in over-representing voters that are interested in politics due to disproportionate self-selection in survey samples (Voogt and Saris 2003). This problem can be linked to two factors: the inclusion of actual non-voters who are not willing to declare they did not cast a vote for reasons of social desirability (Belli et al. 1999) or a sampling error consisting in selecting a sample that systematically over-represents voters and under-represents non-voters (Sciarini and Goldberg 2016). Once again, ecological inference models to cross-validate the survey data can be useful tools in this matter (Russo 2014a).

Aggregate data and aggregate concepts

Turnout, electoral volatility, nationalization

As the excellent argument put forward by Welzel and Inglehart (2007) suggests, certain phenomena are best observed at the aggregate level. In fact, these phenomena are aggregate by nature and definition. In this section, we offer three examples: turnout, electoral volatility and nationalization. Of course, these subjects are not even nearly an exhaustive list, but they do offer a clear illustration.

Turnout is one of the most investigated topics in political science. The phenomenon of turnout can obviously be studied from both an individual perspective (as the individual decision to cast a vote) and an aggregate one (e.g., the turnout of a municipality/region/country). As Franklin (2004) highlights:

> While voting is a matter of individual decisions, turnout is an aggregate-level phenomenon. It is a feature of an electorate not a voter. And, while it is true that electorates are made up of aggregates of voters, the process of aggregation is not simply one of adding up relevant features of the individuals who form part of it.
>
> *(Franklin 2004: 16)*

The study of turnout from an aggregate perspective is in fact rich in substantive prominent contributions (for a review on turnout literature at the aggregate level, see Geys 2006; for a theoretical overview on turnout on the aggregate level, see Blais 2007: 621–630).

Strictly connected to turnout, it is possible to identify another phenomenon that can be studied as aggregate: electoral volatility. Electoral volatility is also a very widely investigated phenomenon (Dalton 1984; Bartolini and Mair 1990; Dalton, McAllister and Wattenberg 2000; Mair 2002; Mair, Müller and Plasser 2004; Mair 2008, among others). Since the 1970s, when a process of voter de-alignment started, increasingly voters have shown to change their vote choice for parties from one election to another (Dalton and Wattenberg 2000; Franklin, Mackie and Valen 1992). As for turnout, if the decision of changing party is an individual attribute (see, for example, Dalton, McAllister and Wattenberg 2000; Lachat 2007), the level of volatility in, for example, a country, is an aggregate attribute (see, for example, Bartolini and Mair 1990; Tavits 2005).

Electoral volatility at the aggregate level can be studied as net volatility or total volatility. Net volatility entails the gains and losses of political parties participating in two consecutive elections (i.e., the change in vote share for each party). Total (or gross) volatility is the total proportion of voters who switched party (assuming a stable population of voters – which is an assumption that is almost impossible to maintain). It is evident that total volatility is less informative than the net one, but both share the problem of an almost certain underestimation of the real volatility. Consider the following (extreme) scenario: in a two-party system 50 percent of the electorate votes for party A and the other 50 percent votes for party B; at the consecutive election the two electorates make a perfect switch. In that case, both the estimated total and net volatility would (erroneously) be estimated as zero. Nonetheless, using a volatility index has the great advantage of potentially working with a large number of observations, as the data needed to compute the indexes (which will be presented in the next section) are easily obtainable (at the country, and often also at the sub-country level). This allows working with large comparative and longitudinal datasets.

Finally, another topic that is intrinsically aggregate is the nationalization of politics, generally defined as a long-term process resulting in the uniformity or universality of attitudes and political behavior within nations (Caramani 1996, 2004).The underlying logic of this process is that, as a result of the emergence of national electorates and national electoral systems (which in turn are due to the development of mass politics), the differences between the areas within a country gradually decrease, and eventually become minimal. In other words, as the local dimension of the cleavages decreases, national politics substitutes local politics (Caramani 1996, 2004). This nationalization process has been observed widely, both in Europe (Caramani 2004) and in the Americas (Alemán and Kellam 2008).

The whole process of the nationalization of politics can be conceptually divided into two related dynamics: the nationalization of the party offer and the nationalization of voters' electoral behavior. As both Morgenstern and Potthoff (2005) and Lago and Montero (2014) noticed, because of its intrinsically multidimensional nature, the concept of the nationalization of the party system has suffered from ambiguity.

The nationalization of the vote can be conceptualized and, consequently, measured in several different ways. Claggett, Flanigan and Zingale (1984) propose a comprehensive classification that distinguishes three different dimensions of nationalization:

1   *the homogeneity of the electoral support*, which implies that an election is nationalized when support for the parties is homogenous across the units of a country (Kasuya and Moenius 2008);
2   *the source (or level) of political forces*, that is, the tendency of the electorate to vote for national parties rather than local ones – this is a dynamic observed, for instance, in Italy (Caramani 2004);
3   *the type of the answer*, which entails a dynamic/time element: the election is considered to be a stimulus to which voters will respond and nationalization is operationalized as a uniform change across territorial units of a country between two elections (Russo 2014b).

Irrespective of which type of nationalization one wishes to study, none of them are observable at the individual level: the nationalization of the offer because it does not involve individuals but parties, and the nationalization of the vote because it is a phenomenon that is only observable in its aggregate nature.

Beyond ecological inference: other uses of aggregate data

When analyzing data of aggregate nature without wishing to make inferences about the behavior of individuals, the statistical techniques that are possible to apply are almost limitless. Aggregate data are normally interval-level data, therefore correlations, regressions and so forth can be used.

Turnout at the aggregate level has been used as a dependent or independent variable in regression models in a large amount of literature (see, for example, Powell 1986; Fornos, Power and Garand 2004; Fowler 2006; Riera and Russo 2016).

Unlike turnout, electoral volatility needs to be calculated as an index. The most famous index to calculate net electoral volatility is the index of dissimilarity (Pedersen 1979), which is the sum of the absolute changes in vote shares for each party divided by two, but several alternatives are available (see Taagepera and Grofman 2003).

Nationalization is also computed as an index, in case one wishes to measure nationalization both of the offer and of the vote. The indexes available for both kinds are very numerous (for a review, see Bochsler 2010; Lago and Montero 2014; Russo and Deschouwer 2015). In the field of the nationalization of the vote, the *standardized Party Nationalization Score* (Bochsler 2010) is the most widely accepted, whilst with regard to the nationalization of the offer Lago and Montero (2014) have elaborated the *local entrant measure* (E^1) that tries to overcome the limits of previously proposed indexes.

Finally, another interesting possibility that aggregate data offer is to analyze geographical patterns (see, for example, Rentfrow, Jokela and Lamb 2015, who investigates the existence of similar personality characteristics in neighboring regions), and to test geographical hypotheses (for example, as in Dejaeghere and Vanhoutte 2016, where the main assumption is that characteristics such as population density and immigration rate will influence turnout in local elections). In fact, as aforementioned, aggregate data can often be available at fine aggregation levels such as municipalities (as in Riera and Russo 2016) or even polling stations (Russo 2014a, 2014b). With fine sub-country data it is possible to apply advanced techniques (i.e., spatial lag models) that allow to verify whether the outcome observed in one area/unit is influenced by characteristics of the surrounding territorial units.[3] With regards to the aggregation level, one important aspect to take into account is that research has shown that the level of aggregation has an important impact on the quality of the estimates: the lower the aggregation level, the more reliable the estimates (Russo and Beauguitte 2014).

Conclusion

Aggregate data have multiple applications and great potential. They do not hold some of the great potential of individual-level data, but they can be a valid resource when there is a lack of individual-level data, and, more importantly, aggregate data are the right level of aggregation when one needs to study a phenomenon that is aggregate per se.

In this chapter, both scenarios have been illustrated. In the first part of the chapter, the main rationale of the ecological inference problem and the proposed solutions have been discussed. Then, the ecological (and individualistic) fallacy concept and the related debate have been presented. On this matter, it is important to stress once more that when analyzing a problem and commenting on the results, it is not the level of the data (aggregate or individual) that makes the quality of the findings, but the rigor in implementing and interpreting the analysis. The first part closes with an overview of possible settings in which the use of aggregate data can be the only or the best approach. The second part of the chapter focuses on the use of aggregate data when the topic under scrutiny is of an aggregate nature. Three examples have been offered: turnout, electoral volatility and nationalization. These topics do not represent an exhaustive list, but they have been selected (in this precise order of presentation) because they entail different levels of conceptualization and estimation. While turnout is a quite straightforward concept and not hard to measure – even though, as Geys (2006) notices, a certain level of clarification is required – electoral volatility needs to be computed as an index, and nationalization (also an index) involves a finer level of conceptualization. Many of the considerations made concerning the ecological fallacy apply to the second part of the chapter as well, especially the idea that certain attributes can be considered aggregate attributes of the population, and need to be examined at the aggregate level.

Finally, aggregate data seem to be the only viable solution when one is interested in exploring the geographical patterns of certain phenomena – at least until representative survey data are collected at a more local level.

Notes

1 For a more detailed explanation of some of the models, see Tam Cho and Manski (2008) and Elff, Gschwend and Johnston (2008).
2 Several authors argue that political behavior is not sufficiently informed about the role of territorial context. Franklin and Wlezien (2002) have noted that many of the factors that influence voting behavior are in fact geographically based and need to be incorporated into the analysis for us to be able to gain a better understanding. Despite the scholarly interest for the dimension of space and its analytical implications (Clark and Jones 2013), studies that have employed a territorial perspective are relatively few (Agnew 2002; Johnston and Pattie 2006) and lacking a comparative perspective, as they produced only "a large number of isolated findings but few generalizations" (Taylor and Flint 2000: 236).
3 For a technical overview of the mathematical operation of spatial models, see Franzese and Hays (2008).

References

Agnew, J. A. (1994) "The National Versus the Contextual: The Controversy Over Measuring Electoral Change in Italy Using Goodman Flow-Of-Vote Estimates," *Political Geography*, vol. 13, no. 3, May, 245–254.

Agnew, J. (1996) "Mapping Politics: How Context Counts in Electoral Geography," *Political Geography*, vol. 15, no. 2, February, 129–146.

Agnew, J. A. (2002) *Place and Politics in Modern Italy*, Chicago: University of Chicago Press.

Alemán, E., and Kellman, M. (2008) "The Nationalization of Electoral Change in the Americas," *Electoral Studies*, vol. 27, no. 2, June, 193–212.

Alford, R. R. and Lee, E. C. (1968) "Voting Turnout in American Cities," *American Political Science Review*, vol. 62, no. 3, September, 796–813.

Alker, H. R. (1969) "A Typology of Ecological Fallacies," in Dogan, M. and Rokkan, S. (eds.) *Quantitative Ecological Analysis in the Social Sciences*, Cambridge, MA: MIT Press: 69–86.

Ansolabehere, S. and Hersh, E. (2012) "Validation: What Big Data Reveal About Survey Misreporting and the Real Electorate," *Political Analysis*, vol. 20, no. 4, Autumn, 437–549.

Bartolini, S. and Mair, P. (1990) *Identity, Competition and Electoral Availability: The Stability of European Electorates 1885–1985*, Cambridge: Cambridge University Press.

Belli, R. F., Traugott, M. W., Young, M. and McGonagle, K. A. (1999) "Reducing Vote Overreporting In Surveys: Social Desirability, Memory Failure, and Source Monitoring," *Public Opinion Quarterly*, vol. 63, no. 1, Spring, 90–108.

Benoit, K., Laver, M. and Giannetti, D. (2004) "14 Multiparty Split-Ticket Voting Estimation as an Ecological Inference Problem," in King, G., Rosen, O. and Tanner, M. A. (eds.) *Ecological Inference: New Methodological Strategies*, Cambridge: Cambridge University Press: 333–350.

Blais, A. (2007) "Turnout in Elections," in Dalton, R. J. and Klingemann, H. D. (ed.) *The Oxford Handbook of Political Behavior*, New York: Oxford University Press: 621–635.

Bochsler, R. (2010) "Measuring Party Nationalization: A New Gini-based Indicator that Corrects for the Number of Unit," *Electoral Studies*, vol. 29, no. 1, March, 155–168.

Brunell, T. L. and Grofman, B. (2009) "Testing Sincere Versus Strategic Split-Ticket Voting at the Aggregate Level: Evidence from Split House–President Outcomes, 1900–2004," *Electoral Studies*, vol. 28, no. 1, March, 62–69.

Campbell, A., Converse, P. E., Miller, W. E. and Stokes, D. E. (1960) *The American Voter*, New York: Willey.

Caramani, D. (1996) "The Nationalisation of Electoral Politics: A Conceptual Reconstruction and Review of the Literature," *West European Politics*, vol. 19, no. 2, 205–224.

Caramani, D. (2004) *The Nationalization of Politics: The Formation of National Electorates and Party Systems in Western Europe*, Cambridge: Cambridge University Press.

Claggett, W., Flanigan, W. and Zingale, N. (1984) "Nationalization of the American Electorate," *American Political Science Review*, vol. 78, no. 1, March, 77–91.

Clark, J. and Jones, A. (2013) "The Great Implications of Spatialisation: Grounds for Closer Engagement Between Political Geography and Political Science?," *Geoforum*, vol. 45, March, 305–314.

Dalton, R. J. (1984) "Cognitive Mobilization and Partisan Dealignment in Advanced Industrial Democracies," *Journal of Politics*, vol. 46, no. 2, February, 264–284.

Dalton, R. J. and Wattenberg, M. P. (2000) *Parties Without Partisans: Political Change in Advanced Industrial Democracies*, New York: Oxford University Press.

Dalton, R. J., McAllister, I. and Wattenberg. M. P. (2000) "The Consequences of Partisan Dealignment," in Dalton, R. J. and Wattenberg, M. P. (eds.) *Parties Without Partisans: Political Change in Advanced Industrial Democracies*, Oxford: Oxford University Press: 37–63.

De Sio, L. (2008) *Elettori In Movimento: Nuove Tecniche di Inferenza Ecologica Per Lo Studio Dei Flussi Elettorali*, Firenze: Edizioni Polistampa.

Dejaeghere, Y. and Vanhoutte, B. (2016) "Virtuous Villages and Sinful Cities? A Spatial Analysis into the Effects of Community Characteristics on Turnout and Blank/Invalid Voting in Local Elections in Belgium 2006–2012," *Acta Politica*, vol. 51, no. 1, January, 80–101.

Downs, A. (1957) *An Economic Theory of Democracy*, New York: Harper Collins.

Duncan, O. D. and Davis, B. (1953) "An Alternative to Ecological Correlation," *American Sociological Review*, vol. 18, no. 6, December, 665–666.

Elff, M., Gschwend, T. and Johnston, R. J. (2008) "Ignoramus, Ignorabimus? On Uncertainty in Ecological Inference," *Political Analysis*, vol. 16, no. 1, Winter, 70–92.

Falter, J. (1991) *Hitler Wähler*, Munich: C. H. Beck.

Forcina, A., Gnaldi, M. and Bracalente, B. (2012) "A Revised Brown and Payne Model of Voting Behaviour Applied to the 2009 Elections in Italy," *Statistical Methods and Applications*, vol. 21, no. 1, March, 109–119.

Fornos, C. A., Power, T. J. and Garand, J. C. (2004) "Explaining Voter Turnout in Latin America, 1980 to 2000," *Comparative Political Studies*, vol. 37, no. 8, October, 909–940.

Fowler, J. H. (2006) "Habitual Voting and Behavioral Turnout," *Journal of Politics*, vol. 68, no. 2, May, 335–344.

Franklin, M. N. (2004) *Voter Turnout and the Dynamics of Electoral Competition in Established Democracies Since 1945*, Cambridge: Cambridge University Press.

Franklin, M. and Wlezien, C. (2002) "Reinventing Election Studies," *Electoral Studies*, vol. 21, no. 2, June, 331–338.

Franklin, M., Mackie, T. T. and Valen, H. (1992) *Electoral Change: Responses to Evolving Social and Attitudinal Structures in Western Nations*, Cambridge: Cambridge University Press.

Franzese, R. J. and Hays, J. C. (2008) "Empirical Models of Spatial Interdependence," in Box-Steffensmeier, J. M., Brady, H. E. and Collier, D. (eds.) *Oxford Handbook of Political Methodology*, New York: Oxford University Press: 570–604.

Freedman, D. A., Klein, S. P., Sacks, J., Smyth, C. A. and Everett, C. G. (1991) "Ecological Regression and Voting Rights," *Evaluation Review*, vol. 15, no. 6, December, 673–711.

Geys, B. (2006) "Explaining Voter Turnout: A Review of Aggregate-Level Research," *Electoral Studies*, vol. 25, no. 4, December, 637–663.

Goodman, L. A. (1953) "Ecological Regressions and Behavior of Individuals," *American Sociological Review*, vol. 18, no. 6, December, 663–664.

Johnston, R. and Pattie, C. (2000) "Ecological Inference and Entropy-Maximizing: An Alternative Estimation Procedure for Split-Ticket Voting," *Political Analysis*, vol. 8, no. 4, Autumn, 333–345.

Johnston, R. and Pattie, C. (2006) *Putting Voters in their Place: Geography and Elections in Great Britain*, New York: Oxford University Press.

Katz, J. N. and King, G. (1999) "A Statistical Model for Multiparty Electoral Data," *American Political Science Review*, vol. 93, no. 1, March, 15–32.

Kasuya, Y. and Moenius, J. (2008) "The Nationalization of Party Systems: Conceptual Issues and Alternative District-Focused Measures," *Electoral Studies*, vol. 27, no. 1, March, 126–135.

King, G. (1997) *A Solution to the Ecological Inference Problem*, Princeton: Princeton University Press.

Lachat, R. (2007) *A Heterogeneous Electorate: Political Sophistication, Predisposition Strength and the Voting Decision Process*, Baden-Baden: Nomos.

Lago, I. and Montero, J. R. (2014) "Defining and Measuring Party System Nationalization," *European Political Science Review*, vol. 6, no. 2, May, 191–211.

Landa, J., Copeland, M. and Grofman, B. (1995) "Ethnic Voting Patterns: A Case Study of Metropolitan Toronto," *Political Geography*, vol. 14, no. 5, July, 435–449.

Lazarsfeld, P. F., Berelson, B. and Gaudet, H. (1944) *The People's Choice: How the Voter Makes Up His Mind in a Presidential Campaign*, New York: Columbia University Press.

Liu, B. and Vanderleeuw, J. M. (2001) "Racial Transition and White-Voter Support for Black Candidates in Urban Elections," *Journal of Urban Affairs*, vol. 23, no. 4, Autumn, 309–322.

Mair, P. (2002) "In the Aggregate: Mass Electoral Behaviour in Western Europe, 1950–2000," in Keman, H. (ed.) *Comparative Democratic Politics*, London: Sage: 122–140.

Mair, P. (2008) "Electoral Volatility and the Dutch Party System: A Comparative Perspective," *Acta Politica*, vol. 43, no. 2, July, 235–253.

Mair, P., Müller, W. and Plasser, F. (2004) *Political Change and Electoral Change*, London: Thousand Oaks.

Morgenstern, S. and Potthoff, R. (2005) "The Components of Elections: District Heterogeneity, District-Time Effects, and Volatility," *Electoral Studies*, vol. 24, no. 1, March, 17–40.

Pedersen, M. N. (1979) "The Dynamics of European Party Systems: Changing Patterns of Electoral Volatility," *European Journal of Political Research*, vol. 7, no. 1, March, 1–26.

Powell, G. B. (1986) "American Voter Turnout in Comparative Perspective," *American Political Science Review*, vol. 80, no. 1, March, 17–43.

Rentfrow, P. J., Jokela, M. and Lamb, M. E. (2015) "Regional Personality Differences in Great Britain," *PLoS ONE*, vol. 10, no. 3, e0122245.

Riera, P. and Russo, L. (2016) "Breaking the Cartel: The Geography of the Electoral Support of New Parties in Italy and Spain," *Italian Political Science Review*, vol. 46, no. 2, July, 219–241.

Robinson, W. S. (1950) "Ecological Correlations and the Behavior of Individuals," *American Sociological Review*, vol. 15, no. 2, April, 351–357.

Russo, L. (2014a) "Estimating Floating Voters: A Comparison Between the Ecological Inference and the Survey Methods," *Quality and Quantity*, vol. 48, no. 3, May, 1667–1683.

Russo, L. (2014b) "The Nationalization of Electoral Change in a Geographical Perspective: The Case of Italy (2006–2008)," *GeoJournal*, vol. 79, no. 1, February, 73–87.

Russo, L. and Beauguitte, L. (2014) "Aggregation Level Matters: Evidence from French Electoral Data," *Quality and Quantity*, vol. 48, no. 2, March, 923–938.

Russo, L. and Deschouwer, K. (2015) "Split Offer and Homogenous Response: The (De)-Nationalization of Electoral Politics in Belgium," Unpublished Manuscript, Maastricht University.

Sciarini, P. and Goldberg, A. C. (2016) "Turnout Bias in Postelection Surveys: Political Involvement, Survey Participation, and Vote Overreporting," *Journal of Survey Statistics and Methodology*, vol. 4, no. 1, March, 110–137.

Selb, P. and Munzert, S. (2013) "Voter Overrepresentation, Vote Misreporting, and Turnout Bias in Postelection Surveys," *Electoral Studies*, vol. 32, no. 1, March, 186–196.

Shin, M. E. and Agnew, J. (2002) "The Geography of Party Replacement in Italy, 1987–1996," *Political Geography*, vol. 21, no. 2, February, 221–242.

Shin, M. E. and Agnew, J. A. (2008) *Berlusconi's Italy: Mapping Contemporary Italian Politics*, Philadelphia: Temple University Press.

Taagepera, R. and Grofman, B. (2003) "Mapping the Indices of Seats–Votes Disproportionality and Inter-Election Volatility," *Party Politics*, vol. 9, no. 6, November, 659–677.

Tam Cho, W. K. and Gaines, B. J. (2004) "The Limits of Ecological Inference: The Case of Split-Ticket Voting," *American Journal of Political Science*, vol. 48, no. 1, January, 152–171.

Tam Cho, W. K. and Manski, C. F. (2008) "Cross Level/Ecological Inference," in Box-Steffensmeier, J. M., Brady, H. E. and Collier, D. (eds.) *Oxford Handbook of Political Methodology*, New York: Oxford University Press: 547–569.

Tavits, M. (2005) "The Development of Stable Party Support: Electoral Dynamics in Post-Communist Europe," *American Journal of Political Science*, vol. 49, no. 2, April, 283–298.

Taylor, P. J. and Flint, C. (2000) *Political Geography: World-System, Nation-State and Locality*, Harlow: Prentice Hall.

Voogt, R. J. and Saris, W. E. (2003) "To Participate or Not to Participate: The Link Between Survey Participation, Electoral Participation, and Political Interest," *Political Analysis*, vol. 11, no. 2, Spring, 164–179.

Welzel, C. and Inglehart, R. (2007) "Mass Beliefs and Democratic Institutions," in Boix, C. and Stokes, S. C. (eds.) *The Oxford Handbook of Comparative Politics*, New York: Oxford University Press: 297–313.

Whiteley, P., Sanders, D., Stewart, M. and Clarke, H. (2011) "Aggregate Level Forecasting of the 2010 General Election in Britain: The Seats–Votes Model," *Electoral Studies*, vol. 30, no. 2, June, 278–283.

Wright, G. C. (1977) "Contextual Models of Electoral Behavior: The Southern Wallace Vote," *American Political Science Review*, vol. 71, no. 2, June, 497–508.

39

ELECTION FORECASTING[1]

Stephen D. Fisher

Introduction

Election forecasting is a mug's game, so I'm often told. Maybe. But it is fun, people will do it and it is important enough to try to do well. Election forecasts, even if they are not much reported directly in the media, do get noticed and influence the tone of media election coverage. They set expectations so strongly that people are shocked if the forecasting consensus is seriously wrong and substantial amounts of money are made or lost on various markets.

People both inside and outside academia do election forecasting and this is an area where academics learn a lot from non-academics and vice versa. Sadly much of the non-academic forecasting is not well documented. Descriptions of methods tend to be thin on detail and often disappear after elections with little or no postmortems. For this reason the references in this chapter are dominated by the academic literature, but most of the principles and issues discussed apply to the non- and semi-academic forecasting too.

The bulk of the chapter reviews various different methods being deployed at the time of writing. For reasons of space and because the chapter is required to focus on the state-of-the-art material, older literature and debates have been neglected in favor of citing recent examples of applications of well-established methods. Readers can follow citations within citations to identify the origins and development of particular approaches. Also there are several recent reviews, albeit they are on specific elections, collections or methods (Lewis-Beck and Bélanger 2012; Linzer and Lewis-Beck 2015; Fisher and Lewis-Beck 2016; Ford et al. 2017; Murr 2017; Graefe 2017).

The discussion here is dominated by Britain and the US mainly because those countries are where there has been most methodological innovation that is also documented in scholarly journals. But developments in these countries do not always travel well to other countries with different institutions, politics and especially different data availability. There are significant and fascinating developments across Europe and elsewhere that deserve more attention outside those countries, just some of which have been reviewed here.

This chapter does not cover amusing historical correlations between election outcomes and obviously irrelevant variables, such as the color of cup-winning football tops (Mortimore 2014). No matter how strong they are, such relationships are almost certainly spurious and eventually break down. Instead this chapter covers methods of election forecasting that are of most interest either from a substantive electoral behavior point of view or from broader social scientific and methodological perspectives.

After reflecting a little on what forecasting is used for, the bulk of this chapter reviews election forecasting methods. This section is organized somewhat by method and somewhat by information type. Issues of seat forecasting are dealt with in a separate section later. The concluding discussion makes some observations on what more could be learnt and what could be done to improve forecasting further.

What is election forecasting for?

Election forecasts constitute data for analyzing current political situations, performance of political actors and the effect of substantive events. For instance, Berg, Penney and Rietz (2015) use prediction market data to analyze the "political impact" of events. For this approach to be valid requires forecasts to constitute meaningful measures of current political standings for candidates and parties – that is, they have to be based on consistently reliably good forecasting methods.

But what political scientists want to learn from election forecasting is often something more than or different from how to get the most accurate predictions. Election forecasting is also about trying to understand how elections work and how good political science theories are at predicting the future as well as explaining the past. For instance, Lewis-Beck and Stegmaier (2014) provide a list of five main substantive lessons from the experience of forecasting US presidential elections: electoral cycles exist, campaigns matter, the economy matters a lot, voters are retrospective and myopic, and voters cannot easily be swayed.

In truth this list could be disputed, but even to the extent that the forecasting literature does show us these things, they have also been established without forecasting. What is not clear is what scholars are learning from the experience of forecasting that they cannot or are not learning from traditional theory testing research. The idea that there are some things that can only be learnt from forecasting is perhaps too tall an order. But forecasting does help focus the mind as to what is important for really influencing election outcomes. While traditional post-election survey research points to many powerful predictors of vote choice at the individual-level that suggest macro-level predictors such as partisanship, it turns out that changing macro-partisanship is not necessarily a powerful predictor for forecasting election outcomes (Campbell and Garand 2000). This has important implications for the ways in which we should interpret findings from individual-level analysis. Predicted probabilities from individual-level regression models cannot necessarily be interpreted as estimates of effects on election outcomes.

Rightly or wrongly, the demand for forecasts sets an academic agenda. For example, key to some debates on US election forecasting is the question of how much weight to put on vote intention polls at what stage in the campaign. This problem is part of the motivation for some of the research on campaign dynamics. This may be the tail wagging the dog for some, but it is useful knowledge generation for others.

How is election forecasting done?

This section starts with more traditional social science theory based models before turning to models based on vote-intention polls, primarily because the most prominent vote-intention models now build on the traditional models. We then turn to prediction markets, citizen forecasting, experts and other more diverse sources. Processes of synthesizing different methods and combining forecasts are also discussed in this section, but some methodological issues are held over to the following section on seats forecasting.

Structural models and the "fundamentals"

Structural models are the archetypal political science forecasting models. They are traditionally based on fitting a parsimonious theoretically informed regression model to an historical set of elections and then using the resulting equation for prediction. The most common predictors are economic and political factors: the fundamentals. The term structural refers to the fact that the predictors structure the vote in the sense of there being a causal relationship.

The predictors in structural models are referred to as the "fundamentals" on the basis that they are powerful exogenous factors driving election outcomes. However, the term fundamentals is increasingly used very loosely to refer to any variable in a forecasting model that might possibly be related to vote choice. This may not matter for forecasting purposes but it does undermine the idea that the models are simultaneously telling us something about causal processes. Many so-called fundamentals are either not very powerful predictors (Lauderdale and Linzer 2015), or not mainly exgenous and so not really fundamental to vote choice.

Electoral pendulum, election cycles, incumbency and the cost of governing

Shakespeare wrote about "a tide in the affairs of men." The notion that there is an electoral pendulum that swings back and forth between the two main parties/blocks competing for power has a long heritage and is commonly assumed among political elites and commentators. Helmut Norpoth and his colleagues have shown that in Britain and the US the pendulum swings between the two main parties roughly every two and half elections (Norpoth 2014; Lebo and Norpoth 2016). By this account, it is entirely unsurprising that Cameron and Obama should have won re-election.

For some the pendulum is driven by the "costs of governing" (the accumulation of resentment), which is often operationalized as just time in office. But note that some versions of the pendulum model involve not steady deterioration but a positive incumbency advantage for the head of government for first re-election, turning to disadvantage in subsequent attempts.

Incumbency effects at the district level are vital to forecasting in the US congressional elections (Cox and Katz 2014) and important components in some other majoritarian systems (Fisher 2016). They too have their own dynamics over elections, but different from those affecting heads of government.

The pendulum effect is often referred to as an election cycle, but that term is also used to refer to the period between two elections. In Britain, at least, there is common folklore that governments have a honeymoon just after winning an election, then suffer mid-term blues, from which they recover (somewhat) in the final months. These kinds of cyclical dynamics can be used in forecasting, but to different effect from the multiple-term pendulum model (Fisher 2015).

Moreover, the word cycle has been used to refer to poor government performance in mid-term and/or second-order elections (Bellucci 2010). In US mid-term election forecasting the same idea is used but without the same language of cycles (Silver 2014).

Economic voting models

The main idea behind these is that the voters' tendency to reward or punish governments based on the performance of the economy is so strong that we can anticipate election outcomes on the basis of objective macro-economic indicators. Economic evaluations are also used but they do raise questions about endogeneity when it comes to interpretation.

Economic indicators have been particularly popular for forecasts of US presidential elections, especially more than a couple of months in advance because the identity of both main candidates is not (well) known and opinion polls are still relatively uninformative (Jerôme and Jerôme-Speziari 2012).

In parliamentary democracies, the polls are generally much more informative about the eventual result earlier on (Jennings and Wlezien 2016), and so there may be less need to use economic indicators instead of polls. Furthermore, retrospective economic voting depends on the kind of clarity of responsibility that is in relatively short supply in more consensual proportional systems. So forecasting models in these places may struggle to identify who will be held accountable for economic outcomes.

There are various intriguing forecasting papers that address these issues. In Norway, low unemployment helps the social democrats whether they are in or out of government (Arnesen 2012). In Spain it is just the center-right in government that is affected (Magalhães, Aguiar-Conraria and Lewis-Beck 2012). More strikingly in Austria the combined share of the two main parties (at least one of which is always in government, sometimes both) drops with rising unemployment (Aichholzer and Willmann 2014). Economic indicators even work for forecasting in francophone Belgium for a long period when voters did not have the opportunity of voting for the (Dutch-speaking) prime minister's party (Dassonneville and Hooghe 2012). A key lesson here is that the appropriate forecasting model with economic indicators is highly context dependent.

Leadership evaluations

No party has lost a British general election when it was ahead on both leadership and economic competence evaluations (Kellner 2014). In the run-up to an election, we expect the party with the best thought of leader to be most likely to win and some forecasting models use leader ratings to capture this – for example, in Germany (Norpoth and Gschwend 2010) and Britain (Lebo and Norpoth 2016). Similarly government evaluations are successful predictors in Italy (Bellucci 2010), but this measure comes closer to being effectively a proxy for vote intention than do leadership ratings.

A rather different approach uses primaries and internal party leadership contests as measures of relative candidate qualities. Those candidates and leaders who won their party competition more comfortably are more likely to be clear election winners. Thus the "primary model" for US presidential elections is based on evidence that those candidates that win their early primaries most emphatically are more likely to win the general election (Norpoth and Bednarczuk 2012). In Britain the party leader who won their internal leadership among MPs contest most clearly tends to become prime minister (Murr 2015a).

Vote-intention poll-based forecasting

The prevalence of vote-intention polls and the media demand for continually updated forecasts mean that aggregation of opinion polls is the main (but usually not sole) basis for the most high-profile election forecasts. In the US, these include Drew Linzer's votamatic.com, Sam Wang's Princeton Election Consortium (election.princeton.edu), Simon Jackman's HuffPollster forecasts and most famously Nate Silver's fivethirtyeight.com. There have similarly been poll aggregation based forecasts in Britain (electionforecast.co.uk, electionsetc.com and Polling Observatory), Germany and elsewhere. This broad approach was also applied to the UK's referendum on EU membership (Fisher and Renwick 2016).

Naturally, forecasting based on poll aggregation faces two main challenges: how to aggregate and how to forecast. Poll aggregation ranges from simple averaging of recent polls to technically sophisticated Bayesian state-space models. There are a lot of modeling choices to be made in the process, including whether and how to measure pollster quality, how to weight pollsters, how to estimate differences between pollsters (house effects) and how much they change, how to forecast overall polling industry accuracy and how to estimate uncertainty in all these things. Much of the analysis of these things is inherently technical with conclusions highly contingent on historical experience and context rather than on theoretical grounds. Perhaps the most important of these issues is the extent to which polls are on average right, or wrong, in a predictable manner.

For instance, the successful poll aggregation based forecasts of the 2012 US presidential election are rightly acclaimed (see, for example, Linzer 2013). But it is worth noting that they relied on there being no significant bias for the average pollster; a reasonable assumption given the historical experience in the US. By contrast the same assumption was disastrous in the 2015 British general election, which saw massive industry bias which was only partially anticipated and only by some (Fisher and Lewis-Beck 2016).

Another salutary lesson from recent British politics regards house effects. Most state-of-the-art poll aggregators use some variation of the Kalman filter or Bayesian state space model. These models treat polls as noisy indictors of true public opinion. In trying to estimate levels of party support they take into account the sample size of polls and corresponding sampling variation, and they simultaneously estimate the extent to which different pollsters tend to produce systematically high or low estimates for particular parties (house effects). Such differences typically exist because of methodological choices by pollsters, not least the mode of interview (face-to-face, telephone or online). To estimate these models, house effects need to be assumed to be stable, or at least evolve only slowly. It takes quite a few polls to distinguish between a modest change in house effect from statistical noise. However, both the 2014 Scottish independence referendum and the 2015 British general election saw house effects collapse with apparent herding at the end of the campaign (Fisher 2016; Sturgis et al. 2016). In the UK's EU referendum there were many methodological changes within the final weeks, and especially for the final polls (Curtice 2016), which meant that house effects could not adequately be estimated. All three of these events also saw a dwindling in the final weeks of what were earlier in the campaign relatively stable differences between telephone and internet polls (Fisher and Renwick 2016; Sturgis et al. 2016). With significant risk of rapidly changing and unidentifiable house effects, more simple poll averaging is likely to be more robust than a model which assumes stable house effects.

Aggregating polls to form estimates of current vote intention provides a now-cast. There remains the question as to how to forecast the future. Information about how things are likely to change by election day essentially comes from history, including some structural models of the kind discussed in the previous section. So while the prominent poll aggregator forecasts are almost entirely dominated by polls close to the election, they usually depend substantially on a structural model when forecasting from several months out. So while they are often called aggregators, they are actually synthesizers.

Synthetic models

Synthetic models typically seek to incorporate the best of both the polling and the structural models. They are typically built using historical evidence of the relative weight to put on economic data and polling data, which varies according to how far away the election is (Linzer 2013; Lewis-Beck and Dassonneville 2015; Lewis-Beck, Nadeau and Bélanger 2016). Arguably many structural models comprised various different components (e.g., economic and political) and so could be thought of as synthetic models. But this term is not used in that way.

There was considerable debate in the run-up to the 2014 US Midterms as to whether a synthetic or polls-only model would be best (Blumenthal, Edwards-Levy and Lienesch 2014; Wang 2015). Given that the case for a synthetic model is stronger further out from the election, this debate raises important questions about how to evaluate dynamically updated forecasts. Some methods may be better at making forecasts at some times than others.

Betting and prediction markets

Prediction markets are a favored source of forecasts by many economists and business people who believe in the power of markets to aggregate information. Betting markets are similar but involve a bookmaker setting odds rather than participants trading directly with each other. With enough participants, betting odds are primarily driven by what the punters think collectively about the relative chances of different outcomes, once you account for the bookmaker's over round (setting odds with implied probabilities that sum to greater than 100 percent).

The theoretical argument for political prediction markets is that they involve people staking their own money, sometimes serious amounts of it, and, if they are rational actors, they will be taking account of all the information available to them. One of the intriguing issues for election forecasters is that the information punters use partly comes from opinion polls. So it is not clear that betting and prediction markets do any better than polls properly interpreted (Erikson and Wlezien 2012). UK constituency betting markets have been found to have various systematic biases (Wall, Sudulich and Cunningham 2012), and there are examples of poor performance of markets, such as Germany in 2013 (Graefe 2015b) and the UK's EU referendum (Fisher and Shorrocks 2016). One concern when they do go wrong is that we typically do not know why. More research is needed on who bets, why and on what basis. However, while acknowledging that they can sometimes be manipulated, Graefe (2017) argues that prediction markets have a better track record than forecasts based on opinion polls or structural models.

Citizen and expert forecasting

While the implied forecasts from betting markets are based on the money staked on each side winning, a related process of aggregating individual forecasts is known as citizen forecasting. The central theoretical idea here is that the average (or median) guess from a large (ideally representative) sample, referred to as a voter expectation survey, will be close to the truth even if most guesses are wide of the mark. This "wisdom of crowds" principle works if people on average have a better chance of getting the answer right than wrong. Citizen forecasting has a very good track record in a number of countries (Murr 2017), including Britain (Murr 2016) and especially the United States. Expectation surveys in the US arguably outperform vote intention polls, prediction markets, structural models and expert judgments across the final 100 days of the seven presidential elections between 1988 and 2012 (Graefe 2014).

The relative performance of expectation surveys and prediction forecasts raises particularly interesting questions about information aggregation. Advocates of betting markets suggest that the risks that bets involve concentrate the mind and people are only willing to place them if they feel they know enough to think that the bet is worthwhile. The supposed advantages of betting markets depend on the participants being unrepresentative and exclusive of the ignorant. Citizen forecasts by contrast make a virtue of having a much more representative sample of the population at the expense of numerous potentially poor quality responses.

What meta-analyses there are suggest that citizen forecasts are typically more accurate than prediction markets (Graefe 2014, 2017; Murr 2017). This finding would seem to vindicate those who argue for collective democratic decision making against those who worry about voter ignorance.

This is not to say that some citizens are not better than others at forecasting elections. Some are and forecasts can be improved by identifying the better forecasters and weighting their forecasts according to a measure of competence (Murr 2015b). Amongst other characteristics, Murr found that better forecasters tended to be older and more educated and less likely to have a strong party identification.

Intriguingly, interest in politics was not consistently linked to forecasting success among citizens and professional political experts are not necessarily the best. Indeed the meta-analyses typically show voter expectation surveys out-performing expert surveys (Graefe 2014, 2017; Murr 2017). At the 2015 British general election expectations of academics, pollsters and journalists were very similarly wrong, perhaps because of looking at the same sets of polls and forecasts on social media, but journalists were slightly less wrong than the other two groups (Hanretty and Jennings 2015). In a similar expert survey before the UK's EU referendum in 2016 it was the academics who were slightly less wrong than the journalists (Jennings and Fisher 2016).

One of the issues that this EU referendum expert survey raises is whether respondents should be asked who is more likely to win or what the probability is of each side/candidate/party winning. Eighty-seven percent of the experts thought that Remain was most likely to win, but the average probability was assessed to be just 62 percent. More research is needed to see if citizen forecasts might be similarly more informative and improved if citizens too were asked to assess probabilities. Also, as with prediction markets, it would be helpful to know more about how people make their forecasts and on what basis. Currently we know little about why citizen forecasts sometimes do well and sometimes do not.

Big data

With the growth of social media there have been recent attempts to forecast elections with content from Twitter and other platforms, but with little success (Huberty 2015; Burnap et al. 2016). A lot of learning about the relationships between online content and election outcomes is still needed, presumably involving cross-national analysis because of the paucity of elections with enough online content in any single country. However, since this is a fast-changing area with changing platforms and participants, what holds about social media for one election may not do so for the next.

Combining forecasts

What aggregators are to pollsters, combiners are to forecasters. Whereas synthetic models include different kinds of predictors in one model, combining forecasts is a process of averaging the forecasts of different models (often based on different predictors). For example, PollyVote.com averages forecasts from polls, prediction markets, expert judgments, citizen forecasts and various quantitative models with considerable success in the US (Silver 2012; Graefe 2015a; Rothschild 2015) and Germany (Graefe 2015b). A similar approach was also taken at ElectionsEtc.com to forecasting the UK's EU referendum (Fisher and Shorrocks 2016).

Naturally it matters how forecasts are combined. Both PollyVote and ElectionsEtc first identified categories of forecast type (e.g., betting markets, prediction markets, citizen forecasts, etc.) and averaged the forecasts within each type before averaging across types. This can effectively mean that various different econometric models each carry very little weight in the overall forecast. The advantage of this approach should be that it ensures that lots of forecasts based on just one source of information do not swamp a series of individual forecasts each based on its own particular source. However, there are major judgment calls required regarding when to consider two forecasting methods sufficiently similar to constitute examples of one type, or when they should be considered instances of two different types.

Another related issue is what weight to give each forecast (or forecast type). Montgomery, Hollenbach and Ward (2015) advocate ensemble Bayesian model averaging whereby forecasts are weighted according to prior performance. This is not always possible, but even when it is Graefe et al. (2015) argue that weights should only be used if there is strong evidence for them.

How to balance forecasts based on recent information with those that are older is another important issue. There is plenty of scope for fruitful work in this area, perhaps also more broadly in thinking about how to combine both forecasts and raw information, maybe with a neural network approach (Borisyuk et al. 2005).

Forecasting seat outcomes

The audience for election forecasts is much more interested in who gets elected and who ends up governing than they are in the share of the vote. So this section discusses how seat forecasting is done.

Votes-to-seats and multi-level votes and seats forecasting

In most proportional representation systems, forecasting the number of seats for each party nationally is relatively straightforward given a forecast of the number of votes for each party nationally. For single member district systems, uniform change (or swing) is a traditional model that, for all its imperfections, is not a bad starting point (Jackman 2014; Fisher and Lewis-Beck 2016). Arguably uniform change is not a simple votes-to-seats translation because it relies on constituency-specific information, but that information is static and prior to the campaign.

Many of the most complicated forecasting models in Britain and the US generate probabilistic seat (or electoral college) forecasts by having vote forecasts at different levels based on dynamic data at different levels. We might term these multi-level votes-to-seats forecasting methods. At recent US presidential and senate elections, there have been enough state-level polls to predict each state outcome separately but borrow strength from information from others and the national level (Linzer 2013). For the US House of Representatives, a different approach is needed (Bafumi, Erikson and Wlezien 2014).

In Britain, constituency polls were rare until 2015 but were still not ubiquitous. Still it was possible to model the GB share of the vote at the constituency level. A further complication was that in 2015 changes in party support were so different in Scotland from the rest of Britain that forecasts needed to respect this and use information from Scotland-only polls. Reconciling information at these different levels is tricky, but Hanretty, Lauderdale and Vivyan (2016) present a thoughtful and sensible solution. They adjust a predicted constituency pattern to fit the national forecast by assuming the same pattern of turnout at the previous election and shifting the vote shares in each constituency using a generalized normal distribution. Most of the time the effect of this is close to that from applying a uniform change adjustment, but for small parties it ensures against predicting negative vote shares.

To the extent that multi-level forecasting models use individual-level data, they typically model it to inform their district-level models, perhaps along with district-level opinion polls

(Fisher 2016; Ford et al. 2016; Hanretty, Lauderdale and Vivyan 2016). However, Mellon and Fieldhouse (2016) present a model which reconciles district-level variation in individual voter transitions with national-level vote share forecasts.

There is still more potential to develop this framework for national elections. For example, the results of local/municipal elections have been used to forecast national elections (Prosser 2016; Rallings, Thrasher and Borisyuk 2016), but not simultaneously with national-level polling data.

A multi-level strategy, together with sub-national election modeling, has been advocated as a solution to the small N problem for estimating structural models for recently democratized countries (Turgeon and Rennó 2012). Taking the multi-level approach to a level above the national, Simon Hix and Michael Marsh use both national and Europe-wide factors to forecast outcomes of European Parliament elections for the whole of the EU (Hix and Marsh 2011; Hix, Marsh and Cunningham 2014).

Seats bypassing votes

It is possible to forecast seat outcomes without forecasting vote shares. In the case of citizen forecasting, this is unavoidable: surveys ask who will win, not what the shares of the vote for each party in their constituency will be (Murr 2017). In some other models, vote shares are essentially bypassed on the basis that the main target of the forecast should be modeled directly (Whiteley et al. 2016; Lebo and Norpoth 2016). What is not clear are the circumstances under which this is a more successful strategy than providing an equivalent model for votes and then translating votes to seats. This would seem to be a safer strategy, respecting the logic of elections that seats depend on votes.

Forecasting government formation

While the public are most interested in who will form the next government, forecasters rarely attempt to tell them this when there is a significant chance that no party will win a majority. In multi-party systems where coalition government is common, uncertainty over seat outcomes implies uncertainty over governing outcomes, even if there is assumed to be certainty over government formation conditional on any particular seats outcome. While there are examples of this kind of government forecast (see, for example, Fisher 2016), there are none that I know of which allow for the possibility that different governments might form out of the same election outcome. It is not clear what models would inform the estimates of the conditional probabilities required for such a forecast, and they may need to be partially subjective.

Conclusion

Philip Tetlock is famous for dismissing "expert" forecasters as worse than dart-throwing chimps. His most recent book makes it clear that he does not intend this remark to apply to those, including "polling analysts like Nate Silver," with forecasting models that have been tested and revised to calibrate accuracy (Tetlock and Gardner 2015). While Tetlock is right to try to distinguish systematic scientific forecasting from the more ad hoc kind, it is not clear that any election forecasters have models they can confidently say are well calibrated for future political events.

For most there is a lot of room for improvement in uncertainty estimation. Lauderdale and Linzer (2015) make a powerful argument that established structural models in the US understate prediction uncertainty in various ways. Correcting for these problems they show that, "there is not sufficient historical evidence to warrant strong, early-campaign assessments about the probable outcome of a presidential election." This is a major challenge for all structural models to improve our understanding of how much election outcomes can really be said to be predictable from particular factors.

More generally, uncertainty estimation is important for well-calibrated forecast probabilities for all methods. Ultimately though, forecasting, including uncertainty calibration, is about assuming the future will be like the past. There is plenty of reason to expect that electoral politics, surveys and markets will not continue to operate just as always. This additional uncertainty is something producers and consumers of forecasts need to be aware of.

There is hope for more accurate and precise forecasts though. The academic literature reviewed above shows increasing methodological sophistication, richer data becoming more available, understanding of relative advantages of different methods becoming stronger and forecasting quality improving. Election forecasting should continue to improve with more research.

Not least of the priorities should be more meta-analysis. Those that have been conducted so far have been helpful for giving us a broad overview of the relative performance of different methods. For example, looking across forty-four elections from eight countries, Graefe (2017) argues that prediction markets beat structural models and opinion polls, but not citizen forecasts, with combination forecasts doing best of all. Further meta-analyses would be helpful for understanding the circumstances under which particular methods do relatively well. We need to know more about the extent to which particular political systems are best served by particular forecasting methods and how much the answers depend on how close the election is. The well-known idea that opinion polls are best very close to an election but citizen forecast and prediction markets do better further out could do with more systematic assessment.

While the performance of synthetic models and particularly combined forecasts is impressive overall, it is not yet clear when and why these forecasts go seriously wrong. Many election forecasts do worse than assuming the election outcome will be the same as the last one. We need to understand the contextual factors influencing the absolute performance of forecasting methods better. While some methods did better than others in forecasting the 2015 British general election, the main problem was that all the models, methods and markets were way out, failing to predict the Conservative majority by a large margin (Fisher and Lewis-Beck 2016). Similarly, all the forecasting methods before the UK's EU referendum pointed toward Remain (Fisher and Shorrocks 2016). Forecasts from different methods should be more like Tolstoy's happy and unhappy families: they should either be accurate in the same way or inaccurate each in their own particular ways. It is easy to see how the serious 2015 British polling miss affected all poll-based forecasts, but more difficult to identify is how and why the betting markets and expert and citizen surveys were similarly misleading. What matters in this context is not who did best but why they all failed, and how the failures of different methods are related to each other.

Despite this and other major failures that loom large in the public mind, election forecasts are still much better than Tetlock's dart-throwing chimps. Most of the time they manage to predict the right winner and get the flavor of the outcome well enough. There is an interesting question here as to how good forecasts ought to be. Forecasts the day before ought to be spot on; there shouldn't be much if anything left to change minds and generate late swing. Sadly final forecasts often fail to come as close as they should to eventual outcomes. Forecasts further out from an election should stand a high chance of being indicative of the outcome. But they should not be expected to be spot on. Voters are not and should not be entirely predictable.

Note

1 Thanks to Andreas Murr for comments and to John Kenny and Eilidh Macfarlane for help compiling literature searches.

References

Aichholzer, J. and Willmann, J. (2014) "Forecasting Austrian National Elections: The Grand Coalition Model," *International Journal of Forecasting*, vol. 30, no. 1, March, 55–64.

Arnesen, S. (2012) "Forecasting Norwegian Elections: Out of Work and Out of Office," *International Journal of Forecasting*, vol. 28, no. 4, December, 789–796.

Bafumi, J., Erikson, R. S. and Wlezien, C. (2014) "National Polls, District Information, and House Seats: Forecasting the 2014 Midterm Election," *PS: Political Science and Politics*, vol. 47, no. 4, October, 775–778.

Bellucci, P. (2010) "Election Cycles and Electoral Forecasting in Italy, 1994–2008," *International Journal of Forecasting*, vol. 26, no. 1, March, 54–67.

Berg, J. E., Penney, C. E. and Rietz, T. A. (2015) "Partisan Politics and Congressional Election Prospects: Evidence from the Iowa Electronic Markets," *PS: Political Science and Politics*, vol. 48, no. 4, October, 573–578.

Blumenthal, M., Edwards-Levy, A. and Lienesch, R. (2014) "What You Need To Know About That 'Nerd Fight'," *The Huffington Post*, September 19, 2014, available online: www.huffingtonpost.com/2014/09/19/senate-models_n_5848920.html [accessed March 23, 2016].

Borisyuk, R., Borisyuk, G., Rallings, C. and Thrasher, M. (2005) "Forecasting the 2005 General Election: A Neural Network Approach," *The British Journal of Politics and International Relations*, vol. 7, no. 2, May, 199–209.

Burnap, P., Gibson, R., Sloan, L., Southern, R. and Williams, M. (2016) "140 Characters to Victory?: Using Twitter to Predict the UK 2015 General Election," *Electoral Studies*, vol. 41, March, 230–233.

Campbell, J. E. and Garand, J. C. (2000) *Before the Vote*, London: Sage.

Cox, A. and Katz, J. (2014) "NYTimes Senate Forecasting Model," *New York Times*, available online: www.nytimes.com/newsgraphics/2014/senate-model/methodology.html [accessed October 24, 2014].

Curtice, J. (2016) "How Leave Won the Battle but Remain May Still Win the War," whatukthinks.org, June 30, 2016, available online: http://whatukthinks.org/eu/how-leave-won-the-battle-but-remain-may-still-win-the-war/ [accessed June 30, 2016].

Dassonneville, R. and Hooghe, M. (2012) "Election Forecasting Under Opaque Conditions: A Model for Francophone Belgium, 1981–2010," *International Journal of Forecasting*, vol. 28, no. 4, December, 777–788.

Erikson, R. S. and Wlezien, C. (2012) "Markets vs. Polls as Election Predictors: An Historical Assessment," *Electoral Studies*, vol. 31, no. 3, September, 532–539.

Fisher, S. D. (2015) "Predictable and Unpredictable Changes in Party Support: A Method for Long-Range Daily Election Forecasting from Opinion Polls," *Journal of Elections, Public Opinion and Parties*, vol. 25, no. 2, April, 137–158.

Fisher, S. D. (2016) "Piecing it All Together and Forecasting Who Governs: The 2015 British General Election," *Electoral Studies*, vol. 41, March, 234–238.

Fisher, S. D. and Lewis-Beck, M. S. (2016) "Forecasting the 2015 British General Election: The 1992 Debacle All Over Again?," *Electoral Studies*, vol. 41, March, 225–229.

Fisher, S. D. and Renwick, A. (2016) "Final Forecast from the Historical Referendums and Polls Based Method," ElectionsEtc.com, June 23, 2016, available online: https://electionsetc.com/2016/06/23/final-forecast-from-the-historical-referendums-and-polls-based-method/ [accessed June 30, 2016].

Fisher, S. D. and Shorrocks, R. (2016) "Final Combined EU Referendum Forecast," ElectionsEtc.com, June 23, 2016, available online: https://electionsetc.com/2016/06/23/final-combined-eu-referendum-forecast/ [accessed June 30, 2016].

Ford, R., Jennings, W., Pickup, M. and Wlezien, C. (2016) "From Polls to Votes to Seats: Forecasting the 2015 British General Election," *Electoral Studies*, vol. 41, March, 244–249.

Ford, R., Wlezien, C., Pickup, M. and Jennings, W. (2017) "Polls and Votes," in Arzheimer, K., Evans, J. and Lewis-Beck, M. S. (eds.) *The SAGE Handbook of Electoral Behaviour*, London: Sage: 787–812.

Graefe, A. (2014) "Accuracy of Vote Expectation Surveys in Forecasting Elections," *Public Opinion Quarterly*, vol. 78, no. S1, June, 204–232.

Graefe, A. (2015a) "Accuracy Gains of Adding Vote Expectation Surveys to a Combined Forecast of US Presidential Election Outcomes," *Research and Politics*, vol. 2, no. 1, March, 1–5.

Graefe, A. (2015b) "German Election Forecasting: Comparing and Combining Methods for 2013," *German Politics*, vol. 24, no. 2, April, 195–204.

Graefe, A. (2017) "Political Markets," in Arzheimer, K., Evans, J. and Lewis-Beck, M. S. (eds.) *The SAGE Handbook of Electoral Behaviour*, London: Sage: 861–882.

Graefe, A., Küchenhoff, H., Stierle, V. and Riedl, B. (2015) "Limitations of Ensemble Bayesian Model Averaging for Forecasting Social Science Problems," *International Journal of Forecasting*, vol. 31, no. 3, September, 943–951.

Hanretty, C. and Jennings, W. (2015) "Expert Predictions of the 2015 General Election," London: Political Studies Association. Available online: www.psa.ac.uk/sites/default/files/PSA%20GE%20Election%20Predictions%20Report.pdf [accessed April 30, 2015].

Hanretty, C., Lauderdale, B. and Vivyan, N. (2016) "Combining National and Constituency Polling for Forecasting," *Electoral Studies*, vol. 41, March, 239–243.

Hix, S. and Marsh, M. (2011) "Second-Order Effects Plus Pan-European Political Swings: An Analysis of European Parliament Elections Across Time," *Electoral Studies*, vol. 30, no. 1, March, 4–15.

Hix, S., Marsh, M. and Cunningham, K. (2014) "PollWatch2014 Methodology," electio2014.eu, available online: www.electio2014.eu/pollsandscenarios/pollsabout [accessed May 15, 2014].

Huberty, M. (2015) "Can We Vote with Our Tweet? On the Perennial Difficulty of Election Forecasting with Social Media," *International Journal of Forecasting*, vol. 31, no. 3, September, 992–1007.

Jackman, S. (2014) "The Predictive Power of Uniform Swing," *PS: Political Science and Politics*, vol. 47, no. 2, April, 317–321.

Jennings, W. and Fisher, S. D. (2016) "Expert Predictions of the 2016 EU Referendum," London: Political Studies Association, available online: www.psa.ac.uk/sites/default/files/PSA%20EU2016%20Report.pdf [accessed June 2, 2016].

Jennings, W. and Wlezien, C. (2016) "The Timeline of Elections: A Comparative Perspective," *American Journal of Political Science*, vol. 60, no. 1, January, 219–233.

Jérôme, B. and Jérôme-Speziari, V. (2012) "Forecasting the 2012 US Presidential Election: Lessons from a State-by-State Political Economy Model," *PS: Political Science and Politics*, vol. 45, no. 4, October, 663–668.

Kellner, P. (2014) "The Fundamentals Favour Cameron," YouGov, available online: https://yougov.co.uk/news/2014/04/14/fundamentals-favour-cameron/ [accessed March 22, 2016].

Lauderdale, B. E. and Linzer, D. (2015) "Under-Performing, Over-Performing, or Just Performing? The Limitations of Fundamentals-Based Presidential Election Forecasting," *International Journal of Forecasting*, vol. 31, no. 3, September, 965–979.

Lebo, M. J. and Norpoth, H. (2016) "Victory Without Power: The Pm-Pendulum Forecast," *Electoral Studies*, vol. 41, March, 255–259.

Lewis-Beck, M. S. and Bélanger, É. (2012) "Election Forecasting in Neglected Democracies: An Introduction," *International Journal of Forecasting*, vol. 28, no. 4, 767–768.

Lewis-Beck, M. S. and Dassonneville, R. (2015) "Forecasting Elections in Europe: Synthetic Models," *Research and Politics*, vol. 2, no. 1, March, 1–11.

Lewis-Beck, M. S. and Stegmaier, M. (2014) "US Presidential Election Forecasting," *PS: Political Science and Politics*, vol. 47, no. 2, April, 284–288.

Lewis-Beck, M. S., Nadeau, R. and Bélanger, É. (2016) "The British General Election: Synthetic Forecasts," *Electoral Studies*, vol. 41, March, 264–268.

Linzer, D. A. (2013) "Dynamic Bayesian Forecasting of Presidential Elections in the States," *Journal of the American Statistical Association*, vol. 108, no. 501, March, 124–134.

Linzer, D. and Lewis-Beck, M. S. (2015) "Forecasting US Presidential Elections: New Approaches (An Introduction)," *International Journal of Forecasting*, vol. 31, no. 3, April, 895–897.

Magalhães, P. C., Aguiar-Conraria, L. and Lewis-Beck, M. S. (2012) "Forecasting Spanish Elections," *International Journal of Forecasting*, vol. 28, no. 4, December, 769–776.

Mellon, J. and Fieldhouse, E. (2016) "The British Election Study 2015 General Election Constituency Forecast," *Electoral Studies*, vol. 41, March, 250–254.

Montgomery, J. M., Hollenbach, F. M. and Ward, M. D. (2015) "Calibrating Ensemble Forecasting Models with Sparse Data in the Social Sciences," *International Journal of Forecasting*, vol. 31, no. 3, September, 930–942.

Mortimore, R. (2014) "Sweet FA," ipsos-mori.com, 1–3. Available online: www.ipsos.com/ipsos-mori/en-uk/sweet-fa?language_content_entity=en-uk [accessed March 24, 2016].

Murr, A. E. (2015a) "The Party Leadership Model: An Early Forecast of the 2015 British General Election," *Research and Politics*, vol. 2, no. 2, June, 1–9.

Murr, A. E. (2015b) "The Wisdom of Crowds: Applying Condorcet's Jury Theorem to Forecasting US Presidential Elections," *International Journal of Forecasting*, vol. 31, no. 3, September, 916–929.

Murr, A. E. (2016) "The Wisdom of Crowds: What do Citizens Forecast for the 2015 British General Election?," *Electoral Studies*, vol. 41, March, 283–288.

Murr, A. E. (2017) "Wisdom of Crowds," in Arzheimer, K., Evans, J. and Lewis-Beck, M. S. (eds.) *The SAGE Handbook of Electoral Behaviour*, London: Sage: 835–860.

Norpoth, H. (2014) "The Electoral Cycle," *PS: Political Science and Politics*, vol. 47, no. 2, April, 332–335.

Norpoth, H. and Bednarczuk, M. (2012) "History and Primary: The Obama Reelection," *PS: Political Science and Politics*, vol. 45, no. 4, October, 614–617.

Norpoth, H. and Gschwend, T. (2010) "The Chancellor Model: Forecasting German Elections," *International Journal of Forecasting*, vol. 26, no. 1, March, 42–53.

Prosser, C. (2016) "Do Local Elections Predict the Outcome of the Next General Election? Forecasting British General Elections from Local Election National Vote Share Estimates," *Electoral Studies*, vol. 41, March, 274–278.

Rallings, C., Thrasher, M. and Borisyuk, G. (2016) "Forecasting the 2015 General Election Using Aggregate Local Election Data," *Electoral Studies*, vol. 41, March, 279–282.

Rothschild, D. (2015) "Combining Forecasts for Elections: Accurate, Relevant, and Timely," *International Journal of Forecasting*, vol. 31, no. 3, September, 952–964.

Silver, N. (2012) "Models, Models, Everywhere," FiveThirtyEight, available online: http://fivethirtyeight.com/features/models-models-everywhere/ [accessed March 1, 2015].

Silver, N. (2014) "How The FiveThirtyEight Senate Forecast Model Works," FiveThirtyEight, available online: http://fivethirtyeight.com/features/how-the-fivethirtyeight-senate-forecast-model-works/ [accessed March 24, 2016].

Sturgis, P., Baker, N., Callegaro, M., Fisher, S. D., Green, J., Jennings, W., Kuha, J., Lauderdale, B. E. and Smith, P. G. (2016) *Report of the Inquiry into the 2015 British General Election Opinion Polls*, London: Market Research Society and British Polling Council.

Tetlock, P. and Gardner, D. (2015) *Superforecasting*, New York: Random House.

Turgeon, M. and Rennó, L. (2012) "Forecasting Brazilian Presidential Elections: Solving the N Problem," *International Journal of Forecasting*, vol. 28, no. 4, December, 804–812.

Wall, M., Sudulich, M. L. and Cunningham, K. (2012) "What are the Odds? Using Constituency-Level Betting Markets to Forecast Seat Shares in the 2010 UK General Elections," *Journal of Elections, Public Opinion and Parties*, vol. 22, no. 1, February, 3–26.

Wang, S. S. H. (2015) "Origins of Presidential Poll Aggregation: A Perspective from 2004 to 2012," *International Journal of Forecasting*, vol. 31, no. 3, September, 898–909.

Whiteley, P., Clarke, H. D., Sanders, D. and Stewart, M. C. (2016) "Forecasting the 2015 British General Election: The Seats-Votes Model," *Electoral Studies*, vol. 41, March, 269–273.

40

FIELD EXPERIMENTS IN POLITICAL BEHAVIOR

Donald P. Green and Erin A. York

The study of political behavior is broad in scope, encompassing both conduct in political settings and the psychological, sociological, and economic precursors that lead people to value different things, harbor different beliefs, and pursue different objectives. Much of the scholarship in this domain is descriptive. Researchers measure quantities such as the proportion of the public that feels a sense of attachment to a political party, assess whether these proportions have changed over time, and estimate correlations among variables such as conservatism and party affiliation. Other scholarly investigations focus on cause-and-effect relationships. For example, does exposure to political campaigns make voters more knowledgeable about the candidates' stances on policy issues?

During the latter half of the twentieth century, both descriptive and causal questions such as these were addressed using a single research method: opinion surveys. For example, Huckfeldt and Sprague used panel surveys of residents of South Bend, Indiana during the 1984 election campaign to demonstrate that people hold political attitudes that are correlated with those held by others in their social network, a descriptive fact that they interpret causally to mean that "vote preferences are socially structured ... by the characteristics and preferences of others with whom the voter discusses politics," such as an individual's friends and family (Huckfeldt and Sprague 1995: 189). Similarly, Almond and Verba (1963: 133) and Wolfinger and Rosenstone (1980: 17) observe a strong correlation between education and participatory attitudes and voting, respectively, and both argue that this correlation reflects the causal influence of education and the outlook and skills that it imparts.

Although these authors make cogent arguments on behalf of their causal interpretations, the survey evidence they adduce is subject to competing interpretations. The correlation between the political views among those in the same friendship or family networks that Huckfeldt and Sprague observe might arise if members of these networks share unmeasured attributes, such as similar pre-adult socialization experiences (Fowler et al. 2011). Education might be predictive of participatory orientations not because schooling imparts them but rather because education is a marker for other unmeasured attributes, such as social position or norms conveyed by parents, that are causal. The correlation that Rosenstone and Hansen (1993) observe between voter turnout and reported exposure to mobilization activity may reflect the fact that strategic campaigns target likely voters for persuasive communication; we might observe this correlation even in the absence of any mobilizing effects.

One way to overcome the concern that "correlation is not causation" is to study propositions such as these using experimental designs. We use the term experiment to refer to studies in which subjects are randomly assigned to treatment or control conditions (Gerber and Green 2012). Random assignment implies that subjects in the treatment group have the same expected potential outcomes as subjects in the control group. Any given random assignment may produce groups that differ in some measured or unmeasured way, but there is no systematic tendency for one group to be favored over the other in terms of outcomes, as may be the case when subjects self-select into the treatment group or are targeted for treatment by strategic actors.

The 1980s and 1990s saw increasing use of experimental designs in studies of political behavior. Technological developments, such as computer-assisted interviewing, allowed survey researchers to randomly manipulate question wording, order, and response options. Survey experimentation, which had been used sporadically to settle debates about over-time trends in survey responses (Sullivan, Piereson, and Marcus 1978) and required years of data collection (Schuman and Presser 1981), now became an area of rapid growth, especially as a tool to explore hard-to-measure attitudes on subjects such as race (Kuklinski, Cobb, and Gilens 1997). Use of survey experimentation was spurred by further developments, such as the advent of cooperative surveys that subsidized researchers' access to experimental opportunities (Mutz 2011) and online survey platforms that allowed researchers to make inexpensive use of nonprobability samples (Berinsky, Huber, and Lenz 2012). This era also witnessed new interest in laboratory experimentation, which had largely been the province of psychology. An especially influential study was Iyengar, Peters, and Kinder (1982), which recruited participants from the New Haven community to view a series of doctored news broadcasts that randomly stressed different national issues (inflation, defense, and environmental pollution). The researchers found that the treatments had no detectable effect on subjects' policy views but did change the importance that they accorded different issues. Evidently, news broadcasts do not change what people think but do affect what they think about (Iyengar, Peters, and Kinder 1982: 852). Subsequent lab experiments have used this research paradigm to study the effects of negative advertising (Ansolabehere and Iyengar 1997), confrontational public affairs programs (Mutz 2015), and ideologically slanted news (Arceneaux and Johnson 2013). Many recent experiments blend ingredients from lab and survey experiments, such as studies in which subjects deliberate over policy questions (Karpowitz, Mendelberg, and Shaker 2012; Farrar et al. 2010), sometimes after discussion with public officials or policy experts (Minozzi et al. 2015).

Survey experiments and lab experiments have many attractive features but also some important limitations. The principal advantage is that random allocation allows researchers to draw unbiased causal inferences that are free from "omitted variables bias." Another advantage is that the researcher is (usually) in full control of the stimuli that subjects receive and may deploy creative and carefully controlled interventions across multiple treatment arms in order to isolate causal mechanisms (Druckman et al. 2011; Gerber and Green 2012). Finally, the logistics of executing a study are typically manageable. Noncompliance with the assigned treatment, missing outcome data, and contamination across treatment conditions rarely afflict lab experiments. On the other hand, survey and lab experiments are often criticized for features that limit the generalizations that can be drawn from the results. Subjects in lab experiments are often college undergraduates (Sears 1986). The treatments that subjects receive are often contrived (e.g., campaign advertisements by hypothetical candidates), and the same may be said of the context in which subjects receive the treatment (e.g., amid an opinion survey or, in lab studies, in a faux living room where subjects are asked to watch television programs – without a remote control). Finally, outcomes tend to be measured shortly after the intervention occurs, usually at the end of the survey or lab session.

Field experimentation represents an attempt to address these concerns. Ideally, field experiments deploy interventions and measure outcomes in a manner that is both realistic and unobtrusive. The subjects are the very people who would ordinarily be targeted for an intervention; the treatment is the kind of intervention that would ordinarily be deployed in the real world (e.g., an actual political ad); subjects receive the intervention in a naturalistic context; the intervention and outcome measurement are unobtrusive in that subjects are unaware that their behavior is being studied. In practice, field experiments vary in terms of the extent to which they satisfy these criteria. On the ideal end of the spectrum are studies such as Rogers and Middleton (2015), in which persuasive mailings concerning five ballot propositions were sent by an advocacy campaign to randomly assigned voting precincts prior to an election. Outcomes were assessed unobtrusively using precinct-level voting returns. Somewhat more obtrusive are studies such as Gerber et al. (2011), in which a gubernatorial campaign deployed television ads in randomly assigned media markets, but voters' preferences in each market were assessed using opinion surveys. In this case, subjects were unaware of the connection between the media campaign and the survey. More obtrusive is Paluck's (2009) experimental evaluation of a Rwandan radio soap opera. Rwandan villages were randomly assigned to listen to an ethnic reconciliation soap opera or a control radio program that focused on health. Villagers were brought together every few weeks to listen to the radio programs and interviewed at the end of the year. Here, the treatment is a real program broadcast in the rest of the country, but the context in which the audience listened to the shows was somewhat lab-like, and it is possible that some respondents saw the connection between the content of the radio intervention and the end-line survey.[1]

The use of field experiments in political science is by no means new. The pioneering work of Gosnell (1927) and Eldersveld (1956) used controlled experiments to assess the effectiveness of voter mobilization tactics. The pace of field experimental developments slowed, however, after the 1950s, and only a handful of field experiments found their way into print during the remainder of the twentieth century (see Green and Gerber 2002a, 2002b). Remarkably, not a single field experiment appeared in any political science journal during the 1990s.

The current wave of field experimentation in political science began at the turn of the twenty-first century, reflecting the "credibility revolution" that was brewing across the social sciences. The large-scale voter turnout experiments conducted by Gerber and Green (2000) not only revived interest in randomized experimentation in real-world settings; this study also ushered in an era of growing methodological sophistication in analyzing field experiments, especially regarding issues posed by noncompliance, spillovers, and attrition.

Field experimentation may therefore be viewed as a two-pronged strategy to improve the credibility of causal inferences: experimental assignment is used to isolate cause-and-effect by eliminating systematic differences between treatment and control groups, and unobtrusive field-based designs narrow the gap between the research protocol and the political world to which the research is applied. The challenge is, of course, to design and execute this kind of research in a way that is theoretically illuminating. To do so requires an extensive research program that not only tests the effects of different interventions on a given subject pool and political setting but also tests whether the results hold across different subject pools and political settings. The remainder of this chapter therefore devotes special attention to the growth and development of the field experimental literature, which started with studies of voter turnout in the United States but rapidly branched out to other forms of political behavior and to a variety of political contexts. Accordingly, we begin our literature review by discussing voter mobilization experiments and then turn our attention to studies of persuasive messaging, attempts to induce non-electoral participation, and efforts to bolster the accountability of public officials through anti-corruption initiatives and mobilization of underserved populations. We conclude by speculating about the future of field experimentation in political behavior, discussing the growing body of work that focuses on the behavior of elites.

Voter turnout

Since the 1920s, scholars have sought to understand the conditions under which people vote. Scholarly interest in this question reflects a combination of political, normative, and theoretical motivations. Many political scientists have worked closely with political campaigns, and their research on voter mobilization grew out of efforts to gain a competitive advantage during an election campaign (Issenberg 2012). Others are drawn to the study of voter turnout on account of its distributive implications. In countries such as the United States, the socioeconomic and ethnic composition of the voting electorate often differs markedly from that of the eligible electorate, especially in low-salience elections where overall turnout rates tend to be well below 50 percent. Many scholars have expressed concern that affluent whites have disproportionate influence on politics due to their relatively high voting rates (Bedolla and Michelson 2012). Voter turnout also represents a theoretical puzzle for rational choice models of political behavior. In any large electorate, a given voter has an infinitesimal chance of casting the decisive vote; the instrumental value of voting is therefore negligible even when the election has enormous political implications (Downs 1957). To the extent that rational actors cast ballots, they must do so because of what Olson (1965) calls "selective incentives," the utility they receive from the act of voting itself. These selective incentives could include outright bribes, but in the contemporary American context more often comprise the intrinsic satisfaction voters receive from doing their civic duty and the social approbation they receive when others see them vote (Riker and Ordeshook 1968). Drawing on this theoretical framework, much of the experimental literature has probed the extent to which turnout is affected by interventions that affect the direct costs and benefits of voting. Conversely, in an effort to critically evaluate the assumptions of this theoretical model, many researchers conduct experiments designed to emphasize the closeness of the election or its importance for policy, two factors that should be irrelevant in a model where citizens rationally weigh the costs and benefits of voting.

Experiments on the costs and benefits of voting fall into four broad categories. First, several studies conducted in collaboration with non-partisan organizations have sought to raise turnout by lowering information costs.[2] In these experiments, voters are reminded by mail, phone call, email, or text message that Election Day is approaching, and in some cases they are also provided information about the location of their polling place. The many experiments that have sent reminders via mail or email have uniformly found null effects (Green and Gerber 2015: 58, 99). Brief recorded phone call reminders have also proven ineffective; live reminder calls have fared slightly better, generating a modest turnout increase among those who are successfully reached by phone (Green and Gerber 2015: 82–83). The one mode that seems to generate reliable effects is text messaging. Messages from a non-partisan group to an opt-in list of recipients raised turnout by about four percentage points in an early study (Dale and Strauss 2009); messages from the local registrar of voters generated a small percentage-point increase in turnout but one comparable to Dale and Strauss (2009) in percentage terms (Malhotra, Michelson, and Valenzuela 2012); and a series of large-scale experiments in Denmark found statistically significant effects among the young voters targeted by the campaign (Bhatti et al. 2014). Although Dale and Strauss (2009) attribute these effects to the fact that text messages are "noticeable reminders," it remains unclear why these reminders are so much more effective than those delivered via a live phone call. Another interesting puzzle concerns the fact that turnout does not respond in any consistent way to the content or urgency of the message. Bhatti et al. (2014), for example, find that messages delivered a few days prior to Election Day are more effective than those delivered on Election Day itself.

A second line of research assesses whether turnout rises when voting is made more convenient. Several experiments in the United States assess whether turnout increases when eligible citizens are encouraged to register as "permanent absentees," which means that the ballot is mailed to them weeks in advance of the election. Another set of experiments test whether turnout rises when voters are reminded that their jurisdiction allows for early in-person voting, enabling them to vote when it suits their schedule. Results seem to suggest that these appeals do induce recipients to cast ballots using more convenient options, but the net turnout rate rises only slightly (Mann 2011; Mann and Mayhew 2015). The lack of effect calls into question the hypothesis that low turnout rates in the United States reflect onerous registration requirements (Piven and Cloward 1989; Powell 1986), although experimental evidence does suggest that encouraging registration increases turnout in both the United States (Nickerson 2015) and France (Bracconier, Dormagen, and Pons 2017).

A third line of research offers people direct incentives to vote. Surprisingly, some state and municipal laws in the US permit cash inducements to vote in non-federal elections provided that recipients are not encouraged to vote for any particular candidate or cause. Panagopoulos (2013) randomly varied the incentives offered to voters from zero to $25 in two experiments conducted in municipal elections and found overall that turnout rises 1.5 percentage points for every $10 offered (roughly 15 to 20 percent of the control group voted in these elections). Although statistically significant, this estimated effect is not particularly large, perhaps because voters were incredulous about whether they would actually be paid.

A final strand of this literature focuses on social incentives. Here, the core proposition is that voters widely subscribe to the prescriptive social norm that one ought to vote and that one can induce compliance with this norm through social pressure. Social pressure may be exerted through the forceful assertion of norms ("Do your civic duty and vote!"), by monitoring of compliance with the norm, and by promising to disclose future (non)compliance to others. In the context of voter turnout, monitoring and disclosure are facilitated by the fact that voter turnout is a matter of public record – some states even post this information online. Experiments testing the turnout effects of social pressure date back to Gosnell (1927) and Gross et al. (1974); this research agenda was revived by Gerber, Green, and Larimer (2008), who showed that turnout rises substantially as larger doses of social pressure are applied via direct mail. The strong effects of social pressure seem to hold across an array of low- and medium-salience elections (Gerber, Green, and Larimer 2010; Mann 2010; Panagopoulos 2010; Sinclair, McConnell, and Michelson 2013), but the effects appear to be much weaker in high-salience races (Rogers et al. 2017), perhaps because non-voters in such elections tend to be less sensitive to the enforcement of voting norms. Interestingly, the effects also appear to be weaker when voters are presented with their record of past turnout but not scolded to do their civic duty (Murray and Matland 2014).

Social incentives arguably play a role in two related experimental literatures. The first concerns the effects of door-to-door canvassing. Dozens of studies in the United States (see Green and Gerber 2015: 31–35) as well as studies in the United Kingdom (Foos and de Rooij 2013; John and Brannan 2008; John and Foos 2014), China (Guan and Green 2006), Pakistan (Giné and Mansuri 2011), Sweden (Nyman 2017), and Italy (Cantoni and Pons 2016) show that turnout increases when canvassers converse with eligible voters. Interestingly, these settings are ones in which door-to-door mobilization is a common political practice. Comparable studies on the European continent where canvassing is uncommon have failed to find effects; see Pons

(2016) on turnout effects in France, Ramiro, Morales, and Jiménez-Buedo (2012) in Spain, and Bhatti et al. (2016) in Denmark. Another experimental finding that suggests the role of social incentives concerns volunteer phone-banking campaigns in which, several days before the election, voters are urged to vote and asked whether they can be counted on to vote on Election Day. Voters who pledge to vote are called back on the eve of the election and reminded to make good on their promise to vote. The results from three such experiments seem to suggest strong mobilization effects (Michelson, Bedolla, and McConnell 2009).

Overall, the literature offers a mixed verdict on efforts to change voting rates by altering the costs and benefits. Some evidence suggests that voting rates can be increased through cash payments and text message reminders, but other forms of reminders produce disappointing results, and offering more convenient voting options seems to do little to lure non-voters to the polls. The most powerful effects seem to stem from social pressure, especially when stern admonitions are coupled with monitoring and disclosure, suggesting that the costs that matter most are those that are socially imposed. At the same time, more gentle messages that urge voting face-to-face or through repeated interaction with voters who have pledged to vote also raise turnout substantially – at least in polities where such practices are common.

Persuasion

Non-partisan information

A growing body of scholarship addresses the impact of non-partisan information provision on electoral accountability. Interventions in this area are motivated by the theoretical assumption that limited political knowledge reduces voters' ability to hold politicians accountable, which in turn contributes to low-quality politicians and poor performance while in office (Pande 2011). A large formal literature on the link between information and voting behavior predicts that voters should punish politicians who do badly and reward good performers with another term in office (Besley 2006). However, the difficulty in identifying the impact of information has led to an increasing focus on experimental treatments that augment what voters know about public officials and the electoral process.

One strand of this experimental literature distributes non-partisan information about candidate performance. These interventions often involve the development and distribution of politician "report cards" intended to grade their integrity or performance while in office. Incumbents might be judged according to their attendance in lawmaking sessions or productivity in office. An analogous approach, intended to address corruption in office, provides voters with reports on candidates' inappropriate behavior, such as irregularities in spending or allegations of criminal conduct. Outcomes are often measured using hard electoral indicators, such as vote shares or incumbent reelection rates.

The several experiments conducted in this category have found effects that often vary depending on the context in which the information is deployed. An early natural experiment taking advantage of randomized rollout of municipal audits in Brazil found that reelection rates were sensitive to incumbent performance: for incumbents with few violations, electoral outcomes improved, while for incumbents with many violations, likelihood of reelection was reduced (Ferraz and Finan 2008). The impact of revelation varied according to the level of media present in a municipality; effects were larger where results could be disseminated via local radio.

Some findings have conflicted with theoretical predictions. In another experiment in Brazil, Figueiredo, Hidalgo, and Kasahara (2010) distributed fliers informing voters that the incumbent and challenger in a mayoral election had been cited for corruption convictions. The results suggest that this type of information can have different effects for different politicians: exposing bad behavior by the incumbent had no effect on his vote share, but the challenger's prospects were reduced by the intervention. In a similar field experiment implemented in Mexico, Chong et al. (2015) found that distributing fliers detailing mayoral corruption had the effect of reducing votes for *both* the incumbent and challenger party (producing an overall decrease in turnout). Finally, a report card experiment conducted in Uganda suggests that while effects of positive and negative information are in the predicted directions, their impact is short-lived in practice: an information treatment had large effects when administered via survey experiment but no discernable impact on electoral returns (Humphreys and Weinstein 2012).

Another line of research addresses the methods by which voters obtain information, studying the impact of different types of citizen–candidate interactions on a set of outcomes including turnout, candidate vote share, or voter knowledge. In these studies, the intervention is typically implemented with the cooperation of politicians, and the treatment involves some deviation from a normal campaign strategy in a given context. The motivation for this research stems in part from the politics of developing countries, where voters tend to be less informed about candidates and political campaigns often revolve around the distribution of private goods rather than policy platforms (Keefer and Khemani 2005).

This line of research was inspired by an early study that randomly varied campaign platforms in Benin (Wantchekon 2003). In these studies, researchers often coordinate directly with political parties in order to devise and deliver varying campaign messages. The deviation from "politics as usual" is expected to change voter perceptions of the candidates or parties involved in some context-specific manner. For example, voters may derive additional information about the options on the ballot by observing candidate performance in debates, which allows for more complex interactions between politicians. This in turn should cause them to reward strong performers and punish those who do poorly. Testing this hypothesis in Sierra Leone, Bidwell, Casey, and Glennerster (2015) randomly vary voters' exposure to candidate debates in the 2012 parliamentary elections. The authors found that watching the debates increased citizens' knowledge of candidates and their policy platforms and produced a bump in vote share for the debate "best performers." MPs involved in the debates also exhibited strengthened constituent engagement once in office.

This ambitious line of research offers new opportunities to learn about the relationship between voter knowledge and political outcomes, particularly in the developing world. At the same time, experimental interventions are difficult to implement with fidelity to random assignment when researchers depend on the cooperation of political actors, whose incentives may not be fully aligned with the goals of the study.

Persuasion designed to build voter support for a candidate or cause

A small but growing literature examines the extent to which voters' preferences for candidates or policies change in the wake of communication from campaigns. Several experiments focus on the effects of the face-to-face communication that occurs when canvassers visit voters at their doorstep. Some of the early studies looked at the persuasive effects of canvassing by advocacy groups (Arceneaux 2005; Nickerson 2007) and political campaigns (Nickerson, Friedrichs, and King 2006), sometimes featuring canvassing by candidates themselves (Arceneaux 2007). This literature has grown rapidly outside the United States, with large-scale experiments conducted in Benin (Wantchekon 2003), Canada (Dewan, Humphreys, and Rubenson 2014), France (Pons 2016), and Italy (Cantoni and Pons 2016; Kendall, Nannicini, and Trebbi 2015). Many of the more recent studies have looked at large-scale persuasion efforts using direct mail (Rogers and Middleton 2015), Facebook advertising (Broockman and Green 2014), automated phone messages (Shaw et al. 2012), or television commercials (Gerber et al. 2011). Results from these studies have ranged widely. Rogers and Middleton (2015) found their mailings to have a strong effect on vote outcomes (but see Cubbison 2015 and Doherty and Adler 2014); Broockman and Green (2014) found Facebook ads to have no effect; and Gerber et al. (2011) found televised ads to have a strong initial effect that dissipated quickly.

In sum, recent years have seen rapid growth in the rigorous evaluation of persuasive communication. This line of research is branching out to different countries and modes of communication. At this stage, it is too early to say why certain kinds of advertising campaigns tend to be more persuasive than others. A simple dichotomy between personal and impersonal seems not to work as an explanation: personal tactics such as canvassing sometimes produce weak results, while impersonal tactics such as direct mail sometimes produce substantial effects. Systematic variation of factors such as source credibility (see, for example, Shaw et al. 2012) and "dosage" of communication (Cubbison 2015) have sometimes also produced counterintuitive results, with endorsements from credible sources and high volumes of mail failing to shift vote preferences. Another interesting puzzle is that persuasive communications typically fail to increase voter turnout even when the persuasive effects are large (see, for example, Rogers and Middleton 2015). One of the more intriguing experimental results suggests that one-sided persuasive communication from a single campaign fails to increase turnout, but two-sided communication from opposing campaigns does raise turnout (Loewen and Rubenson 2010).

Conclusion

This chapter has presented a brief overview of the main lines of field experimental research in political behavior, notably studies of voter turnout and persuasive communication. Many other lines of inquiry have been given short shrift, and we conclude by describing several important and growing areas of investigation.

Field experiments are increasingly directed at forms of political participation other than voting in elections. Early studies of contributing to campaigns or political organizations (Miller and Krosnick 2004) paved the way for similar experiments in economics (Rondeau and List 2008; Perez-Truglia and Cruces 2017) and political science (Green et al. 2015; Schwam-Baird et al. 2016), with increasing emphasis on head-to-head comparisons of different kinds of messaging appeals. Another form of participation less specific to the American context than fundraising is participation in political meetings and rallies. Recent works in the US and Honduras have accentuated the role of social ties in promoting this form of participation (McClendon 2014; Stafford and Hughes 2012).

Another important strand of experimental inquiry focuses on the behavior of public officials rather than voters. Several studies have borrowed the "audit study" paradigm commonly used to study the labor market or housing discrimination to assess whether public officials respond differently to requests made by majority or minority constituents (Butler and Broockman 2011; Butler 2014; Distelhorst and Hou 2014) or by citizens inside or outside their own constituency (Broockman 2014). The question of differential treatment also pertains to the question of whether campaign donors enjoy greater access to public officials than ordinary constituents (Kalla and Broockman 2015). Other recent studies have sought to assess the effects of factchecking (Nyhan and Reifler 2015), lobbying by citizen organizations (Bergan 2009), or providing information about constituent opinion on pending legislation (Butler and Nickerson 2011). The growing use of experiments to study elite behavior complements the growing use of naturally-occurring randomizations, such as lotteries that determine seniority on legislative committees (Broockman and Butler 2015; Kellerman and Shepsle 2009), term length (Titiunik 2016), or the ability to offer legislative proposals to the Canadian House of Commons (Loewen et al. 2014). Although elite behavior remains less widely studied than mass behavior, field experiments have brought about something of a renaissance of research on elites, and the years to come are likely to see growing use of this research approach in studies of comparative politics.

Notes

1 Paluck points out that it is common for Rwandans to listen to radio in groups. This study also featured unobtrusive outcome measures that were reported in Paluck and Green (2009).
2 A related hypothesis is that turnout increases when voters become informed about the stakes of an upcoming election. A noteworthy leafleting experiment randomly varied the distribution of persuasive messages by one or both sides of a referendum campaign (Loewen and Rubenson 2010) and found that only two-sided communication raised turnout.

References

Almond, G. A. and Verba, S. (1963) *The Civic Culture: Political Attitudes and Democracy in Five Nations*, Princeton: Princeton University Press.

Ansolabehere, S. and Iyengar, S. (1997) *Going Negative: How Political Advertising Divides and Shrinks the American Electorate*, New York: Free Press.

Arceneaux, K. (2005) "Using Cluster Randomized Field Experiments to Study Voting Behavior," *The ANNALS of the American Academy of Political and Social Science*, vol. 601, no. 1, September, 169–179.

Arceneaux, K. (2007) "I'm Asking for Your Support: The Effects of Personally Delivered Campaign Messages on Voting Decisions and Opinion Formation," *Quarterly Journal of Political Science*, vol. 2, no. 1, March, 43–65.

Arceneaux, K. and Johnson, M. (2013) *Changing Minds Or Changing Channels?: Partisan News in an Age of Choice*, Chicago: University of Chicago Press.

Bedolla, L. G. and Michelson, M. R. (2012) *Mobilizing Inclusion: Transforming the Electorate Through Get-Out-The-Vote Campaigns*, New Haven: Yale University Press.

Bergan, D. E. (2009) "Does Grassroots Lobbying Work? A Field Experiment Measuring the Effects of an E-Mail Lobbying Campaign on Legislative Behavior," *American Politics Research*, vol. 37, no. 2, March, 327–352.

Berinsky, A. J., Huber, G. A., and Lenz, G. S. (2012) "Evaluating Online Labor Markets for Experimental Research: Amazon.com's Mechanical Turk," *Political Analysis*, vol. 20, no. 3, Summer, 351–368.

Besley, T. J. (2006) *Principled Agents? The Political Economy of Good Government*, Oxford: Oxford University Press.

Bhatti, Y., Dahlgaard, J. O., Hansen, J. H., and Hansen, K. (2014) "How Voter Mobilization Spread in Households and Families: The Use of Short Text Messages on Cell Phones to Boost Turnout," Paper presented at the 2014 Annual Meeting of the American Political Science Association, Washington, DC, August 28–31.

Bhatti, Y., Dahlgaard, J. O., Hansen, J. H., and Hansen, K. M. (2016) "Is Door-to-Door Canvassing Effective in Europe? Evidence from a Meta-study Across Six European Countries," *British Journal of Political Science*, First View, 1–12.

Bidwell, K., Casey, K., and Glennerster, R. (2015) *Debates: Voter and Politician Response to Political Communication in Sierra Leone*, Stanford: Stanford University Graduate School of Business. Available online: www.barcelona-ipeg.eu/wp-content/uploads/2015/09/Debates_24August2015.pdf.

Braconnier, C., Dormagen, J. Y., and Pons, V. (2017) "Voter Registration Costs and Disenfranchisement: Experimental Evidence from France," *American Political Science Review*, First View, 1–21.

Broockman, D. E. (2014) "Distorted Communication, Unequal Representation: Constituents Communicate Less to Representatives Not of Their Race," *American Journal of Political Science*, vol. 58, no. 2, April, 307–321.

Broockman, D. E. and Butler, D. M. (2015) "Do Better Committee Assignments Meaningfully Benefit Legislators? Evidence from a Randomized Experiment in the Arkansas State Legislature," *Journal of Experimental Political Science*, vol. 2, no. 2, January, 152–163.

Broockman, D. E. and Green, D. P. (2014) "Do Online Advertisements Increase Political Candidates' Name Recognition or Favorability? Evidence from Randomized Field Experiments," *Political Behavior*, vol. 36, no. 2, June, 263–289.

Butler, D. M. (2014) *Representing the Advantaged: How Politicians Reinforce Inequality*, New York: Cambridge University Press.

Butler, D. M. and Broockman, D. E. (2011) "Do Politicians Racially Discriminate Against Constituents? A Field Experiment on State Legislators," *American Journal of Political Science*, vol. 55, no. 3, July, 463–477.

Butler, D. M. and Nickerson, D. W. (2011) "Can Learning Constituency Opinion Affect How Legislators Vote? Results From a Field Experiment," *Quarterly Journal of Political Science*, vol. 6, no. 1, 55–83.

Cantoni, E., and Pons, V. (2016) *Do Interactions with Candidates Increase Voter Support and Participation? Experimental Evidence from Italy*, Cambridge, MA: Harvard Business School. Available online: www.hbs.edu/faculty/Publication%20Files/16-080_559d110b-4b31-467c-9d14-5cd08083a527.pdf.

Chong, A., Ana, L., Karlan, D., and Wantchekon, L. (2015) "Does Corruption Information Inspire the Fight or Quash the Hope? A Field Experiment in Mexico on Voter Turnout, Choice, and Party Identification," *Journal of Politics*, vol. 77, no. 1, January, 55–71.

Cubbison, W. (2015) "The Marginal Effects of Direct Mail on Vote Choice," Paper presented at the 2015 Annual Meeting of the Midwest Political Science Association, Chicago, April 16–19.

Dale, A. and Strauss, A. (2009) "Don't Forget to Vote: Text Message Reminders as a Mobilization Tool," *American Journal of Political Science*, vol. 53, no. 4, October, 787–804.

Dewan, T., Humphreys, M., and Rubenson, D. (2014) "The Elements of Political Persuasion: Content, Charisma and Cue," *Economic Journal*, vol. 124, no. 574, February, 257–292.

Distelhorst, G. and Hou, Y. (2014) "Ingroup Bias in Official Behavior: A National Field Experiment in China," *Quarterly Journal of Political Science*, vol. 9, no. 2, June, 203–230.

Doherty, D. and Adler, E. S. (2014) "The Persuasive Effects of Partisan Campaign Mailers," *Political Research Quarterly*, vol. 67, no. 3, September, 562–573.

Downs, A. (1957) "An Economic Theory of Political Action in a Democracy," *The Journal of Political Economy*, vol. 65, no. 2, April, 135–150.

Druckman, J. N., Green, D. P., Kuklinski, J. H., and Lupia, A. (2011) *Cambridge Handbook of Experimental Political Science*, New York: Cambridge University Press.

Eldersveld, S. (1956) "Experimental Propaganda Techniques and Voting Behavior," *American Political Science Review*, vol. 50, no. 1, March, 154–166.

Farrar, C., Fishkin, J. S., Green, D. P., List, C., Luskin, R. C., and Levy Paluck, E. (2010) "Disaggregating Deliberation's Effects: An Experiment Within a Deliberative Poll," *British Journal of Political Science*, vol. 40, no. 2, April, 333–347.

Ferraz, C. and Finan, F. (2008) "Exposing Corrupt Politicians: The Effects of Brazil's Publicly Released Audits on Electoral Outcomes," *The Quarterly Journal of Economics*, vol. 123, no. 2, May, 703–745.

Figueiredo, M. F. P. D., Hidalgo, F. D., and Kasahara, Y. (2010) "When Do Voters Punish Corrupt Politicians? Experimental Evidence from Brazil," Unpublished Manuscript, University of Connecticut.

Foos, F. and de Rooij, E. (2013) "The Asymmetrical Mobilization Effects of Partisan GOTV Campaigns: Evidence from a Randomised Field Experiment in the UK," Working Paper, University of Zurich.

Fowler, J. H., Heaney, M. T., Nickerson, D. W., Padgett, J. F., and Sinclair, B. (2011) "Causality in Political Networks," *American Politics Research*, vol. 39, no. 2, March, 437–480.

Gerber, A. S. and Green, D. P. (2000) "The Effects of Canvassing, Telephone Calls, and Direct Mail on Voter Turnout: A Field Experiment," *American Political Science Review*, vol. 94, no. 3, September, 653–663.

Gerber, A. S. and Green, D. P. (2012) *Field Experiments: Design, Analysis, and Interpretation*, New York: W. W. Norton.

Gerber, A. S., Gimpel, J. G., Green, D. P., and Shaw, D. R. (2011) "How Large and Long-Lasting are the Persuasive Effects of Televised Campaign Ads? Results from a Randomized Field Experiment," *American Political Science Review*, vol. 105, no. 1, February, 135–150.

Gerber, A. S., Green, D. P., and Larimer, C. W. (2008) "Social Pressure and Voter Turnout: Evidence from a Large-Scale Field Experiment," *American Political Science Review*, vol. 102, no. 1, February, 33–48.

Gerber, A. S., Green, D. P., and Larimer, C. W. (2010) "An Experiment Testing the Relative Effectiveness of Encouraging Voter Participation by Inducing Feelings of Pride or Shame," *Political Behavior*, vol. 32, no. 3, September, 409–422.

Giné, X. and Mansuri, G. (2011) "Together We Will: Experimental Evidence on Female Voting Behavior in Pakistan," Working Paper, Development Research Group, The World Bank.

Gosnell, H. F. (1927) *Getting Out the Vote: An Experiment in the Stimulation of Voting*, Chicago: University of Chicago Press.

Green, D. P. and Gerber, A. S. (2002a) "The Downstream Benefits of Experimentation," *Political Analysis*, vol. 10, no. 4, Autumn, 394–402.

Green, D. P. and Gerber, A. S. (2002b) "Reclaiming the Experimental Tradition in Political Science," in Milner, H. and Katznelson, I. (eds.) *Political Science: The State of the Discipline*, 3rd Edition, New York: W. W. Norton & Co: 805–832.

Green, D. P., and Gerber, A. S. (2015) *Get Out the Vote*, Washington, DC: Brookings Institution Press.

Green, D. P., Krasno, J. S., Panagopoulos, C., Farrer, B., and Schwam-Baird, M. (2015) "Encouraging Small Donor Contributions: A Field Experiment Testing the Effects of Nonpartisan Messages," *Journal of Experimental Political Science*, vol. 2, no. 2, January, 183–191.

Gross, A. E., Schmidt, M. J., Keating, J. P., and Saks, M. J. (1974) "Persuasion, Surveillance, and Voting Behavior," *Journal of Experimental Social Psychology*, vol. 10, no. 5, September, 451–460.

Guan, M. and Green, D. P. (2006) "Noncoercive Mobilization in State-Controlled Elections: An Experimental Study in Beijing," *Comparative Political Studies*, vol. 39, no. 10, December, 5–8.

Huckfeldt, R. R. and Sprague, J. (1995) *Citizens, Politics and Social Communication: Information and Influence in an Election Campaign*, New York: Cambridge University Press.

Humphreys, M. and Weinstein, J. (2012) "Policing Politicians: Citizen Empowerment and Political Accountability in Uganda, Preliminary Analysis," Unpublished Manuscript, Columbia University.

Issenberg, S. (2012) *The Victory Lab: The Secret Science of Winning Campaigns*, New York: Crown.

Iyengar, S., Peters, M. D., and Kinder, D. R. (1982) "Experimental Demonstrations of the "Not-So-Minimal" Consequences of Television News Programs," *American Political Science Review*, vol. 76, no. 4, December, 848–858.

John, P. and Brannan, T. (2008) "How Different are Telephoning and Canvassing? Results from a 'Get Out the Vote' Field Experiment in the British 2005 General Election," *British Journal of Political Science*, vol. 38, no. 3, July, 565–574.

John, P. and Foos, F. (2014) "How to Get Out the Vote of Your Supporters While Putting Off Your Opponents: A Partisan Mobilisation Experiment in the 2014 European Elections," Unpublished Manuscript, University College London.

Kalla, J. L. and Broockman, D. E. (2015) "Campaign Contributions Facilitate Access to Congressional Officials: A Randomized Field Experiment," *American Journal of Political Science*, vol. 60, no. 3, July, 545–558.

Karpowitz, C. F., Mendelberg, T., and Shaker, L. (2012) "Gender Inequality in Deliberative Participation," *American Political Science Review*, vol. 106, no. 3, August, 533–547.

Keefer, P. and Khemani, S. (2005) "Democracy, Public Expenditures, and the Poor: Understanding Political Incentives for Providing Public Services," *The World Bank Research Observer*, vol. 20, no. 1, Spring, 1–27.

Kellermann, M. and Shepsle, K. A. (2009) "Congressional Careers, Committee Assignments, and Seniority Randomization in the US House of Representatives," *Quarterly Journal of Political Science*, vol. 4, no. 2, July, 87–101.

Kendall, C., Nannicini, T., and Trebbi, F. (2015) "How Do Voters Respond to Information? Evidence from a Randomized Campaign," *American Economic Review*, vol. 105, no. 1, January, 322–353.

Kuklinski, J. H., Cobb, M. D., and Gilens, M. (1997) "Racial Attitudes and the 'New South'," *Journal of Politics*, vol. 59, no. 2, May, 323–349.

Loewen, P. J. and Rubenson, D. (2010) "Democratic Competition Increases Voter Participation," Unpublished Manuscript, University of Toronto.

Loewen, P. J., Koop, R., Settle, J., and Fowler, J. H. (2014) "A Natural Experiment in Proposal Power and Electoral Success," *American Journal of Political Science*, vol. 58, no. 1, January, 189–196.

Malhotra, N., Michelson, M. R., and Valenzuela, A. A. (2012) "Emails from Official Sources Can Increase Turnout," *Quarterly Journal of Political Science*, vol. 7, no. 3, June, 321–332.

Mann, C. B. (2010) "Is There Backlash to Social Pressure? A Large-Scale Field Experiment on Voter Mobilization," *Political Behavior*, vol. 32, no. 3, September, 387–407.

Mann, C. B. (2011) "Looking Beyond Election Day: Voter Mobilization Experiments and Pre-Election Day Voting," *Newsletter of the APSA Experimental Section*, vol. 2, no. 2, Autumn, 3–4.

Mann, C. B. and Mayhew, G. (2015) "Voter Mobilization Meets eGovernment: Turnout and Voting by Mail From Online or Paper Ballot Request," *Journal of Political Marketing*, vol. 14, no. 4, October, 352–380.

McClendon, G. H. (2014) "Social Esteem and Participation in Contentious Politics: A Field Experiment at an LGBT Pride Rally," *American Journal of Political Science*, vol. 58, no. 2, April, 279–290.

Michelson, M. R., Bedolla, L. G., and McConnell, M. A. (2009) "Heeding the Call: The Effect of Targeted Two-Round Phone Banks on Voter Turnout," *Journal of Politics*, vol. 71, no. 4, October, 1549–1563.

Miller, J. M. and Krosnick, J. A. (2004) "Threat as a Motivator of Political Activism: A Field Experiment," *Political Psychology*, vol. 25, no. 4, August, 507–523.

Minozzi, W., Neblo, M. A., Esterling, K. M., and Lazer, D. M. (2015) "Field Experiment Evidence of Substantive, Attributional, and Behavioral Persuasion by Members of Congress in Online Town Halls," *Proceedings of the National Academy of Sciences*, vol. 112, no. 13, March, 3937–3942.

Murray, G. R. and Matland, R. E. (2014) "Mobilization Effects Using Mail Social Pressure, Descriptive Norms, and Timing," *Political Research Quarterly*, vol. 67, no. 2, June, 304–319.

Mutz, D. C. (2011) *Population-Based Survey Experiments*, Princeton: Princeton University Press.

Mutz, D. C. (2015) *In-Your-Face Politics: The Consequences of Uncivil Media*, Princeton: Princeton University Press.

Nickerson, D. W. (2007) "Don't Talk to Strangers: Experimental Evidence of the Need for Targeting," Working Paper, Temple University.

Nickerson, D. W. (2015) "Do Voter Registration Drives Increase Participation? For Whom and When?" *Journal of Politics*, vol. 77, no. 1, January, 88–101.

Nickerson, D. W., Friedrichs, R. D., and King, D. C. (2006) "Partisan Mobilization Campaigns in the Field: Results from a Statewide Turnout Experiment in Michigan," *Political Research Quarterly*, vol. 59, no. 1, March, 85–97.

Nyhan, B. and Reifler, J. (2015) "The Effect of Fact-Checking on Elites: A Field Experiment on US State Legislators," *American Journal of Political Science*, vol. 59, no. 3, July, 628–640.

Nyman, P. (2017) "Door-to-Door Canvassing in the European Elections: Evidence from a Swedish Field Experiment," *Electoral Studies*, vol. 45, February, 110–118.

Olson, M. (1965) *The Logic of Collective Action*, Cambridge, MA: Harvard University Press.

Paluck, E. L. (2009) "Reducing Intergroup Prejudice and Conflict Using the Media: A Field Experiment in Rwanda," *Journal of Personality and Social Psychology*, vol. 96, no. 3, March, 574–587.

Paluck, E. L. and Green, D. P. (2009) "Prejudice Reduction: What Works? A Review and Assessment of Research and Practice," *Annual Review of Psychology*, vol. 60, January, 339–367.

Panagopoulos, C. (2010) "Affect, Social Pressure and Prosocial Motivation: Field Experimental Evidence of the Mobilizing Effects of Pride, Shame and Publicizing Voting Behavior," *Political Behavior*, vol. 32, no. 3, September, 369–386.

Panagopoulos, C. (2013) "Extrinsic Rewards, Intrinsic Motivation and Voting," *Journal of Politics*, vol. 75, no. 1, January, 266–280.

Pande, R. (2011) "Can Informed Voters Enforce Better Governance? Experiments in Low-Income Democracies," *Annual Review of Economics*, vol. 3, September, 215–237.

Perez-Truglia, R. and Cruces, G. (2017) "Partisan Interactions: Evidence from a Field Experiment in the United States," *Journal of Political Economy*, 125 (4), doi.org/10.1086/692711.

Piven, F. F. and Cloward, R. A. (1989) "Government Statistics and Conflicting Explanations of Nonvoting," *PS: Political Science and Politics*, vol. 22, no. 3, September, 580–588.

Pons, V. (2016) "Will a Five-Minute Discussion Change Your Mind? A Countrywide Experiment on Voter Choice in France," Cambridge, MA: Harvard Business School. Available online: www.hbs.edu/faculty/Publication%20Files/16-079_a06efc8e-7efa-400c-b983-4fe56e042394.pdf.

Powell, G. B. (1986) "American Voter Turnout in Comparative Perspective," *American Political Science Review*, vol. 80, no. 1, March, 17–43.

Ramiro, L., Morales, L., and Jiménez-Buedo, M. (2012) "The Effects of Party Mobilization on Electoral Results: An Experimental Study of the 2011 Spanish Local Elections," Unpublished Manuscript, University of Leicester.

Riker, W. H. and Ordeshook, P. C. (1968) "A Theory of the Calculus of Voting," *American Political Science Review*, vol. 62, no. 1, March, 25–42.

Rogers, T. and Middleton, J. (2015) "Are Ballot Initiative Outcomes Influenced by the Campaigns of Independent Groups? A Precinct-Randomized Field Experiment Showing That They Are," *Political Behavior*, vol. 37, no. 3, September, 567–593.

Rogers, T., Green, D., Ternovski, J., and Ferrerosa-Young, C. (2017) "Social Pressure and Voting: A Field Experiment Conducted in a High-Salience Election," Electoral Studies 46:87-100.

Rondeau, D. and List, J. A. (2008) "Matching and Challenge Gifts to Charity: Evidence from Laboratory and Natural Field Experiments," *Experimental Economics*, vol. 11, no. 3, September, 253–267.

Rosenstone, S. and Hansen, J. M. (1993) *Mobilization, Participation and Democracy in America*, New York: Macmillan.

Schuman, H. and Presser, S. (1981) *Questions and Answers in Attitude Surveys: Experiments on Question Form, Wording, and Context*, New York: Academic Press.

Schwam-Baird, M., Panagopoulos, C., Krasno, J. S., and Green, D. P. (2016) "Do Public Matching Funds and Tax Credits Encourage Political Contributions? Evidence from Three Field Experiments Using Nonpartisan Messages," Working Paper, Columbia University.

Sears, D. O. (1986) "College Sophomores in the Laboratory: Influences of a Narrow Data Base on Social Psychology's View of Human Nature," *Journal of Personality and Social Psychology*, vol. 51, no. 3, September, 515–530.

Shaw, D. R., Green, D. P., Gimpel, J. G., and Gerber, A. S. (2012) "Do Robotic Calls from Credible Sources Influence Voter Turnout or Vote Choice? Evidence from a Randomized Field Experiment," *Journal of Political Marketing*, vol. 11, no. 4, November, 231–245.

Sinclair, B., McConnell, M., and Michelson, M. R. (2013) "Local Canvassing: The Efficacy of Grassroots Voter Mobilization," *Political Communication*, vol. 30, no. 1, January, 42–57.

Stafford, D. K. and Hughes, D. A. (2012) "Mobilization, Participation, and Social Influence," Unpublished Manuscript, University of California, San Diego.

Sullivan, J. L., Piereson, J. E., and Marcus, G. E. (1978) "Ideological Constraint in the Mass Public: A Methodological Critique and Some New Findings," *American Journal of Political Science*, vol. 22, no. 2, May, 233–249.

Titiunik, R. (2016) "Drawing Your Senator from a Jar: Term Length and Legislative Behavior," *Political Science Research and Methods*, vol. 4, no. 2, May, 293–316.

Wantchekon, L. (2003) "Clientelism and Voting Behavior: Evidence from a Field Experiment in Benin," *World Politics*, vol. 55, no. 3, April, 399–422.

Wolfinger, R. E. and Rosenstone, S. J. (1980) *Who Votes?* New Haven: Yale University Press.

41

MAKING INFERENCES ABOUT ELECTIONS AND PUBLIC OPINION USING INCIDENTALLY COLLECTED DATA

Jonathan Mellon

Introduction

This chapter discusses the use of large quantities of incidentally collected data (ICD) to make inferences about elections and public opinion. ICD is data that was created or collected primarily for a purpose other than analysis (Sjoberg, Mellon, and Peixoto 2017). The internet has expanded the availability and reduced the cost of ICD with data sources including internet searches, social media data, and civic platforms. This chapter focuses on the uses of ICD in elections and public opinion (EPOP) research and the challenges that researchers face in using it effectively.

ICD is often categorized as "big data." This chapter doesn't use that term for several reasons. First, the term big data has at least six commonly used definitions that are often incompatible with each other (Monroe 2012; Ward and Barker 2013). The most common definitions focus on the amount of data (for instance, Intel uses a cutoff of 300 terabytes of weekly data). Data size is an important criterion when looking at storage or technological requirements for running an analysis (e.g., which database software or cloud service to use), but is less important when considering questions of what types of inference can be made from data. Looking merely in terms of size, both anonymized census records and large sets of tweets are big data. However, census records are some of the least problematic data to draw inferences to the general population from (because they are near complete information on the population), whereas drawing valid inferences from social media data is much more difficult.

Other big data definitions focus on the velocity of the data (how quickly it is produced), on the computing power required to analyze the data, on the extent to which the data is structured in a complex way, or whether particular tools are used to analyze the data (e.g., machine learning, NoSQL databases, or Hadoop). A particular dataset or analysis can easily fit different sets of these definitions, meaning the term big data is uninformative without further explanation. Rather than trying to solve this semantic debate, this chapter focuses on the analysis and inferential issues that political scientists face when studying data that was collected for purposes other than analysis.

This chapter proceeds in four sections. The first focuses on the different types of inferences that elections and public opinion researchers have made from ICD: point estimates of public opinion or party behavior, election forecasts, and estimates of causal relationships. The second discusses how researchers should think about representativeness and validation when using ICD. The third section discusses other common problems that researchers face when analyzing ICD, including dealing with spam and automation. The fourth section applies the ICD framework to a paper analyzing the ideology of Twitter users.

Inferences with ICD

Several uses of ICD are especially relevant to the study of elections and public opinion: making point estimates, election forecasting, and estimating causal relationships. This section reviews the ways in which researchers have used ICD to do each of these.

Point estimates

One way in which ICD EPOP researchers use ICD is making point estimates of public opinion within particular populations. The most commonly used form of ICD for this purpose is internet search data, particularly from Google Trends. Google Trends provides aggregated time series counting the number of searches for a particular search term within a specified geographic area. The time series are available daily or weekly.

Google data has been used in public opinion research to study issue salience. These studies include studying agenda setting by the media (Weeks and Southwell 2010; Ripberger 2011; Granka 2010; Ragas and Tran 2013) and identifying trends in public interest in various environmental issues (Wilde and Pope 2012; Oltra 2011; Anderegg and Goldsmith 2014). Other studies using search data have shown how interest in candidates affects fundraising for that candidate (Ellis, Swearingen, and Ripberger 2011), and the effect of racist attitudes on Barack Obama's 2008 vote share (Stephens-Davidowitz 2012).

Some studies have also used text analysis of tweets as proxies for public opinion. Studies using Twitter have studied the reaction of the public to presidential debates (Wang et al. 2012), including using spikes in tweets to identify key moments within a debate, and analyzed the effect of political events on the public mood (Bollen and Pepe 2011) and the public's engagement with politicians (Raynauld and Greenberg 2014).

Most of the studies using ICD to track public opinion do not conduct any validation of the measures they use to track public opinion and it is therefore not clear whether the results of these studies are valid. The representativeness and ICD section of this chapter discusses some studies which have conducted validation and the extent to which unvalidated data is likely to lead to false inferences.

ICD has also been used to describe the behavior of parties. This analysis tends to be much less problematic as it is relatively straightforward to sample either all the relevant online behavior of parties or a representative subset of it. Examples of this type of analysis include Gibson and Ward's (2003) analysis of Australian party websites using automated content analysis. During that period, this could be seen as a reasonably representative sample of how the political parties used the internet. If the aim had been to make an inference about party behavior in general, the inference would have required more assumptions or validation, but the approach was well suited for the narrower question of how parties use the internet. Similar studies have looked at elections in Germany and Austria (Russmann 2011), Norway (Enli and Skogerbø 2013), and other Australian elections (Bruns and Highfield 2013). Recent studies have also documented the rapid rise in political parties' use of social media across many electoral contexts (Jungherr 2015; Bode and Epstein 2015; Karlsen 2011; Van Dalen et al. 2015; Larsson 2015).

Forecasting

Another major use of ICD is election forecasting. Many papers have used data on the number of times different candidates are mentioned on Twitter to forecast elections, with the assumption that more Twitter mentions is associated with a higher vote share (Tumasjan et al. 2010; Sang and Bos 2012; O'Connor et al. 2010; McKelvey, DiGrazia, and Rojas 2014; Marchetti-Bowick and Chambers 2012; Choy et al. 2012; Digrazia et al. 2013). Election forecasting has also been attempted using Google Trends data on the number of searches for candidate and party names (Graefe and Armstrong 2012; Granka 2013; Polykalas, Prezerakos, and Konidaris 2013a, 2013b). While all of these papers claimed success in this process, they are all based on retrospective forecasts of elections.

Subsequent research has suggested that these "forecasts" succeeded only due to arbitrary decisions (Gayo-Avello 2012) and that when their methods are applied to elections other than the one where success is claimed they perform no better than chance (Gayo-Avello, Metaxas, and Mustafaraj 2011; Metaxas, Mustafaraj, and Gayo-Avello 2011). Additionally, a pre-registered Twitter forecast of the 2015 UK election did not replicate the success of retrospective "forecasts" (Burnap et al. 2016).[1]

Causal relationships

Another form of inference that is sometimes used with ICD is to argue that even though the sample is unrepresentative, the social mechanisms that the authors are testing are not likely to be affected by the sample's unrepresentativeness. This is essentially the same logic that governs external validity in laboratory experiments. As with experiments, the extent to which this is a convincing argument will vary dramatically across studies. This logic of inference is rarely convincing when trying to get exact point estimates of a proportion (e.g., the proportion of voters who will vote for the Democrats), but can be more convincing when trying to understand how two variables will be correlated (e.g., whether consumption of left-wing media content correlates with voting democrat).

One example of this logic is a 61 million person get-out-the-vote experiment that was run on Facebook users by showing them a message about their friends' voting (Bond et al. 2012). Given the size of Facebook, this is interesting in its own right, but it is also plausible that such subtle social nudges are influential outside of Facebook, helping to justify the wider conclusions that the authors drew.

In another example, Mellon, Sjoberg, and Peixoto (2016) examine predictors of petition success on the change.org platform. They argue that the mechanisms tested are sufficiently broad (level of mobilization, institutional support, and regime type) that they are likely to apply to settings beyond the change.org platform. While the analysis itself makes inferences about petitions on the platform, the conclusions are drawn more widely.

In another example, Reddit data was used to examine the types of arguments that are most convincing to other people (Tan et al. 2016). While the data is specific to the Reddit platform, the authors explicitly make wider claims about the mechanisms behind persuasion. In this case, the generalizability of the findings is more difficult to assess. The data the paper uses is based on the ChangeMyView Reddit forum where users specifically ask for people to try and change their minds. It is therefore unclear whether data from this setting is relevant to opinion change more generally. In each of these cases, the mechanisms are argued to be sufficiently similar in the available ICD, that wider conclusions can be drawn.

Drawing useful inferences from ICD

There are two main ways that scholars can draw inferences from ICD: representativeness and proxy validation. Representativeness makes sure that the sample is sufficiently representative of the population that a researcher wants to make inferences about. Proxy validation takes a black box approach, where the key question is whether we can be confident that, for whatever reason, a trend in ICD reliably tracks a real-world phenomenon of interest.

Representativeness

Researchers using ICD need to consider representativeness in two ways. First, whether the platform the ICD is taken from is representative of the wider population that the research is interested in (voters, politicians, the general population, etc.). Second, regardless of the population of interest, researchers have to consider whether the ICD is organized at the correct unit of analysis for the research question.

Representativeness of users

When looking at ICD, the first threat to representativeness is the composition of the platform's users. In the case of social media data, Facebook users tend to be more demographically and politically representative of the general population than Twitter users (Mellon and Prosser 2017), but both groups would take considerable adjustment to make them representative of the general population. As with survey data, when an initial sample is not representative, it is sometimes possible to achieve representativeness using weighting; however, this still assumes the sample is representative within the weighting strata.

Most studies that attempt to make point estimates do not assume that ICD is a sample of the general population of a country, but many studies do try to make inferences about subpopulations. On the other hand, many studies that focus on causal relationships implicitly assume that social media users are sufficiently representative of the general population to draw inferences outside of social media users.

Choosing the correct unit of analysis

Most datasets used by scholars of elections and public opinion are either directly collected by them or by someone who collected it to make inferences about political phenomena. In standard social science data collection, the sampling procedure will generally reflect the analysis to be conducted. If a research question is about countries, data will be collected at the country level and if a question is about the behavior of individual voters, then data will be sampled at the individual level.

By definition, ICD is not collected in this way and instead reflects the priorities of the platform. Consequently, researchers may need to adjust the data in order to make inferences about the phenomena of interest. With ICD, the data will generally be organized at whatever level was most useful for the original purpose. Often this is in the form of event logs, which take an event as the unit of analysis. However, making inferences about the universe of events is often not the aim of a political scientist.

In public opinion research and elections research, the individual is generally treated as the fundamental unit of analysis. That is, we want to know something about the average individual in a population. In most survey research, we are interested in knowing something about the distribution of a variable across individuals. In the case of media analysis, we are usually ultimately interested in understanding the distribution of exposure to possible influences across individuals – for example, how much pro-Labour media is a typical voter exposed to?

Twitter data can be used to make inferences about these different populations. If we are, for instance, interested in using Twitter data in the run-up to a UK election, we could be interested in making inferences about any of the following (even before we consider making inferences beyond Twitter):

1   UK tweets
2   The consumption of Twitter content in the UK
3   The behavior of UK Twitter users

These choices are non-trivial because Twitter usage is highly skewed. The median Twitter account has just one follower (Bruner 2013). The first option is often the default way in which researchers receive Twitter data: a chronological stream of tweets written that match certain criteria (such as location, time, and topic), gathered by storing tweets matching a certain criteria in the streaming API for a certain time period. However, it is not immediately clear why we should care about tweets as a population to make inferences about. If we think that Twitter is politically relevant because it is an important source of campaign information, then we should be focused on the second option: what Twitter users consume, and if we are interested in Twitter as a source of data on the political behavior of individuals, then we should be interested in the third option. A stream of tweets is essentially a measure of individual behavior (tweeting) weighted proportionally to the level of activity of each individual. However, many articles using Twitter data (Jungherr 2014; Raynauld and Greenberg 2014; Jungherr, Jurgens, and Schoen 2011; Christensen 2013; Caldarelli et al. 2014) take it is as given that the content of Twitter as a whole is the most relevant analysis frame.

The second option (the consumption of Twitter content in the UK) is most useful for research looking at Twitter as a medium for media consumption. Obtaining a representative sample of what content is consumed on Twitter is possible using weighting: a researcher simply needs to capture a stream of tweets fitting particular criteria and then subsequently reweight or resample according to the number of followers the creator of each tweet has. This means that a tweet seen by 10,000 followers is weighted 500 times as highly as a tweet seen by 20 followers. While there are some simplifying assumptions[2] in this process, it will create a collection of tweets that much more closely resembles what people see on Twitter. If we are interested in Twitter as a source of information, then this is the most relevant universe.

The difference between what is consumed and what is tweeted is likely to be important. While Twitter users as a whole are numerous enough that they span many sections of society, popular Twitter users tend to be more reflective of existing sources of political influence: for example, celebrities, media figures, academics, and political figures. Focusing on everything that is tweeted would be likely to give the impression that Twitter consumption looks less like traditional media than is actually the case.

The third potential population of interest is Twitter users themselves or a particular subset of the users. Samples of Twitter users can be obtained in a number of ways. It is possible to scrape a random sample of users from the Twitter API by randomly sampling ID numbers from a uniform distribution (Bruner 2013), as user IDs are assigned more or less sequentially over time. As of 2013, around 63 percent of randomly chosen ID numbers resolved to a Twitter user. The downside of this approach is that it is not possible to filter users by particular criteria, so researchers would have to sample the whole of Twitter and then discard all non-relevant users.

Alternatively, a researcher could obtain a representative sample of active users (i.e., users who tweeted at least once in a time period), by collecting all tweets matching particular criteria (e.g., in the UK and mentioning political terms). The researcher can then use the Twitter search API to collect the full tweeting behavior of these users in this time period. This approach is relatively rare in the literature, although Boyadjian and Neihouser (2014) do demonstrate how to collect a panel of Twitter users.

Another approach that has been taken is to define a core set of political Twitter users such as politicians from other sources. Politically interested users can then be further identified by looking at the followers of these core political users (Barberá 2014). Similarly, other studies have looked at all users who tweeted using a particular hashtag (Larsson and Moe 2011).

In light of this discussion, it is perhaps not surprising that Twitter election forecasts have a poor track record, given that: (1) almost all papers on this topic use tweet counts, which (as noted above) neither track Twitter user behavior nor what Twitter users are exposed to, and (2) Twitter users are highly unrepresentative of the general public in every country studied (Vaccari et al. 2013; Mellon and Prosser 2017; Barberá and Rivero 2014).

This is not to say that researchers should never analyze a stream of tweets, simply that they should articulate why doing so answers their research question. While this section has focused primarily on Twitter, these same concerns apply to any ICD analysis.

Proxy validation

Another form of logic that researchers use to make inferences about a population on the basis of ICD is proxy validation. In this case, it is considered sufficient to use the ICD to measure public opinion if we can be confident that there is a strong relationship between the underlying variable in the population and a particular measurement using ICD, even if the mechanism driving the link is not necessarily clear.

An example of the validation logic comes from work using Google Trends. Mellon (2013b) outlines a three-step procedure for determining the extent to which a Google Trends time series can be considered a valid proxy for the salience of a particular issue: face validity, content validity, and criterion validity.

Face validity simply refers to whether or not a Google Trends term initially looks plausible as a proxy for a given variable. For instance, the search term "council housing" seems plausible as a measure of the issue salience of housing in the UK.

Content validity goes a step further and examines the actual search terms used within searches that make up the trend for a keyword. For instance, are Google Trends for "jobs" about searches for employment or the new Steve Jobs biopic? Google Trends allows the top terms for a trend to be downloaded and examined. Problematic terms can then be iteratively removed, to leave only relevant searches.

Criterion validity refers to the extent to which a measure can be shown to correlate with an existing gold standard measure. Given the widespread concerns about traditional data collection techniques such as polling data (Sturgis et al. 2016; Mokrzycki, Keeter, and Kennedy 2009), it is doubtful whether we truly have a gold standard for many public opinion measures, but traditional techniques at least have established standards for assessing their likely quality and unambiguous tests of their accuracy around elections.

When applying these steps to Google Trends series in the US, just 5 out of 20 trends with face validity were shown to possess both content validity and criterion validity (Mellon 2013b). A similarly low validation rate was seen in Spain (5 out of 12) and the United Kingdom (14 out of 39) (Mellon 2013a). In none of the three countries was an initially plausible Google Trends series more likely to turn out to be valid than not. While these steps are designed around using internet search data, many other sources of ICD could potentially benefit from similar steps of validation.

A limited amount of work has been conducted validating trends in Twitter data against public opinion (O'Connor et al. 2010). While the authors of this work are optimistic about the potential for tracking public opinion using Twitter, their results show that the strength of the relationship between public opinion and Twitter sentiment varies greatly over time, sometimes reaching as high as a 0.8 correlation but often showing zero or even negative correlations. This study also therefore casts doubt on the efficacy of Twitter data for making point estimates of public opinion.

Measurement challenges associated with ICD

In addition to the issues about making inferences from the sample themselves, researchers using ICD also need to consider other measurement concerns that are inherent to analyzing these forms of data.

Inferring attitudes from behavior

Survey research generally gathers a large quantity of systematic data about respondents' attitudes, but has relatively limited directly observed behavioral data (vote validation is a notable exception in electoral research). With ICD, the situation is usually reversed: there are large quantities of non-systematic behavioral data with little systematic attitudinal data. The issue for analyzing ICD is therefore how to interpret behaviors.

One example of this problem is Google Trends data. Researchers observe normalized counts of searches for a given term, but have to assume the reasons why these people searched for the terms they did. Are people searching for "Trump" because they plan to vote for Donald Trump in the Republican primary, because they want to find negative information about him, or because they plan to stay at a Trump hotel? With Google Trends data, it is possible to see what other terms are being combined with a search term which can help to disambiguate these meanings (Mellon 2013b), but the meaning of behavioral data will often be ambiguous.

Non-behavior and self-selection

While any survey response is technically behavioral, the fact that the survey respondents are proactively collected by the researcher reduces the impact of self-selection. By contrast, ICD events are proactively generated by the research subjects themselves. Consequently, we only observe any behavior (such as tweeting, posting, or even reading) for people who are sufficiently motivated to take this action. Making inferences about what people in general think on the basis of the actions of the most motivated can therefore be potentially misleading. Consequently, researchers need to make explicit how they are considering the large number of potential subjects in their study who did not take an action. While there may be unprecedented numbers of people searching for Donald Trump, the vast majority of people on any given day will not be doing so. Researchers need to consider whether it is valid to make inferences about people who did not take an action on the basis of the behavior of those people who did take an action.

Artifacts of the platform

Another potential problem with ICD is the extent to which certain behaviors are encouraged or even automated by the platform itself. Google auto-completes searches with suggestions, Facebook and Twitter suggest possible people to connect with, and change.org emails users with suggested petitions to sign. Even email clients will automatically include all previous recipients in a message when a user clicks "reply all." Consequently, it is easy for research to conflate the design of the platform itself with the behavior of users on that platform.

This problem has become more acute with the introduction of algorithmic timelines on several platforms. This means that users are exposed to content on the basis of a proprietary algorithm rather than chronologically. This has led to controversy when the Facebook algorithm was alleged to reduce the visibility of conservative-leaning news outlets (LaCapria 2016) and further highlights the role that a platform's algorithms play in the behavior of its users.

Spam and fake data

Since the collection of ICD is generally not determined by the researcher, there are fewer protections against fake or duplicate information. Twitter and Facebook are both frequently targeted by advertising bots. These may even end up contaminating political data if they make use of popular hashtags, or retweet political information to help hide their tracks. Researchers should proactively look for this kind of contamination when using social media data.

Case study

Despite the challenges that using ICD presents to the researcher, it can and has been used to conduct novel and important analyses of political phenomena. This section briefly describes one such successful attempt conducted by Pablo Barberá, who studied the interactions of politicians and citizens on Twitter with a view to testing the extent to which such ICD could be used to infer ideological orientations. Here we concentrate particularly on how he navigated the concerns of representativeness and drawing valid inferences (Barberá 2014).

Estimating ideology from Twitter

In this study, Barberá aims to make inferences about the ideology of elite political actors (politicians, media outlets, and think tanks) based on the composition of users they interact with and who follows them. While legislators have long been classified on the basis of ideology, Barberá points out that other types of political actors have generally not been able to be rated on the same scale. Developing a method that can estimate ideology for any political actor (providing they are on Twitter) thus offers a potentially very useful new resource for political scientists.

Barberá correctly samples at the level of the user by first choosing several hundred political Twitter accounts in each of the countries in the study. He then downloads the information for each Twitter user who follows at least one of these target accounts. These users then allow the position of the elites and general users to be simultaneously estimated on the basis of their connections to each other. Barberá uses the logic of validation at both the standard user and the elite level. For normal users, he validates the ideal point estimates against matched data on users' campaign contributions and party registration. At the elite level he validates the ideal point estimates against DW-nominate scores in the US and expert survey measures of ideology in other countries. Barberá also accounts for potential contamination of measurement by spam on Twitter by excluding accounts with low levels of activity.

Barberá is also clear in outlining what population he intends to make inferences about: political actors in general at the elite level and Twitter users at the mass level, finding that most exchanges on Twitter take place between users with similar ideological positions and that a small cohort of highly engaged right-wing users disproportionately drive the public conversation on Twitter. This analysis exemplifies good practice for analyzing ICD by combining ICD with traditional data sources, appropriately choosing the unit of analysis, and accounting for potential biases in the data caused by the platform.

Conclusions

This chapter has outlined the sources of incidentally collected data (ICD) that have been used in public opinion and elections research. The nature of the data necessitates a careful consideration of what population is being researched and how the behavior on these platforms can be interpreted.

While ICD sources are highly varied, researchers would be advised to consider the following questions when deciding whether to use ICD in their research. The first question is whether the research question is best answered using ICD or is there another data source that would work better? The second question researchers should ask is how the ICD they are using was collected and make sure that this process is accounted for in the analysis process. Finally, researchers should ask what population they want to make inferences about and whether the data they have is structured appropriately to make these inferences.

While this chapter has emphasized the limitations of ICD in political analysis, this should not distract from the substantial research possibilities that ICD opens up. There are very limited possibilities for collecting large-scale network data outside of ICD, for instance. It fact it is precisely because of the increasing use of ICD in political science that it is important for researchers to understand how to best make use of these data sources and understand their limitations.

Notes

1 It should be noted that all the forecasts in the 2015 UK forecasting symposium performed poorly (Fisher and Lewis-Beck 2015), so Twitter forecasting was certainly not the only method called into question.
2 In particular, we assume that all Twitter followers are equally likely to read a tweet and that the follower count attached to a tweet that matches a certain criterion (such as originating from the UK) is representative of the number of UK followers.

References

Anderegg, W. R. L. and Goldsmith, G. R. (2014) "Public Interest in Climate Change over the Past Decade and the Effects of the 'Climategate' Media Event," *Environmental Research Letters*, vol. 9, no. 5, May, 1–8.

Barberá, P. (2014) "Birds of the Same Feather Tweet Together: Bayesian Ideal Point Estimation Using Twitter Data," *Political Analysis*, vol. 23, no. 1, January, 76–91.

Barberá, P. and Rivero, G. (2014) "Understanding the Political Representativeness of Twitter Users," *Social Science Computer Review*, vol. 33, no. 6, December, 712–729.

Bode, L. and Epstein, B. (2015) "Campaign Klout: Measuring Online Influence During the 2012 Election," *Journal of Information Technology and Politics*, vol. 12, no. 2, April, 133–148.

Bollen, J. and Pepe, A. (2011) "Modeling Public Mood and Emotion: Twitter Sentiment and Socio-Economic Phenomena," Paper presented at the 2011 Conference on Weblogs and Social Media, Barcelona, July 17–21.

Bond, R. M., Fariss, C. J., Jones, J. J., Kramer, A. D. I., Marlow, C., Settle, J. E., and Fowler, J. H. (2012) "A 61-Million-Person Experiment in Social Influence and Political Mobilization," *Nature*, vol. 489, no. 7415, September, 295–298.

Boyadjian, J. and Neihouser, M. (2014) "Why and How to Create a Panel of Twitter Users," in Skoric, M. M., Parycek, P., and Sachs, M. (eds.) *CeDEM Asia 2014: Conference for E-Democracy an Open Government*, Krems: Donau-Universität Krems, 247–252.

Bruner, J. (2013) "Tweets Loud and Quiet," *O'Reilly Radar*, December 18, 2013, available online: www.oreilly.com/ideas/tweets-loud-and-quiet [accessed February 17, 2017].

Bruns, A. and Highfield, T. (2013) "Political Networks on Twitter: Tweeting the Queensland State Election," *Information, Communication and Society*, vol. 16, no. 5, June, 667–691.

Burnap, P., Gibson, R., Sloan, L., Southern, R., and Williams, M. (2016) "140 Characters to Victory?: Using Twitter to Predict the UK 2015 General Election," *Electoral Studies*, vol. 41, March, 230–233.

Caldarelli, G., Chessa, A., Pammolli, F., Pompa, G., Puliga, M., Riccaboni, M., and Riotta, G. (2014) "A Multi-Level Geographical Study of Italian Political Elections from Twitter Data," *PLoS ONE*, vol. 9, no. 5, May, e95809.

Choy, M., Cheong, M., Laik, M. N., and Shung, K. P. (2012) "US Presidential Election 2012 Prediction Using Census Corrected Twitter Model," *ArXiv.org: Applications; Computers and Society*, November.

Christensen, C. (2013) "Wave-Riding and Hashtag-Jumping: Twitter, Minority 'Third Parties,' and the 2012 US Election," *Information, Communication and Society*, vol. 16, no. 5, June, 646–666.

Digrazia, J., McKelvey, K., Bollen, J., and Rojas, F. (2013) "More Tweets, More Votes: Social Media as a Quantitative Indicator of Political Behavior," *PLoS One*, vol. 8, no. 11, November, e79449.

Ellis, C., Swearingen, C., and Ripberger, J. T. (2011) "Examining the Impact of Public Attention on Fundraising in U.S. Senate Elections," Paper presented to the 2011 Annual Meeting of the American Political Science Association, Seattle, September 1–4.

Enli, G. S. and Skogerbø, E. (2013) "Personalized Campaigns in Party-Centered Politics," *Information, Communication and Society*, vol. 16, no. 5, June, 757–774.

Fisher, S. D. and Lewis-Beck, M. S. (2015) "Forecasting the 2015 British General Election: The 1992 Debacle All Over Again?," *Electoral Studies*, vol. 41, March, 225–229.

Gayo-Avello, D. (2012) "'I Wanted to Predict Elections with Twitter and All I Got Was This Lousy Paper' – A Balanced Survey on Election Prediction Using Twitter Data," *ArXiv.org: Computers and Society; Computation and Language; Physics and Society*, April, 13.

Gayo-Avello, D., Metaxas, P. T., and Mustafaraj, E. (2011) "Limits of Electoral Predictions Using Twitter," *Association for the Advancement of Artificial Intelligence*, 490–493, available online: http://citeseerx.ist.psu.edu/viewdoc/download?doi=10.1.1.221.5177&rep=rep1&type=pdf [accessed November 1, 2016]. In Proceedings of the International AAAI Conference on Weblogs and Social Media. Barcelona, Spain, AAAI.

Gibson, R. and Ward, S. (2003) "Letting the Daylight in? Australian Parties' Use of the World Wide Web at the State and Territory Level," in Gibson, R., Nixon, P. and Ward, S. (eds.) *Political Parties and the Internet: Net Gain?*, London: Routledge: 161–174.

Graefe, A., and Armstrong, J. S. (2012) "Predicting Elections from the Most Important Issue: A Test of the Take-the-Best Heuristic," *Journal of Behavioral Decision Making*, vol. 25, no. 1, July, 41–48.

Granka, L. (2010) "Measuring Agenda Setting with Online Search Traffic: Influences of Online and Traditional Media," Paper presented at the 2010 Annual Meeting of the American Political Science Association, Washington, DC, September 2–5.

Granka, L. (2013) "Using Online Search Traffic to Predict US Presidential Elections," *PS: Political Science and Politics*, vol. 46, no. 2, April, 271–279.

Jungherr, A. (2014) "The Logic of Political Coverage on Twitter: Temporal Dynamics and Content," *Journal of Communication*, vol. 64, no. 2, April, 239–259.

Jungherr, A. (2015) "Twitter Use in Election Campaigns: A Systematic Literature Review," *Journal of Information Technology and Politics*, vol. 13, no. 5, December, 72–91.

Jungherr, A., Jurgens, P., and Schoen, H. (2011) "Why the Pirate Party Won the German Election of 2009 or The Trouble with Predictions: A Response to Tumasjan, A., Sprenger, T. O., Sander, P. G. and Welpe, I. M. 'Predicting Elections with Twitter: What 140 Characters Reveal About Political Sentiment'," *Social Science Computer Review*, vol. 30, no. 2, May, 229–234.

Karlsen, R. (2011) "A Platform for Individualized Campaigning? Social Media and Parliamentary Candidates in the 2009 Norwegian Election Campaign," *Policy and Internet*, vol. 3, no. 4, December, 1–25.

LaCapria, K. (2016) "The Algorithm is Gonna Get You," *The Technosceptic*, January 21, 2016, available online: https://thetechnoskeptic.com/algorithm-is-gonna-get-you/ [accessed February 17, 2017].

Larsson, A. O. (2015) "The EU Parliament on Twitter – Assessing the Permanent Online Practices of Parliamentarians," *Journal of Information Technology and Politics*, vol. 12, no. 2, April, 149–166.

Larsson, A. O., and Moe, H. (2011) "Studying Political Microblogging: Twitter Users in the 2010 Swedish Election Campaign," *New Media and Society*, vol. 14, no. 5, August, 729–747.

Marchetti-Bowick, M. and Chambers, N. (2012) "Learning for Microblogs with Distant Supervision: Political Forecasting with Twitter," Paper presented at the 2012 Annual Conference of the European Chapter of the Association for Computational Linguistics, Avignon, April 23–27.

McKelvey, K., DiGrazia, J., and Rojas, F. (2014) "Twitter Publics: How Online Political Communities Signaled Electoral Outcomes in the 2010 US House Election," *Information, Communication and Society*, vol. 17, no. 4, April, 436–450.

Mellon, J. (2013a) "Where and When Can We Use Google Trends to Measure Issue Salience?," *PS: Political Science and Politics*, vol. 46, no. 2, April, 280–290.

Mellon, J. (2013b) "Internet Search Data and Issue Salience: The Properties of Google Trends as a Measure of Issue Salience," *Journal of Elections, Public Opinion and Parties*, vol. 24, no. 1, February, 45–72.

Mellon, J. and Prosser, C. (2017) "Twitter and Facebook Are Not Representative of the General Population: Political Attitudes and Demographics of British Social Media Users," Research and Politics, Jul–Sep: 1–9.

Mellon, J., Sjoberg, F. M., and Peixoto, T. (2016) "Connective Action: The Prevalence and Effects of Large Scale Transnational Activism," Working Paper, The World Bank.

Metaxas, P. T., Mustafaraj, E., and Gayo-Avello, D. (2011) "How (Not) to Predict Elections," Paper presented at the 2012 International Conference on Social Computing, Amsterdam, September 3–5.

Mokrzycki, M., Keeter, S., and Kennedy, C. (2009) "Cell-Phone-Only Voters in the 2008 Exit Poll and Implications for Future Noncoverage Bias," *Public Opinion Quarterly*, vol. 73, no. 5, December, 845–865.

Monroe, B. L. (2012) "The Five Vs of Big Data Political Science: Introduction to the Virtual Issue on Big Data in Political Science," *Political Analysis*, vol. 21, no. 5, April, 1–9.

O'Connor, B., Balasubramanyan, R., Routledge, B., and Smith, N. (2010) "From Tweets to Polls: Linking Text Sentiment to Public Opinion Time Series," Paper presented at the 2010 International AAAI Conference on Weblogs and Social Media, Washington, DC, May 23–26.

Oltra, C. (2011) "Stakeholder Perceptions of Biofuels from Microalgae," *Energy Policy*, vol. 39, no. 3, March, 1774–1781.

Polykalas, S., Prezerakos, G., and Konidaris, A. (2013a) "A General Purpose Model for Future Prediction Based on Web Search Data: Predicting Greek and Spanish Election," Paper presented at the 2013 International Conference on Advanced Information Networking and Applications Workshops, Barcelona, March 25–28.

Polykalas, S., Prezerakos, G., and Konidaris, A. (2013b) "An Algorithm Based on Google Trends' Data for Future Prediction. Case Study: German Elections," Paper presented at the 2013 International Symposium on Signal Processing and Information Technology, Athens, December 12–15.

Ragas, M. W. and Tran, H. (2013) "Beyond Cognitions: A Longitudinal Study of Online Search Salience and Media Coverage of the President," *Journalism and Mass Communication Quarterly*, vol. 90, no. 3, September, 478–499.

Raynauld, V. and Greenberg, J. (2014) "Tweet, Click, Vote: Twitter and the 2010 Ottawa Municipal Election," *Journal of Information Technology and Politics*, vol. 11, no. 4, 412–434.

Ripberger, J. T. (2011) "Capturing Curiosity: Using Internet Search Trends to Measure Public Attentiveness," *Policy Studies Journal*, vol. 39, no. 2, May, 239–259.

Russmann, U. (2011) "Targeting Voters via the Web – A Comparative Structural Analysis of Austrian and German Party Websites," *Policy and Internet*, vol. 3, no. 3, September, 26–48.

Sang, E. T. K. and Bos, J. (2012) "Predicting the 2011 Dutch Senate Election Results with Twitter," Paper presented at the 2012 Workshop on Semantical Analysis in Social Media, Avignon, April 23.

Sjoberg, F. M., Mellon, J., and Peixoto, T. (2017) "The Effect of Bureaucratic Responsiveness on Citizen Participation," *Public Administration Review*, vol. 77, no. 3, May/June, 340–351.

Stephens-Davidowitz, S. I. (2012) "The Effects of Racial Animus on a Black Presidential Candidate: Using Google Search Data to Find What Surveys Miss," Working Paper, Harvard University.

Sturgis, P., Baker, N., Callegaro, M., Fisher, S. D., Green, J., Jennings, W., Kuha, J., Lauderdale, B. E., and Smith, P. G. (2016) *Report of the Inquiry into the 2015 British General Election Opinion Polls*, London: Market Research Society and British Polling Council.

Tan, C., Niculae, V., Danescu-Niculescu-Mizil, C., and Lee, L. (2016) "Winning Arguments: Interaction Dynamics and Persuasion Strategies in Good-Faith Online Discussions," Paper presented at the 2016 Conference on the World Wide Web, Montreal, April 11–15.

Tumasjan, A., Sprenger, T. O., Sandner, P. G., and Welpe, I. M. (2010) "Predicting Elections with Twitter: What 140 Characters Reveal about Political Sentiment," Paper presented at the 2010 Conference on Weblogs and Social Media, Washington, DC, May 23–25.

Vaccari, C., Valeriani, A., Barberá, P., Bonneau, R., Jost, J. T., Nagler, J., and Tucker, J. A. (2013) "Social Media and Political Communication: A Survey of Twitter Users during the 2013 Italian General Election," *Rivista Italiana di Scienza Politica*, vol. 43, no. 3, December, 381–409.

Van Dalen, A., Fazekas, Z., Klemmensen, R., and Hansen, K. M. (2015) "Policy Considerations on Facebook: Agendas, Coherence, and Communication Patterns in the 2011 Danish Parliamentary Elections," *Journal of Information Technology and Politics*, vol. 12, no. 3, July, 303–324.

Wang, H., Can, D., Kazemzadeh, A., Bar, F., and Narayanan, S. (2012) "A System for Real-Time Twitter Sentiment Analysis of 2012 U.S. Presidential Election Cycle," Paper presented at the 2012 Annual Meeting of the Association for Computational Linguistics, Jeju, July 8–14.

Ward, J. S. and Barker, A. (2013) "Undefined by Data: A Survey of Big Data Definitions," *ArXiv.org: Databases*, September, 2.

Weeks, B. and Southwell, B. (2010) "The Symbiosis of News Coverage and Aggregate Online Search Behavior: Obama, Rumors, and Presidential Politics," *Mass Communication and Society*, vol. 13, no. 4, September, 341–360.

Wilde, G. R. and Pope, K. L. (2012) "Worldwide Trends in Fishing Interest Indicated by Internet Search Volume," *Fisheries Management and Ecology*, vol. 20, no. 3, April, 211–222.

INDEX

Page numbers in *italics* denote tables, those in **bold** denote figures.